DEFINING DOCUMENTS
IN AMERICAN HISTORY

Voters' Rights

Editor
Michael Shally-Jensen, PhD

SALEM PRESS
A Division of EBSCO Information Services, Inc.
Ipswich, Massachusetts

GREY HOUSE PUBLISHING

Cover: Image via iStock.com

Copyright © 2024 by EBSCO Information Services, Inc., and Grey House Publishing, Inc.

Defining Documents in American History: Voters' Rights, published by Grey House Publishing, Inc., Amenia, NY, under exclusive license from EBSCO Information Services, Inc.

All rights reserved. No part of this work may be used or reproduced in any manner whatsoever or transmitted in any form or by any means, electronic or mechanical, including photocopy, recording, or any information storage and retrieval system, without written permission from the copyright owner. For information, contact Grey House Publishing/Salem Press, 4919 Route 22, PO Box 56, Amenia, NY 12501.

∞ The paper used in these volumes conforms to the American National Standard for Permanence of Paper for Printed Library Materials, Z39.48 1992 (R2009).

Publisher's Cataloging-in-Publication Data
(Prepared by Parlew Associates, LLC)

Names: Shally-Jensen, Michael, editor.
Title: Voters' rights / editor, Michael Shally-Jensen, PhD.
Other titles: Defining documents in American history (Salem Press)
Description: Ipswich, MA : Salem Press, a division of EBSCO Information Services, Inc. ; Amenia, NY : Grey House Publishing, 2024. | Includes bibliographical references and index. | Includes b&w and color photos and prints.
Identifiers: ISBN 9798891790582 (hardback) | ISBN 9798891790599 (ebook)
Subjects: LCSH: Suffrage — United States — History. | Voting — United States — History. Election law — United States — History. | Election law — United States — Sources. | BISAC: POLITICAL SCIENCE / Political Process / Campaigns & Elections. | POLITICAL SCIENCE / Civics & Citizenship. | HISTORY / United States / General.
Classification: LCC JK1846 S53 2024 (print) | LCC JK1846 (ebook) | DDC 324.6209—dc23

FIRST PRINTING
PRINTED IN THE UNITED STATES OF AMERICA

■ Table of Contents

Publisher's Note vii
Introduction—Voting Rights and Challenges. ix
Contributors xv

Voting and Dissent in the Early Republic. 1
Federalist Paper No. 52 2
Twelfth Amendment to the U.S. Constitution 10
The "People's Constitution" and Dorr's Rebellion 17
Henry David Thoreau: "Civil Disobedience" 22

Votes for Women! 35
Seneca Falls Convention: Declaration of Sentiments. 36
Susan B. Anthony: "Is It a Crime for a Citizen of the United States to Vote?". 49
Petition to U.S. Congress for Women's Suffrage 62
Jane Addams: "Why Women Should Vote". 70
Alice Paul: Testimony before the House Judiciary Committee 79
Anna Howard Shaw: "Women's Suffrage in a Democratic Republic". 91
Prison Writings of a Radical Suffragist 102
Nineteenth Amendment to the U.S. Constitution 108

Voter Rights and Civil Rights 117
Fourteenth and Fifteenth Amendments to the Constitution 120
A Contested Election: Report to Congress on the Activities of the Ku Klux Klan 131
Booker T. Washington: "Statement on Suffrage" 144
Guinn v. United States 154
Indian Citizenship Act 172
Alice Moore Dunbar-Nelson: "The Negro Woman and the Ballot" 176
Smith v. Allwright 186
Malcolm X: "The Ballot or the Bullet" 198
Twenty-Fourth Amendment to the U.S. Constitution 218
Speech before Congress on Voting Rights 224
Voting Rights Act of 1965. 237

Voting Changes in the Modern Era 243
Seventeenth Amendment to the U.S. Constitution 244
Twenty-Sixth Amendment to the U.S. Constitution. 250
National Voter Registration Act of 1993 (NVRA). 255
Help America Vote Act of 2002 (HAVA) 263
Americans with Disabilities Act (ADA) Polling Place Accessibility Checklist 270
Civics Test for Naturalization. 283
Electoral Count Reform Act of 2022 299

Voting in Dispute 305
Baker v. Carr. 307
Reynolds v. Sims 315
Red Lion Broadcasting v. FCC 325
Richardson v. Ramirez. 337
Buckley v. Valeo 344
Shaw v. Reno. 384
Bush v. Gore 393
Citizens United v. Federal Election Commission 404
Shelby County v. Holder 424
Cooper v. Harris 443
Rucho v. Common Cause 456

Voting and Political Division Today 465
Statement to the U.S. Senate Judiciary Committee concerning Cambridge Analytica 467
Remarks by President Biden One Year after the January 6 Assault on the U.S. Capitol 483
"Texas Limits Mail Voting, Adds ID Requirements After Surge in Turnout" 497
"Republican Resolution Would Declare Trump the Winner in 2024, Regardless of What Voters Say" 507

Appendixes
Chronological List 515
Web Resources. 517
Bibliography 521

Index 531

■ Publisher's Note

The *Defining Documents in American History* series, produced by Salem Press, offers a closer look at important historical documents by pairing primary source documents on a broad range of subjects with essays written especially for the series by expert writers, including historians, professors, researchers, and other authorities in the subject under examination. This established series now includes forty-eight titles that present documents selected to illuminate specific eras in American history—including the Great Migration, the Constitution, and Civil Rights—or to explore significant themes and developments in American society—The Free Press, Prison Reform, Slavery, and Workers' Rights.

This set, *Defining Documents in American History: Voters' Rights*, offers in-depth analysis of forty-five documents, including articles, constitutional documents, court opinions, essays, laws, letters, political tracts, reports, speeches, and testimonies, as well as a checklist from the Americans with Disabilities Act, and an example naturalization test. These selections help define events surrounding the passionate and controversial history of voters' rights in the United States, including important milestones and landmark court cases.

The material is organized into six sections, each beginning with a brief introduction that examines the importance of the topic through a variety of historical documents.

Essays appear under the following topics:
- Voting and Dissent in the Early Republic
- Votes for Women!
- Voter Rights and Civil Rights
- Voting Changes in the Modern Era
- Voting in Dispute
- Voting and Political Division Today

The documents contained within these sections provide an overview of the history and significance of the evolution of voters' rights in the U.S., and the many challenges, legal battles, and conflicting interests that occurred along the way, shaping American history in the process.

Essay Format

Each Historical Document is supported by a critical essay, written by historians and teachers, that includes a Summary Overview, Defining Moment, About the Author, Document Analysis, and Essential Themes. An important feature of each essay is a close reading of the primary source that develops broader themes, such as the author's rhetorical purpose, social or class position, point of view, and other relevant issues. Each essay also includes a section entitled Bibliography and Additional Reading that provides suggestions for further readings and research.

Appendixes

- **Chronological List** arranges all documents by date.
- **Web Resources** is an annotated list of websites that offer valuable supplemental resources.
- **Bibliography** lists helpful articles and books for further study.

Contributors

Salem Press would like to extend its appreciation to all involved in the development and production of this work, in particular Editor Michael Shally-Jensen, who compiled the volume and oversaw the creation of new content. In general, the essays have been written and signed by scholars of history, humanities, and other disciplines related to the essays' topics. Without these expert contributions, a project of this nature would not be possible. A full list of the contributors to this set with their affiliations appears following the Editor's Introduction.

Introduction—Voting Rights and Challenges

Voting is the core process in any democratic society. Whether at the local, state, or federal level, voting is the primary tool that American citizens have at their disposal to shape the future of their country, its laws, and its politics. The outcome of American elections can profoundly change American culture and can influence the nation's development many years into the future. For these reasons, voting rights has been a key battleground for activists in the United States since the beginning.

The History of American Voting Rights

In 1787, when the United States Constitution was accepted by constitutional delegates and the ratification process began, the U.S. was unique among the societies descended from European colonialism. At the time, most of the Eurocentric world consisted of principalities and kingdoms, few of which allowed for much in the way of popular input on the development of the state. However, the shift from monarchy to constitutional republic was not a sudden innovation. There had been activism ongoing in Britain for centuries pushing for a higher level of popular representation, and this ultimately led Britain to shift from an absolute monarchy, in which monarchs have absolute control over the laws, to a constitutional monarchy, in which power is split between the monarchy and a civilian government. When Britain became a constitutional monarchy in 1688–89, the British government also expanded the influence of the citizenry over the development of the government by allowing for the formation of local representative groups that could lobby landowning aristocrats or the parliament. Despite these changes, democratic influence would remain limited in Britain for many more years as aristocrats and the monarchy guarded their privilege.

Overseas, in Britain's colonial properties, similar reforms resulted in the establishment of the first representative assemblies, political organizations that were populated with elected or appointed representatives of the citizenry and helped to represent the interests of the general public in meetings to determine policies and laws. The comparative independence of the overseas colonies allowed for a higher degree of popular influence, but many of the colonists, particularly those who were wealthy or independent businessmen and producers, still resented their financial obligations to England. This is the debate, over taxation and economic autonomy, that saw the colonies go to war with England for control and ultimately resulted in the establishment of the United States.

Seeking to avoid another situation where a powerful executive administration was able to dominate the citizenry, the United States adopted a system inspired by the ancient democracies of the classical world, resulting in an indirect quasi-democratic system in which citizens of the state were empowered to vote for their leaders and, in some cases, directly on certain laws and/or policies. Because of the representative assemblies that existed in the colonies, American citizens were already familiar with the idea of voting, but the establishment of the American republic necessitated a whole host of new voting rules.

Nothing in the U.S. Constitution guarantees American citizens a right to vote in American elections. This omission was intentional, as the most libertarian of the Framers fought to retain a high degree of state autonomy and to prevent the formation of an executive branch strong enough to dominate the populace. As a result, however, there is no federal "right to vote" in the United States. This means that voting can either be a right of citizenship, or a privilege, but this is a determination that occurs at the level of the state, and not at the federal level. Because voting is not a constitutional right, many states immediately enacted limitations on voting privileges that benefitted the dominant group but denied the vast majority of citizens any input as to the formation of laws and policies in the states or the nation.

In the beginning, the state governments were largely under the control of a relatively small group of wealthy white landowners, and the initial voting laws in American culture not only favored this group, but, in most states, prohibited anyone who was not a white, property-owning male, from casting a vote in almost any election. As a result, less than 2 percent of the adult population voted in the nation's first federal election, and state elections often had even fewer voters. Originally, the idea that only white males could vote was a matter of state law, but the 1790 Naturalization Act made this explicit by officially stating that only white males were citizens of the state. Women and slaves were legally considered the property of white men, and other nonwhite individuals were simply residents without any citizenship rights.

American women were denied access to the political franchise for most of American history. It was frequently argued that women lacked the experience, knowledge, or intelligence to make informed voting decisions, misogynistic arguments that are still frequently made with regard to women holding political office or other leadership positions. Half of the population was disenfranchised right from the beginning. Initially, the founding fathers also felt that poor people lacked the experience or knowledge to vote effectively. Many wealthy white men and allied politicians argued that only property-owning men were invested enough in the republic to deserve a political voice, and this attitude motivated laws that effectively banned working-class votes, either by limiting votes to property owners or by instituting fees and taxes that made it prohibitively expensive for poor persons to participate in elections.

The journey from these profoundly undemocratic beginnings to the more egalitarian though still imperfect modern political system was long and fraught with difficulty and conflict. The expansion of voting rights to the poor came gradually, as political parties fought to increase the voting population as a way to gain an advantage in new election cycles. The expansion of voting rights for African Americans came only after a Civil War that left much of America in ruins and decimated the economy. Women's suffrage was achieved after more than a century of passionate activism and campaigning and came only during the tumultuous period surrounding the First World War when the conservative party of the era sought to solidify power by attracting women voters.

Even after women and people of color were officially allowed to vote, those who embrace misogynistic attitudes about gender roles or who have embraced white supremacist ideology used their power, influence, and resources to limit the political rights afforded to women and people of color. In the case of African Americans, white supremacists in the southern states, and in the Midwest and West, enacted many laws that were meant to disenfranchise black voters or to discourage African Americans from exercising their political privileges as citizens. Armed white supremacist terrorist groups like the Ku Klux Klan attacked, murdered, and terrorized African Americans who tried to exercise their rights despite state-sanctioned discrimination. For women, winning the right to vote was a crucial step toward equality, but women still faced significant barriers in the professional and political realm that prevented them from expressing their political views and will. Women activists continued to campaign for inclusion in political and economic leadership.

The key federal legislation in the realm of voting rights was the 1965 Voting Rights Act which, for the first time, prohibited prejudicial voting policies and laws that discriminated against individuals on the basis of race or gender. This landmark legislation was a true turning point in America, with the federal government for the first time asserting dominance over the states in the realm of determining voting rights and privileges. Federal voting rights campaigns did not end here, of course, as the Voting Rights Act was really only a crucial first step in combating voting rights inequities.

Advancements and Existing Challenges

While America has come a long way from the time when wealthy white landowners used the laws that they created to dominate the American political landscape entirely, from the Voting Rights Act to the twenty-first century, Americans have continued to grapple with important issues. There remains a facet of the American people who consider themselves and those like them to be the only Americans with the right and ability to handle voting rights, or to make decisions about the future of their country, and these individuals have used their power and political influence to continue searching for ways to exclude those they see as "unfit" to vote.

One of the major issues in voting law that came to a head in 1971, was the age at which Americans could enjoy the privilege of voting. During the Vietnam War, many young adults complained that they were eligible to be forcibly conscripted into the armed forces at the age of 18, but were not given the right to participate in deciding on the nation's laws, as the voting age was then set at 21. This resulted in a major campaign that successfully, in 1971, reduced the voting age to 18, but questions still linger about whether or not persons as young as 16 or 15 should also be given a voice in American politics given the complex responsibilities that many in this age range experience. Some activists argue that it is unfair for individuals to be able to hold jobs and to be held responsible in the court of law, but still be denied voting rights.

Another major issue in the realm of voting concerns the languages that Americans use and understand. For many years, conservatives used "literacy tests" to prohibit people from voting, meaning that a person needed to be able to pass a written English test to be able to vote. This technique was promoted by nativists seeking to prevent immigrants from having political influence, and it was argued that the literacy tests guaranteed that only Americans with a certain level of education would have their voices heard. In 1975, a relatively progressive congress added language to the Voting Rights Act that protected individuals who lacked or had limited proficiency in English. Polling places were therefore required to provide language assistance to citizens who wanted to vote, to ensure that linguistic barriers did not stand in the way of engagement. Since that time, activists have been working to increase the number of languages accepted as appropriate languages for American voters. For instance, polling places are not required to provide translated ballots in Arabic, despite the increasing prominence of the language in American culture.

In 1982, America took another major step forward by adding additional detail to the Voting Rights Act that required polling places to provide services and assistance for people with disabilities. This victory was part of what became a new prong of voting rights activism in the decades that followed, because states still have the right, under the Federal Voting Rights Act, to deny permission to vote to person's based on "mental incapacity." What this means has been a major topic of debate among experts, with states still placing limitations on voting by people with certain kinds of neurodivergence.

While activists and voting rights advocates have successfully used the Voting Rights Act to challenge various inequities in the voting system, there remains some Americans who seek to limit voting rights as a way to gain a perceived advantage for those who look or think like them. Those who think this way gained a major advantage in the 2013 case of *Shelby County v. Holder*, in which the Supreme Court essentially eliminated a provision of the Voting Rights Act that forced states to get "preclearance" of any new voting law, to ensure that the laws met with the requirements of the Voting Right Act.4 As soon as this decision was passed, the state of Texas passed a new law requiring photo identification, immediately disenfranchising many citizens of the state—primarily the poor—who did not use photo identification. The ruling in the *Shelby* decision allegedly came down to balancing state interests with the interests of the federal government, but the ruling resulted in a situation in which any state could pass a law that limited voting rights and, even if that law was later overturned by a legal challenge, the law would temporarily give the dominant party in the state legislature an advantage.

Suppression and Security

In the early days of the American republic, it was considered acceptable for a white male citizen to openly express opposition to voting among people of color or women. However, shifting trends in American pop culture over the years gradually meant that it was no longer as socially acceptable for Americans to express openly sexist, classist, or racist views. As a result, those who still wished to limit rights for everyone except wealthy white men needed to use subterfuge and misinformation to pursue their agendas. Conservative politicians seized on the threat of voter fraud and electoral security to pass laws that were, in fact, meant to limit voting access to women, people of color, or those who typically support a specific political party other than the existing conservative party. This strategy became popular after the Civil War, when white supremacists wanted to limit the impact of African American voters but could not openly state their intention to deny black voters access to the franchise, because the Fifteenth Amendment explicitly granted African American men the privilege of voting. As a result, white supremacist legislators passed laws allegedly meant to enhance "voting security" but that were actually meant to allow them to make it more difficult for black voters to cast their votes.

The most current example of how this works can be seen in the political career of Donald Trump between 2016 and 2020. In both elections, Trump failed to win the popular vote, and in 2016 he won a technical victory only by securing a sufficient number of voting districts.. Because Trump lacks enough popular support to win an outright democratic victory, higher levels of voter turnout are bad for him. It therefore benefits him to limit voting access, especially in urban areas, areas with high levels of minority residents, and poor neighborhoods. Conservative legislatures therefore engage in practices like closing polling places in minority or poor neighborhoods, or limiting polling access in cities, which leads to long lines and, they hope, lower levels of engagement for urban voters. These policy changes, closures of polling places, and similar measures, are often justified by the need to ensure electoral security or to preserve funds, but they actually serve to give conservative candidates an advan- tage. Donald Trump won in 2016 because of these advantages, despite losing the popular vote by more than 3 million votes.

In the wake of his 2016 popular vote loss, Trump claimed that the three million votes had been fraudulent, despite providing no evidence to support this claim. Over the ensuing four years, Trump did not increase his level of support among the populace, and when the 2020 election came, he lost by a large margin. This loss was, despite the emotions expressed by supporters who had been misled to feel otherwise, not surprising given his polling numbers and overall inability to gain supporters over the previous years. Despite this, Trump vociferously and without evidence claimed that he had won the election and that President Joe Biden's victory had been fraudulent. Trump then raised millions from supporters who believed his claims that the election had been fraudulent, and who donated their money to an alleged effort to prove that this had happened. Meanwhile, conservative politicians allied with Trump began proposing a whole slew of new electoral security measures, including limitations on early voting, online voting, and other measures that enable people with limitations to engage in the process. Meanwhile, Trump tried to use his unvalidated and evidence-less claims of fraud to engage in a legal effort to overturn the results of the election.

While Trump's strategy was controversial, it was not wholly unprecedented. Politicians have long used the alleged threat of voter fraud to engage in suppression, and Trump allies were attempting to do the same thing in the wake of President Biden's defeat of Trump in the national election. Proposed changes to voting rights were not, in any realistic way, connected to actual fraud or the threat of fraud, as evidenced by numerous studies failing to find evidence of fraud sufficient of significantly altering the outcome of the election, but were meant, instead, to limit voting access, reducing engagement and therefore giving conservative candidates a better chance of winning technical victories like Trump's in 2016.

Beyond Trump, conservative politicians have participated in this same strategy for their own benefit, proposing new security measures and laws that are actually meant to suppress the votes of a certain portion of the American public, primarily including people of color, poor voters, elderly urban voters, and other groups that typically favor progressive or liberal political candidates. Defenders of the Republican Party's push for tighter electoral restrictions argue that voter fraud is a major threat and that new measures are needed both to protect elections and to reassure American voters that the electoral system will remain safe and secure. Despite many independent reviews of American elections indicating that fraud plays no serious role in elections at either the state or federal level, the large number of conservative voters who continue to believe that this is occurring continue to motivate new security measures to address the alleged problem and to "restore confidence" the voting system.

Major Issues in Voting Rights

Because the illusion of fraud still motivates many conservative voters and politicians, voter security remains an important issue. In the 2020s, this manifested in calls for new voting identification requirements, including state voter identification (ID) laws that have been passed or debated around the country. Advocates argue that voter ID laws are necessary to protect against fraud or to ensure trust in the system, while critics argue that voter ID laws disproportionately impact the poor and underserved. The American Civil Liberties Union (ACLU) reports that around 7 percent of Americans lack government-issued photo IDs, many of whom are poor or have other challenges in obtaining or maintaining identification. The ACLU opposes photo ID requirements as unnecessary, and argues that the federal government should need to prove that voter fraud is a problem in order to justify new identification requirements.

Also controversial were a whole series of other laws and municipal developments that voting rights activists claimed might limit voting capabilities for segments of the population. This includes the decision to eliminate or restrict at-home voting, absentee voting, and mail-in voting, which disproportionately impacts the elderly, people with disabilities, and the poor. In a similar vein, the closure and consolidation of polling places in many cities is another issue that activists claim reduced voting capabilities for a segment of the population.

Another voting rights issue that has remained relevant in this debate for many years is the disenfranchisement of Americans convicted on felony charges. Laws that deprive felons of voting privileges have been part of the American system since before the Civil War, but these laws have become more and more contentious as felon enfranchisement became a key issue for civil rights and social democrat reformers. Conservatives continue to see felon disenfranchisement as an appropriate punishment for those who are convicted of felony crimes, while activists argue that felon disenfranchisement laws have always been motivated by racial prejudice, and unfairly restrict key political powers from citizens based on past actions. Opinions on voting rights for felons depend on whether one believes that disenfranchisement is an appropriate punishment for those who violate felony laws, but activists have argued that this facet of voting law serves no legitimate purpose for the state and, further, that felon political participation might encourage more successful integration for those released after imprisonment on felony charges.

In all, many journalists and political analysts noted that the issue of voting rights divided Americans along ideological lines like few other issues in American politics. Some political scientists have argued, on a deeper level, that politics in America is becoming more and more divisive and politically polarized.6 Some have suggested that the impending and unavoidable end to the white majority in America has motivated a more radicalized and politically active effort to protect white political dominance. The shrinking of the middle class and the loss of working-class jobs is another factor that some analysts have suggested as a driver of more radical political attitudes as Americans struggle to find the best strategies to protect those threatened by the nation's increasing income and wealth inequality.

Another important factor has been the rise and spread of digital and social media, which has limited the influence of legitimate political journalism and has facilitated the spread of propaganda and misinformation. The political and ideological dangers of this era are perhaps best represented by the efforts of the Russian government to disrupt and damage the American political system by flooding American social media with false claims against then presidential candidate Hillary Clinton, an effort that fueled and exacerbated radical right-wing conspiracy theories and violence. Social media likewise provided the main channel for the amplification of voter fraud theories, and mainstream journalistic, educational, and research organization refused to support Trump's claim of widespread fraud. Even conservative publications and news organizations would not endorse the stolen election narrative that Trump promoted, and continued faith in this false claim therefore demonstrates the impact of social media in the political environment as it affects voting rights and attitudes.

All of these factors have combined to create a political system in which many Americans are increasingly perceiving very different versions of reality, and this colors how Americans feel about issues within the spectrum of voting rights. For those who embrace the idea that Donald Trump was the target of a political conspiracy and that the 2020 election was marred by all manner of illegal voting, it may appear that the American election system is in deep disarray and so that potentially radical changes may be called for. Those who embrace mainstream consensus on the election may be far less concerned about election security, but may now be concerned that the new conservative effort to enact new voter restrictions will make it difficult for many citizens to cast their votes. Attitudes about voting rights and laws, as well as peripheral issues such as whether or not to allow former felons to vote or whether the voting system should be upgraded with modern digital technology, therefore depend on what highly politicized version of reality Americans have embraced, but also depend on what kind of priorities appeal to each individual.

The effort to expand access to voting appeals to those who believe that voting should be a basic right of citizenship, rather than a privilege reserved only for certain classes, and to those who have accepted that many of the voting practices, policies, and laws that the nation has adopted over the years were intended to deny some facet of the American people access to the elective franchise. On the other hand, the effort to restrict voting access appeals to those who wish to prioritize their own sense of electoral safety over the potential risk of denying voting access to some facet of the population, and who have embraced the political claim that America's electoral system is vulnerable and fraught with fraud and corruption.

—*Micah L. Issitt*

Bibliography and Additional Reading

Bailyn, Bernard. *The Ideological Origins of the American Revolution*. Cambridge, MA: Harvard University Press, 1992.

"Fact Check: Trump lies about voter fraud while states, CDC, encourage voting-by-mail as pandemic-friendly option." *CNN*. Facts First. www.cnn.com/factsfirst/politics/factcheck_33b225f3-5d02-4f2c-abca-41e694c90b4f.

Holloway, Pippa. *Living in Infamy: Felon Disenfranchisement and the History of American Citizenship*. New York: Oxford University Press, 2014.

Laconte, Joseph. "An American Defense of Britain's Constitutional Monarchy." *The Heritage Foundation*. 19 Mar. 2021. www.heritage.org/europe/commentary/american-defense-britains-constitutional-monarchy.

Lucas, Ryan. "Senate Releases Final Report on Russia's Interference in 2016 Election." *NPR*. 18 Aug. 2020. www.npr.org/2020/08/18/903616315/senate-releases-final-report-on-russias-interference-in-2016-election.

"Oppose Voter ID Legislation—Fact Sheet." *ACLU*. Jul 21, 2011. www.aclu.org/documents/oppose-voter-id-legislation-fact-sheet

Rawnsley, Adam. "Trump's Voter Fraud Expert Shot Down Campaign's Election Lies." *Rolling Stone*. Mar 12, 2024.

"Reflecting On the 10th Anniversary of Shelby County v. Holder." *Office of Public Affairs*. U.S. DOJ. Jun 23, 2023. www.justice.gov/opa/blog/reflecting-10th-anniversary-shelby-county-v-holder#:~:text=The%20Shelby%20County%20ruling%20marked,were%20covered%20under%20Section%205.

"The Right to Vote." *Disability Justice*. disabilityjustice.org/right-to-vote.

"The 26th Amendment: An Explainer." *Rock the Vote*. 2024. www.rockthevote.org/explainers/the-26th-amendment-and-the-youth-vote.

"U.S. Voting Rights Timeline." *Northern California Citizenship Project*. 2004. a.s.kqed.net/pdf/education/digitalmedia/us-voting-rights-timeline.pdf.

Van Duyn, Emily. *Democracy Lives in Darkness: How and Why People Keep Their Politics a Secret*. New York: Oxford University Press, 2022.

"Voting Rights: A Short History." *Carnegie*. 18 Nov. 2019. www.carnegie.org/our-work/article/voting-rights-timeline/.

Wang, Hansi Lo. "A federal law requires translated voting ballots, but not in Arabic or Haitian Creole."

■ Contributors

Angela M. Alexander, MA
University of Georgia

Michael P. Auerbach, MA
Independent Scholar

James A. Baer, PhD
Northern Virginia Community College

Adam Berger, PhD
Independent Scholar

Amanda Beyer-Purvis, MA
University of Florida

Chris Bingley, PhD
Independent Scholar

Steven L. Danver, PhD
Mesa Verde Publishing

Donna M. DeBlasio, PhD
Youngstown State University

Amber R. Dickinson, PhD
University of California, Los Angeles

Marcia B. Dinneen, PhD
Bridgewater State College

Bethany Groff Dorau, MA
Historic New England

Ashleigh Fata, MA
University of California, Los Angeles

Aaron George, PhD
Tarleton State University

Gerald F. Goodwin, PhD
Independent Scholar

Aaron John Gulyas, MA
Mott Community College

Micah L. Issitt
Independent Scholar

Kay Lemay, MA
Independent Scholar

Karen Linkletter, PhD
California State University-Fullerton

Laurence W. Mazzeno, PhD
Alvernia College

Scott A. Merriman, PhD
Troy University

Michael J. O'Neal, PhD
Independent Scholar

Martha Pallante, PhD
Youngstown State University

Luca Prono, PhD
Independent Scholar

Michael Shally-Jensen, PhD
Independent Scholar

Michele McBride Simonelli, JD
Independent Scholar

Noëlle Sinclair, JD, MLS
Independent Scholar

Contributors

Robert Surbrug, PhD
Bay Path University

Lee Tunstall, PhD
Independent Scholar

Vanessa E. Vaughn, MA
Independent Scholar

Anthony Vivian, PhD
University of California, Los Angeles

Donald A. Watt, PhD
Dakota Wesleyan University

Cary D. Wintz, PhD
Texas Southern University

Charles L. Zelden, PhD
Nova Southeastern University

Voting and Dissent in the Early Republic

Government in the United States is based on the doctrine of popular consent, meaning a legitimate government derives its just powers from the consent of its citizens through their vote in elections. In the early days of the United States, however, only about 120,000 people in a total population of over 4 million could vote. The U.S. Constitution did not originally contain any explicit guarantee of a right to vote. Instead, each state determined voter qualifications, and those qualifications differed widely from state to state. Voting was generally limited to free white men who owned property and met certain religious qualifications. Eventually, the right to vote became more widespread. By 1860 almost every state allowed all white men over twenty-one to vote. African Americans became eligible to vote, by constitutional amendment, following the American Civil War. Women, however, still had another half century to wait for their turn.

In this section we look at an early statement, *Federalist Paper* No. 52, written by either James Madison or Alexander Hamilton, about the "right to suffrage." The author says that voting "is very justly regarded as a fundamental article of republican government." Of course, the meaning of republican government at the time was essentially patrician government, or rule by proper "gentlemen." The use of electors in what would come to be known as the Electoral College was one reflection of the gentlemanly atmosphere that was obtained. This body, whose members were selected by the states, initially voted more or less at will for their preferred presidential and vice-presidential candidates, resulting in two troublesome elections in 1796 and 1800. (In both cases, the president and vice president were at odds with each other.) The Twelfth Amendment to the Constitution, ratified in 1804, rectified the situation while still retaining the Electoral College.

Efforts to *democratize* the vote began early on, as well. One such effort was an uprising in Rhode Island in 1841 called Dorr's Rebellion. The rebels objected to the fact that the state government was run by a small clique of wealthy rural landowners. Supporters of widespread suffrage—a popular vote—went so far as to set up a separate, parallel government. The "Dorrites" attempted an attack on the arsenal in Providence but were put down. Despite the defeat, the protestors succeeded in advancing the cause of having a new state constitution written, one that extended the vote to all native-born adult men who could pay a poll tax of $1.

Another way of protesting, one that was not very widespread then, was civil disobedience, or "resistance to civil government" as the noted writer and activist Henry David Thoreau phrased it. In his famous essay on the topic, from 1849, Thoreau notes that he was inspired to protest precisely because of a poll tax he was required to pay. In this case, he objected less to the poll tax as such and more to the uses to which the collected funds might be put. Slavery was still practiced in the United States, and Thoreau preferred not to contribute one dime toward supporting it. He also objected to U.S. aims in the Mexican-American War (1846–1848). He was briefly jailed for his refusal to pay the tax.

Poll taxes remained on the books in many states until the advent of the Twenty-Fourth Amendment to the U.S. Constitution in 1964.

Federalist Paper No. 52

Date: 1788
Authors: Alexander Hamilton or James Madison
Genre: essay

Summary Overview

Part of The Federalist Papers, Federalist Paper *No. 52 discusses the House of Representatives and the election of its members. As the lower house of the proposed bicameral legislature in the U.S. Constitution, the House needed to have rules appropriate to its role. Written by either Alexander Hamilton or James Madison during the time of the ratification of the Constitution, as with all* Federalist Papers, Federalist Paper *No. 52 recommends two-year periods of service for representatives and focuses on the right to vote as laid out in the Constitution.*

Defining Moment

The Constitutional Convention was held in Philadelphia from May to September 1787 to correct errors of the Articles of Confederation and draft a new governing document for the country. The Articles of Confederation had organized a unicameral legislature with equal representation for each state, and delegates at the Convention were concerned with the legislature's shape in the new United States government. The central debates concerned state power in the legislature and whether the body would employ proportional or equal representation for its members. The main camps were generally divided between large and small states. Delegates supported either the Virginia Plan, in which the upper and lower houses of Congress would have proportional representation but differing means of election, or the New Jersey Plan, in which a single house would continue to have equal representation for the states.

On July 5, 1787, a committee of delegates from each state proposed a compromise to this ongoing issue of representation. The Great Compromise—or "Connecticut Compromise" for the agreement's author, the delegate from Connecticut Roger Sherman—created a bicameral legislature, in which two bodies would represent the people. The Senate gave equal representation to the states (with two members each), while the House gave more power to larger states (with the number of its members based on a state's population). With this organization of Congress in place, the Constitution was signed by the delegates on September 17, 1787.

Authors' Biographies

Alexander Hamilton (1757–1804) was a prominent statesman and considered a Founding Father of the United States. Born in Nevis, British West Indies, Hamilton rose to prominence in New York as a pam-

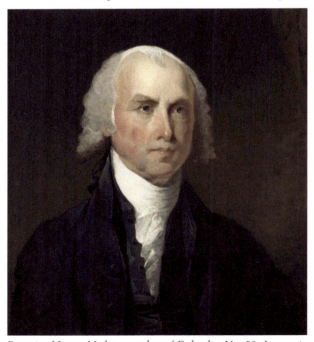

Portrait of James Madison, author of Federalist No. 52. Image via Wikimedia Commons. [Public domain.]

phleteer. He joined the revolutionary cause and served in the military, including as an aide to General George Washington. After playing a key part in the drafting of the Constitution as the delegate from New York, and as an author of *The Federalist Papers*, Hamilton served as the first secretary of the treasury of the United States (1789–1795). He died during a duel with his political rival Aaron Burr.

James Madison (1751–1836), also considered a Founding Father, was Hamilton's main collaborator in *The Federalist Papers*. Born in Virginia, Madison served as that state's delegate at the Constitutional Convention where he favored a strong federal government and proposed the Virginia Plan. In the years after ratification, Madison served in numerous political offices. He came to be a leader in the House of Representatives and was secretary of state during Thomas Jefferson's presidency. Madison's political career culminated in his election as the fourth president of the United States (1809–1817).

Historical Document

The Federalist Papers: No. 52

(Suffrage and the House of Representatives)

From the *New York Packet*, Friday, February 8, 1788.

To the People of the State of New York:

FROM the more general inquiries pursued in the four last papers, I pass on to a more particular examination of the several parts of the government. I shall begin with the House of Representatives. The first view to be taken of this part of the government relates to the qualifications of the electors and the elected. Those of the former are to be the same with those of the electors of the most numerous branch of the State legislatures. The definition of the right of suffrage is very justly regarded as a fundamental article of republican government. It was incumbent on the convention, therefore, to define and establish this right in the Constitution. To have left it open for the occasional regulation of the Congress, would have been improper for the reason just mentioned. To have submitted it to the legislative discretion of the States, would have been improper for the same reason; and for the additional reason that it would have rendered too dependent on the State governments that branch of the federal government which ought to be dependent on the people alone. To have reduced the different qualifications in the different States to one uniform rule, would probably have been as dissatisfactory to some of the States as it would have been difficult to the convention. The provision made by the convention appears, therefore, to be the best that lay within their option.

It must be satisfactory to every State, because it is conformable to the standard already established, or which may be established, by the State itself. It will be safe to the United States, because, being fixed by the State constitutions, it is not alterable by the State governments, and it cannot be feared that the people of the States will alter this part of their constitutions in such a manner as to abridge the rights secured to them by the federal Constitution. The qualifications of the elected, being less carefully and properly defined by the State constitutions, and being at the same time more susceptible of uniformity, have been very properly considered and regulated by the convention. A representative of the United States must be of the age of twenty-five years; must have been seven years a citizen of the United States; must, at the time of his election, be an inhabitant of the State he is to represent; and, during the time of his service, must be in no office under the United States. Under these reasonable limitations, the door of this part of the federal government is open to merit of every description, whether native or adoptive, whether young or old, and without regard to poverty or wealth, or to any particular profession of religious faith.

The term for which the representatives are to be elected falls under a second view which may be taken of this branch. In order to decide on the propriety of this article, two questions must be considered: first, whether biennial elections will, in this case, be safe; secondly, whether they be necessary or useful. First. As it is essential to liberty that the government in general should have a common interest with the people, so it is particularly essential that the branch of it under consideration should have an immediate dependence on, and an intimate sympathy with, the people. Frequent elections are unquestionably the only policy by which this dependence and sympathy can be effectually secured. But what particular degree of frequency may be absolutely necessary for the purpose, does not appear to be susceptible of any precise calculation, and must depend on a variety of circumstances with which it may be connected.

Let us consult experience, the guide that ought always to be followed whenever it can be found. The scheme of representation, as a substitute for a meeting of the citizens in person, being at most but very imperfectly known to ancient polity, it is in more modern times only that we are to expect instructive examples. And even here, in order to avoid a research too vague and diffusive, it will be proper to confine ourselves to the few examples which are best known, and which bear the greatest analogy to our particular case. The first to which this character ought to be applied, is the House of Commons in Great Britain. The history of this branch of the English Constitution, anterior to the date of Magna Charta, is too obscure to yield instruction. The very existence of it has been made a question among political antiquaries. The earliest records of subsequent date prove that parliaments were to SIT only every year; not that they were to be ELECTED every year. And even these annual sessions were left so much at the discretion of the monarch, that, under various pretexts, very long and dangerous intermissions were often contrived by royal ambition. To remedy this grievance, it was provided by a statute in the reign of Charles II. , that the intermissions should not be protracted beyond a period of three years. On the accession of William III. , when a revolution took place in the government, the subject was still more seriously resumed, and it was declared to be among the fundamental rights of the people that parliaments ought to be held FREQUENTLY. By another statute, which passed a few years later in the same reign, the term "frequently," which had alluded to the triennial period settled in the time of Charles II. , is reduced to a precise meaning, it being expressly enacted that a new parliament shall be called within three years after the termination of the former. The last change, from three to seven years, is well known to have been introduced pretty early in the present century, under on alarm for the Hanoverian succession.

From these facts it appears that the greatest frequency of elections which has been deemed necessary in that kingdom, for binding the representatives to their constituents, does not exceed a triennial return of them. And if we may argue from the degree of liberty retained even under septennial elections, and all the other vicious ingredients in the parliamentary constitution, we cannot doubt that a reduction of the period from seven to three years, with the other necessary reforms, would so far extend the influence of the people over their representatives as to satisfy us that biennial elections, under the federal system, cannot possibly be dangerous to the requisite dependence of the House of Representatives on their constituents. Elections in Ireland, till of late, were regulated entirely by the discretion of the crown, and were seldom repeated, except on the accession of a new prince, or some other contingent event. The parliament which commenced with George II. was continued throughout his whole reign, a period of about thirty-five years. The only dependence of the representatives on the people consisted in the right of the latter to supply occasional vacancies by the election of new members, and in the chance of some event which might produce a general new election. The ability also of the Irish parliament to maintain the rights of their constituents, so far as the disposition might exist, was extremely shackled by the control of the crown over the subjects of their deliberation. Of late these shackles, if I mistake not, have been broken; and octennial parliaments have besides been established. What effect may be produced by this partial reform, must be left to further experience. The example of Ireland, from this view of it, can throw but little light on the subject. As far as we can draw any conclusion from it, it must be that if the people of that country have been able under all these disadvantages to retain any liberty whatever, the advantage of biennial elections would secure to them every degree of liberty, which might depend on a due connection between their representatives and themselves. Let us bring our inquiries nearer home. The example of these States, when British colonies, claims particular attention, at the same time that it is so well known as to require little to be said on it. The principle of representation, in one branch of the legislature at least, was established in all of them. But the periods of election were different. They varied from one to seven years. Have we any reason to infer, from the spirit and conduct of the representatives of the people, prior to the Revolution, that biennial elections would have been dangerous to the public liberties? The spirit which everywhere displayed itself at the commencement of the struggle, and which vanquished the obstacles to independence, is the best of proofs that a sufficient portion of liberty had been everywhere enjoyed to inspire both a sense of its worth and a zeal for its proper enlargement This remark holds good, as well with regard to the then colonies whose elections were least frequent, as to those whose elections were most frequent Virginia was the colony which stood first in resisting the parliamentary usurpations of Great Britain; it was the first also in espousing, by public act, the resolution of independence.

In Virginia, nevertheless, if I have not been misinformed, elections under the former government were septennial. This particular example is brought into view, not as a proof of any peculiar merit, for the priority in those instances was probably accidental; and still less of any advantage in SEPTENNIAL elections, for when compared with a greater frequency they are inadmissible; but merely as a proof, and I conceive it to be a very substantial proof, that the liberties of the people can be in no danger from BIENNIAL elections. The conclusion resulting from these examples will be not a little strengthened by recollecting three circumstances. The first is, that the federal legislature will possess a part only of that supreme legislative authority which is vested completely in the British Parliament; and which, with a few exceptions, was exercised by the colonial assemblies and the Irish legislature. It is a received and well-founded maxim, that where no other circumstances affect the case, the greater the power is, the shorter ought to be its duration; and, conversely, the smaller the power, the more safely may its duration be protracted. In the second place, it has, on another occasion, been shown that the federal legislature will not only be restrained by its dependence on its people, as other legislative bodies are, but that it will be, moreover, watched and controlled by the several collateral legislatures, which other legislative bodies are not. And in the third place, no comparison can be made between the means that will be possessed by the more permanent branches of the federal government for seducing, if they should be disposed to seduce, the House of Representatives from their duty to the people, and the means of influence over the popular branch possessed by the other branches of the government above cited. With less power, therefore, to abuse, the federal representatives can be less tempted on one side, and will be doubly watched on the other.

PUBLIUS.

Document Analysis

During the ratification process, *The Federalist Papers* were published in major newspapers to make the case for endorsing the Constitution to the public. The *New York Packet* newspaper published *Federalist Paper* No. 52 on February 8, 1788. Written under the pseudonym Publius (used for all *The Federalist Papers*), the author—Hamilton or Madison—lays out the requirements for membership in the House of Representatives.

The author notes the hope to avoid the inconsistent rules set out by each state in their requirements for members of the House: "The qualifications of the elected, being less carefully and properly defined by the State constitutions, and being at the same time more susceptible of uniformity, have been very properly considered and regulated by the convention." Furthermore, it should not be the role of Congress to make these rules; rather, they should be laid out in the Constitution itself. Representatives must be at least twenty-five years old and a citizen of the United States for seven years. The author mentions that aside from residency in the state the House member represents, there are few other barriers to running for office. Clearly at this time only white men were able to run for office, but the author's emphasis on there being few other qualifications to serve in the House reflects the ideas of liberty and freedom that were cornerstones of the newly drafted Constitution. This theme of liberty serves as the justification for many of the author's other points throughout the essay.

Elections would be held every two years for representatives, clearing up any irregularity among the states. Up to this point, state elections had been held every one to seven years, with little consistency. A normal cycle of elections and the right to vote is only fair to the citizens themselves, who will be represented in the new government (and not directly participating in it). The author argues that "biennial elections, under the federal system, cannot possibly be dangerous to the requisite dependence of the House of Representatives on their constituents." In other words, representatives must seek the approval of their constituents because they face elections so regularly.

This form of representative government, however, differs from that of other nations. The author describes how for the English House of Commons, "[t]he earliest records of subsequent date prove that parliaments were to SIT only every year; not that they were to be ELECTED every year." And these sessions would only occur by royal decree, with great intervals in between. That is, the British monarch's interference only briefly brought about positive change, with an agreement that Parliament would meet at least every three years. In Ireland as well, meetings of Parliament were inconsistent and often only convened during seminal events. According to the author, the volatility of this system should not be emulated in the United States.

Three principles unique to the United States mentioned at the end of *Federalist Paper* No. 52 lay out how the House, and the federal legislature more broadly, will not have unlimited power. First, its power will not be as broad as other legislative bodies in foreign countries. Second, "several collateral legislatures"—namely the different state legislatures—will be able to check federal power. And finally, because House members will face election every two years, they cannot be unduly influenced or seduced by those that are not their constituents.

Essential Themes

The Anti-Federalist Papers refer to the numerous treatises written in response to *The Federalist Papers* and against the ratification of the Constitution. Apprehensive about the formation of a strong central government, the Anti-Federalists addressed specific aspects of the proposed Constitution. In response to the organization of the House of Representatives, the authors of *Anti-Federalist Paper* No. 52 (published as "On the Guarantee of Congressional Biennial Elections" on April 9, 1788) focused on the election of House members. The opponents were preoccupied with the possibility that House members might delay elections and not be held to the biennial schedule. That there was no direct provision against this in the U.S. Constitution meant that bad actors elected to the House had the potential to "burden and oppress the people."

Despite these misgivings, the Constitution became the governing document of the United States on June

21, 1788, when nine of the thirteen states had officially ratified it. After elections later that year, the first session of the House of Representatives began on April 1, 1789.

—*Chris Bingley, PhD*

Bibliography and Additional Reading

Allen, W. B., with Kevin A. Cloonan. *The Federalist Papers: A Commentary*. New York: Peter Lang, 2000.

Coenen, Dan T. *The Story of* The Federalist: *How Hamilton and Madison Reconceived America*. New York: Twelve Tables Press, 2007.

Rakove, Jack N. "The Great Compromise: Ideas, Interests, and the Politics of Constitution Making." *William and Mary Quarterly* 44 (1987): 424–457.

Storing, Herbert J. *What the Anti-Federalists Were For: The Political Thought of the Opponents of the Constitution*. Chicago: University of Chicago Press, 1981.

■ Twelfth Amendment to the U.S. Constitution

Date: June 15, 1804
Author: U.S. Congress
Genre: constitutional amendment

Summary Overview

The Twelfth Amendment to the U.S. Constitution served to change the way in which the president and vice president are elected. Prior to 1804, when the amendment was ratified, each member of the Electoral College voted for two candidates, and the candidate with the most votes won the presidency while the candidate earning second place won the vice presidency. This proved awkward in the elections of 1796 and 1800, and so a change was proposed in the form of a Constitutional amendment. Once approved by Congress and ratified by three-fourths of the states, the Twelfth Amendment took effect. It established a system in which the president and vice president were to be voted for separately by electors. The new system proved durable and remains in place to this day, albeit with refinements set in place in 1887 and 2022 through legislative acts.

Defining Moment

Under the terms of Article II, Section 1, of the Constitution, as originally written, the electors of each state were to cast their votes for both the president and the vice president on a single ballot, without specifying which of the two candidates was preferred as president and which as vice president. The candidate receiving the highest number of electoral votes would then become president, and the runner-up would become vice president.

However, the formation of political parties in the late eighteenth century altered the dynamic of the results of the voting process. In 1796, the Electoral College chose a president and vice president from different parties using the original method: John Adams, of the Federalist Party, and Thomas Jefferson, of the Democratic-Republican party. Their political differences created undue tensions in the Executive Office.

In the 1800 election, both major parties attempted to address the problem that surfaced in 1796 by nominating separate presidential and vice presidential candidates on a party ticket. However, because of the constitutional provision in place at the time there was no way for the electors to distinguish between the two offices when they cast their votes; so if all the electors voted for their party tickets, the election would end in a tie between the two candidates from the most popular ticket. Thus, the casting of two ballots for the same ticket of candidates resulted in a tie between presidential candidate Thomas Jefferson and his own running mate, Aaron Burr. After a protracted deadlock, the House of Representatives eventually voted in what is called a contingent election for Jefferson; it took thirty-five ballots to reach that result. This event more than anything lay behind the demand for the Twelfth Amendment. (Meanwhile, relations between Jefferson and Burr deteriorated to the point where the two men could barely tolerate each other.)

Document Information

In January 1797, Representative William L. Smith of South Carolina presented a resolution on the floor of the House of Representatives for an amendment to the Constitution under which the presidential electors would designate which candidate would be president and which vice president. However, no action was taken on Smith's proposal, setting the stage for the deadlocked election of 1800.

Following that election, DeWitt Clinton of New York won (1802) a vacant seat in the U.S. Senate. Clinton was instrumental in bringing the "designation amendment" to Congress. However, the Democratic-Republicans decided to wait for the next,

Twelfth Amendment in the National Archives. Photo via Wikimedia Commons. [Public domain.]

Eighth Congress to take up the matter because it would allow them a better chance to meet the two-thirds vote requirement to approve a Constitutional amendment and send it to the states for ratification.

In early 1803, the Eighth Congress considered the proposed amendment. After several formulations and refinements to the bill, the final version of the Twelfth Amendment was approved by the House of Representatives on December 9, 1803, by vote of 84–42; it had been previously passed by the Senate, by a vote of 22–10. The amendment was submitted to the seventeen states on December 12, 1803, and had been ratified by three-fourths of them by June 15, 1804.

Historical Document

The Electors shall meet in their respective states, and vote by ballot for President and Vice-President, one of whom, at least, shall not be an inhabitant of the same state with themselves; they shall name in their ballots the person voted for as President, and in distinct ballots the person voted for as Vice-President, and they shall make distinct lists of all persons voted for as President, and all persons voted for as Vice-President and of the number of votes for each, which lists they shall sign and certify, and transmit sealed to the seat of the government of the United States, directed to the President of the Senate;

The President of the Senate shall, in the presence of the Senate and House of Representatives, open all the certificates and the votes shall then be counted;

The person having the greatest number of votes for President, shall be the President, if such number be a majority of the whole number of Electors appointed; and if no person have such majority, then from the persons having the highest numbers not exceeding three on the list of those voted for as President, the House of Representatives shall choose immediately, by ballot, the President. But in choosing the President, the votes shall be taken by states, the representation from each state having one vote; a quorum for this purpose shall consist of a member or members from two-thirds of the states, and a majority of all the states shall be necessary to a choice. *And if the House of Representatives shall not choose a President whenever the right of choice shall devolve upon them, before the fourth day of March next following, then the Vice-President shall act as President, as in the case of the death or other constitutional disability of the President.*[1]

The person having the greatest number of votes as Vice-President, shall be the Vice-President, if such number be a majority of the whole number of Electors appointed, and if no person have a majority, then from the two highest numbers on the list, the Senate shall choose the Vice-President; a quorum for the purpose shall consist of two-thirds of the whole number of Senators, and a majority of the whole number shall be necessary to a choice. But no person constitutionally ineligible to the office of President shall be eligible to that of Vice-President of the United States.[1]

[1] *(Note: This provision was superseded by Sections 1, 2, and 3 of the Twentieth Amendment in 1933, which moved the date from March to January.)*

Document Themes and Analysis

The Twelfth Amendment provides the following:

1. electors are to use separate ballots in voting for each office (president and vice-president);
2. candidates with the greatest number of votes for each office are elected if that number represents a majority of the total electors;
3. if no such majority is met for either or both of the two highest offices, the House of Representatives then votes for the president from among the three highest candidates and the Senate votes for the vice-president from among the two highest candidates;
4. no person constitutionally ineligible to be president can be vice-president;
5. the results of the vote by the electors (i.e., the Electoral College vote) are to be signed, sealed, and securely delivered to Congress ("the seat of government") and then counted by the President of the Senate (i.e., the Vice-President of the United States).

One of the central subjects of the amendment is the electors of the Electoral College and the balloting done by them in choosing the holders of the nation's two highest offices. The Electoral College is, simply put, the body that elects the president and vice president of the United States every four years, generally reflecting the will of the voters. Article II, Section 1, of the Constitution provides that each state shall appoint as many presidential electors as the state has members of Congress. Thus, a state with two senators (as all states have) and ten representatives produces twelve votes in the Electoral College. Although the Constitution gives the legislature of each state the authority to decide how a state's presidential electors are to be chosen, every state now provides that the electors shall be directly elected by the voters. (This was not the case in earlier periods of American history.) When one votes in a presidential election, one is actually voting for *the electors* of the candidates one prefers, not the candidates themselves.

After the electors have been chosen, they meet in their respective state capitals to cast their ballots for president and vice president, based on the majority vote in their state as determined by voters. The only constitutional restriction is that an elector may vote for only one candidate who is a resident of the same state as that of the elector. This reflects the original premise that the electors might exercise a choice. In practice, electors pledge to support the party and candidate chosen by the majority of voters in their state.

In other words, in order to be elected president or vice president, a candidate must receive a majority of all the electoral votes cast. If no candidate receives a majority, it is up to the House of Representatives to choose the president from among the three candidates receiving the highest number of electoral votes. For this purpose each state has one vote; for the House to make a choice, a majority of states must agree on one candidate. When no candidate for vice president receives a majority, the Senate chooses the vice president from the two highest-ranked candidates. Each senator has one vote; to win, a candidate must receive a majority of the votes cast in the Senate.

Again, in practice, especially after the Twelfth Amendment took hold, the presidential electors are chosen through the political parties. Each party in each state nominates a slate of presidential electors for that state. In most states this means that the voters choose one party's slate over another's; the result is that one party wins all of the state's electoral votes. An exception to this practice developed in the states of Maine and Nebraska; they choose their electors through a proportional voting system. This means that the electoral vote for those two states can be split between contending parties and candidates. The choosing of electors by slates makes it difficult for a third party to challenge the major parties, unless it has strength across a number of states. The Twelfth Amendment did not lock in this result but, over the years, it made it more likely in practice as major parties contended for political power.

In recent decades arguments have been made to do away with the Electoral College and have voters vote directly for presidents and vice presidents. Such arguments gained prominence following the election of 2000. In that election, one candidate (Al Gore) won the popular vote (by 543,895, or 0.51 percent) while another (George W. Bush) won the Electoral College vote (by five votes). Under the provisions of the Constitution, Bush became president (after a contest in the Supreme Court regarding faulty ballots in

The Twelfth Amendment, which clarifies the role of the vice-president in counting electoral votes, was formalized by Congress in 1887. In the 2020 election, Donald Trump refused to accept the results and called on Vice-President Mike Pence to not certify the votes. Despite threats of violence, Pence upheld the law and the certification of Joe Biden as president proceeded. Photo via Wikimedia Commons. [Public domain.]

Florida). A similar outcome was produced in the election of 2016. Hillary Rodham Clinton won the popular vote (by 2,848,090, or 2.1 percent) but Donald J. Trump won the electoral vote (by seventy-four votes). Again, critics advocated eliminating the Electoral College and relying solely on the outcome of the popular vote. Others have proposed giving each party the same proportion of a state's electoral vote that it receives of the state's popular vote. A third option supported by some is to elect individual presidential electors in each congressional district and two electors-at-large in each state. That is the system used by Maine and Nebraska, which results in split Electoral College votes rather than "winner-take-all" results.

The present system gives disproportionate weight to the smaller, less populous states, as it was intended to do by the Founding Fathers in order to balance out the weight of the larger, more populace states. Because these same small states would need to ratify any constitutional change, it seems unlikely that the Electoral College will be abolished anytime soon.

One provision of the Twelfth Amendment, that concerning the "count" of votes conducted by the vice president serving in his or her role as president of the Senate, was clarified by Congress in 1887, ten years after the disputed election of 1876. The Electoral Count Act of 1887 formalized the counting procedure in terms of deadlines that electoral votes from the states were to be submitted by and the procedures to be used in certifying the vote. It remained uncontroversial until the election of 2020. In that election, Donald Trump refused to admit defeat to Joe Biden and worked to undo the results of the election. One of Trump's tactics was to call on his vice president, Mike

Pence, to *not* certify the results by performing the standard count. Pence, for his part, said he would follow the Constitution. On the day the certification was to take place, January 6, 2021, violent Trump supporters outside the Capitol shouted "Hang Mike Pence!" and erected a mock gallows. The official count was interrupted that day by these same protestors, who breached the Capitol Building and made threats to lawmakers who participated in the certification process. After the violent incident was quelled, the count proceeded and Joe Biden was declared president.

As a result of the January 6 incident, proposals were made in Congress to further shore-up the provision regarding the electoral count, to make certain that it could not be interpreted as being anything but a straightforward count as mandated by the Twelfth Amendment. (The new law also addressed the matter of "slates" of electors and the issue of "alternative slates" as advocated by unofficial Trump "electors.") The result of the January 6 controversy was the Electoral Count Reform and Presidential Transition Improvement Act, passed in 2022 and signed into law that same year. (*See* article on same in the present volume.)

—Michael Shally-Jensen, PhD

Bibliography and Additional Reading

Congressional Research Service. *The Electoral College: How It Works in Contemporary Presidential Elections.* Washington, DC: CRS, 2024.

Delahunty, Robert J., and John Yoo. "Who Counts? The Twelfth Amendment, the Vice President, and the Electoral College." *Case Western Reserve Law Review* 73, no. 1 (2022): 27–138.

Kuroda, Tadahisa. *The Origins of the Twelfth Amendment: The Electoral College in the Early Republic, 1787–1804.* Westport, CT: Praeger, 1994.

Muller, Derek T. "The President of the Senate, the Original Public Meaning of the Twelfth Amendment, and the Electoral Count Reform Act." *Case Western Reserve Law Review* 73, no. 4 (2023): 1023–1046.

Toller, Eric T. "A More Perfect Electoral College: Challenging Winner-Take-All Provisions under the Twelfth Amendment." *Legislation & Policy Brief* 9, no. 1 (2020): 4–36.

■ The "People's Constitution" and Dorr's Rebellion

Date: 1841–1842
Author: Thomas Wilson Dorr
Genre: constitution document

Summary Overview

In the 1840s, Rhode Island witnessed a period of violence over the extension of suffrage to disenfranchised male citizens. Because voting rights up to this period were still tied to land ownership, many men were barred from voting in state elections. (Nonwhite men and all women were barred completely.) Under the leadership of Thomas William Dorr, these disenfranchised voters set about to seize power from a landed elite that had come to dominate Rhode Island state politics. In 1841, the reformers held a convention and issued a constitution that precipitated a violent conflict between Dorr's followers and state forces. In the end, the rebellion led to Rhode Island adopting a new constitution in 1843 that extended voting rights in the state.

Defining Moment

As late as the mid-nineteenth century, Rhode Island continued to use its 1663 colonial charter as its governing document, requiring that voters own land and giving sparsely populated farming communities the same amount of governmental representation as those in cities. Yet, in the years since the earlier era, Rhode Island had witnessed a gradual reduction in the size of the landed class as the state became more urbanized with population centers like Providence growing at a rapid pace. In addition, an immigrant class attracted to factory work and predominately living on tenements did not own any land. Thus, while aristocratic landowners(who paid a hefty tax to the state) felt that they were entitled to control the Rhode Island government, many other men resented that they had been barred from the political process.

Most other states had by this time done away with property requirements in order to vote, but attempts at reform in Rhode Island had been unsuccessful. The Rhode Island General Assembly, made up of landed men in the state, refused to amend the charter (which some believed to be unconstitutional in itself, since it was signed by the British monarch). In response, state representative Thomas William Dorr led a diverse group of laborers and reformers, dubbed

Thomas W. Dorr from an 1844 book's frontispiece. Image via Wikimedia Commons. [Public domain.]

A polemic applauding Democratic support of the Dorrite cause in Rhode Island, 1844. Image via Wikimedia Commons. [Public domain.]

"Dorrites," in a campaign to have the charter changed and a new constitution adopted.

In 1841, Rhode Island suffragists held their own constitutional convention and tasked Dorr with drafting the People's Constitution. The new constitution expanded the right to vote in the state and was met with a positive response. In December 1841, the Dorrites organized a statewide referendum in which newly eligible voters approved the new constitution. Still, the standing government chose not to recognize the results of the referendum, and political chaos ensued.

Author Biography

Born in Providence, Rhode Island, Thomas Wilson Dorr (1805–1854) was a lawyer and politician. After graduating from Harvard College and studying law in New York City, he returned to his home state to practice law. Dorr was elected to the Rhode Island General Assembly in 1834. During the rebellion, he spent periods of time in exile from Rhode Island. Following these events, Dorr returned to the state in October 1843 and was charged with treason. Handed down a life sentence in 1844, Dorr served only part of the sentence and was released the next year.

Historical Document

Citizens of Rhode—Island! Read! Mark! learn! From the following extract from Article 2d of the so called "People's Constitution," it will be seen who have and who have not a right to vote under that Constitution ... Providence, Feb. 18, 1842.

"Of Electors and the Right of Suffrage.

"1. Every white male citizen of the United States, of the age of twenty-one years, who has resided in this State for one year, and, in the town, city, or district where he offers to vote, for three months, next preceding an election, shall be an elector of all officers, who are elected, or may hereafter be made eligible by the People. But persons in the military, naval, or marine service of the United States shall not be considered as having such established residence, by being stationed in any garrison, barrack, or military place, in any town or city in this State.

"2. Paupers and persons under guardianship, insane, or lunatic are excluded from the electoral right; and the same shall be forfeited on conviction of bribery, forgery, perjury, theft, or other infamous crime; and shall not be restored unless by an act of the General Assembly."

The other provisions relative to Suffrage in this Constitution are unimportant, and are substantially the same as those in the other Constitution.

Under the provisions of the so called "People's Constitution," the whole body of naturalized foreigners in this State, amounting to several THOUSANDS, are placed on an equality with our native-born citizens; and at every election they will be sure to outvote them. In other words, the foreign population of the State will govern the State, and they will govern it in all time! Does any man desire such a state of things in Rhode Island!

[Source: www.loc.gov/static/js/lib/pdf-2.6-es5/web/viewer.html?file=https://tile.loc.gov/storage-services/service/rbc/rbpe/rbpe16/rbpe169/16901000/16901000.pdf]

Document Analysis

The People's Constitution focuses on the concept of liberty and adapts many of the tenets of the United States Constitution, specifically guaranteeing free education and representation based on population. In the section excerpted here, the land ownership requirement is rescinded in favor of a one-year residency in the state for white male citizens. At the convention, Dorr disagreed with this provision, intending to fight for both white and black men's right to vote. His followers, however, eventually overruled him, promising to address the matter at the anticipated first meeting of the People's Legislature. Black suffragists eventually sided with the landed class in opposing Dorr's aims during this period.

This section also focuses on residency in the state as a guarantee to vote, including for natural- and foreign-born citizens. "Naturalized foreigners" are given special mention by Dorr in this section for being a sizeable group worthy of having the power to vote. And Dorr in fact claims that they will outvote natural-born citizens in the state. The growing population of predominately Irish immigrants was centered in cities, where they worked in factories. This class came to outgrow Rhode Islanders working on farms in rural communities, who had an affinity with the aristocratic class who owned the land worked by these citizens.

One key takeaway from this section on voting rights is that the Dorrites are not aiming at universal suffrage. Black people and women still had not gained the right to vote in the United States, and the Dorrites focus a sizeable portion of the text on who is barred from voting: those on military deployment in the state, the mentally ill, criminals, and other supposed reprobates. This exclusion no doubt is intended to persuade more Rhode Islanders to the reasonableness of the provisions included in the new constitution, clearly reflected in its popularity in the initial referendum in 1841.

Essential Themes

The charter government did not sanction the Convention's new constitution, and in April 1842 Rhode Island held two separate elections. Dorr was elected governor under the People's Constitution, while Samuel Ward King was elected under the state charter. Viewing the Dorrites skeptically, the state subsequently decided to arrest the leaders of the competing government. In response, Dorr chose to take up arms, encouraging his followers that violent resistance was the only means to combat what they saw as an attack on their newly adopted rights. The state sought to put down the rebellion by assembling its military forces.

The subsequent conflict lasted several months. In May, after stealing cannons from a military outpost, Dorr led a small force against the state arsenal in Providence. Following his forces' defeat there, and seeing no alternative, Dorr went into exile in New York. In July, he returned to Rhode Island with another small group of men to reconvene the rebellion's legislature. With a force sent against the Dorrites by Governor King, Dorr disbanded his forces and again fled the state, realizing that he could not win.

Still, the suffrage movement in Rhode Island gained steam and the state soon drafted a new constitution that was enacted in May 1843. Under the new constitution, any man born in the state gained the right to vote as long as he could pay a poll tax, a $1 provision that greatly expanded voting in the state. Importantly, this provision extended the right to vote to both black and white Rhode Islanders, but the landholding requirement still applied to immigrants.

The People's Constitution and subsequent rebellion presaged many of the political issues that would come to define the nineteenth century as the country raced toward civil war. Though the Dorrites were not overtly concerned with slavery, their debates while drafting the constitution centered on liberty and equality, issues that would come to the fore in the abolition movement. In fact, the enfranchisement of black men in the 1843 constitution was the first of its kind in the United States. Finally, whether citizens had the right to disband their current government and form a new one would also be a central matter as southern states seceded during the American Civil War period.

—*Chris Bingley, PhD*

Bibliography and Additional Reading

Chaput, Erik J. *The People's Martyr: Thomas Wilson Dorr and His 1842 Rhode Island Rebellion.* Lawrence: UP of Kansas, 2013.

Gettleman, Marvin E. *The Dorr Rebellion: A Study in American Radicalism, 1833–1849.* New York: Random House, 1973.

Raven, Rory. *The Dorr War: Treason, Rebellion, and the Fight for Reform in Rhode Island.* Charleston, SC: Arcadia Publishing, 2015.

■ Henry David Thoreau: "Civil Disobedience"

Date: 1849
Author: Thoreau, Henry David
Genre: essay

Summary Overview

The writer and philosopher Henry David Thoreau is known for a number of works on different subjects. Walden (1854), a meditation on nature and living, is perhaps his most famous work. Another notable writing of Thoreau's is the essay "Civil Disobedience" (1849), excerpted here. Originally titled "Resistance to Civil Government," the piece describes the natural propensity of governments to act in unethical ways, the need for individuals to be vigilant critics of government actions, and, most important, the idea that righteous people should not participate in the workings of unrighteous governments. In Thoreau's account, civil disobedience occurs when speaking out or voting in opposition are inadequate—or when the vote is barred to you.

The essay arose out of the following circumstances. On July 23, 1846, during a sojourn to the isolated Walden Pond, Thoreau walked into Concord, Massachusetts, to get his shoe fixed. He ran into the local law-enforcement official, Sam Staples, who was in charge of collecting taxes. Thoreau owed six years of outstanding poll taxes—i.e., taxes levied on all individuals within a town or district and usually required to be paid before voting. He had chosen not to pay the tax as a way of protesting the fact that slavery remained legal in part of the United States. When Thoreau again refused to pay the poll tax, restating his opposition to slavery and saying that he was also disgusted by the Mexican-American War, Staples placed him under arrest and put him in jail.

Thoreau was bailed out the following day, against his will, possibly by his aunt. However, the experience left a mark on the author. For the next few years, he delivered spoken addresses about the matter. "Resistance to Civil Government" was published in 1849. After Thoreau's death the title was changed to "Civil Disobedience," to reflect the common understanding of the subject.

Defining Moment

Although Henry David Thoreau was clearly a man of great inspiration, acting from a strong sense of iconoclastic creativity, he was also a product of his times. Events on an international, national, and regional scale helped to shape his personal character and the

Henry David Thoreau. Photo via Wikimedia Commons. [Public domain.]

content of his work. Understanding these forces is the key to making sense of Thoreau as a person and an author and appreciating what "Resistance to Civil Government" meant to him.

The Industrial Revolution, which began in the middle of the eighteenth century, had dramatically transformed American and European society by the mid-nineteenth century, when Thoreau did the bulk of his writing. It shifted the base of the economy from agricultural to manufacturing activities and led to a large-scale movement of people from rural to urban settings. While most people of his day had a purely positive view of the Industrial Revolution's impact, Thoreau was more critical in his reactions to it. He was concerned that people were growing out of touch with the power of nature and the ways of life associated with traditional agrarian rural communities, which he considered to be healthier and more authentic than those that came from living in large cities.

He shared these atypical beliefs with another important writer in the region, Ralph Waldo Emerson (1803–82). Beginning around 1836, Emerson gained fame as a touring lecturer in the northeastern United States. He expounded on a loosely congruous set of topics, including the divine character of nature, the importance of individual creativity, and the superiority of rural life to urban life. This general philosophy came to be known as transcendentalism. As a young man, freshly graduated from Harvard and working as a schoolteacher, Thoreau became close friends with Emerson, and he lived with Emerson's family on and off through much of his adult life. Thoreau's inclusion in the circle of philosophers, essayists, and poets who published the transcendentalist journal the *Dial* must be considered one of the great influences on his writing career.

At the same time, Thoreau was more frankly political than many other transcendentalists, and he was always known to be concerned about the key issues of his day. He developed the ideas expressed in "Resistance to Civil Government" after being briefly jailed in 1846 for refusing six years of outstanding poll tax. He claimed he did so as a protest against slavery and the Mexican-American War.

The northeastern states banned slavery in the decades after the Revolutionary War, but it remained a thriving and lucrative institution in the South until the Emancipation Proclamation of 1863. Thoreau's was among an increasing number of Northern voices calling for a federal ban on slavery, and in his later life, he supported controversial antislavery activists such as John Brown, who led slaves in a violent rebellion against proslavery white Southerners.

Thoreau was staunchly against the Mexican-American War, which lasted from 1846 to 1848, from its outset. The war was fundamentally a dispute over where the borders of the two countries should be drawn, especially in Texas. It was opposed by many Americans, particularly in the North. Abolitionists considered the American incursion into Mexico to be a ploy by Southern proslavery activists to expand the area of legalized slavery in the United States. Many others simply felt it was an unnecessary act of aggression, and costly in terms of American lives and resources.

Author Biography

Henry David Thoreau was born as David Henry Thoreau on July 12, 1817. His parents, John Thoreau and Cynthia Dunbar, were of modest financial means, as his father worked as a pencil manufacturer. However, the Thoreau family enjoyed a good reputation for hard work and honesty in their Concord, Massachusetts, community.

Thoreau was a keen student in his early years, and he drew attention to himself for his wit and intellect at Concord Academy. After secondary school, he began his studies at Harvard College, which he attended from 1833 to 1837. After graduating from Harvard, he became a schoolteacher at a public school in Concord. He soon found that he did not agree with administering corporal punishment to misbehaving students as directed by his superiors and resigned from his post in protest. In the following years, he worked alongside his brother John in an alternative private school in Concord. His brother died of tetanus after cutting himself shaving, and this tragedy deeply impacted Thoreau.

During this time, Henry David Thoreau, as he was now calling himself, became acquainted with several members of the locally flourishing transcendentalist movement, including the patriarch of the philosophy, Ralph Waldo Emerson. Emerson became convinced of the younger man's literary talent and encouraged him to write essays for the transcendentalist journal the *Dial*. Starting with an initial essay in 1840, Thoreau soon became a favorite contributor to the periodical. Thoreau grew very close to Emerson and lived with his family from 1841 to1843, both in Massachusetts and at Emerson's brother's home on Staten Island, New York. Thoreau became a tutor and caretaker for Emerson's children, as well as a sort of groundskeeper for the Emerson estates.

In 1843, Thoreau returned to his hometown of Concord and took over the family pencil-manufacturing business, which he ran on and off for the rest of his life. However, he continued to take sojourns to pursue his writing and lecturing interests. The most famous of these took place from 1845 to 1847, when he moved to a small cabin on the edge of Walden Pond and built a cabin on land owned by Emerson. This experience, which Thoreau considered a great experiment in simple living away from society, resulted in the celebrated *Walden*, eventually published in 1854.

During his stay at Walden Pond, Thoreau had an altercation with the law when a tax collector demanded that he pay six years of delinquent poll taxes. Thoreau refused, saying that he was opposed to slavery and the Mexican-American War, and was thrown in jail for the night of July 23, 1846. Although he was freed when his aunt paid the taxes without his knowledge, the arrest shaped Thoreau's political opinions, which he expressed in a series of lectures and papers. These thoughts were ultimately published as the essay "Resistance to Civil Government" in 1849.

Thoreau moved back to Concord in the autumn of 1847. He first lived at the Emerson's home but had two subsequent homes of his own in town. For the decade of the 1850s, Thoreau ran his family's pencil-manufacturing business. He occasionally traveled throughout the northeastern United States and Canada to give popular lectures and pursue his passionate interest in the natural history of the region.

Henry David Thoreau died on May 6, 1862, finally succumbing to complications from tuberculosis, which he had contracted decades earlier in college. He is remembered as one of the leading voices in early American literature. As a poet, essayist, and social activist, he gave voice to a philosophical radicalism developing in the New England region in the middle of the nineteenth century. Like his close friend Ralph Waldo Emerson, Thoreau used his prowess as a writer and speaker to challenge the status quo of New England society and encourage new ways of understanding what it meant to be American.

Historical Document

"Resistance to Civil Government"

I heartily accept the motto, "That government is best which governs least"; and I should like to see it acted up to more rapidly and systematically. Carried out, it finally amounts to this, which also I believe—"That government is best which governs not at all"; and when men are prepared for it, that will be the kind of government which they will have. Government is at best but an expedient; but most governments are usually, and all governments are sometimes, inexpedient. The objections which have been brought against a standing army, and they are many and weighty, and deserve to prevail, may also at last be brought against a standing government. The standing army is only an arm of the standing government. The government itself, which is only the mode which the people have chosen to execute their will, is equally liable to be abused and perverted before the people can act through it. Witness the present Mexican war, the work of comparatively a few individuals using the standing government as their tool; for in the outset, the people would not have consented to this measure.

This American government—what is it but a tradition, though a recent one, endeavoring to transmit itself unimpaired to posterity, but each instant losing some of its integrity? It has not the vitality and force of a single living man; for a single man can bend it to his will. It is a sort of wooden gun to the people themselves. But it is not the less necessary for this; for the people must have some complicated machinery or other, and hear its din, to satisfy that idea of government which they have. Governments show thus how successfully men can be imposed upon, even impose on themselves, for their own advantage. It is excellent, we must all allow. Yet this government never of itself furthered any enterprise, but by the alacrity with which it got out of its way. It does not keep the country free. It does not settle the West. It does not educate. The character inherent in the American people has done all that has been accomplished; and it would have done somewhat more, if the government had not sometimes got in its way. For government is an expedient, by which men would fain succeed in letting one another alone; and, as has been said, when it is most expedient, the governed are most let alone by it. Trade and commerce, if they were not made of india-rubber, would never manage to bounce over obstacles which legislators are continually putting in their way; and if one were to judge these men wholly by the effects of their actions and not partly by their intentions, they would deserve to be classed and punished with those mischievous persons who put obstructions on the railroads.

But, to speak practically and as a citizen, unlike those who call themselves no-government men, I ask for, not at once no govern-ment, but at once a better government. Let every man make known what kind of government would command his respect, and that will be one step toward obtaining it.

After all, the practical reason why, when the power is once in the hands of the people, a majority are permitted, and for a long period continue, to rule is not because they are most likely to be in the right, nor because this seems fairest to the minority, but because they are physically the strongest. But a government in which the majority rule in all cases cannot be based on justice, even as far as men understand it. Can there not be a government in which the majorities do not virtually decide right and wrong, but conscience?—in which majorities decide only those questions to which the rule of expediency is applicable? Must the citizen ever for a moment, or in the least degree, resign his conscience to the legislator? Why has every man a conscience then? I think that we should be men first, and subjects afterward. It is not desirable to cultivate a respect for the law, so much as for the right. The only obligation which I have a right to assume is to do at any time what I think right. . . .

The mass of men serve the state thus, not as men mainly, but as machines, with their bodies. They are the standing army, and the militia, jailers, constables, posse comitatus, etc. In most cases there is no free exercise whatever of the judgment or of the moral sense; but they put themselves on a level with wood and earth and stones; and wooden men can perhaps be manufactured that will serve the purpose as well. Such command no more respect than men of straw or a lump of dirt. They have the same sort of worth only as horses and dogs. Yet such as these even are commonly esteemed good citizens. Others—as most legislators, politicians, lawyers, ministers, and office-holders—serve the state chiefly with their heads; and, as the rarely make any moral distinctions, they are as likely to serve the devil, without intending it, as God. A very few—as heroes, patriots, martyrs, reformers in the great sense, and men—serve the state with their consciences also, and so necessarily resist it for the most part; and they are commonly treated as enemies by it. A wise man will only be useful as a man, and will not submit to be "clay," and "stop a hole to keep the wind away," but leave that office to his dust at least:

"I am too high-born to be propertied,
To be a second at control,
Or useful serving-man and instrument
To any sovereign state throughout the world."

He who gives himself entirely to his fellow men appears to them useless and selfish; but he who gives himself partially to them in pronounced a benefactor and philanthropist.

How does it become a man to behave toward the American government today? I answer, that he cannot without disgrace be associated with it. I cannot for an instant recognize that political organization as my government which is the slave's government also.

All men recognize the right of revolution; that is, the right to refuse allegiance to, and to resist, the government, when its tyranny or its inefficiency are great and unendurable. But almost all say that such is not the case now. But such was the case, they think, in the Revolution of '75. If one were to tell me that this was a bad government because it taxed certain foreign commodities brought to its ports, it is most probable that I should not make an ado about it, for I can do without them. All machines have their friction; and possibly this does enough good to counter-balance the evil. At any rate, it is a great evil to make a stir about it. But when the friction comes to have its machine, and oppression and robbery are organized, I say, let us not have such a machine any longer. In other words, when a sixth of the population of a nation which has undertaken to be the refuge of liberty are slaves, and a whole country is unjustly overrun and conquered by a foreign army, and subjected to military law, I think that it is not too soon for honest men to rebel and revolutionize. What makes this duty the more urgent is that fact that the country so overrun is not our own, but ours is the invading army. . . .

Practically speaking, the opponents to a reform in Massachusetts are not a hundred thousand politicians at the South, but a hundred thousand merchants and farmers here, who are more interested in commerce and agriculture than they are in humanity, and are not prepared to do justice to the slave and to Mexico, cost what it may. I quarrel not with far-off foes, but with those who, neat at home, co-operate with, and do the bidding of, those far away, and without whom the latter would be harmless. We are accustomed to say, that the mass of men are unprepared; but improvement is slow, because the few are not as materially wiser or better than the many. It is not so important that many should be good as you, as that there be some absolute goodness somewhere; for that will leaven the whole lump. There are thousands who are in opinion opposed to slavery and to the war, who yet in effect do nothing to put an end to them; who, esteeming themselves children of Washington and Franklin, sit down with their hands in their pockets, and say that they know not what to do, and do nothing; who even postpone the question of freedom to the question of free trade, and quietly read the prices-current along with the latest advices from Mexico, after dinner, and, it may be, fall asleep over them both. What is the price-current of an honest man and patriot today? They hesitate, and they regret, and sometimes they petition; but they do nothing in earnest and with effect. They will wait, well disposed, for other to remedy the evil that they may no longer have it to regret. At most, they give up only a cheap vote, and a feeble countenance and Godspeed, to the right, as it goes by them. There are nine hundred and ninety-nine patrons of virtue to one virtuous man. But it is easier to deal with the real possessor of a thing than with the temporary guardian of it.

All voting is a sort of gaming, like checkers or backgammon, with a slight moral tinge to it, a playing with right and wrong, with moral questions; and betting naturally accompanies it. The character of the voters is not staked. I cast my vote, perchance, as I think right; but I am not vitally concerned that that right should prevail. I am willing to leave it to the majority. Its obligation, therefore, never exceeds that of expediency. Even voting for the right is doing nothing for it. It is only expressing to men feebly your desire that it should prevail. A wise man will not leave the right to the mercy of chance, nor wish it to prevail through the power of the majority. There is but little virtue in the action of masses of men. When the majority shall at length vote for the abolition of slavery, it will be because they are indifferent to slavery, or because there is but little slavery left to be abolished by their vote. They will then be the only slaves. Only his vote can hasten the abolition of slavery who asserts his own freedom by his vote. . . .

Under a government which imprisons unjustly, the true place for a just man is also in prison. The proper place today, the only place which Massachusetts has provided for her freer and less desponding spirits, is in her prisons, to be put out and locked out of the State by her own act, as they have already put themselves out by their principles. It is there that the fugitive slave, and the Mexican prisoner on parole, and the Indian come to plead the wrongs of his race, should find them; on that separate, but more free and honorable ground, where the State places those who are not with her, but against her,—the only house in a slave State in which a free man can abide with honor. If any think that their influence would be lost there, and their voices no longer afflict the ear of the State, that they would not be as an enemy within its walls, they do not know by how much truth is stronger than error, nor how much more eloquently and effectively he can combat injustice who has experienced a little in his own person. Cast your whole vote, not a strip of paper merely, but your whole influence. A minority is powerless while it conforms to the majority; it is not even a minority then; but it is irresistible when it clogs by its whole weight. If the alternative is to keep all just men in prison, or give up war and slavery, the State will not hesitate which to choose. If a thousand men were not to pay their tax bills this year that would not be a violent and bloody measure, as it would be to pay them, and enable the State to commit violence and shed innocent blood. This is, in fact, the definition of a peaceable revolution, if any such is possible. If the tax-gatherer, or any other public officer, asks me, as one has done, "But what shall I do?" my answer is, "If you really wish to do anything, resign your office." When the subject has refused allegiance, and the officer has resigned his office, then the revolution is accomplished. But even suppose blood should flow. Is there not a sort of blood shed when the conscience is wounded? Through this wound a man's real manhood and immortality flow out, and he bleeds to an everlasting death. I see this blood flowing now.

Glossary

constable: a local law-enforcement officer similar to a sheriff

expedient: something that serves a purpose or makes a course of action easier

posse comitatus: a local militia force

Revolution of '75: an early nineteenth-century way of referring to the American Revolutionary War, which in fact began in 1775

standing army: a military that exists even in times of peace

Document Analysis

The first line of "Resistance to Civil Disobedience" is clearly its most famous. Specifically, the quoted phrase, "That government is best which governs least," is remembered as most forcefully communicating the point of the essay. The origin of this quote is unclear, however. It is commonly considered to be a phrase coined by Thomas Jefferson, but this has not been documented by historians. It may be the case that the phrase was attributed without evidence to Jefferson in Thoreau's day, just as it is now, and Thoreau believed that he was in fact quoting the author of the Declaration of Independence, even if he was incorrect in this belief.

Whatever the authenticity of this alleged Jefferson quote, Thoreau is clearly using it as a response to his friend Ralph Waldo Emerson. In an 1844 essay entitled "Politics," Emerson stated, "The less government we have the better." Although Thoreau was a more outspoken political activist, the theme of mistrust of government was a staple of transcendentalist philosophy, since government control was antithetical to individual freedom.

In the next several passages, Thoreau states the point even more forcefully, saying, "That government is best which governs not at all." Although he writes the phrase as though as though he is quoting an outside source again, this line is clearly of his own invention. He goes on to explain his position, saying that the whole point of government is that it is supposed to make life easier for its citizens, but in reality it makes life more difficult.

Next, he relates that there is a controversy about governments having standing armies. Many Americans of his day were opposed to such a military institution, preferring that a suitable military be formed to meet challenges as they occurred and disbanded when these challenges passed. Thoreau argues that it is equally unnecessary to have a standing government that continues to exist even in times when it is not required by the people of the nation.

Thoreau couches his main objection to a standing government in the observation that it can be "abused and perverted" by people with special interests. He gives the example of the Mexican-American War, which was largely unpopular, especially in the North. Many abolitionists considered it to be driven by the Southern slaveholding lobby, which sought to create a larger Southern zone in which slavery was legal and thereby increase their power on a national level. According to Thoreau, the Mexican-American War would not have occurred except that "a few individuals using the standing government as their tool" forced it on the American people.

He continues by saying that the American government, a relatively new institution, is changing in character, shifting from merely reflecting the will of the people to imposing its own will on the people. Thoreau passionately exclaims that it is not government that keeps people free, pushes the western frontier, and educates the citizens. These achievements, he argues, must be acknowledged as the achievements of the American people themselves.

He next takes a more economic approach to furthering his argument against government. According to Thoreau, the American government has recently imposed so many complicated regulations on trade that it is a wonder that commerce has continued at all. The author contends that if they were to be judged on the actual impact of their actions rather than their good intentions, the men who drafted the laws concerning trade would be found to be criminally obstructive.

In the following section of the essay, Thoreau significantly tempers the tone of his argument. He steps back from his radically anarchistic position, saying that he knows it is not actually possible for the nation to exist without any government at all. As a responsible citizen, then, what he is truly calling for is for his fellow Americans to demand a better government than the one that is currently developing.

Notably, he is against the idea of a government acting based solely on the will of the majority of its citizens. Such a system, he explains, will not automatically result in a government that makes the right decisions. Such a government will often commit injustices against the minorities within the nation. The only way to prevent a government ruled by majority opinion from becoming a destructive force is for all of the citizens who shape the actions of the government to always listen to their consciences when making decisions that impact their fellow Americans. Law alone, Thoreau, states, will not make people act better toward one another; that can only come from people individually acting according to a well-developed sense of morality.

Thoreau points out that one result of too much blind adherence to the law is unthinking militarism. When men do what they think is expected of them by their government, rather than what they know to be right, they become part of a dehumanizing military machine. Even though the men assembled in a military procession are alive, they may as well be ready to be buried with military ceremony. Thoreau caps off his point by quoting a famous dirge by the poet Charles Wolfe (1791–1823) entitled "The Burial of Sir John Moore after Corruna," which is about the British fighting the French in Spain in 1809. Men who serve out of a sense of duty to the state, whether in the army and navy or as constables or jailers, are of no more actual value, according to Thoreau, than dogs or horses.

Other people serve with their minds rather than with their bodies. Instead of serving in a military capacity, these people act as lawyers and politicians. They are just as likely, in Thoreau's view, to unintentionally do evil, even if they perceive themselves as doing good for the country.

Only rarely do people who truly deserve respect participate in the functioning of the state. Indeed, people who are honest and true to their own sense of morality will soon find that they have a difficult time remaining in office, since many within the government will have disdain for them and consider them enemies of the state. However, these are the true "heroes, patriots," and "martyrs." Thoreau again uses a literary allusion to underscore his point, this time quoting Shakespeare's play *King John*, in which the king's son Lewis proclaims, "I am too high born to be propertied, / To be a secondary at control, / Or useful serving-man and instrument, / To any sovereign state throughout the world."

Thoreau then rhetorically asks how a righteous person should interact with the government. He responds by saying that a decent person should not participate at all in the government, since it is also the government that allows the institution of slavery to continue. Although Americans recognized the right to rebel against the British government during the Revolutionary War, many of Thoreau's readers would not have thought revolution appropriate at this juncture. Thoreau argues that it is worth contemplating revolutionary change because the current government keeps a sixth of its population enslaved and acts like an occupying army toward the rest of its citizens.

In the section of the essay that follows, Thoreau directly responds to the ideas of an English Enlightenment philosopher named William Paley (1743–1805). In several essays that appeared in his 1785 tome *Principles of Moral and Political Philosophy*, Paley put forth the argument that it is God's will that a government be obeyed as long as it is acting in the interest of the overall society. As a utilitarian philosopher, Paley believed that the benefits of a government should be measured by how it benefits the majority of its citizens. Thoreau takes issue with this mode of judging actions, saying that even if the acts of a government are good for the majority of people, they can still be morally wrong if they negatively impact some of the people in the governed society. The examples he gives of this, not surprisingly, are slavery and the Mexican-American War.

The reality is, Thoreau states, that the reason that slavery continues and the Mexican-American War is being fought is not only because the Southern slaveholders are protecting their interests but also because the far larger number of Northern merchants simply do not want to hobble their own incomes by disrupting farming or trade by pressing for emancipation. Even though the majority of people might be against slavery or the war in theoretical terms, they are unwilling to risk their own temporary well-being by taking principled stands against the immoral institutions of slavery and aggressive wars. In Thoreau's view, there are simply far too few real patriots willing to act to make America a true land of freedom.

Thoreau cautions against putting too much faith in the ballot. He compares voting to a kind of gambling or gaming, with voters placing bets on the side they think will win. Although it has some elements of moral judgment, is it a weak substitute, in Thoreau's view, for people actually voicing their opinions about the issues of the day. He even goes so far as to say that voting is actually doing nothing.

Thoreau clarifies that he does not intend this essay to mean that it is the responsibility of every good person to singlehandedly take on all the moral wrongs of the day. Instead, what he means is that decent people must find a way to avoid participating in the immoral acts, directly or indirectly. As he says, he knows many people who would not serve if ordered to fight in Mexico or put down a slave rebellion, yet still willingly pay their taxes, thus sending people in their place to commit these immoral acts. Instead of seeking to dissolve the government, Thoreau advocates that people of conscience dissolve the connections between themselves and an immoral government.

It is not enough, Thoreau continues, for people merely to have opinions on political matters; they must act. He states as fact that there are unjust laws, then asks his audience to think about the best way to proceed in such a context. Should a person follow unfair laws, speak out against them but continue to obey them, or simply break them? For Thoreau, the last option is clearly the right choice.

Not participating in the operation of an unjust government seems to Thoreau to be the strategy that most confounds those within it. This is evidenced, in his opinion, by the state's eagerness to indefinitely jail even a very poor man if he does not pay his taxes to the government. Meanwhile, the government barely does anything to those people who siphon off government funds for private gain, allowing them to remain free.

In a metaphor that he repeats throughout the essay, Thoreau compares the government to a machine. He says that injustice may indeed be the friction of the machine. If that is the case, he advises, it is best to simply disengage from it. There is a chance that the machine itself may "wear smooth," and it will definitely "wear out" in time. In fact, it may be best to work to stop the machine if the injustice is too great to tolerate.

Thoreau asserts that it is not up to an individual to do everything to improve the world. However, it is necessary for decent people to do something to work for a better future. He is dismissive of the possibility that there are ways of working within the government to make this happen, stating that the entire basis of the government is flawed.

He next suggests a specific course of action for abolitionists living in the state of Massachusetts, saying that if they wish to end the institution of slavery in the United States, they should effectively cut off their involvement with the government on all levels, starting with the state government. Thoreau writes that the only way that he ever encounters the state government is in the person of the tax collector, so it is against this person that he must struggle for freedom from a corrupt government. Even though it might seem like a very small act of conscience, Thoreau proposes that all true revolutions start in this way, with a single determined individual acting in a morally upright manner.

Thoreau next puts forth his famous argument that the only true place for an honest man living in a society ruled by an unjust government is in prison. He explains that incarceration is the main tactic that the state knows to use to combat those who are against it, and anyone who honestly opposes the immoral actions of the state should be willing to be arrested. He asserts that being locked up as a prisoner of conscience is a way to clog up the prison system and convince those people charged with administering the functions of the state that they should quit their positions.

Thoreau envisions this as a nonviolent revolutionary tactic. However, he is quick to point out that he is not altogether opposed to the use of violence in reforming the government. He argues that it is a kind of violence to make people live contrary to their consciences, and this kind of metaphorical bloodshed is already taking place.

After acknowledging that the state sometimes chooses to take away property instead of incarcerating individuals who do not pay tax, Thoreau segues into a brief but powerful discussion of wealth in general. Overall, he believes, wealth is a corrupting force. As he puts it, "the more money, the less virtue," meaning that people of economic means often forget the importance of living according to their principles as they accumulate wealth by working within a corrupt state.

Thoreau devotes a significant portion of the essay to recounting his own experience with not paying taxes. He first mentions that he refused to pay a tax that was being collected on behalf of the church. Although the tax man threatened him with jail if he did not pay, Thoreau wrote a letter to the town clerk stating that he did not wish to be known as a member of the church and that he would not pay any taxes to it.

The next incident Thoreau describes is his far more famous run-in with the law over his refusal to pay poll taxes for six years. He says that during the night he spent in jail, he did not feel constrained and in fact considered himself to be freer than the people on the outside. He recounts how he talked at length with his cellmate, learning all he could about the people who had previously dwelt within the cell, and was surprised to learn what a rich history the modest jail cell had. He describes it as a lot like traveling a foreign country, with unusual things to see and experience.

When he was released the next day because someone "interfered" and paid his tax, he writes, he felt himself to be a changed man. His resolve to resist the state was strengthened rather than weakened, and he no longer felt he could tolerate the company of his neighbors who professed to be against slavery and the Mexican-American War but were not willing to do anything about it. He recounts how he found solace from his ill feelings toward his fellow townspeople by going off into the countryside and picking berries.

Thoreau concludes "Resistance to Civil Government" by discussing the actual role that government can play in effecting meaningful change. He says that the American government, though it bears significant flaws, such as a constitution that allows slavery, is not a particularly bad one. However, he argues, it is not possible to rely on government alone to make a better world. Although the citizens of the United States should insist on improvements to their government, politicians are too limited in their understanding of what matters in life to bring about true reforms. Ultimately, Thoreau asserts, meaningful change comes from the creative force of individuals. Someday government may progress to the point that it respects the individual as the basis of its power, but such a state has yet to exist.

Essential Themes

Thoreau wrote "Resistance to Civil Government" with two specific, related grievances in mind: the continuation of the slave trade in the United States and the Mexican-American War. However, the impact of this work transcended his lifetime and the particular issues of his day. Later activists drew upon the main concepts he laid out in this groundbreaking work to further their own movements. As such, it is possible to consider Thoreau as an important pioneer in the field of social activism.

The key lesson of "Resistance to Civil Government" is that people of conscience should not simply work within the existing political system to change legislation but should instead disengage from an immoral government altogether. Thoreau envisioned government as a kind of machine and insisted that it is important for socially conscious people to refuse to be part of the machine if it is causing harm to society. By completely withdrawing their support from the machine, by not giving it their labor or taxes, morally astute individuals can help break down the corrupt machine.

Of course, Thoreau acknowledged that governments do not approve of people who refuse to participate in their smooth functioning. They will invariably react by punishing such activists, usually by placing them under arrest. As he learned from his own experience of being briefly incarcerated for refusing to pay poll tax, being put in prison is not necessarily such a terrible fate, and a person of strong convictions should take pride in being jailed by an immoral government, since this is the most honorable place for an honest person living in a corrupt state.

Although Thoreau did not entirely reject the possibility of supporting a violent revolution, his essay laid out a sort of template for nonviolent social protest that was used by some of the best-known social activists of the twentieth century. For instance, Mahatma Gandhi (1869–1948), who was the most influential leader of the movement to free India from British rule, was an avid reader of Thoreau's work. Gandhi first gained experience in the social-justice field through his civil rights work in South Africa. He described Thoreau as an important teacher in this period of his life, stating that "Resistance to Civil Government" affirmed the work he was doing to end racial oppression by the white South African government.

Another prominent figure in the history of nonviolent social change who greatly admired Thoreau was Martin Luther King Jr. (1929–68). America's best-known civil rights activist, King worked in the 1960s to improve conditions for African Americans. Like Gandhi, King was explicit about the important role that Thoreau's "Resistance to Civil Government" played in helping to shape his own philosophy and celebrated quest for social justice. King's struggle, Gandhi's, and the struggles of so many other activists who have been touched by "Resistance to Civil Government" and used the tactic of nonparticipation in corrupt governments stand as evidence of Henry David Thoreau's lasting legacy of innovative political philosophy.

—*Adam Berger, PhD*

Bibliography and Additional Reading

Cain, William. *A Historical Guide to Henry David Thoreau*. Oxford: Oxford UP, 2000.

Dassow, Laura. *Henry David Thoreau: A Life*. Chicago: University of Chicago Press, 2017.

McKenzie, Jonathan. *The Political Thought of Henry David Thoreau: Privatism and the Practice of Philosophy*. Lexington: UP of Kentucky, 2016.

Moller, Mary Elkins. *Thoreau in the Human Community*. Amherst: University of Massachusetts Press 1980.

Votes for Women!

During the nineteenth century, for a variety of reasons, most states prohibited women from voting. The formal movement for female suffrage began in the 1840s at the first Women's Rights Convention, which was held in Seneca Falls, New York, in 1848. The campaign for women's suffrage lasted nearly eighty years, involving a variety of strategies and spanning at least two generations of leaders. It was not until the aftermath of World War I that the long-anticipated passage of a constitutional amendment legalizing suffrage for women in the United States finally occurred. Its author, Susan B. Anthony, and its proponents had hoped the amendment would follow on the heels of the Fifteenth Amendment, providing for universal male suffrage in 1870. Their hope for a sixteenth amendment allowing women to vote was frustrated, however, and they had to settle for a fifty-year wait in opposition until the Nineteenth Amendment was proposed.

In 1869, the Wyoming Territory became the first jurisdiction to permit women to vote. But when the U.S. Supreme Court, in 1875, rejected a Fourteenth Amendment challenge to a Missouri law that limited the franchise to men, it became clear that female suffrage was a law-based privilege and not a constitutional right. By the end of the nineteenth century, only five states—Wyoming (1869), Montana (1887), Colorado (1893), Utah (1896), and Idaho (1896)—had embraced full female suffrage.

The strategy of women's rights organizations was twofold: lobby individual states to confer voting rights on women and push for a suffrage amendment to the Constitution. Congress rejected amendment proposals in 1914 and 1915. By 1917, however, more members of Congress were elected from states that permitted women to vote than from states that did not, and the following year, President Woodrow Wilson articulated his support for a constitutional amendment. On May 21, 1919, the House of Representatives passed a proposed constitutional amendment that read in part, "The right of citizens of the United States to vote shall not be denied or abridged by the United States or by any State on account of sex." The Senate voted favorably on June 4, 1919. The proposed amendment was then sent to the states for ratification. On August 18, 1920, Tennessee became the thirty-sixth state to ratify the proposed amendment, thus achieving the constitutionally required three-fourths of the states voting in support. Eight days later, the Nineteenth Amendment went in effect.

■ Seneca Falls Convention: Declaration of Sentiments

Date: July 19–20, 1848
Author: Elizabeth Cady Stanton
Genre: charter; political tract

Summary Overview

This Declaration of Sentiments was drafted by the early women's rights writer and activist Elizabeth Cady Stanton and read at the historically notable Seneca Falls Convention in upstate New York on July 19–20, 1848. Modeling her work on the Declaration of Independence, the author sought to address the wrongs perpetrated against womankind and called for redress of those wrongs. The Seneca Falls meeting was the first convention specifically devoted to the issue of women's rights. Organized by Stanton, Lucretia Coffin Mott, Mary Ann McClintock, Martha Wright, and Jane Hunt, the convention's goal was to address "the social, civil and religious rights of women," according to the Seneca County Courier of July 14, 1848. The Declaration of Sentiments summed up the current state of women's rights in the United States and served notice that women would no longer stand for being treated inequitably.

The Declaration was considered radical for its time, especially in the clause calling for suffrage (voting) of women. While antebellum reformers, many of whom were abolitionists, connected the situation of women with that of slaves, in that neither could vote, hold office, sit on juries, or have property rights, the Seneca Falls Convention marked the first time that men and women publicly discussed the issue of women's rights. The people who gathered at Seneca Falls realized that they were taking an unprecedented—not to mention controversial—step in calling for full citizenship for American women. In the context of antebellum America, this document is indeed a radical one. While it took seventy-two years for women to get the vote and even longer to abolish other forms of discrimination, the Declaration of Sentiments marked the first step in the long struggle for women's rights.

Defining Moment

The United States in the 1840s seethed with a variety of reform movements, inspired by the religious upheaval known as the Second Great Awakening as well as the rise of transcendentalism. (Transcendentalism was a new way of looking at life, spirituality, and religion that emerged in the mid-nineteenth century. Transcendentalists, among them Ralph Waldo Emerson, generally believed that they could gain knowledge of spiritual reality through the use of intuition rather than through established religion.) The men and women reformers thought they could improve American society by changing some of the ills they

Elizabeth Cady Stanton and two of her three sons, 1848. Photo via Library of Congress. [Public domain.]

Our Roll of Honor

Containing all the Signatures to the "Declaration of Sentiments" Set Forth by the First

Woman's Rights Convention,

held at

Seneca Falls, New York
July 19-20, 1848

This card was issued for the celebration held at Seneca Falls in 1908 and is added to the book by Harriot Stanton Blatch

LADIES:

Lucretia Mott
Harriet Cady Eaton
Margaret Pryor
Elizabeth Cady Stanton
Eunice Newton Foote
Mary Ann M'Clintock
Margaret Schooley
Martha C. Wright
Jane C. Hunt
Amy Post
Catherine F. Stebbins
Mary Ann Frink
Lydia Mount
Delia Mathews
Catherine C. Paine
Elizabeth W. M'Clintock
Malvina Seymour
Phebe Mosher
Catherine Shaw
Deborah Scott
Sarah Hallowell
Mary M'Clintock
Mary Gilbert

Sophronia Taylor
Cynthia Davis
Hannah Plant
Lucy Jones
Sarah Whitney
Mary H. Hallowell
Elizabeth Conklin
Sally Pitcher
Mary Conklin
Susan Quinn
Mary S. Mirror
Phebe King
Julia Ann Drake
Charlotte Woodward
Martha Underhill
Dorothy Mathews
Eunice Barker
Sarah R. Woods
Lydia Gild
Sarah Hoffman
Elizabeth Leslie
Martha Ridley

Rachel D. Bonnel
Betsey Tewksbury
Rhoda Palmer
Margaret Jenkins
Cynthia Fuller
Mary Martin
P. A. Culvert
Susan R. Doty
Rebecca Race
Sarah A. Mosher
Mary E. Vail
Lucy Spalding
Lovina Latham
Sarah Smith
Eliza Martin
Maria E. Wilbur
Elizabeth D. Smith
Caroline Barker
Ann Porter
Experience Gibbs
Antoinette E. Segur
Hannah J. Latham
Sarah Sisson

GENTLEMEN:

Richard P. Hunt
Samuel D. Tillman
Justin Williams
Elisha Foote
Frederick Douglass
Henry W. Seymour
Henry Seymour
David Spalding
William G. Barker
Elias J. Doty
John Jones

William S. Dell
James Mott
William Burroughs
Robert Smallbridge
Jacob Mathews
Charles L. Hoskins
Thomas M'Clintock
Saron Phillips
Jacob P. Chamberlain
Jonathan Metcalf

Nathan J. Milliken
S. E. Woodworth
Edward F. Underhill
George W. Pryor
Joel Bunker
Isaac VanTassel
Thomas Dell
E. W. Capron
Stephen Shear
Henry Hatley
Azaliah Schooley

Signers of the Declaration of Sentiments at Seneca Falls in order: Lucretia Coffin Mott is on top of the list. Photo courtesy of PBS, via Wikimedia Commons.

perceived as plagues upon the nation. Some of the reformers' causes included better treatment of the mentally ill, opposition to capital punishment and war, temperance, and most notably, abolitionism. The first publication of William Lloyd Garrison's antislavery newspaper the *Liberator* on January 1, 1831, traditionally marks the beginning of the American abolitionist movement. Garrison's newspaper proclaimed on its masthead that there should "no union with slaveholders" and demanded the end of slavery immediately. This call for immediate abolition set the abolitionists apart from antislavery advocates who were more moderate and willing to accept the gradual dismantling of the slave system. The formation of the American Anti-Slavery Society in 1833 created an organization committed to the immediate abolition of slavery. Throughout the North activists formed antislavery organizations loosely affiliated with the American Anti-Slavery Society.

Men of conscience, however, were not the only ones who wanted to free the enslaved. Organized antislavery encouraged women to participate in the movement, although the more conservative preferred that women form auxiliary organizations rather than joining with the men in the same group. Others, like Garrison and his friend Stephen S. Foster, believed that women should participate in the same organizations alongside the men. The role of women in the American Anti-Slavery Society became one of several issues that finally split the organization in 1840. Those who supported full participation of women stayed in the American Anti-Slavery Society, while the dissenters formed the American and Foreign Anti-Slavery Society. Those who stayed in the American Anti-Slavery Society also viewed the U.S. Constitution as a proslavery document and eschewed involvement with political parties.

Female abolitionists played a number of roles in the fight to end slavery, circulating petitions to Congress, holding antislavery fairs, contributing articles to antislavery publications, and organizing antislavery societies. Some even took the daring step of speaking out publicly against slavery. The sisters Sarah and Angelina Grimké were among the first women who gave public orations to mixed-gender audiences on the issue of abolition. This was considered so

James and Lucretia Mott, c. 1842. Photo via Wikimedia Commons. [Public domain.]

outrageous that they were often on the receiving end of abuse, both verbal and physical. The Grimkés paved the way for other women orators such as Abby Kelley Foster. The abolitionist movement, as well as other contemporary reform movements such as temperance and anti-capital punishment, was fertile ground for inspiring women's activity beyond the home. Their work in reform motivated many women to question their role in society and begin to work to improve their own lot. It was in this atmosphere that Elizabeth Cady Stanton, Lucretia Coffin Mott, Jane Hunt, Mary Ann McClintock, and Martha Wright called for a convention to discuss the issue of women's rights.

The seed for what became the Seneca Falls Convention in 1848 was actually planted several years earlier at the 1840 World Anti-Slavery Convention in London. Mott and Stanton met for the first time at the London convention. Stanton was accompanying her husband,

Henry, who was a delegate to the convention. Mott was actually a delegate herself but, because of her gender, was denied a seat at the convention. This blatant discrimination forced the women to rethink their treatment in American society and call for their rights as free citizens of the United States.

The immediate impetus for the Seneca Falls Convention was the impending passage of a married women's property law in New York State. Traditionally women had no legal rights to property; once married, everything from the clothes on their backs to their children belonged to the husband. The New York legislature was considering legislation to give married women some property rights. The convention's organizers hoped that by meeting they would bring awareness to the inequitable treatment of women and gain support for passage of the law. Mott's husband, James, chaired the convention; the participants feared that having a woman preside would only increase hostility toward their cause. Seneca Falls was the last time that a male presided over a women's rights convention. The Declaration of Sentiments was one of two documents produced at the convention. The other was a preamble followed by a series of eleven resolutions making various demands for women's rights. Resolution number nine was the most radical—it called for the right of women to vote. All eleven resolutions passed, ten of them unanimously. Only the demand for the vote was not passed unanimously. Indeed, even Lucretia Mott felt that asking for votes for women would harm their cause.

Author Biography

Elizabeth Cady Stanton was born on November 12, 1815, in Johnstown, New York, the daughter of Margaret Livingstone and Daniel Cady. Stanton's father was a distinguished lawyer and jurist who ultimately served on the state's highest court. Stanton was one of eleven of children, many of whom did not survive to adulthood. Young Elizabeth received tutoring in Greek and mathematics; she also became an accomplished equestrian. Judge Cady allowed her free run of his library, giving her access to any book she wished to read, including law books. Cady alternated praising his daughter's accomplishments with telling her he wished she had been born male, creating in her a determination to succeed at academic as well as domestic activities. By reading her father's law books, she also learned that women were accorded a second-class status in the legal realm, planting the seed that eventually matured into her campaign for women's rights.

Stanton furthered her education at Emma Willard's Troy Female Seminary in Troy, New York. Willard's school provided the best female education available for its time. Stanton studied the classics, algebra, geometry, philosophy, and history as well as proper female deportment and etiquette. After her graduation in 1833, Stanton lived with a cousin, the abolitionist Gerrit Smith, in whose circle she was exposed to reformist sentiment. It was at Smith's residence that she met a fellow abolitionist, Henry Stanton, whom she married in 1840. Stanton accompanied her husband to London in that year, where he was a delegate to the World Anti-Slavery Convention. She met another American delegate, Lucretia Coffin Mott, who, because of her gender, could not take her seat at the convention. All the female delegates were allowed only to observe the proceedings in silence. Mott and Stanton commiserated about the injustice dealt the women and vowed to do something about it. This fateful meeting eventually culminated in the Seneca Falls Convention.

Upon their return from Europe, the Stantons settled with her family so that Henry could study to law. They moved to Boston in 1842, where Henry practiced law. The couple also began their family in 1842; their last of six children was born in 1856. Elizabeth became an avid participant in Boston's intellectual life, where she met luminaries such as Frederick Douglass, Louisa May Alcott, and Ralph Waldo Emerson. Henry actively participated in antislavery activities, although he was more closely allied with the conservative wing of abolitionism, rather than the Garrisonian wing. He and Elizabeth disagreed on a number of issues, particularly that of women's rights. Indeed, throughout her life she refused to refer to herself as "Mrs. Henry Stanton"; instead she used "Elizabeth Cady Stanton" or "E. C. Stanton." In 1847 the Stantons left Boston for Seneca Falls, in Upstate New York, because of Henry's health.

Seneca Falls was a small community in the Finger Lakes region. While children and her household occupied some of Stanton's time, she missed the intellectual stimulation of city life. As she became involved in her new home, Stanton made the acquaintance of women who agreed that something needed to be done to improve the rights of women. Stanton, Lucretia Mott, Jane Hunt, Martha Wright, and Mary Ann McClintock organized a convention to discuss the rights of women. The Seneca Falls Convention, where Stanton presented her Declaration of Sentiments, gave birth to other women's rights conventions around the country, including the first national convention, in Worcester, Massachusetts, in 1850. The conventions continued until the outbreak of the Civil War.

In 1851 Amelia Bloomer introduced Stanton to the woman who would become her lifelong friend, Susan B. Anthony. The two women had complementary gifts; Stanton was the better writer and Anthony the superior organizer. The unmarried Anthony was free to travel and speak out on women's rights, while Stanton stayed home and saw to her family but wrote Anthony's speeches. Together Stanton and Anthony provided decades of leadership for the nascent feminist movement. Following the Civil War, Stanton and Anthony formed the Equal Rights Association supporting universal suffrage and tried to get women included in the Fourteenth Amendment, which defined citizens as exclusively male for the first time in the Constitution. Stanton took a hard-line stance that neither the Fourteenth nor the Fifteenth Amendment (which gave black men the right to vote) should be passed unless woman suffrage was included. The women were told that it was "the Negro's hour," and both amendments passed without provisions for woman suffrage, but some of the feminists embarked on their own crusade to gain the vote for women.

Stanton and Anthony split from the more conservative feminists like Lucy Stone and Julia Ward Howe, differing on passage of the Fourteenth and Fifteenth Amendments as well as the approach to organizing the suffrage movement. Stanton and Anthony organized the National Woman Suffrage Association (NWSA) and Stone and Howe the American Woman Suffrage Association (AWSA), both in 1869. The NWSA believed that the goal should be an amendment to the U.S. Constitution, with the Fifteenth Amendment as the model. The organization also propounded a broader agenda of women's rights in general, not just the vote. The AWSA, on the other hand, supported the Fourteenth and Fifteenth Amendments and worked on gaining votes for women state by state. The NWSA counted among its supporters Sojourner Truth and Matilda Joslyn Gage, who became a leader in the suffrage movement and, in an interesting aside, was the mother-in-law of L. Frank Baum, author of *The Wizard of Oz*.

Stanton put her writing skills to good use on behalf of the feminist movement. Together with Anthony and the feminist Parker Pillsbury, she wrote and edited a feminist periodical called *Revolution* in 1868. She also published a number of works including her autobiography, *Eighty Years and More* (1898). With Anthony and Gage she wrote volumes 1 through 3 of *The History of Woman Suffrage* (published in six volumes 1881–1922, with the later volumes completed by Anthony, Gage, and Ida Husted

Frederick Douglass championed the Declaration of Sentiment in the North Star. Photo via Wikimedia Commons. [Public domain.]

National Anti-Suffrage Association. (Library of Congress)

Harper). Stanton's *Woman's Bible* (1895) is an intriguing publication, offering a feminist interpretation of scripture.

As Stanton's children matured, she was able to more actively pursue the cause of women's rights. She made speeches and worked to pass suffrage laws in several states, including New York, Michigan, and Kansas. Senator Aaron A. Sargent of California introduced the woman suffrage amendment to the U.S. Senate for the first time in 1878 at the behest of Stanton and Anthony. It contained the exact wording that would finally become law in 1920.

The suffrage movement gained strength when the NWSA and AWSA merged in 1890 to form the National American Woman Suffrage Association and elected Stanton its first president. Stanton served the organization until her death on October 26, 1902. Throughout her long life, Stanton worked tirelessly for women's rights. Her ideas were often considered too radical for the mainstream, and eventually it was Anthony who received most of the adulation from young suffragists, whose primary goal was the vote. In a great disservice to Stanton, the Nineteenth Amendment is also referred to as the "Susan B. Anthony amendment." With the revitalization of the feminist movement in the 1960s, Stanton has been restored to her proper place of importance as a founding mother of modern feminism.

Historical Document

Declaration of Sentiments

When, in the course of human events, it becomes necessary for one portion of the family of man to assume among the people of the earth a position different from that which they have hitherto occupied, but one to which the laws of nature and of nature's God entitle them, a decent respect to the opinions of mankind requires that they should declare the causes that impel them to such a course.

We hold these truths to be self-evident: that all men and women are created equal; that they are endowed by their Creator with certain inalienable rights; that among these are life, liberty, and the pursuit of happiness; that to secure these rights governments are instituted, deriving their just powers from the consent of the governed. Whenever any form of government becomes destructive of these ends, it is the right of those who suffer from it to refuse allegiance to it, and to insist upon the institution of a new government, laying its foundation on such principles, and organizing its powers in such form, as to them shall seem most likely to effect their safety and happiness. Prudence, indeed, will dictate that governments long established should not be changed for light and transient causes; and accordingly all experience hath shown that mankind are more disposed to suffer, while evils are sufferable, than to right themselves by abolishing the forms to which they are accustomed. But when a long train of abuses and usurpations, pursuing invariably the same object, evinces a design to reduce them under absolute despotism, it is their duty to throw off such government, and to provide new guards for their future security. Such has been the patient sufferance of the women under this government, and such is now the necessity which constrains them to demand the equal station to which they are entitled. The history of mankind is a history of repeated injuries and usurpations on the part of man toward woman, having in direct object the establishment of an absolute tyranny over her. To prove this, let facts be submitted to a candid world.

The history of mankind is a history of repeated injuries and usurpations on the part of man toward woman, having in direct object the establishment of an absolute tyranny over her. To prove this, let facts be submitted to a candid world.

He has never permitted her to exercise her inalienable right to the elective franchise.

He has compelled her to submit to laws, in the formation of which she had no voice.

He has withheld from her rights which are given to the most ignorant and degraded men—both natives and foreigners.

Having deprived her of this first right of a citizen, the elective franchise, thereby leaving her without representation in the halls of legislation, he has oppressed her on all sides.

He has made her, if married, in the eye of the law, civilly dead.

He has taken from her all right in property, even to the wages she earns.

He has made her, morally, an irresponsible being, as she can commit many crimes with impunity, provided they be done in the presence of her husband. In the covenant of marriage, she is compelled to promise obedience to her husband, he becoming, to all intents and purposes, her master—the law giving him power to deprive her of her liberty, and to administer chastisement.

He has so framed the laws of divorce, as to what shall be the proper causes, and in case of separation, to whom the guardianship of the children shall be given, as to be wholly regardless of the happiness of women—the law, in all cases, going upon a false supposition of the supremacy of man, and giving all power into his hands.

After depriving her of all rights as a married woman, if single, and the owner of property, he has taxed her to support a government which recognizes her only when her property can be made profitable to it.

He has monopolized nearly all the profitable employments, and from those she is permitted to follow, she receives but a scanty remuneration. He closes against her all the avenues to wealth and distinction which he considers most honorable to himself. As a teacher of theology, medicine, or law, she is not known.

He has denied her the facilities for obtaining a thorough education, all colleges being closed against her.

He allows her in church, as well as state, but a subordinate position, claiming apostolic authority for her exclusion from the ministry, and, with some exceptions, from any public participation in the affairs of the church.

He has created a false public sentiment by giving to the world a different code of morals for men and women, by which moral delinquencies which exclude women from society, are not only tolerated, but deemed of little account in man.

He has usurped the prerogative of Jehovah himself, claiming it as his right to assign for her a sphere of action, when that belongs to her conscience and to her God.

He has endeavored, in every way that he could, to destroy her confidence in her own powers, to lessen her self-respect, and to make her willing to lead a dependent and abject life.

Now, in view of this entire disfranchisement of one-half the people of this country, their social and religious degradation—in view of the unjust laws above mentioned, and because women do feel themselves aggrieved, oppressed, and fraudulently deprived of their most sacred rights, we insist that they have immediate admission to all the rights and privileges which belong to them as citizens of the United States.

Glossary

candid: impartial

chastisement: discipline, especially physical punishment

constrains: forces; compels

covenant: formal agreement of legal validity

disfranchisement: denial of a right, especially the right to vote

franchise: the right to vote

hitherto: up to this time; until now

impunity: immunity from punishment

inalienable: incapable of being repudiated or transferred to another

Jehovah: a name for God in the Old Testament

prerogative: exclusive entitlement

prudence: caution regarding practical matters

remuneration: payment or consideration received for services or employment

sufferance: capacity to endure hardship

supposition: an assumption

usurped: used without authority or right; employed wrongfully

Document Analysis

The Declaration of Sentiments echoes the language and structure of the Declaration of Independence's preamble. Its opening justifies the actions of those who support women's rights and prepares the reader for the litany of the wrongs perpetrated against womankind. Stanton uses the religious language of the Declaration of Independence when she refers to "nature's God" and points out that the rights women are demanding come not from government but from "nature" as well as the Supreme Being.

Stanton goes on to state, "We hold these truths to be self-evident: that all men and women are created equal." This ringing proclamation comes directly from the Declaration of Independence, with only the words "and women" added. Women, like men, are entitled to "life, liberty, and the pursuit of happiness," and the government was instituted to make sure that all people are guaranteed these rights. Stanton states that people who have been denied their rights have the right to "refuse allegiance" to their government and "insist upon the institution of a new government." In fact, those who are abused in this way have a responsibility and duty "to throw off such government." These are the words Thomas Jefferson used to justify the American people's break from Great Britain and formation of a new government. Stanton added, however, language stating that women have suffered patiently under the current government, which has denied them their full rights, and "such is now the necessity which constrains them to demand the equal station to which they are entitled."

A statement that the "history of mankind is a history of repeated injustices and usurpations on the part of man toward woman" introduces the lengthy portion of the document that lists the wrongs visited upon womankind. The first five focus on women's political rights—or lack thereof. The list begins with the fact that women are denied the vote. Logically, from lacking the vote, women are subject to laws that they had no say in making. The next item argues that women have been denied simple rights possessed by even the "most ignorant and degraded" men, not only native-born but even foreign. This statement was an appeal to the nativist element that was emerging in the late nineteenth century. The next statement again makes mention of the denial of "the elective franchise" in the context of denying women "representation in the halls of the legislation."

The next set of wrongs deals with marriage and property rights. Stanton observes that the institution of marriage has been particularly destructive to women, given that married women are defined outright as "civilly dead" in the eyes of the law. Because of that, married women have no rights to property, even their own wages. The next clause states that because of the usurpation of these rights, the law has essentially rendered woman "an irresponsible being" who can commit any crime without fear of punishment, as long as it is done "in the presence of her husband." Stanton further notes that women must obey their husbands unquestioningly and that the law gives him the power "to deprive her of her liberty" and physically and emotionally abuse her without recourse. Divorce is the next topic, and here women are denied the guardianship of their children, no matter what the cause for ending the marriage. Single women are mentioned in the next clause, which points out that if a single woman is a property owner, then she is subject to taxes; thus the government "recognizes her only when her property can be made profitable to it."

Clauses on employment, education, and religion make up the next set. Stanton states that men have "monopolized nearly all the profitable employments." Not only that, but in the professions women could enter, they were not equitably paid. At the time the Declaration of Sentiments was written, the only acceptable profession for "respectable" women was teaching—and even that was restricted to educating young children. Stanton believed that women should have access to any profession they wished. The next clause focuses on education, noting that all colleges are "closed against her." Stanton actually slightly exaggerates in this clause, as Oberlin College did admit women equally with men by 1848, but that was the exception rather than the rule. Organized religion comes under attack next, for it keeps women "in a subordinate position," barring them from the ministry and generally from any "public participation in the affairs of the church." Not only are women discriminated against by "the church," but also in the realm of

U.S. commemorative stamp from 1948 titled 100 Years of Progress of Women: 1848–1948. From left to right, Stanton, Carrie Chapman Catt, Lucretia Mott. Image via Wikimedia Commons. [Public domain.]

morals they are subjected to a double standard; as the clause puts it, there is "a different code of morals for men and women." The penultimate clause makes reference to God and states that man has "usurped" the Lord's "prerogative" by assigning woman a sphere of action "when that belongs to her conscience and to her God." Finally, the last clause states that man has decreed women should be submissive and dependent, destroying "her confidence in her own powers" and lessening "her self-respect."

The last paragraph sums up the entire document. Stanton states that in light of the aforementioned grievances, including "the disenfranchisement of one-half the people of this country," American women "insist that they have immediate admission to all the rights and privileges which belong to them as citizens of the United States."

Delivered at Seneca Falls, New York, on July 20, 1848, the Declaration of Sentiments, a woman's rights manifesto primarily written by Stanton, was revolutionary and echoed the ideology behind America's own Revolution. By changing the language of the Declaration of Independence, the basic document proclaiming America's independence from tyranny, Stanton brought focus to the failure of that document to provide rights for half of America's citizens: women. The Declaration of Sentiments was presented at the first woman's rights convention, attended by more than one hundred women and men. It was followed by a set of eleven resolutions, including the resolution that women secure the right to vote. Signing the document to support the sentiments and resolutions were sixty-eight women and thirty-two men, including the abolitionist Frederick Douglass, a former slave.

A week before the convention, a group of woman, including Stanton and Mott, decided it was time to speak for the rights of women. The drafting of an advertisement for the convention, to be held at the Wesleyan Chapel in Seneca Falls, prompted the question of what to say there. Stanton hit on the idea of reconstructing Thomas Jefferson's Declaration of Independence to highlight the position of women. In her preface, she amends Jefferson's "one people" to refer to "one portion of the family of man" needing "to assume ... a position different from that which they have hitherto occupied." Immediately she is pointing out that Jefferson's "one people" did not include women. The second section of Stanton's declaration adds two words (italicized here) to Jefferson's: "We hold these truths to be self-evident: that all men *and women* are created equal." She continues with women meriting the same rights of "life, liberty, and the pursuit of happiness."

In writing her declaration, Stanton wanted to echo Jefferson's eighteen indictments against the king of England. She remarks, like Jefferson, that "the history of mankind is a history of repeated injuries and usurpation." Rather than accusing the king, she states that these acts have been caused by "man toward woman," resulting in "the establishment of an absolute tyranny over her." Her first indictment is "He has never permitted her to exercise her inalienable right to the elective franchise." Stanton, with her familiarity with the law, believed that women's position would change only through their acquiring the vote. Voting would provide the power to make laws needed for political actions. Another indictment is a reference to a woman's position once married: She became bound to her husband, who had control of her and custody of their children. She was also without property rights, "even to the wages she earns." Although New York State had passed the Married Women's Property Act just months before the convention, the law did not allow a woman to keep the wages she earned, just property inherited. Other states had no such laws. Another indictment is "He has made her, morally, an irresponsible being," since according to the law a woman's husband was her master and was responsible for her actions. Stanton brings up divorce, which she would campaign over throughout her career. Under existing laws and irrespective of the reasons for separation, guardianship of children was awarded to the husband, "regardless of the happiness of women."

Another indictment applied to single women, who could own taxable property but had no voice in government, essentially taxation without representation. In employment, wages were not equal between men and women, and many "avenues to wealth" were closed to women. In addition, few women could attend colleges, since almost all admitted men only; Oberlin College, in Ohio, was the exception. Most damaging to women, according to Stanton, was "a different code of morals for men and women," creating a separate "sphere of action" for women. With this double standard, women were made to be of little account in society.

Following the Declaration of Sentiments were eleven resolutions, framed to redress the indictments. In writing the resolutions, Stanton asked for help from her lawyer husband. When she proposed the ninth resolution—"That it is the duty of the women of this country to secure to themselves their sacred right to the elective franchise"—he declined to support it and refused to attend the conference. Mott also thought the resolution would make the convention look "ridiculous," but she and others signed. Stanton felt that the law played a major role in setting men over women and that by demanding the vote women could work together against their repression and have roles in society beyond those of wife and mother. Concluding her declaration, Stanton calls for further actions, including other woman's rights conventions in different parts of the country, to promote the work of this first convention. Although there was a follow-up convention two weeks later in Rochester, New York, not until 1850 did other states begin to hold such conventions.

Essential Themes

Following its adoption at the Seneca Falls Convention, the Declaration of Sentiments became a flash point for criticism and ridicule of the nascent women's rights movement. The newspapers that reported on the convention derided the document and its signers. The press generally expressed fears that by demanding equal rights, women were stepping out of the role ordained for them not only by society but also by God and nature. The only newspaper that actually applauded the Declaration of Sentiments was Frederick Douglass's *North Star*, which called it the "grand basis for attaining the civil, social, political, and religious rights of women" (July 28, 1848). A second women's rights convention met a few weeks later, on August 2, 1848, in Rochester, New York. This convention was the first to have a female president, Abigail Bush. The participants adopted the Declaration of Sentiments from Seneca Falls. The Rochester convention was also subject to ridicule and derision by the general public. By the time that the first women's rights convention was held west of the Alleghenies, at Salem, Ohio, in 1850, supporters of feminism no longer considered the suffrage clause radical. Indeed, the vote was now seen as an essential element in women's rights reform and eventually became the centerpiece of the movement.

From its introduction in 1848 through the present, the Declaration of Sentiments has been a central part of feminist thought. While the women's movement focused solely on the vote following the Civil War, there were still many feminists who had a broader vision of women's rights. Alice Paul and the National Woman's Party, which was founded in 1914 as the Congressional Union, saw beyond the vote to full equality for women, not only in the United States but indeed worldwide. The revitalized feminist movement in the 1960s was more in the spirit of the Declaration of Sentiments, demanding full participation in society. In 1998, at the 150th anniversary of the Seneca Falls Convention, the National Organization for Women issued its own Declaration of Sentiments modeled on the Seneca Falls document. The demands expressed generations ago still have relevance for men and women seeking justice for all in the contemporary world.

—Donna M. DeBlasio, PhD,
Marcia B. Dinneen, PhD

Bibliography and Additional Reading

Baker, Jean H., ed. *Votes for Women: The Struggle for Suffrage Revisited*. New York: Oxford UP, 2002.

DuBois, Ellen Carol. *Feminism and Suffrage: The Emergence of an Independent Women's Movement in the United States, 1848–1869*. Revised edition. Ithaca, N.Y.: Cornell UP, 1999.

Flexner, Eleanor, and Ellen Fitzpatrick. *Century of Struggle: The Woman's Rights Movement in the United States*. Enlarged edition. Cambridge, Mass.: Belknap Press of Harvard UP, 1996.

Ginzberg, Lori. *Untidy Origins: A Story of Woman's Rights in Antebellum New York*. Chapel Hill: University of North Carolina Press, 2005.

Griffith, Elisabeth. *In Her Own Right: The Life of Elizabeth Cady Stanton*. New York: Oxford UP, 1985.

Isenberg, Nancy. *Sex and Citizenship in Antebellum America*. Chapel Hill: University of North Carolina Press, 1998.

Kraditor, Aileen. *The Ideas of the Woman Suffrage Movement, 1890–1920*. Reprint, New York: W. W. Norton, 1981.

McMillen, Sally. *Seneca Falls and the Origins of the Women's Rights Movement*. New York: Oxford UP, 2008.

Ward, Geoffrey C. [based on a documentary film by Ken Burns and Paul Barnes]. *Not for Ourselves Alone: The Story of Elizabeth Cady Stanton and Susan B. Anthony: An Illustrated History*. New York. Alfred A. Knopf, 1999.

Wellman, Judith. *The Road to Seneca Falls: Elizabeth Cady Stanton and the First Woman's Rights Convention*. Urbana: University of Illinois Press, 2004.

Susan B. Anthony: "Is It a Crime for a Citizen of the United States to Vote?"

Date: 1873
Author: Susan B. Anthony
Genre: speech

Summary Overview

In all her speeches and writings, Susan B. Anthony displayed her single-minded devotion to the cause of women's rights—particularly the right to vote. Over the years she honed her arguments, dramatically increasing the chance for women's suffrage to become law. The major shift in public opinion, in the decades following this speech, was the result in large part of Anthony's carefully crafted arguments. This speech was given on numerous occasions throughout the state of New York after having been charged with, and eventually convicted of, voting illegally, in the 1872 election.

By the time she was charged, Anthony, and others, had been working toward the goal of women's suffrage for twenty years, with limited success. Although it would be almost fifty years before women across the United States would be guaranteed the right to vote with the Nineteenth Amendment to the Constitution, many people started taking Anthony and her cause more seriously after the trial alluded to in this speech.

Defining Moment

With the Civil War still a recent memory, three amendments to the Constitution were ratified which were intended to ensure that African-Americans, who had been slaves, were accorded the same rights as white Americans. The goals of the abolitionists had been accomplished. Anthony, and some of her associates, hoped that the new Thirteenth, Fourteenth, and Fifteenth Amendments might assist them in gaining the vote for women. On November 1st, Anthony, followed by fifty other women, intimidated election officials into allowing all of them to register to vote, based on the recently adopted Fourteenth Amendment. Having gained assurance that she would not be physically stopped from voting, Anthony and sixteen other women resolved to vote.

Thus, in Rochester, New York, on November 5, 1872, Anthony cast her ballot for the Republican ticket in the presidential election, as did the other sixteen. Anthony claimed the Fourteenth Amendment put no gender qualification on the right to vote. In response to her arrest and trial for illegally casting a

Susan B. Anthony. Photo via Wikimedia Commons. [Public domain.]

Cover of Life *magazine in 1913. Titled "Ancient History," it shows an Anthony-like figure in classical dress leading a protest for women's rights. Cover by Rea Irvin, via Wikimedia Commons. [Public domain.]*

ballot, Anthony launched a speaking tour throughout the state of New York. The address she delivered, which was included in the record of the trial, was titled "Is It a Crime for a Citizen of the United States to Vote?" Although she invoked the Declaration of Independence, the Constitution, James Madison, Thomas Paine, the Supreme Court, and the Civil War Amendments as justification for a woman's right to vote, she was convicted of civil disobedience in June of 1873.

Anthony was brought to trial, but not given a chance to speak in her own defense, and was found guilty by the judge before the jury even had a chance to deliberate. For many people, the manner in which the trial had been handled made them much more sympathetic to her and her cause. After the verdict, no sentence was enforced, so that Anthony did not have grounds to appeal. Throughout the rest of her life, as she campaigned for women's suffrage, she carried a copy of the court transcript with her in her trademark purse.

Author Biography

Susan Brownell Anthony, who devoted more than a half century to women's suffrage and other social issues, was born into a liberal family in Adams, Massachusetts, on February 15, 1820. Educated at a Quaker boarding school in Philadelphia, she trained to be a teacher. After moving to Rochester, New York, in 1845, she became active in a range of social causes, including abolition of slavery, temperance, the rights of labor, education reform, and particularly women's rights. She signed the Declaration of Sentiments produced by the 1848 Seneca Falls Convention, the first women's rights convention held in the United States. In the early 1850s she met her lifelong friend and fellow suffragist, Elizabeth Cady Stanton—although Stanton adopted a more radical approach to women's rights.

After the Civil War and the abolition of slavery, Anthony, Stanton, and other suffragist leaders were hopeful that the Fifteenth Amendment to the Constitution, which granted voting rights to African Americans, would extend the same rights to women. It did not. In 1868 Anthony launched a weekly journal called the *Revolution* under the motto "The true republic—men, their rights and nothing more; women, their rights and nothing less." For the next four decades Anthony devoted her life to writing and speaking in support of women's rights, particularly the right to vote.

After Anthony and several other women cast ballots in Rochester in the 1872 presidential election, only she was arrested, tried, found guilty, and fined, though she never paid the fine and was never jailed. During the legal proceedings, she recorded her reactions in letters written in 1872 and 1873.

Anthony is often regarded as the author of the Nineteenth Amendment to the U.S. Constitution which recognizes the right of women to vote. She originally wrote the amendment in 1877, using the Fifteenth Amendment as a model. The amendment, which came to be referred to as the Anthony Amendment, was submitted to every session of Congress until 1919. Just one month before her death on March 13, 1906, Anthony concluded her last public speech, delivered at a meeting of the National American Women Suffrage Association, with the words "Failure is impossible"—her final public utterance and a phrase that survived as a rallying cry for women's rights proponents throughout the twentieth century.

Historical Document

"Is It a Crime for a Citizen of the United States to Vote?"

Friends and Fellow-citizens: I stand before you under indictment for the alleged crime of having voted at the last presidential election, without having a lawful right to vote. It shall be my work this evening to prove to you that in thus voting, I not only committed no crime, but instead simply exercised my citizen's right, guaranteed to me and all United States citizens by the National Constitution beyond the power of any State to deny.

Our democratic-republican government is based on the idea of the natural right of every individual member thereof to a voice and a vote in making and executing the laws. We assert the province of government to be to secure the people in the enjoyment of their inalienable rights. We throw to the winds the old dogma that governments can give rights. No one denies that before governments were organized each individual possessed the right to protect his own life, liberty and property. When 100 or 1,000,000 people enter into a free government, they do not barter away their natural rights; they simply pledge themselves to protect each other in the enjoyment of them through prescribed judicial and legislative tribunals. They agree to abandon the methods of brute force in the adjustment of their differences and adopt those of civilization. Nor can you find a word in any of the grand documents left us by the fathers which assumes for government the power to create or to confer rights. The Declaration of Independence, the United States Constitution, the constitutions of the several states and the organic laws of the territories, all alike propose *to protect* the people in the exercise of their God-given rights. Not one of them pretends to bestow rights.

"All men are created equal, and endowed by their Creator with certain inalienable rights. Among these are life, liberty and the pursuit of happiness. That to secure these [rights], governments are instituted among men, deriving their just powers from the consent of the governed."

Here is no shadow of government authority over rights, or exclusion of any class from their full and equal enjoyment. Here is pronounced the right of all men, and "consequently," as the Quaker preacher said, "of all women," to a voice in the government. And here, in this very first paragraph of the declaration, is the assertion of the natural right of all to the ballot; for how can "the consent of the governed" be given, if the right to vote be denied. Again:

"Whenever any form of government becomes destructive of these ends, it is the right of the people to alter or abolish it, and to institute a new government, laying its foundations on such principles, and organizing its powers in such forms as to them shall seem most likely to effect their safety and happiness."

Surely, the right of the whole people to vote is here clearly implied. For however destructive to their happiness this government might become, a disfranchised class could neither alter nor abolish it, nor institute a new one, except by the old brute force method of insurrection and rebellion. One-half of the people of this nation today are utterly powerless to blot from the statute books an unjust law, or to write there a new and a just one....

The preamble of the federal constitution says:

"We, the people of the United States, in order to form a more perfect union, establish justice, insure domestic tranquility, provide for the common defence, promote the general welfare and secure the blessings of liberty to ourselves and our posterity, do ordain and established this Constitution for the United States of America."

It was we, the people, not we, the white male citizens, nor we, the male citizens; but we, the whole people, who formed this Union. We formed it not to give the blessings of liberty but to secure them; not to the half of ourselves and the half of our posterity, but to the whole people—women as well as men. It is downright mockery to talk to women of their enjoyment of the blessings of liberty while they are denied the only means of securing them provided by this democratic-republican government—the ballot....

James Madison said;

"Under every view of the subject, it seems indispensable that the mass of the citizens should not be without a voice in making the laws which they are to obey, and in choosing the magistrates who are to administer them.... Let it be remembered, finally, that it has ever been the pride and the boast of America that the rights for which she contended were the rights of human nature."

These assertions by the framers of the United States Constitution of the equal and natural right of all the people to a voice in the government, have been affirmed and reaffirmed by the leading statesmen of the nation, throughout the entire history of our government....

The clauses of the United States Constitution cited by our opponents as giving power to the States to disfranchise any classes of citizens they shall please are contained in Sections 2 and 4 of Article I. The second says:

"The House of Representatives shall be composed of members chosen every second year by the people of the several States; and the electors in each State shall have the qualifications requisite for electors of the most numerous branch of the State legislature."

This cannot be construed into a concession to the States of the power to destroy the right to become an elector, but simply to prescribe what shall be the qualification, such as competency of intellect, maturity of age, length of residence, that shall be deemed necessary to enable them to make an intelligent choice of candidates. If, as our opponents assert, the last clause of this section makes it the duty of the United States to protect citizens in the several States against higher or different qualifications for electors for representatives in Congress than for members of the Assembly, then it must be equally imperative for the national government to interfere with the States, and forbid them from arbitrarily cutting off the right of one-half of the people to become electors altogether. Section 4 says:

"The times, places and manner of holding elections for senators and representatives shall be prescribed in each State by the legislature thereof; but Congress may at any time, by law, make or alter such regulations, except as to the places of choosing Senators."

Here is conceded to the States the power only to prescribe times, places and manner of holding the elections; and even with these Congress may interfere in all excepting the mere place of choosing senators. Thus, you see, there is not the slightest permission in either section for the States to discriminate against the right of any class of citizens to vote. Surely, to regulate cannot be to annihilate; to qualify cannot be wholly to deprive....

For any State to make sex a qualification, which must ever result in the disfranchisement of one entire half of the people, is to pass a bill of attainder, or an ex post facto law, and is therefore a violation of the supreme law of the land. By it, the blessings of liberty are forever withheld from women and their female posterity. For them, this government has no just powers derived from the consent of the governed. For them this government is not a democracy. It is not a republic. It is the most odious aristocracy ever established on the face of the globe. An oligarchy of wealth, where the rich govern the poor; an oligarchy of learning, where the educated govern the ignorant; or even an oligarchy of race, where the Saxon rules the African, might be endured; but this oligarchy of sex, which makes father, brothers, husband, sons, the oligarchs over the mother and sisters, the wife and daughters of every household; which ordains all men sovereigns, all women subjects, carries dissension, discord and rebellion into every home of the nation. This most odious aristocracy exists, too, in the face of Section 4, of Article IV, which says: "The United States shall guarantee to every State in the Union a republican form of government."

What, I ask you, is the distinctive difference between the inhabitants of a monarchical and those of a republican form of government, save that in the monarchical the people are subjects, helpless, powerless, bound to obey laws made by political superiors—while in the republican, the people are citizens, individual sovereigns, all clothed with equal power, to make and unmake both their laws and law makers. The moment you deprive a person of his right to a voice in the government, you degrade him from the status of a citizen of the republic to that of a subject. It matters very little to him whether his monarch be an individual tyrant, as is the Czar of Russia, or a 15,000,000 headed monster, as here in the United States; he is a powerless subject, serf or slave; not in any sense a free and independent citizen.

It is urged that the use of the masculine pronouns *he*, *his* and *him*, in all the constitutions and laws, is proof that only men were meant to be included in their provisions. If you insist on this version of the letter of the law, we shall insist that you be consistent, and accept the other horn of the dilemma, which would compel you to exempt women from taxation for the support of the government and from penalties for the violation of laws....

Though the words persons, people, inhabitants, electors, citizens, are all used indiscriminately in the national and State constitutions, there was always a conflict of opinion, prior to the war, as to whether they were synonymous terms, but whatever there was for a doubt, under the old regime, the adoption of the Fourteenth Amendment settled that question forever, in its first sentence: "All persons born or naturalized in the United States and subject to the jurisdiction thereof, are citizens of the United States and of the state wherein they reside."

The second settles the equal status of all citizens:

"No State shall make or enforce any law which shall abridge the privileges or immunities of citizens of the United States; nor shall any State deprive any person of life, liberty or property, without due process of law, nor deny to any person within its jurisdiction the equal protection of the laws."

The only question left to be settled, now, is: Are women persons? I scarcely believe any of our opponents will have the hardihood to say they are not. Being persons, then, women are citizens, and no State has a right to make any new law, or to enforce any old law, which shall abridge their privileges or immunities. Hence, every discrimination against women in the constitutions and laws of the several States, is today null and void, precisely as is every one against negroes....

If the Fourteenth Amendment does not secure to all citizens the right to vote, for what purpose was the grand old charter of the fathers lumbered with its unwieldy proportions? The Republican party, and Judges Howard and Bingham, who drafted the document, pretended it was to do something for black men; and if that something were not to secure them in their right to vote and hold office, what could it have been? For, by the Thirteenth Amendment, black men had become people, and hence were entitled to all the privileges and immunities of the government, precisely as were the women of the country, and foreign men not naturalized....

Thus, you see, those newly-freed men were in possession of every possible right, privilege and immunity of the government, except that of suffrage, and hence, needed no constitutional amendment for any other purpose. What right in this country has the Irishman the day after he receives his naturalization papers that he did not possess the day before, save the right to vote and hold office? The Chinamen now crowding our Pacific coast are in precisely the same position. What privilege or immunity has California or Oregon the right to deny them, save that of the ballot? Clearly, then if the Fourteenth Amendment was not to secure to black men their right to vote it did nothing for them, since they possessed everything else before. But if it was intended to prohibit the states from denying or abridging their right to vote, then it did the same for all persons, white women included, born or naturalized in the United States; for the amendment does not say that all male persons of African descent, but that all persons are citizens.

However much the doctors of the law may disagree, as to whether people and citizens, in the original Constitution, were one and the same, or whether the privileges and immunities in the Fourteenth Amendment include the right of suffrage, the question of the citizen's right to vote is forever settled by the Fifteenth Amendment. "The right of citizens of the United States to vote shall not be denied or abridged by the United States or by any State on account of race, color, or previous condition of servitude." How can the State deny or abridge the right of the citizen, if the citizen does not possess it? There is no escape from the conclusion that to vote is the citizen's right, and the specifications of race, color, or previous condition of servitude can in no way impair the force of the emphatic assertion that the citizen's right to vote shall not be denied or abridged.

The political strategy of the second section of the Fourteenth Amendment, failing to coerce the rebel States into enfranchising their negroes, and the necessities of the Republican party demanding their votes throughout the South, to ensure the re-election of Grant in 1872, that party was compelled to place this positive prohibition of the Fifteenth Amendment upon the United States and all the States thereof....

If, however, you will insist that the Fifteenth Amendment's emphatic interdiction against robbing United States citizens of their suffrage "on account of race, color, or previous condition of servitude" is a recognition of the right of either the United States or any State to deprive them of the ballot for any or all other reasons, I will prove to you that the class of citizens for whom I now plead are by all the principles of our government, and many of the laws of the States, included under the term "previous condition of servitude."

Consider first married women and their legal status. What is servitude? "The condition of a slave." What is a slave? "A person who is robbed of the proceeds of his labor; a person who is subject to the will of another." By the laws of Georgia, South Carolina, and all the States of the South, the negro had no right to the custody and control of his person. He belonged to his master. If he were disobedient, the master had the right to use correction. If the negro did not like the correction and ran away, the master had a right to use coercion to bring him back. By the laws of almost every State in this Union today, North as well as South, the married woman has no right to the custody and control of her person. The wife belongs to the husband; and if she refuse obedience, he may use moderate correction, and if she do not like his moderate correction and leave his "bed and board," the husband may use moderate coercion to bring her back. The little word "moderate," you see, is the saving clause for the wife, and would doubtless be overstepped should her offended husband administer his correction with the "cat-o'-nine-tails," or accomplish his coercion with blood-hounds.

Again, the slave had no right to the earnings of his hands, they belonged to his master; no right to the custody of his children, they belonged to his master; no right to sue or be sued, or to testify in the courts. If he committed a crime, it was the master who must sue or be sued....

I submit the question, if the deprivation by law of the ownership of one's own person, wages, property, children, the denial of the right as an individual to sue and be sued and testify in the courts, is not a condition of servitude most bitter and absolute, even though under the sacred name of marriage?

Glossary

Chinamen: a term for Asians in general and persons of Chinese origin in particular common at the time and not considered a racial slur

Doctors of the Law: lawyers

ex post facto: Latin for "after the fact," a term for a retroactive law; a law that changes the consequences for specific acts that occurred prior to the adoption of the law

The Grand Old Charter: the Constitution

horn of the dilemma: the position of being forced to choose between two equally unacceptable alternatives

old regime: the U.S. government prior to the Civil War and the freeing of slaves

oligarchy: a government in which a small group of people exercise dictatorial control

organic laws: original, fundamental laws

prescribed ... tribunals: legally and formally chosen courts of review

province: responsibility

suffrage: the right to vote

Document Analysis

In response to her arrest and trial for voting in the 1872 presidential election, Susan B. Anthony launched a speaking tour throughout New York. The address she delivered and that was included in the records of the trial is titled "Is It a Crime for a Citizen of the United States to Vote?" The address fell roughly into three parts. The first was an appeal to the nation's foundational documents, particularly the Declaration of Independence and the Constitution. The second was an appeal to the language of law as it applies to citizenship and other matters. In the third, Anthony drew an analogy between women's suffrage and the issue of slavery.

In the opening paragraphs of her address, Anthony expressed the view that as a citizen of the United States, living under a "democratic-republican" form of government, she possessed a "natural right" to participate in the nation's political affairs by voting. (The terms *democratic* and *republican* in this context do not refer to modern political parties but to forms of government.) Anthony thus drew a distinction between rights that are granted by the state and those that anyone possessed by virtue of being a citizen.

The concept of natural rights represented a philosophical tradition from the eighteenth-century Age of Enlightenment. Anthony cited the Declaration of Independence, which enshrined the Enlightenment concept of natural rights with its statement that "life, liberty and the pursuit of happiness" are "inalienable rights"—that is to say, rights that cannot be taken away. Rights, then, are not granted by the state, nor can the state deny to citizens their full enjoyment of their rights. People possess rights by virtue of being human. She went on to say that the Declaration's avowal of the "right of the people to alter or abolish" a government that is "destructive of these ends" clearly implied the right to vote. Voting was the only civilized way to form and alter governments; the only alternative was brute force. Disenfranchising half of the population—women—compelled them to obey laws to which they had never consented.

Anthony then cited the U.S. Constitution, noting that it began with the words "We, the people," not "we, the white male citizens" or "we, the male citizens." This was a glancing reference to her bitter disappointment that the Fifteenth Amendment extending suffrage to freed slaves did not also extend suffrage to women. She noted that even James Madison, who earlier in his career had expressed fear of the rabble, came around to a belief in universal suffrage, as expressed in the 1787 debates at the Constitutional Convention.

Anthony referred to the first article of the Constitution, which, her opponents asserted, disenfranchised women because it turned over to the states the power to regulate elections. Anthony replied to this view by noting that all the Constitution did was prescribe procedures to ensure that electors were qualified; these stipulations in no way implied that half the population was to be disenfranchised. She argued that disenfranchisement on the basis of sex amounted to a "bill of attainder." She noted that under current U.S. law, a "monarchy," or at best an "oligarchy" of males ruled females, in direct violation of the Constitution, which required every state to guarantee to its citizens a "republican" form of government, with the concomitant right to vote.

On this basis, Anthony took up the issue of legal language, in the process making an ingenious argument. She noted that laws routinely used the pronouns *he* and *his*, suggesting that women were excluded, just as they were excluded from the voting booth. If that was the case, then, women should be exempted from *all* laws in which *he* and *his* were used, including criminal laws and laws applying to taxation. Anthony extended her discussion of the language of the law to the indiscriminant use of words such as "persons, people, inhabitants, electors," and "citizens" and raised the question of who was included in these terms. She noted that under the Fourteenth Amendment, all "persons" who were born or naturalized in the United States were "citizens." If "persons" were "citizens," then denying women the right to vote was a violation of the federal Constitution.

Making a transition to the third major argument of her address, Anthony drew an analogy between the status of African Americans and that of women. Just as women and black men had both been disenfranchised, Anthony made the argument that the law which applied to black men should also apply to women. She began with a reference to the Fourteenth Amendment, one of the three so-called Civil War, or

Reconstruction, Amendments. Although Section 1 of the amendment does not mention race, the effect of the amendment was to make African Americans "citizens," deny to the states the right to "abridge" the rights of any citizens, and give all citizens due process and equal protection under the law. Anthony made the argument that the earlier Thirteenth Amendment, which banned slavery, had in effect already made African Americans citizens of the nation, thus giving them the right to vote. The Fourteenth Amendment, Anthony suggested, was unnecessary, except for the purpose of granting African Americans equal protection under the law, among other provisions. She concluded the argument by stating, regarding the Fourteenth Amendment, that if it's purpose was to "prohibit states from denying" voting rights for African Americans, then it should do the same for women, since "all persons are citizens."

Anthony turned to the Fifteenth Amendment, which specifically states that the right to vote cannot be denied or abridged on the basis of "race, color, or previous condition of servitude," the last of the three items prohibiting states from denying the vote to former slaves. From this, Anthony made yet another ingenious argument, from a legal perspective. Her key point was that women, like African Americans, lived under the condition of servitude. She pointed out, for example, that a woman, like a slave, had no "control" over her person and could be corrected if she offended her master. Similarly, just as a slave was not entitled to retain his earnings from labor, so, too, any earnings a woman might have were the property of her husband. A corollary to this was that if the wife was guilty of some offense, it was her husband, not her, who was sued, based on the principle that the wife did not own anything that the person who sued could collect; at the same time, a wife could not sue another, but a husband could file suit on her behalf. Simply put, then, women lived under the condition of servitude, holding a position little different from that of slaves. If the Fifteenth Amendment granted the right to vote despite "previous condition of servitude," then it granted women the right to vote.

Essential Themes

It is difficult to overstate the impact of Susan B. Anthony and her ability, through her writings, speeches, and correspondence, to galvanize Americans in the pursuit of women's rights. She recognized, for example, that women could not achieve equal rights until they achieved economic independence and the education they needed for such independence. As long as women were under the economic control of men, legislators had no reason to grant them the right to vote or any other right, for they did not form a constituency. While numerous women in the middle decades of the nineteenth century were proponents of women's rights—and at the same time opposed to slavery—Anthony, along with such other towering figures as Elizabeth Cady Stanton and Lucretia Mott, was able to forge a sustained political movement that led to a series of successes ranging from the landmark 1860 Married Women's Property Act in New York to, eventually, the Nineteenth Amendment, ratified in 1920.

In this speech, Anthony made it clear that she had a solid philosophical foundation in her advocacy of women's suffrage. Using legal and political documents and statements, Anthony pushed the idea that the constitution was for all the people, not just for men. Focusing on the Constitution, she strongly asserted that nothing in it limited citizenship or political activity to just men. She argued that to the contrary, the Constitution was an inclusive document, which did not allow states to limit political participation. Although she was fighting an uphill battle during her lifetime, with limited acceptance by those in power, things changed in the twentieth century. By the turn of the new century, the cause of women's suffrage and the name of "Miss Anthony" were almost synonymous. Although, the nineteenth century featured numerous important women's rights activists, in the twentieth century and beyond it is Susan B. Anthony's name that survives.

—*Michael J. O'Neal, PhD, Donald A. Watt, PhD*

Bibliography and Additional Reading

Burns, Ken and Paul Barnes. "United States vs. Anthony." *Not for Ourselves Alone*. Washington: PBS and WETA, 1999.

Gordon, Ann D. ed. *The Elizabeth Cady Stanton & Susan B. Anthony Papers Project*. New Brunswick NJ: Rutgers, The State University of New Jersey, 2012.

Hull, N.E.H. *The Woman Who Dared to Vote: The Trial of Susan B. Anthony*. Lawrence KS: The UP of Kansas, 2012.

National Park Service. "Notable Women's Rights Leaders." Women's Rights National Historical Park. Washington: National Park Service, 2017.

Sherr, Lynn. *Failure Is Impossible: Susan B. Anthony in Her Own Words*. New York: Random House, 1995.

Susan B. Anthony House. "Biography of Susan B. Anthony." National Susan B. Anthony Museum & House. Rochester NY: Susan B. Anthony House, 2013.

■ Petition to U.S. Congress for Women's Suffrage

Date: January 12, 1874
Author: Susan B. Anthony
Genre: petition; political tract

Summary Overview

Susan B. Anthony, one of the most prominent women's rights campaigners of her time, was particularly interested in winning the right to vote (suffrage) for women. Having spent the better part of her life advocating for such, on November 5, 1872 she and fourteen other women in the first district of Rochester, New York's, Eighth Ward tested the American electoral system by attempting to register and vote in the national election. She and the other women were arrested two weeks after the election and charged with voting illegally, but only Anthony's case was pursued; she was tried in federal court in June 1873. In United States v. Susan B. Anthony *the court eventually decided against Anthony and fined her $100, along with court costs. At this point, Anthony petitioned the U.S. Congress to revoke the fine, which she never paid and which the government never compelled her to pay. In this way, these women were the first to actually vote in a U.S. election, which did not become a legal right for women nationwide until the Nineteenth Amendment came into force in 1920.*

Defining Moment

Although the women's rights movement had been active before the American Civil War, the movement was mainly put on hold as the nation decided its stance on slavery. The 1848 Seneca Falls Convention in New York and the 1850 National Women's Rights Convention in Worcester, Massachusetts, were evidence that the antebellum women's rights movement was gaining momentum. Many women's rights activists had been deeply involved in the abolition movement as well, which gave them invaluable experience in how to organize and communicate their reform platforms. After the Civil War concluded, many women returned their attention to women's rights and, in particular, to women's suffrage. This was a time in American history when many other social reforms and civil rights were emerging. Many fought for more than women's rights to vote, pushing for equal pay and equal access to higher education for women. Others took up the cause of temperance (the abolition of the sale of alcohol and certain drugs), as they were seen as detrimental to stable family life, an issue in which women had a vested interest.

As for suffrage, Anthony, along with other activists, saw the newly enacted Fourteenth Amendment as an opportunity to test the system. This amendment to the Constitution, ratified in 1868, was part of the Reconstruction efforts after the Civil War, and was designed to grant former slaves U.S. citizenship, with due process and equal protection under the law. It

Susan B. Anthony was the first woman to appear on a U.S. dollar coin. Photo via Wikimedia Commons. [Public domain.]

was the citizenship clause of the amendment on which Anthony focused, reasoning that because women were U.S. citizens, they too had the right to vote. The Fifteenth Amendment (1870), which gave the federal government oversight of elections, was also seen to be in their favor, as it too had a clause stipulating that citizen's right to vote "shall not be denied or abridged by the United States or by any state on account of race, color, or previous condition of servitude." Anthony and the National Woman Suffrage Association decided to challenge the new laws through the courts to see if women's suffrage could be gained by such means. As such, in 1872, a group of women including Anthony tried to register to vote in Rochester, New York. As they were successful in this, many returned to actually vote in the election, and they were allowed to do so by the federal election inspectors. Anthony used this challenge as a key theme of one of her speaking tours, which she undertook before her trial in June 1873. At the trial, the judge gave a directed guilty verdict to the jury. Anthony was ordered to pay a fine, but instead, she petitioned Congress to overturn the fine.

Author Biography

Susan Brownell Anthony, born on February 15, 1820, in Adams, Massachusetts, was one of the most prominent civil rights activists in the nineteenth century. She was a particular proponent of women's right to vote (or suffrage) and to higher education and equal pay for equal work, although she was also active in the abolitionist and temperance movements. She had a working partnership for most of her life with Elizabeth Cady Stanton. While Stanton wrote copiously, Anthony traveled and lectured tirelessly, sharing their ideas for reform far and wide, which included petitioning state and federal legislatures. A leader in the suffrage movement, Anthony organized the National Woman Suffrage Association with Stanton, which eventually merged with the American Woman Suffrage Association to form the National American Woman Suffrage Association. With her suffrage colleagues, Anthony ensured the history of the early movement was documented and disseminated to school and university libraries. She died on March 13, 1906.

Historical Document

Petition to U.S. Congress for Women's Suffrage

To the Congress of the United States.

The petition of Susan B. Anthony, of the city of Rochester in the county of Monroe and state of New York, respectfully represents:

That prior to the late Presidential election your petitioner applied to the board of registry in the Eighth ward of the city of Rochester, in which city she had resided for more than 25 years, to have her name placed upon the register of voters, and the board of registry, after consideration of the subject, decided that your petitioner was entitled to have her name placed upon the register, and placed it there accordingly.

On the day of the election, your petitioner, in common with hundreds of other American citizens, her neighbors, whose names had also been registered as voters, offered to the inspectors of election, her ballots for electors of President and Vice President, and for members of Congress, which were received and deposited in the ballot box by the inspectors.

For this act of your petitioner, an indictment was found against her by the grand jury, at the sitting of the District Court of the United States for the Northern District of New York at Albany, charging your petitioner, under the nineteenth section of the Act of Congress of May 31, 1870, entitled, "An act to enforce the rights of citizens of the United States to vote in the several states of this union, and for other purposes," with having *"knowingly* voted without having a lawful right to vote."

To that indictment your petitioner pleaded not guilty, and the trial of the issue thus joined took place at the Circuit Court in Canandaigua, in the county of Ontario, before the Honorable Ward Hunt, one of the Justices of the Supreme Court of the United States, on the eighteenth day of June last.

Upon that trial, the facts of voting by your petitioner, and that she was a woman, were not denied—nor was it claimed on the part of the government, that your petitioner lacked any of the qualifications of a voter, unless disqualified by reason of her sex.

It was shown on behalf of your petitioner on the trial, that before voting she called upon a respectable lawyer and asked his opinion whether she had a right to vote, and he advised her that she had such right; and the lawyer was examined as a witness in her behalf, and testified that he gave her such advice, and that he gave it in good faith, believing that she had such right.

It also appeared that when she offered to vote, the question, whether, as a woman she had a right to vote, was raised by the inspectors, and considered by them in her presence, and they decided that she had a right to vote, and received her vote accordingly.

It was shown on the part of the government, that on the examination of your petitioner before the commissioner on whose warrant she was arrested, your petitioner stated that she should have voted if allowed to vote, without reference to the advice of the attorney whose opinion she had asked; that she was not induced to vote by that opinion; that she had before determined to offer her vote, and had no doubt about her right to vote.

At the close of the testimony, your petitioner's counsel proceeded to address the jury and stated that he desired to present for consideration three propositions, two of law and one of fact:

First—That your petitioner had a lawful right to vote.

Second—That whether she had a right to vote or not, if she honestly believed that she had that right, and voted in good faith in that belief, she was guilty of no crime.

Third—That when your petitioner gave her vote she gave it in good faith, believing that it was her right to do so.

That the two first propositions presented questions for the Court to decide, and the last a question for the jury.

When your petitioner's counsel had proceeded thus far, the Judge suggested that the counsel had better discuss in the first place the questions of law; which the counsel proceeded to do, and having discussed the two legal questions at length, asked leave then to say a few words to the jury on the question of fact. The Judge then said to the counsel that he thought that had better be left until the views of the court upon the legal questions should be made known.

The district attorney thereupon addressed the court at length upon the legal questions, and at the close of his argument the Judge delivered an opinion adverse to the positions of your petitioner's counsel upon both of the legal questions presented, holding, that your petitioner was not entitled to vote; and that if she voted in good faith in the belief in fact that she had a right to vote, it would constitute no defense—the ground of the decision on the last point being that your petitioner was bound to know that by law she was not a legal voter, and that even if she voted in good faith in the contrary belief, it constituted no defence to the crime with which she was charged.

The decision of the Judge upon those questions was read from a written document, and at the close of the reading the Judge said, that the decision of those questions disposed of the case, and left no question of fact for the jury, and that he should therefore direct the jury to find a verdict of guilty. The judge then said to the jury that the decision of the Court had disposed of all there was in the case, and that he directed them to find a verdict of guilty; and he instructed the clerk to enter such a verdict.

At this time, before any entry had been made by the clerk, your petitioner's counsel asked the Judge to submit the case to the jury, and to give to the jury the following several instructions:

First—That if the defendant at the time of voting, believed that she had a right to vote, and voted in good faith in that belief, she was not guilty of the offence charged.

Second—That in determining the question whether she did or did not believe that she had a right to vote, the jury might take into consideration as bearing upon that question, the advice which she received from the counsel to whom she applied.

Third—That they might also take into consideration as bearing upon the same question, the fact that the inspectors considered the question, and came to the conclusion that she had a right to vote.

Fourth—That the jury had a right to find a general verdict of guilty or not guilty, as they should believe that she had or had not been guilty of the offense described in the statute.

The Judge declined to submit the case to the jury upon any question whatever, and directed them to render a verdict of guilty against your petitioner.

Your petitioner's counsel excepted to the decision of the Judge upon the legal questions, and to his direction to the jury to find a verdict of guilty; insisting that it was a direction which no court had a right to give in any criminal case.

The Judge then instructed the clerk to take the verdict, and the clerk said, "Gentlemen of the jury, hearken to your verdict as the court hath recorded it. You say you find the defendant guilty of the offence charged. So say you all."

No response whatever was made by the jury either by word or sign. They had not consulted together in their seats or otherwise. Neither of them had spoken a word, nor had they been asked whether they had or had not agreed upon a verdict.

Your petitioner's counsel then asked that the clerk be requested to poll the jury. The Judge said, "that cannot be allowed, gentlemen of the jury you are discharged," and the jurors left the box. No juror spoke a word during the trial, from the time when they were empannelled to the time of their discharge.

After denying a motion for a new trial, the Judge proceeded upon the conviction thus obtained to pass sentence upon your petitioner, imposing upon her, a fine of one hundred dollars, and the costs of the prosecution.

Your petitioner respectfully submits, that in these proceedings she has been denied the rights guaranteed by the constitution to all persons accused of crime, the right of trial by jury, and the right to have the assistance of counsel for their defence. It is a mockery to call her trial a trial by jury; and unless the assistance of counsel may be limited to the argument of legal questions, without the privilege of saying a word to the jury upon the question of the guilt or innocence in fact of the party charged, or the privilege of ascertaining from the jury whether they do or do not agree to the verdict pronounced by the court in their name, she has been denied the assistance of counsel for her defence.

Your petitioner, also, respectfully insists, that the decision of the Judge, that good faith on the part of your petitioner in offering her vote did not constitute a defence, was not only a violation of the deepest and most sacred principle of the criminal law, that no one can be guilty of crime unless a criminal intent exists; but was also, a palpable violation of the statute under which the conviction was had; not on the ground that good faith could, in this, or in any case justify a criminal act, but on the ground that *bad faith* in voting was an indispensable ingredient in the offence with which your petitioner was charged. Any other interpretation strikes the word "knowingly," out of the statute, the word which alone describes the essence of the offence.

The statute means, as your petitioner is advised, and humbly submits, a *knowledge in fact*, not a knowledge falsely imputed by law to a party not possessing it in fact, as the Judge in this case has held. Crimes cannot either in law, or in morals, be established by judicial falsehood. If there be any crime in the case, your petitioner humbly insists, it is to be found in such an adjudication.

To the decision of the Judge upon the question of the right of your petitioner to vote she makes no complaint. It was a question properly belonging to the court to decide, was fully and fairly submitted to the Judge, and of his decision, whether right or wrong, your petitioner is well aware she cannot here complain.

But in regard to her conviction of crime, which she insists, for the reasons above given, was in violation of the principles of the common law, of common morality, of the statute under which she was charged, and of the Constitution; a crime of which she was as innocent as the Judge by whom, she was convicted, she respectfully asks, inasmuch as the law has provided no means of reviewing the decisions of the Judge, or of correcting his errors, that the fine imposed upon your petitioner be remitted, as an expression of the sense of this high tribunal that her conviction was unjust.

Dated January 12, 1874.

Susan B. Anthony.

Glossary

empanel: (or impanel): to situate on a panel or jury; to establish as a jury

except to: take exception to, disagree with

hearken: listen to, hear

Document Analysis

By the time Anthony sent her petition to Congress in 1874, she had already been found guilty of voting illegally. She felt she had done nothing wrong and did not agree to pay the fine. In this document, Anthony appeals her conviction to Congress and asks for her fine to be overturned. In her appeal, Anthony relies upon legal arguments involving the Fourteenth and Fifteenth Amendments, as well as prior legal arguments made by her lawyer designed to appeal her conviction.

Throughout the document, Anthony addresses members of Congress in language they would easily understand. As they are in charge of making the laws, she speaks to them in legal terms. She quotes verbatim from her lawyer, Henry Selden, at times, knowing that the words of a man, and a lawyer, may well hold more weight with them than the words of a woman found guilty of a crime. Anthony presents the facts of her case, and the history of how her case came before the courts, in a concise, dispassionate, and logical manner, which is in direct opposition to the more passionate tones of her public speeches on suffrage. She makes the point that before attempting to vote, she asked the opinion of a respected (male) lawyer, and that he "advised her that she had such right" (he repeated this when called as a witness at her trial). She also makes the point that the election inspectors also "decided that she had a right to vote, and received her vote accordingly."

Anthony also insists that because of this, she truly believes she has the right to vote and, therefore, voted in good faith. She is also concerned that her verdict and sentence were directed to the jury by the judge in the case and that, therefore, she was denied her constitutional right to a trial by jury. She feels that because of these irregularities, her conviction is unjust. Further, she states that because the court system gives her no access to appeal or "no means of reviewing the decisions of the Judge, or of correcting his errors," she should not have to pay the fine and, therefore, asks Congress to overturn her sentence by remitting the fine.

Essential Themes

As a woman, Anthony could not legally vote in elections in 1872, and yet she dared to do so. Change was in the air, and progressive women and men began advocating for a woman's right to vote. As amendments had been introduced to ensure that some black men were able to vote after the Civil War, many women saw this as an opportunity for them to gain the same right.

Anthony's legal and constitutional challenge for the right of women to vote set the stage for the growth of the suffrage movement over the following several decades. These events also provided her with an opportunity to embark on a speaking tour about suffrage and to sway many other women, and especially men, to her cause. Anthony actually wanted to be arrested, for the sake of publicity, and published three thousand copies of her lawyer's argument in 1873 as pamphlets, mailing them to key newspapers. In 1874, she also published an account of her trial.

After losing her case, Anthony was portrayed as either a martyr for the suffrage cause or as a common criminal. However, Anthony is remembered as a feminist icon and a champion of women's rights. Americans did not forget this trailblazing woman, and she was the first woman to appear on a U.S. dollar coin. Although Anthony died more than a decade before American women finally won the right to vote in 1920, her life's work set the stage for change.

—Lee Tunstall, PhD

Bibliography and Additional Reading

Barry, Kathleen. *Susan B. Anthony: A Biography of a Singular Feminist.* New York: NYUP, 1988.

Gordon, Ann D., ed. *The Selected Papers of Elizabeth Cady Stanton and Susan B. Anthony.* 6 Vols. New Brunswick: Rutgers UP, 1997–2013.

_____. *The Trial of Susan B. Anthony.* Washington, DC: Federal Judicial Center, 2005.

Hull, N. E. H. *The Woman Who Dared to Vote.* Lawrence: U of Kansas P, 2012.

Sherr, Lynn. *Failure Is Impossible: Susan B. Anthony in Her Own Words.* New York: Times Books, 1995.

Stanton, Elizabeth Cady, and Susan Brownell Anthony. *The Elizabeth Cady Stanton–Susan B. Anthony Reader: Correspondence, Writings, Speeches.* Ed. Ellen Carol DuBois. Boston: Northeastern UP, 1992.

■ Jane Addams: "Why Women Should Vote"

Date: 1910
Author: Jane Addams
Genre: essay

Summary Overview

Jane Addams is remembered as a prominent figure in the Progressive movement, a broad and diverse middle-class coalition that, at the turn of the twentieth century, tried to reform American society. The Progressives sought to alter the American capitalist system and its institutions from within, aiming to strike a compromise between politically radical demands on the one hand and the preservation of established interests on the other. The steady industrialization and urbanization of the 1880s and 1890s had deeply transformed American society, spurring harsh conflicts between labor and management. The middle class had supported the process of industrialization by espousing the Victorian values of laissez-faire individualism, domesticity, and self-control. Yet by the 1890s it was apparent that these values had trapped the middle class between the warring demands of big business and the working classes. Growing consumerism, a new wave of immigration, and tensions between the sexes further challenged bourgeois existence. In the face of these confrontations, the Progressives went to work. Addams is known primarily for her work in creating "settlement houses" for immigrant families in Chicago. Yet she also was involved generally in Progressive causes. Her passion for reform is apparent in her strong endorsement of women's suffrage in the essay "Why Women Should Vote," published as an editorial in the Ladies' Home Journal in January 1910.

Defining Moment

Great changes rocked the United States in the second half of the nineteenth century and the beginning of the twentieth. The Civil War had destroyed the South, and many Americans looked westward for new opportunities. Industrialization at the same time was changing the Northern landscape: it moved traditionally domestic production, like textiles, into factories; corporations amassed great amounts of money at the cost of cheap labor. Public education began to overtake private schools, which meant that literacy and certain trade skills were in the hands of those who could afford to learn. Progressive politics in the United States began at the end of the nineteenth century with the goal to target the corruption and excesses of industrialization and expand government

Jane Addams. Photo via Wikimedia Commons. [Public domain.]

Women suffragists demonstrating for the right to vote in 1913. Photo via Wikimedia Commons. [Public domain.]

services to those without the means to procure them themselves.

The primary audience of the *Ladies' Home Journal*, the magazine in which Addams' essay was first published, was middle-class American homemakers. As such, Addams shapes her message to appeal to the sentiments of such an audience that likely had little to no experience of the daily exigencies of poor women. Jane Addams, however, was in a privileged position to explain these experiences: she came from the same background as her readers, but she had spent years working with the less fortunate at her Chicago-based Hull House, which she founded with Ellen Gates Starr in 1889.

Her unique position for typical readers of *Ladies' Home Journal* did not obstruct her ability to push her agenda: Progressive politics. Extending the vote to women was not just a matter of equality but also an issue of great practicality. Traditionally, women managed the house and children, but many issues outside of the home affected women as housekeepers. Men regulated the politics that administered services such as garbage, plumbing, and food regulation, but they had no idea how the policies they enacted actually affected the home. For this pragmatic reason, Addams appeals to her female readership that women ought to have a voice. Addams' diplomacy and pragmatic writing contributed to the respected position she held in the American mind by the time of her death in 1935.

In some of her other writings, Jane Addams more ostensibly ascribes to an evolutionary model of history. In this view, enfranchisement expands to different social classes in stages as human society changes what it needs. At first, the middle class revolted against the nobility; next, Addams imagined that women, a social class in their own right according to her, would necessarily receive the right to vote. In this evolutionary model, it was only natural, since industrialization had changed the needs of human society. No longer did women's domestic lives have to revolve around the work of textile production such as wool spinning and rearing children: women could make money in textile factories while public institutions took over education. Since larger institutions and the government abrogated these functions, it was only right that women have some voice in the management of their traditional spheres of influence.

Additionally, for a thinker such as Addams, it would be impossible to ignore the rise of first-wave feminism. This movement began at the Seneca Falls Convention in 1848, when Elizabeth Cady Stanton and Lucretia Mott organized a conference that culminated in writing the Declaration of Sentiments. This document, modeled on the Declaration of Independence, called for a number of economic reforms for women's rights, such as the right for married women to own property and earn their own wages, in addition to suffrage. The work these early feminists did influenced the rise of the "New Woman" in the later part of the nineteenth century. Jane Addams fit the model of New Woman well: she was a well-educated social activist who eschewed traditional marriage to form Hull House, a settlement house on Chicago's West Side. As new states joined the Union, many of them included provisions that permitted women's full suffrage: Wyoming was first in 1869, followed by Utah in 1970 and Washington in 1883. Addams was a product of all these trends affecting all the contemporary American middle-class women who were beginning to think about the plight of less privileged women.

Author Biography

Jane Addams, the eighth of nine children, was born on September 6, 1860, in Cedarville, Illinois, into a wealthy family of Quaker background. Addams was a member of the first generation of American women to attend college. She graduated in 1881 from Rockford Female Seminary, in Illinois, which the following year became Rockford College for Women, allowing Addams to obtain her bachelor's degree. In the 1880s Addams began studying medicine at the Women's Medical College of Philadelphia, but she had to suspend her studies because of poor health. Throughout the decade Addams also suffered from depression owing to her father's sudden death in 1881. Her physical and mental conditions, however, did not prevent her from traveling extensively in Europe. During one of her voyages, Addams visited London's original settlement house of Toynbee Hall, established in 1884, with her companion, Ellen Gates Starr. The visit led the two women to establish the Chicago settlement house of Hull House in 1889, the second such house to be established in America. (Dr. Stanton Coit and Charles B. Stover had founded the first American settlement house, the Neighborhood Guild of New York City, in 1886.) Through Hull House, Addams found a vocation for her adult life, overcoming the sense of uselessness that had besieged her for most of the 1880s.

Addams campaigned for every major reform issue of her era, such as fairer workplace conditions for men and women, tenement regulation, juvenile-court law, women's suffrage, and women's rights. She worked closely with social workers, politicians, and labor and immigrant groups to achieve her purposes, and she was not afraid to take controversial stances, as when she decided to campaign against U.S. entry into World War I. While in the first part of her life Addams was mainly involved in social work in Hull House, in the twentieth century she used her notoriety to advance political causes and became a well-known public figure. In 1910 she was the first woman president of the National Conference of Social Work, and in 1912 she actively campaigned for the Progressive presidential candidate, Theodore Roosevelt, becoming the first woman to give a nominating speech at a party convention. Addams was also a founding member of the National Association for the Advancement of Colored People.

In conjunction with her antiwar efforts, she became the president of the Woman's Peace Party in 1915 and chaired the International Women's Congress for Peace and Freedom at The Hague, Netherlands. That congress led to the foundation of the

Women's International League for Peace and Freedom, which Addams chaired until 1929, when she was made honorary president for the remainder of her life. Americans were not unanimous in their praise for Addams's campaigning for peace. On the contrary, she was bitterly attacked by the press and was expelled from the Daughters of the American Revolution. In 1931, however, Addams's antiwar efforts won her the Nobel Peace Prize, which she shared with Nicholas Murray Butler. Because of her declining health, she was unable to collect the prize in person. Addams died in Chicago on May 21, 1935, three days after being diagnosed with cancer.

Addams's life, speeches, and writings are typical of middle-class reformers at the turn of the century. She was widely acknowledged as a pioneer social worker, and she spoke vigorously in favor of social reform. Her addresses and public interventions show her to have been idealistic yet committed to concrete action. Like other Progressive thinkers, such as John Dewey, Herbert Croly, Walter Lippmann, and Charlotte Perkins Gilman, Addams was deeply concerned with the changing nature of human ties and the meaning of community in an increasingly industrialized and urbanized world. Taking a critical stance toward the laissez-faire capitalism that had characterized the Gilded Age, a period of excessive displays of wealth in the late nineteenth century, Progressives like Addams expanded the authority to solve private and public problems to include not only the individual but also the government. They charged the state with the task of intervening in social and economic matters when appropriate, to defeat self-interest in the name of the common good.

Historical Document

"Why Women Should Vote"

For many generations it has been believed that woman's place is within the walls of her home, and it is indeed impossible to imagine the time when her duty there shall be ended or to forecast any social change which shall release her from that paramount obligation....

Many women today are failing to discharge their duties to their own households properly simply because they do not perceive that as society grows more complicated it is necessary that woman shall extend her sense of responsibility to many things outside of her own home if she would continue to preserve the home in its entirety.... A woman's simplest duty, one would say, is to keep her house clean and wholesome and to feed her children properly. Yet if she lives in a tenement house ... she cannot fulfill these simple obligations by her own efforts because she is utterly dependent upon the city administration for the conditions which render decent living possible. Her basement will not be dry, her stairways will not be fireproof, her house will not be provided with sufficient windows to give light and air, nor will it be equipped with sanitary plumbing, unless the Public Works Department sends inspectors who constantly insist that these elementary decencies be provided. Women who live in the country sweep their own dooryards and may either feed the refuse of the table to a flock of chickens or allow it innocently to decay in the open air and sunshine. In a crowded city quarter, however, if the street is not cleaned by the city authorities no amount of private sweeping will keep the tenement free from grime; if the garbage is not properly collected and destroyed a tenement-house mother may see her children sicken and die of diseases from which she alone is powerless to shield them, although her tenderness and devotion are unbounded. She cannot even secure untainted meat for her household, she cannot provide fresh fruit, unless the meat has been inspected by city officials, and the decayed fruit, which is so often placed upon sale in the tenement districts, has been destroyed in the interests of public health. In short, if woman would keep on with her old business of caring for her house and rearing her children she will have to have some conscience in regard to public affairs lying quite outside of her immediate household. The individual conscience and devotion are no longer effective....

In other words, if women would effectively continue their old avocations they must take part in the slow upbuilding of that code of legislation which is alone sufficient to protect the home from the dangers incident to modern life....

The more extensively the modern city endeavors on the one hand to control and on the other hand to provide recreational facilities for its young people the more necessary it is that women should assist in their direction and extension. After all, a care for wholesome and innocent amusement is what women have for many years assumed. When the reaction comes on the part of taxpayers women's votes may be necessary to keep the city to its beneficent obligations toward its own young people....

Ever since steam power has been applied to the processes of weaving and spinning woman's traditional work has been carried on largely outside of the home. The clothing and household linen are not only spun and woven, but also usually sewed, by machinery; the preparation of many foods has also passed into the factory and necessarily a certain number of women have been obliged to follow their work there, although it is doubtful, in spite of the large numbers of factory girls, whether women now are doing as large a proportion of the world's work as they used to do. Because many thousands of those working in factories and shops are girls between the ages of fourteen and twenty-two there is a necessity that older women should be interested in the conditions of industry. The very fact that these girls are not going to remain in industry permanently makes it more important that someone should see to it that they shall not be incapacitated for their future family life because they work for exhausting hours and under insanitary conditions.

If woman's sense of obligation had enlarged as the industrial conditions changed she might naturally and almost imperceptibly have inaugurated the movements for social amelioration in the line of factory legislation and shop sanitation. That she has not done so is doubtless due to the fact that her conscience is slow to recognize any obligation outside of her own family circle, and because she was so absorbed in her own household that she failed to see what the conditions outside actually were. It would be interesting to know how far the consciousness that she had no vote and could not change matters operated in this direction. After all, we see only those things to which our attention has been drawn, we feel responsibility for those things which are brought to us as matters of responsibility. If conscientious women were convinced that it was a civic duty to be informed in regard to these grave industrial affairs, and then to express the conclusions which they had reached by depositing a piece of paper in a ballot box, one cannot imagine that they would shirk simply because the action ran counter to old traditions....

To turn the administration of our civic affairs wholly over to men may mean that the American city will continue to push forward in its commercial and industrial development, and continue to lag behind in those things which make a city healthful and beautiful. After all, woman's traditional function has been to make her dwelling-place both clean and fair. Is that dreariness in city life, that lack of domesticity which the humblest farm dwelling presents, due to a withdrawal of one of the naturally cooperating forces? If women have in any sense been responsible for the gentler side of life which softens and blurs some of its harsher conditions, may they not have a duty to perform in our American cities?

In closing, may I recapitulate that if woman would fulfill her traditional responsibility to her own children; if she would educate and protect from danger factory children who must find their recreation on the street; if she would bring the cultural forces to bear upon our materialistic civilization; and if she would do it all with the dignity and directness fitting one who carries on her immemorial duties, then she must bring herself to the use of the ballot—that latest implement for self government. May we not fairly say that American women need this implement in order to preserve the home?

Glossary

dooryards: small front yards

incident to: related to, or following from

tenement house: a slum dwelling

this implement: the vote

Document Analysis

Addams's essay on women's suffrage, "Why Women Should Vote," published as an editorial in the *Ladies' Home Journal* in January 1910, inscribes itself in the intense debate on the topic that took place at the beginning of the twentieth century in America. The women's movement was a crucial part of Progressivism, and one of its most pressing questions was how women could attain equality with men and reform a society dominated by them. Many women's rights advocates claimed that voting was essential for women to achieve their reformist goals. Addams shared this belief. Yet, contrary to other women's rights campaigners, she rooted her support for female suffrage within the values of domesticity. While many within the movement argued that suffrage would be instrumental in helping women move beyond the narrow boundaries of the home, Addams begins her essay by situating women's place firmly within the home. She finds that no social change will release women from their domestic obligations. However, for women to fulfill such obligations, it is crucial that they can vote so that they can "take part in the slow upbuilding of that code of legislation which is alone sufficient to protect the home from the dangers incident to modern life."

Because the essay apparently embraces the traditional domestic role that Victorian society ascribed to women, Addams was criticized by her contemporaries as bowing to the popular and conservative perceptions of gender and womanhood. Yet, as Victoria Bissell Brown has pointed out, "Why Women Should Vote" is indicative of Addams's "unusual ability to weave [her] concern [for economic and political democracy] with her own mediating temperament, diplomatic style, and genuine respect for domesticity into a pro-suffrage argument that appealed to mainstream sensibilities." Addams's rhetorical ability is apparent not only in what she includes in her essay but also in what she leaves out. While many pro-suffrage writings took direct issue with arguments against women's voting rights, Addams never once cites her adversaries in her speech, such that her style comes across as completely nonconfrontational.

To Addams, the quest for women's suffrage represents an opportunity to hear women's voices in matters that are fundamental to the improvement of family life and to the struggle against urban vices. In its focus on the enhancement of living conditions within the urban environment, "Why Women Should Vote" ties the question of women's suffrage to the larger Progressive agenda, clearly stating that the two mutually reinforce each other. Because women have deep knowledge of the needs of youth, they can provide unique insights into effective ways "on the one hand to control and on the other hand to provide recreational facilities for its young people." Defining voting rights for women as a potential service toward the entire community, the essay is typical of the Progressives' affirmation of collective over individual concerns. As Brown writes, Addams assigns domesticity a crucial place in women's life not to "placate the patriarchs," but "because her daily experience taught her that domesticity was ... a utilitarian reality for her working-class neighbors, and one that could be powerful if deployed in the political arena against America's individualistic patriarchs."

Essential Themes

This document exemplifies the pragmatic philosophy that typified Jane Addams' social thought. She appeals to women who might still have embraced a conservative mindset or been unaware of the benefits of suffrage: it is the women who have not gone out to forge their own career like Addams did with Hull House that Addams addresses. Her diplomatic and peaceful methods found a home in the National American Woman Suffrage Association (NAWSA), in which she served as vice president from 1911-14 in addition to her many other activities. NAWSA was instrumental in securing the passage of the Nineteenth Amendment, which gave women the right to vote; Addams' dedication to achieving social change through peaceful means was well-suited to NAWSA, which did not favor militant protests or violence.

There are traces in this document of principles that drove the creation of a later organization that Addams helped found, the American Civil Liberties Union (ACLU). Addams cared about the right for women to vote, but suffrage was part of a larger array of civil injustices affecting women and children. Although Addams' essay ultimately achieved her desired goal of making women's suffrage a widespread phenomenon in the United States, the ACLU still carries on much of Addams' legacy in campaigning for better living conditions for women.

—Ashleigh Fata, MA, Luca Prono, PhD

Bibliography and Additional Reading

Fradin, Judith Bloom and Dennis Brindell Fradin. *Jane Addams: Champion of Democracy.* New York: Clarion, 2006.

Hamington, Maurice. *The Social Philosophy of Jane Addams.* Chicago: University of Illinois Press, 2009.

Lasch, Christopher, ed. *The Social Thought of Jane Addams.* 2nd ed. New York: Irvington, 1997.

McGerr, Michael. *A Fierce Discontent: The Rise and Fall of the Progressive Movement in America, 1870-1920.* New York: Free Press, 2003.

Schneider, Dorothy and Carl J. Schneider. *American Women in the Progressive Era, 1900-1920.* New York: Facts on File, 1993.

Stebner, Eleanor J. *The Women of Hull House: A Study in Spirituality, Vocation, and Friendship.* Albany: State University of New York Press, 1997.

Alice Paul: Testimony before the House Judiciary Committee

Date: December 16. 1915
Author: Alice Paul; members of the House Judiciary Committee (Congressmen William Ezra Williams, Joseph Taggart, Andrew Volstead, Edwin Webb, Ralph Moss, Warren Gard)
Genre: testimony

Summary Overview

The suffragist, feminist, and women's rights activist Alice Paul did not produce a large body of written documents. Modern students of the woman's suffrage and early feminist movements can gain insight into Paul's values and beliefs from oral sources, including her Testimony to the House Judiciary Committee on the question of female suffrage. Along with three of her fellow suffragists, Paul appeared before the committee on December 16, 1915, to speak on behalf of the Congressional Union for Woman Suffrage in support of an amendment to the U.S. Constitution granting voting rights to women.

Earlier that month, the so-called Anthony Amendment (named for Susan B. Anthony) had been introduced (not for the first time) in the House by Franklin Wheeler Mondell and in the Senate by George Sutherland. In the ensuing years, the amendment was repeatedly tabled, postponed, or rejected. It was not until June of 1919 that Congress voted fifty-six to twenty-five to pass the Nineteenth Amendment. It took effect on August 18, 1920, when Tennessee became the thirty-sixth state to ratify it.

Defining Moment

The women's rights movement started in 1848 at the Seneca Falls Convention. At this groundbreaking meeting of minds, one hundred people signed the Declaration of Sentiments, in which a revolutionary idea was proposed: votes for women. Thirty years later, Senator Sargent of California introduced the "Anthony Amendment," which prohibited denial of suffrage based on sex. Delaying the proposal for years, Congress ultimately struck down women's suffrage in 1887.

This did not stop the growth of the women's rights movement. Similar proposals to Sargent's were introduced yearly, although the disaster of the Civil War intervened, and in the meantime the number of states in the union grew. Since the limitation on suffrage was left unclear by the Constitution, new states in the West could define the boundaries of enfranchisement.

Alice Paul. Photo via Wikimedia Commons. [Public domain.]

Legislators in Wyoming drafted the first state constitution in 1870 that permitted women to vote in 1869. Following in Wyoming's lead, Utah was the next state to extend women the vote in 1870, followed by Washington in 1883. At the same time, the organizational power of women's groups expanded. In 1890, leaders of the women's rights movement formed the National American Woman Suffrage Association (NAWSA) out of two similar associations. Susan B. Anthony and Carrie Chapman Catt were the first two presidents of this new association; Anna Howard Shaw took over in 1904 and held the position until 1915, when tensions between the activist philosophies of the NAWSA and Alice Paul's group became too great.

This disagreement reflected fundamental differences between two camps within the women's rights movement. On one side, NAWSA and Shaw believed that they would best attain suffrage through peaceful means and pushing for suffrage on a state-by-state basis. However, Alice Paul and her supporters used more militant means of protest, which included protesting President Wilson during World War I and getting women in enfranchised states to vote out any congressman who did not support national voting rights for women. Paul had been part of NAWSA since 1910, but her methods started to meet resistance from leaders in the association as of 1913.

The year 1913 marked a shift in suffragist politics. First, on March 3, 1913, Paul organized for NAWSA a great march through the streets of Washington, D.C., which was a day before President Wilson was to be inaugurated. The resulting disturbances from angry crowds put a great deal attention back on the suffragists' cause. In 1913, Paul created the Congressional Union (CU) and began to use a British tactic she had learned: opposing the candidacies of any politician against suffrage. Paul's campaign to oppose the party in power started in the same year Illinois opened up votes to women in the Presidential and Municipal Voting Act: this was the first state east of the Mississippi to enfranchise women in presidential elections and it meant that Paul's group could appeal to a large new contingent of women voters. In the next two years, NAWSA's competing branch, the Congressional Committee, suffered several setbacks: the Senate struck down a proposal on women's suffrage for the first time since 1887, and then New York, Pennsylvania, New Jersey, and Massachusetts all struck down state amendments for suffrage. Additionally, in 1915, a German submarine torpedoed the Lusitania; the dozens of American deaths, while tragic, also threatened to draw attention away from the new fire in the struggle for women's right to vote.

Paul's CU continued campaigning, even as war broke out overseas. At the same time as President Wilson was attempting to solidify American support for the war effort, the suffragists were following his campaign to press him on support for their cause. At the end of the 1915, Paul hinted to the House Judiciary Committee that her group would continue to campaign against any congressmen opposing national enfranchisement. A day after Paul gave her testimony, she and several colleagues met the new president of NAWSA, Carrie Chapman Catt, along with a few board members to explore reconciliation between the CU and NAWSA. The rift was not to be healed, and by July 1916, Paul would form her own rival organization, the National Women's Party (NWP). Although this conflict would mark out disaster for any other organized movement, the formation of the NWP initiated a new and fiery phase of the suffrage movement that would culminate in a national amendment in 1919 and the official extension of voting rights.

Since the 1870s, advocates for women's suffrage tirelessly petitioned Congress to consider a constitutional amendment that prohibited voter discrimination on account of sex. In order to change federal law, any proposal had to pass the House Judiciary Committee, which, among other duties, has jurisdiction over matters of constitutional amendments and federal civil rights. In fact, the first woman to address a congressional committee was Victoria Woodhull, who spoke in 1871 before this committee on the issue of women's suffrage. Woodhull's testimony did not secure a majority vote from the Committee at the time. At the end of the year in 1915, Alice Paul would offer her testimony once again in front of the House Judiciary Committee in another attempt to ratify a national amendment.

After a season of encouraging enfranchised women in the western states to vote against any Congressional candidates who opposed women's suffrage, the House of Representatives was more amenable to hearing the testimony of suffragists again in order to recoup campaign losses. Paul faced an uphill battle in her testimony to the House Judiciary Committee in 1915, since the majority were Democratic, a party that at the time did not wholly support the cause of Paul and her colleagues. It would take several more years and finally President Wilson's support for the suffragists to break the cycle of delaying, postponing, and rejection from Congress.

Author Biography

Alice Paul, one of the nation's most outspoken suffragists and feminists in the early twentieth century and beyond, was born to a Quaker family at their Paulsdale estate in Mount Laurel, New Jersey, on January 11, 1885. Her religious background is relevant because the Hicksite Quakerism the family practiced placed a great deal of emphasis on gender equality. She came from a prominent family, with ancestors who included William Penn on her mother's side and the Massachusetts Winthrops on her father's. Her maternal grandfather was one of the founders of Swarthmore College, where Paul earned a bachelor's degree in biology in 1905. After attending the New York School of Philanthropy, she earned a master's degree from the University of Pennsylvania in 1907 and then went on to study at England's University of Birmingham and the London School of Economics before returning to the University of Pennsylvania, where she earned a PhD in sociology in 1912.

Her years in England, 1907 to 1910, were eventful. It was there that she served her apprenticeship in the struggle for women's rights. She came under the influence of the militant feminists Emmeline Pankhurst and her daughters, Christabel and Sylvia, and during those years she earned her stripes as an activist through demonstrations, arrests, imprisonment, hunger strikes, and force-feeding. On her return to the United States, she enlisted in the suffrage movement, first with the National American Woman Suffrage Association, though she and the young women she attracted to the movement were impatient with the association's conservative tactics. Accordingly, she broke with the association to found the Congressional Union for Woman Suffrage in 1913. The purpose of the new organization was to seek a federal constitutional amendment granting women the right to vote. In 1915 she appeared before the Judiciary Committee of the U.S. House of Representatives to testify on behalf of the proposed amendment.

In 1916 the Congressional Union evolved into the National Woman's Party. Paul and her followers, dubbed the Silent Sentinels, gained notoriety by launching a two-and-a-half-year picket (with Sundays off) of the White House, urging President Woodrow Wilson to support a suffrage amendment. After the United States entered World War I in 1917, few people believed that the picketers would continue. They did, often writing such incendiary phrases as "Kaiser Wilson" on placards, leading many people to conclude that the women were unpatriotic. (The reference was to Kaiser Wilhelm, ruler of Germany, America's enemy in the war.) Public opinion began to sway in favor of the suffragists when it was learned that more than 150 picketers had been arrested and sentenced to jail, usually on thin charges of obstructing traffic, and that the conditions the jailed women endured were often brutal. Paul, in particular, was subjected to inhuman treatment and launched a hunger strike in protest until she and the other protestors were released after a court of appeals ruled the arrests illegal. Meanwhile, the National Woman's Party continued to campaign against U.S. legislators who opposed the suffrage amendment.

After the passage by Congress (1919) and successful ratification (1920) of the Nineteenth Amendment recognizing the right of women to vote, Paul remained active in the woman's rights movement. In 1921 she wrote an equal rights amendment in the face of opposition from more conservative women's groups, who feared that such an amendment might strip women of protective legislation—in such areas as labor conditions—that had been passed during the Progressive Era. Nevertheless, she campaigned to make an equal rights amendment a plank in the platforms of both major political parties, which she succeeded in doing by 1944. In

November 1972 and May 1973 she shared her reflections on the women's movement with an interviewer as part of an oral history project conducted by the University of California, Berkeley. She lived long enough to see Congress approve the Equal Rights Amendment in 1972, though the amendment was not ratified by enough states to allow it to become part of the Constitution. Paul died on July 9, 1977.

Historical Document

Miss Paul: In closing the argument before this committee, may I summarize our position? We have come here to ask one simple thing: that the Judiciary Committee refer this Suffrage Amendment, known as the Susan B. Anthony Amendment, to the House of Representatives. We are simply asking you to do what you can do—that you let the House of Representatives decide this question. We have tried to bring people to this hearing from all over the United States to show the desire of women that this should be done.

I want to emphasize just one point, in addition, that we are absolutely non-partisan. We are made up of women who are strong Democrats, women who are strong Republicans, women who are Socialists, Progressives—every type of women. We are all united on this one thing—that we put Suffrage before everything else. In every election, if we ever go into any future elections, we simply pledge ourselves to this—that we will consider the furtherance of Suffrage and not our party affiliations in deciding what action we shall take.

Mr. Williams, of Illinois: Is it your policy to fight this question out only as a national issue? Do you make any attempt to secure relief through the States?

Miss Paul: The Congressional Union is organized to work for an Amendment to the National Constitution. We feel that the time has come, because of the winning of so many Suffrage States in the West, to use the votes of women to get Suffrage nationally. In the earlier days in this country, all the Suffrage work was done in the States, but the winning of the Western States has given us a power which we did not have before, so we have now turned from State work to national work. We are concentrating on the national government.

Mr. Gard: Miss Paul, is it true that you prefer to approach this through the State legislatures than to approach it directly through the people?

Miss Paul: We prefer the quickest way, which we believe is by Congressional action.

Mr. Taggart: Why did you oppose the Democrats in the last election?

Miss Paul: We came into existence when the administration of President Wilson first came in. We appealed to all members of Congress to have this Amendment put through at once. We did get that measure out upon the floor of the House and Senate, but when it came to getting a vote in the House we found we were absolutely blocked. We went again and again, week after week, and month after month to the Democratic members of the Rules Committee, who controlled the apportioning of the time of the House, and asked them to give us five or ten minutes for the discussion of Suffrage. Every time they refused. They told us that they were powerless to act because the Democrats had met in caucus and decided that Suffrage was a matter to be decided in the States and should not be brought up in Congress. (Here Miss Paul, moving the papers in front of her, deftly extracted a letter.) I have here a letter from Mr. Henry, Chairman of the Rules Committee, in which he says: "It would give me great pleasure to report the Resolution to the House, except for the fact that the Democratic caucus, by its direct action, has tied my hands and placed me in a position where I will not be authorized to do so unless the caucus is reconvened and changes its decision. I am sure your good judgment will cause you to thoroughly understand my attitude."...

After we had been met for months with the statement that the Democratic Party had decided in caucus not to let Suffrage come up in Congress, we said, "We will go out to the women voters in the West and tell them how we are blocked in Washington, and ask them if they will use their vote for the very highest purpose for which they can use it—to help get votes for other women."

We campaigned against every one of the forty-three men who were running for Congress on the Democratic ticket in any of the Suffrage States; and only nineteen of those we campaigned against came back to Washington. In December, at the close of the election, we went back to the Rules Committee. They told us then that they had no greater desire in the world than to bring the Suffrage Amendment out. They told us that we had misunderstood them in thinking that they were opposed to having Suffrage come up in Congress. They voted at once to bring Suffrage upon the floor for the first time in history. The whole opposition of the Democratic Party melted away and the decision of the party caucus was reversed.

The part we played in the last election was simply to tell the women voters of the West of the way the Democratic Party had blocked us at Washington and of the way the individual members of the Party, from the West, had supported their Party in blocking us. As soon as we told this record they ceased blocking us and we trust they will never block us again.

Question: But what about next time?

Miss Paul: We hope we will never have to go into another election. We are appealing to all Parties and to all men to put this Amendment through this Congress and send it on to the State Legislatures. What we are doing is giving the Democrats their opportunity. We did pursue a certain policy which we have outlined to you as you requested. As to what we may do we cannot say. It depends upon the future situation.

Question: But we want to know what you will do in the 1916 election?

Miss Paul: Can you possibly tell us what will be in the platform of the Democratic Party in 1916?

Mr. Webb: I can tell one plank that will not be there, and that is a plank in favor of Woman Suffrage.

Question: If conditions are the same, do you not propose to fight Democrats just the same as you did a year ago?

Miss Paul: We have come to ask your help in this Congress. But in asking it we have ventured to remind you that in the next election one-fifth of the vote for President comes from Suffrage States. What we shall do in that election depends upon what you do.

Mr. Webb: We would know better what to do if we knew what you were going to do.

Mr. Gard: We should not approach this bearing in any partisan sense. What I would like is to be informed about some facts. I asked Mrs. Field what reason your organization had for asking Congress to submit this question to States that have already acted upon it. Why should there be a resubmission to the voters by national action in States which have either voted for or against it, when the machinery exists in these same States to vote for it again?

Miss Paul: They have never voted on the question of a National Amendment.

Mr. Gard: The States can only ratify it. You would prefer that course to having it taken directly to the people?

Miss Paul: Simply because we have the power of women's votes to back up this method.

Mr. Gard: You are using this method because you think you have power to enforce it?

Miss Paul: Because we know we have power.

Mr. Taggart: The women who have the vote in the West are not worrying about what women are doing in the East. You will have to get more States before you try this nationally.

Miss Paul: We think that this repeated advice to go back to the States proves beyond all cavil that we are on the right track.

Mr. Taggart: Suppose you get fewer votes this time? Do you think it is fair to those members of Congress who voted for Woman Suffrage and have stood for Woman Suffrage, to oppose them merely because a majority of their Party were not in favor of Woman Suffrage?

Miss Paul: Every man that we opposed stood by his Party caucus in its opposition to Suffrage.

Mr. Volstead: This inquiry is absolutely unfair and improper. It is cheap politics, and I have gotten awfully tired listening to it.

Mr. Taggart: Have your services been bespoken by the Republican committee of Kansas for the next campaign?

Miss Paul: We are greatly gratified by this tribute to our value.

Mr. Moss: State just whether or not it is a fact that the question is, What is right? and not, What will be the reward or punishment of the members of this committee? Is not that the only question that is pending before this committee?

Miss Paul: Yes, as we have said over and over today. We have come simply to ask that this committee report this measure to the House, that the House may consider the question.

Mr. Moss: Can you explain to the committee what the question of what you are going to do to a member of this committee or a Congressman in regard to his vote has to do with the question of what we should do as our duty?

Miss Paul: As I have said, we don't see any reason for discussing that.

Mr. Webb: You have no blacklist, have you, Miss Paul?

Miss Paul: No.

Mr. Taggart: You are organized, are you not, for the chastisement of political Parties that do not do your bidding at once?

Miss Paul: We are organized to win votes for women and our method of doing this is to organize the women who have the vote to help other women to get it.

Glossary

bring the Suffrage Amendment out: the act whereby legislators vote a bill, in this case the one on woman suffrage, out of committee for a vote

caucus: any group of members in the House of Representatives who meet to pursue common legislative interests

Congressional Union: the Congressional Union for Woman Suffrage, founded in 1913 by Alice Paul and her associates

Mrs. Field: Sara Bard Field, prominent suffragist and feminist orator

plank: a figure of speech referring to a goal expressed in a political party's platform, or agenda

Document Analysis

The suffrage movement at the end of the nineteenth century and during the first two decades of the twentieth century was an amalgam of high ideals of justice and equality and more practical, mundane politics. Throughout these years, various organizations were formed, re-formed, and combined to pursue the right to vote through a variety of methods.

The mainstream suffrage organization was the National American Woman Suffrage Association, formed in 1890 by the combination of two predecessor organizations, the National Woman Suffrage Association and the American Woman Suffrage Association. The leaders of this group included such towering figures as Susan B. Anthony, Carrie Chapman Catt, Elizabeth Cady Stanton, and Frances Willard. Many of these women, however, had been fighting in the trenches for decades—Susan B. Anthony, for example, died in 1906 at the age of eighty-six—and a new generation of suffragists was growing impatient with the slow pace of progress. Among them was Alice Paul, who had absorbed the more radical tactics of militant feminists during the years she lived and studied in England, where she joined the Women's Social and Political Union. As a member, Paul urged the National American Woman Suffrage Association to adopt more militant tactics, but the more conservative organization resisted her pleas and forced her and her protégées out. Accordingly, Paul joined forces with such women as Lucy Burns, Olympia Brown, Mabel Vernon, Belle La Follette, Mary Ritter Beard, Maria Montessori, Doris Stevens, and Crystal Eastman to form the Congressional Union for Woman Suffrage (CUWS) in 1913.

During these years one of the principal issues faced by the suffragist movement was whether to pursue voting rights on a state-by-state basis or to seek an amendment to the Constitution. Already a number of states, led by Colorado, Idaho, Utah, and Wyoming and followed by Washington, California, Kansas, Oregon, Arizona, Montana, Nevada, and the Alaska Territory, had granted suffrage to women not only in municipal and state elections but in federal elections as well. Various other states had considered suffrage amendments to their state constitutions at different times. Approaching the matter one state at a time, though, was exhausting work, and it was generally believed that extending the franchise to women in the states of the highly conservative South would be next to impossible, particularly because of fears among many southerners that doing so would give black women the vote. For this reason, the new generation of suffragists focused on an amendment to the national Constitution.

One of the tactics the CUWS pursued was to target and defeat members of Congress who were up for reelection in 1914. Since 1878 the so-called Anthony Amendment had been proposed in every session of Congress. This was the original suffrage amendment formulated by Susan B. Anthony and other suffrage leaders in that year and which in 1920 would be ratified as the Nineteenth Amendment to the Constitution. In the intervening years, however, the amendment had been blocked, primarily by members of the Democratic Party, a party that was particularly strong in the South. In such states as Alabama, Georgia, and Louisiana every senator and congressman was a Democrat. Although Democrats also represented states in which suffrage had been granted, the CUWS targeted them in the 1914 election because, according to Paul, they had stood with the party in blocking efforts to bring a national amendment up for a vote on the floor of the Senate and House. The CUWS wanted to demonstrate that in states where women had the vote, they could use that power to chastise their congressional representatives and to demonstrate support for a national amendment.

It was in this context that Alice Paul testified before the House Judiciary Committee on the suffrage question on December 16, 1915. In her remarks she summarizes the position of the CUWS—simply that its members wanted the House Judiciary Committee to refer the Anthony Amendment to the floor of the House of Representatives for a vote. (Congressional procedure dictates that any bill has to be referred by an appropriate committee for consideration on the floor.) Paul adds that her organization was "absolutely non-partisan," even though it had targeted Democrats in the previous year's election. She emphasizes that women of all political parties supported the goal of suffrage.

At this point the Democrat William Ezra Williams of Illinois interrupted the proceedings and asked Paul about the issue of pursuing suffrage through the states rather than nationally. Paul makes clear in her remarks that the goal of the Congressional Union was to pursue an amendment to the federal Constitution, noting that the western states, where suffrage was a reality, gave women a power base from which to urge a national amendment. She emphasizes the same point in a brief exchange with the Democratic Representative Warren Gard of Ohio.

Then the Democrat Joseph Taggart of Kansas asked Paul a pointed question—why the group opposed Democrats in the last election. In her reply Paul puts forward the position of the CUWS. The organization, she says, tried repeatedly, "again and again, week after week, and month after month," to bring the matter of suffrage to a vote in Congress. Repeatedly the effort was blocked. The culprits, in Paul's view, were congressional Democrats on the Rules Committee who refused to vote the measure out of committee and onto the floor of the House. These Democrats argued that the matter was one for the individual states to decide. Accordingly, the CUWS took a bold step: The organization went to the women of the West—the states where suffrage had been granted were all in the Midwest, the Rocky Mountain region, and the West Coast—and persuaded them that they could use their votes to defeat Democrats. The campaign was successful in defeating twenty-four of the forty-three Democratic candidates who were up for reelection in those states. This campaign, Paul notes, had the desired effect. When Congress reconvened, the Rules Committee, claiming that it had been "misunderstood," voted to bring the suffrage amendment to the floor of the House, and Democratic opposition to the measure "melted away."

The remainder of the committee's proceedings betrayed a certain level of irritation on the part of some members of the committee—irritation that Paul met with clear, measured responses. When asked about the CUWS's plans for the next election, Paul says that the answer to that depended on the actions of Congress and on the Democratic Party's platform in 1916. The Democrat Edwin Webb of North Carolina flatly gave his opinion that the platform would not include a suffrage amendment. In reply, Paul pointedly mentions that one-fifth of the vote in the next year's presidential election would come from states with woman's suffrage and says that "what we shall do in that election depends upon what you do." Congressman Gard questioned why the suffrage issue should come up for a vote in states that already had a suffrage amendment. Paul replies that those states "had never voted on the question of a National Amendment." Congressman Taggart suggested that the best way for the CUWS to proceed was to increase its power base by getting suffrage amendments passed in more states. Paul answers that the organization had repeatedly been given this advice, proving "beyond all cavil" that the organization was "on the right track." Taggart then raised the question of whether it was fair to target men from the party who had supported women's suffrage; Paul replies that in every case these men had stood by their party in blocking efforts to bring the amendment to a vote.

After the committee's chairman, Minnesota Republican Andrew Volstead, expressed the view that the inquiry was improper, Taggart and the Indiana Democrat Ralph Moss attempted to pin Paul down on her motives and future plans, including the question of whether the CUWS had a "blacklist." Paul, a slender, delicate woman who on this occasion appeared in a violet dress, refused to buckle under this interrogation and insisted that her only motive was to win the vote for women.

Essential Themes

This document reveals only the beginning of Alice Paul's campaign against the politically powerful men who refused to support the right to vote for women. This campaign in 1914 secured for Paul the ability to approach the House Judiciary Committee again on women's suffrage, since it had resulted in the loss of some seats for the Democratic Party. Following a lack of progress in Congress after this testimony, Paul renewed her campaign of "punishing the party in power." Although the efforts of Paul and the NWP could not prevent the re-election of the intransigent President Wilson, they did succeed in the defeat of

Representative Joseph Taggart, the combative committee member from Paul's testimony.

The absence of any substantive progress from the House Judiciary Committee did not deter Paul, however. After a year of campaigning and organizing in 1916, Paul and her suffragists began picketing the White House at the start of 1917. This was also the same year that Jeanette Rankin took her seat in the House of Representatives as the first elected congresswoman. The suffragists attacked President Wilson for his rhetoric on freedom and democracy in World War I, while at the same time refusing to support women's suffrage. In August 1917, Lucy Burns unfurled a notorious banner calling the president "Kaiser Wilson," comparing the president to the leader of the United States' enemy at the time, Kaiser Wilhelm II. Paul and many of her fellow suffragists suffered beatings, force-feeding, contaminated food and water, and solitary confinement while jailed for protesting during the year. Attacks on these picketers and the deplorable conditions they suffered when jailed encouraged an eventual reconciliation between the two factions of suffragists who had split shortly after Paul's 1915 testimony.

Finally, President Wilson could avoid the topic of women's suffrage no longer by 1918. Britain, Russia, Germany, and Canada had already extended the vote to women; if Wilson had not encouraged his country to the same goal, he would be demonstrably a hypocrite. After months of tireless outreach from the women's organizations and Paul, the Anthony Amendment was finally brought to a vote in Congress: it passed in the House and Senate as of May 21, 1919. By the end of August 1920, thirty-six states had finally ratified what became the Nineteenth Amendment, and the right for women to vote was at long last the law of the nation.

Paul's grassroots tactics, while shocking at the time, quickly became the norm for future civil rights struggles. Her work did not end with the Nineteenth Amendment, though. She went on to propose an early form of the Equal Rights Amendment (ERA), which would ultimately fail to secure the required number of ratifications from the states by 1982. As perhaps a subtle nod to the enduring struggle of women's rights, Hillary Clinton wore white, the favored color of suffragists like Alice Paul, when she accepted her nomination as the first female nominee of a major U.S. political party in 2016.

—*Ashleigh Fata, MA, Michael J. O'Neal, PhD*

Bibliography and Additional Reading

Barber, Lucy G. *Marching on Washington: the Forging of an American Political Tradition.* Berkeley: University of California Press, 2002.

Cahill, Bernadette. *Alice Paul, the National Women's Party and the Vote.* Jefferson, NC: McFarland & Company, 2015.

Ford, Linda G. *Iron-Jawed Angels: The Suffrage Militancy of the National Women's Party, 1912-1920.* Lanham, NY: UP of America, 1991.

Kraditor, Aileen S. *The Ideas of the Woman Suffrage Movement, 1890-1920.* New York: Anchor, 1971.

Tilly, Louise A., and Patricia Gurin, eds. *Women, Politics, and Change.* New York: Russell Sage Foundation, 1990.

Walton, Mary. *A Woman's Crusade: Alice Paul and the Battle for the Ballot.* New York: Palgrave MacMillan, 2010.

Anna Howard Shaw: "Women's Suffrage in a Democratic Republic"

Date: June 21, 1915
Author: Anna Howard Shaw
Genre: speech

Summary Overview

In June 1915, the suffragist and social reformer Anna Howard Shaw delivered one of many similarly themed speeches she gave across New York State. Speaking in Ogdensburg, in the far north of the state, Shaw argued that the United States could not be considered a true democratic republic when not all of its citizens could participate in the democratic process. With World War I raging in Europe, Shaw proposed that women's suffrage could help foster future peace.

Defining Moment

The women's movement in the United States, which began in earnest in the mid-nineteenth century and continued through the twentieth century, coincided with (and in many cases was overshadowed by) some of the key events of this pivotal period. Early in its life, the movement linked women's empowerment with social issues, such as temperance and family matters. Prior to the Civil War, however, two key figures in the movement—Susan B. Anthony and Elizabeth Cady Stanton—met to launch a formal, national campaign for women's rights. The two led an unsuccessful push to include women in the Fourteenth and Fifteenth Amendments, which were already controversial by granting citizenship and suffrage to freed slaves.

During the post–Civil War era, the movement found new life, but it was marred by a disagreement over how to achieve suffrage. Anthony, Stanton, and Anna Howard Shaw believed that change should occur at the federal level, while activists like Lucy Stone pushed for a state-level approach. Neither approach gained much traction, despite garnering some sympathy from leaders in Congress and some state legislatures. This trend changed during the last decade of the nineteenth century. Anthony, Stanton, and Shaw's National American Women's Suffrage Association (NAWSA)—created in 1889 by the merger of the Anthony and Stanton's National Women's Suffrage Association with the American Woman Suffrage Association with which Shaw had been affiliated—returned to the movement's roots, recruiting new supporters by focusing on social issues that were in the eye of the general public, such as labor, child protection, and temperance.

Stanton died in 1902 and Anthony in 1906. Leadership of NAWSA fell to Shaw in 1904, whose exceptional oratory skills had been well known since the late nineteenth century. Shaw was able to attract more than 150,000 new suffrage activists to NAWSA during her tenure and tripled the number of states in which NAWSA sought legislative changes. During

Anna Howard Shaw, c. 1919. Photo via Wikimedia Commons. [Public domain.]

"The Awakening: Votes for Women" in Puck *Magazine, 1915. Image via Wikimedia Commons. [Public domain.]*

this period of growth, however, war broke out in Europe. Americans' attention was diverted from domestic issues to foreign matters—specifically, whether the United States should enter the war.

U.S. neutrality was called into question in 1915, when German U-boats sank the British ocean liner *Lusitania* on May 7, 1915, shortly after it departed New York for Liverpool, England, with a large number of American passengers aboard—128 of them were among the nearly 1,200 people killed in the tragedy. Shaw was delivering presentations across New York State at the time. With Americans focused on the Great War, Shaw modified her speeches to suggest that a truly unified United States—with men, women, and people of all races sharing equal power in the spirit of democracy—would see the greatest success in the war and in the future establishment of world peace. Her speech—dubbed "The Fundamental Principle of a Republic"—was never written down verbatim. However, she echoed its verbiage throughout the state, including on June 21, 1915, when she delivered it in Ogdensburg as part of the New York state equal suffrage campaign.

Author Biography

Anna Howard Shaw was born in Newcastle-on-Tyne, England, on February 14, 1847. She and her parents immigrated to Massachusetts in 1851 and, in 1859, moved to the wilderness in Michigan. Shaw began her career as a teacher at the age of fifteen. She paid her way through Albion College in Michigan until 1875 and then attended the Theological School at Boston University, graduating in 1878. She was a pastor in East Dennis, Massachusetts, and sought ordination in the Methodist Episcopal Church before being ordained as a Methodist Protestant elder in 1880. She also went on to earn her medical degree in 1886 and worked as a paramedic for the poor in South Boston.

During the late 1880s, she became involved in the suffrage and temperance movements, joining the Massachusetts Women's Suffrage Association and the Women's Christian Temperance Union. In 1900, when Anthony resigned as president of NAWSA, Carrie B. Chapman became NAWSA's president and Shaw was named vice president at large. Shaw later became the association's president, serving from 1904 to 1915. During World War I, she was an outspoken advocate for the American effort, receiving numerous honors for her leadership. She died from pneumonia on July 2, 1919, in Moylan, Pennsylvania.

Historical Document

"Women's Suffrage in a Democratic Republic"

When I came into your hall tonight, I thought of the last time I was in your city. Twenty-one years ago I came here with Susan B. Anthony, and we came for exactly the same purpose as that for which we are here tonight. Boys have been born since that time and have become voters, and the women are still trying to persuade American men to believe in the fundamental principles of democracy, and I never quite feel as if it was a fair field to argue this question with men, because in doing it you have to assume that a man who professes to believe in a Republican form of government does not believe in a Republican form of government, for the only thing that woman's enfranchisement means at all is that a government which claims to be a Republic should be a Republic, and not an aristocracy. The difficulty with discussing this question with those who oppose us is that they make any number of arguments but none of them have anything to do with Woman's Suffrage; they always have something to do with something else, therefore the arguments which we have to make rarely ever have anything to do with the subject, because we have to answer our opponents who always escape the subject as far as possible in order to have any sort of reason in connection with what they say.

Now one of two things is true: either a Republic is a desirable form of government, or else it is not. If it is, then we should have it, if it is not then we ought not to pretend that we have it. We ought at least to be true to our ideals, and the men of New York have, for the first time in their lives, the rare opportunity, on the second day of next November, of making the state truly a part of a Republic. It is the greatest opportunity which has ever come to the men of the state. If Woman's Suffrage is wrong, it is a great wrong; if it is right, it is a profound and fundamental principle, and we all know, if we know what a Republic is, that it is the fundamental principle upon which a Republic must rise. Let us see where we are as a people; how we act here and what we think we are. The difficulty with the men of this country is that they are so consistent in their inconsistency that they are not aware of having been inconsistent; because their consistency has been so continuous and their inconsistency so consecutive that it has never been broken, from the beginning of our Nation's life to the present time. If we trace our history back we will find that from the very dawn of our existence as a people, men have been imbued with a spirit and a vision more lofty than they have been able to live; they have been led by visions of the sublimest truth, both in regard to religion and in regard to government that ever inspired the souls of men from the time the Puritans left the old world to come to this country, led by the Divine ideal which is the sublimest and supremest ideal in religious freedom which men have ever known, the theory that a man has a right to worship God according to the dictates of his own conscience, without the intervention of any other man or any other group of men. And it was this theory, this vision of the right of the human soul which led men first to the shores of this country.

Now, nobody can deny that they are sincere, honest and earnest men. No one can deny that the Puritans were men of profound conviction, and yet these men who gave up everything in behalf of an ideal, hardly established their communities in this new country before they began to practice exactly the same sort of persecutions on other men which had been practiced upon them. They settled in their communities on the New England shores and when they formed their compacts by which they governed their local societies, they permitted no man to have a voice in the affairs unless he was a member of the church, and not a member of any church, but a member of the particular church which dominated the particular community in which he happened to be. In Massachusetts they drove the Baptists down to Rhode Island; in Connecticut they drove the Presbyterians over to New Jersey; they burned the Quakers in Massachusetts and ducked the witches, and no colony, either Catholic or Protestant allowed a Jew to have a voice. And so a man must worship God according to the conscience of the particular community in which he was located, and yet they called that religious freedom, they were not able to live the ideal of religious liberty, and from that time to this the men of this government have been following along the same line of inconsistency, while they too have been following a vision of equal grandeur and power.

And God said in the beginning, "It is not good for man to stand alone." That is why we are here tonight, and that is all that woman's suffrage means; just to repeat again and again that first declaration of the Divine, "It is not good for man to stand alone," and so the women of this state are asking that the word "male" shall be stricken out of the constitution altogether and that the constitution stand as it ought to have stood in the beginning and as it must before this state is any part of a Republic. Every citizen possessing the necessary qualifications shall be entitled to cast one vote at every election, and have that vote counted. We are not asking, as our Anti-Suffrage friends think we are, for any of the awful things that we hear will happen if we are allowed to vote: we are simply asking that that government which professes to be a Republic shall be a Republic and not pretend to be what it is not.

Now what is a Republic? Take your dictionary, encyclopedia, lexicon or anything else you like and look up the definition and you will find that a Republic is a form of government in which the laws are enacted by representatives elected by the people. Now when did the people of New York ever elect their representatives? Never in the world. The men of New York have, and I grant you that men are people, admirable people, as far as they go, but they only go half way. There is still another half of the people who have not elected representatives, and you never read a definition of a Republic in which half of the people elect representatives to govern the whole of the people. That is an aristocracy and that is just what we are. We have been many kinds of aristocracies. We have been a hierarchy of church members, [then] an oligarchy of sex.

There are two old theories which are dying today. Dying hard but dying. One of them is dying on the plains of Flanders and the Mountains of Galicia and Austria, and that is the theory of the divine right of kings. The other is dying here in the state of New York and Massachusetts and New Jersey and Pennsylvania and that is the divine right of sex. Neither of them had a foundation in reason, or justice or common sense.

Now I want to make this proposition, and I believe every man will accept it. Of course he will if he is intelligent. Whenever a Republic prescribes the qualifications as applying equally to all the citizens of the Republic, when the Republic says in order to vote, a citizen must be twenty-one years of age, it applies to all alike, there is no discrimination against any race or sex. When the government says that a citizen must be a native born citizen or a naturalized citizen, that applies to all; we are either born or naturalized, somehow or other we are here. Whenever the government says that a citizen, in order to vote, must be a resident of a community a certain length of time, and of the state a certain length of time and of the nation a certain length of time, that applies to all equally. There is no discrimination. We might go further and we might say that in order to vote the citizen must be able to read his ballot. We have not gone that far yet. We have been very careful of male ignorance in these United States. I was much interested, as perhaps many of you, in reading the Congressional Record this last winter over the debate over the immigration bill, and when that illiteracy clause was introduced into the immigration bill, what fear there was in the souls of men for fear we would do injustice to some of the people who might want to come to our shores, and I was much interested in the language in which the President vetoed the bill, when he declared that by inserting the clause we would keep out of our shores a large body of very excellent people. I could not help wondering then how it happens that male ignorance is so much less ignorant than female ignorance. When I hear people say that if women were permitted to vote a large body of ignorant people would vote, and therefore because an ignorant woman would vote, no intelligent women should be allowed to vote. I wonder why we have made it so easy for male ignorance and so hard for female ignorance.

Where is the difficulty? Just in one thing and one thing only, that men are so sentimental. We used to believe that women were the sentimental sex, but they cannot hold a tallow candle compared with the arc light of the men. Men are so sentimental in their attitude about women that they cannot reason about them. Now men are usually very fair to each other. I think the average man recognizes that he has no more right to anything at the hands of the government than has every other man. He has no right at all to anything to which every other man has not an equal right with himself. He says why have I a right to certain things in the government; why have I a right to life and liberty; why have I a right to this or this? Does he say because I am a man? Not at all, because I am human, and being human I have a right to everything which belongs to humanity, and every right which any other human being has, I have. And then he says of his neighbor, and my neighbor he also is human, therefore every right which belongs to me as a human being, belongs to him as a human being, and I have no right to anything under the government to which he is not equally entitled. And then up comes a woman, and then they say now she's a woman; she is not quite human, but she is my wife, or my sister, or my daughter or an aunt, or my cousin. She is not quite human, she is only related to a human, and being related to a human a human will take care of her. So we have had that care taking human being to look after us and they have not recognized that women too are equally human with men. Now if men could forget for a minute—I believe the anti-suffragists say that we want men to forget that we are related to them, they don't know me—if for a minute they could forget our relationship and remember that we are equally human with themselves, then they would say—yes, and this human being, not because she is a woman, but because she is human is entitled to every privilege and every right under the government which I, as a human being am entitled to. The only reason men do not see as fairly in regard to women as they do in regard to each other is because they have looked upon us from an altogether different plane than what they have looked at men; that is because women have been the homemakers while men have been the so-called protectors, in the period of the world's civilization when people needed to be protected. I know that they say that men protect us now and when we ask them what they are protecting us from the only answer they can give is from themselves. I do not think that men need any very great credit for protecting us from themselves. They are not protecting us from any special thing from which we could not protect ourselves except themselves. Now this old time idea of protection was all right when the world needed this protection, but today the protection in civilization comes from within and not from without. . .

When suffragettes are feminists, and when I ask what that is no one is able to tell me. I would give anything to know what a feminist is. They say, would you like to be a feminist? If I could find out I would, you either have to be masculine or feminine and I prefer feminine. Then they cry that we are socialists, and anarchists. Just how a human can be both at the same time, I really do not know. If I know what socialism means it means absolute government and anarchism means no government at all. So we are feminists, socialists, anarchists and mormons or spinsters. Now that is about the list. I have not heard the last speech. Now as a matter of fact, as a unit we are nothing, as individuals we are like all other individuals.

We have our theories, our beliefs, but as suffragettes we have but one belief, but one principle, but one theory and this is the right of a human being to have a voice in the government under which he or she lives, on that we agree, if on nothing else. Whether we agree or not on religion or politics we are not concerned. . . .

Now what does it matter whether the women will vote as their husbands do or will not vote; whether they have time or have not; or whether they will vote for prohibition or not. What has that to do with the fundamental question of democracy, no one has yet discovered. But they cannot argue on that; they cannot argue on the fundamental basis of our existence so that they have to get off on all these side tricks to get anything approaching an argument. So they tell you that democracy is a form of government. It is not. It was before governments were; it will prevail when governments cease to be; it is more than a form of government; it is a great spiritual force emanating from the heart of the Infinite, transforming human character until some day, some day in the distant future, man by the power of the spirit of democracy, will be able to look back into the face of the Infinite and answer, as man cannot answer today, "One is our Father, even God, and all we people are the children of one family." And when democracy has taken possession of human lives no man will ask for him to grant to his neighbor, whether that neighbor be a man or a woman; no man will then be willing to allow another man to rise to power on his shoulders, nor will he be willing to rise to power on the shoulders of another prostrate human being. But that has not yet taken possession of us, but some day we will be free, and we are getting nearer and nearer to it all the time; and never in the history of our country had the men and women of this nation a better right to approach it than they have today; never in the history of the nation did it stand out so splendidly as it stands today, and never ought we men and women to be more grateful for anything than that there presides in the White House today a man of peace.

The other resolution was on peace. We believed then and many of us believe today, notwithstanding all the discussion that is going on, we believe and we will continue to believe that preparedness for war is an incentive to war, and the only hope of permanent peace is the systematic and scientific disarmament of all the nations of the world, and we passed a resolution and passed it unanimously to that effect. A few days afterward I attended a large reception given by the American Ambassador and there was an Italian diplomat there and he spoke rather superciliously and said, "You women think you have been having a very remarkable convention, and I understand that a resolution on peace was offered by the Germans, the French women seconded it, and the British presiding officer presented it and it was carried unanimously." We none of us dreamed what was taking place at that time, but he knew and we learned it before we arrived home, that awful, awful thing that was about to sweep over the nations of the world. The American ambassador replied to the Italian diplomat and said, "Yes Prince, it was a remarkable convention, and it is a remarkable thing that the only people who can get together internationally and discuss their various problems without acrimony and without a sword at their side are the women of the world, but we men, even when we go to The

Hague to discuss peace, we go with a sword dangling at our side." It is remarkable that even at this age men cannot discuss international problems and discuss them in peace.

No we women do not want the ballot in order that we may fight, but we do want the ballot in order that we may help men to keep from fighting, whether it is in the home or in the state, just as the home is not without the man, so the state is not without the woman, and you can no more build up homes without men than you can build up the state without women. We are needed everywhere where human life is. We are needed everywhere where human problems are to be solved. Men and women must go through this world together from the cradle to the grave, it is God's way and it is the fundamental principle of a Republican form of government.

Document Analysis

Speaking before her New York state audience, Anna Howard Shaw linked the women's rights movement—which she said had taken place over decades of her own life—to the idea of a true democratic republic. She argued that the nation was founded and developed by men, who were initially well-meaning and earnest but who eventually succumbed to the same sorts of prejudices that had driven them from Europe. Through universal suffrage, she said, the country would be stronger and free from discrimination. It was time, therefore, for men to share governance of the country with the rest of its citizens. Women in particular, she said, could help promote peace and stability in the postwar era.

In her speech, Shaw reminds the audience of how long it has been since the women's suffrage movement began (she and Anthony stood on that very stage twenty-one years earlier, she said, addressing this very issue) and how much had changed during that period. Men, who centuries earlier had established the colonies and then founded the nation, continued to entrench themselves in positions of leadership, promoting the idea of the nation as a democratic republic. However, she said, men had given in to many of the same prejudices that they escaped while under British rule—male religious leaders had driven out different-minded people from New England during the colonial era, and had excluded other religious and social groups from power throughout history.

The central issue, Shaw said, was whether the nation wished to be a democratic republic. Such a political structure, she argued, was designed to be all-inclusive, fed by the votes and participation of every citizen. The present form of government, Shaw said, strayed considerably from this ideal and more resembled an "aristocracy"—the male-dominated political machines, for example, limited open political participation. The notions that fueled this approach to male-dominated government—the divine right of kings and the divine right of sex—were slowly "dying," she said. Leadership was starting to take note of the need to embrace a more literal idea of a republic.

Standing in the way of this progress, however, were "sentimental" men who were unwilling to change the country's ways. Men clung to the notions of women as homemakers and wives and not as citizens, she said (adding that some men even saw women as lesser humans). Suffragists, women's rights activists, and feminists, she said, were seen by men as threats. Thus, the men confronted with such groups would label them "socialists" and "anarchists" and seek to keep them out of mainstream politics.

An acceptance of women's suffrage, Shaw said, posed little risk. Women would not necessarily vote in a way that would disrupt the government. However, she said, their vote on any number of topics would represent a greater sample of Americans' preferences. Still, the issues of interest to women would be brought to light and addressed, she said. One such issue was world peace; she suggested that the intransigence of men had created the ongoing war, while the initiative of multinational women's groups resulted in peaceful resolutions (which had not been adopted by the warring nations' governments, however). Women were created to provide a balance for men. In this case, she said, the balance created by acceptance of women's suffrage could keep men from fighting and instead foster international peace.

Essential Themes

Anna Howard Shaw recognized the fact that the women's rights movement—specifically in the area of suffrage—had been developing slowly since the mid-1800s and yet had produced few tangible results. Men, as they had throughout American history, continued to dominate the U.S. political system. In the shadow of World War I, Shaw spoke to the ideals of the democratic republic to which Americans were endeared, and said that if these ideals were indeed invaluable to Americans, women should be allowed to vote and participate in government.

Shaw was one of the last living icons of the women's suffrage movement when she delivered this address (with Stanton and Anthony dying during the previous decade). Shaw said that the reason why women had not yet accomplished suffrage (and why the movement itself was consistently met with resistance) was simple: men would not relinquish power. Men had long been America's primary leaders, she said, while women and people of color were relegated to subordinate positions. Men continued to hold all seats in Congress and in other legislative bodies. When faced with the increased influence of suffragists, she added, these men would resist. In fact, in a desperate attempt to defend a male-dominated United States system, Shaw said, men would inevitably dub these activists anarchists or socialists as the rising voice of women captured the nation's attention.

Because men held fast to their positions, Shaw said, the nation was not a true democratic republic, instead resembling an aristocracy. Still, Shaw said, the "divine right" of kings and gender that men presumed to enjoy in the past was slowly dying as women and minority groups sought the opportunity to participate. Ironically, Americans were considering entering a war in an effort to defeat the ideals of discrimination and royalty while America itself was clinging to some of these virtues in its own political system. If given a chance to vote, she added, women would play a role in finally defeating these principles and promoting the peaceful democratic ideals Americans professed to embrace.

—*Michael P. Auerbach, MA*

Bibliography and Additional Reading

Bausum, Ann. *With Courage and Cloth: Winning the Fight for a Woman's Right to Vote.* Washington, DC: Natl. Geographic, 2004.

Crawford, Elizabeth. *The Women's Suffrage Movement: A Reference Guide, 1866–1928.* London: Routledge, 2001.

Franzen, Trisha. *Anna Howard Shaw: The Work of Woman Suffrage.* Champaign: U of Illinois P, 2014.

Frost-Knappman, Elizabeth, and Kathryn Cullen-DuPont. *Women's Suffrage in America: An Eyewitness History.* New York: Facts on File, 1992.

Shaw, Anna Howard. The Story of a Pioneer. Teddington: Echo Lib., 2006.

■ Prison Writings of a Radical Suffragist

Date: 1920 (describing events of 1917)
Author: Rose Winslow
Genre: diary; letter

Summary Overview

Rose Winslow was a member of the National Women's Party (NWP), an organization founded by Alice Paul and Lucy Burns in 1913 to advocate for voting rights for women. The NWP broke away from the National American Woman Suffrage Association, which some women viewed as too conservative. The NWP decided to focus its energy on appealing directly to the president, Woodrow Wilson, who had not committed his support to suffrage in 1917. Winslow and others participated in picketing in front of the White House, agitation that was initially ignored. When the nation began mobilizing for war in Europe, however, the picketers were arrested and imprisoned. When they refused to eat in protest, picketers were force-fed, a process that caused significant pain and distress to them. In scraps of paper smuggled out of the prison, Winslow described conditions in the Occoquan Workhouse in Virginia, focusing particularly on the torturous process of force-feeding.

Defining Moment

The NWP began its life as a radical organization, founded by a group of women who believed that direct, public agitation would be an effective strategy to win women the right to vote. Alice Paul, the leader of the NWP, was an intelligent, savvy, and combative strategist who understood public relations. She organized a large suffrage parade on March 3, 1913, the day before Wilson's first inauguration, and over five thousand people took part. In January 1917, Paul organized the Silent Sentinels, a group of women who picketed in front of the White House around the clock, every day but Sunday. She understood that the publicity gained from picketing would force the president to action. At first, Wilson and the police ignored the picketers, considering them curiosities rather than serious agitators. As the United States readied for war against Germany, however, the mood changed. Picket signs became increasingly incendiary (one compared Wilson to the hated kaiser of Germany), and the women were increasingly attacked and harassed. Beginning on June 25, picketers began to be arrested, ostensibly for obstructing traffic. At first, most were offered jail or a fine. If they chose jail, they were released after a few days, or pardoned. Wil-

Rose Winslow. Photo via Wikimedia Commons. [Public domain.]

son, a progressive reformer, did not wish to be seen as a brute by his European allies, but also did not want to appear weak. As the picketing continued, the sentences for these women grew. Winslow was arrested on October 15 and Paul was arrested on October 20. The women were sentenced to seven months and six months in jail, respectively, and were sent to the Occoquan Workhouse in Virginia.

Once in jail, Winslow and her fellow picketers were threatened, assaulted, and abused. Paul was sentenced to solitary confinement, with only bread and water to eat for two weeks. When she became so weak she could no longer stand, she was sent to the prison hospital, where she refused to eat. Winslow and several others went on hunger strike as well, a practical and symbolic tactic that forced the authorities to either release them or torture them by force-feeding. It was also intended to identify the picketers as political rather than criminal prisoners. On other occasions, women were beaten, choked, knocked unconscious, and chained to their cells. Women were threatened with commitment to insane asylums. Newspapers carried sensational stories of the treatment of women like Winslow, who fainted from hunger on several occasions, and supporters smuggled out information describing brutal force-feedings and terrible treatment. Though there was certainly strong anti-suffrage sentiment in the United States, the treatment of the picketers, many of whom were middle- and upper-class women, began to galvanize support for suffrage. All of the picketers were released on November 27 and 28, and their convictions later erased. Wilson himself came out in favor of votes for women in early 1918, and the Nineteenth Amendment, outlawing voting discrimination on the basis of gender, was finally ratified in August 1920.

Author Biography

Rose Winslow was born Ruza Wenclawska in Poland and immigrated to the United States with her family as an infant. Winslow's father worked as a coal miner and steel worker in Pennsylvania. Winslow began working at a hosiery mill in Pittsburgh at age eleven and also worked in factories in Philadelphia. She con-

"Kaiser Wilson" banner held by an NWP member picketing the White House, 1917. Photo via Wikimedia Commons. [Public domain.]

tracted tuberculosis when she was nineteen and was unable to work for two years. Despite her fragile health, Winslow became a factory inspector and labor organizer in New York City, working with both the National Consumers' League and the National Women's Trade Union League.

Winslow became an excellent public speaker during her years of union activism, and she brought this skill with her when she joined the NWP in 1916. Winslow traveled across the country speaking to suffrage rallies, often with NWP founder Paul, with whom she sometimes clashed. Winslow advocated for the inclusion of working-class women and men in the NWP, while Paul did not wish to organize men and did not encourage a prolabor message in her platform.

Winslow was a lead picketer of the White House in 1917, and she was arrested on October 15, 1917, and sent to the DC jail and the Occoquan Workhouse. Like Paul, she was placed in solitary confinement. She joined Paul on a hunger strike in October and was freed in November. Her actions helped convince Wilson to support a suffrage amendment. Little is known of Winslow's later life. She died in 1977.

Nina Allender political cartoon aimed at President Wilson published in The Suffragist on October 3, 1917. Image via Wikimedia Commons. [Public domain.]

Historical Document

Prison Writings of a Radical Suffragist

If this thing is necessary we will naturally go through with it. Force is so stupid a weapon. I feel so happy doing my bit for decency—for *our* war, which is after all, real and fundamental.

The women are all so magnificent, so beautiful. Alice Paul is as thin as ever, pale and large-eyed. We have been in solitary for five weeks. There is nothing to tell but that the days go by somehow. I have felt quite feeble the last few days—faint, so that I could hardly get my hair brushed, my arms ached so. But to-day I'm well again. Alice Paul and I talk back and forth though we are at opposite ends of the building and a hall door also shuts us apart. But occasionally—thrills—we escape from behind our iron-barred doors and visit. Great laughter and rejoicing!

[to her husband]

My fainting probably means nothing except that I am not strong after these weeks. I know YOU won't be alarmed.

I told about a syphilitic colored woman with one leg. The other one was cut off, having rotted so that it was alive with maggots when she came in. The remaining one is now getting as bad. They are so short of nurses that a little colored girl of twelve, who is here waiting to have her tonsils removed, waits on her. This child and two others share a ward with a syphilitic child of three or four years, whose mother refused to have it at home. It makes you absolutely ill to see it....

Alice Paul is in the psychopathetic ward. She dreaded forcible feeding frightfully, and I hate to think how she must be feeling. I had a nervous time of it, gasping a long time afterward, and my stomach rejecting during the process. I spent a bad, restless night, but otherwise I am all right. The poor soul who fed me got liberally besprinkled during the process. I heard myself making the most hideous sounds.... One feels so forsaken when one lies prone and people shove a pipe down one's stomach.

This morning but for an astounding tiredness, I am all right. I am waiting to see what happens when the President realizes that brutal bullying isn't quite a statesmanlike method for settling a demand for justice at home. At least, if men are supine enough to endure, women—to their eternal glory—are not....

Don't let them tell you we take this well. Miss Paul vomits much. I do, too.... We think of the coming feeding all day. It is horrible. The doctor thinks I take it well. I hate the thought of Alice Paul and the others if I take it well....

All the officers here know we are making this hunger strike that women fighting for liberty may be considered political prisoners; we have told them. God knows we don't want other women ever to have to do this over again.

Document Analysis

The passages in this selection were taken from scraps of Winslow's diary that were smuggled out of the Occoquan Workhouse in 1917 and were, therefore, intended to be shared not only with the supporters of the prisoners, but also with the public, whose interest in the plight of the women was piqued. Doris Stevens published excerpts of these smuggled diary scraps in *Jailed for Freedom* (1920), a history of militant suffragists in the United States between 1913 and 1919.

In her account, Winslow describes the harrowing experience of hunger-striking and being force-fed, but also demonstrates her admiration for the other picketers in prison and her pride in her role in the movement. She is "happy doing my bit for decency" and views their fight for the vote as "war, which is after all, real and fundamental." Despite being in solitary confinement, Winslow is sometimes able to see Paul, who is "thin as ever, pale and large-eyed." Although they are held at opposite ends of the prison, they are able to hear each other, and when they are able to visit, there is "great laughter and rejoicing." Winslow is impressed with the other prisoners as well. "The women are all so magnificent, so beautiful," and she is determined to make her stance as a political prisoner clear, and win her fight so that "other women [don't] ever have to do this over again."

Winslow describes her physical state in detail in these passages, as well as the brutal process of force-feeding. In the context of her time, when women were considered fragile and delicate, these descriptions were a powerful way to gain sympathy for the plight of these women. Winslow emphasized her physical weakness, but also her resilience. "I have felt quite feeble the last few days—faint, so that I could hardly get my hair brushed, my arms ached so. But to-day I am well again."

Winslow describes force-feeding as "brutal bullying" and predicts, correctly, that President Wilson will realize that "isn't quite a statesmanlike method for settling a demand for justice at home." Winslow worries about Paul, who is locked up in a "psychopathic ward" and "dreaded forcible feeding frightfully." Winslow herself describes spending the day anticipating the torturous practice and the choking and vomiting that she knows will follow. "One feels so forsaken when one lies prone and people shove a pipe down one's stomach." Winslow is aware that the prison and the government are downplaying their suffering in a way that could hurt the prisoners' cause. "Don't let them tell you we take this well." Her words show that she wants the strikers to be perceived as political prisoners who are willing to endure pain and bodily harm as part of their struggle for suffrage.

Essential Themes

Winslow was determined to accurately portray both the frailty and the determination of the picketers held in the Occoquan Workhouse and to describe the hunger strike as a political, not criminal, action. American feelings about the delicacy of womanhood were offended by the idea of holding down women—primarily middle- and upper-class white women—and shoving hoses down their throats while they choked and vomited. The willingness of these women to risk their health was shown to be evidence of their determination to win their fight and impressed many political leaders, including Wilson, who was forced to face mounting opposition to their imprisonment and ill-treatment. As difficult and painful as these experiences were for suffragettes, information leaked to the outside world was crucial in turning the tide of public opinion in their favor.

—*Bethany Groff Dorau, MA*

Bibliography and Additional Reading

Buchanan, Paul D. *The American Women's Rights Movement: A Chronology of Events and Opportunities from 1600 to 2008*. Boston: Branden, 2009.

Dubois, E. C. *Feminism and Suffrage: The Emergence of an Independent Women's Movement in America, 1848–1869*. Ithaca: Cornell UP, 1978.

Flexner, Eleanor. *Century of Struggle: The Woman's Rights Movement in the United States*. Cambridge: Belknap, 1996.

Library of Congress. "Profiles: Selected Leaders of the National Woman's Party." *Library of Congress*. Library of Congress, n.d.

Stevens, Doris. *Jailed for Freedom*. 1920: n.p. Project Gutenberg, 2003.

Nineteenth Amendment to the U.S. Constitution

Date: August 18, 1920
Authors: Susan B. Anthony; U.S. Congress
Genre: law; constitutional provision

Summary Overview

After a long and protracted struggle by suffragists and women's rights advocates, on June 4, 1919 the United States Congress voted to approve the Nineteenth Amendment to the Constitution, guaranteeing women the right to vote. The campaign for women's suffrage began in the 1840s and lasted nearly eighty years. The battle embraced a multitude of strategies and spanned two generations of leaders. It was not until the aftermath of World War I (1914–1918) that the long-anticipated passage of a constitutional amendment legalizing suffrage for women in the United States finally occurred. Its author, Susan B. Anthony, and its proponents had hoped the amendment would follow on the heels of the Fifteenth Amendment, providing for universal male suffrage in 1870. Their hope for a sixteenth amendment allowing women to vote was frustrated, however, and they had to settle for a fifty-year struggle in opposition before the Nineteenth Amendment was proposed.

The Nineteenth Amendment was approved by the House of Representatives in a vote of 304 to 89 and by the Senate in a vote of 56 to 25. The Sixty-sixth Congress proceeded to send the bill to the states for ratification. During the following fourteen months, thirty-six state legislatures voted in favor of the amendment, leading to its acceptance on August 18, 1920. As expected, the greatest support for the amendment derived from the Midwest and trans-Mississippi regions of the United States, with the states of the Northeast lagging behind only slightly. The strongest opposition came primarily from the South.

Anthony, the author of the amendment, did not live to see the passage or ratification of her proposal. Her death in 1906 followed a long career as a suffragist and general reformer. She wrote a women's suffrage amendment in 1878 and persuaded a sympathetic senator from California, Aaron Augustus Sargent, to introduce the measure in Congress that year. Although Congress failed to act on the resolution, it became a focal point for suffragist activity and public attention. Anthony's resolution, also known as the "Anthony Amendment," was reintroduced in every session of Congress with its wording unchanged until its passage forty-one years later, in 1919.

Carrie Chapman Catt, President of the National American Woman Suffrage Association, organized the "Winning Plan" that helped secure passage of the Nineteenth Amendment. Photo via Wikimedia Commons. [Public domain.]

Final acceptance of the amendment can be attributed primarily to the plan introduced by Carrie Chapman Catt, president of the National American Woman Suffrage Association (NAWSA), at that organization's annual meeting in 1916 at Atlantic City, New Jersey. She called for cooperation across the suffragists' spectrum and the mobilization of state and local organizations for the cause. The plan also suggested the targeting of unsympathetic legislators at all levels. By 1918 she had secured the endorsement of President Woodrow Wilson. Although it required another eighteen months of diligence, the goal was accomplished, and women across the United States voted in the presidential election of 1920.

Defining Moment

The movement for women's suffrage in the United States can trace its beginnings to the eighteenth century and the period of the American Revolution. Women such as the playwright and historian Mercy Otis Warren; the writer and educational reformer Judith Sargent Murray; and Abigail Adams, the wife of President John Adams, questioned the traditional roles and limitations placed on American women. While Adams wrote to her husband advising him not to forget women at the same time that American male leaders were deliberating the rights of men, Murray contemplated the inequality of educational opportunities extended to male and female children. She argued, "How is the one exalted and the other depressed, by the contrary modes of education that are adopted! The one is taught to aspire, the other is early confined and limited". An Englishwoman, Mary Wollstonecraft, laid the theoretical bases and raised the fundamental questions pursued by American women's rights advocates for the next 120 years. The most fundamental and, at times, controversial tenet of her work *A Vindication of the Rights of Woman* was that the rights of men and of women were identical.

In the 1840s, during a period of more generalized reform efforts, the issue of women's rights emerged as a concerted cause. In the midst of earlier movements advocating reforms in education and prisons, abolition, and temperance, women began to question their status. Many outspoken advocates of reforms in education and for the abolition of slavery, such as Sarah Grimké, Elizabeth Cady Stanton, and Anthony, found the suppression of their voices on the ground of their femininity frustrating and indicative of their larger problems. The exclusion of women from the World Anti-Slavery Conference in London in 1840 resulted in the direct comparison of slaves' and women's lack of freedoms. The Women's Rights Convention that met at Seneca Falls, New York, in July 1848 marks the official beginning of the women's rights movement in the United States. More than three hundred individuals, including Stanton, the Quaker social reformer Lucretia Coffin Mott, and the former slave and abolitionist Frederick Douglass, attended the conference, and at its conclusion sixty-eight women and

Poster by the League of Women Voters, 1920. Image via Wikimedia Commons. [Public domain.]

thirty-two men signed the Declaration of Sentiments. Over the next decade the movement advocated not only for woman suffrage but also for more radical ideals, such as women's property rights, the abolition of a double standard in divorce laws, and the rights of women to testify and to sign contracts. The movement attracted supporters to the cause, most notably Anthony, who attended the annual convention in Syracuse in 1852. During the late 1850s and 1860s the movement's leaders and grassroots supporters channeled their efforts into Civil War work and the strident advocacy of abolition. They also conjectured that along with African Americans they would be legally recognized at the end of the struggle.

Although their hopes did not materialize, the training and experiences garnered during this period served them well during the decades that followed the war. In 1866 Stanton and Anthony established the American Equal Rights Association, an organization open to white and African American women whose aim was universal suffrage. The suffragists suffered a setback in 1868 when the states ratified the Fourteenth Amendment, which extended the protections of the Constitution to all citizens but defined a citizen as specifically male. Disputes over how to deal with crises created by the amendment's ratification and the proposed Fifteenth Amendment created a breach in the movement resulting in the establishment of two rival organizations. In 1869 Stanton and Anthony founded the National Woman Suffrage Association (NWSA) in New York. The more radical of two organizations, the NWSA limited its membership to women only and campaigned for a variety of women's social and economic issues in addition to suffrage. Its rival organization, the American Woman Suffrage Association (AWSA), was more conservative in nature. Its founders, Lucy Stone, Julia Ward Howe, and Henry Browne Blackwell, limited participation in national meetings to recognized delegates and its mission solely to suffrage. Its members believed that social and economic issues distracted their energies and alienated influential supporters. Rather than working for a national resolution, the group advocated a state-by-state approach to accomplishing its goal.

In 1878 Anthony wrote what would become known as the Anthony Amendment. Modeled on the recently ratified Fifteenth Amendment guaranteeing suffrage to all men regardless of race, this resolution would remove gender as a qualification for suffrage. Anthony and her colleagues in the NWSA persuaded a sympathetic senator from California, Aaron A. Sargent, to introduce it to Congress on January 10, 1878. Congress declined to act on the proposal, but its supporters continued to reintroduce it at every session of Congress until its eventual passage forty-one years later.

During that period the woman suffrage and rights movements underwent a multitude of changes and challenges. Perhaps most significant was the reconciliation of the NWSA and AWSA in 1890. Initiated in 1887 by members of the AWSA and negotiated by Alice Stone Blackwell (the daughter of Lucy Stone and Henry Browne Blackwell), their merger into the National American Woman Suffrage Association marked an important turning point in the movement. While the early leaders of both factions remained visible, younger women took up the standards and continued the fight. Anthony was among the last of the earlier generation and carefully cultivated her successors, Catt and Anna Howard Shaw. By 1910 all of the first generation had passed from the scene. Between 1890 and the passage of the Anthony Amendment by Congress in 1919 a variety of organizations joined the fight. The Woman's Christian Temperance Union had from its inception in 1878 supported woman suffrage as a tool for promoting temperance. The National Council of Jewish Women (1893), the National Association of Colored Women (1896), and the Women's Trade Union League (1903) broadened the movement's base of support and drew in women left at the fringes by the NAWSA, which tended to represent white, Protestant women of the middle and upper classes. The movement also had it opponents, including mainstream politicians, businessmen, liquor manufacturers, factions of the Catholic Church, and other women. The best-organized dissenting faction, the National Association Opposed to Woman Suffrage, emerged in 1911, led by Mrs. Arthur Dodge.

By the 1910s the question concerning woman suffrage became when and not if it would be achieved. In 1916 the NAWSA president, Catt, introduced her plan at the group's annual meeting in Atlantic City.

She called on her membership to mobilize women at all levels of society, to curry support from all sources, and to target politicians whose positions were antithetical to the goal of woman suffrage. At the state level, a number of legislatures authorized partial or state suffrage. Another factor that worked in their favor was the growing anti-immigration sentiment across the nation. Ironically, many white, Protestant men of the middle and upper classes saw the suffragists and the allied causes as sympathetic to their interests and a way of balancing out the growing pool of naturalized immigrants joining the cadre of voters.

While the United States's entry into World War I temporarily dampened the suffragists' efforts as the majority of suffragists put their energies into war work, their patriotism and service ultimately had great benefits. Their efforts swayed many of their opponents to the cause. The most significant convert was President Woodrow Wilson, who voiced his support for the amendment in 1918.

It took an additional eighteen months to unseat some of the suffragists' staunchest opponents in Congress. The Anthony Amendment passed through the House in May 1919 and was approved by the Senate on June 4 by a vote of fifty-six to thirty-two. Fourteen months later, on August 18, 1920, the state of Tennessee became the thirty-sixth state legislature to ratify the resolution, and the Nineteenth Amendment became law.

Author Biography

Defining exactly who authored the Nineteenth Amendment is somewhat difficult. Susan B. Anthony is generally credited for its initial submission to Congress through her friend and sympathizer Aaron Sargent. After its first reading it became known as the Anthony Amendment in her honor. The amendment, itself, however, is a rewording of the earlier Fifteenth Amendment, which guaranteed universal male suffrage. Anthony, Stanton, and other leaders of the NWSA contributed to the cause.

Susan Brownell Anthony was born to Quaker parents, Daniel and Lucy, in Adams, Massachusetts, on February 15, 1820. Honoring the Quaker sensitivity for gender equality, her parents provided all of their children, male and female, an advanced education at a private Quaker boarding school in Philadelphia. There Anthony trained as a teacher and acquired her lifelong zeal for activism and reform. When Anthony's family relocated to Rochester, New York, in 1845, they continued to engage in a broad range of reform movements, including abolition, temperance,

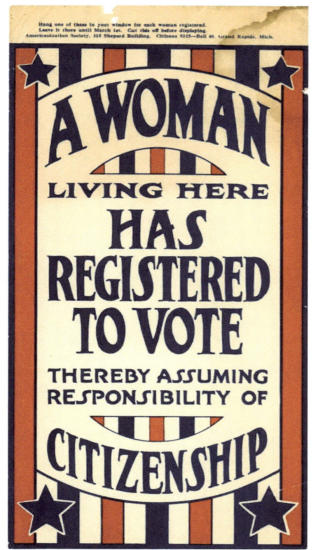

Get-Out-the-Vote activists used advertising and education campaigns to boost women's flagging turnout in the early 1920s. In Grand Rapids, Michigan, local advocates asked women to demonstrate that they had registered to vote by displaying window posters like the one above. Photo via the National Museum of American History/National Park Service (nps.gov). [Public domain.]

education, labor, and women's rights. Both of her parents and her sister Mary signed the Declaration of Sentiments at Seneca Falls in 1848. It was through this connection that Anthony met Elizabeth Cady Stanton and attended her first women's rights convention in Syracuse in 1852. Anthony became involved in work for women's rights through her engagement in the temperance movement. Active in the Daughters of Temperance, Anthony was refused the right to speak at a Sons of Temperance meeting in 1853, and the New York state legislature refused to recognize a petition limiting sale of alcohol circulated by Stanton and herself because most of the 28,000 signatures were by women.

Anthony, who never married, worked tirelessly for the suffragist movement for more than fifty years. During the 1850s Stanton, Anthony, and others allied themselves with the abolitionist movement and ultimately the Republican Party because they believed that their support would be rewarded by the extension of suffrage to women along with African American men. In the aftermath of the Civil War, frustrated and angered by their deliberate exclusion, they established the American Equal Rights Association in 1866 and an affiliated newspaper, the *Revolution*, in 1868. When the suffrage movement split in 1869, Anthony and Stanton established the NWSA to advocate not only suffrage but also broader social and economic reforms for women. Anthony and several others were arrested in Rochester in 1872 when they attempted to test the limits of the Fifteenth Amendment by voting in the presidential election. Although they successfully cast their ballots, they were later arrested, convicted, and fined. Anthony refused to pay the fine, hoping to take the case to the Supreme Court. Her plans were foiled by her lawyer, who paid the costs himself to keep Anthony out of jail.

In 1877, using the Fifteenth Amendment as model, she authored the Anthony Amendment, and Senator Sargent submitted it to Congress on January 10, 1878. Although both the House and the Senate refused to consider the action, Anthony saw its presentation at every session of Congress until her death in 1916. The tradition of the Anthony Amendment continued until its eventual passage in 1919.

Between 1878 and her death in 1906, Anthony continued to promote her cause. She participated in the reunion of the NWSA and the AWSA in 1890 and served as the NAWSA's second president (after Stanton) until 1900. She also broadened her horizons to establish the International Council of Women in 1888 and the International Woman Suffrage Council in 1904. To celebrate her eighty-sixth birthday, Anthony delivered the "Failure Is Impossible" speech, the title of which became the rallying cry of the woman suffrage movement. She returned to Rochester, New York, and on March 13, 1906, at her home, Anthony succumbed to congestive heart failure.

Historical Document

Nineteenth Amendment to the U.S. Constitution

Sixty-sixth Congress of the United States of America; At the First Session,

Begun and held at the City of Washington on Monday, the nine-teenth day of May, one thousand nine hundred and nineteen.

Joint Resolution Proposing an Amendment to the Constitution Ex-tending the Right of Suffrage to Women.

Resolved by the Senate and House of Representatives of the United States of America in Congress assembled (two-thirds of each House concurring therein), That the following article is proposed as an amendment to the Constitution, which shall be valid to all intents and purposes as part of the Constitution when ratified by the legislature of three-fourths of the several States.

ARTICLE .

"The right of citizens of the United States to vote shall not be denied or abridged by the United States or by any State on account of sex.

Congress shall have power to enforce this article by appropriate legislation."

Glossary

abridged: reduced or limited

account of sex: by reason of gender

Joint Resolution: resolution to both houses of Congress

ratified: approved or sanctioned, in this case by state legislatures

suffrage: right to vote

H. J. Res. 1.

Sixty-sixth Congress of the United States of America;

At the First Session,

Begun and held at the City of Washington on Monday, the nineteenth day of May, one thousand nine hundred and nineteen.

JOINT RESOLUTION

Proposing an amendment to the Constitution extending the right of suffrage to women.

Resolved by the Senate and House of Representatives of the United States of America in Congress assembled (two-thirds of each House concurring therein), That the following article is proposed as an amendment to the Constitution, which shall be valid to all intents and purposes as part of the Constitution when ratified by the legislatures of three-fourths of the several States.

"ARTICLE ———.

"The right of citizens of the United States to vote shall not be denied or abridged by the United States or by any State on account of sex.

"Congress shall have power to enforce this article by appropriate legislation."

F. H. Gillett
Speaker of the House of Representatives.

Thos. R. Marshall
Vice President of the United States and
President of the Senate.

The Nineteenth Amendment in the National Archives. Photo via Wikimedia Commons. [Public domain.]

Document Analysis

The document is divided into three parts: a preface, a definition of the desired goal, and the amendment itself. The amendment itself contains two sections.

The preface explains that the resolution is before the first session of the Sixty-Sixth Congress. (This count refers to the number of different Houses of Representatives elected since 1787.) The preface also includes the date, May 1919, and the location of the meeting, Washington, D.C.

The second portion of the document describes the resolution and the process of congressional approval and ratification by the states. The proposed amendment mandates a change in the U.S. Constitution to permit women to vote. It also indicates that in a joint session, both the House of Representatives and the Senate must approve by at least a two-thirds majority the resolution on the floor. It proceeds to state that the resolution becomes law when legislatures in "three-fourths" of the states (thirty-six) ratify it.

The final part of the document is the amendment itself. It states that gender does not constitute a basis for the denial of suffrage and thus defines women as citizens. It also affirms the right of the federal government to pass other legislation to enforce the suffrage provision.

Anthony is usually credited with authorship of the Nineteenth Amendment. She wrote a version of the amendment in 1877, basing its wording on the Fifteenth Amendment, which said that the right to vote could not be denied on the basis of race, color, or previous condition of servitude (that is, slavery). A sympathetic California senator, Aaron Sargent, submitted the amendment to the U.S. Congress, which refused to take action on it. As the proposal was resubmitted in every session of Congress in the decades that followed, it came to be referred to as the Anthony Amendment.

After Anthony's death in 1906, pressure for passage of the amendment began to mount. It culminated in 1917 after the United States entered World War I. Early that year, the so-called Silent Sentinels, a group of suffragists led by Alice Paul, among others, began a two-and-a-half-year picket (with Sundays off) of the White House, urging President Woodrow Wilson to support a suffrage amendment. Public opinion began to sway in favor of the suffragists when it was learned that many of the picketers had been arrested and sentenced to jail, usually on thin charges of obstructing traffic, and that the conditions the jailed women endured were often brutal. Alice Paul, in particular, was subjected to inhuman treatment and launched a hunger strike in protest until she and the other protestors were released after a court of appeals ruled the arrests illegal.

Finally, on January 9, 1918, Wilson announced that he supported the amendment. On January 10, 1918, the House of Representatives narrowly passed the amendment, but the Senate refused to consider the matter until October, when the measure failed by just three votes. In response, the newly formed National Women's Party, led by Alice Paul, mounted a campaign against legislators who supported the Democratic Party's resistance to bringing the suffrage amendment to a vote in Congress and were up for re-election—as she and her supporters had done in 1914. These efforts, along with efforts to mold public opinion, were successful, for on May 21, 1919, after the House of Representatives passed the measure by a vote of 304 to 89, the Senate, on June 4, passed it by a vote of fifty-six to twenty-five. The amendment was then submitted to the states for ratification. The first state to ratify it was Illinois. Thirty-six states needed to ratify the amendment for it to become part of the Constitution. That number was reached on August 18, 1920, when Tennessee, following contentious debate and two deadlocked roll calls, ratified it after one legislator, Harry Burn, changed his vote on the urging of his mother. Oddly, several states throughout the South initially rejected the amendment and were quite slow to ratify it later, the last being Mississippi in 1984.

The language of the amendment is simple and straightforward. A preface notes that the resolution, dated May 1919, is before the first session of the Sixty-sixth Congress in Washington, D.C. The preface is followed by a description of the resolution and the process of approving it, including congressional approval and ratification by the states. In particular, it says that the resolution has to be approved by a two-thirds majority in both the House of

Representatives and the Senate and that it must be ratified, or approved, by three fourths of the states—at that time, thirty-six states (out of forty-eight). The third part of the document is the text of the amendment itself, stating that citizens cannot be denied the right to vote on the basis of sex and that Congress has the power to enforce the amendment by legislation.

Essential Themes

Despite the many predictions made concerning the effects of woman suffrage, the actual impact was relatively mild. While politicians now paid greater attention to women's issues, political activity and legislation did not become more feminine in nature, as both detractors and advocates had predicted. The welfare and social causes perceived as falling into women's spheres found only slightly more favor than they had prior to the passage of the Nineteenth Amendment. The suffragists also faced a difficult question: what was next.

After ratification, one particular transformation occurred rapidly. The NAWSA ceased to exist and reconstituted as the League of Women Voters. The avowed purpose of the organization was to provide responsible leadership and information for women who were new to political activity. Among their challenges was to chart a path between allying with existing political parties and forming an independent political organization. Catt and others felt that the only way to accomplish their larger goals was to work through existing party structures. Other women, such as the social reformer Jane Addams, advocated policies of continued separate activity and independence. In the end, the league plotted a policy of nonpartisan activity aimed at keeping members informed and politicians honest in their approaches and promises to female voters.

Politicians at all levels reacted to their new female constituents cautiously. During the early 1920s local, state, and national legislators enacted laws favorable to women. Female lobbies and information campaigns had enough impact to affect legislative decisions. These concerned issues of maternity, length of the workday, and safety concerns. The predicted humanitarian transformation of politics caused by the infusion of feminine values, however, did not materialize, and by mid-decade their influence waned. The majority of women voted along lines that had more to do with their diverse socioeconomic statuses and their racial and ethnic backgrounds than any perceived nurturing instincts.

As American politics in general grew more conservative, women's rights advocates began to reconsider some issues deemed too radical only a decade earlier. Suffrage alone did not resolve the inequities still visited upon women; gender discrimination continued to exist. In 1923 Alice Paul of the National Woman's Party introduced the Equal Rights Amendment that would eventually bear her name. The Paul Amendment, or ERA, contended that equal rights could not be limited on the basis of gender. For Paul and those who were like-minded, the Nineteenth Amendment was merely the first step in the battle for equity.

—*Martha Pallante, PhD, Michael J. O'Neal, PhD*

Bibliography and Additional Reading

Bunting, Luke, ed. *Symposium Commemorating the 100th Anniversary of the Nineteenth Amendment.* Special issue of Georgetown Journal of Law & Public Policy 20, no. 1 (2022).

Chafe, William H. *The Paradox of Change: American Women in the Twentieth Century.* New York: Oxford UP, 1991.

Clift, Eleanor. *Founding Sisters and the Nineteenth Amendment.* New York: Wiley, 2003.

Cott, Nancy F. *The Grounding of Modern Feminism.* New Haven, Conn.: Yale UP, 1987.

Roydhouse, Marion W. *Votes for Women! The American Suffrage Movement and the Nineteenth Amendment: A Reference Guide.* Santa Barbara, CA: ABC-CLIO, 2020.

Woloch, Nancy. *Women and the American Experience.* New York: Alfred A. Knopf, 1984.

Voter Rights and Civil Rights

The Fourteenth and Fifteenth Amendments to the Constitution, ratified in 1868 and 1870, respectively, made illegal all attempts to prevent individuals from exercising their voting rights on the basis of race. However, these amendments were in practice ineffective because the white people who controlled the political system and social institutions created impediments such as literacy tests, residency requirements, and poll taxes to block Black citizens' access to political participation. Additionally, white supremacist groups such as the Ku Klux Klan employed terrorism to intimidate those African Americans who wanted to exercise their voting rights.

In the 1950s, the emerging civil rights movement created a backlash in the South. Opponents of the movement responded with violence, firebombing homes, churches, and other buildings associated with civil rights activities. The implicit threat of violence intimidated African Americans and prevented many from registering to vote.

The Civil Rights Act of 1957, designed to protect a person's right to exercise the right to vote, authorized the attorney general of the United States to intervene through court action whenever citizens were illegally excluded from voter registration. However, the case-by-case suits proved to be time-consuming and hard to resolve.

In 1959, the U.S. Commission on Civil Rights presented a report documenting numerous incidents in which African Americans had been denied the right to vote in southern states. The commission recommended that voter registration be handled by the federal government, but Attorney General William P. Rogers proposed instead that referees handle citizen complaints filed with federal courts. A bill based on the attorney general's referee plan passed in the House and gained passage in the Senate with the aid of Majority Leader Lyndon B. Johnson and Minority Leader Everett Dirksen. The Civil Rights Act of 1960 became law on May 6, 1960, and was later known as the Voting Rights Act of 1960. The act sought to protect every citizen's right to vote by empowering the attorney general to appoint voting referees to investigate and act, using federal courts, on complaints that state officials denied people the right to exercise their right to vote on the basis of their race or color. However, the 1960 act did not address impediments to voting such as literacy tests but simply mandated that the requirements be applied equally to voters, regardless of their race. Although the act represented an advance over previous civil rights legislation, it proved to be ineffective because in every case of alleged discrimination, the attorney general, in concert with federal courts, had to establish that an individual was denied the right to vote solely on the basis of the person's race or color.

It took the Voting Rights Act of 1965, the preeminent piece of voting rights legislation of the century, to finish the job. It affirmed the principles regarding the elimination and prohibition of open practices of racial discrimination in voting in earlier legislation along with the Twenty-Fourth Amendment (1964) to the Constitution of the United States.

The Twenty-Fourth Amendment sought to protect the right of U.S. citizens to vote by banning any poll tax or other voting tax. It also provided Congress with the power to enforce the amendment using appropriate legislation. Although this and other laws had been passed to protect the rights of African American and other minority voters, these groups remained disenfranchised and continued to have difficulty registering to vote in many sections of the country. The Voting Rights Act of 1965 was designed to address the denial of minority citizens of the most basic right of U.S. citizenship the right to vote.

The right to vote is central to the full political participation of all citizens because it gives them the power to elect officials who make decisions affecting their rights. However, many minority citizens had not been able to exercise their right to vote freely because state and local officials and private citizens had made efforts to prevent them from casting their ballots.

African Americans, Mexican Americans, Asian Americans, some Caucasian Americans, and various ethnic and racial minority groups backed the Voting Rights Act of 1965. Major civil rights organizations lending support included the National Association for the Advancement of Colored People (NAACP) and the Student Nonviolent Coordinating Committee (SNCC). Politicians and leaders such as Martin Luther King Jr., Ralph Abernathy, Hubert Humphrey, and President Lyndon B. Johnson also championed the act. These organizations and individuals were deeply involved in trying to get legislation enacted that would prohibit the numerous practices used to deny minority citizens the right to vote. These tactics included physical intimidation and harassment, the use of literacy tests, a poll tax, English-only elections, and racial gerrymandering. The results of these practices were low voter registration and turnout among minorities and the election of only a few officials who were members of racial or ethnic minorities. In many areas, minorities were almost totally excluded from the political process.

Opponents of the act were mainly southern politicians such as Governor George Wallace, Senator Allen Ellender, Senator Sam Ervin, and Governor J. P. Coleman and private citizens' groups such as the White Citizens Council, the Ku Klux Klan, and the Council of Federated Organizations (COFO).

The U.S. Congress responded to the demands of civil rights activists who were demonstrating during the 1960s by passing the Voting Rights Act of 1965. President Johnson signed it into law in August, 1965. The act overcame some of the weaknesses in the Civil Rights Act of 1964. It authorized federal voting examiners to register voters for federal and state elections, suspended literacy tests, banned the use of poll taxes, and provided limited federal approval of new state registration laws and voting statutes. Penalties were also established for those who sought to deny any person the right to vote.

The general provisions of the act protected the voting right of American citizens in several important ways. These provisions prohibited voting qualifications or procedures that would deny or abridge a person's right to vote because of race, color, or inclusion in a minority language group. The general provisions made it a crime for a public official to refuse to allow a qualified person to vote or for any person to use threats or intimidation to prevent someone from voting or helping another to vote. The act also contained special provisions that provided additional voting protections to citizens in certain jurisdictions. Unlike the general provisions, which are permanent and apply nationwide, the special provisions were temporary and applied only to those jurisdictions that met certain criteria.

Section II of the Voting Rights Act of 1965 prohibited the use of voting laws, practices, or procedures that discriminate in either purpose or effect on the basis of race, color, or membership in a minority language group. Section V was designed to prevent states and other governmental entities with a history of voting discrimination from continuing to devise new ways to discriminate and prevent citizens from voting. These jurisdictions were required to submit any proposed voting changes in their election practices prior to implementation for federal approval by either the attorney general or the federal district court for the district of Columbia. They had to demonstrate that the proposed voting changes would not have the purpose or effect of discrimination against protected racial or language minorities. This process was referred to as the preclearance process. Minority language groups protected by the act were Native Americans, Asian Americans, Alaskan natives, and persons of Spanish heritage.

The law had an immediate impact. By the end of 1965, a quarter of a million new African American voters had been registered, one-third by federal examiners. Although passage of the Voting Rights Act of 1965 resulted in an increase in minority voter registration from approximately 29 percent to 52 percent of the minority population by the end of the decade, some persistent and serious obstacles remained. For example, some jurisdictions resisted provisions requiring the printing of materials related to registration and voting in the applicable minority language and the providing of oral assistance.

The Voting Rights Act of 1965 was subsequently readopted and strengthened in 1970, 1975, and 1982. Over the years, however, several Supreme Court decisions came to limit various provisions of the law. The strongest such rulings, such as that in *Shelby County v. Holder* (2013), have limited the federal government's power to approve/disapprove electoral districts prior to their implementation, based on the government's understanding of how and why the electoral lines were established. With this provision being declared unconstitutional in 2013, only challenges by individuals who believe their constitutional rights have been violated can file a complaint, with the burden of proof falling to the individual filing the case.

Fourteenth and Fifteenth Amendments to the Constitution

Date: July 9, 1868; February 3, 1870
Author: Fortieth and Forty-first U.S. Congresses
Genre: constitution; law

Summary Overview

At the conclusion of the Civil War, the government of the United States, dominated by Northern Republicans, began to propose and pass legislation to transform the Southern states. Faced with the task of rebuilding the political, economic, and societal structures that had been devastated in the war, legislators also had to work with the president (Andrew Johnson, followed by Ulysses S. Grant) to reunite the nation. This period, known as Reconstruction, established profound legal change. In instituting unprecedented laws, acts, and constitutional amendments, the Fortieth and Forty-First Congresses not only redefined the citizenship status and legal rights of former slaves and other free blacks, but they also expanded the authority of the national government over the states. The redefinition of the federal and state relationship codified in the Fourteenth and Fifteenth Amendments was a highly controversial yet crucial aspect of Reconstruction that allowed the U.S. government to institute and defend the newly established rights of black Americans. The Fifteenth Amendment, for example, required the implementation of suffrage for black (male) citizens in the South. Other provisions were similarly new to the traditional Southern way of life—and were resisted at every turn.

Defining Moment

Signed in 1863, two years before the conclusion of the war, the Emancipation Proclamation declared the slave population of the Confederate states free from the bondage of slavery. In December 1865, the Thirty-Eighth Congress passed the Thirteenth Amendment, which abolished slavery throughout the rest of the Union, including the border slave states of Missouri, Kentucky, Delaware, and Maryland that had remained in the Union and were previously exempted from the dictates of the Proclamation. With almost four million newly freed African Americans, the majority of whom resided in Southern states that were hostile to their new status; the U.S. government knew that a permanent solution was needed to ensure the rights of former slaves. The government became determined to enact new legislation to ensure that the rights of freedmen would not be immediately abridged as soon as Southern states were reintegrated into the Union.

The government was also facing the question of what criteria Confederate states would have to meet in order to be allowed back into the Union. At the conclusion of the Civil War, Union troops remained an occupying force in the Southern states and the South had no federal representation in Congress. The federal government was in a position to wield unprecedented power over the rebuilding of Southern state governments. Congress also had the power to dictate the conditions under which these states could receive reinstatement to full federal representation. Seen as an affront by some to the critical issue of state rights, much debate ensued concerning what proof of loyalty or other qualifications rebel states would have to meet to be fully readmitted to the Union. Another crucial question for Reconstruction legislators was how to enforce these legal changes and requirements on the states without violating the constitutional limitations on the federal government. The writing and passing of the Fourteenth and Fifteenth Amendments reflects the struggles and attempted solutions by the Reconstruction-era Congress to establish legal equality between blacks and whites in the United States. Beyond these immediate goals, however, the Reconstruction amendments redefined the balance of power between the individual states and the federal government.

Author Biography

The Thirty-Ninth through the Forty-First Congresses of the United States were convened during one of the most unstable and demanding times in American political history. The Union victory in the Civil War provided a remarkable opportunity for Congress to institute sweeping legal, social, and constitutional changes, not only over the defeated Southern states, but over the nation as a whole. The efforts to bring these changes to fruition, however, were disrupted and marred by a presidential assassination, uncooperative Southern states, and repeated presidential vetoes to their legislative efforts.

In the aftermath of the Civil War, the Thirty-Ninth Congress was composed only of representatives from states loyal to the Union; Alabama, Arkansas, Florida, Georgia, North Carolina, South Carolina, Texas, Virginia, and Mississippi were all denied federal representation. Tennessee, though having seceded from the Union during the Civil War, became the only Southern state to regain congressional seats during the session. The Thirty-Ninth Congress was only assembled for one month before Abraham Lincoln's assassination, which shook the foundation of the newly victorious federal government. Andrew Johnson, Lincoln's successor to the presidency, vetoed nearly every bill, act, and amendment proposed by the Congress. Despite these hurdles, however, the Thirty-Ninth Congress used a two-thirds majority vote to override Johnson's presidential vetoes in order to pass landmark legislation. During its tenure, the Thirty-Ninth Congress debated and passed the Civil Rights Act of 1866, the Freedmen's Bureau Bill, and the Fourteenth Amendment to the Constitution. It would be an additional two years before the amendment was ratified.

The Fortieth Congress convened in March of 1867 and was populated largely by a political faction known as the Radical Republicans. The Radical Republicans pushed hard for the implementation of Reconstruction policies, which gave substantial civil rights to former slaves and doled out tough guidelines to govern Southern states. The Radical Republicans often clashed with President Andrew Johnson, who was much more conciliatory toward the ex-Confederate states. These tensions came to a head in 1868, when the Fortieth Congress impeached Johnson on charges of violating congressional policy (he was acquitted and finished his term). Despite these intragovernmental tensions, the Fortieth Congress was able to compose and pass three Reconstruction Acts and the Fifteenth Amendment to the Constitution, which would be ratified within the next year.

The Forty-First Congress convened in March of 1869 and contained the first African American member of Congress, Hiram Rhodes Revels from Mississippi, and the first African American member of the House of Representatives, Joseph H. Rainey from South Carolina. Ulysses S. Grant, the former Civil War general, was elected president of the United States during Congress's first session, and the following year, the four remaining Southern states were readmitted to the Union: Virginia (January), Mississippi (February), Texas (March), and Georgia (July) were once again granted federal representation.

Although the Fifteenth Amendment was passed by the Fortieth Congress one month before its final session, several states resisted ratification. The Forty-First Congress ruled, therefore, that in order for the remaining four Southern states to be readmitted to the Union, they had to accept both the Fourteenth and Fifteenth amendments, which, having no other choice, they eventually did. For many, this was the final step in Reconstruction.

Historical Document

The Fourteenth and Fifteenth Amendments to the U.S. Constitution

AMENDMENT XIV

Passed by Congress June 13, 1866. Ratified July 9, 1868.

Note: Article I, Section 2, of the Constitution was modified by Section 2 of the 14th amendment.

Section 1.

All persons born or naturalized in the United States, and subject to the jurisdiction thereof, are citizens of the United States and of the State wherein they reside. No State shall make or enforce any law which shall abridge the privileges or make or enforce any law which shall abridge the privileges or immunities of citizens of the United States; nor shall any State deprive any person of life, liberty, or property, without due process of law; nor deny to any person within its jurisdiction the equal protection of the laws.

Section 2.

Representatives shall be apportioned among the several States according to their respective numbers, counting the whole number of persons in each State, excluding Indians not taxed. But when the right to vote at any election for the choice of electors for President and Vice-President of the United States, Representatives in Congress, the Executive and Judicial officers of a State, or the members of the Legislature thereof, is denied to any of the male inhabitants of such State, being twenty-one years of age,* and citizens of the United States, or in any way abridged, except for participation in rebellion, or other crime, the basis of representation therein shall be reduced in the proportion which the number of such male citizens shall bear to the whole number of male citizens twenty-one years of age in such State.

Section 3.

No person shall be a Senator or Representative in Congress, or elector of President and Vice-President, or hold any office, civil or military, under the United States, or under any State, who, having previously taken an oath, as a member of Congress, or as an officer of the United States, or as a member of any State legislature, or as an executive or judicial officer of any State, to

The Fifteenth Amendment in the National Archives. Photo via Wikimedia Commons. [Public domain.]

support the Constitution of the United States, shall have engaged in insurrection or rebellion against the same, or given aid or comfort to the enemies thereof. But Congress may by a vote of two-thirds of each House, remove such disability.

Section 4.

The validity of the public debt of the United States, authorized by law, including debts incurred for payment of pensions and bounties for services in suppressing insurrection or rebellion, shall not be questioned. But neither the United States nor any State shall assume or pay any debt or obligation incurred in aid of insurrection or rebellion against the United States, or any claim for the loss or emancipation of any slave; but all such debts, obligations and claims shall be held illegal and void.

Section 5.

The Congress shall have the power to enforce, by appropriate legislation, the provisions of this article.

*Changed by Section 1 of the 26th amendment.

AMENDMENT XV

Passed by Congress February 26, 1869. Ratified February 3, 1870.

Section 1.

The right of citizens of the United States to vote shall not be denied or abridged by the United States or by any State on account of race, color, or previous condition of servitude.

Section 2.

The Congress shall have the power to enforce this article by appropriate legislation.

Proposal and Ratification of 14th Amendment

Ratification was completed on July 9, 1868.

The amendment was subsequently ratified by Alabama, July 13, 1868; Georgia, July 21, 1868 (after having rejected it on November 9, 1866); Virginia, October 8, 1869 (after having rejected it on January 9, 1867); Mississippi, January 17, 1870; Texas, February 18, 1870 (after having rejected it on October 27, 1866); Delaware, February 12, 1901 (after having rejected it on

February 8, 1867); Maryland, April 4, 1959 (after having rejected it on March 23, 1867); California, May 6, 1959; Kentucky, March 18, 1976 (after having rejected it on January 8, 1867).

Proposal and Ratification of 15th Amendment

The fifteenth amendment to the Constitution of the United States was proposed to the legislatures of the several States by the Fortieth Congress, on the 26th of February, 1869, and was declared, in a proclamation of the Secretary of State, dated March 30, 1870, to have been ratified by the legislatures of twenty-nine of the thirty-seven States. The dates of ratification were: Nevada, March 1, 1869; West Virginia, March 3, 1869; Illinois, March 5, 1869; Louisiana, March 5, 1869; North Carolina, March 5, 1869; Michigan, March 8, 1869; Wisconsin, March 9, 1869; Maine, March 11, 1869; Massachusetts, March 12, 1869; Arkansas, March 15, 1869; South Carolina, March 15, 1869; Pennsylvania, March 25, 1869; New York, April 14, 1869 (and the legislature of the same State passed a resolution January 5, 1870, to withdraw its consent to it, which action it rescinded on March 30, 1970); Indiana, May 14, 1869; Connecticut, May 19, 1869; Florida, June 14, 1869; New Hampshire, July 1, 1869; Virginia, October 8, 1869; Vermont, October 20, 1869; Missouri, January 7, 1870; Minnesota, January 13, 1870; Mississippi, January 17, 1870; Rhode Island, January 18, 1870; Kansas, January 19, 1870; Ohio, January 27, 1870 (after having rejected it on April 30, 1869); Georgia, February 2, 1870; Iowa, February 3, 1870.

Ratification was completed on February 3, 1870, unless the withdrawal of ratification by New York was effective; in which event ratification was completed on February 17, 1870, when Nebraska ratified.

The amendment was subsequently ratified by Texas, February 18, 1870; New Jersey, February 15, 1871 (after having rejected it on February 7, 1870); Delaware, February 12, 1901 (after having rejected it on March 18, 1869); Oregon, February 24, 1959; California, April 3, 1962 (after having rejected it on January 28, 1870); Kentucky, March 18, 1976 (after having rejected it on March 12, 1869).

The amendment was approved by the Governor of Maryland, May 7, 1973; Maryland having previously rejected it on February 26, 1870.

The amendment was rejected (and not subsequently ratified) by Tennessee, November 16, 1869.

Glossary

abridge: diminish the extent of

due process: an established system of legal procedures that ensure compliance with accepted rules and ideologies

equal protection: the concept that principles of law must be applied equally in all comparable situations

immunities: exemptions

insurrection: an uprising against an established regime

ratification: formal confirmation

Document Analysis

Throughout the South during the Civil War, both the rumored and real proximity of Union forces often resulted in slaves refusing to work, abandoning their plantations, or demanding to be paid wages by their masters. Even in yet unoccupied areas, slaves began fleeing to the Northern lines in substantial numbers. Eventually runaway slaves were permitted to join the Union Army to assist in combat. Military service had long been understood in the United States as linked to rights of citizenship. In enlisting with Union forces, escaped slaves were manifestly claiming access to rights —an issue with which the federal government was soon forced to grapple. Simultaneously, the social philosophy and governmental theory of equal rights for slaves, long championed by abolitionist groups, was becoming increasingly influential in the halls of power. Many of the abolitionists' calls for equality under the law worked to inform the ideas ultimately contained in the Reconstruction amendments. Though a controversial and barely articulated goal at the start of the war, by the conclusion of the conflict, the freeing of slaves and the codification of their equal status became a defining objective of the Union forces as well as a political and legal goal of the U.S. government. After the passage of the Thirteenth Amendment outlawing slavery, the Thirty-Ninth through the Forty-First Congresses set about writing and passing amendments to the Constitution that empowered the government to enact and enforce among all the states the equality of African Americans before the law. In doing so, the Reconstruction Congress expanded the definition of United States citizenship, the authority of the federal government over the states, and the legal status of African Americans.

The Fourteenth Amendment

The first section of the Fourteenth Amendment served to define the parameters of national citizenship. In 1857, the Supreme Court's decision in *Dred Scott v. Sandford* had classified people of African ancestry, slave or free, as noncitizens. Within the jurisdiction of the United States, blacks had no citizenship rights and enjoyed no constitutional protections. The Fourteenth Amendment directly refuted this decision by declaring all people born in the United States to be U.S. citizens. Citizenship rights would henceforth be determined at the national level and the enumerated rights of citizens were to be considered unalterable by the states. This codification of citizenship was noted by Congressman Wendell Phillips, who participated in its passage, as being a profound step for the United States, a country that had previously left undefined the parameters of what constituted a citizen. The clause guaranteeing the "privileges and immunities" of citizenship, however, had a contested meaning almost from the moment of its writing. Crafted by the Joint Committee on Reconstruction and principally authored by John Bingham, a representative from Ohio, the clause likely sought to constitutionally protect the Civil Rights Act, which dictated that rights extended to whites must likewise be extended to all citizens. By constitutionalizing the equal rights of citizens within states, Congress sought to prevent a repeal of the acts that enumerated the civil liberties states were required to provide for all of their citizens. The guarantees of "due process of law" and "equal protection under the law" were clauses that, at the time of their writing, were primarily concerned with guaranteeing that no citizen could be denied his or her liberty without just cause. Additionally, "just cause" could only derive from the applied rights and legal structures that operated equally for all citizens of the day.

The second section of the Fourteenth Amendment was written specifically to address the limitations on population representation in the Constitution's first article. When writing the original Constitution, Southern states were profoundly concerned that their seats in the House of Representatives could easily be overwhelmed by Northern states if they were prevented from including slave numbers into their overall population. As a result of vigorous negotiating over the manner in which populations should be calculated for the purpose of representation and taxation, Northern and Southern states came to a compromise regarding how to count Southern slaves. Article 1, section 2 of the Constitution states, "Representatives and direct Taxes shall be apportioned among the several States which may be included within this Union, according to their respective Numbers, which shall be determined by adding to the whole Number of free Persons, including those bound to Service for a Term of Years, and excluding Indians not taxed, three fifths of all other Persons." The section denoting "three fifths of all other persons" was a reference to slaves' inclusion in determining the amount of federal representation allowed to Southern states. Though every five slaves would count as three additional people in the South's representative populous, the slaves were barred from ever contributing to the selection of the representatives their numbers allowed. In the wake of the Civil War, the Fourteenth Amendment sought to reverse this constitutional edict. The second section of the amendment mandated that former slaves be counted as whole people. Additionally, the amendment dictated that if a state denied any men of voting age access to the vote, the number of representatives claimed by that state in Congress must likewise be reduced. This clause served the purpose of preserving federalism by keeping the right to create voting laws in the hands of the states while also attempting to prevent Southern states from instituting legislation specifically preventing former slaves from voting. According to the section, if states did institute such targeted discriminatory legislation, they would lose representation proportional to the population excluded from voting, thereby weakening their influence at the federal level.

The third section of the Fourteenth Amendment sought to deal with the reestablishment of Southern state governments as well as the reintegration of Southern delegates into the federal government. Of major concern to the Reconstruction Congress was the possibility of the immediate return of Confederate officials to positions of political and legal authority and thus a rapid return to the racial dynamics of Southern slavery and the immediate oppression of freedmen. Additionally, Congress feared that rebel leaders would escape punishment by simply retaking their positions of power without any apparent consequences for their betrayal of the Union. Congress' concern was well-founded: Andrew Johnson had already begun to assemble new state governments in the South that were replete with former Confederate leaders. To prevent a de-facto reenslavement of the African American population in the South, the Fourteenth Amendment precluded from holding office at the state or federal level those who had "engaged in insurrection or rebellion" against the government as well as those who had "given aid or comfort to [its] enemies."

The fourth section of the amendment expressed the commitment of the federal government to paying all Union debts and pensions, but it prohibited not only the federal government but also states from paying off debts to those who had supported the Confederacy. Most importantly, neither the government nor the states were permitted to reimburse former slaveholders for the value of their slaves. The majority of Southern wealth before the Civil War was located in the value of their slave population. When slaves were emancipated, the vast majority of the wealth held by slaveholders was instantly eliminated. Early in the war, President Lincoln had proposed that slave states still in the Union participate in "compensated emancipation," in which slaves residing within Union borders would be gradually freed in exchange for the government providing slave owners monetary compensation for the freed slaves' value. Though Lincoln's proposal was rejected by the slaveholding border states, the concept of "compensated emancipation" continued to be debated by those concerned about the postwar decimation of the South's economy. The Fourteenth Amendment prevented either the federal government or the states from compensating former slave owners for the slaves that had been emancipated.

Finally, and considered of paramount importance by the Reconstruction Congress, the Fourteenth Amendment granted Congress the right to make compulsory the provisions of the amendment. The Fourteenth Amendment clearly located the political authority to generate and enforce civil rights laws in the hands of the federal government. Prior to the passage of the Fourteenth Amendment, states retained authority over all aspects of the general welfare, heath, and safety of those citizens who resided within its borders. The federal government's powers over state action were restricted exclusively to issues of commerce, taxation, interstate disputes, and foreign relations. All other powers were reserved for the states. The Fourteenth Amendment was a defining moment in which the federal government was given license to override any state law or action that violated the rights of national citizenship.

The Fifteenth Amendment

The Fifteenth Amendment addressed the issue of political citizenship rights that had been largely ignored not only by the Thirteenth and Fourteenth Amendments, but also by the Reconstruction bills Congress had passed during its Thirty-Ninth session. Although no legislation had been put into place guaranteeing freedmen's voting rights, a precedent had already been set by the federal government in making black suffrage a requirement for Southern states seeking readmission to the Union. The Fortieth congressional session, which was comprised of a significant number of Radical Republicans, first attempted to remedy this oversight by implementing a voting rights bill. Constitutional debates soon began, however, over the right of the federal government to dictate voting parameters that were widely understood to be reserved to the states. Additionally, questions concerning the second section of the Fourteenth Amendment, which allowed states to restrict voting rights as long as they abdicated the right to added representation, was understood to indicate that states retained the right to create parameters around what part of their state population was allowed to vote. As a result, the Congress turned once again to the task of making constitutional the political rights of former slaves.

In debating the form the amendment would take, several congressmen proposed including additional disenfranchised groups into the amendment's guarantee of voting rights. It was proposed that the amendment protect from voting discrimination the Irish, women, religious dissenters, nonpropertied citizens, and immigrants. There was also concern that if race were the only protection mentioned by the amendment, states could find indirect means of excluding blacks from voting, such as requiring educational tests or proof of property ownership—problems that would indeed arise after the era of Reconstruction ended. Despite these more comprehensive proposals, the final result was direct and succinct. The amendment simply prohibited the federal and state government from denying any citizen the right to vote on "account of race, color, or previous condition of servitude." Additionally, just as in the Fourteenth Amendment, the Fifteenth conferred on Congress the ability to enforce African American voting rights through legislation. Though soon to face massive resistance by state law and even the federal judiciary, the protection of voting rights by the Fifteenth Amendment gave freedmen full political rights for the first time in United States history.

Essential Themes

The Due Process Clause of the Fourteenth Amendment had a profound and long-term legal effect in protecting the rights of the people outlined in the Bill of Rights against infringement by the states. Additionally, as a result of the federal enforcement of the amendments and acts implemented during the era of Reconstruction, African Americans experienced unprecedented access to political participation in the South. By the end of the nineteenth century, however, the gains of citizenship rights for African Americans began to experience a rapid and devastating decline. The Jim Crow era of social and legal subordination of the black population of the South began to emerge in full force. Jim Crow laws effectively functioned to dismantle the authority of the Fourteenth and Fifteenth Amendments over civil rights law in the South. The federal Congress and judiciary did little to prevent these racially discriminatory laws and, indeed, upheld many of their tenets. For example, the Supreme Court case of *Plessy v. Ferguson*, decided in 1896, made constitutional the doctrine of "separate but equal" and is an unambiguous example of just how quickly the Reconstruction amendments were taken apart through political and legal means. It would take nearly one hundred years for civil rights enforcement to receive federal support once more, and only as a result of mounting pressure from the activism of the civil rights movement.

—*Amanda Beyer-Purvis, MA*

Bibliography and Additional Reading

Barnett, Randy E., and Evan D. Bernick. *The Original Meaning of the Fourteenth Amendment: Its Letter and Spirit.* Cambridge, MA: Belknap Press/Harvard UP, 2021.

Epps, Garrett. *Democracy Reborn: The Fourteenth Amendment and the Fight for Equal Rights in Post–Civil War America.* New York: Holt, 2006.

Foner, Eric. *Reconstruction: America's Unfinished Revolution, 1863–1877.* New York: Perennial, 2002.

Goldstone, Lawrence. *Inherently Unequal: The Betrayal of Equal Rights by the Supreme Court, 1865–1903.* New York: Walker, 2011.

Meyer, Howard N. *The Amendment That Refused to Die: Equality and Justice Deferred: The History of the Fourteenth Amendment.* Lanham: Madison, 2000.

Perry, Michael J. *We the People: The Fourteenth Amendment and the Supreme Court.* New York: Oxford UP, 1999.

Reconstruction: The Second Civil War." *American Experience.* PBS Online/WGBH, 2004.

A Contested Election: Report to Congress on the Activities of the Ku Klux Klan

Date: February 11, 1870
Author: United States House of Representatives
Genre: report

Summary Overview

The activities of the newly organized Ku Klux Klan in Tennessee so disrupted the 1868 election in the Fourth Congressional District that Governor William Brownlow invalidated the election results and declared Republican candidate Lewis Tillman the winner. Conservative candidate C. A. Sheafe, who received the majority of votes, contested the decision and petitioned the U.S. House of Representatives to reverse Brownlow's ruling. The House committee tasked with investigating the matter took extensive testimony, which revealed the nature and extent of the Klan's efforts to intimidate African Americans and their white supporters. As a result, the House of Representatives decided that Tillman should be awarded the seat in Congress. The committee's inquiry prompted widespread interest in Klan activities and was instrumental in the establishment of a joint committee of Congress to investigate the Klan's influence across the South.

Defining Moment

In August 1868 the Tennessee state legislature had initiated its own investigation into the activities of the Ku Klux Klan as part of an ongoing campaign by Radical Republican Governor William Brownlow to reactivate the Tennessee State Guard, a militia under his control. The Guard was established in 1867 and used effectively to keep peace during elections that year; however, early in 1868 it was deactivated. Reports during the spring of 1868 of growing violence against African Americans and white Americans who supported Republicans made Brownlow fearful that congressional elections in November would be disrupted. Convinced that federal troops would be unavailable to stop Klan violence, Brownlow called a special session of the Tennessee legislature in July 1868 to push through legislation reactivating the Guard.

During the session, a joint military committee conducted an inquiry into Klan activities. Led by Tennessee state senator William J. Smith and state representative William F. Prosser, former Union officers and staunch supporters of Reconstruction, the committee took testimony from dozens of witnesses who told horrifying stories of intimidation, physical

Governor William Brownlow. Photo via Wikimedia Commons. [Public domain.]

Lewis Tillman. Photo via Wikimedia Commons. [Public domain.]

abuse, rape, and murder. The committee's report was printed in September 1868. To Brownlow's dismay, however, the bill authorizing reestablishment of the Guard did not pass in time for him to deploy troops to areas where Klan violence was likely to be highest during the November election.

Initial results in Tennessee's Fourth Congressional District indicated that conservative C. A. Sheafe defeated Republican Lewis Tillman by a comfortable majority. Governor Brownlow was convinced that Klan intimidation kept many of the district's nearly eight thousand African Americans from voting; he declared the results invalid and certified Tillman as the winner. Sheafe contested the decision, and in 1869 the matter was taken up in the U.S. House of Representatives, which has the power to seat its members.

The House committee adjudicating Sheafe's claim heard testimony from individuals who had been subject to Klan intimidation. Also testifying was Tennessee state senator William J. Wisener, another member of the state legislature's joint military committee. Through him, extracts from the joint military committee's report were made part of the House investigation. The House committee also incorporated into its report information from an 1868 account of Klan activities in Tennessee submitted by Major General William P. Carlin, assistant commissioner of the Tennessee Freedmen's Bureau, to Major General Oliver O. Howard, commissioner of the Freedmen's Bureau in Washington, D.C., as well as accounts from other bureau agents. Their reports confirmed the testimony of witnesses to both the Tennessee legislature in 1868 and the House committee in 1869 that the Ku Klux Klan was a growing menace, posing a serious threat to the restoration of democracy and the guarantee of equal rights in former Confederate states.

Author Biography

The principals in the 1868 election in Tennessee's Fourth Congressional District were little more than pawns in the chess game between Southerners intent on restoring the social and political order as it had existed before the war and Radicals bent on reconstructing the state in the image of its Northern neighbors. Ironically, Republican candidate Lewis Tillman was a Tennessee native who had spent his career in the state's court system and as a newspaper editor, while his conservative opponent, C. A. Sheafe, was an Ohioan who had served in the federal army before moving to Tennessee.

That the Ku Klux Klan played a role in keeping Tillman's supporters from the polls seems indisputable, yet it is in some ways remarkable. Founded in 1866, the Klan had no strong formal organization; many bands of miscreants rode through the countryside calling themselves Klansmen. While the perpetrators of violence were most often members of the working classes, a number of prominent Southerners had ties to the Klan, helping to protect other Klansmen accused of crimes. The Klan remained active throughout the South until the mid-1870s.

In Tennessee the fight against the Klan was led by William G. Brownlow. Born in 1805 in Virginia, Brownlow became a minister and was a traveling preacher throughout Appalachia before settling in Elizabethton, Tennessee, in 1836. Before the Civil War he was editor of a pro-Union newspaper. He left

"Ku-Klux Mode of Torture" from *Experience of a northern man among the Ku-Klux; or, The condition of the South* (1872). Image via Wikimedia Commons. [Public domain.]

the state after Tennessee seceded but returned in 1863 when Union troops established an occupation force there. He was elected governor in 1865 and was reelected in 1867, largely on votes of his new constituency, freed slaves. Shortly after the 1868 elections, he began lobbying the legislature to appoint him U.S. senator for Tennessee, a position he assumed in March 1869. After serving one term, he returned to Tennessee and resumed his newspaper career until his death in 1877.

Among the groups that gathered information on atrocities committed by the Ku Klux Klan and other reactionary groups in the South, none was more important than the Bureau of Refugees, Freedmen, and Abandoned Lands. Established by Congress in 1865, the Freedmen's Bureau, as it was popularly known, assisted freed slaves with a variety of economic and political issues. Led by Union General Oliver O. Howard, a native of Maine, the Bureau placed agents throughout the South to carry out its mission. These agents were often targets of Klan violence themselves, and their reports to the Bureau's headquarters in Washington, D.C., provided further evidence of the difficulties African Americans faced in becoming fully integrated into postwar society.

Historical Document

Report to Congress on the Activities of the Ku Klux Klan

This pertains to the deposition of William H. Wisener in case of C. A. Sheafe vs. Lewis Tillman, contested election.

WM. GALBREATH, *Mayor.*

Report of the joint military committee of the two houses in relation to the organization of the militia of the State of Tennessee, submitted to the extra session of the thirty-fifth general assembly, September 2, 1868.

Mr. Speaker: Your committee to whom was referred that part of the governor's message relating to outrages perpetrated by an organization known as the Ku-Klux Klan, and the necessity of organizing the militia for the protection of the loyal people of the State of Tennessee, have had the same under consideration; and after summoning a great many witnesses before them, are satisfied that there exists an organization of armed men going abroad disguised, robbing poor negroes of their fire-arms, taking them out of their houses at night, hanging, shooting, and whipping them in a most cruel manner, and driving them from their homes. Nor is this confined to the colored men alone. Women and children have been subjected to the torture of the lash, and brutal assaults have been committed upon them by these night-prowlers, and in many instances, the persons of females have been violated, and when the husband or father complained, he has been obliged to flee to save his own life.

Nor has this been confined to one county or one section of the State alone. Your committee find, that, after a careful investigation of all the facts, that these depredations have been committed all over Middle and West Tennessee, and in some parts of East Tennessee; particularly has this been the case in Maury, Lincoln, Giles, Marshall, Obion, Hardeman, Fayette and Gibson Counties. In Lincoln County, they took Senator Wm. Wyatt from his house in the night, and inflicted all sorts of indignities upon him. They beat him over the head with their pistols, cutting a frightful gash, and saturating his shirt with blood, leaving him insensible. Senator Wyatt is a Christian gentleman, and sixty-five years of age; his only offense being that he is a Union man and a member of the State legislature.

We also find that the same spirit exists in Obion County; that it was rife there, indeed, one year and a half ago, when the disloyalists so inhumanly and brutally murdered Senator Case and his son. Since then, depredations have been committed all over the country that calls loudly for redress. No loyal man is safe in that country at the present time.

Your committee's attention has also been directed to Maury County. We find that a perfect reign of terror exists there; that some two hundred colored men have had to flee from their homes, and take refuge in the city of Nashville; afraid to return, although here they are destitute of food, or any means of subsistence. In this county, school-houses have been burned down, teachers driven away, and colored men shot, whipped, and murdered at will. Hon. S. M. Arnell, congressman from that district, was sought for, when he was at home on a visit, by members of the Ku-Klux Klan, who were thirsting for his blood.

In Fayette County, the teacher of colored children has been assaulted and driven away by the Ku-Klux Klan.

Your committee find, that to enumerate all the outrages committed by this organization of outlaws, would take more time than can be spared. They would most respectfully direct your attention to a synopsis of the evidence taken before your committee; remarking at the same time, that much valuable information is necessarily left out on account of the witnesses fearing to have their names mentioned in this report, lest they should hereafter, on account of their testimony, lose their lives.

One of the most brutal assaults perhaps, that had been committed, was on the person of a school teacher, in Shelbyville, Bedford County, Tennessee. Mr. Dunlap, a white instructor, was taken from his house in the night by the Ku-Klux Klan, and most inhumanly whipped; and for no other reason than he was a white man, teaching a colored school. One witness testified that he was a confederate soldier, a native Tennessean; has been with negroes all his life, and seen them whipped by different persons; but never saw any one beaten as this man, Dunlap, was. It is in evidence that Mr. Dunlap is a member of the Methodist Church, and a very quiet, inoffensive man. Attention is especially directed to the evidence in this case.

Your committee also find that there has been a determined effort and is still a determined purpose all over Middle and West Tennessee, to keep colored men from the polls, and thus secure the election to office of candidates of the democratic party. Very many of the outrages committed have been against men who were formerly soldiers in the national army. The proof shows that there is an eternal hatred existing against all men that voted the republican ticket, or who belong to the Loyal League, or are engaged in teaching schools, and giving instruction to the humbler classes of their fellow-men.

The committee are compelled to conclude, from the evidence before them, that the ultimate object of the Ku-Klux Klan is, to intimidate Union men, both black and white, keep them from the polls on election day, and, by a system of anti-lawry and terrorism, carry the State in November next for Seymour and Blair.

Your committee would again call the attention of the general assembly to the following synopsis of testimony, as better calculated to show the true condition of the country than anything your committee could say:

We are permitted to make the following extracts from the report of Major General Carlin to General Howard, for the month of June, 1868:

"General: I have the honor to submit the following report on the condition of affairs pertaining to this department, during the month of June last. It is with deep regret that I am compelled to begin this report with the statement, that, since my connection with the bureau, no such discouraging state of affairs has prevailed in Tennessee, during any one month, as that for the month of June last. I say discouraging, because it is totally beyond the powers of myself and subordinates to remedy evils that cry aloud for redress."

"In the counties of Marshall, Rutherford, Maury, and Giles, it may be said that a reign of terror has been established, and will doubtless remain, unless the State, or United States, should provide a military force to be stationed in those counties."

"The hostility of the implacable pro-slavery people to colored education has manifested itself in numerous instances of violence toward teachers of colored schools."

"Your attention is called especially to the case of Mr. Newton, who was assaulted and badly wounded at Somerville. He would doubtless have been slain if he had not escaped in time. The case was reported by the undersigned to Major General Thomas, commanding the department, and troops were asked for to protect the school and teachers. Mr. Newton was escorted back by them to his school-house, where he has continued to conduct his school."

"This affair is more particularly described in the extracts from the report of Lieutenant Colonel Palmer, sub-assistant commissioner of the sub-district of Memphis."

"There will doubtless be great excitement and frequent disturbances in the State during the present political canvass for President and State officers. Nearly every day furnishes additional evidence of the determination of the Ku-Klux Klan and their friends to bring about a state of affairs that will preclude the possibility of personal liberty for the colored people, and the active, out-spoken Union men. I doubt if any measure, short of martial law, will preserve peace and insure safety till after the next election."

A. H. Eastman, agent at Columbia, Tennessee, reports the following extracts:

"The Ku-Klux Klan appear to be on the 'war path.' Complaints of visitations by night, all over my district, of the breaking into of houses and assaults upon the inmates, are very frequent. The Klan went to the house of Joshua Ferrell, an old and quiet colored man, on the night of the 12th instant, called him from his bed, and, while he was unfastening the door, they jumped in upon him and beat his head with a pistol, cutting a gash half an inch wide, four inches long, and to the skull. Then they asked him for fire-arms, which he said he had not. They then took him into a field and whipped him so badly that it nearly killed him. They also tore up everything in the house, and then went to his son's house, took him from his bed, smashed a large looking-glass over the head of his sick wife, who was in bed. They then whipped the man with stirrup-straps and buckles, which cut long and deep gashes into the flesh, and all because, they said, he was a 'big-feeling nigger, voted for Brownlow, and belonged to the Union League.'

J. K. Nelson, agent at Murfreesboro, Tennessee, says the Ku-Klux Klan took from his house, about midnight, Bill Carlton, (colored) living in Middleton district, and beat him very severely, giving him, as he says, one hundred and fifty lashes with a heavy leather strap.

"On Thursday night last, the Klan went to the house of Minor Fletcher, living eight miles from here, on the Shelbyville pike, rode into his front and back porches on their horses, and called him out. They then proceeded to the house of D. Webb, about ten or twelve in number, and, as he reports, called to him to come out. This he refused to do, until they assured him that he should not be hurt, and threatened him with violence in case of his refusal. He went out; they then accused him of being a radical, and a Loyal Leaguer. He denied being a member of the league, but told them that he was a Union man and always had been. They called him a liar, and threatened to hang him, calling at the same time for a halter. His wife, who was in a critical condition, screamed and plead for him, and begged them to spare him on her account. They then told him to go back to his wife. He turned to go, when one of them caught him by the hair, jerked him to the ground, sprang upon him, and beat him in the face in a shocking manner, at the same time holding a pistol to his head, and threatening to shoot him. They then left him in an almost insensible condition, scarcely able to crawl to his house."

"More than half the outrages perpetrated by this Klan are not reported to me. The parties are afraid, or have a want of confidence in the bureau. There is a feeling of insecurity among the people (Unionists) that has not been equaled since 1861. I am so impressed with my own inability to fully understand the exact condition of affairs that I will be excused for not making the same comprehensible to you."

"This I do know, that I have been sleeping for months with a revolver under my pillow, and a double-barreled shot-gun, heavily charged with buck shot, at one hand, and a hatchet at the other, with an inclination to sell the little piece of mortality with which I am entrusted as dearly as possible. I have had to submit to insults, which make a man despise himself for bearing, and which I cannot submit to any longer. Many freedmen are afraid to sleep in their own houses. Many have already been driven from the country." ...

Rev. H. O. Hoffman, Shelbyville, Tenn.:

"Have never seen any of the Klan, but that it exists in our county no one doubts. Several have been harmed by this secret organization. Mr. Dunlap and a colored man by the name of Jeff were badly whipped on the night of the 4th of July. His person was cut in great gashes, from the middle of his back to his knees. Mr. Dunlap's offense was teaching a colored school. I have been repeatedly threatened, and was told that the Ku-Klux Klan had a list made of men they designed driving from the country. Found the following note in my yard:

"In Ku-klux Council, July 24, 1868.

Rev. Mr. Hoffman: Your name is before the council. Beware! We will attend to you. You shall not call us villains—damn you. Ku-Klux."

"I believe the object of the Klan is to whip unarmed negroes, scare timid white men, break up elections, and interfere with the State government, and steal and plunder the goods of the people." ...

Glossary

Blair: Francis Blair; politician, Union Army general, and unsuccessful candidate for vice president of the United States on the Democratic ticket in 1868

Galbreath, William: mayor of Shelbyville, Tennessee, in 1869

Mr. Speaker: DeWitt C. Senter, speaker of the Tennessee State Legislature in 1868

radical: term generally used by Southerners after the Civil War to describe those who supported Reconstruction policies and equal rights for former slaves

Seymour: Horatio Seymour, two-term governor of New York (1853–1854 and 1863–1864) and unsuccessful Democratic candidate for president of the United States in 1868

stirrup-straps: leather loops attached to a saddle to assist riders in mounting

Thomas, George Henry: U.S. Army major general, a career soldier and in 1868 commander of the Department of the Cumberland (Tennessee and Kentucky)

Document Analysis

The excerpt above is part of an official report of a committee of the U.S. House of Representatives appointed in 1869 to investigate a contested election that took place the previous November in Tennessee's Fourth Congressional District. The committee was charged with making recommendations to the full House regarding a challenge filed by C. A. Sheafe, who had won the popular vote. Governor William Brownlow, determining that voter intimidation had been rampant in the district, certified Sheafe's opponent, Republican candidate Lewis Tillman, as the winner. The committee's report is contained in the Miscellaneous Documents of the Forty-First Congress (1869–71) under the title *Papers in the Contested Election Case of Sheafe vs. Tillman in the Fourth Congressional District of Tennessee*, which has an official printing date of February 11, 1870. The excerpted passages are taken from official reports and witness testimony that describe conditions in Tennessee during the spring and summer of 1868. The initial selection provides a summary and findings from a joint military committee appointed in August 1868 by the Tennessee legislature to investigate activities of the Ku Klux Klan. The Klan was thought to be responsible for an ongoing campaign of intimidation directed at recently freed slaves and their white supporters in order to keep those in the state supportive of Radical Republicans from voting or exercising other civil rights. Reports written by agents or managers of the Freedmen's Bureau provide information to superiors about the conditions of freed slaves in regions for which the agents were responsible. The brief excerpt from testimony by Reverend H. O. Hoffman describes his experience with the Klan.

Like most reports, the document prepared by the House of Representatives has a formal organization that reflects the conduct of the investigation. In the full report, transcripts of questions posed to each witness and witnesses' responses are recorded verbatim. Among those testifying before the House committee was Tennessee state senator William Wisener, who provided information about his own experiences with the Klan as well as information from reports he had received while serving as a member of the joint military committee. As a supplement to Wisener's testimony, the congressional committee authorized the printing of an appendix that offers further evidence of the scope and characteristics of activities being conducted by the Klan. The excerpts above are taken from this appendix, which provides graphic details of the Klan's activities throughout Tennessee.

Founded as a social club in Pulaski, Tennessee, the Ku Klux Klan quickly transformed into an agency of white supremacists and former secessionists disgruntled with Radical Republican efforts to give African Americans equal rights. At a meeting held in Nashville in 1867, former Confederate General Nathan Bedford Forrest was selected as national head of the organization. Despite some attempt to create a structure and hierarchy (complete with mysterious titles for leaders such as "Grand Wizard," "Grand Dragon," and "Grand Cyclops," to name a few), the Klan remained only loosely organized and its leaders had little control over individual groups operating locally under its aegis. In keeping with the secretive nature of the organization, Klan members tended to act at night and nearly always wore disguises. Many Southerners insisted that the Ku Klux Klan did not exist at all. Supporters claimed that much of the violence attributed to the Klan was imagined by its supposed victims, and that night riders who might have caused injury on occasion were simply vigilantes or misguided fun-seeking youth who meant no real harm.

The Testimony

The excerpts from the House of Representatives report represent a sampling of firsthand testimony describing encounters between the Ku Klux Klan and its many victims, and secondhand accounts from officials who routinely received reports of acts of violence. In the first passage, the authors of the joint military committee's report to the Tennessee legislature make clear that, despite protests from many white citizens that the Klan was not really dangerous, this "organization of armed men" posed a serious threat to the safety and well-being of the state's African American population. The summary statement that "poor negroes" were being robbed of their firearms, whipped, hanged, shot, and driven from their homes is based on testimony from numerous African American victims and from white Americans who either witnessed the atrocities or learned of them shortly after they occurred.

The committee seems to go out of its way to stress the widespread nature of the Klan's reign of terror. Traditionally, Tennesseans viewed their state as being divided into three broad regions. When talk of secession grew in 1861, West and Middle Tennessee, areas with many slaveholders, sided with the newly forming Confederacy. East Tennessee, populated by small farmers, was inclined to remain in the Union. While one might have expected trouble in the western and middle regions of the state, the authors of the report make it explicit that all three sections were experiencing an upsurge of Klan violence. After claiming that the "depredations" caused by the Klan extended across the entire state, the committee lists specific counties in which violence was especially prevalent. This list actually served a second purpose: it provided Governor Brownlow a reason for declaring martial law in particularly troubled areas and for deploying troops from the Tennessee State Guard there. Although the governor was unable to send troops in before the November election, after the State Guard was finally reactivated early in 1869, Brownlow declared martial law in nine counties in February.

Particularly noteworthy, too, is the report's stress on the violence committed against white Americans in Tennessee who were working to advance the improvement of the African American population. Virtually every person identified in the excerpt from the joint military committee report is white, including numerous individuals teaching in African American schools who had been intimidated, beaten, or otherwise threatened simply for wanting to educate former slaves. The report's authors also play upon a fear common among Southerners, the desecration of the family ("women and children have been subjected to the torture of the lash") and especially of women ("the persons of females have been violated"). Though perhaps not intentional, there is a note of irony in this behavior. One of the principal arguments of white supremacists was that, if not checked, African Americans would take advantage of white women and adulterate the purity of the race.

Because the joint military committee report was being submitted to colleagues in the legislature, the authors include incidents in which elected officials have suffered at the hands of Klansmen who have no respect for the law or those sworn to uphold it. The extensive description of the treatment of the aging Senator William Wyatt is intended to make fellow legislators realize that the danger posed by the Klan could easily be visited upon them. The allusion to State Senator Almon Case and his son would have also caused consternation among Radical legislators. Case was murdered in January 1867, his son four months earlier. Case's assailant was known but escaped prosecution because he enjoyed the protection of white Americans sympathetic to the Klan's activities. The committee may have been looking toward the upcoming congressional elections when they cited the case of Samuel M. Arnell, who had been elected to the U.S. House of Representatives in a contested election a year earlier. Arnell's experience makes it clear that even members of Congress had much to fear from Klansmen "thirsting" for their blood.

Reports from various officials of the Freedmen's Bureau corroborate the testimony of witnesses before the joint military committee and the congressional committee investigating the contested election. The Freedmen's Bureau was established as the Civil War was coming to a close by President Abraham Lincoln, who foresaw that former slaves would need assistance in becoming independent citizens. Designed to provide legal, medical, educational, and economic aid, the Bureau established offices and deployed agents throughout the South. Their efforts met with stiff resistance from the white population, and many agents found themselves subjected to harassment and intimidation similar to that suffered by the clients they were supposed to be serving. Major General William Carlin's report on conditions in West Tennessee highlights several cases of brutality that had occurred recently in this region, among them the ongoing hostility toward education for African Americans exhibited by "pro-slavery people," by which he means former secessionists who had adopted the mantle of white supremacists. Throughout the South, many white Americans were fearful that, once educated,

African Americans would become a powerful political force in communities where they outnumbered white people, and therefore posed a threat to their former masters. Few in the South believed that the races could coexist harmoniously; white Americans especially feared that educating and arming the African American population would inevitably lead to a revolution aimed at wiping out all white people.

Undoubtedly many of the attacks on African Americans perpetrated by the Klan were launched randomly against any African American unfortunate enough to be spotted by night riders out to cause mayhem and create terror. As the reports by agents A. H. Eastman and J. K. Nelson indicate, however, some African Americans were targeted for their political activity. Both Joshua Ferrell and D. Webb were told they were chosen by the Klan because they supported the Union League or the Loyal League, held Radical sympathies, or voted for the Radical Republican candidate for governor in the most recent election. The activities of the Union League (sometimes called the Loyal League) were particularly vexing to former secessionists and white supremacists. Founded in 1862 in Northern cities to support the Union cause, the Union League organized chapters in the South after the war to promote the Republican political agenda and to encourage African Americans to vote and become involved in politics. Many former slaves joined the Union League even if they were not political activists.

As every witness testifies, the Klan's actions ranged from simple intimidation to significant physical violence, sometimes resulting in murder. In many cases threats alone were enough to cause white and African Americans alike to submit to the Klan's will. One intimidation technique typical of many groups of Klansmen is described by the Reverend H. O. Hoffman, who reports having received threats himself, including one delivered in a fashion typical of Klansmen at the time: a note left in his yard warning him that his "name is before the Council" and that the Klan "will attend to you." Such notes alone were often sufficient to deter whites from continuing to support African Americans, and in some cases caused them to leave the region rather than face the prospect of reprisal for their actions.

A number of whites were forced to submit to public insult, which, coupled with secondhand reports of violence, caused them to behave like agent J. K. Nelson, who slept with firearms nearby. Many African Americans, fearing for their lives and wishing to keep themselves and their families safe from Klan attacks, simply fled to what they perceived to be safer regions. As the joint military committee report indicates, this posed new problems: the "two hundred colored men" who fled to Nashville ended up "destitute of food, or any means of subsistence." This early instance of African American flight to urban centers is a harbinger of what would come for many who left the harsh life of the segregated rural South only to end up no better off in crowded cities, where they remained victims of inequality and prejudice.

Language and Rhetoric

Some of the hyperbolic language in these excerpts can be attributed to a general tendency during the nineteenth century for Americans to assume an oratorical posture in their writing. A comparison of these reports with contemporary sermons might reveal striking similarities. Words such as "outrage," "depredation," and "reign of terror" appear regularly in written communications from this period, particularly in newspapers. While some accounts are emotionally charged and may be exaggerated, the sheer volume of reporting makes it evident that the Klan's campaign of terror was effective in keeping freed slaves and their white supporters from exercising their civil rights.

The inclusion of lengthy descriptions of specific acts of mayhem and torture, however, would have had immediate impact on readers of these reports, and would have convinced even the most skeptical to agree that strong countermeasures were required to curb the Klan's activities. Reverend Hoffman's description of the injuries suffered by the "colored man by the name of Jeff," agent Eastman's testimony about the treatment Joshua Ferrell received simply because he supported Governor Brownlow and the Union League, and the manhandling of Minor Fletcher and D. Webb described by agent J. K. Nelson contain little overblown rhetoric. Instead, the graphic language used in a series of declarative sentences filled with strong action verbs conveys without exaggeration the horror of the circumstances in which these men found themselves. The detail with which incidents of brutality are described is clearly intended to provoke both fear and outrage. The elderly Senator Wyatt was pistol-whipped so badly that he suffered a "frightful gash, saturating his shirt with blood, leaving him insensible." Joshua Ferrell, also old and apparently harmless, was similarly beaten, the pistol "cutting a gash half an inch wide, four inches long" into his skull. Little is left to the imagination except the unstated conclusion that incidents like these will continue to occur unless the Klan is neutralized.

Also common among these reports is the tendency to establish clear political and moral differences between perpetrators and victims in the attacks. For example, Senator Wyatt is described as "a Christian gentleman" and "a Union Man." The schoolteacher Dunlap is "a member of the Methodist Church," quiet and inoffensive. Many of the victims are former members of the Union Army. Those who threaten these honest, law-abiding, loyal citizens of the United States are violent, lawless bands intent on sedition. The attack on Senator Case indicates to the writers of the joint committee report that "no loyal man" is safe at present. Additionally, there is a sense running through these reports that these individual groups of "night-prowlers" are part of a larger, sinister organization that was creating a "system of anti-lawry and terrorism" for political motives: to deliver votes in the upcoming presidential election to the Democratic ticket.

The testimony recorded in these reports displays the power of anecdotal evidence in supporting an argument for government support of victims. The specific action sought by both state and federal officials was armed intervention. In his June 1868 report, Carlin makes it clear that Freedmen's Bureau agents were powerless to "remedy" the "evils that cry out for redress," and he predicts exactly what Governor Brownlow feared. The level of Klan activity in the early months of 1868 strongly suggested that "frequent disturbances" would continue to occur during the fall campaigns for president and seats in Congress. The Klan's activities were certain to "bring about a state of affairs that will preclude the possibility for the colored people, and the active, out-spoken Union men" to vote in the November election. Carlin is clear in his belief that nothing short of martial law "will preserve the peace and insure safety." No doubt in the summer of 1868 Governor Brownlow was pleased to see this kind of support for his own position against the Klan. For members of Congress receiving this report in 1870, the message was equally clear: some definite action was needed to ameliorate or eliminate Klan violence, or the country as a whole might slip back into anarchy and civil strife.

Essential Themes

The importance of congressional investigations into the activities of the Ku Klux Klan during the first decade following the end of the Civil War can hardly be overstated. Between 1866 and 1870 the Klan had spread to virtually every state in the former Confederacy. Its brutal campaign to intimidate the African American population in those states not only affected the political climate, but also caused many former slaves to fear for their lives and their property. The ability of Klansmen to act with impunity, knowing that sympathetic white officials in law enforcement and government would do little to prosecute them for any crimes they committed, created a virtual state of anarchy that many then and later would equate with terrorism. Although it is impossible to speculate on what might have happened, many scholars agree with those who witnessed Klan violence that the United States may well have slipped back into civil war had the Klan's activities not been checked. Hence, reports that document the Klan's systematic assault on equal rights were instrumental in bringing about action at the federal level to suppress the organization and restore order and the rule of law in the South.

Various investigations led to decisions that influenced the future of the nation. Undoubtedly the 1868 report prompted Tennessee legislators to reestablish the State Guard. In 1870 the House of Representatives was convinced by its committee's report that the African American population in Tennessee had been denied their civil rights; it voted to allow Tillman to retain the disputed Fourth District seat in Congress. Widespread accounts of Klan violence such as the ones documented in the House committee's report were instrumental in generating further action at the federal level. In 1871, Senator John Scott of Pennsylvania convened a congressional committee to investigate Klan activities in the South. The extensive testimony presented before Smith's committee was published in thirteen volumes in 1872 as *Report of the Joint Select Committee Appointed to Inquire in to the Condition of Affairs in the Late Insurrectionary States*. It became the most important contemporary document outlining the nature and extent of Klan violence during the early years of Reconstruction. The report also prompted passage of a stronger law allowing the federal government to counter Klan activities, which were identified as supporting a specific political agenda, that of the Democratic Party.

As a result of strong enforcement by President Ulysses S. Grant, the Ku Klux Klan's influence was almost completely nullified by 1877, when Reconstruction ended and former Confederate states were once again allowed to participate as full partners in the national government. Unfortunately, once free to act without federal supervision, many Southern states enacted laws that brought about the same result that the Klan had sought through violence: a segregated society in which African Americans remained separate and decidedly unequal.

—*Laurence W. Mazzeno, PhD*

Bibliography and Additional Reading

Bergeron, Paul H., Stephen V. Ash, and Jeanette Keith. *Tennesseans and Their History*. Knoxville: U of Tennessee P, 1999.

Budiansky, Stephen. *The Bloody Shirt: Terror after Appomattox*. New York: Viking, 2008.

Foner, Eric. *Reconstruction: America's Unfinished Revolution, 1863–1877*. New York: Harper, 1988.

Martinez, J. Michael. *Carpetbaggers, Cavalry, and the Ku Klux Klan: Exposing the Invisible Empire during Reconstruction*. Lanham: Rowman, 2007.

Newton, Michael. *The Ku Klux Klan: History, Organization, Language, Influence, and Activities of America's Most Notorious Secret Society*. Jefferson: McFarland, 2007.

Parsons, Elaine Frantz. *Ku Klux: The Birth of the Klan during Reconstruction*. Chapel Hill: U of North Carolina P, 2016.

Rable, George C. *But There Was No Peace: The Role of Violence in the Politics of Reconstruction*. Athens: U of Georgia P, 2007.

Summers, Mark W. *A Dangerous Stir: Fear, Paranoia, and the Making of Reconstruction*. Chapel Hill: U of North Carolina P, 2009.

Booker T. Washington: "Statement on Suffrage"

Date: 1903
Author: Booker T. Washington
Genre: address; speech

Summary Overview

As he addressed the concerns of his race, the black educator and head of the Tuskegee Institute, Booker T. Washington, sought to balance his attack on the injustice of segregation and racial violence with his institution's need to survive in an increasingly racist and violent South. Washington was an astute politician. He developed associations with northern business leaders and southern politicians that enabled him to successfully operate Tuskegee as a black educational institution. Although not known for his fiery rhetoric, Washington spoke out about the injustice of discrimination, biased suffrage laws, and the horror of lynching. He retained the belief that logic would prevail and that if they were shown that it was in their interest to promote the development of blacks, the leadership of the South and educated and cultured southerners would support the cause of racial justice.

Washington used a variety of means to express his views. His most famous statements were public speeches, but he also published "letters to the editor" in southern and northern newspapers, gave interviews, and wrote articles and private letters to powerful and influential white men to express his political and racial views. His "Statement on Suffrage" was made in a letter published in the Philadelphia North American. In it, Washington takes the position that voting laws passed in the South were largely unjust and discriminatory and that blacks' right to vote should be part of an overall process of education.

Defining Moment

Booker T. Washington's "Statement on Suffrage" sought to speak to the interests of both white southerners and African Americans. He encouraged African Americans to seek an industrial education because he believed that both blacks and whites would benefit. A more academically focused education for blacks would give rise to controversy and a white backlash. By deemphasizing the importance of civil and political rights, Washington hoped to attract the support of southern whites who favored social segregation and black disenfranchisement, but who might be convinced to support African Americans learning a trade. Similarly, Washington's suggestion that blacks seek the advice of whites when voting was

Booker T. Washington, c. 1905. Photo via Wikimedia Commons. [Public domain.]

almost certainly intended to appease whites who were hostile to black political participation.

At the same time, Washington was addressing a black audience. He assured the black community that he, too, opposed voting laws that disenfranchised the majority of black voters on the basis of race. However, the attainment of voting rights would be a long process. African Americans should concentrate on gaining an industrial education, which would not only increase educational levels in the black community but would also lead to greater economic prosperity and self-sufficiency. When blacks had accumulated more wealth and property they would be better prepared to fight for civil and political equality. Black suffrage would then be more acceptable to whites.

Author Biography

Booker Taliaferro Washington was born on a farm near Hale's Ford in the foothills of the Blue Ridge Mountains in Franklin County, Virginia, most likely on April 5, 1856. Washington spent the first eight years of his childhood as a slave. Following emancipation, he moved with his mother, brother, and sister to join his stepfather, who had found employment in the saltworks in Malden, West Virginia. Emancipation did not significantly raise the economic well-being of the family. The young Washington alternated between working in the saltworks and attending school.

At the age of sixteen, Washington left home for Virginia to further his education at Hampton Institute, under the influence of General Samuel C. Armstrong and his theory of industrial education. Three years later, he graduated as one of the school's top students and a protégé of General Armstrong. After a short stint as a schoolteacher in Malden, Washington returned to Hampton as a member of the faculty and for additional education. In May 1881, Armstrong arranged for his prize student to be named principal of a recently authorized Alabama state normal and industrial school for black students.

When Washington arrived in Tuskegee, he discovered that the school existed only on paper. Despite his youth and inexperience, he managed to create the school—acquiring land, erecting the buildings, and recruiting the faculty. More impressively, he mastered the political, administrative, and financial skills that he needed to form a black institution in the inhospitable hills of northern Alabama. By the early 1890s, Tuskegee Institute was a success, and Washington was beginning to address the broader political and economic issues that confronted African Americans.

In 1895, Washington was asked to speak at the opening ceremonies of the Atlanta Exposition. This speech was a phenomenal success and transformed Washington from a southern educator to the most influential and powerful African American in the United States. He consulted with presidents and corporate leaders and headed a political machine that dispersed funds and political patronage throughout the black community. In 1901, his status brought him an invitation to lunch at the White House with President Theodore Roosevelt.

Washington confronted the task of devising a strategy for blacks to successfully move from slavery to citizenship, a process made more difficult by the rise in racism, discrimination, and violence characterizing the beginning of the twentieth century. Washington's strategy addressed the needs of the vast majority of African Americans who resided in the South. It focused on education, self-reliance, hard work, and economic success. While his critics accused him of accepting discrimination and white supremacy, Washington consistently spoke out against segregation, lynching, and the restrictions placed on black suffrage. Nevertheless, in the early twentieth century, W. E. B. Du Bois and other African American leaders, especially in the North, became increasingly dissatisfied with Washington's program and his political power. The Niagara Movement, founded in 1905, and later, the National Association for the Advancement of Colored People (NAACP), founded in 1909, challenged his leadership. Still, at the time of his death in November 1915, Washington was still the most widely known and respected African American leader in the United States.

Historical Document

"Statement on Suffrage"

MR. PRESIDENT AND GENTLEMEN OF THE BOARD OF DIRECTORS AND CITIZENS.

One-third of the population of the South is of the Negro race. No enterprise seeking the material, civil, or moral welfare of this section can disregard this element of our population and reach the highest success. I but convey to you, Mr. President and Directors, the sentiment of the masses of my race when I say that in no way have the value and manhood of the American Negro been more fittingly and generously recognized than by the managers of this magnificent Exposition at every stage of its progress. It is a recognition that will do more to cement the friendship of the two races than any occurrence since the dawn of our freedom.

Not only this, but the opportunity here afforded will awaken among us a new era of industrial progress. Ignorant and inexperienced, it is not strange that in the first years of our new life we began at the top instead of at the bottom; that a seat in Congress or the state legislature was more sought than real estate or industrial skill; that the political convention of stump speaking had more attraction than starting a dairy farm or truck garden.

A ship lost at sea for many days suddenly sighted a friendly vessel. From the mast of the unfortunate vessel was seen a signal, "Water, water; we die of thirst!" The answer from the friendly vessel at once came back, "Cast down your bucket where you are." A second time the signal, "Water, water; send us water!" ran up from the distressed vessel, and was answered, "Cast down your bucket where you are." And a third and fourth signal for water was answered, "Cast down your bucket where you are." The captain of the distressed vessel, at last heeding the injunction, cast down his bucket, and it came up full of fresh, sparkling water from the mouth of the Amazon River. To those of my race who depend on bettering their condition in a foreign land or who underestimate the importance of cultivating friendly relations with the southern white man, who is their next-door neighbour, I would say: "Cast down your bucket where you are"—cast it down in making friends in every manly way of the people of all races by whom we are surrounded.

Cast it down in agriculture, mechanics, in commerce, in domestic service, and in the professions. And in this connection it is well to bear in mind that whatever other sins the South may be called to bear, when it comes to business, pure and simple, it is in the South that the Negro is given a man's chance in the commercial world, and in nothing is this Exposition more eloquent than in emphasizing this chance. Our greatest danger is that in the great leap from slavery to freedom we may overlook the fact that the masses of us are to live by the productions of our hands, and fail to keep in mind that we shall prosper in proportion as we learn to dignify and glorify common labor and put brains and skill into the common occupations of life; shall prosper in proportion as we learn to draw the line between the superficial and the substantial, the ornamental gewgaws of life and the useful. No race can prosper till it learns that there is as much dignity in tilling a field as in writing a poem. It is at the bottom of life we must begin, and not at the top. Nor should we permit our grievances to overshadow our opportunities.

To those of the white race who look to the incoming of those of foreign birth and strange tongue and habits for the prosperity of the South, were I permitted I would repeat what I say to my own race, "Cast down your bucket where you are." Cast it down among the eight millions of Negroes whose habits you know, whose fidelity and love you have tested in days when to have proved treacherous meant the ruin of your firesides. Cast down your bucket among these people who have, without strikes and labor wars, tilled your fields, cleared your forests, built your railroads and cities, and brought forth treasures from the bowels of the earth, and helped make possible this magnificent representation of the progress of the South. Casting down your bucket among my people, helping and encouraging them as you are doing on these grounds, and to education of head, hand, and heart, you will find that they will buy your surplus land, make blossom the waste places in your fields, and run your factories. While doing this, you can be sure in the future, as in the past, that you and your families will be surrounded by the most patient, faithful, law-abiding, and unresentful people that the world has seen. As we have proved our loyalty to you in the past, in nursing your children, watching by the sick-bed of your mothers and fathers, and often following them with tear-dimmed eyes to their graves, so in the future, in our humble way, we shall stand by you with a devotion that no foreigner can approach, ready to lay down our lives, if need be, in defense of yours, interlacing our industrial, commercial, civil, and religious life with yours in a way that shall make the interests of both races one. In all things that are purely social we can be as separate as the fingers, yet one as the hand in all things essential to mutual progress.

There is no defense or security for any of us except in the highest intelligence and development of all. If anywhere there are efforts tending to curtail the fullest growth of the Negro, let these efforts be turned into stimulating, encouraging, and making him the most useful and intelligent citizen. Effort or means so invested will pay a thousand per cent. interest. These efforts will be twice blessed—"blessing him that gives and him that takes."

There is no escape through law of man or God from the inevitable:—

The laws of changeless justice bind
Oppressor with oppressed;
And close as sin and suffering joined
We march to fate abreast.

Nearly sixteen millions of hands will aid you in pulling the load upward, or they will pull against you the load downward. We shall constitute one-third and more of the ignorance and crime of the South, or one-third its intelligence and progress; we shall contribute one-third to the business and industrial prosperity of the South, or we shall prove a veritable body of death, stagnating, depressing, retarding every effort to advance the body politic.

Gentlemen of the Exposition, as we present to you our humble effort at an exhibition of our progress, you must not expect overmuch. Starting thirty years ago with ownership here and there in a few quilts and pumpkins and chickens (gathered from miscellaneous sources), remember the path that has led from these to the inventions and production of agricultural implements, buggies, steam-engines, newspapers, books, statuary, carving, paintings, the management of drug-stores and banks, has not been trodden without contact with thorns and thistles. While we take pride in what we exhibit as a result of our independent efforts, we do not for a moment forget that our part in this exhibition would fall far short of your expectations but for the constant help that has come to our educational life, not only from the southern states, but especially from Northern philanthropists, who have made their gifts a constant stream of blessing and encouragement.

The wisest among my race understand that the agitation of questions of social equality is the extremest folly, and that progress in the enjoyment of all the privileges that will come to us must be the result of severe and constant struggle rather than of artificial forcing. No race that has anything to contribute to the markets of the world is long in any degree ostracized. It is important and right that all privileges of the law be ours, but it is vastly more important that we be prepared for the exercises of these privileges. The opportunity to earn a dollar in a factory just now is worth infinitely more than the opportunity to spend a dollar in an opera-house.

In conclusion, may I repeat that nothing in thirty years has given us more hope and encouragement, and drawn us so near to you of the white race, as this opportunity offered by the Exposition; and here bending, as it were, over the altar that represents the results of the struggles of your race and mine, both starting practically empty-handed three decades ago, I pledge that in your effort to work out the great and intricate problem which God has laid at the doors of the South, you shall have at all times the patient, sympathetic help of my race; only let this be constantly in mind, that, while from representations in these buildings of the product of field, of forest, of mine, of factory, letters, and art, much good will come, yet far above and beyond material benefits will be that higher good, that, let us pray God, will come, in a blotting out of sectional differences and racial animosities and suspicions, in a determination to administer absolute justice, in a willing obedience among all classes to the mandates of law. This, this, coupled with our material prosperity, will bring into our beloved South a new heaven and a new earth. . . .

Negro and the White

I believe it is the duty of the negro—as the greater part of the race is already doing—to deport himself modestly in regard to political claims, depending on the slow but sure influences that proceed from the possession of property, intelligence and high character for the full recognition of his political rights.

I think that the according of the full exercise of political rights is going to be a matter of natural, slow growth, not an over-night, gourd-vine affair. I do not believe that the negro should cease voting, for a man cannot learn the exercise of self-government by ceasing to vote, any more than a boy can learn to swim by keeping out of the water; but I do believe that in his voting he should more and more be influenced by those of intelligence and character who are his next-door neighbors.

I know colored men who, through the encouragement, help and advice of southern white people, have accumulated thousands of dollars worth of property, but who, at the same time, would never think of going to those same persons for advice concerning the casting of their ballots. This, it seems to me, is unwise and unreasonable, and should cease. In saying this, I do not mean that the negro should truckle, or not vote from principle, for the instant he ceases to vote from principle he loses the confidence and respect of the southern white man even.

Suffrage Laws Unjust

I do not believe that any State should make a law that permits an ignorant and poverty-stricken white man to vote and prevents a black man in the same condition from voting.

Such a law is not only unjust, but it will react, as all unjust laws do, in time; for the effect of such a law is to encourage the negro to secure education and property, and at the same time it encourages the white man to remain in ignorance and poverty. I believe that in time, through the operation of intelligence and friendly race relations, all cheating at the ballot-box in the South will cease.

It will become apparent that the white man who begins by cheating a negro out of his ballot soon learns to cheat a white man out of his, and that man who does this ends his career of dishonesty by the theft of property or by some equally serious crime.

In my opinion, the time will come when the South will encourage all of its citizens to vote. It will see that it pays better, from every standpoint, to have healthy, vigorous life than to have that political stagnation which always results when one-half the population has no share and no interest in the government.

As a rule, I believe in universal, free suffrage, but I believe that in the South we are confronted with peculiar conditions that justify the protection of the ballot in many of the States, for a while at least, either by an educational test, a property test, or by both combined; but whatever tests are required they should be made to apply with equal and exact justice to both races.

Glossary

gewgaws: trinkets, showy but worthless toys

The laws of changeless justice bind... : from "At Point Royal" (1862) by American poet John Greenleaf Whittier

Document Analysis

In the years that followed the Atlanta address, Washington's power grew. In 1901, he lunched with President Theodore Roosevelt at the White House. He counted many top industrialists, such as Andrew Carnegie, as his supporters. Nonetheless, racial conditions grew steadily worse as segregation became entrenched and southern states deprived black citizens of their right to vote. Washington's prestige allowed him access to the media to voice his concerns about these developments, and he did so repeatedly. In June 1903, he addressed the suffrage issue in a letter published in the Philadelphia *North American*.

Washington began his letter with a discussion of black political rights. He argued that African Americans had a "duty" to be "modest" in their desire for political equality and should instead concentrate on accumulating property, gaining an education, and behaving with "high character." The attainment of these goals would effectively prove to white southerners that African Americans were deserving of the rights and freedoms guaranteed to them in the Constitution. It was Washington's belief that the granting of political rights would occur naturally after African Americans were able to gain more education and property. Black behavior could play a significant role in determining how whites viewed African Americans. If African Americans behaved like whites and adopted white, middle-class values, they would be more likely to be accepted by whites. Political rights would not come overnight but as a "matter of natural, slow growth," that is, the acquisition of white, middle class values.

To Washington, this did not mean that blacks should forego suffrage; but that they should concentrate on other issues and not force that issue with whites. The fight for political rights would increase racial tensions and limit opportunities for African Americans to obtain an education at industrial and agricultural schools. Washington was essentially arguing that blacks should fight for rights they were most likely to receive and that would provoke the least amount of opposition from whites.

Washington suggested that blacks who were able to vote should seek the guidance and support of knowledgeable and trusted southern whites. Washington stated that he knew many African Americans "who, through the encouragement, help, and advice of southern white people, have accumulated thousands of dollars-worth of property," and yet these same people would never think to ask southern whites "for advice concerning the casting of their ballots," a situation that Washington labeled "unwise and unreasonable."

Washington raised the issue of the unjust suffrage laws that discriminated against blacks. These laws had proliferated across the South in the years between 1895 and 1903 and been upheld by the Supreme Court in *Williams v. Mississippi* in 1898. He noted that these laws were unjust, discriminatory, and clearly targeted at African Americans. They did not prevent "ignorant and poverty-stricken white men" from participating in elections. These laws should serve as a further motivation for African Americans to concentrate on gaining property and an education. Ironically, they encouraged whites to remain poor and uneducated since they had the vote anyway.

Washington argued that whites who were willing to deny blacks the right to vote would eventually decide to deny other whites their voting rights as well. The denial of black rights established a precedent. However, Washington expressed confidence that the South would eventually have universal suffrage.

While Washington expressed support for universal suffrage, he also acknowledged that states have the right to protect the ballot "for a while at least, either by educational test, a property test, or both combined." However, these tests should be applied equally to African Americans and whites. He seemed to support some restrictions on the right to vote, but not their application solely to African Americans.

As was his style, Washington here presents logical arguments appealing to both the reason and the self-interest of his white audience. He is not confrontational. While this approach displeased many of his black critics, it allowed him to make his arguments in a way that did not undermine his position among whites and protected the security of Tuskegee and his family in rural Alabama. As persuasive as his arguments were, they did not have any immediate impact on the movement to deny blacks their political rights. However, even more aggressive attacks on disfranchisement did not bear fruit for many years.

During his lifetime, Washington witnessed the widespread erosion of black rights and freedoms. While the Fifteenth Amendment officially guaranteed African Americans the right to vote, it wasn't long after its passage that white southern Democrats began trying to undermine its effects. In 1882, South Carolina passed the Eight Box Law, which required voters to deposit a series of ballots in the proper ballot boxes before voting. Illiterate voters proved unable to identify the "correct" boxes without the help of white officials. Not surprisingly, African American voters were the primary victims of this new law. In 1889, Mississippi altered its constitution by including a number of complex voting requirements. Without mentioning race, Mississippi required voters to provide proof of residency, payment of taxes, and a $2 poll tax. Literacy was required, but illiterate men could still vote if they were able to demonstrate an understanding of the Constitution to voting officials. Officials almost universally accepted all white applicants while rejecting the vast majority of black voters. Similarly, in 1895, South Carolina changed their constitution to include an "understanding clause," which disenfranchised the majority of black voters.

In 1898, Louisiana created a new method for disenfranchising black voters called the grandfather clause. This clause stipulated that only men who had been eligible to vote or whose fathers or grandfathers were eligible to vote before 1867 could vote. As the vast majority of blacks had only recently been freed from slavery in 1867 and the Fifteenth Amendment had not yet been passed, this disenfranchised hundreds of thousands of black voters. In 1896, 130,000 thousand African Americans voted, but by 1904, as a result of the grandfather clause, only 1,342 voted. By the end of the nineteenth century, every southern state except Kentucky and West Virginia had enacted a series of elaborate voting laws meant to disenfranchise black voters.

During this same period, southern states enacted laws requiring segregation of the races in public places. In 1891, Louisiana passed a law that required segregation of the races on trains. Homer A. Plessy, who was one-eighth black and who had been arrested for using a railcar reserved for whites, sought to have the law declared unconstitutional. In 1896, the case—*Plessy v. Ferguson*—reached the Supreme Court, which ruled 8 to 1 to uphold the Louisiana law. A legal precedent having been established, southern states rushed to pass hundreds of laws requiring segregation of the races in railroad stations, theatres, auditoriums, bathrooms, and drinking fountains. While *Plessy v. Ferguson* permitted separate facilities for African Americans and whites as long as facilities of equal quality were provided for both, black facilities were generally substandard and, in many cases, nonexistent. Almost all hotels, restaurants, libraries, public and private parks, swimming pools, golf and tennis courses, refused to admit black people altogether.

At the same time that black voting rights were being eroded and segregation laws were being enacted, African Americans also faced increasing levels of violence in the form of mob attacks and lynchings. In 1898, a white mob attacked a black-owned newspaper, *The Daily Record*, in Wilmington, North Carolina, murdering at least twelve black men and causing 1,500 black residents to flee. A similar riot occurred in New Orleans two years later, leading to the death of more than thirty African Americans. However, more often than not, violence against African Americans came in the form of lynchings. Beginning in 1889, an average of two to three people, the majority of them black men, were lynched every week for the next thirty years, often with the tacit approval of white officials. In 1900 alone, 100 African Americans were lynched.

Within this environment of disenfranchisement, segregation, and racial violence, Washington arose to a position of leadership. He believed wholeheartedly that his message of accommodation towards segregation and disenfranchisement in favor of industrial education would eventually lead blacks towards progress and success. He also hoped that his policies would ease tensions between blacks and whites and, most importantly, reduce the increasing levels of violence.

Essential Themes

Washington's efforts to attract black and white support by emphasizing his industrial program and downplaying political and social rights revealed a pragmatic approach. Industrial education was a far less controversial issue than civil and political rights for blacks and as a result much less likely to excite opposition or violence from whites. White philanthropists in both the North and South were willing to provide financial support for black colleges offering an industrial education. Few of these white supporters would not have supported Washington had he advocated more aggressively for black political and civil rights. By 1915, there were sixteen black land-grant colleges including Florida A&M, Alcorn A&M in Mississippi, Southern University in Louisiana, and Washington's Tuskegee Institute, which received both public and private funding. Without these schools, southern blacks would have had few opportunities to receive any sort of higher education.

Yet, despite his support for industrial education and his attempts to placate suspicious whites, racial tension and violence against blacks continued unabated. In fairness, there was likely nothing Washington or any other black leader could have done to prevent continued violence, but the advocacy of industrial education did little if anything to protect African Americans from discrimination or violence.

Washington's insistence that African Americans concentrate on industrial education, forego liberal arts education, and postpone demands for political or civil rights engendered significant criticism and opposition from such prominent black leaders as Harvard-trained scholar W. E. B. Du Bois, African Methodist Episcopal Bishop Henry M. Bishop, and journalist Ida B. Wells. They argued that African Americans should not limit themselves only to an industrial education. There was an inherent value to a liberal education which included the learning of mathematics, literature, science, and languages. A number of private black colleges like Fisk, Morris Brown, and Paul Quinn continued to emphasize a liberal arts education and resisted pressures to switch to an industrial and agricultural-based curriculum.

Leaders like Du Bois and Bishop also strongly resented Washington's seeming indifference to the loss of political and civil rights. These leaders linked their support for a liberal education to their support for black civil and political rights arguing that such an education would create leaders more capable of leading the black masses towards greater equality. While Washington sought to create greater educational opportunities for African Americans, his efforts were criticized by other African American leaders who argued that he sacrificed too much for too little.

—*Gerald F. Goodwin, PhD, Cary D. Wintz, PhD*

Bibliography and Additional Reading

Brundage, W. Fitzhugh, ed. *Booker T. Washington and Black Progress: Up from Slavery 100 Years Later.* Gainesville: UP of Florida, 2003.

Harlan, Louis R. *Booker T. Washington: The Wizard of Tuskegee, 1901–1915.* Vol. 2. Oxford, UK: Oxford UP, 1983.

Hine, Darlene Clark, William C. Hine, and Stanley C. Harrold. *African Americans: A Concise History,* Combined Volume. Boston: Pearson, 2011.

Norrell, Robert J. *Up from History: The Life of Booker T. Washington.* Cambridge, MA: Harvard UP, 2009.

Smock, Raymond W. *Booker T. Washington: Black Leadership in the Age of Jim Crow.* Chicago: Ivan R. Dee, 2009.

Washington, Booker T. *Up from Slavery.* Mineola, NY: Dover Publications, 1995.

Guinn v. United States

Date: 1915
Author: Edward Douglass White, Jr.
Genre: court decision

Summary Overview

In the 1915 Supreme Court case Frank Guinn and J. J. Beal v. United States, *Chief Justice Edward White held that the grandfather clause, an amendment to Oklahoma's constitution, limited black suffrage and was therefore invalid. The case also applied to Maryland's constitution, which had a similar clause. The grandfather clause had worked in conjunction with a literacy test to deprive African Americans of the right to vote. The literacy test stipulated that all voters be able to read, but the grandfather clause lifted literacy test requirements for anyone who was otherwise qualified to vote anywhere in the United States on January 1, 1866. The clause was particularly galling to African Americans in Oklahoma, as that state had not even existed in 1866. The literacy test additionally discriminated against African Americans, since it was very subjective and was applied unfairly by white southern registrars.*

The U.S. Supreme Court held that Oklahoma's grandfather clause was unconstitutional, because it violated the spirit of the Fifteenth Amendment, ratified in 1870, which granted former slaves the right to vote. The Court's ruling had little direct effect on the extension of voting rights to African Americans in Oklahoma, however: The state simply passed a new statute, disenfranchising all those who did not register to vote during a brief, two-week window in 1916, except those who had voted in 1914. Thus, all voting whites could still vote, but all of the previously disenfranchised blacks were still disenfranchised, unless they had been able to work their way through the system in a two-week period.

Defining Moment

The *Guinn* case was one of the first major court cases in which the National Association for the Advancement of Colored People (NAACP) played a role, filing a brief, and represented one of the few times in the early twentieth century when the federal government appeared on the side of African Americans in a legal battle. *Guinn* was also one of the first challenges to discriminatory voting laws, which had been restricting voting rights to certain segments of American society for more than forty years. The first such laws appeared in the post–Civil War Reconstruction pe-

Chief Justice White wrote the opinion. Photo via Wikimedia Commons. [Public domain.]

riod. African Americans and poor whites gained allies in the White House when the Republican Party—the party of Abraham Lincoln—took power in 1860; meanwhile, southern Democrats—supporters of segregationist policies at that time—vowed to wrest their power back using any and all means to achieve their ends. Despite the fact that the ratification of the Fifteenth Amendment to the U.S. Constitution in the spring of 1870 had granted all male citizens the right to vote regardless of race, color, or prior slave status, violence and threats of violence were often used and suggested by Democrats over the next decade to keep Republicans, particularly black Republicans, from voting. As a result, all of the southern states had Democratic legislatures by the late 1870s.

Efforts continued in subsequent years to eliminate all African Americans and many poor whites from the voting ranks, leading to the growth of the Populist movement. This biracial groundswell stemmed from a financial crisis and labor unrest in the United States that resulted in the failure of businesses throughout the country, particularly many small farms in the South and the West. Channeling the anger of America's small farmers and other laborers who wanted reform, the Populist movement pushed for policy changes that would empower the nation's workers, both black and white, and protect small businesses from corrupt corporate interests. Reform and Fusion tickets won often in the South (and the West) in the early 1890s. Fusion politics refers to the combined power of the Republican and Populist parties at the end of the nineteenth century. In response, wealthy whites interested in seeing a resurgence of the Democratic Party organized mobs to drive African Americans from the polls. Many states adopted constitutional amendments in the late 1890s and early 1900s designed specifically to disenfranchise blacks and to limit the voting of poor whites. All of the previous restrictions on voting rights were retained and even more were added.

It was in the midst of this political clash that Oklahoma became the forty-sixth state in the Union in late 1907. The region came late into statehood, because much of its land had been set aside for Native American reservations until the 1890s. In 1910 Oklahoma adopted a constitutional amendment that tied the voting rights of its citizens to the successful completion of a literacy test. However, certain individuals—almost always whites—were able to circumvent the literacy test requirement because of an exception known as the grandfather clause, which guaranteed descendants of eligible voters the right to vote without question. The amendment used a date of January 1 of the year after the end of the Civil War as the date for which a voter was required to prove that an ancestor—presumably a grandfather—was qualified to vote. Prospective voters who were unable to satisfy the terms of the grandfather clause were forced to prove their literacy. Maryland's grandfather clause, tested also in the case of *Guinn v. United States*, was adopted in 1908, just a couple of years before Oklahoma's.

The grandfather clause had little effect on the right to vote for most whites, but it served as a barrier to the ballot box for African American voters. Freedmen and all men of color were not guaranteed the right to vote until the passage of the Fifteenth Amendment in 1870—four years after the date specified in the grandfather clause. The Oklahoma state government claimed that the clause did not discriminate against voters on the basis of their race; the term *race* was not even mentioned in the text. Clearly, however, the voting rights of African Americans, not whites, were most threatened by the terms of the statute. In fact, the grandfather clause and similar voting restrictions generally had loopholes to protect white voters. Typically, a person who owned property or paid sufficient taxes was considered exempt from the clause; because the rate of property ownership was higher among whites than blacks, this exception adversely affected potential black voters.

It should be noted, however, that the grandfather clause (and the literacy test used in Oklahoma) were not the only methods employed to disenfranchise blacks. Among other techniques was the poll tax, an annual per-person fee that had to be paid before a ballot could be cast in any election. In effect, the poll tax added an economic dimension to the social inequities encountered by African Americans seeking to exercise their right to vote. At about a dollar per person, the tax placed a financial burden on a segment of the population with little or no money to spare. In addition to making the payment, voters were required to prove that they had paid the tax each year for as long as they had resided in the state; however, records and receipts for those members of the black community who managed to pay the poll tax were often lost or never entered in official logs. Taken together, these provisions effectively denied the right of suffrage to African Americans in the South.

It was in this context that the case of *Guinn v. United States* came to the Supreme Court. Black citizens of Oklahoma had voiced complaints to the U.S. Justice Department concerning the enormous amount of racial violence surrounding the Oklahoma elections of 1910, which served to discourage blacks from voting. In light of the brutal and discriminatory atmosphere of the elections, U.S. Attorney John Embry, along with fellow U.S. Attorney William R. Gregg, indicted two Oklahoma elections officials, J. J. Beal and Frank Guinn, on criminal charges of depriving people of their rights under the Constitution and federal law. Contrary to most expectations, the officials were convicted of civil rights violations on September 29, 1911—despite the fact that they had been enforcing an amendment to the Oklahoma state constitution. The two officials took the case to the U.S. Court of Appeals, claiming that they should not be prosecuted for upholding the law of their state. The Court of Appeals sent the case on to the Supreme Court in 1913, and it was decided on June 21, 1915.

There are several different audiences for this Supreme Court decision, the most obvious being the parties involved: the U.S. government and the two Oklahoma election officials named in the case, Frank Guinn and J. J. Beal, who had been convicted of civil rights violations. A broader audience was the South as a whole as well as the state of Maryland, which also had a grandfather clause. The nation's black community and the lawyers and members of the NAACP (who, as noted, had filed a brief) were no doubt interested parties, and this case stands as the first twentieth-century victory for African Americans at the Supreme Court level. Historians, scholars, and students of African American culture represent a modern-day audience, one that can see how the nation took its first halting steps toward equality and how limited those steps really were.

Author Biography

Chief Justice Edward Douglass White, Jr., was born November 3, 1845, in Louisiana and served in the Confederate army during the Civil War. After that service, he returned to his parents' sugarcane plantation and began to study law. Practicing in Louisiana after joining the bar in 1868, he briefly served in the state senate and then on the Louisiana Supreme Court before returning to his legal practice in 1880. In 1891, White was elected to the U.S. Senate; three years later he was appointed to the U.S. Supreme Court, and in 1910 he became the Court's chief justice. A southern Democrat, White was the second Catholic to serve as a Supreme Court justice.

Although White had sided with the majority in the 1896 case of *Plessy v. Ferguson*, which upheld segregation in public transportation and in general by establishing the "separate but equal" clause, he went on to author the *Guinn v. United States* decision in 1915. In 1917, White agreed with the majority in *Buchanan v. Warley*, a decision that held a residential segregation law in Louisville, Kentucky, illegal. The common thread between the latter two cases, and the difference between them and *Plessy*, is that the law in the cases of both *Buchanan* and *Guinn* directly and clearly discriminated against African Americans, whereas in *Plessy* the law was explained away by the majority as being unbiased on its face. After *Guinn*, White served as chief justice for another six years. He died on May 19, 1921.

Historical Document

Guinn v. United States

Syllabus

The so-called Grandfather Clause of the amendment to the constitution of Oklahoma of 1910 is void because it violates the Fifteenth Amendment to the Constitution of the United States.

The Grandfather Clause being unconstitutional, and not being separable from the remainder of the amendment to the constitution of Oklahoma of 1910, that amendment as a whole is invalid.

The Fifteenth Amendment does not, in a general sense, take from the States the power over suffrage possessed by the States from the beginning, but it does restrict the power of the United States or the States to abridge or deny the right of a citizen of the United States to vote on account of race, color or previous condition of servitude. While the Fifteenth Amendment gives no right of suffrage, as its command is self-executing, rights of suffrage may be enjoyed by reason of the striking out of discriminations against the exercise of the right.

A provision in a state constitution recurring to conditions existing before the adoption of the Fifteenth Amendment and the continuance of which conditions that amendment prohibited, and making those conditions the test of the right to the suffrage, is in conflict with, and void under, the Fifteenth Amendment.

The establishment of a literacy test for exercising the suffrage is an exercise by the State of a lawful power vested in it not subject to the supervision of the Federal courts.

Whether a provision in a suffrage statute may be valid under the Federal Constitution if it is so connected with other provisions that are invalid as to make the whole statute unconstitutional is a question of state law, but, in the absence of any decision by the state court, this court may, in a case coming from the Federal courts, determine it for itself.

The suffrage and literacy tests in the amendment of 1910 to the constitution of Oklahoma are so connected with each other that the unconstitutionality of the former renders the whole amendment invalid.

The facts, which involve the constitutionality under the Fifteenth Amendment of the Constitution of the United States of the suffrage amendment to the constitution of Oklahoma, known as the Grandfather Clause, and the responsibility of election officers under §5508, Rev. Stat., and §19 of the Penal Code for preventing people from voting who have the right to vote, are stated in the opinion.

Mr. Chief Justice White delivered the opinion of the court

This case is before us on a certificate drawn by the court below as the basis of two questions which are submitted for our solution in order to enable the court correctly to decide issues in a case which it has under consideration. Those issues arose from an indictment and conviction of certain election officers of the State of Oklahoma (the plaintiffs in error) of the crime of having conspired unlawfully, willfully and fraudulently to deprive certain negro citizens, on account of their race and color, of a right to vote at a general election held in that State in 1910, they being entitled to vote under the state law and which right was secured to them by the Fifteenth Amendment to the Constitution of the United States. The prosecution was directly concerned with §5508, Rev. Stat., now §19 of the Penal Code which is as follows:

"If two or more persons conspire to injure, oppress, threaten, or intimidate any citizen in the free exercise or enjoyment of any right or privilege secured to him by the Constitution or laws of the United States, or because of his having so exercised the same, or if two or more persons go in disguise on the highway, or on the premises of another, with intent to prevent or hinder his free exercise or enjoyment of any right or privilege so secured, they shall be fined not more than five thousand dollars and imprisoned not more than ten years, and shall, moreover, be thereafter ineligible to any office or place of honor, profit, or trust created by the Constitution or laws of the United States."

We concentrate and state from the certificate only matters which we deem essential to dispose of the questions asked.

Suffrage in Oklahoma was regulated by §1, Article III of the Constitution under which the State was admitted into the Union. Shortly after the admission, there was submitted an amendment to the Constitution making a radical change in that article which was adopted prior to November 8, 1910. At an election for members of Congress which followed the adoption of this Amendment, certain election officers, in enforcing its provisions, refused to allow certain negro citizens to vote who were clearly entitled to vote under the provision of the Constitution under which the State was admitted, that is, before the amendment, and who, it is equally clear, were not entitled to vote under the provision of the suffrage amendment if that amendment governed. The persons so excluded based their claim of right to vote upon the original Constitution and upon the assertion that the suffrage amendment was void because in conflict with the prohibitions of the Fifteenth Amendment, and therefore afforded no basis for denying them the right guaranteed and protected by that Amendment. And upon the assumption that this claim was justified and that the election officers had violated the Fifteenth Amendment in denying the right to vote, this prosecution, as we have said, was commenced. At the trial, the court instructed that, by the Fifteenth Amendment, the States were prohibited from discriminating as to suffrage because of race, color, or previous condition of servitude, and that Congress, in pursuance of the authority which was conferred upon it by the very terms of the Amendment to enforce its provisions, had enacted the following (Rev. Stat., §2004):

"All citizens of the United States who are otherwise qualified by law to vote at any election by the people of any State, Territory, district, ... municipality, ... or other territorial subdivision, shall be entitled and allowed to vote at all such elections, without distinction of race, color, or previous condition of servitude; any constitution, law, custom, usage, or regulation of any State or Territory, or by or under its authority to the contrary notwithstanding."

It then instructed as follows:

"The State amendment which imposes the test of reading and writing any section of the State constitution as a condition to voting to persons not on or prior to January 1, 1866, entitled to vote under some form of government, or then resident in some foreign nation, or a lineal descendant of such person, is not valid, but you may consider it insofar as it was in good faith relied and acted upon by the defendants in ascertaining their intent and motive. If you believe from the evidence that the defendants formed a common design and cooperated in denying the colored voters of Union Township precinct, or any of them, entitled to vote, the privilege of voting, but this was due to a mistaken belief sincerely entertained by the defendants as to the qualifications of the voters—that is, if the motive actuating the defendants was honest, and they simply erred in the conception of their duty—then the criminal intent requisite to their guilt is wanting, and they cannot be convicted. On the other hand, if they knew or believed these colored persons were entitled to vote, and their purpose was to unfairly and fraudulently deny the right of suffrage to them, or any of them entitled thereto, on account of their race and color, then their purpose was a corrupt one, and they cannot be shielded by their official positions."

The questions which the court below asks are these:

"1. Was the amendment to the constitution of Oklahoma, heretofore set forth, valid?"

"2. Was that amendment void insofar as it attempted to debar from the right or privilege of voting for a qualified candidate for a Member of Congress in

Oklahoma, unless they were able to read and write any section of the constitution of Oklahoma, negro citizens of the United States who were otherwise qualified to vote for a qualified candidate for a Member of Congress in that State, but who were not, and none of whose lineal ancestors was entitled to vote under any form of government on January 1, 1866, or at any time prior thereto, because they were then slaves?"

As these questions obviously relate to the provisions concerning suffrage in the original constitution and the amendment to those provisions which forms the basis of the controversy, we state the text of both. The original clause, so far as material, was this:

"The qualified electors of the State shall be male citizens of the United States, male citizens of the State, and male persons of Indian descent native of the United States, who are over the age of twenty-one years, who have resided in the State one year, in the county six months, and in the election precinct thirty days, next preceding the election at which any such elector offers to vote."

And this is the amendment:

"No person shall be registered as an elector of this State or be allowed to vote in any election herein, unless he be able to read and write any section of the constitution of the State of Oklahoma; but no person who was, on January 1, 1866, or at any time prior thereto, entitled to vote under any form of government, or who at that time resided in some foreign nation, and no lineal descendant of such person, shall be denied the right to register and vote because of his inability to so read and write sections of such constitution. Precinct election inspectors having in charge the registration of electors shall enforce the provisions of this section at the time of registration, provided registration be required. Should registration be dispensed with, the provisions of this section shall be enforced by the precinct election officer when electors apply for ballots to vote."

Considering the questions in the right of the text of the suffrage amendment, it is apparent that they are two-fold, because of the two-fold character of the provisions as to suffrage which the amendment contains. The first question is concerned with that provision of the amendment which fixes a standard by which the right to vote is given upon conditions existing on January 1, 1866, and relieves those coming within that standard from the standard based on a literacy test which is established by the other provision of the amendment. The second question asks as to the validity of the literacy test and how far, if intrinsically valid, it would continue to exist and be operative in the event the standard based upon January 1, 1866, should be held to be illegal as violative of the Fifteenth Amendment.

To avoid that which is unnecessary, let us at once consider and sift the propositions of the United States, on the one hand, and of the plaintiffs in error, on the other, in order to reach with precision the real and final question to be considered. The United States insists that the provision of the amendment which fixes a standard based upon January 1, 1866, is repugnant to the prohibitions of the Fifteenth Amendment because, in substance and effect, that provision, if not an express, is certainly an open, repudiation of the Fifteenth Amendment, and hence the provision in question was stricken with nullity in its inception by the self-operative force of the Amendment, and, as the result of the same power, was at all subsequent times devoid of any vitality whatever.

For the plaintiffs in error, on the other hand, it is said the States have the power to fix standards for suffrage, and that power was not taken away by the Fifteenth Amendment, but only limited to the extent of the prohibitions which that Amendment established. This being true, as the standard fixed does not in terms make any discrimination on account of race, color, or previous condition of servitude, since all, whether negro or white, who come within its requirements enjoy the privilege of voting, there is no ground upon which to rest the contention that the provision violates the Fifteenth Amendment. This, it is insisted, must be the case unless it is intended to expressly deny the State's right to provide a standard for suffrage, or, what is equivalent thereto, to assert: a, that the judgment of the State exercised in the exertion of that power is subject to Federal judicial review or supervision, or b, that it may be questioned and be brought within the prohibitions of the Amendment by attributing to the legislative authority an occult motive to violate the Amendment or by assuming that an exercise of the otherwise lawful power may be invalidated because of conclusions concerning its operation in practical execution and resulting discrimination arising therefrom, albeit such discrimination was not expressed in the standard fixed or fairly to be implied, but simply arose from inequalities naturally inhering in those who must come within the standard in order to enjoy the right to vote.

On the other hand, the United States denies the relevancy of these contentions. It says state power to provide for suffrage is not disputed, although, of course, the authority of the Fifteenth Amendment and the limit on that power which it imposes is insisted upon. Hence, no assertion denying the right of a State to exert judgment and discretion in fixing the qualification of suffrage is advanced, and no right to question the motive of the State in establishing a standard as to such subjects under such circumstances or to review or supervise the same is relied upon, and no power to destroy an otherwise valid exertion of authority upon the mere ultimate operation of the power exercised is asserted. And, applying these principles to the very case in hand, the argument of the Government, in substance, says: no question is raised by the Government concerning the validity of the literacy test provided for in the amendment under consideration as an independent standard, since the conclusion is plain that that test rests on the exercise of state judgment, and therefore cannot be here assailed either by disregarding the State's power to judge on the subject or by testing its motive in enacting the provision. The real question involved, so the argument of the Government insists, is the repugnancy of the standard which the amendment makes, based upon the conditions existing on January 1, 1866, because, on its face and inherently, considering the substance of things, that standard is a mere denial of the restrictions imposed by the prohibitions of the Fifteenth Amendment, and by necessary result, recreates and perpetuates the very conditions which the Amendment was intended to destroy. From this, it is urged that no legitimate discretion could have entered into the fixing of such standard which involved only the determination to directly set at naught or by indirection avoid the commands of the Amendment. And it is insisted that nothing contrary to these propositions is involved in the contention of the Government that, if the standard which the suffrage amendment fixes based upon the conditions existing on January 1, 1866, be found to be void for the reasons urged, the other and literacy test is also void, since that contention rests not upon any assertion on the part of the Government of any abstract repugnancy of the literacy test to the prohibitions of the Fifteenth Amendment, but upon the relation between that test and the other as formulated in the suffrage amendment, and the inevitable result which it is deemed must follow from holding it to be void if the other is so declared to be.

Looking comprehensively at these contentions of the parties, it plainly results that the conflict between them is much narrower than it would seem to be because the premise which the arguments of the plaintiffs in error attribute to the propositions of the United States is by it denied. On the very face of things, it is clear that the United States disclaims the gloss put upon its contentions by limiting them to the propositions which we have hitherto pointed out, since it rests the contentions which it makes as to the assailed provision of the suffrage amendment solely upon the ground that it involves an unmistakable, although it may be a somewhat disguised, refusal to give effect to the prohibitions of the Fifteenth Amendment by creating a standard which it is repeated, but calls to life the very conditions which that Amendment was adopted to destroy and which it had destroyed.

The questions then are: (1) giving to the propositions of the Government the interpretation which the Government puts upon them and assuming that the suffrage provision has the significance which the Government assumes it to have, is that provision, as a matter of law, repugnant to the Fifteenth Amendment? which leads us, of course, to consider the operation and effect of the Fifteenth Amendment. (2) If yes, has the assailed amendment, insofar as it fixes a standard for voting as of January 1, 1866, the meaning which the Government attributes to it? which leads us to analyze and interpret that provision of the amendment. (3) If the investigation as to the two prior subjects establishes that the standard fixed as of January 1, 1866, is void, what, if any, effect does that conclusion have upon the literacy standard otherwise established by the amendment? which involves determining whether that standard, if legal, may survive the recognition of the fact that the other or 1866 standard has not, and never had, any legal existence. Let us consider these subjects under separate headings.

1. The operation and effect of the Fifteenth Amendment. This is its text:

"Section 1. The right of citizens of the United States to vote shall not be denied or abridged by the United States or by any State on account of race, color, or previous condition of servitude."

"Section 2. The Congress shall have power to enforce this article by appropriate legislation."

(a) Beyond doubt, the Amendment does not take away from the state governments in a general sense the power over suffrage which has belonged to those governments from the beginning, and without the possession of which power the whole fabric upon which the division of state and national authority under the Constitution and the organization of both governments rest would be without support and both the authority of the nation and the State would fall to the ground. In fact, the very command of the Amendment recognizes the possession of the general power by the State, since the Amendment seeks to regulate its exercise as to the particular subject with which it deals.

(b) But it is equally beyond the possibility of question that the Amendment, in express terms, restricts the power of the United States or the States to abridge or deny the right of a citizen of the United States to vote on account of race, color or previous condition of servitude. The restriction is coincident with the power, and prevents its exertion in disregard of the command of the Amendment.

But, while this is true, it is true also that the Amendment does not change, modify or deprive the States of their full power as to suffrage except, of course, as to the subject with which the Amendment deals and to the extent that obedience to its command is necessary. Thus, the authority over suffrage which the States possess and the limitation which the Amendment imposes are coordinate, and one may not destroy the other without bringing about the destruction of both.

(c) While, in the true sense, therefore, the Amendment gives no right of suffrage, it was long ago recognized that, in operation, its prohibition might measurably have that effect; that is to say, that, as the command of the Amendment was self-executing and reached without legislative action the conditions of discrimination against which it was aimed, the result might arise that as a consequence of the striking down of a discriminating clause a right of suffrage would be enjoyed by reason of the generic character of the provision which would remain after the discrimination was stricken out. Ex parte Yarbrough; Neal v. Delaware. A familiar illustration of this doctrine resulted from the effect of the adoption of the Amendment on state constitutions in which, at the time of the adoption of the Amendment, the right of suffrage was conferred on all white male citizens, since, by the inherent power of the Amendment, the word white disappeared, and therefore all male citizens, without discrimination on account of race, color or previous condition of servitude, came under the generic grant of suffrage made by the State.

With these principles before us, how can there be room for any serious dispute concerning the repugnancy of the standard based upon January 1, 1866 (a date which preceded the adoption of the Fifteenth Amendment), if the suffrage provision fixing that standard is susceptible of the significance which the Government attributes to it? Indeed, there seems no escape from the conclusion that to hold that there was even possibility for dispute on the subject would be but to declare that the Fifteenth Amendment not only had not the self-executing power which it has been recognized to have from the beginning, but that its provisions were wholly inoperative, because susceptible of being rendered inapplicable by mere forms of expression embodying no exercise of judgment and resting upon no discernible reason other than the purpose to disregard the prohibitions of the Amendment by creating a standard of voting which on its face was, in substance, but a revitalization of conditions which, when they prevailed in the past, had been destroyed by the self-operative force of the Amendment.

2. The standard of January 1, 1866, fixed in the suffrage amendment and its significance.

The inquiry, of course, here is, does the amendment as to the particular standard which this heading embraces involve the mere refusal to comply with the commands of the Fifteenth Amendment as previously stated? This leads us for the purpose of the analysis to recur to the text of the suffrage amendment. Its opening sentence fixes the literacy standard, which is all-inclusive, since it is general in its expression and contains no word of discrimination on account of race or color or any other reason. This, however, is immediately followed by the provisions creating the standard based upon the condition existing on January 1, 1866, and carving out those coming under that standard from the inclusion in the literacy test which would have controlled them but for the exclusion thus expressly provided for. The provision is this:

"But no person who was, on January 1, 1866, or at any time prior thereto, entitled to vote under any form of government, or who at that time resided in some foreign nation, and no lineal descendant of such person, shall be denied the right to register and vote because of his inability to so read and write sections of such constitution."

We have difficulty in finding words to more clearly demonstrate the conviction we entertain that this standard has the characteristics which the Government attributes to it than does the mere statement of the text. It is true it contains no express words of an exclusion from the standard which it establishes of any person on account of race, color, or previous condition of servitude prohibited by the Fifteenth Amendment, but the standard itself inherently brings that result into existence, since it is based purely upon a period of time before the enactment of the Fifteenth Amendment, and makes that period the controlling and dominant test of the right of suffrage. In other words, we seek in vain for any ground which would sustain any other interpretation but that the provision, recurring to the conditions existing before the Fifteenth Amendment was adopted and the continuance of which the Fifteenth Amendment prohibited, proposed by, in substance and effect, lifting those conditions over to a period of time after the Amendment to make them the basis of the right to suffrage conferred in direct and positive disregard of the Fifteenth Amendment. And the same result, we are of opinion, is demonstrated by considering whether it is possible to discover any basis of reason for the standard thus fixed other than the purpose above stated. We say this because we are unable to discover how, unless the prohibitions of the Fifteenth Amendment were considered, the slightest reason was afforded for basing the classification upon a period of time prior to the Fifteenth Amendment. Certainly it cannot be said that there was any peculiar necromancy in the time named which engendered attributes affecting the qualification to vote which would not exist at another and different period unless the Fifteenth Amendment was in view.

While these considerations establish that the standard fixed on the basis of the 1866 test is void, they do not enable us to reply even to the first question asked by the court below, since, to do so, we must consider the literacy standard established by the suffrage amendment and the possibility of its surviving the determination of the fact that the 1866 standard never took life, since it was void from the beginning because of the operation upon it of the prohibitions of the Fifteenth Amendment. And this brings us to the last heading:

3. The determination of the validity of the literacy test and the possibility of its surviving the disappearance of the 1866 standard with which it is associated in the suffrage amendment.

No time need be spent on the question of the validity of the literacy test, considered alone, since, as we have seen, its establishment was but the exercise by the State of a lawful power vested in it not subject to our supervision, and, indeed, its validity is admitted. Whether this test is so connected with the other one relating to the situation on January 1, 1866, that the invalidity of the latter requires the rejection of the former, is really a question of state law, but, in the absence of any decision on the subject by the Supreme Court of the State, we must determine it for ourselves. We are of opinion that neither forms of classification nor methods of enumeration should be made the basis of striking down a provision which was independently legal, and therefore was lawfully enacted because of the removal of an illegal provision with which the legal provision or provisions may have been associated. We state what we hold to be the rule thus strongly because we are of opinion that, on a subject like the one under consideration, involving the establishment of a right whose exercise lies at the very basis of government, a much more exacting standard is required than would ordinarily obtain where the influence of the declared unconstitutionality of one provision of a statute upon another and constitutional provision is required to be fixed. Of course, rigorous as is this rule and imperative as is the duty not to violate it, it does not mean that it applies in a case where it expressly appears that a contrary conclusion must be reached if the plain letter and necessary intendment of the provision under consideration so compels, or where such a result is rendered necessary because to follow the contrary course would give rise to such an extreme and anomalous situation as would cause it to be impossible to conclude that it could have been upon any hypothesis whatever within the mind of the lawmaking power.

Does the general rule here govern, or is the case controlled by one or the other of the exceptional conditions which we have just stated, is then the remaining question to be decided. Coming to solve it, we are of opinion that, by a consideration of the text of the suffrage amendment insofar as it deals with the literacy test, and to the extent that it creates the standard based upon conditions existing on January 1, 1866, the case is taken out of the general rule and brought under the first of the exceptions stated. We say this because, in our opinion, the very language of the suffrage amendment expresses, not by implication nor by forms of classification nor by the order in which they are made, but by direct and positive language, the command that the persons embraced in the 1866 standard should not be under any conditions subjected to the literacy test, a command which would be virtually set at naught if on the obliteration of the one standard by the force of the Fifteenth Amendment the other standard should be held to continue in force.

The reasons previously stated dispose of the case and make it plain that it is our duty to answer the first question No, and the second Yes; but before we direct the entry of an order to that effect, we come briefly to dispose of an issue the consideration of which we have hitherto postponed from a desire not to break the continuity of discussion as to the general and important subject before us.

In various forms of statement not challenging the instructions given by the trial court, concretely considered, concerning the liability of the election officers for their official conduct, it is insisted that as, in connection with the instructions, the jury was charged that the suffrage amendment was unconstitutional because of its repugnancy to the Fifteenth Amendment, therefore, taken as a whole, the charge was erroneous. But we are of opinion that this contention is without merit, especially in view of the doctrine long since settled concerning the self-executing power of the Fifteenth Amendment, and of what we have held to be the nature and character of the suffrage amendment in question. The contention concerning the inapplicability of §5508, Rev. Stat., now §19 of the Penal Code, or of its repeal by implication, is fully answered by the ruling this day made in United States v. Mosley, No. 180, post.

We answer the first question, No, and the second question, Yes.

And it will be so certified.

Glossary

ex parte: a Latin term referring to a legal proceeding in which only one party is represented

necromancy: sorcery, usually involving the dead

nullity: the condition of being void

occult: secret or hidden

plaintiff in error: the plaintiff in a case on appeal, who may or may not be the plaintiff in the lower court case whose decision is being appealed

self-executing: a law that does not require further legislative or court action to take effect

Syllabus: the portion of a Supreme Court decision that summarizes the key findings and rulings

Document Analysis

At issue in the U.S. Supreme Court case of *Guinn v. United States* was whether grandfather clauses had been deliberately enacted by state governments to deny African Americans their right to vote. Two Oklahoma election officials, Frank Guinn and J. J. Beal, had been charged with violating federal law by conspiring to deprive black Oklahomans of their voting rights in a general election held in 1910. Following the convictions of both men by a jury in an Oklahoma district court a year later, the *Guinn* case was brought before the Supreme Court on appeal in 1913. *Guinn v. United States* forced the highest court in the nation to examine the combined use of grandfather clauses and literacy tests as prerequisites to voting; specifically, the application of such tests in Oklahoma and Maryland was analyzed for fairness amid charges that black voters had been subjected to racial discrimination at the ballot box.

Before voting, a black voter had to prove his literacy to the satisfaction of a white registrar. Whites were generally exempt from the test by the grandfather clause, which waived the need for a voter to display his literacy if his grandfather had been eligible to vote in 1866. African American voters could not satisfy this requirement because suffrage had not yet been granted to freedmen in 1866. And so blacks, at the discretion of a white registrar, might be asked to read a book in Greek or submit to a general knowledge test about a provision in either the state's constitution or the U.S. Constitution. In some southern states, general knowledge provisions were imposed by election officials, with registrars asking prospective voters such questions as "How many bubbles are there in a bar of soap?" The adequacy of a black voter's response to such questions was determined solely by the registrar.

Before the text of Chief Justice Edward White's opinion in *Guinn v. United States* is a syllabus summarizing the key points of the lower court's decision. Justice White then quotes the laws backing up the Fifteenth Amendment, discusses the election officials' trial, reiterates the jury instructions given at that trial, and lays out the responsibility of the Supreme Court in the case: "Let us at once consider and sift the propositions of the United States, on the one hand, and of the plaintiffs in error, on the other, in order to reach with precision the real and final question to be considered." That question, according to White, boils down to whether or not the state amendment creating the grandfather clause was valid and whether the law itself was invalid because it violated the Fifteenth Amendment. White examines the arguments on each side of the case and ends with justifications for his conclusions.

Justice White's opinion begins by noting that two election officials were charged with violating the federal law by denying "certain negro citizens" the right to vote based on the color of their skin. The Thirteenth Amendment, passed in late 1865, had abolished slavery in the United States, but the South's refusal to guarantee basic human rights to emancipated slaves forced the adoption of the Fourteenth Amendment, granting citizenship to all freedmen. Abuses continued, however, and the Republican Party in the South was seriously weakened because its large African American voting base was being denied the right to vote on a variety of technicalities. The Fifteenth Amendment to the U.S. Constitution was designed to further safeguard the rights of newly freed slaves by removing obstacles to their voting. The chief justice quotes the language of the Fifteenth Amendment, which was ratified soon after the end of the Civil War: "The right of citizens of the United States to vote shall not be denied or abridged by the United States or by any State on account of race, color, or previous condition of servitude." Black suffrage seems to be spelled out quite clearly by the text of this amendment, but that was not the case. *Guinn v. United States* tested the power of the Fifteenth Amendment against the rights of states to establish their own standards for suffrage.

After stating the law, the Court then looks back at the claims of each side represented in the original case. Representing the United States was U.S. solicitor general John Davis, who appeared before the Court to challenge the Oklahoma amendment. Davis argued that Oklahoma's provision had the effect of denying the right to vote based on race and should be struck down as a violation of the Fifteenth Amendment, regardless of whether the law was explicitly in violation of that constitutional provision. The defense, however, argued for state sovereignty—not state sovereignty in terms of states being allowed to ignore the Fifteenth Amendment, but sovereignty in terms of their being able to set their own qualifications for voting. As the law in question did not specifically use race as a standard, the state contended that it should be allowed. The federal government, the defendants argued, should not be able to read a motive into the act or state that the effect of the law made an otherwise lawful act invalid. The defendants also claimed that the fact that no blacks qualified to vote under the law was not due to the law but due to their inability to read. It should be noted that no defense was noted by the Supreme Court as to why a date of January 1, 1866, was picked if the point were not to force all black voters to take the test.

The Supreme Court argues here that suffrage and qualifications put upon suffrage were state issues and that their position in this case did not limit that state power in any way. Of course, state regulations like this one that blatantly violated the Fifteenth Amendment were still being challenged, but otherwise the federal government left most decisions to the states alone. The Court then considers the literacy test, stating that it would not challenge the state's right to administer such a test. The only challenge was the use of the law to try to bypass the intended meaning of the Fifteenth Amendment.

Justice White continues his opinion with the enumeration of three key questions: Did the grandfather clause law violate the Fifteenth Amendment? Did the amendment, choosing January 1, 1866 as the date to use for the grandfather clause, mean what the government said it did? And would the striking down of the grandfather clause make the rest of the literacy test invalid? The rest of Justice White's opinion sought to answer to those questions.

The Court, in answering the first question, notes that the Fifteenth Amendment still allows room for the state to manage the business of voting; state-imposed literacy tests, then, remain lawful. It is important to evaluate this decision in the proper context: It embodies an era during which states wielded great power. The reach of the Fourteenth Amendment to prohibit racial bias at the state level was still very limited, and the use of the amendment to curtail the actions of state legislatures, unless they were directly and blatantly biased, did not occur for another three decades, when the Supreme Court decided *Shelley v. Kraemer* (1948), holding that courts could not enforce racially based private restrictive covenants.

In his explanation of what the Fifteenth Amendment says about suffrage, White holds that the state still has full power over suffrage qualifications, with the exception of those qualifications based on "race, color, or previous condition of servitude." He goes on to say that while no right to vote is directly created by the amendment, that right might still result when discriminatory rules are struck down by the amendment, which the Court held to be self-executing. White takes exception to the intent of Oklahoma's grandfather clause, pointing out that for a brief period of time prior to the adoption of the clause the hurdles to African American suffrage, while still present, were actually lower. According to White, there was no doubt that the statute had been adopted as an attempt to get around the Fifteenth Amendment. For that reason, the amendment to the Oklahoma Constitution ran into direct conflict with the federal constitutional amendment.

Regarding the date the amendment to the Oklahoma Constitution was adopted, White again theorizes that the only possible reason for using the date of January 1, 1866, was to bypass the rights implied in the Fifteenth Amendment. Although the language of the grandfather clause does not refer to skin color or prior slave status, its clear purpose was to avoid granting suffrage to former slaves. As White puts it, the very use of that date shows a "direct and positive disregard of the Fifteenth Amendment." The Court also considered whether anything had occurred in 1866 other than the granting of the right to vote to blacks in some areas (and throughout the nation four years later with the passage of the Fifteenth Amendment) that would cause a state to return its voting status to a time prior to that date. In other words, the opinion states that there was no legal change to suffrage in 1866 other than granting slaves the right to vote. If the date had been based on some other, potentially more reasonable (in the eyes of the Court) state intention, the Court might still have considered the grandfather clause law valid. No such reason was found, however.

Finally the Court examined the literacy test, but not to determine whether it disparately affected African Americans, as that was not a concern of the Court at the time. Actually, at this point in history, the Court also ignored laws that produced obvious disadvantages for black voters, such as the white primary created in Texas and other states. There, the Democratic Party was by far the majority party, and so the primary to nominate party candidates was even more important than the election, in which candidates from the various parties squared off against each other. In other decisions, the Supreme Court allowed the Democratic Party to limit primary voting to whites and ignored the connection of the party to the state. It was not until 1944 that the white primary was finally struck down. Thus, the court's decision here to consider the literacy test in the abstract is not surprising.

In *Guinn v. United States*, the literacy test used in Oklahoma was directly intertwined with the state's grandfather clause, and so the question was whether the grandfather clause could be struck down while allowing the literacy test to still operate. Justice White states that, in general, the Court would rely on state court decisions in areas like this, but he also points out that no such decision had yet been made. He asks what the impact of the decision already announced—striking down the grandfather clause—would be on the literacy test. The Court holds that the statute contradicted itself once the grandfather clause was removed, as without the grandfather clause all people would be subjected to the literacy test, which was the exact opposite of the stated goal of the legislation. The stated goal of the legislation was to limit the number of people who had to take the literacy test, and the elimination of the grandfather clause would have once again forced everyone to take the literacy test. Thus, since the legislation, as necessarily amended by the Supreme Court decision, contradicted itself, it must be struck down as a whole, even though literacy tests generally would be allowed.

Literacy tests were used to deprive African Americans of their right to suffrage through the early 1960s, as were comprehension tests covering the federal and state constitutions. Employed unfairly and disproportionately against blacks but rarely given to whites, these tests swayed the results of elections for decades. A half century after the 1915 decision in *Guinn v. United States*, the Voting Rights Act of 1965 did away with impediments to voting by allowing the federal government to appoint registrars in any state where a significant racial disparity in voting registration existed. After the passage of this law, millions more African Americans registered to vote. In 1915, though, such advances were still fifty years in the future.

At the end of his opinion, Justice White addresses an objection made by the defendants to the charge made against them in court. This argument basically states that since the charge had presumed that the suffrage amendment to the Oklahoma constitution was unconstitutional, it should be thrown out because it had presumed their guilt. However, the Supreme Court replies that since the Fifteenth Amendment was self-executing and clearly in conflict with the suffrage amendment to the Oklahoma constitution, the charge would be allowed. The final complaint was against a conspiracy statute under which the men were arrested. However, that same day the U.S. Supreme Court had upheld the same statute in another case dealing with Oklahoma—one concerning election officials who refused to count the votes cast by African Americans. The officials were convicted, and the conviction was upheld, which in turn meant that the statute was acceptable; therefore, the conviction of the defendants in the *Guinn* case was also upheld. It should be noted that the aforementioned cases involving Oklahoma election officials were rooted somewhat in political considerations. The Republican Party was losing political ground, so party officials pushed for the thorough investigation of alleged voting rights abuses. By the end of the nineteenth century, the Republican Party had practically died out throughout the South; the adoption of new constitutions by some southern states around 1900 compounded the party's woes and proved that their concern was not an idle one. Whether motivated by the fear of the party's demise or by a real concern for the rights of those not being allowed to vote, the Republican Party's escalation of suffrage cases to the

U.S. Supreme Court was a necessary step in black enfranchisement.

Essential Themes

The decision in the case of *Guinn v. United States* had a limited impact on black voting rights at the time it was handed down. Only a few states had such grandfather clauses, as most preferred to restrict African American suffrage more subtly. Even national leaders who supported segregation were opposed to these clauses owing to their deliberate disregard for the spirit of the law. The voters in Oklahoma were not affected by the decision; the Oklahoma state government simply adopted a law allowing all people who had voted in 1914 to vote again, along with whoever could survive a rigorous registration process that was open for only two weeks. Those states with literacy tests could breathe a sigh of relief as well, since the Supreme Court refused to challenge them directly and generally granted full rights to the state to create their own standards for suffrage, as long as they did not blatantly challenge the Fifteenth Amendment.

The more important effect was a long-term one, as the NAACP and others saw that they could win at the Supreme Court level and so continued to press cases to the highest court. *Guinn* also saw the first brief filed by the NAACP, which helped to validate the group's efforts. The NAACP would come to be the premier organization fighting for African Americans' rights through the court system.

—Scott A. Merriman, PhD

Bibliography and Additional Reading

Kotz, Nick. *Judgment Days: Lyndon Baines Johnson, Martin Luther King, Jr., and the Laws That Changed America.* Boston: Houghton Mifflin, 2005.

Pratt, Walter F., Jr. *The Supreme Court under Edward Douglass White, 1910–1921.* Columbia: University of South Carolina Press, 1999.

Rush, Mark E., ed. *Voting Rights and Redistricting in the United States.* Westport, Conn.: Praeger, 1998.

Shoemaker, Rebecca S. *The White Court: Justices, Rulings, and Legacy.* Santa Barbara, Calif.: ABC-CLIO, 2004.

Valley, Richard M. *The Two Reconstructions: The Struggle for Black Enfranchisement.* Chicago: University of Chicago Press, 2004.

Zelden, Charles. *Voting Rights on Trial.* Indianapolis, Ind.: Hackett, 2004.

Indian Citizenship Act

Date: June 2, 1924
Author: Homer P. Snyder
Genre: law; legislation

Summary Overview

The Indian Citizenship Act, also known as the Snyder Act, passed by the U.S. Congress in 1924, granted U.S. citizenship to the approximately 125,000 American Indians who did not own enough property off of reservation lands to be considered taxable, which had been the bar for Native citizenship before the act.

Defining Moment

A public effort to grant Indians citizenship arose at the end of World War I, as many Indian Nations had supported the war effort and those Indians who had served honorably had been granted citizenship. However, the Indian Citizenship Act can also be viewed in the context of the continual effort to encourage the assimilation of Indian peoples based upon American economic, religious, and cultural norms.

Though the act did make all Indian (or Native American) people eligible for citizenship, it did not impact the "trust relationship" that exists between the federal government and the tribes. Indian people retain their tribal memberships and most federally recognized tribal governments kept their status as "domestic dependent nations" that had been established in the U.S. Supreme Court's 1832 *Cherokee Nation v. Georgia* decision. These distinctions would lead to further confusion and litigation, as local and state governments saw Indian citizenship as bringing Native peoples under their jurisdiction.

Author Biography

Representative Homer P. Snyder (R-New York) was born in Amsterdam, New York, in 1863 and served in the U.S. House of Representatives from 1915 until 1925. While a congressman, Snyder chaired the Committee on Indian Affairs from 1921 until 1925, shepherding a number of reforms including the establishment of what would become the Indian Health Service. Under pressure from the so-called Friends of the Indian, who met annually at the Lake Mohonk Conference, Snyder pushed for the extension of the rights and protections that had been granted to African Americans by the Fourteenth Amendment to American Indian peoples, who up until that point could only be U.S. citizens if they had less than half Indian blood quantum and were subject to off-reservation taxation. The move was supported by many Indian reformers, both Native and white, including then-Senator Charles Curtis, who was a member of the Kaw tribe in Kansas and the Republican Senate Majority Whip. He would go on to become vice president of the United States during 1929–33 under Herbert Hoover.

President Calvin Coolidge stands with four Osage Indians at the White House after signing the bill. Photo via Wikimedia Commons. [Public domain.]

Historical Document

Indian Citizenship Act

Sixty-eighth Congress of the United States of America;

At the First Session,

Begun and held at the City of Washington on Monday, the third day of December, one thousand nine hundred and twenty-three.

An Act

To authorize the Secretary of the Interior to issue certificates of citizenship to Indians.

Be it enacted by the Senate and house of Representatives of the United States of America in Congress assembled, That all non-citizen Indians born within the territorial limits of the United States be, and they are hereby, declared to be citizens of the United States: *Provided,* That the granting of such citizenship shall not in any manner impair or otherwise affect the right of any Indian to tribal or other property.

Approved June 2, 1924.

Document Analysis

Although exceedingly brief, the Indian Citizenship Act of 1924 was vast in its assumptions of the proper path for American Indian peoples as well as in its ramifications for the future of American Indian sovereignty. To American Indian "reformers"—those who wanted a departure from the constitutionally-enshrined practice of relating to tribes on a nation-to-nation basis—citizenship was a vital part of the process of the assimilation of Indian peoples into Euro-American economic, cultural, and religious norms.

However, some Indian people were already United States citizens before the act, though the privilege was unevenly applied and came with many strings attached. Some treaties in the mid-nineteenth century included citizenship as compensation for the tribe giving up self-government and their land base. Although the U.S. Supreme Court's 1884 decision in the case of *Elk v. Wilkins* denied American Indians the protections of the Fourteenth Amendment, which stated that "[a]ll persons born or naturalized in the United States, and subject to the jurisdiction thereof, are citizens of the United States and of the state wherein they reside," arguing that their status as "domestic dependent nations" precluded tribal members from U.S. citizenship, within the communities of reformers of Indian policy, the so-called Friends of the Indian, momentum was building to place citizenship alongside land ownership and the practice of Christian religion as the hallmarks of whether or not an Indian could be considered civilized.

Individual Indians who took ownership of parcels of tribal land as a result of the Dawes Act of 1887 were granted citizenship. Some individual Indians were given citizenship in return for their service in the U.S. military. However, the typical means of naturalization that were granted to immigrants from Europe were not available to American Indian peoples during the nineteenth century. In 1890, the Indian Territory Naturalization Act was passed by Congress, allowing Indians living in Indian Territory (present-day Oklahoma) to apply for citizenship. Many in Congress saw citizenship for Indians as a goal that would not only move Indian people further toward the goal of assimilation into American society but would also speed the process for Indian Territory to be done away with, in order for a new state to be formed and with it, new lands for white settlers to farm.

As the twentieth century dawned, the voices calling for citizenship as a tool for assimilation only grew louder. Many Indians fought in the U.S. forces during World War I, which led to increased calls for citizenship. In Congress, Charles Curtis, a man of Kansa and Osage backgrounds who was a staunch proponent of assimilation and citizenship, had become a very influential Republican in the U.S. Senate, chairing the Senate Committee on Indian Affairs and sponsoring the Indian Citizenship Act. In following years, he would go on to become Senate majority leader and vice president of the United States. Additionally, Secretary of the Interior Hubert Work created what was called the Committee of One Hundred, made up of business and religious leaders, to help reshape Indian policy. With staunch support in government, in the business community, and from religious leaders, Congress passed the Indian Citizenship Act on June 4, 1924.

Essential Themes

The Indian Citizenship Act accomplished many of its goals. Along with the entire chain of Indian policy from the 1860s through the 1920s, it succeeded in dividing many Indian communities between traditionalists and assimilationists. The amount of land held by Indian peoples and nations continued to shrink. At the same time, it exacerbated many questions of national allegiance. Some Indian people have refused the rights and liabilities that come with citizenship, such as voting and paying taxes. Tribes such as the seven nations of the Haudenosaunee (or Iroquois) have issued their own passports under which their citizens can travel internationally, though the U.S. government and many of its allies refuse to honor them as valid. Most Indian people, however, have managed to find a sometimes-uneasy balance between their tribal nation allegiance and their allegiance to the United States.

Throughout the rest of the twentieth century, federal Indian policy would vacillate between the push for Indian sovereignty and assimilation. During the 1930s, the arrival of the Indian New Deal would help many tribal nations establish new governments with a larger degree of sovereignty than they had previously. However, much of that ground was lost when, during the 1950s, the federal government returned to a policy of encouraging assimilation through the termination of the trust relationship between the tribes and the federal government. Self-determination as a goal returned during the Red Power movement of the 1970s and has remained a priority for most Indian nations ever since.

—*Steven L. Danver, PhD*

Bibliography and Additional Reading

Deloria, Vine, Jr., and Clifford M. Lytle. *The Nations Within: The Past and Future of American Indian Sovereignty*. Austin: University of Texas Press, 1984.

Deloria, Vine, Jr., ed. *American Indian Policy in the Twentieth Century*. Norman: University of Oklahoma Press, 1985.

Deloria, Vine, Jr., and David E. Wilkins. *Tribes, Treaties, and Constitutional Tribulations*. Austin: University of Texas Press, 1999.

McCool, Daniel, Susan M. Olson, and Jennifer L. Robinson. *Native Vote: American Indians, the Voting Rights Act, and the Right to Vote*. New York: Cambridge UP, 2007.

Prucha, Francis Paul. *American Indian Policy in Crisis: Christian Reformers and the Indian, 1865–1900*. Norman: University of Oklahoma Press, 1964.

_____. *The Great Father: The United States Government and the American Indians*. Lincoln: University of Nebraska Press, 1984.

Alice Moore Dunbar-Nelson: "The Negro Woman and the Ballot"

Date: 1927
Author: Alice Moore Dunbar-Nelson
Genre: article

Summary Overview

The writer, educator, and activist Alice Moore Dunbar-Nelson published the article "The Negro Woman and the Ballot" in 1927 in the African American magazine The Messenger. *In it, she posed the question What have black women done with their vote? Dunbar-Nelson believed that black women had accomplished not nearly enough as a result of their enfranchisement (along with all other adult women) in 1920, and she encouraged them to start exercising their power as voters without bowing to pressure from their male peers or loyalty to the Republican Party. She noted that African American women had already demonstrated their power as a group in the congressional elections of 1922, in which their votes had helped oust Republican legislators in Delaware, New Jersey, and Michigan who had failed to support the antilynching legislation known as the Dyer bill. Dunbar-Nelson concluded her article by positing that when black women have realized that their children's futures could be helped or hindered by the way they voted, perhaps they would set aside allegiance to the Republican Party and use their ballot power to better the condition of all African Americans.*

Defining Moment

Women in the United States had been agitating for the right to vote since the early nineteenth century. By mid-century, Lucretia Mott, Elizabeth Cady Stanton, Susan B. Anthony, and others had emerged as leading advocates for women's suffrage. In their nationwide movement, suffragists marched and picketed, gave lectures, published articles, submitted petitions, faced verbal and physical abuse, and sometimes even went to prison. In 1870 the Fifteenth Amendment to the Constitution extended the right to vote to African American men but not to women of any race. Women would still have to wait and work toward their enfranchisement. And work they did, although different factions went about it in different ways. Some worked for state voting rights, while others pressed for a national constitutional amendment. By 1918, fifteen states, most of them in the West, had granted women full suffrage (the right to vote in all

Alice Dunbar Nelson, c. early 1920s. Photo via Wikimedia Commons. [Public domain.]

elections), and women had limited voting rights in about two dozen other states. However, by this time most national women's suffrage organizations had become united behind the push for a constitutional amendment that would grant full suffrage to women.

When President Woodrow Wilson changed his stance and announced his support of the women's suffrage amendment in early 1918, the political atmosphere began to shift. In 1919 Congress passed the Nineteenth Amendment, which granted full suffrage to women. In August 1920 Tennessee became the thirty-sixth and final state needed to ratify the amendment. On August 26, Secretary of State Bainbridge Colby certified the amendment's adoption. Finally, women had been granted the right to vote in all elections nationwide.

In the congressional elections of 1922, women were given the opportunity to make a broad-based statement in support of the Dyer bill, the first piece of antilynching legislation ever to have reached the Senate for a vote. After the Civil War, white supremacists had sought ways to infringe upon the newly won rights of African Americans. Lynching had existed since the days of British rule, and its victims had included many white people and Native Americans. In the South during the late nineteenth and early twentieth centuries, lynching became one of the cruelest and more frequent forms of violence practiced against African Americans, who comprised the majority of its victims. In April 1918, Leonidas C. Dyer, a Republican congressman from Missouri, introduced a bill in the House of Representatives that would prohibit lynching and make it a federal offense. He was motivated by the horrible riots—including lynching and other violent acts—that took place in July of 1917 in East St. Louis, Illinois—directly across the Mississippi River from Dyer's district in St. Louis. The Dyer bill was sponsored by the National Association for the Advancement of Colored People (NAACP). Despite bitter opposition, the House passed a somewhat modified form of the Dyer bill by a substantial majority on January 26, 1922, and it moved on to the Senate for consideration.

A women's organization called the Anti-Lynching Crusaders was founded in the late spring of 1922, and that summer it launched a national campaign that pressed for passage of the Dyer bill in the Senate. The Anti-Lynching Crusaders set forth to raise money for its parent organization, the NAACP, and to educate the American public about the horrific practice of lynching. The campaign was to be completed on or before January 1, 1923. The organization was headed by the president of the National Association of Colored Women, Mary B. Talbert (referred to as "Mrs. Mary B. Talbot" in "The Negro Woman and the Ballot"). Although the Anti-Lynching Crusaders consisted largely of African American women, white women were encouraged to join, and some worked for the cause. At the end of a five-month campaign, all funds were turned over to the NAACP.

Because of the inaction of Republican senators and a filibuster by Democratic Senate minority leader Oscar W. Underwood of Alabama, the Senate did not vote on the Dyer bill in 1922. Congressman Dyer reintroduced the bill in the House of Representatives in 1923 and again in every succeeding congressional session in the 1920s but failed to gain congressional support. Further interest in antilynching legislation had to wait until the 1930s. But the Republican failure to secure passage of the Dyer bill in the Senate had not come without a political price.

In the early 1920s, most African American voters still were members of the Republican Party, the party of Abraham Lincoln, who had issued the Emancipation Proclamation in 1863. Because Lincoln, the first Republican president, had taken up the cause of emancipation, many African Americans felt they owed allegiance to his party. During Reconstruction some black Republicans were voted into Congress. The Republican Party also kept blacks' allegiance because Republicans seemed to be the only ones who cared anything for African American issues or helping to secure their rights, especially through the Civil Rights Act of 1875. However, the seeming indifference of Republican politicians toward the fate of the Dyer bill in the Senate disheartened many African Americans. The filibuster by a southern Democrat had not been surprising, since many politicians from the Deep South touted white-supremacist views.

Many African American women, as Dunbar-Nelson noted in "The Negro Woman and the Ballot," made their disappointment known in the congressional elections of 1922, especially in Delaware, New Jersey, and Michigan, by voting down those Republican legislators who had let the Dyer bill fade away. Indeed, Republican apathy about the Dyer bill caused many African Americans, a good number of them women, to switch their support to the Democratic Party, which at the national level had begun to embrace progressive values regardless of the views of some reactionary Democrats, mostly from the South. Dunbar-Nelson freely admitted that her own disappointment in her Republican congressional representatives had caused her to become a Democrat.

Women, both white and black, had worked tirelessly for the right to vote, and black women in particular had urged the passage of antilynching legislation. After the failure of the Dyer bill in the Senate, women proved that their vote counted when those legislators seen as careless with the power vested in them by their constituents were sent home. Several years later in "The Negro Woman and the Ballot," Dunbar-Nelson examined what she thought it would take for African American women to build upon their display of political strength in 1922.

Author Biography

Alice Moore Dunbar-Nelson was born Alice Ruth Moore, on July 19, 1875, in New Orleans, Louisiana. Her father, Joseph Moore, was a seaman who had some white ancestry. Her mother, Patricia Wright, a former slave turned seamstress, had Native American and African American blood. In Creole society, the light skin and reddish hair that Alice had inherited helped her socially and allowed her sometimes to pass for white when she desired to partake of the activities of high culture limited to whites.

After Dunbar-Nelson graduated from a two-year teaching program at Straight College (now Dillard University) in 1892, she taught at a New Orleans elementary school. In 1895, when she was just twenty, she published her first book, a collection of poetry, short stories, reviews, and essays titled *Violets and Other Tales*. Poetry from this book, along with her picture, was featured in the *Boston Monthly Review*, a literary magazine, and attracted the attention of the prominent African American poet Paul Laurence Dunbar. At first the two maintained an epistolary relationship, but they finally met in person in 1897. They were wed in March 1898 in New York City.

The Dunbars moved to Washington, D.C., where they became a celebrated literary couple. In 1899, Dunbar-Nelson published another collection of short fiction, *The Goodness of St. Rocque and Other Stories*, as the companion volume to her husband's *Poems of Cabin and Field*. In 1902 the couple separated after four tumultuous years. Because Paul Dunbar suffered from medically induced alcoholism and drug addiction, he occasionally flew into rages during which he physically abused his wife. That Dunbar-Nelson sometimes critiqued her husband's poetry written in African American dialect hardly eased tensions between the two. Four years after his separation from his wife, Dunbar died of tuberculosis. While Dunbar-Nelson's relationship with her husband at his death was not amicable, she would be honored for the rest of her life as the widow of Paul Dunbar.

After Dunbar-Nelson separated from her husband, she moved to Wilmington, Delaware, where she was joined by her mother, sister, and her sister's children. She started teaching at Howard High School, and in addition to teaching and administrative duties there, she studied at Cornell University, Columbia University, and the University of Pennsylvania. She edited two works, *Masterpieces of Negro Eloquence* (1914) and *The Dunbar Speaker and Entertainer* (1920). During these years, Dunbar-Nelson was involved in several relationships, including one with the principal of Howard High School, Edwina B. Kruse, and a secret marriage to fellow teacher Henry Arthur Callis on January 19, 1910. Callis was younger than Dunbar-Nelson by twelve years, and the marriage did not last long.

In 1916 Dunbar-Nelson married the journalist Robert J. Nelson. This union would last for the rest of her life, even though she would continue to have romantic affairs with both women and men. Dunbar-Nelson became even more of a political and social activist after she married Nelson. She participated in the movement for women's suffrage and World War I relief efforts. Together, the couple published the *Wilmington Advocate*, a liberal black newspaper, from 1920 to 1922. During this period, Dunbar-Nelson was also a member of the

State Republican Committee of Delaware, and she chaired the Delaware branch of the Anti-Lynching Crusaders. She also became active in the Federation of Colored Women's Clubs. After the demise of the Dyer bill in the Senate, Dunbar-Nelson switched her allegiance to the Democratic Party and encouraged other African Americans to do the same. Beginning in 1924, she started to organize Democratic black women voters.

Dunbar-Nelson cofounded the Industrial School for Colored Girls in Marshallton, Delaware, where from 1924 to 1928 she served on the staff. From 1926 to 1930 she wrote columns regularly for various newspapers. Instead of the society gossip typical of female columnists of that time, Dunbar-Nelson wrote incisive pieces that addressed politics and cultural issues. She also traveled extensively as a public speaker, in part because of her position as executive secretary from 1928 to 1931 of the American Friends Inter-Racial Peace Committee.

In 1928 Dunbar-Nelson, along with many other middle-class African American women who previously had been Republicans, worked for the nomination of Alfred E. Smith as the Democratic presidential candidate. She gave speeches in support of Smith, whom she saw as the best presidential candidate for African Americans. One can only wonder how she must have viewed the victory of the Republican candidate Herbert Hoover that November.

In 1921 and again from 1926 to 1931, Dunbar-Nelson kept a diary in which she expressed her frustration with her literary career and other matters. She continued to write poetry and short fiction and completed two novels, and she was welcomed into the circle of Harlem Renaissance writers; however, she never found the success as an author that she had achieved as a journalist. In her diary she also gave voice to her concerns about personal financial instability. In 1932 Robert Nelson obtained a political appointment to the Pennsylvania Athletic Commission, a position that offered him a more steady income. The couple moved to Pennsylvania, where Dunbar-Nelson, finally living comfortably, continued to be active socially and politically. Her health, however, began to fail, and she died of a heart condition on September 18, 1935, at the University of Pennsylvania Hospital.

Historical Document

"The Negro Woman and the Ballot"

It has been six years since the franchise as a national measure has been granted women. The Negro woman has had the ballot in conjunction with her white sister, and friend and foe alike are asking the question, What has she done with it?

Six years is a very short time in which to ask for results from any measure or condition, no matter how simple. In six years a human being is barely able to make itself intelligible to listeners; is a feeble, puny thing at best, with undeveloped understanding, no power of reasoning, with a slight contributory value to the human race, except in a sentimental fashion. Nations in six years are but the beginnings of an idea. It is barely possible to erect a structure of any permanent value in six years, and only the most ephemeral trees have reached any size in six years.

So perhaps it is hardly fair to ask with a cynic's sneer, What has the Negro woman done with the ballot since she has had it? But, since the question continues to be hurled at the woman, she must needs be nettled into reply.

To those colored women who worked, fought, spoke, sacrificed, traveled, pleaded, wept, cajoled, all but died for the right of suffrage for themselves and their peers, it seemed as if the ballot would be the great objective of life. That with its granting, all the economic, political, and social problems to which the race had been subject would be solved. They did not hesitate to say—those militantly gentle workers for the vote—that with the granting of the ballot the women would step into the dominant place, politically, of the race. That all the mistakes which the men had made would be rectified. The men have sold their birthright for a mess of pottage, said the women. Cheap political office and little political preferment had dazzled their eyes so that they could not see the great issues affecting the race. They had been fooled by specious lies, fair promises and large-sounding words. Pre-election promises had inflated their chests, so that they could not see the post-election failures at their feet.

And thus on and on during all the bitter campaign of votes for women.

One of the strange phases of the situation was the rather violent objection of the Negro man to the Negro woman's having the vote. Just what his objection racially was, he did not say, preferring to hide behind the grandiloquent platitude of his white political boss. He had probably not thought the matter through; if he had, remembering how precious the ballot was to the race, he would have hesitated at withholding its privilege from another one of his own people.

But all that is neither here nor there. The Negro woman got the vote along with some tens of million other women in the country. And has it made any appreciable difference in the status of the race? ... The Negro woman was going to be independent, she had averred. She came into the political game with a clean slate. No Civil War memories for her, and no deadening sense of gratitude to influence her vote. She would vote men and measures, not parties. She could scan each candidate's record and give him her support according to how he had stood in the past on the question of race. She owed no party allegiance. The name of Abraham Lincoln was not synonymous with her for blind G.O.P. allegiance. She would show the Negro man how to make his vote a power, and not a joke. She would break up the tradition that one could tell a black man's politics by the color of his skin.

And when she got the ballot she slipped quietly, safely, easily, and conservatively into the political party of her male relatives.

Which is to say, that with the exception of New York City, and a sporadic break here and there, she became a Republican. Not a conservative one, however. She was virulent and zealous. Prone to stop speaking to her friends who might disagree with her findings on the political issue, and vituperative in campaigns.

In other words the Negro woman has by and large been a disappointment in her handling of the ballot. She has added to the overhead charges of the political machinery, without solving racial problems.

One of two bright lights in the story hearten the reader. In the congressional campaign of 1922 the Negro woman cut adrift from party allegiance and took up the cudgel (if one may mix metaphors) for the cause of the Dyer Bill. The Anti-Lynching Crusaders, led by Mrs. Mary B. Talbot, found in several states—New Jersey, Delaware, and Michigan particularly—that its cause was involved in the congressional election. Sundry gentlemen had voted against the Dyer Bill in the House and had come up for re-election. They were properly castigated by being kept at home. The women's votes unquestionably had the deciding influence in the three states mentioned and the campaign conducted by them was of a most commendable kind.

School bond issues here and there have been decided by the colored woman's votes—but so slight is the ripple on the smooth surface of conservatism that it has attracted no attention from the deadly monotony of the blind faith in the "Party of Massa Linkun."

As the younger generation becomes of age it is apt to be independent in thought and in act. But it is soon whipped into line by the elders, and by the promise of plums of preferment or of an amicable position in the community or of easy social relations—for we still persecute socially those who disagree with us politically. What is true of the men is true of the women. The very young is apt to let father, sweetheart, brother, or uncle decide her vote....

Whether women have been influenced and corrupted by their male relatives and friends is a moot question. Were I to judge by my personal experience I would say unquestionably so, I mean a personal experience with some hundreds of women in the North Atlantic, Middle Atlantic, and Middle Western States. High ideals are laughed at, and women confess with drooping wings how they have been scoffed at for working for nothing, for voting for nothing, for supporting a candidate before having first been "seen." In the face of this sinister influence it is difficult to see how the Negro woman could have been anything else but "just another vote."

All this is rather a gloomy presentment of a well-known situation. But it is not altogether hopeless. The fact that the Negro woman CAN be roused when something near and dear to her is touched and threatened is cheering. Then she throws off the influence of her male companion and strikes out for herself. Whatever the Negro may hope to gain for himself must be won at the ballot box, and quiet "going along" will never gain his end. When the Negro woman finds that the future of her children lies in her own hands—if she can be made to see this—she will strike off the political shackles she has allowed to be hung upon her, and win the economic freedom of her race.

Perhaps some Joan of Arc will lead the way.

Glossary

Anti-Lynching Crusaders: a women's group organized to stop lynching

Dyer Bill: a bill first introduced in the U.S. House of Representatives, aimed at making lynching a federal offense

G.O.P.: "Grand Old Party," the nickname of the Republican Party

Joan of Arc: a French peasant girl who, in the early fifteenth century, led the French army to several important victories during the Hundred Years' War

Massa Linkun: mimicking southern black dialect, a reference to President Abraham Lincoln

"sold their birthright for a mess of pottage": exchanged something of value for immediate gain, a reference to the story of Jacob and Esau in Genesis 25:29–34

Document Analysis

In late August 1920, the Nineteenth Amendment to the Constitution, which gave women the right to vote, was ratified. In the first paragraph of "The Negro Woman and the Ballot," Dunbar-Nelson puts forth the question that "friend and foe alike are asking": What has the African American woman done with her right to vote in the six years she has had it? Dunbar-Nelson's aim in posing this question was to encourage African American women not to waste this right by being "just another vote" for the Republicans without evaluating issues and candidates for themselves. Blind Republican faith, according to her, was not the way to go.

In paragraph 2, Dunbar-Nelson acknowledges that "six years is a very short time in which to ask for results from any measure or condition, no matter how simple." She gives the examples of how at six a human being is still a mere child and how structures meant to last centuries could rarely be finished within six years. Likewise, she notes that most trees would not reach anything approaching their potential size in six years and that a nation only six years old stands for "but the beginnings of an idea." Was it fair, then, Dunbar-Nelson asks, to expect much of the African American woman in the six years she has been able to vote? Regardless of the question's fairness, people have persisted in asking it, and Dunbar-Nelson therefore offers an answer.

Before proceeding to her answer, Dunbar-Nelson in paragraph 4 asks what African American women who worked to gain the vote thought would be achieved by having this right. Dunbar-Nelson says that for these women "it seemed as if the ballot would be the great objective of life." All their social, economic, and racial troubles—stemming from political decisions made for them by men—would be overcome by gaining the right to vote. They would "step into the dominant place, politically, of the race" and rectify the injustices that African American men had allowed to stand. According to Dunbar-Nelson, African American men had given up their political power in return for "cheap political office and little political preferment," while the "great issues affecting the race" had taken a backseat. Women, it would seem, would not let this happen if they got the vote.

In paragraph 6, Dunbar-Nelson observes that as a rule black men had not wanted black women to have the vote. Although she is unsure exactly why, she accuses the black man of having hidden "behind the grandiloquent platitude of his white political boss." If black men had been thinking about the progress of African Americans, surely they would not have kept half of their race from voting. This was not the point, though, says Dunbar-Nelson. The point was that women, both white and black, had been given the franchise. Here she revisits a facet of her original question: How has the African American woman exercised her right to vote such that she has made an "appreciable difference" in bettering the situation of all African Americans? In paragraph 7, Dunbar-Nelson recalls that ideally the African American woman, when she got the vote, should not have been swayed in ways that the black man had been. She would be "independent," since she had come "into the political game with a clean slate." She would not allow Republican political pressure to influence her vote, since gratitude to Abraham Lincoln did not require "blind G.O.P. allegiance." Unquestioning loyalty to the Republican Party, according to Dunbar-Nelson, was what had made African American men's votes "a joke" instead of a bastion of political strength and had led everyone to believe all black men were Republicans by default.

Nevertheless, many African American women, like their male peers, became Republicans. As Dunbar-Nelson eloquently puts it in paragraph 8, they "slipped quietly, safely, easily, and conservatively into the political party of [their] male relatives." In the next paragraph, Dunbar-Nelson names only black women in New York City and "a sporadic break here and there" by voters elsewhere as exceptions. However, she notes that the flavor of Republicanism of many black women was often not particularly conservative. Dunbar-Nelson uses the word *conservative* to mean "restrained." Rather than restrained, these women were often "zealous," "virulent," and even "vituperative" when they expressed their political views. Some even might have forsaken a friendship over a difference of political opinion. These observations notwithstanding, Dunbar-Nelson states in paragraph 10 that the answer to her opening question as to what

African American women have done with their right to vote must be that thus far their voting record has "by and large been a disappointment." Their votes in accordance with the Republican Party's policies may even have contributed to the problems facing their communities.

Still, Dunbar-Nelson maintains that there was room for hope in the form of "two bright lights." One of them, the brightest by far, was the ballot power demonstrated by African American women during the congressional elections of 1922. Dunbar-Nelson claims that their votes helped decide the outcome of elections in New Jersey, Delaware, and Michigan, in which legislators who had not actively supported the Dyer bill failed to be reelected. The other "bright light" Dunbar-Nelson characterizes as dim in comparison with the show of strength in the 1922 congressional elections—support for school bond measures. In elections involving school bond measures, many African American women had voted for what was best for their communities and had not allowed party pressure to sway them. However, Dunbar-Nelson observes, "the ripple" resulting from these elections was "so slight" that it barely stirred up discontent with the Republican Party.

In paragraph 13, Dunbar-Nelson laments that all too often young voters have submitted to the political status quo in exchange for preferred places in their communities and "easy social relations." Quite pointedly, she observes that "we still persecute socially those who disagree with us politically." Dunbar-Nelson views this as having been as true of women as of men and hardly limited to African Americans. As she notes, young women living with fathers, brothers, and uncles tended to defer to their political preferences. In the following paragraph, she adds that women's deference to men's political views was often true for older voters as well, judging by her encounters with hundreds of women across the United States. She blames men for having repeatedly mocked women's ideas, hopes, and "high ideals."

Nevertheless, Dunbar-Nelson in paragraph 15 expresses hope that African American women might break out of the confines of party allegiance and male influence and vote for what they believe, particularly if something "near and dear" to them were to be threatened. Blind party allegiance could not help African Americans, and the ballot was one of the few instruments by which they could assert their power: "Whatever the Negro may hope to gain ... must be won at the ballot box." Dunbar-Nelson states that once black women have realized that with their votes they might control the future of their children, they would cast votes in the best interest of their families and communities.

In her concluding paragraph, Dunbar-Nelson calls for "some Joan of Arc" to "lead the way." In other words, she was hoping for a leader like the "Maid of Orléans"—the peasant girl Joan of Arc, who, in the early fifteenth century, led the French army to several important victories during the Hundred Years' War, thus contributing to the coronation of Charles VII. Perhaps a woman of courage and divine inspiration would come forth to lead African American women in their struggle for economic freedom and political empowerment.

Essential Themes

Dunbar-Nelson's work, although popular among African American publishers at the time, did not attract the attention of white publishers. Nonetheless, Dunbar-Nelson became one of the older and more traditional voices of the Harlem Renaissance of the 1920s and 1930s. She also is considered one of the founders of the African American short-story tradition. Her contributions to literature and journalism as well as education, politics, and social activism continue to attest to the varied abilities and achievements of educated African American women and men during the late nineteenth and early twentieth centuries.

—*Angela M. Alexander, MA*

Bibliography and Additional Reading

Dray, Philip. *At the Hands of Persons Unknown: The Lynching of Black America.* New York: Random House, 2002.

Dunbar-Nelson, Alice. *Give Us Each Day: The Diary of Alice Dunbar-Nelson,* ed. Gloria T. Hull. New York: W. W. Norton, 1984.

Gordon, Ann D., et al., eds. *African American Women and the Vote, 1837–1965.* Amherst: University of Massachusetts Press, 1997.

Hull, Gloria T. "Alice Dunbar-Nelson (1875–1935)." Cengage Learning Web site. college.cengage.com/dunbarnelson_al.html.

Johnson, Wilma J. "Dunbar-Nelson, Alice Ruth Moore (1875–1935)." BlackPast.org Web site. blackpast.com/dunbar-nelson-alice-ruth-moore-1875-1935.

Marable, Manning, and Leith Mullings, eds. *Let Nobody Turn Us Around: An African American Anthology.* Lanham, Md: Rowman & Littlefield, 2009.

Mungarro, Angelica, et al. "How Did Black Women in the NAACP Promote the Dyer Anti-Lynching Bill, 1918–1923?" Women and Social Movements in the United States, 1600–2000, Web site. womhist.alexanderstreet.com/lynch/intro.htm.

■ Smith v. Allwright

Date: April 3, 1944
Author: Stanley F. Reed
Genre: court opinion

Summary Overview

On April 3, 1944, the U.S. Supreme Court issued a pivotal ruling, Smith v. Allwright, *regarding the constitutionality of all-white primaries. The decision, written by Associate Justice Stanley F. Reed, involved a Texas law that allowed the Democratic Party to ban African Americans from voting in primary elections. This meant that African Americans could not participate in the selection of Democratic candidates for office. All-white primaries were commonly used throughout the South to disenfranchise black voters. The practice had previously been upheld by the Supreme Court in* Grovey v. Townsend *(1935). However, in* Smith v. Allwright, *the Court overturned its previous decision, concluding that primaries existed under the authority of the state government and all-white primaries were a direct violation of the Fourteenth and Fifteenth Amendments to the U.S. Constitution.*

Defining Moment

As the last of the Reconstruction Era amendments, the Fifteenth Amendment (1870) asserted that the right to vote "shall not be denied or abridged by the United States or by any state on account of race, color, or previous condition of servitude," officially guaranteeing the right to vote for all African American males. However, black enfranchisement in the post–Reconstruction Era was heavily contested and brief. The withdrawal of federal troops from the South in 1877 accelerated the return of white supremacist control of state governments, which over the next forty years passed laws designed to prevent African Americans from voting.

Poll taxes, or the requirement of a fee to vote, and literacy tests, which asked potential voters to read, recite, or interpret political texts to the satisfaction of local white registrars were among the most common and effective forms of disenfranchising African Americans.

Less studied by historians, but equally as effective, were the establishment of all-white party primaries. Collectively, these legal efforts ensured that in 1940 fewer than 5 percent of all African Americans of voting age were registered to vote in the eleven former Confederate states. The widespread disenfranchise- ment of African Americans was a vital

Houston dentist Lonnie E. Smith casts his ballot in the 1944 Texas Democratic primary election (July 22, 1944). Photo via Wikimedia Commons. [Public domain.]

component of a larger system of racial segregation in the South.

Smith v. Allwright also occurred within the context of growing black activism. World War II and the American fight against German fascism and Japanese imperialism led many African Americans to note the hypocrisy of their own country, which represented itself as a democracy but denied African Americans both suffrage and basic human rights. Increasingly African Americans, many of whom had served in the military during World War II, began to organize. Membership in the National Association for the Advancement of Colored People (NAACP) skyrocketed from 50,000 to around 400,000 during the war. Other civil rights organizations—most notably the Congress of Racial Equality (CORE)—emerged during this period. Energized by the same political-ideological currents, many white liberals and northern politicians from both parties, who hoped to gain black votes, lent support to the cause of African American voting rights.

In this climate of activism, important first steps were made to gain and protect black suffrage. The Soldier Voting Act of 1942 (amended in 1944) allowed military personnel, regardless of race, to vote when stationed away from home and exempted them from poll taxes and registration requirements. By ruling that white primaries were unconstitutional, the Supreme Court not only reversed its previous decision in *Grovey v. Townsend* (1935) but also encouraged African Americans to continue to organize against laws that disenfranchised them.

Author Biography

Stanley F. Reed was born on December 31, 1884, in Mason County, Kentucky. He received undergraduate degrees at both Kentucky Wesleyan College (1902) and Yale University (1906). He attended law school at both the University of Virginia and Columbia University but did not graduate from either. After passing the bar exam, he practiced law in Marysville, Kentucky, before joining the military in World War I. Once his military service ended, he served as general counsel for the Federal Farm Board and Reconstruction Finance Corporation. In 1935, President Franklin Delano Roosevelt appointed Reed solicitor general of the United States. In January 1938, he was appointed associate justice to the U.S. Supreme Court, retiring from the position nearly twenty years later in 1958.

Historical Document

Smith v. Allwright (1944)

Argued: January 12, 1944. Decided: April 03, 1944

Messrs. Thurgood Marshall, of Baltimore, Md., and William H. Hastie, of Washington, D.C., for petitioner.

Mr. George W. Barcus, of Austin, Tex., for Gerald C. Mann, Attorney General of Texas, as amicus curiae, by special leave of Court.

No. appearance for respondents.

Mr. Justice REED delivered the opinion of the Court.

This writ of certiorari brings here for review a claim for damages in the sum of $5,000 on the part of petitioner, a Negro citizen of the 48th precinct of Harris County, Texas, [321 U.S. 649, 651] for the refusal of respondents, election and associate election judges respectively of that precinct, to give petitioner a ballot or to permit him to cast a ballot in the primary election of July 27, 1940, for the nomination of Democratic candidates for the United States Senate and House of Representatives, and Governor and other state officers. The refusal is alleged to have been solely because of the race and color of the proposed voter.

The actions of respondents are said to violate Sections 31 and 43 of Title 81 of the United States Code, 8 U.S.C.A. 31 and 43, in that petitioner was deprived of rights secured by Sections 2 and 4 of Article 12 and the Fourteenth, Fifteenth and Seventeenth Amend- [321 U.S. 649, 652] ments to the United States Constitution. 3 The suit was filed in the District Court of the United States for the Southern District of Texas, which had jurisdiction under Judicial Code Section 24, subsection 14, 28 U. S.C.A. 41 (14).4

The District Court denied the relief sought and the Circuit Court of Appeals quite properly affirmed its action on the authority of Grovey v. Townsend, 295 U.S. 45 , 55 S.Ct. 622, 97 A.L.R. 680.5 We granted the petition for certiorari to resolve a claimed inconsistency between the decision in the Grovey case and that of United States v. Classic, 313 U.S. 299 , 61 S.Ct. 1031. 319 U.S. 738 , 63 S.Ct. 1325.

The State of Texas by its Constitution and statutes provides that every person, if certain other requirements are met which are not here in issue, qualified by residence [321 U.S. 649, 653] in the district or county 'shall be deemed a qualified elector.' Constitution of Texas, Article VI, Section 2 Vernon's Ann.St.; Vernon's Civil Statutes (1939 ed.), Article 2955. Primary elections for United States Senators, Congressmen and state officers are provided for by Chapters Twelve and Thirteen of the statutes. Under these chapters, the Democratic Party was required to hold the primary which was the occasion of the alleged wrong to petitioner. A summary of the state statutes regulating primaries appears in the footnote. 6 These nominations are to be made by the qualified voters of the party. Art. 3101. [321 U.S. 649, 654] The Democratic Party of Texas is held by the Supreme Court of that state to be a 'voluntary association,' Bell v. Hill, 123 Tex. 531, 534, 74 S.W.2d 113, protected by Section 27 of the Bill of Rights, Art. 1, Constitution of Texas, from interference by the state except that:

'In the interest of fair methods and a fair expression by their members of their preferences in the selection of their [321 U.S. 649, 655] nominees, the State may regulate such elections by proper laws.' Page 545 of 123 Tex., page 120 of 74 S.W.2d. That court stated further:

'Since the right to organize and maintain a political party is one guaranteed by the Bill of Rights of this state, it necessarily follows that every privilege essential or reasonably appropriate to the exercise of that right is likewise [321 U.S. 649, 656] guaranteed, including, of course, the privilege of determining the policies of the party and its membership. Without the privilege of determining the policy of a political association and its membership, the right to organize such an association would be a mere mockery. We think these rights, that is, the right to determine the membership of a political party and to determine its policies, of necessity are to be exercised by the State Convention of such party, and cannot, under any circumstances, be conferred upon a state or governmental agency.' Page 546 of 123 Tex., page 120 of 74 S.W.2d Cf. Waples v. Marrast, 108 Tex. 5, 184 S.W. 180, L.R.A.1917A, 253.

The Democratic party on May 24, 1932, in a State Convention adopted the following resolution, which has not since been 'amended, abrogated, annulled or avoided':

'Be it resolved that all white citizens of the State of Texas who are qualified to vote under the Constitution and laws of the State shall be eligible to membership in the [321 U.S. 649, 657] Democratic party and, as such, entitled to participate in its deliberations.' It was by virtue of this resolution that the respondents refused to permit the petitioner to vote.

Texas is free to conduct her elections and limit her electorate as she may deem wise, save only as her action may be affected by the prohibitions of the United States Constitution or in conflict with powers delegated to and exercised by the National Government. 7 The Fourteenth Amendment forbids a state from making or enforcing any law which abridges the privileges or immunities of citizens of the United States and the Fifteenth Amendment specifically interdicts any denial or abridgement by a state of the right of citizens to vote on account of color. Respondents appeared in the District Court and the Circuit Court of Appeals and defended on the ground that the Democratic party of Texas is a voluntary organization with members banded together for the purpose of selecting individuals of the group representing the common political beliefs as candidates in the general election. As such a voluntary organization, it was claimed, the Democratic party is free to select its own membership and limit to whites participation in the party primary. Such action, the answer asserted, does not violate the Fourteenth, Fifteenth or Seventeenth Amendment as officers of government cannot be chosen at primaries and the Amendments are applicable only to general elections where governmental officers are actually elected. Primaries, it is said, are political party affairs, handled by party not governmental officers. No appearance for respondents is made in this Court. Arguments presented here by the Attorney General of Texas and the Chairman of the State Democratic Executive Committee of Texas, as amici [321 U.S. 649, 658] curiae, urged substantially the same grounds as those advanced by the respondents.

The right of a Negro to vote in the Texas primary has been considered heretofore by this Court. The first case was Nixon v. Herndon, 273 U.S. 536 , 47 S.Ct. 446. At that time, 1924, the Texas statute, Art. 3093a, Acts 1923, 2d Called Sess., c. 32, afterwards numbered Art. 3107, Rev.Stat.1925, declared 'in no event shall a Negro be eligible to participate in a Democratic party primary election ... in the State of Texas.' Nixon was refused the right to vote in a Democratic primary and brought a suit for damages against the election officers under R.S. 1979 and 2004, the present sections 43 and 31 of Title 8, U.S.C., 8 U.S.C.A. 43 and 31, respectively. It was urged to this Court that the denial of the franchise the Nixon violated his Constitutional rights under the Fourteenth and Fifteenth Amendments. Without consideration of the Fifteenth, this Court held that the action of Texas in denying the ballot to Negroes by statute was in violation of the equal protection clause of the Fourteenth Amendment and reversed the dismissal of the suit.

The legislature of Texas reenacted the article but gave the State Executive Committee of a party the power to prescribe the qualifications of its members for voting or other participation. This article remains in the statutes. The State Executive Committee of the Democratic party adopted a resolution that white Democrats and none other might participate in the primaries of that party. Nixon was refused again the privilege of voting in a primary and again brought suit for damages by virtue of Section 31, Title 8 U.S.C., 18 U.S.C.A. 31. This Court again reversed the dismissal of the suit for the reason that the Committee action was deemed to be State action and invalid as discriminatory under the Fourteenth Amendment. The test was said to be whether the Committee operated as representative of the State in the discharge of the

State's authority. Nixon v. Condon, 286 U.S. 73 , 52 S.Ct. 484, 88 A. L.R. 458. The question of the inherent power [321 U.S. 649, 659] of a political party in Texas 'without restraint by any law to determine its own membership' was lift open. Id., 286 U.S. 83, 84 , 85 S., 52 S.Ct. 485.

In Grovey v. Townsend, 295 U.S. 45 , 55 S.Ct. 622, 97 A. L.R. 680, this Court had before it another suit for damages for the refusal in a primary of a county clerk, a Texas officer with only public functions to perform, to furnish petitioner, a Negro, an absentee ballot. The refusal was solely on the ground of race. This case differed from Nixon v. Condon, supra, in that a state convention of the Democratic party had passed the resolution of May 24, 1932, hereinbefore quoted. It was decided that the determination by the state convention of the membership of the Democratic party made a significant change from a determination by the Executive Committee. The former was party action, voluntary in character. The latter, as had been held in the Condon case, was action by authority of the State. The managers of the primary election were therefore declared not to be state officials in such sense that their action was state action. A state convention of a party was said not to be an organ of the state. This Court went on to announce that to deny a vote in a primary was a mere refusal of party membership with which 'the state need have no concern,' 295 U.S. loc.cit. 55, 55 S.Ct.loc.cit. 626, while for a state to deny a vote in a general election on the ground of race or color violated the Constitution. Consequently, there was found no ground for holding that the county clerk's refusal of a ballot because of racial ineligibility for party membership denied the petitioner any right under the Fourteenth or Fifteenth Amendments.

Since Grovey v. Townsend and prior to the present suit, no case from Texas involving primary elections has been before this Court. We did decide, however, United States v. Classic, 313 U.S. 299 , 61 S.Ct. 1031. We there held that Section 4 of Article I of the Constitution authorized Congress to regulate primary as well as general elections, 313 U.S. at pages 316, 317, 61 S.Ct. at page 1038, [321 U.S. 649, 660] 'where the primary is by law made an integral part of the election machinery.' 313 U.S. at page 318, 61 S.Ct. at page 1039. Consequently, in the Classic case, we upheld the applicability to frauds in a Louisiana primary of 19 and 20 of the Criminal Code, 18 U.S.C.A. 51, 52 Thereby corrupt acts of election officers were subjected to Congressional sanctions because that body had power to protect rights of Federal suffrage secured by the Constitution in primary as in general elections. 313 U.S. at page 323, 61 S.Ct. at page 1041. This decision depended, too, on the determination that under the Louisiana statutes the primary was a part of the procedure for choice of Federal officials. By this decision the doubt as to whether or not such primaries were a part of 'elections' subject to Federal control, which had remained unanswered since Newberry v. United States, 256 U.S. 232 , 41 S.Ct. 469, was erased. The Nixon cases were decided under the equal protection clause of the Fourteenth Amendment without a determination of the status of the primary as a part of the electoral process. The exclusion of Negroes from the primaries by action of the State was held invalid under that Amendment. The fusing by the Classic case of the primary and general elections into a single instrumentality for choice of officers has a definite bearing on the permissibility under the Constitution of excluding Negroes from primaries. This is not to say that the Classic case cuts directly into the rationale of Grovey v. Townsend. This latter case was not mentioned in the opinion. Classic bears upon Grovey v. Townsend not because exclusion of Negroes from primaries is any more or less state action by reason of the unitary character of the electoral process but because the recognition of the place of the primary in the electoral scheme makes clear that state delegation to a party of the power to fix the qualifications of primary elections is delegation of a state function that may make the party's action the action of the state. When Grovey v. Townsend was written, the Court looked upon the denial of a vote in a primary as a [321 U.S. 649, 661] mere refusal by a party of party membership. 295 U.S. at page 55, 55 S.Ct. at page 626, 97 A.L.R. 680. As the Louisiana statutes for holding primaries are similar to those of Texas, our ruling in Classic as to the unitary character of the electoral process calls for a reexamination as to whether or not the exclusion of Negroes from a Texas party primary was state action.

The statutes of Texas relating to primaries and the resolution of the Democratic party of Texas extending the privileges of membership to white citizens only are the same in substance and effect today as they were when Grovey v. Townsend was decided by a unanimous Court. The question as to whether the exclusionary action of the party was the action of the State persists as the determinative factor. In again entering upon consideration of the inference to be drawn as to state action from a substantially similar factual situation, it should be noted that Grovey v. Townsend upheld exclusion of Negroes from primaries through the denial of party membership by a party convention. A few years before this Court refused approval of exclusion by the State Executive Committee of the party. A different result was reached on the theory that the Committee action was state authorized and the Convention action was unfettered by statutory control. Such a variation in the result from so slight a change in form influences us to consider anew the legal validity of the distinction which has resulted in barring Negroes from participating in the nominations of candidates of the Democratic party in Texas. Other precedents of this Court forbid the abridgement of the right to vote. United States v. Reese, 92 U.S. 214, 217; Neal v. Delaware, 103 U.S. 370, 388; Guinn v. United States, 238 U.S. 347, 361, 35 S.Ct. 926, 930, L.R.A.1916A, 1124; Myers v. Anderson, 238 U.S. 368, 379, 35 S. Ct. 932, 934, 59 L.ed. 1349; Lane v. Wilson, 307 U.S. 268, 59 S.Ct. 872.

It may now be taken as a postulate that the right to vote in such a primary for the nomination of candidates without discrimination by the State, like the right to vote [321 U.S. 649, 662] in a general election, is a right secured by the

Constitution. United States v. Classic, 313 U.S. at page 314, 61 S.Ct. at page 1037; Myers v. Anderson, 238 U.S. 368 , 35 S.Ct. 932; Ex parte Yarbrough, 110 U.S. 651 , 663 et seq., 4 S.Ct. 152, 158. By the terms of the Fifteenth Amendment that right may not be abridged by any state on account of race. Under our Constitution the great privilege of the ballot may not be denied a man by the State because of his color.

We are thus brought to an examination of the qualifications for Democratic primary electors in Texas, to determine whether state action or private action has excluded Negroes from participation. Despite Texas' decision that the exclusion is produced by private or party action, Bell v. Hill, supra, Federal courts must for themselves appraise the facts leading to that conclusion. It is only by the performance of this obligation that a final and uniform interpretation can be given to the Constitution, the 'supreme Law of the Land.' Nixon v. Condon, 286 U.S. 73, 88 , 52 S.Ct. 484, 88 A.L.R. 458; Standard Oil Co. v. Johnson, 316 U.S. 481, 483 , 62 S.Ct. 1168, 1169; Bridges v. California, 314 U.S. 252 , 62 S.Ct. 190; Lisenba v. California, 314 U.S. 219, 238 , 62 S.Ct. 280, 290; Union Pacific R. Co. v. United States, 313 U.S. 450, 467 , 61 S.Ct. 1064, 1074; Milk Wagon Drivers Union v. Meadowmoor Dairies, 312 U.S. 287, 294 , 61 S.Ct. 552, 555, 132 A.L.R. 1200; Chambers v. Florida, 309 U.S. 227, 228 , 60 S.Ct. 472, 473. Texas requires electors in a primary to pay a poll tax. Every person who does so pay and who has the qualifications of age and residence is an acceptable voter for the primary. Art. 2955. As appears above in the summary of the statutory provisions set out in note 6, Texas requires by the law the election of the county officers of a party. These compose the county executive committee. The county chairmen so selected are members of the district executive committee and choose the chairman for the district. Precinct primary election officers are named by the county executive committee. Statutes provide for the election by the voters of precinct [321 U.S. 649, 663] delegates to the county convention of a party and the selection of delegates to the district and state conventions by the county convention. The state convention selects the state executive committee. No convention may place in platform or resolution any demand for specific legislation without endorsement of such legislation by the voters in a primary. Texas thus directs the selection of all party officers.

Primary elections are conducted by the party under state statutory authority. The county executive committee selects precinct election officials and the county, district or state executive committees, respectively, canvass the returns. These party committees or the state convention certify the party's candidates to the appropriate officers for inclusion on the official ballot for the general election. No name which has not been so certified may appear upon the ballot for the general election as a candidate of a political party. No other name may be printed on the ballot which has not been placed in nomination by qualified voters who must take oath that they did not participate in a primary for the selection of a candidate for the office for which the nomination is made.

The state courts are given exclusive original jurisdiction of contested elections and of mandamus proceedings to compel party officers to perform their statutory duties.

We think that this statutory system for the selection of party nominees for inclusion on the general election ballot makes the party which is required to follow these legislative directions an agency of the state in so far as it determines the participants in a primary election. The party takes its character as a state agency from the duties imposed upon it by state statutes; the duties do not become matters of private law because they are performed by a political party. The plan of the Texas primary follows substantially that of Louisiana, with the exception that in [321 U.S. 649, 664] Louisiana the state pays the cost of the primary while Texas assesses the cost against candidates. In numerous instances, the Texas statutes fix or limit the fees to be charged. Whether paid directly by the state or through state requirements, it is state action which compels. When primaries become a part of the machinery for choosing officials, state and national, as they have here, the same tests to determine the character of discrimination or abridgement should be applied to the primary as are applied to the general election. If the state requires a certain electoral procedure, prescribes a general election ballot made up of party nominees so chosen and limits the choice of the electorate in general elections for state offices, practically speaking, to those whose names appear on such a ballot, it endorses, adopts and enforces the discrimination against Negroes, practiced by a party entrusted by Texas law with the determination of the qualifications of participants in the primary. This is state action within the meaning of the Fifteenth Amendment. Guinn v. United States, 238 U.S. 347, 362, 35 S.Ct. 926, 930, L.R.A. 1916A, 1124.

The United States is a constitutional democracy. Its organic law grants to all citizens a right to participate in the choice of elected officials without restriction by any state because of race. This grant to the people of the opportunity for choice is not to be nulified by a state through casting its electoral process in a form which permits a private organization to practice racial discrimination in the election. Constitutional rights would be of little value if they could be thus indirectly denied. Lane v. Wilson, 307 U.S. 268, 275, 59 S.Ct. 872, 876.

The privilege of membership in a party may be, as this Court said in Grovey v. Townsend, 295 U.S. 45, 55, 55 S.Ct. 622, 626, 97 A.L.R. 680, no concern of a state. But when, as here, that privilege is also the essential qualification for voting in a primary to select nominees for a general election, the state makes the action [321 U.S. 649, 665] of the party the action of the state. In reaching this conclusion we are not unmindful of the desirability of continuity of decision in constitutional questions. 8 However, when convinced of former error, this Court has never felt constrained to follow precedent. In constitutional questions, where correction depends upon amendment and not upon legislative action this Court throughout its history has freely exercised its power to reexamine the basis of its constitutional decisions. This has long been accepted practice,9 and this practice has continued to this day. 10 This is particularly true when the decision believed erroneous is the application of a constitutional principle rather [321 U.S. 649, 666] than an interpretation of the Constitution to extract the principle itself. 11 Here we are applying, contrary to the recent decision in Grovey v. Townsend, the well established principle of the Fifteenth Amendment, forbidding the abridgement by a state of a citizen's right to vote. Grovey v. Townsend is overruled.

Judgment reversed.

Document Analysis

Smith v. Allwright (1944) considered a Texas law that gave state political parties the authority to determine primary voting requirements. The Texas Democratic Party, which dominated the state politically, established white-only primaries that banned African American participation.

The Supreme Court ruling began by examining the particulars of the case. The petitioner, Lonnie E. Smith, an African American man from Harris County, Texas, was seeking $5,000 in damages after he was denied a ballot in the Democratic party primary election of July 27, 1940. It was alleged that he had been denied a ballot "solely because of the race and color of the proposed voter," a violation of the Fourteenth, Fifteenth, and Seventeenth Amendments to the Constitution.

Smith had previously been denied relief by the District Court of the United States for the Southern District of Texas and the United States Circuit Courts of Appeals, in large part because of the previous Supreme Court ruling, *Grovey v. Townsend*, which both courts interpreted as allowing political parties to make their own rules on voting in primaries. However, in his decision, Justice Reed noted that the Texas Constitution requires parties to hold primary elections, "including the primary which was the occasion of the alleged wrong to the petitioner." Democratic Party membership was voluntary, but Texas law required the party to hold primaries.

The Texas Constitution noted that every citizen, provided "other requirements are met which are not here in issue," is "deemed a qualified elector." However, the State Convention for the Texas Democratic Party adopted a resolution May 24, 1932, restricting membership in the party to "all white citizens of the state of Texas." Reed noted that while Texas had the legal authority to "conduct her elections and limit her electorate as she may deem wise," they could not establish rules or procedures that violate the U.S. Constitution. Of particular concern, was whether all-white primaries violated the Fourteenth Amendment, which guarantees equal protection before the law, and the Fifteenth Amendment, which stipulates that American citizens cannot be denied the right to vote on the basis of race or skin color.

Democratic Party officials, with the support of the attorney general of Texas, argued that the Democratic Party had not violated these amendments because it was a voluntary organization and "officers of the government cannot be chosen at primaries and the Amendments are applicable only to general elections where governmental officers are actually elected."

The Supreme Court had previously ruled in *Nixon v. Herndon* (1924) that a statute banning African American from participation in a Democratic primary violated the Fourteenth Amendment. In contrast, in *Grovey v. Townsend* (1935) the Court ruled that black voters could be banned from participating in primaries provided the decision was made by a state convention viewing it as a "mere refusal by a party of membership."

Complicating matters further, *United States v. Classic* (1941) established that Congress had the authority to regulate primary elections, suggesting that the court had reconsidered the relationship between voting in a primary and voting in the general election.

In *Smith v. Allwright*, then, Reed argued that "the right to vote in such a primary for the nomination of candidates without discrimination by the State, like the right to vote in a general election, is a right secured by the Constitution," and that under the Fifteenth Amendment that right cannot be denied on the basis of race. While primary elections are conducted by parties, they do so under the auspices of state authority and state law. Given that primaries are instrumental in choosing state and federal officials, "the same tests to determine the character of discrimination or abridgement should be applied to the primary as are applied to the general election."

Essential Themes

The *Smith v. Allwright* decision panicked white southerners and renewed optimism among African Americans. Not surprisingly, many white politicians in the South, as well as their supporters, refused to honor the *Smith* decision and continued to resist black efforts to gain the vote.

In contrast, African Americans saw the decision as a victory and a reason to continue to mobilize in support of black enfranchisement. In 1940, roughly 3 percent of African Americans were registered to vote in the South, but by 1947 the number quadrupled to 12 percent. While the vast majority of African Americans remained disenfranchised, *Smith v. Allwright* was a milestone in the movement to gain black suffrage that would eventually culminate in the passage of the Twenty-Fourth Amendment (1964), banning poll taxes, and the Voting Rights Act of 1965, which provided federal oversight of voting and effectively ended racially discriminatory southern state laws designed to disenfranchise African Americans.

—*Gerald F. Goodwin, PhD*

Bibliography and Additional Reading

Anderson, Carol. *One Person, No Vote: How Voter Suppression Is Destroying Our Democracy*. New York: Bloomsbury Publishing, 2018.

Payne, Charles M. *I've Got the Light of Freedom: The Organizing Tradition and the Mississippi Freedom Struggle.* Berkeley: University of California Press, 1995.

Zeldin, Charles Z. *The Battle for the Black Ballot: Smith v. Allwright and the Defeat of the Texas All-White Primary.* Lawrence: UP of Kansas, 2004.

Malcolm X: "The Ballot or the Bullet"

Date: April 3, 1964
Author: Malcolm X
Genre: speech

Summary Overview

Arguably the most famous of the noted black nationalist leader Malcolm X's speeches, "The Ballot or the Bullet" stands as a declaration of both the frustration and anger felt by African Americans denied civil rights and of the power of voting to enact the political changes needed to secure those rights. Malcolm X delivered the speech shortly after parting ways with the separatist Nation of Islam, and his advocacy of political participation as a means to attaining equality represented a turning point in his public position on the civil rights movement. In the speech, he sought to reframe the struggle for civil rights as one for simple human rights, declaring that the continued denial of these essential liberties presented African Americans with a choice between political action or armed resistance. The oration became the definitive statement of Malcolm X's ideology and inspired black nationalists for years to come.

Defining Moment

The first black residents of the lands that became the United States arrived as slaves during colonial times. Over the centuries that followed, the position of African Americans—even those who gained their freedom from bondage and their free descendants—remained an unequivocally inferior one. Colonial and later state laws sometimes banned enslaved and free blacks from exercising even what white Americans considered the most basic rights, and violence against African Americans often went unpunished. The U.S. Constitution initially accepted the institution of slavery and established rules for counting three-fifths of the enslaved residents of a state toward its population for representation.

Amendments following the Civil War ended slavery and extended citizenship and voting guarantees, but Reconstruction policies failed to unite the nation as one racially integrated people. Racial tension continued, and African American leaders such as Booker T. Washington and W. E. B. Du Bois disagreed on the best methods for an oppressed people to seek justice and equality. By the 1920s, a sense of black pride had begun to develop in some segments of the African American community. Black nationalist leaders who urged African Americans to see themselves and their

Malcolm X, c. 1964. Photo via Wikimedia Commons. [Public domain.]

culture as vibrant and important helped support this shift. So, too, did the cultural and social interest in black artistic achievement brought about by the Harlem Renaissance.

During the 1930s, a new black nationalist organization called the Nation of Islam began to attract African American supporters. Although not a traditional Muslim sect, the Nation of Islam blended Islamic tenets with Black Nationalism to form its own distinctive ideology. Led by Elijah Muhammad, the Nation of Islam urged African Americans to separate from white American society. It spoke against integration and intermarriage and rejected black political engagement with the mainstream U.S. government as counterproductive. The organization also firmly asserted black supremacy, earning accusations of racism. Membership in the Nation of Islam grew rapidly during the 1950s even as public attention to civil rights increased as the results of the protests, boycotts, and marches of less radical groups such as the Southern Christian Leadership Conference.

Civil rights became a public concern during the early 1960s. Violence in parts of the South heightened the passions of those on all sides of the debate. White segregationists saw their cause as moral and necessary to the southern way of life; pro-civil rights activists saw continued inequality as a national embarrassment at best and a sign of pure evil at worst. Meanwhile, African American activists were divided into those who strove for civil rights through nonviolent means—most famously led by Martin Luther King Jr.—and those who felt more extreme measures were justified and perhaps necessary.

Author Biography and Document Information

Born Malcolm Little in 1925, Malcolm X grew up mostly in Lansing, Michigan. His parents had been supporters of black nationalist leader Marcus Garvey, serving as organizers for the Omaha, Nebraska, chapter of the Universal Negro Improvement Association during the 1920s. Ku Klux Klan members harassed the family, and it was widely rumored that his father's death after being hit by a street car was an assassination. Malcolm X's childhood and teen years were turbulent ones, and in 1946, he was imprisoned for robbery.

While in prison Malcolm X read widely and converted to Islam. He became a member of the Nation of Islam and after his release from prison in 1952 emerged as one of its most influential leaders. A charismatic and powerful speaker, he was the leading voice supporting an alternative pathway to civil rights beyond the moderate, nonviolent approach advocated by Dr. Martin Luther King Jr. However, he split from the Nation of Islam in 1964 and the following year was assassinated by members of that organization.

Historical Document

"The Ballot or the Bullet"

Mr. Moderator, Brother Lomax, brothers and sisters, friends and enemies: I just can't believe everyone in here is a friend, and I don't want to leave anybody out. The question tonight, as I understand it, is "The Negro Revolt, and Where Do We Go From Here?" or What Next?" In my little humble way of understanding it, it points toward either the ballot or the bullet.

Before we try and explain what is meant by the ballot or the bullet, I would like to clarify something concerning myself. I'm still a Muslim; my religion is still Islam. That's my personal belief. Just as Adam Clayton Powell is a Christian minister who heads the Abyssinian Baptist Church in New York, but at the same time takes part in the political struggles to try and bring about rights to the black people in this country; and Dr. Martin Luther King is a Christian minister down in Atlanta, Georgia, who heads another organization fighting for the civil rights of black people in this country; and Reverend Galamison, I guess you've heard of him, is another Christian minister in New York who has been deeply involved in the school boycotts to eliminate segregated education; well, I myself am a minister, not a Christian minister, but a Muslim minister; and I believe in action on all fronts by whatever means necessary.

Although I'm still a Muslim, I'm not here tonight to discuss my religion. I'm not here to try and change your religion. I'm not here to argue or discuss anything that we differ about, because it's time for us to submerge our differences and realize that it is best for us to first see that we have the same problem, a common problem, a problem that will make you catch hell whether you're a Baptist, or a Methodist, or a Muslim, or a nationalist. Whether you're educated or illiterate, whether you live on the boulevard or in the alley, you're going to catch hell just like I am. We're all in the same boat and we all are going to catch the same hell from the same man. He just happens to be a white man. All of us have suffered here, in this country, political oppression at the hands of the white man, economic exploitation at the hands of the white man, and social degradation at the hands of the white man.

Now in speaking like this, it doesn't mean that we're anti-white, but it does mean we're anti-exploitation, we're anti-degradation, we're anti-oppression. And if the white man doesn't want us to be anti-him, let him stop oppressing and exploiting and degrading us. Whether we are Christians or Muslims or nationalists or agnostics or atheists, we must first learn to forget our differences. If we have differences, let us differ in the closet; when we come out in front, let us not have anything to argue about until we get finished arguing with the man. If the late President Kennedy could get together with Khrushchev and exchange some wheat, we certainly have more in common with each other than Kennedy and Khrushchev had with each other.

If we don't do something real soon, I think you'll have to agree that we're going to be forced either to use the ballot or the bullet. It's one or the other in 1964. It isn't that time is running out—time has run out!

1964 threatens to be the most explosive year America has ever witnessed. The most explosive year. Why? It's also a political year. It's the year when all of the white politicians will be back in the so-called Negro community jiving you and me for some votes. The year when all of the white political crooks will be right back in your and my community with their false promises, building up our hopes for a letdown, with their trickery and their treachery, with their false promises which they don't intend to keep. As they nourish these dissatisfactions, it can only lead to one thing, an explosion; and now we have the type of black man on the scene in America today—I'm sorry, Brother Lomax—who just doesn't intend to turn the other cheek any longer.

Don't let anybody tell you anything about the odds are against you. If they draft you, they send you to Korea and make you face 800 million Chinese. If you can be brave over there, you can be brave right here. These odds aren't as great as those odds. And if you fight here, you will at least know what you're fighting for.

I'm not a politician, not even a student of politics; in fact, I'm not a student of much of anything. I'm not a Democrat. I'm not a Republican, and I don't even consider myself an American. If you and I were Americans, there'd be no problem. Those Honkies that just got off the boat, they're already Americans; Polacks are already Americans; the Italian refugees are already Americans. Everything that came out of Europe, every blue-eyed thing, is already an American. And as long as you and I have been over here, we aren't Americans yet.

Well, I am one who doesn't believe in deluding myself. I'm not going to sit at your table and watch you eat, with nothing on my plate, and call myself a diner. Sitting at the table doesn't make you a diner, unless you eat some of what's on that plate. Being here in America doesn't make you an American. Being born here in America doesn't make you an American. Why, if birth made you American, you wouldn't need any legislation; you wouldn't need any amendments to the Constitution; you wouldn't be faced with civil-rights filibustering in Washington, D.C., right now. They don't have to pass civil-rights legislation to make a Polack an American.

No, I'm not an American. I'm one of the 22 million black people who are the victims of Americanism. One of the 22 million black people who are the victims of democracy, nothing but disguised hypocrisy. So, I'm not standing here speaking to you as an American, or a patriot, or a flag-saluter, or a flag-waver—no, not I. I'm speaking as a victim of this American system. And I see America through the eyes of the victim. I don't see any American dream; I see an American nightmare.

These 22 million victims are waking up. Their eyes are coming open. They're beginning to see what they used to only look at. They're becoming politically mature. They are realizing that there are new political trends from coast to coast. As they see these new political trends, it's possible for them to see that every time there's an election the races are so close that they have to have a recount. They had to recount in Massachusetts to see who was going to be governor, it was so close. It was the same way in Rhode Island, in Minnesota, and in many other parts of the country. And the same with Kennedy and Nixon when they ran for president. It was so close they had to count all over again. Well, what does this mean? It means that when white people are evenly divided, and black people have a bloc of votes of their own, it is left up to them to determine who's going to sit in the White House and who's going to be in the dog house.

It was the black man's vote that put the present administration in Washington, D.C. Your vote, your dumb vote, your ignorant vote, your wasted vote put in an administration in Washington, D.C., that has seen fit to pass every kind of legislation imaginable, saving you until last, then filibustering on top of that. And your and my leaders have the audacity to run around clapping their hands and talk about how much progress we're making. And what a good president we have. If he wasn't good in Texas, he sure can't be good in Washington, D.C. Because Texas is a lynch state. It is in the same breath as Mississippi, no different; only they lynch you in Texas with a Texas accent and lynch you in Mississippi with a Mississippi accent. And these Negro leaders have the audacity to go and have some coffee in the White House with a Texan, a Southern cracker—that's all he is—and then come out and tell you and me that he's going to be better for us because, since he's from the South, he knows how to deal with the Southerners. What kind of logic is that? Let Eastland be president, he's from the South too. He should be better able to deal with them than Johnson.

In this present administration they have in the House of Representatives 257 Democrats to only 177 Republicans. They control two-thirds of the House vote. Why can't they pass something that will help you and me? In the Senate, there are 67 senators who are of the Democratic Party. Only 33 of them are Republicans. Why, the Democrats have got the government sewed up, and you're the one who sewed it up for them. And what have they given you for it? Four years in office, and just now getting around to some civil-rights legislation. Just now, after everything else is gone, out of the way, they're going to sit down now and play with you all summer long—the same old giant con game that they call filibuster. All those are in cahoots together. Don't you ever think they're not in cahoots together, for the man that is heading the civil-rights filibuster is a man from Georgia named Richard Russell. When Johnson became president, the first man he asked for when he got back to Washington, D.C., was "Dicky"—that's how tight they are. That's his boy, that's his pal, that's his buddy. But they're playing that old con game. One of them makes believe he's for you, and he's got it fixed where the other one is so tight against you, he never has to keep his promise.

So it's time in 1964 to wake up. And when you see them coming up with that kind of conspiracy, let them know your eyes are open. And let them know you—something else that's wide open too. It's got to be the ballot or the bullet. The ballot or the bullet. If you're afraid to use an expression like that, you should get on out of the country; you should get back in the cotton patch; you should get back in the alley. They get all the Negro vote, and after they get it, the Negro gets nothing in return. All they did when they got to Washington was give a few big Negroes big jobs. Those big Negroes didn't need big jobs, they already had jobs. That's camouflage, that's trickery, that's treachery, window-dressing. I'm not trying to knock out the Democrats for the Republicans. We'll get to them in a minute. But it is true; you put the Democrats first and the Democrats put you last.

Look at it the way it is. What alibis do they use, since they control Congress and the Senate? What alibi do they use when you and I ask, "Well, when are you going to keep your promise?" They blame the Dixiecrats. What is a Dixiecrat? A Democrat. A Dixiecrat is nothing but a Democrat in disguise. The titular head of the Democrats is also the head of the Dixiecrats, because the Dixiecrats are a part of the Democratic Party. The Democrats have never kicked the Dixiecrats out of the party. The Dixiecrats bolted themselves once, but the Democrats didn't put them out. Imagine, these lowdown Southern segregationists put the Northern Democrats down. But the Northern Democrats have never put the Dixiecrats down. No, look at that thing the way it is. They have got a con game going on, a political con game, and you and I are in the middle. It's time for you and me to wake up and start looking at it like it is, and trying to understand it like it is; and then we can deal with it like it is.

The Dixiecrats in Washington, D.C., control the key committees that run the government. The only reason the Dixiecrats control these committees is because they have seniority. The only reason they have seniority is because they come from states where Negroes can't vote. This is not even a government that's based on democracy. It. is not a government that is made up of representatives of the people. Half of the people in the South can't even vote. Eastland is not even supposed to be in Washington. Half of the senators and congressmen who occupy these key positions in Washington, D.C., are there illegally, are there unconstitutionally.

I was in Washington, D.C., a week ago Thursday, when they were debating whether or not they should let the bill come onto the floor. And in the back of the room where the Senate meets, there's a huge map of the United States, and on that map it shows the location of Negroes throughout the country. And it shows that the Southern section of the country, the states that are most heavily concentrated with Negroes, are the ones that have senators and congressmen standing up filibustering and doing all other kinds of trickery to keep the Negro from being able to vote. This is pitiful. But it's not pitiful for us any longer; it's actually pitiful for the white man, because soon now, as the Negro awakens a little more and sees the vise that he's in, sees the bag that he's in, sees the real game that he's in, then the Negro's going to develop a new tactic.

These senators and congressmen actually violate the constitutional amendments that guarantee the people of that particular state or county the right to vote. And the Constitution itself has within it the machinery to expel any representative from a state where the voting rights of the people are violated. You don't even need new legislation. Any person in Congress right now, who is there from a state or a district where the voting rights of the people are violated, that particular person should be expelled from Congress. And when you expel him, you've removed one of the obstacles in the path of any real meaningful legislation in this country. In fact, when you expel them, you don't need new legislation, because they will be replaced by black representatives from counties and districts where the black man is in the majority, not in the minority.

If the black man in these Southern states had his full voting rights, the key Dixiecrats in Washington, D. C., which means the key Democrats in Washington, D.C., would lose their seats. The Democratic Party itself would lose its power. It would cease to be powerful as a party. When you see the amount of power that would be lost by the Democratic Party if it were to lose the Dixiecrat wing, or branch, or element, you can see where it's against the interests of the Democrats to give voting rights to Negroes in states where the Democrats have been in complete power and authority ever since the Civil War. You just can't belong to that Party without analyzing it.

I say again, I'm not anti-Democrat, I'm not anti-Republican, I'm not anti-anything. I'm just questioning their sincerity, and some of the strategy that they've been using on our people by promising them promises that they don't intend to keep. When you keep the Democrats in power, you're keeping the Dixiecrats in power. I doubt that my good Brother Lomax will deny that. A vote for a Democrat is a vote for a Dixiecrat. That's why, in 1964, it's time now for you and me to become more politically mature and realize what the ballot is for; what we're supposed to get when we cast a ballot; and that if we don't cast a ballot, it's going to end up in a situation where we're going to have to cast a bullet. It's either a ballot or a bullet.

In the North, they do it a different way. They have a system that's known as gerrymandering, whatever that means. It means when Negroes become too heavily concentrated in a certain area, and begin to gain too much political power, the white man comes along and changes the district lines. You may say, "Why do you keep saying white man?" Because it's the white man who does it. I haven't ever seen any Negro changing any lines. They don't let him get near the line. It's the white man who does this. And usually, it's the white man who grins at you the most, and pats you on the back, and is supposed to be your friend. He may be friendly, but he's not your friend.

So, what I'm trying to impress upon you, in essence, is this: You and I in America are faced not with a segregationist conspiracy, we're faced with a government conspiracy. Everyone who's filibustering is a senator—that's the government. Everyone who's finagling in Washington, D.C., is a congressman—that's the government. You don't have anybody putting blocks in your path but people who are a part of the government. The same government that you go abroad to fight for and die for is the government that is in a conspiracy to deprive you of your voting rights, deprive you of your economic opportunities, deprive you of decent housing, deprive you of decent education. You don't need to go to the employer alone, it is the government itself, the government of America, that is responsible for the oppression and exploitation and degradation of black people in this country. And you should drop it in their lap. This government has failed the Negro. This so-called democracy has failed the Negro. And all these white liberals have definitely failed the Negro.

So, where do we go from here? First, we need some friends. We need some new allies. The entire civil-rights struggle needs a new interpretation, a broader interpretation. We need to look at this civil-rights thing from another angle—from the inside as well as from the outside. To those of us whose philosophy is black nationalism, the only way you can get involved in the civil-rights struggle is give it a new interpretation. That old interpretation excluded us. It kept us out. So, we're giving a new interpretation to the civil-rights struggle, an interpretation that will enable us to come into it, take part in it. And these handkerchief-heads who have been dilly-dallying and pussy footing and compromising—we don't intend to let them pussyfoot and dillydally and compromise any longer.

How can you thank a man for giving you what's already yours? How then can you thank him for giving you only part of what's already yours? You haven't even made progress, if what's being given to you, you should have had already. That's not progress. And I love my Brother Lomax, the way he pointed out we're right back where we were in 1954. We're not even as far up as we were in 1954. We're behind where we were in 1954. There's more segregation now than there was in 1954. There's more racial animosity, more racial hatred, more racial violence today in 1964, than there was in 1954. Where is the progress?

And now you're facing a situation where the young Negro's coming up. They don't want to hear that "turn the-other-cheek" stuff, no. In Jacksonville, those were teenagers, they were throwing Molotov cocktails. Negroes have never done that before. But it shows you there's a new deal coming in. There's new thinking coming in. There's new strategy coming in. It'll be Molotov cocktails this month, hand grenades next month, and something else next month. It'll be ballots, or it'll be bullets. It'll be liberty, or it will be death. The only difference about this kind of death—it'll be reciprocal. You know what is meant by "reciprocal?" That's one of Brother Lomax's words. I stole it from him. I don't usually deal with those big words because I don't usually deal with big people. I deal with small people. I find you can get a whole lot of small people and whip hell out of a whole lot of big people. They haven't got anything to lose, and they've got every thing to gain. And they'll let you know in a minute: "It takes two to tango; when I go, you go."

The black nationalists, those whose philosophy is black nationalism, in bringing about this new interpretation of the entire meaning of civil rights, look upon it as meaning, as Brother Lomax has pointed out, equality of opportunity. Well, we're justified in seeking civil rights, if it means equality of opportunity, because all we're doing there is trying to collect for our investment. Our mothers and fathers invested sweat and blood. Three hundred and ten years we worked in this country without a dime in return—I mean without a dime in return. You let the white man walk around here talking about how rich this country is, but you never stop to think how it got rich so quick. It got rich because you made it rich.

You take the people who are in this audience right now. They're poor. We're all poor as individuals. Our weekly salary individually amounts to hardly anything. But if you take the salary of everyone in here collectively, it'll fill up a whole lot of baskets. It's a lot of wealth. If you can collect the wages of just these people right here for a year, you'll be rich—richer than rich. When you look at it like that, think how rich Uncle Sam had to become, not with this handful, but millions of black people. Your and my mother and father, who didn't work an eight-hour shift, but worked from "can't see" in the morning until "can't see" at night, and worked for nothing, making the white man rich, making Uncle Sam rich. This is our investment. This is our contribution, our blood.

Not only did we give of our free labor, we gave of our blood. Every time he had a call to arms, we were the first ones in uniform. We died on every battlefield the white man had. We have made a greater sacrifice than anybody who's standing up in America today. We have made a greater contribution and have collected less. Civil rights, for those of us whose philosophy is black nationalism, means: "Give it to us now. Don't wait for next year. Give it to us yesterday, and that's not fast enough."

I might stop right here to point out one thing. Whenever you're going after something that belongs to you, anyone who's depriving you of the right to have it is a criminal. Understand that. Whenever you are going after something that is yours, you are within your legal rights to lay claim to it. And anyone who puts forth any effort to deprive you of that which is yours, is breaking the law, is a criminal. And this was pointed out by the Supreme Court decision. It outlawed segregation.

Which means segregation is against the law. Which means a segregationist is breaking the law. A segregationist is a criminal. You can't label him as anything other than that. And when you demonstrate against segregation, the law is on your side. The Supreme Court is on your side.

Now, who is it that opposes you in carrying out the law? The police department itself. With police dogs and clubs. Whenever you demonstrate against segregation, whether it is segregated education, segregated housing, or anything else, the law is on your side, and anyone who stands in the way is not the law any longer. They are breaking the law; they are not representatives of the law. Any time you demonstrate against segregation and a man has the audacity to put a police dog on you, kill that dog, kill him, I'm telling you, kill that dog. I say it if they put me in jail tomorrow, kill that dog. Then you'll put a stop to it. Now, if these white people in here don't want to see that kind of action, get down and tell the mayor to tell the police department to pull the dogs in. That's all you have to do. If you don't do it, someone else will.

If you don't take this kind of stand, your little children will grow up and look at you and think "shame." If you don't take an uncompromising stand, I don't mean go out and get violent; but at the same time you should never be nonviolent unless you run into some nonviolence. I'm nonviolent with those who are nonviolent with me. But when you drop that violence on me, then you've made me go insane, and I'm not responsible for what I do. And that's the way every Negro should get. Any time you know you're within the law, within your legal rights, within your moral rights, in accord with justice, then die for what you believe in. But don't die alone. Let your dying be reciprocal. This is what is meant by equality. What's good for the goose is good for the gander.

When we begin to get in this area, we need new friends, we need new allies. We need to expand the civil-rights struggle to a higher level—to the level of human rights. Whenever you are in a civil-rights struggle, whether you know it or not, you are confining yourself to the jurisdiction of Uncle Sam. No one from the outside world can speak out in your behalf as long as your struggle is a civil-rights struggle. Civil rights comes within the domestic affairs of this country. All of our African brothers and our Asian brothers and our Latin-American brothers cannot open their mouths and interfere in the domestic affairs of the United States. And as long as it's civil rights, this comes under the jurisdiction of Uncle Sam.

But the United Nations has what's known as the charter of human rights; it has a committee that deals in human rights. You may wonder why all of the atrocities that have been committed in Africa and in Hungary and in Asia, and in Latin America are brought before the UN, and the Negro problem is never brought before the UN. This is part of the conspiracy. This old, tricky blue-eyed liberal who is supposed to be your and my friend, supposed to be in our corner, supposed to be subsidizing our struggle, and supposed to be acting in the capacity of an adviser, never tells you anything about human rights. They keep you wrapped up in civil rights. And you spend so much time barking up the civil-rights tree, you don't even know there's a human-rights tree on the same floor.

When you expand the civil-rights struggle to the level of human rights, you can then take the case of the black man in this country before the nations in the UN. You can take it before the General Assembly. You can take Uncle Sam before a world court. But the only level you can do it on is the level of human rights. Civil rights keeps you under his restrictions, under his jurisdiction. Civil rights keeps you in his pocket. Civil rights means you're asking Uncle Sam to treat you right. Human rights are something you were born with. Human rights are your God-given rights. Human rights are the rights that are recognized by all nations of this earth. And any time any one violates your human rights, you can take them to the world court.

Uncle Sam's hands are dripping with blood, dripping with the blood of the black man in this country. He's the earth's number-one hypocrite. He has the audacity—yes, he has—imagine him posing as the leader of the free world. The free world! And you over here singing "We Shall Overcome." Expand the civil-rights struggle to the level of human rights. Take it into the United Nations, where our African brothers can throw their weight on our side, where our Asian brothers can throw their weight on our side, where our Latin-American brothers can throw their weight on our side, and where 800 million Chinamen are sitting there waiting to throw their weight on our side.

Let the world know how bloody his hands are. Let the world know the hypocrisy that's practiced over here. Let it be the ballot or the bullet. Let him know that it must be the ballot or the bullet.

When you take your case to Washington, D.C., you're taking it to the criminal who's responsible; it's like running from the wolf to the fox. They're all in cahoots together. They all work political chicanery and make you look like a chump before the eyes of the world. Here you are walking around in America, getting ready to be drafted and sent abroad, like a tin soldier, and when you get over there, people ask you what are you fighting for, and you have to stick your tongue in your cheek. No, take Uncle Sam to court, take him before the world.

By ballot I only mean freedom. Don't you know—I disagree with Lomax on this issue—that the ballot is more important than the dollar? Can I prove it? Yes. Look in the UN. There are poor nations in the UN; yet those poor nations can get together with their voting power and keep the rich nations from making a move. They have one nation—one vote, everyone has an equal vote. And when those brothers from Asia, and Africa and the darker parts of this earth get together, their voting power is sufficient to hold Sam in check. Or Russia in check. Or some other section of the earth in check. So, the ballot is most important.

Right now, in this country, if you and I, 22 million African-Americans—that's what we are—Africans who are in America. You're nothing but Africans. Nothing but Africans. In fact, you'd get farther calling yourself African instead of Negro. Africans don't catch hell. You're the only one catching hell. They don't have to pass civil-rights bills for Africans. An African can go anywhere he wants right now. All you've got to do is tie your head up. That's right, go anywhere you want. Just stop being a Negro. Change your name to Hoogagagooba. That'll show you how silly the white man is. You're dealing with a silly man. A friend of mine who's very dark put a turban on his head and went into a restaurant in Atlanta before they called themselves desegregated. He went into a white restaurant, he sat down, they served him, and he said, "What would happen if a Negro came in here? And there he's sitting, black as night, but because he had his head wrapped up the waitress looked back at him and says, "Why, there wouldn't no nigger dare come in here."

So, you're dealing with a man whose bias and prejudice are making him lose his mind, his intelligence, every day. He's frightened. He looks around and sees what's taking place on this earth, and he sees that the pendulum of time is swinging in your direction. The dark people are waking up. They're losing their fear of the white man. No place where he's fighting right now is he winning. Everywhere he's fighting, he's fighting someone your and my complexion. And they're beating him. He can't win any more. He's won his last battle. He failed to win the Korean War. He couldn't win it. He had to sign a truce. That's a loss.

Any time Uncle Sam, with all his machinery for warfare, is held to a draw by some rice eaters, he's lost the battle. He had to sign a truce. America's not supposed to sign a truce. She's supposed to be bad. But she's not bad any more. She's bad as long as she can use her hydrogen bomb, but she can't use hers for fear Russia might use hers. Russia can't use hers, for fear that Sam might use his. So, both of them are weapon-less. They can't use the weapon because each's weapon nullifies the other's. So the only place where action can take place is on the ground. And the white man can't win another war fighting on the ground. Those days are over. The black man knows it, the brown man knows it, the red man knows it, and the yellow man knows it. So they engage him in guerrilla warfare. That's not his style. You've got to have heart to be a guerrilla warrior, and he hasn't got any heart. I'm telling you now.

I just want to give you a little briefing on guerrilla warfare because, before you know it, before you know it. It takes heart to be a guerrilla warrior because you're on your own. In conventional warfare you have tanks and a whole lot of other people with you to back you up—planes over your head and all that kind of stuff. But a guerrilla is on his own. All you have is a rifle, some sneakers and a bowl of rice, and that's all you need—and a lot of heart. The Japanese on some of those islands in the Pacific, when the American soldiers landed, one Japanese sometimes could hold the whole army off. He'd just wait until the sun went down, and when the sun went down they were all equal. He would take his little blade and slip from bush to bush, and from American to American. The white soldiers couldn't cope with that. Whenever you see a white soldier that fought in the Pacific, he has the shakes, he has a nervous condition, because they scared him to death.

The same thing happened to the French up in French Indochina. People who just a few years previously were rice farmers got together and ran the heavily-mechanized French army out of Indochina. You don't need it—modern warfare today won't work. This is the day of the guerrilla. They did the same thing in Algeria. Algerians, who were nothing but Bedouins, took a rine and sneaked off to the hills, and de Gaulle and all of his highfalutin' war machinery couldn't defeat those guerrillas. Nowhere on this earth does the white man win in a guerrilla warfare. It's not his speed. Just as guerrilla warfare is prevailing in Asia and in parts of Africa and in parts of Latin America, you've got to be mighty naive, or you've got to play the black man cheap, if you don't think some day he's going to wake up and find that it's got to be the ballot or the bullet.

I would like to say, in closing, a few things concerning the Muslim Mosque, Inc., which we established recently in New York City. It's true we're Muslims and our religion is Islam, but we don't mix our religion with our politics and our economics and our social and civil activities—not any more. We keep our religion in our mosque. After our religious services are over, then as Muslims we become involved in political action, economic action and social and civic action. We become involved with anybody, any where, any time and in any manner that's designed to eliminate the evils, the political, economic and social evils that are afflicting the people of our community.

The political philosophy of black nationalism means that the black man should control the politics and the politicians in his own community; no more. The black man in the black community has to be re-educated into the science of politics so he will know what politics is supposed to bring him in return. Don't be throwing out any ballots. A ballot is like a bullet. You don't throw your ballots until you see a target, and if that target is not within your reach, keep your ballot in your pocket.

The political philosophy of black nationalism is being taught in the Christian church. It's being taught in the NAACP. It's being taught in CORE meetings. It's being taught in SNCC Student Nonviolent Coordinating Committee meetings. It's being taught in Muslim meetings. It's being taught where nothing but atheists and agnostics come together. It's being taught everywhere. Black people are fed up with the dillydallying, pussyfooting, compromising approach that we've been using toward getting our freedom. We want freedom now, but we're not going to get it saying "We Shall Overcome." We've got to fight until we overcome.

The economic philosophy of black nationalism is pure and simple. It only means that we should control the economy of our community. Why should white people be running all the stores in our community? Why should white people be running the banks of our community? Why should the economy of our community be in the hands of the white man? Why? If a black man can't move his store into a white community, you tell me why a white man should move his store into a black community. The philosophy of black nationalism involves a re-education program in the black community in regards to economics. Our people have to be made to see that any time you take your dollar out of your community and spend it in a community where you don't live, the community where you live will get poorer and poorer, and the community where you spend your money will get richer and richer.

Then you wonder why where you live is always a ghetto or a slum area. And where you and I are concerned, not only do we lose it when we spend it out of the community, but the white man has got all our stores in the community tied up; so that though we spend it in the community, at sundown the man who runs the store takes it over across town somewhere. He's got us in a vise.

So the economic philosophy of black nationalism means in every church, in every civic organization, in every fraternal order, it's time now for our people to become conscious of the importance of controlling the economy of our community. If we own the stores, if we operate the businesses, if we try and establish some industry in our own community, then we're developing to the position where we are creating employment for our own kind. Once you gain control of the economy of your own community, then you don't have to picket and boycott and beg some cracker downtown for a job in his business.

The social philosophy of black nationalism only means that we have to get together and remove the evils, the vices, alcoholism, drug addiction, and other evils that are destroying the moral fiber of our community. We our selves have to lift the level of our community, the standard of our community to a higher level, make our own society beautiful so that we will be satisfied in our own social circles and won't be running around here trying to knock our way into a social circle where we're not wanted. So I say, in spreading a gospel such as black nationalism, it is not designed to make the black man re-evaluate the white man—you know him already—but to make the black man re-evaluate himself. Don't change the white man's mind—you can't change his mind, and that whole thing about appealing to the moral conscience of America—America's conscience is bankrupt. She lost all conscience a long time ago. Uncle Sam has no conscience.

They don't know what morals are. They don't try and eliminate an evil because it's evil, or because it's illegal, or because it's immoral; they eliminate it only when it threatens their existence. So you're wasting your time appealing to the moral conscience of a bankrupt man like Uncle Sam. If he had a conscience, he'd straighten this thing out with no more pressure being put upon him. So it is not necessary to change the white man's mind. We have to change our own mind. You can't change his mind about us. We've got to change our own minds about each other. We have to see each other with new eyes. We have to see each other as brothers and sisters. We have to come together with warmth so we can develop unity and harmony that's necessary to get this problem solved ourselves. How can we do this? How can we avoid jealousy? How can we avoid the suspicion and the divisions that exist in the community? I'll tell you how.

I have watched how Billy Graham comes into a city, spreading what he calls the gospel of Christ, which is only white nationalism. That's what he is. Billy Graham is a white nationalist; I'm a black nationalist. But since it's the natural tendency for leaders to be jealous and look upon a powerful figure like Graham with suspicion and envy, how is it possible for him to come into a city and get all the cooperation of the church leaders? Don't think because they're church leaders that they don't have weaknesses that make them envious and jealous—no, everybody's got it. It's not an accident that when they want to choose a cardinal, as Pope I over there in Rome, they get in a closet so you can't hear them cussing and fighting and carrying on.

Billy Graham comes in preaching the gospel of Christ. He evangelizes the gospel. He stirs everybody up, but he never tries to start a church. If he came in trying to start a church, all the churches would be against him. So, he just comes in talking about Christ and tells everybody who gets Christ to go to any church where Christ is; and in this way the church cooperates with him. So we're going to take a page from his book.

Our gospel is black nationalism. We're not trying to threaten the existence of any organization, but we're spreading the gospel of black nationalism. Anywhere there's a church that is also preaching and practicing the gospel of black nationalism, join that church. If the NAACP is preaching and practicing the gospel of black nationalism, join the NAACP. If CORE is spreading and practicing the gospel of black nationalism, join CORE. Join any organization that has a gospel that's for the uplift of the black man. And when you get into it and see them pussyfooting or compromising, pull out of it because that's not black nationalism. We'll find another one.

And in this manner, the organizations will increase in number and in quantity and in quality, and by August, it is then our intention to have a black nationalist convention which will consist of delegates from all over the country who are interested in the political, economic and social philosophy of black nationalism. After these delegates convene, we will hold a seminar; we will hold discussions; we will listen to everyone. We want to hear new ideas and new solutions and new answers. And at that time, if we see fit then to form a black nationalist party, we'll form a black nationalist party. If it's necessary to form a black nationalist army, we'll form a black nationalist army. It'll be the ballot or the bullet. It'll be liberty or it'll be death.

It's time for you and me to stop sitting in this country, letting some cracker senators, Northern crackers and Southern crackers, sit there in Washington, D.C., and come to a conclusion in their mind that you and I are supposed to have civil rights. There's no white man going to tell me anything about my rights. Brothers and sisters, always remember, if it doesn't take senators and congressmen and presidential proclamations to give freedom to the white man, it is not necessary for legislation or proclamation or Supreme Court decisions to give freedom to the black man. You let that white man know, if this is a country of freedom, let it be a country of freedom; and if it's not a country of freedom, change it.

We will work with anybody, anywhere, at any time, who is genuinely interested in tackling the problem head-on, nonviolently as long as the enemy is nonviolent, but violent when the enemy gets violent. We'll work with you on the voter-registration drive, we'll work with you on rent strikes, we'll work with you on school boycotts. I don't believe in any kind of integration. I'm not even worried about it, because I know you're not going to get it anyway; you're not going to get it because you're afraid to die. You've got to be ready to die if you try and force yourself on the white man, because he'll get just as violent as those crackers in Mississippi, right here in Cleveland. But we will still work with you on the school boycotts because we're against a segregated school system. A segregated school system produces children who, when they graduate, graduate with crippled minds. But this does not mean that a school is segregated because it's all black. A segregated school means a school that is controlled by people who have no real interest in it whatsoever.

Let me explain what I mean. A segregated district or community is a community in which people live, but outsiders control the politics and the economy of that community. They never refer to the white section as a segregated community. It's the all-Negro section that's a segregated community. Why? The white man controls his own school, his own bank, his own economy, his own politics, his own everything, his own community; but he also controls yours. When you're under someone else's control, you're segregated. They'll always give you the lowest or the worst that there is to offer, but it doesn't mean you're segregated just because you have your own. You've got to control your own. Just like the white man has control of his, you need to control yours.

You know the best way to get rid of segregation? The white man is more afraid of separation than he is of integration. Segregation means that he puts you away from him, but not far enough for you to be out of his jurisdiction; separation means you're gone. And the white man will integrate faster than he'll let you separate. So we will work with you against the segregated school system because it's criminal, because it is absolutely destructive, in every way imaginable, to the minds of the children who have to be exposed to that type of crippling education.

Last but not least, I must say this concerning the great controversy over rifles and shotguns. The only thing that I've ever said is that in areas where the government has proven itself either unwilling or unable to defend the lives and the property of Negroes, it's time for Negroes to defend themselves. Article number two of the constitutional amendments provides you and me the right to own a rifle or a shotgun. It is constitutionally legal to own a shotgun or a rifle. This doesn't mean you're going to get a rifle and form battalions and go out looking for white folks, although you'd be within your rights—I mean, you'd be justified; but that would be illegal and we don't do anything illegal. If the white man doesn't want the black man buying rifles and shotguns, then let the government do its job.

That's all. And don't let the white man come to you and ask you what you think about what Malcolm says—why, you old Uncle Tom. He would never ask you if he thought you were going to say, "Amen!" No, he is making a Tom out of you." So, this doesn't mean forming rifle clubs and going out looking for people, but it is time, in 1964, if you are a man, to let that man know.

If he's not going to do his job in running the government and providing you and me with the protection that our taxes are supposed to be for, since he spends all those billions for his defense budget, he certainly can't begrudge you and me spending $12 or $15 for a single-shot, or double-action. I hope you understand. Don't go out shooting people, but any time—brothers and sisters, and especially the men in this audience; some of you wearing Congressional Medals of Honor, with shoulders this wide, chests this big, muscles that big—any time you and I sit around and read where they bomb a church and murder in cold blood, not some grownups, but four little girls while they were praying to the same God the white man taught them to pray to, and you and I see the government go down and can't find who did it.

Why, this man—he can find Eichmann hiding down in Argentina somewhere. Let two or three American soldiers, who are minding somebody else's business way over in South Vietnam, get killed, and he'll send battleships, sticking his nose in their business. He wanted to send troops down to Cuba and make them have what he calls free elections—this old cracker who doesn't have free elections in his own country.

No, if you never see me another time in your life, if I die in the morning, I'll die saying one thing: the ballot or the bullet, the ballot or the bullet.

If a Negro in 1964 has to sit around and wait for some cracker senator to filibuster when it comes to the rights of black people, why, you and I should hang our heads in shame. You talk about a march on Washington in 1963, you haven't seen anything. There's some more going down in '64.

And this time they're not going like they went last year. They're not going singing "We Shall Overcome." They're not going with white friends. They're not going with placards already painted for them. They're not going with round-trip tickets. They're going with one way tickets. And if they don't want that non-nonviolent army going down there, tell them to bring the filibuster to a halt.

The black nationalists aren't going to wait. Lyndon B. Johnson is the head of the Democratic Party. If he's for civil rights, let him go into the Senate next week and declare himself. Let him go in there right now and declare himself. Let him go in there and denounce the Southern branch of his party. Let him go in there right now and take a moral stand—right now, not later. Tell him don't wait until election time. If he waits too long, brothers and sisters, he will be responsible for letting a condition develop in this country which will create a climate that will bring seeds up out of the ground with vegetation on the end of them looking like something these people never dreamed of. In 1964, it's the ballot or the bullet.

Thank you.

Document Analysis

Given just a few weeks after Malcolm X's public split with the Nation of Islam, the "Ballot or the Bullet" shows the activist's evolving perspective on civil rights efforts and his continued vision of a powerful but separate African American society. Thus, his speech cuts across numerous related topics: his own personal identity as a black man and a Muslim; advocacy of a shared Black Nationalist movement; and the pivotal choice in U.S. society to either accept African American civil and human rights or face the consequences. "It'll be ballots, or it'll be bullets. It'll be liberty, or it will be death," he declares.

Malcolm X warns that historical revolutions have been bloody and asserts that white Americans must realize that black Americans will no longer tolerate being denied true equality. He suggests that nonviolence has been ineffective, and that the immediate and legitimate expansion and application of true political rights—the ballot—provides the only alternative to unleashing a violent uprising of the oppressed—the bullet. He recommends that African Americans own weapons, not to seek out violence but to defend themselves as necessary in the face of racial attacks such as lynching and the bombing of black churches. He claims that the U.S. government has failed African Americans—lambasting American military involvement in Korea and Vietnam while blacks are killed at home, for example—and calls for white leaders such as President Lyndon B. Johnson to finally declare firm support for civil rights or face social upheaval or even guerrilla warfare.

Regardless of the approach, however, Malcolm X argues that Black Nationalism is a movement that transcends other divisions within the African American community, promoting the health and security of black people as a whole. Ultimately, he suggests, Black Nationalism is the key to achieving civil rights and human rights in the United States. It is the necessary reaction to the white nationalism that has permitted institutionalized economic, legal, and social discrimination against African Americans for centuries.

The speech is notable for its wordplay, as when Malcolm X develops an extended metaphor discussing the use of police dogs against protestors in which he urges listeners to "kill that dog." It is implied that the "dog" is both the animal and the human controlling its actions. Nor does Malcolm X refrain from using racially charged language in his condemnation of oppressors. He refers to whites with the derogatory terms "honkies" and "crackers" and skewers white perception of the "so-called Negro community." These language choices emphasize the differences between Malcolm X's Black Nationalist movement, which sought to shore up African American pride and assert the power of black society, and King's nonviolent civil rights movement, which encouraged the integration of African Americans into mainstream white-dominated society. They also reflect a frustration with the racism endemic in U.S. society.

Essential Themes

Malcolm X's assessment of 1964 as a critical year for the civil rights cause was an accurate one. The Civil Rights Act of 1964, passed and signed into law by President Johnson months after the speech, put the weight of the federal government behind civil rights action. So did the following year's Voting Rights Act, which expanded African American access to the ballot and paved the way for increased representation of black communities. However, while these laws perhaps helped prevent the mass revolt Malcolm X warned of, the social tension he discussed did not simply evaporate. Racism remained a roadblock to African Americans and other minorities despite government efforts, and controversies such as the Vietnam War continued to divide the country.

Malcom X's assassination in 1965 was further proof of the ongoing conflict between not only races but also different sects of the civil rights movement. His philosophy had continued to evolve; soon after the "Ballot or the Bullet" speech he completed the Hajj pilgrimage to Mecca. The experience convinced him to move away from his earlier separatist message. While he still supported Black Nationalism and self defense, his more cooperative stance put him at ever further odds with the Nation of Islam, leading to his murder.

Though Malcolm X did not live to see the later stages of the civil rights movement, his ideas helped inspire the Black Power movement throughout the 1960s and 1970s. The Black Panther Party for Self-Defense, a militant civil rights organization that began in California in 1966, drew heavily on Malcolm's ideology. The Black Panthers included members who visibly armed themselves to protect communities against police brutality and other forms of white oppression. At the same time, the movement spearheaded community support initiatives such as a free breakfast program for school children. Just as Malcolm X's openness to use any means necessary to achieve African American rights terrified some white Americans, the Panthers' overt militancy generated great controversy.

Echoes of Black Nationalism as promoted by Malcolm X reached into the first decades of the twenty-first century. While less separatist than the nationalist ideology of the 1960s, the Black Lives Matter movement called on African Americans to unite and support one another in the face of violence and discrimination. The movement also asserted the need of African Americans to attain basic human rights, with or without government support.

—*Vanessa E. Vaughn, MA*

Bibliography and Additional Reading

Malcolm X, and Alex Haley. *The Autobiography of Malcolm X*. 1965. New York: Ballantine, 2015.

Perry, Theresa, ed. *Teaching Malcolm X*. New York: Routledge, 1996.

Pinkney, Alphonso. *Red, Black, and Green: Black Nationalism in the United States*. New York: Cambridge UP, 1976.

Terrill, Robert E., ed. *The Cambridge Companion to Malcolm X*. New York: Cambridge UP, 2010.

Twenty-Fourth Amendment to the U.S. Constitution

Date: January 23, 1964
Author: Eighty-Seventh U.S. Congress
Genre: constitutional amendment

Summary Overview

Poll taxes, or taxes on individuals living within a town or district, were one of the means Southern whites employed to circumvent the Fifteenth Amendment and disenfranchise large numbers of African Americans in the years after Reconstruction. The taxes were typically required to be paid up prior to voting. In 1962, at the height of the African American civil rights movement, the U.S. Congress passed a constitutional amendment banning the use of poll taxes in federal elections. Two years later, on January 23, 1964, South Dakota became the thirty-eighth state to ratify the amendment, making it part of the United States Constitution. It required a ruling by the Supreme Court in 1966 to outlaw the use of poll taxes in state elections.

Defining Moment

The poll tax—also known as the "head tax"—went back to colonial times in America and was regarded primarily as a source of revenue. In the early Republic, the poll tax, along with property taxes in some states, was also a means to limit the franchise to the economically better-off. Over time, however, many states eliminated the poll tax and all other voter qualifications for white men, a process accelerated during the era of Jacksonian democracy.

Nevertheless, the poll tax persisted in a few states such as Pennsylvania even after the Civil War. It was the aftermath of the Civil War and the gains made by African Americans during Reconstruction, especially the Fifteenth Amendment that barred making race a disqualification for voting, that led to the revival of the poll tax in the eleven former states of the Confederacy. During Reconstruction, after 1867 voting by black men was high in the South, and numerous African Americans were elected to state and federal offices. Black gains during Reconstruction, especially the franchise, led to extensive white terrorism in the South against African Americans and their white allies. President Ulysses S. Grant redeployed federal troops to the South in the early 1870s to protect black voters and crush the Ku Klux Klan and other terrorist organizations.

After 1876, however, white northerners lost interest in the South and became increasingly racist themselves; and with the removal of federal protections, white southerners moved to impose a system of racial segregation known as "Jim Crow" and to disenfranchise African Americans. Beyond terrorism, white southerners crafted several legal means to get around the Fifteenth Amendment. The Constitution left voting qualifications and the conduct of elections to the states, and other than the limitations placed on states by the Fifteenth Amendment (and later the Nineteenth Amendment), states were free to set their own rules. Thus, after Reconstruction southern states created new requirements like the "literacy test" in which voters were required to answer specific questions—for example, interpreting clauses from the state constitution. White election officials could then evaluate white voters leniently and black voters stringently and thereby reduce the number of black voters.

In the 1890s Mississippi was the first southern state to implement the poll tax, which was upheld by the U.S. Supreme Court in *Williams v. Mississippi*, (1898). The rest of the former states of the Confederacy followed suit.

Poll taxes were typically not exorbitantly high; however, because most African Americans were sharecroppers or low-wage laborers, few could afford even a modest poll tax. Furthermore, many southern states required the poll tax to be paid months before an election, making it easier for the targeted voters to overlook paying the tax on time. The poll tax also purged many poor white voters. Some southern states found that amenable, especially after the Populist farmer insurgency of the 1890s. But others, beginning with Louisiana, found a way to mitigate the poll tax's impact on low-income white male voters, namely, the "Grandfather Clause," in which any voter who could vote before January 1867, or whose lineal descendants could vote by that date, would be exempt from the poll tax. Since African American voters only began voting with the Military Reconstruction Acts of that year, the Grandfather Clause loophole consequently only exempted white voters from the poll tax. (The Supreme Court ruled the Grandfather Clause unconstitutional in 1915.) After the Nineteenth Amendment enfranchised women in 1920, the poll tax had the further effect of keeping many women of all races off the voting rolls, as many families only had money to pay for one poll tax. In some states like Alabama the poll tax was even more pernicious, because voters were required to pay "back poll taxes" to vote. This meant that if, say, a forty-one-year-old voter sought to register for the first time, he/she would be required to pay a poll tax for every year in which they had been eligible to vote but did not—or, in this example, twenty years of accumulated poll taxes.

The Supreme Court upheld the poll tax again in 1937 in a case brought by a white man from Georgia, *Breedlove v. Suttles*. The Court heard another case by an African American woman in 1951 and again ruled, in *Butler v. Thompson*, that the poll tax did not violate the Fourteenth Amendment's equal protection clause.

The movement to abolish the poll tax gathered steam in the 1940s as the Supreme Court overturned certain southern voting restrictions like the all-white primary. During World War II, Congress voted to waive the poll tax for those in military service for the duration of the conflict. In 1946 President Harry S. Truman appointed the President's Committee on Civil Rights, whose 1948 report, "To Secure These Rights," included poll taxes among the many injustices against black citizens that needed redress. Meanwhile, the National Association for the Advancement of Colored People (NAACP) and the National Committee to Abolish the Poll Tax intensified their campaigns against the poll tax. Labor unions also enlisted in the fight against the poll tax, believing it to be one means by which reactionary antiunion southern members of Congress continued to be reelected and accumulate seniority.

Poll Tax receipt for Rosa Boyles of Jefferson County, Alabama, October 22, 1920. Image via Wikimedia Commons. [Public domain.]

The official Joint Resolution of Congress proposing what became the Twenty-Fourth Amendment as contained in the National Archives. Photo via Wikimedia Commons. [Public domain.]

Southern white members of Congress used their chairmanships on key committees to block civil rights bills, including antilynching legislation. When antipoll tax bills made it through the House of Representatives, the southern minority in the Senate employed the filibuster to block it. They argued that they did not want to set a precedent of Congress dictating voting standards to the states, and insisted they would not filibuster a constitutional amendment proposal, believing such an amendment would not be ratified by three-fourths of the states as required.

But the civil rights struggle that accelerated after the 1954 *Brown v. Board of Education* decision and 1955-1956 Montgomery Bus Boycott, breathed new life into the campaign to abolish the poll tax. In 1962, during the presidency of John F. Kennedy, Congress attained the two-thirds vote necessary to send a poll tax amendment to the states. However, the amendment applied only to federal elections, for example, for the presidency, the Senate, and the House of Representatives. Liberal New York Republican Congressman John V. Lindsay criticized the amendment, declaring, "If we're going to have a constitutional amendment, let's have a meaningful one." Nevertheless, in 1964, South Dakota put the amendment over the three-fourths state-approval threshold for ratification.

Author Biography

The Eighty-Seventh U.S. Congress was sworn in on January 3, 1961, and met until January 3, 1963. It thus overlapped with the last few weeks of the presidency of Dwight D. Eisenhower and the first two years of the presidency of John F. Kennedy. Both the Senate and the House of Representatives enjoyed Democratic majorities, and with Kennedy in the White House the Democrats were able to pass significant legislation as well as to oversee two constitutional amendments. The Twenty-Third Amendment, ratified on March 29, 1961, extended the right to vote in presidential elections to citizens of the District of Columbia. The Twenty-Fourth Amendment, approved by Congress on August 27, 1962, and ratified on January 23, 1964, ended the poll tax in federal elections.

Historical Document

The Twenty-Fourth Amendment

Amendment XXIV

Section 1

The right of citizens of the United States to vote in any primary or other election for President or Vice President, for electors for President or Vice President, or for Senator or Representative in Congress, shall not be denied or abridged by the United States or any State by reason of failure to pay any poll tax or other tax.

Section 2

The Congress shall have power to enforce this article by appropriate legislation.

Document Themes

When the Twenty-Fourth Amendment was ratified, there were only five states still using the poll tax: Alabama, Arkansas, Mississippi, Texas, and Virginia. The Twenty-Fourth Amendment is succinct and clear. It directs that no poll tax shall be required for voting in federal elections, and specifies those offices. Despite the logistical problems of maintaining different qualifications for state and federal elections, the poll tax persisted after the Twenty-Fourth Amendment in states like Virginia. Since southern African Americans were deeply impacted by state and local government, the need to rid the poll tax from those elections was still urgent. During debate on President Lyndon B. Johnson's Voting Rights bill in 1965, liberal Democratic senators such as Phil Hart of Michigan and Edward M. Kennedy of Massachusetts argued strenuously for including abolition of poll taxes in state elections in the bill. The Johnson administration feared that that provision would be unconstitutional, and successfully had the state-election poll tax provision stripped from the Voting Rights bill. Finally, in *Harper v. Virginia Board of Elections* (1966), the Supreme Court struck down the poll tax once and for all as a violation of the Fourteenth Amendment. In the majority decision in the case, Justice William O. Douglass declared, "Voter qualifications have no relation to wealth nor to paying or not paying this or any other tax."

In recent years there has been debate over what some call "voter suppression" efforts directed mainly against African American voters. Critics argue that some states' voter identification (ID) laws are tailored to reduce black voting participation and are reminiscent of similar efforts prior to the Twenty-Fourth Amendment and the Voting Rights Act of 1965 (which the Supreme Court partially overturned in *Shelby v. Holder* in 2013). They note that urban African Americans are less likely to have drivers' licenses, for example, and that other forms of ID frequently require travel and cost to procure, constituting what they charge is "a hidden poll tax."

—*Robert Surbrug, PhD*

Bibliography and Additional Reading

Goldstone, Lawrence. *Stolen Justice: The Struggle for African American Voting Rights.* New York: Scholastic Focus, 2020.

Lawson, Steven F. *Black Ballots: Voting Rights in the South, 1944-1969.* New York: Columbia UP, 1976.

Summers, Mark Wahlgren. *Party Games: Getting, Keeping, and Using Power in the Gilded Age.* Chapel Hill: University of North Carolina Press, 2004.

Woodward, C. Vann. *The Strange Career of Jim Crow: A Commemorative Edition.* New York and Oxford: Oxford UP, 2002.

Speech before Congress on Voting Rights

Date: March 15, 1965
Author: President Lyndon B. Johnson
Genre: speech

Summary Overview

By early 1965, substantial gains had been made in the push for equality for all Americans. However, there were many regions of the country where significant roadblocks prevented full equality from being realized. In most southern states, these roadblocks included efforts to keep African Americans from becoming eligible to vote and, when eligible, from registering to vote or participating in the electoral process. For months, civil rights leaders had been trying to register voters in Alabama. On March 7, 1965, a small group of marchers who supported voting rights left Selma with the aim of walking the fifty-four miles to the capital, Montgomery. The actions that Alabama law enforcement officials took to turn back the demonstrators were televised nationally, exposing police violence and producing sympathy for the marchers and their cause. The time seemed ripe for the introduction of legislation that would give federal officials the authority to intervene in situations where voting rights were being denied on the basis of race. President Lyndon Johnson appeared before Congress and delivered the speech included here two days before sending the bill to Congress. The speech identifies the president's set of priorities regarding the right to vote.

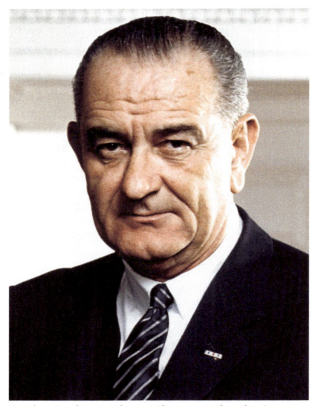

President Lyndon B. Johnson. Photo via Wikimedia Commons. [Public domain.]

Defining Moment

African Americans were given their freedom in 1865 (following the Civil War), granted equal rights in 1868 (Fourteenth Amendment), and the right to vote in 1870 (Fifteenth Amendment). However, for many African American citizens, these rights and freedoms were only words on paper. After the end of Reconstruction, southern states slowly made African Americans second-class citizens and instituted a system of racial segregation. The latter was ratified at the national level by the U.S. Supreme Court in its 1896 ruling *Plessy v. Ferguson,* which allowed that the doctrine of "separate but equal" was acceptable. Not all Americans, and particularly not African-Americans, found the practice acceptable. Throughout the first half of the twentieth century, efforts were made to change such laws, especially through legal proceedings. The landmark case *Brown v. Board of Education* (1954) not only invalidated segregated schools, but also ruled that the "separate but equal" doctrine was flawed.

Emerging from that case were a series of additional civil rights cases as well as the beginnings of efforts to change the system through public demonstrations. The Birmingham Bus Boycott of 1955–56, for example, proved that nonviolent demonstrations and pressure tactics could work to draw attention and turn matters around.

From that time forward, demonstrations and community-wide efforts were used to try to obtain equal rights for all people throughout the land. In 1964, the Civil Rights Act became the first major piece of Congressional legislation to advance the cause of broad equality regardless of race. Because voting rights were already covered under the Fifteenth Amendment, consideration of voting rights was dropped from the 1964 law. But as 1965 opened, the strong effort to register African American voters in Selma proved that state laws and local attitudes still hindered the process. A march to the state capital was planned by civil rights leaders to focus on these laws. Yet, the marchers were attacked by state and local police and by mobs wielding rocks. The brutal response pushed many moderates, citizens, and lawmakers alike, toward supporting a federal voting rights bill. Senate leaders of the Democratic and Republican Parties joined as co-sponsors in an attempt to overcome a possible filibuster by southern senators. President Johnson gave a televised address to a joint session of Congress, thus indicating the strength of his commitment to the bill. Johnson's speech, in fact, is regarded by many as one of his best as president. He understood that this was a pivotal moment and that, without the right to vote, the broader cause of equal rights generally might not be attained.

Author Biography

Lyndon Baines Johnson (1908–1973) was raised in central Texas, a member of a poor, but influential, family. He graduated from high school at fifteen, but alternated work and college until earning his degree at twenty-two. An influential congressional aide, he was then elected to and entered the House of Representatives in 1937, the Senate in 1949, and the vice presidency in 1961. He became president when John F. Kennedy was assassinated, serving from 1963 to 1969. Johnson sponsored what is called "The Great Society" legislation, which included anti-poverty measures in addition to civil rights laws. Outside of civil rights, his most influential pieces of legislation included Medicare, Head Start, work-study for students, and the Gulf of Tonkin Resolution, which legitimized America's expanded participation in the Vietnam War. Although willing to use virtually any means to prevail in politics, Johnson also held a basic belief in the equality of all people.

Historical Document

LBJ's Speech Before Congress on Voting Rights

[Note: This transcript contains the published text of the speech, not the actual words spoken. Thus, there may be some differences between the transcript and the audio content.]

Mr. Speaker, Mr. President, Members of the Congress:

I speak tonight for the dignity of man and the destiny of democracy.

I urge every member of both parties, Americans of all religions and of all colors, from every section of this country, to join me in that cause.

At times history and fate meet at a single time in a single place to shape a turning point in man's unending search for freedom. So it was at Lexington and Concord. So it was a century ago at Appomattox. So it was last week in Selma, Alabama.

There, long-suffering men and women peacefully protested the denial of their rights as Americans. Many were brutally assaulted. One good man, a man of God, was killed.

There is no cause for pride in what has happened in Selma. There is no cause for self-satisfaction in the long denial of equal rights of millions of Americans. But there is cause for hope and for faith in our democracy in what is happening here tonight.

For the cries of pain and the hymns and protests of oppressed people have summoned into convocation all the majesty of this great Government—the Government of the greatest Nation on earth.

Our mission is at once the oldest and the most basic of this country: to right wrong, to do justice, to serve man.

In our time we have come to live with moments of great crisis. Our lives have been marked with debate about great issues; issues of war and peace, issues of prosperity and depression. But rarely in any time does an issue lay bare the secret heart of America itself. Rarely are we met with a challenge, not to our growth or abundance, our welfare or our security, but rather to the values and the purposes and the meaning of our beloved Nation.

The issue of equal rights for American Negroes is such an issue. And should we defeat every enemy, should we double our wealth and conquer the stars, and still be unequal to this issue, then we will have failed as a people and as a nation.

For with a country as with a person, "What is a man profited, if he shall gain the whole world, and lose his own soul ?"

There is no Negro problem. There is no Southern problem. There is no Northern problem. There is only an American problem. And we are met here tonight as Americans—not as Democrats or Republicans—we are met here as Americans to solve that problem.

This was the first nation in the history of the world to be founded with a purpose. The great phrases of that purpose still sound in every American heart, North and South: "All men are created equal"—"government by consent of the governed"—"give me liberty or give me death." Well, those are not just clever words, or those are not just empty theories. In their name Americans have fought and died for two centuries, and tonight around the world they stand there as guardians of our liberty, risking their lives.

Those words are a promise to every citizen that he shall share in the dignity of man. This dignity cannot be found in a man's possessions; it cannot be found in his power, or in his position. It really rests on his right to be treated as a man equal in opportunity to all others. It says that he shall share in freedom, he shall choose his leaders, educate his children, and provide for his family according to his ability and his merits as a human being.

To apply any other test—to deny a man his hopes because of his color or race, his religion or the place of his birth—is not only to do injustice, it is to deny America and to dishonor the dead who gave their lives for American freedom.

Our fathers believed that if this noble view of the rights of man was to flourish, it must be rooted in democracy. The most basic right of all was the right to choose your own leaders. The history of this country, in large measure, is the history of the expansion of that right to all of our people.

Many of the issues of civil rights are very complex and most difficult. But about this there can and should be no argument. Every American citizen must have an equal right to vote. There is no reason which can excuse the denial of that right. There is no duty which weighs more heavily on us than the duty we have to ensure that right.

Yet the harsh fact is that in many places in this country men and women are kept from voting simply because they are Negroes.

Every device of which human ingenuity is capable has been used to deny this right. The Negro citizen may go to register only to be told that the day is wrong, or the hour is late, or the official in charge is absent. And if he persists, and if he manages to present himself to the registrar, he may be disqualified because he did not spell out his middle name or because he abbreviated a word on the application.

And if he manages to fill out an application he is given a test. The registrar is the sole judge of whether he passes this test. He may be asked to recite the entire Constitution, or explain the most complex provisions of State law. And even a college degree cannot be used to prove that he can read and write.

For the fact is that the only way to pass these barriers is to show a white skin.

Experience has clearly shown that the existing process of law cannot overcome systematic and ingenious discrimination. No law that we now have on the books—and I have helped to put three of them there—can ensure the right to vote when local officials are determined to deny it.

In such a case our duty must be clear to all of us. The Constitution says that no person shall be kept from voting because of his race or his color. We have all sworn an oath before God to support and to defend that Constitution. We must now act in obedience to that oath.

Wednesday I will send to Congress a law designed to eliminate illegal barriers to the right to vote.

The broad principles of that bill will be in the hands of the Democratic and Republican leaders tomorrow. After they have reviewed it, it will come here formally as a bill. I am grateful for this opportunity to come here tonight at the invitation of the leadership to reason with my friends, to give them my views, and to visit with my former colleagues.

I have had prepared a more comprehensive analysis of the legislation which I had intended to transmit to the clerk tomorrow but which I will submit to the clerks tonight. But I want to really discuss with you now briefly the main proposals of this legislation.

This bill will strike down restrictions to voting in all elections—federal, state, and local—which have been used to deny Negroes the right to vote.

This bill will establish a simple, uniform standard which cannot be used, however ingenious the effort, to flout our Constitution.

It will provide for citizens to be registered by officials of the United States Government if the State officials refuse to register them.

It will eliminate tedious, unnecessary lawsuits which delay the right to vote.

Finally, this legislation will ensure that properly registered individuals are not prohibited from voting.

I will welcome the suggestions from all of the Members of Congress—I have no doubt that I will get some—on ways and means to strengthen this law and to make it effective. But experience has plainly shown that this is the only path to carry out the command of the Constitution.

To those who seek to avoid action by their National Government in their own communities; who want to and who seek to maintain purely local control over elections, the answer is simple:

Open your polling places to all your people.

Allow men and women to register and vote whatever the color of their skin.

Extend the rights of citizenship to every citizen of this land.

There is no constitutional issue here. The command of the Constitution is plain.

There is no moral issue. It is wrong—deadly wrong—to deny any of your fellow Americans the right to vote in this country.

There is no issue of States rights or national rights. There is only the struggle for human rights.

I have not the slightest doubt what will be your answer.

The last time a President sent a civil rights bill to the Congress it contained a provision to protect voting rights in federal elections. That civil rights bill was passed after eight long months of debate. And when that bill came to my desk from the Congress for my signature, the heart of the voting provision had been eliminated.

This time, on this issue, there must be no delay, no hesitation and no compromise with our purpose.

We cannot, we must not, refuse to protect the right of every American to vote in every election that he may desire to participate in. And we ought not and we cannot and we must not wait another 8 months before we get a bill. We have already waited a hundred years and more, and the time for waiting is gone.

So I ask you to join me in working long hours—nights and weekends, if necessary—to pass this bill. And I don't make that request lightly. For from the window where I sit with the problems of our country I recognize that outside this chamber is the outraged conscience of a nation, the grave concern of many nations, and the harsh judgment of history on our acts.

But even if we pass this bill, the battle will not be over. What happened in Selma is part of a far larger movement which reaches into every section and State of America. It is the effort of American Negroes to secure for themselves the full blessings of American life.

Their cause must be our cause too. Because it is not just Negroes, but really it is all of us, who must overcome the crippling legacy of bigotry and injustice. And we shall overcome.

As a man whose roots go deeply into Southern soil, I know how agonizing racial feelings are. I know how difficult it is to reshape the attitudes and the structure of our society.

But a century has passed, more than a hundred years, since the Negro was freed. And he is not fully free tonight.

It was more than a hundred years ago that Abraham Lincoln, a great President of another party, signed the Emancipation Proclamation, but emancipation is a proclamation and not a fact.

A century has passed, more than a hundred years, since equality was promised. And yet the Negro is not equal.

A century has passed since the day of promise. And the promise is unkept.

The time of justice has now come. I tell you that I believe sincerely that no force can hold it back. It is right in the eyes of man and God that it should come. And when it does, I think that day will brighten the lives of every American.

For Negroes are not the only victims. How many white children have gone uneducated, how many white families have lived in stark poverty, how many white lives have been scarred by fear, because we have wasted our energy and our substance to maintain the barriers of hatred and terror?

So I say to all of you here, and to all in the Nation tonight, that those who appeal to you to hold on to the past do so at the cost of denying you your future.

This great, rich, restless country can offer opportunity and education and hope to all: black and white, North and South, sharecropper and city dweller.

These are the enemies: poverty, ignorance, disease. They are the enemies and not our fellow man, not our neighbor. And these enemies too, poverty, disease and ignorance, we shall overcome.

Now let none of us in any sections look with prideful righteousness on the troubles in another section, or on the problems of our neighbors. There is really no part of America where the promise of equality has been fully kept. In Buffalo as well as in Birmingham, in Philadelphia as well as in Selma, Americans are struggling for the fruits of freedom.

This is one Nation. What happens in Selma or in Cincinnati is a matter of legitimate concern to every American. But let each of us look within our own hearts and our own communities, and let each of us put our shoulder to the wheel to root out injustice wherever it exists.

As we meet here in this peaceful, historic chamber tonight, men from the South, some of whom were at Iwo Jima, men from the North who have carried Old Glory to far corners of the world and brought it back without a stain on it, men from the East and from the West, are all fighting together without regard to religion, or color, or region, in Viet-Nam. Men from every region fought for us across the world 20 years ago.

And in these common dangers and these common sacrifices the South made its contribution of honor and gallantry no less than any other region of the great Republic—and in some instances, a great many of them, more.

And I have not the slightest doubt that good men from everywhere in this country, from the Great Lakes to the Gulf of Mexico, from the Golden Gate to the harbors along the Atlantic, will rally together now in this cause to vindicate the freedom of all Americans. For all of us owe this duty; and I believe that all of us will respond to it.

Your President makes that request of every American.

The real hero of this struggle is the American Negro. His actions and protests, his courage to risk safety and even to risk his life, have awakened the conscience of this Nation. His demonstrations have been designed to call attention to injustice, designed to provoke change, designed to stir reform.

He has called upon us to make good the promise of America. And who among us can say that we would have made the same progress were it not for his persistent bravery, and his faith in American democracy.

For at the real heart of battle for equality is a deep-seated belief in the democratic process. Equality depends not on the force of arms or tear gas but upon the force of moral right; not on recourse to violence but on respect for law and order.

There have been many pressures upon your President and there will be others as the days come and go. But I pledge you tonight that we intend to fight this battle where it should be fought: in the courts, and in the Congress, and in the hearts of men.

We must preserve the right of free speech and the right of free assembly. But the right of free speech does not carry with it, as has been said, the right to holler fire in a crowded theater. We must preserve the right to free assembly, but free assembly does not carry with it the right to block public thoroughfares to traffic.

We do have a right to protest, and a right to march under conditions that do not infringe the constitutional rights of our neighbors. And I intend to protect all those rights as long as I am permitted to serve in this office.

We will guard against violence, knowing it strikes from our hands the very weapons which we seek—progress, obedience to law, and belief in American values.

In Selma as elsewhere we seek and pray for peace. We seek order. We seek unity. But we will not accept the peace of stifled rights, or the order imposed by fear, or the unity that stifles protest. For peace cannot be purchased at the cost of liberty.

In Selma tonight, as in every—and we had a good day there—as in every city, we are working for just and peaceful settlement. We must all remember that after this speech I am making tonight, after the police and the FBI and the Marshals have all gone, and after you have promptly passed this bill, the people of Selma and the other cities of the Nation must still live and work together. And when the attention of the Nation has gone elsewhere they must try to heal the wounds and to build a new community.

This cannot be easily done on a battleground of violence, as the history of the South itself shows. It is in recognition of this that men of both races have shown such an outstandingly impressive responsibility in recent days—last Tuesday, again today.

The bill that I am presenting to you will be known as a civil rights bill. But, in a larger sense, most of the program I am recommending is a civil rights program. Its object is to open the city of hope to all people of all races.

Because all Americans just must have the right to vote. And we are going to give them that right.

All Americans must have the privileges of citizenship regardless of race. And they are going to have those privileges of citizenship regardless of race.

But I would like to caution you and remind you that to exercise these privileges takes much more than just legal right. It requires a trained mind and a healthy body. It requires a decent home, and the chance to find a job, and the opportunity to escape from the clutches of poverty.

Of course, people cannot contribute to the Nation if they are never taught to read or write, if their bodies are stunted from hunger, if their sickness goes untended, if their life is spent in hopeless poverty just drawing a welfare check.

So we want to open the gates to opportunity. But we are also going to give all our people, black and white, the help that they need to walk through those gates.

My first job after college was as a teacher in Cotulla, Texas, in a small Mexican-American school. Few of them could speak English, and I couldn't speak much Spanish. My students were poor and they often came to class without breakfast, hungry. They knew even in their youth the pain of prejudice. They never seemed to know why people disliked them. But they knew it was so, because I saw it in their eyes. I often walked home late in the afternoon, after the classes were finished, wishing there was more that I could do. But all I knew was to teach them the little that I knew, hoping that it might help them against the hardships that lay ahead.

Somehow you never forget what poverty and hatred can do when you see its scars on the hopeful face of a young child.

I never thought then, in 1928, that I would be standing here in 1965. It never even occurred to me in my fondest dreams that I might have the chance to help the sons and daughters of those students and to help people like them all over this country.

But now I do have that chance—and I'll let you in on a secret—I mean to use it. And I hope that you will use it with me.

This is the richest and most powerful country which ever occupied the globe. The might of past empires is little compared to ours. But I do not want to be the President who built empires, or sought grandeur, or extended dominion.

I want to be the President who educated young children to the wonders of their world. I want to be the President who helped to feed the hungry and to prepare them to be taxpayers instead of tax-eaters.

I want to be the President who helped the poor to find their own way and who protected the right of every citizen to vote in every election.

I want to be the President who helped to end hatred among his fellow men and who promoted love among the people of all races and all regions and all parties.

I want to be the President who helped to end war among the brothers of this earth.

And so at the request of your beloved Speaker and the Senator from Montana; the majority leader, the Senator from Illinois; the minority leader, Mr. McCulloch, and other Members of both parties, I came here tonight—not as President Roosevelt came down one time in person to veto a bonus bill, not as President Truman came down one time to urge the passage of a railroad bill—but I came down here to ask you to share this task with me and to share it with the people that we both work for. I want this to be the Congress, Republicans and Democrats alike, which did all these things for all these people.

Beyond this great chamber, out yonder in 50 States, are the people that we serve. Who can tell what deep and unspoken hopes are in their hearts tonight as they sit there and listen. We all can guess, from our own lives, how difficult they often find their own pursuit of happiness, how many problems each little family has. They look most of all to themselves for their futures. But I think that they also look to each of us.

Above the pyramid on the great seal of the United States it says—in Latin—"God has favored our undertaking."

God will not favor everything that we do. It is rather our duty to divine His will. But I cannot help believing that He truly understands and that He really favors the undertaking that we begin here tonight.

Document Analysis

As President Johnson points out, this is not the first civil rights bill to be submitted with a provision guaranteeing voting rights. However, in his mind, the time is right for finally enacting such legislation. Johnson believes that events in Alabama have made it clear that voting rights are not going to be granted unless the federal government steps in. The lack of equal rights for any one group in the United States makes the matter "an American problem." Johnson contrasts the eloquent statements of the Founding Fathers with the situation in which non-white citizens find themselves in many southern states. He states that the time has come for full equality, in all aspects of life, for all American citizens. The shocking images of police assaulting peaceful demonstrators is something that Johnson knows will eventually fade from awareness. Thus, he is adamant that the new legislation must be passed quickly, or else it could languish forever in congressional committees.

Although, from a twenty-first-century perspective, the language of the speech might seem a bit archaic (e.g., the use of the word Negro and referring to groups using only male terms), Johnson takes a somewhat extreme position to reflect his strong support of the right of non-white citizens to vote. Johnson understands that what is at stake here are the "values and the purposes" of America. Quoting the Declaration of Independence, the president sees that there has been a failure in living up to the phrase "All men are created equal." He suggests that this expression will be validated when all people have access to the vote.

The fact that the Civil Rights Act of 1964 had been stripped, during the legislative process, of any provisions regarding voting rights, is an indication to Johnson that quick action is needed. Outlining the history from 1865 to the present, he is able to demonstrate that even the most patient person would be worn thin by events. He continually refers to what took place during the first two Selma marches, as well as to the murder of a New England minister, to remind listeners of the urgency of redressing these wrongs. Although most of the laws restricting voting by non-whites had been passed in the South, Johnson presents his case that given the unity of the country, the march in Selma and the larger struggle for which it stands "reaches into every section" of the United States.

Using biblical and American images and references, Johnson strengthens his case for action. He believes that failure in obtaining equal rights for all citizens is more important than any physical or monetary gains the nation might make. He states that if the only way a person can gain equality, including the right to vote, is to "show a white skin," then the nation is a failure. It is that simple for Johnson. He sees substantial resources being wasted on segregation, resources that could help whites as well as members of minority groups to move out of poverty. In Johnson's mind, this is part of the unity of the nation and of all its citizens.

Essential Themes

In this speech, President Johnson presents a vision of justice and equality for all Americans without qualification. Participation in the political process is a basic part of what it means to be an American. Thus, he speaks about the need to treat a person on the "merits" of his (or her) status as a human being, regardless of what color or ethnicity the person might be. To denigrate anyone because of his or her race or color, from Johnson's perspective, is to deny all that Americans have struggled for in the preceding centuries. Although he was confronting some in the South who seemed to deny such a view, he insists that the matter is part of the great American tradition. Speaking to Congress and to the nation, Johnson seeks to bring that tradition into focus. All must share equally in opportunity, or all will be harmed.

Once signed into law, the Voting Rights Act was quickly implemented. By the end of 1966, nine of the thirteen southern states had more than half their African American citizens registered to vote, two-thirds of them by local officials. However, this did not mean that opponents of the law stopped their efforts completely. The matter, rather, moved to the courts. Initially, the Supreme Court upheld the basic provisions of the law. Over the years, however, seven Supreme Court decisions have come to limited various provisions of the law. The strongest such rulings have limited the federal government's power to approve/disapprove electoral districts prior to their implementation, based on the government's understanding of how and why the electoral lines were established. With this provision being declared unconstitutional in 2013, only challenges by individuals who believe their constitutional rights have been violated can be file a complaint, with the burden of proof falling to the individual filing the case.

President Johnson sought to move the nation toward political equality for all people by adding this legislation to his Great Society quiver. Fifty years later, the issue is still a subject of political and legal debate, some of it quite heated. Advocates for voting rights and similar laws believe that historic injustices have not yet been fully redressed, while opponents believe that institutionalized injustices from the past are dead history as far as current concerns go. President Johnson intentionally drew on words from the civil rights movement when he stated that "we shall overcome" the problems that he describes. Yet, whether the nation has indeed overcome these problems or whether they linger as continuing concerns, remains, it seems, unsettled.

—Donald A. Watt, PhD

Bibliography and Additional Reading

"100 Milestone Documents: Voting Rights Act (1965)." *OurDocuments.Gov.* National Archives and Records Administration, 2015.

Ellis, Sylvia. Freedom's Pragmatist: Lyndon Johnson and Civil Rights. Gainesville: University of Florida Press, 2013.

Kearns, Doris. Lyndon Johnson and the American Dream. New York: St. Martins Griffin, 1991.

"LBJ and Civil Rights." *Lyndon Baines Johnson Library and Museum.* LBJ Presidential Library, 2015.

"Selma Movement." *National Voting Rights Museum and Institute.* National Voting Rights Museum and Institute, 2015.

Voting Rights Act of 1965

Date: August 6, 1965
Author: U.S. Congress
Genre: legislation; law

Summary Overview

The Voting Rights Act of 1965 has been described as one of the most successful pieces of civil rights legislation ever adopted by the U.S. Congress. Coming at a time when, despite decades of reform efforts, African Americans were still substantially disenfranchised in many southern states, the act employed various measures and procedures to restore suffrage to excluded minority voters in the South and later in the nation as a whole.

In doing this, the Voting Rights Act permitted, and even required, the federal government to intrude in matters previously reserved to the individual states, significantly reworking the balance between state and federal powers. Furthermore, the act gave reformers the tools they needed to radically transform election laws and procedures. The result was the rapid integration of African Americans and, later on, members of language minorities, into the electoral process. In time, the act brought about a transformation in politics and the election of thousands of African Americans, Hispanics, and Asian Americans to political office. It represented a reshaping of politics first in the South and eventually across the nation.

Defining Moment

By the 1960s, southern efforts to disenfranchise African American voters had been in place for the better part of a century; blacks had been denied the vote by southern election officials through means both fair and foul. Among the obstacles placed before black voters were unfairly applied literacy and comprehension tests, in which voters had to read, understand, or interpret sections of state constitutions to the satisfaction of white (and usually hostile) election officials; complicated registration requirements that excluded minority voters on technical grounds; and financial barriers such as poll taxes. Intimidation and threats of violence were also effective means of keeping southern blacks from attending the polls. One of the simplest ways of undermining the black vote involved setting up polling places in areas inconvenient for blacks. Many polling places were placed in distant locations or in the middle of white sections of the town or county; similarly, some were put in businesses owned by known opponents of African American suffrage. Finally, in efforts to ensure that blacks had as little voice as possible in government through the election process, state legislatures across the South implemented rules prohibiting blacks from voting in the politically dominant Democratic Party primaries. Since Democratic candidates almost always won in the general elections, this particular method of exclusion was extraordinarily effective.

The South's system of race-based vote denial, which was well entrenched by the start of the twentieth century, came under increasing attack from the 1930s onward. By 1944 the National Association for the Advancement of Colored People (NAACP), a leader in the fight against race-based disenfranchisement via the courts, had pushed the Supreme Court to declare the all-white Democratic primary held in Texas—and by implication, similar institutions in other southern states—to be unconstitutional. Political pressure from the civil rights movement in the 1950s, along with further litigation by the NAACP, led to the passage of two civil rights acts—one in 1957 and the other in 1960—each of which empowered the U.S. Department of Justice (DOJ) to bring lawsuits against unconstitutional vote-denial techniques. Finally, the Civil Rights Act of 1964 sped up the ability of three-judge courts to hear voting rights cases, required that any literacy tests employed be given entirely in writing, demanded that black registration be based upon the same voter qualifications as those applied to whites, and allowed for the temporary appointment of federal voting registrars.

Still, despite the best efforts of leaders of the civil rights movement and the federal government, African American disenfranchisement remained largely intact as the 1960s approached the midway point. As late as 1964, black voter registration in the Deep South state of Mississippi stood at only 6.7 percent—which was at least an increase from the rate of 2 percent two years earlier. Conditions were admittedly better in other states; African American registration throughout the Deep South, where the majority of blacks lived, stood at 22.5 percent in 1964, while in the border-state region, which included such states as Florida, Texas, Tennessee, and Arkansas, registration rates averaged 43 percent. Regardless, come Election Day, the majority of southern blacks were yet unable to cast ballots.

The root of this problem lay in white southerners' extreme unwillingness to accept any court orders or administrative programs reversing disenfranchisement laws. Every time the courts or DOJ overturned laws aimed at disenfranchising southern black voters, southern election officials turned to new (or, at the least, different) techniques to achieve the same discriminatory end—techniques not covered by the courts' orders and thus still permissible until invalidated by another court proceeding. Whenever the courts seemed about to invalidate these new procedures, southern election officials simply adopted still other methods of disenfranchisement, starting the whole process over once more. In consequence, opponents of black vote denial were forced to initiate court case after court case in their efforts to gain the vote and to do so with very few practical gains.

The Voting Rights Act, which passed in 1965, was expressly designed to attack the sources of delay in the case-by-case litigation approach, as the nineteen sections of the act imposed a completely new enforcement methodology with respect to voting rights violations. The act not only outlawed vote denial based on race or color—and later ethnicity—but also gave both the executive branch and the federal courts powerful new abilities and regulations. Among them were the power to appoint federal examiners and observers in whatever numbers the president felt necessary, prohibitions on literacy tests and poll taxes, and rules outlawing any action "under color of the law" that prevented qualified citizens from voting or having their votes fairly counted. Most important of all, the Voting Rights Act froze all southern election laws in place as of its passage. If local or state officials wanted to change laws or procedures, they would have to receive clearance from the DOJ or the federal courts beforehand. In this way, the southern strategy of using ever-shifting techniques of voter denial to derail election reforms was effectively ended.

Author Biography

Pressure for reform of voting rights legislation had been growing for years. In 1963 the federal Commission on Civil Rights announced that the only way to guarantee all citizens the right to vote was through federal legislation that spelled out clear and uniform voter standards. When the Civil Rights Act of 1964 did not go far enough to protect black voting, the Southern Christian Leadership Conference (SCLC) took the risky step of staging a voting registration drive that featured an organized march in Selma, Alabama, in early 1965; their hope was that the expected violent response to the march by local officials would increase public pressure for a voting rights act. The state police indeed produced a public spectacle under

Alabama police in 1965 attack voting rights marchers on "Bloody Sunday," the first of the Selma to Montgomery marches. Photo via

United States President Lyndon B. Johnson, Martin Luther King Jr., and Rosa Parks at the signing of the Voting Rights Act on August 6, 1965. Photo via Wikimedia Commons. [Public domain.]

the leadership of the racist Selma sheriff, Jim Clark, using excessive and unjustified violence against the protesters, including frequent beatings of demonstrators and mass arrests. The leaders of the drive were thus successful in putting pressure on President Lyndon B. Johnson to address the need for an effective voting rights act.

The bill that would become the Voting Rights Act of 1965 was sent to Congress by President Johnson on March 15, 1965. Johnson noted in his message to Congress as he submitted the bill, "Every device of which human ingenuity is capable has been used to deny" blacks their right to vote. He continued: "It is wrong—deadly wrong—to deny any of your fellow Americans the right to vote in this country" (millercenter.org). The Senate passed the bill on May 11, after a successful cloture vote on March 23, by a vote of 77 to 19; the House then passed it by a vote of 333 to 85 on July 10; over the following three weeks, the differences between the two bills were resolved in conference. The House passed the conference report on August 3 by a vote of 328 to 74 and the Senate on August 4 by a vote of 79 to 18. President Johnson signed the Voting Rights Act into law on August 6, 1965.

Historical Document

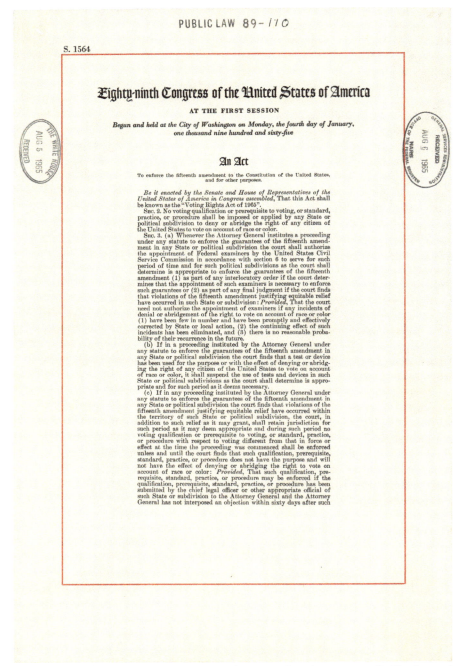

The first page of the Voting Rights Act of 1965. Photo via Wikimedia Commons. [Public domain.]

Document Analysis

Totaling nineteen sections, the full text of the Voting Rights Act of 1965 (not shown in its entirety here) includes both permanent rule changes regulating the voting process nationwide and temporary special provisions designed to attack specific racial injustices in the South (and after 1970, nationwide with respect to language minorities). Before 1980 the temporary provisions—found primarily in Sections 4 to 9 and renewed and amended in 1970, 1974, 1982, and 2006—had the greatest impact on minority voting rights. Designed in direct response to the ongoing problems faced by African Americans and the DOJ in combating southern disenfranchisement, these sections provide for direct federal intervention in the South to protect minority voting rights and place authority to enforce these rights directly in the hands of the executive branch. This dual objective was implemented in three ways.

First, Section 4 creates a triggering formula that imposes federal executive authority over any state that employs such voter-limiting devices as literacy tests to determine voter qualifications and in which, as of November 1, 1964, less than 50 percent of voting-age residents are registered. Those states that meet these criteria—between 1965 and 1975, this group included six southern states in whole and parts of another—automatically fall under the jurisdiction of the act's various temporary requirements.

Second, later in Section 4, comes a direct assault on the tools of vote denial then in use across the South. This portion of the act abolishes the most significant barriers to black voting: literacy tests, exams measuring "good moral character" and "ability to . . . understand," and the requirement that a registered voter vouch for a potential voter. Extended by Congress for another five years in 1970, these prohibitions were made permanent in 1975, at which time another triggering formula was added, applying to states that discriminated against language-minority groups, such as Texas.

Third, Sections 5 through 9 expand the federal government's power and authority to implement these and other reforms. Most important in this regard is Section 5, designed expressly to check the seemingly endless cycle by which southern states replaced one discriminatory law with another every time the old requirements were suspended or declared unconstitutional. To achieve this end, all state voting statutes and procedures in place as of November 1, 1964, are frozen pending federal approval for proposed changes. This meant that any state or county covered by the act's triggering formula that sought to modify its voting laws would first have to gain approval for the changes by submitting proposed revisions to the DOJ and proving that they did "not have the purpose and . . . [would] not have the effect of denying or abridging the right to vote on account of race or color." All changes not cleared ahead of time by the DOJ, which had sixty days to object, were legally barred from implementation. Alternately, a state could file for a declaratory judgment from the district court for the District of Columbia, whose positive response served the same result as preclearance by the DOJ.

Of lesser importance than Section 5 but still significant in promoting change, Sections 6 and 7 grant the attorney general jurisdiction to appoint voting examiners to certify that legally qualified voters are free to register. Section 8 permits the attorney general to assign, as needed, federal observers to oversee the actual voting process in those areas covered by the triggering formula. Elsewhere, passages define the terms *vote* and *voting* for the purposes of the act (Section 14), set out criminal penalties for violating the act (Section 12), prohibit voter fraud and outlaw any action "under color of law" preventing qualified voters from voting or having their votes fairly counted (Section 11), and suggest to the attorney general that he bring suit challenging the poll taxes still in use in four states (Section 10). At the beginning of the document, Section 2 accomplishes the fundamental justice of prohibiting discrimination in voting based on race or color.

Essential Themes

In the years following its passage, the Voting Rights Act of 1965 became one of the most effective tools in the advancement of racial integration across the South. As cited in literally hundreds of separate litigations, the act's provisions forced major changes in the ways that southern states ran their elections. Most states and municipalities were forced to shift away from at-large election formats, whereby all candidates for a similar office (such as county commissioner) ran against one another no matter where they resided in the county, and the top vote-getters county-wide were declared the winners. Further, where possible, every effort was taken to encourage the creation of minority-majority districts, in which minorities made up the majorities. The result in terms of minority officeholding was explosive. In 1965 the number of black public officials nationwide, of any level or significance, numbered fewer than 100. By 1989 the number of African American elected officials stood at 3,265, or 9.8 percent of all offices. By 2000 the number of minority officeholders in any category had increased to almost five thousand. Given that as late as 1944 only about 3 percent of southern blacks were even registered to vote and that none had held elective office since the turn of the century, the changes in southern politics generated by the Voting Rights Act were truly extraordinary. These changes amounted to a reconstruction of southern political power so profound and extensive that it was, in Davidson and Grofman's words, nothing less than a "quiet revolution" in southern politics.

After being augmented in 1970, 1975, and later years, the act continued to function effectively for decades to ensure the proper administration of elections, particularly in districts that had been identified, historically, as being subject to bias and manipulation. However, key portions of the act came to be challenged in 2013, in the case *Shelby County v. Holder*. That year the U.S. Supreme Court concluded that the Voting Rights Act was outmoded and constitutionally unsupported, and therefore must be abandoned in large measure. Specifically, the practice of preclearance was eliminated. Since then, efforts to limit access to the ballot by questioning mail-in ballots, restricting the times and places of voting, requiring valid ID's, and a number of other such measures have taken hold in many states having Republican majorities in the legislatures.

—*Charles L. Zelden, PhD*

Bibliography and Additional Reading

Bullock, Charles S. III, Ronald Keith Gaddie, and Justin J. Wert, eds. *The Rise and Fall of the Voting Rights Act*. Norman, OK: University of Oklahoma Press, 2016.

Davidson, Chandler, and Bernard Grofman, eds. *Quiet Revolution in the South: The Impact of the Voting Rights Act, 1965–1990*. Princeton, NJ: Princeton UP, 1994.

Landsberg, Brian K. *Free at Last to Vote: The Alabama Origins of the 1965 Voting Rights Act*. Lawrence: UP of Kansas, 2007.

Lawson, Steven F. *Black Ballots: Voting Rights in the South, 1944–1969*. Lanham, MD: Lexington Books, 1999.

McCool, Daniel, ed. *The Most Fundamental Right: Contrasting Perspectives on the Voting Rights Act*. Bloomington: Indiana UP, 2012.

Perman, Michael. *Struggle for Mastery: Disfranchisement in the South, 1888–1908*. Chapel Hill: University of North Carolina Press, 2001.

Valelly, Richard M., ed. *The Voting Rights Act: Securing the Ballot*. Washington, DC: CQ Press, 2006.

Voting Changes in the Modern Era

In this section we look at variety of significant changes, primarily legislative, in the area of voting and voters' rights not covered in the previous sections on the suffrage movement or the Civil Rights Era nor in the subsequent section on landmark U.S. Supreme Court decisions. The topics in the present section are as follows:

- Seventeenth Amendment to the U.S. Constitution (1913), which fundamentally changed the way U.S. senators are to be elected (directly by voters as opposed to the old system of state legislatures electing them);
- Twenty-Sixth Amendment (1971), which lowered the voting age in federal elections from twenty-one to eighteen years of age;
- National Voter Registration Act of 1993, also known as the "motor-voter" act because it aimed to make voting procedures and voting registration easier for all, including by offering people the chance to register to vote when they apply for a driver's license (or renew an existing one);
- Help America Vote Act of 2002, a response to the messy presidential election of 2000 between Al Gore (Democrat) and George W. Bush (Republican), where ballot counting problems in selected districts in Florida caused the matter to go to the U.S. Supreme Court, which decided in favor of Bush;
- Americans with Disabilities Act Polling Place Accessibility Checklist, a document from 2016 based on standards set in 2010, themselves based on the 1990 Americans with Disabilities Act, which opened access to public facilities—including voting facilities—to those with disabilities;
- Civics Test for Naturalization (2019), an example of the test given to all those applying for citizenship in the United States—a test that contains many questions regarding voting, elections, and the makeup of the U.S. government; and
- Electoral Count Reform Act (2022), a response to the January 6, 2021 attack on the U.S. Capitol by violent mobs supporting President Donald J. Trump's effort to overturn the results of his election loss (in November 2020) to Joseph R. Biden, in part by seeking to stop the certification of the electoral count by Congress on that day.

Seventeenth Amendment to the U.S. Constitution

Date: April 8, 1913
Author: Proposed by Joseph L. Bristow
Genre: constitutional provision

Summary Overview

During the drafting of the Constitution, one of the initial points of contention concerned the balance between federal and state power. The makeup and functioning of the U.S. Senate was a central topic in that debate. In the final document, the Senate as an institution represented a compromise between large and small states. With each state having two senators regardless of population, the body was designed to ensure that state governments' interests were represented at the federal level. As originally devised, it was state legislatures, not the voting populations of each state, that selected senators.

By the late nineteenth century, this system became increasingly unpopular and, in 1913, the Seventeenth Amendment was ratified. This amendment provides for the people of each state to directly elect their senators and was part of a wider trend toward more directly democratic political systems in the United States.

Defining Moment

The two key issues drove changes to how senators were elected. One of these was the problem of state legislatures not being able to arrive at a consensus on who their senators should be in a timely fashion, delaying that state's representation in the Senate. The other was the perception—and occasional reality—that the senatorial election system originally devised by the Framers created opportunities for corruption. Historians still debate the degree to which corruption was an issue in state legislatures selecting senators; only ten instances of a contested Senate election due to bribery ever arose before the enactment of the Thirteenth Amendment.

While there had been attempts to amend the Constitution to allow for the direct election of senators as early as the 1820s, calls for reform increased during the late nineteenth century. The 1892 Omaha Platform of the Populist Party called for direct election. A number of states already had mechanisms in places to provide for direct election, with popular votes that "instructed" state legislatures to select a particular candidate. The early twentieth century was an era when reformers sought to increase citizen involvement in all levels of government. From changes to the way city governments operated to the increase in the number of states which allowed legislation to be enacted via ballot initiative or provided measures through which voters could recall elected officials, direct democracy was a crucial element of progressive politics. The provisions of the Seventeenth Amendment were as much the result of broader trends in American politics as they were an attempt to address specific perceived shortcomings of the system originally presented in the Constitution. The press—particularly newspaper publisher William Randolph Hearst—also promoted direct election.

State legislatures—perhaps ironically—also began to call for direct election in the first decade of the twentieth century. Proposals for amendments passed the House of Representatives in 1893, 1900, 1904, and 1908. In 1910, ten Republican senators who contributed to an amendment failing in the Senate lost their seats. Clearly, the time was right for reform. The original resolution (House Joint Resolution 39) was introduced in 1911 and reserved for state legislatures the right to establish "the times, places, and manner of" electing senators and was intended to prevent the federal government from combatting voting discrimination based on race. The version that eventually passed in the Senate on April 12 and in the House on May 13, 1912 did not contain this clause and was proposed by Senator Joseph L. Bristow (R-KS). The amendment then when to the states, with Connecticut ratifying it on April 8, 1913, being the final state in the three-fourths necessary for it to go into effect.

Author Biography

Legislation—including proposed Constitutional amendments—is often a collaborative effort, with changes made in conference committees to reconcile variations between language between versions from the House of Representatives and the Senate. In the case of the Seventeenth Amendment, as noted above, we can single out Republican Senator Joseph L. Bristow of Kansas as the originator of the language that would be used.

Bristow was born in Kentucky, in 1861. After getting married in 1879, Bristow and his wife moved to Kansas and briefly farmed before attending college to become a Methodist minister. He would, eventually, work in the newspaper business as an editor. He entered the political field as a secretary to Kansas Governor Edmund Morrill, and would be appointed to an assistant Postmaster General position by President William McKinley. Bristow served one term in the U.S. Senate, from 1909 to 1915, losing in the election of 1914. Following his political career, Bristow moved to a farm in Virginia where he lived until his death in 1944.

Historical Document

Seventeenth Amendment to the U.S. Constitution

Sixty-second Congress of the United States of America; At the Second Session,

Begun and held at the City of Washington on Monday, the fourth day of December, one thousand nine hundred and eleven.

JOINT RESOLUTION

Proposing an amendment to the Constitution providing that Senators shall be elected by the people of the several States.

Resolved by the Senate and House of Representatives of the United States of America in Congress assembled (two-thirds of each House concurring therein), That in lieu of the first paragraph of section three of Article I of the Constitution of the United States, and in lieu of so much of paragraph two of the same section as relates to the filling of vacancies, the following be proposed as an amendment to the Constitution, which shall be valid to all intents and purposes as part of the Constitution when ratified by the legislatures of three-fourths of the States:

"The Senate of the United States shall be composed of two Senators from each State, elected by the people thereof, for six years; and each Senator shall have one vote. The electors in each State shall have the qualifications requisite for electors of the most numerous branch of the State legislatures.

"When vacancies happen in the representation of any State in the Senate, the executive authority of such State shall issue writs of election to fill such vacancies: Provided, That the legislature of any State may empower the executive thereof to make temporary appointments until the people fill the vacancies by election as the legislature may direct.

"This amendment shall not be so construed as to affect the election or term of any Senator chosen before it becomes valid as part of the Constitution."

The Seventeenth Amendment in the National Archives. Photo via Wikimedia Commons. [Public domain.]

Glossary

construed: understood or interpreted

elector: someone with the right to vote in an election

executive authority: the head of the executive branch of a state, such as governor

in lieu of: instead of

Document Analysis

The preamble of the resolution establishes that the Sixty-Second Congress, which opened on December 4, 1911, passed the resolution. The body of the resolution begins by setting out the primary purpose of the amendment, that senators will be elected directly by the people of each state. The resolution continues by confirming that the required two-thirds of each chamber has approved the resolution and detailing which portion of the Constitution (Article 1, Section 3, paragraph 1 and part of paragraph 2) are affected by the amendment.

Then follows the text of the amendment itself, specifying that the senators from each state will be elected by the people of the state will serve six year terms and specifies that electors for the Senate positions should have the same qualifications as those for the state legislatures. The amendment also provides for a means of filling vacant Senate seats, with the "executive authority" (i.e., the governor) of the state having the authority to appoint a replacement, with the provision for the state legislature to mandate a special election.

The amendment closes with the assurance that the terms of existing senators will not be affected by the amendment before it is ratified.

Essential Themes

The Seventeenth Amendment provided a means for the U.S. Senate to be more directly responsible to the voters of each state. Some have argued that the direct election of senators has diminished the power of state legislatures and is not in keeping with the spirit of what the Framers intended, however the fact that several state legislatures delegated Senate selections to the voters prior to the introduction and ratification of the amendment indicates that the political tide was firmly behind more direct participation by the voters.

—*Aaron John Gulyas, MA*

Bibliography and Additional Reading

Bybee, Jay S. "Ulysses at the Mast: Democracy, Federalism, and the Sirens' Song of the Seventeenth Amendment." *Scholarly Works*, 1997. 350. scholars.law.unlv.edu/facpub/350.

Riker, William H. "The Senate and American Federalism." *American Political Science Review* 49, no. 2 (1955): 452-69.

Schiller, Wendy J., and Charles Stewart III. *Electing the Senate: Indirect Democracy before the Seventeenth Amendment.* Princeton, NJ: Princeton UP, 2014.

Zywicki, Todd J. "Beyond the Shell and Husk of History: The History of the Seventeenth Amendment and its Implications for Current Reform Proposals." *Cleveland State Law Review* 45, no. 1 (1997). mason.gmu.edu/~tzywick2/Cleveland%20State%20Senators.pdf.

Twenty-Sixth Amendment to the U.S. Constitution

Date: July 1, 1971
Author: Ninety-second U.S. Congress
Genre: constitution; legislation

Summary Overview

Passed by Congress and ratified by the states in a period of months in 1971, the Twenty-Sixth Amendment established a nationally standardized minimum age of eighteen for participation in state and federal elections. Prior to the ratification of the amendment, states had exercised the right to set their own mandatory minimum voting ages, with twenty-one as the national standard. Federal law made young men eligible for conscription into the military at the age of eighteen. Student activism during the Vietnam War era pushed back against this disparity between the age at which a citizen could be required to fight and possibly die for their nation in wartime and the age at which the same citizen could have a legal say in the government waging that war. The amendment thus represented a significant expansion of the democratic process, if one that has often gone unused due to historically low turnout among young voters.

Defining Moment

The framers of the U.S. Constitution did not include specific criteria for national citizenship or qualification for individual voting in either state or federal elections. The founding document, as written in 1787 and ratified in 1789, guaranteed voting privileges to the states and their representatives in Congress, but not those of the citizenry. And initially, voting was restricted by the states to a relatively small group of property-owning white men.

Between 1792 and 1856, all states removed the voting requirement of property ownership. In 1870 the Fifteenth Amendment officially barred the restriction of voting rights due to race, color, or servitude, though states often continued to use other laws to disenfranchise African Americans and other minorities. State laws also largely restricted the vote to men during the 1800s, with only a few Western territories and states such as Utah granting women's suffrage. A powerful women's rights movement then won the passage of the Nineteenth Amendment, granting women the right to vote nationally in 1920.

A minimum voting age of twenty-one endured throughout this process of gradual expansion of suffrage. Calls for the minimum age to be lowered began after President Franklin D. Roosevelt expanded the military draft to include men as young as eighteen during World War II. A youth rights movement emerged in response, calling for a similarly reduced voting age. West Virginia Congressman Jennings Randolph introduced the first federal bill to make this change in 1942; the following year, Georgia lowered its voting age to eighteen. Randolph's 1942 bill failed to become law, but support for the extension of voting to younger Americans swelled during the 1950s and 1960s.

President Dwight D. Eisenhower, who had led U.S. forces in Europe in World War II, agreed with the argument that a person old enough to fight was old enough to vote. He called for a constitutional amendment affirming suffrage for citizens eighteen and over. The escalation of the conflict in Vietnam during the 1960s heightened the urgency of the issue. Students and youth activists demanded the vote, pointing to the huge numbers of young people drafted to fight in Southeast Asia. Congress debated dozens of measures on the voting age during 1969 alone.

In 1970 Congress passed an extension of the 1965 Voting Rights Act that included an amendment lowering the voting age to eighteen in all states. By this time, only Kentucky, Alaska, and Hawaii had joined Georgia is permitting residents younger than twenty-one to vote. President Richard M. Nixon signed the bill and voiced his support for the lowered voting age, although he expressed concerns that the provision was technically unconstitutional and the issue could only truly by addressed through a constitutional amendment. Soon after, the U.S. Supreme Court heard a challenge to the provision in the case of *Oregon v. Mitchell* (1970). In a narrow decision, the court ruled that Congress lacked the authority to force states to establish a minimum voting age in elections at the state and local level. Agreeing with Nixon, Justice Hugo Black wrote in the court's majority opinion that a constitutional amendment was necessary to enact this change.

The decision left Americans between eighteen and twenty-one years old in an awkward spot. They had the right to vote for president but not necessarily for their local or state leaders. With public pressure mounting, Congress approved a constitutional amendment setting a national minimum age of eighteen for all elections and submitted it to the states for ratification in March 1971. By July of that year enough states had ratified the amendment for it to become part of the Constitution, and it was signed by President Nixon. It was the fastest ratification period for any amendment.

Document Information

The U.S. Constitution establishes two possible ways for new amendments to be considered: approval by both houses of Congress or a constitutional convention. The Twenty-Sixth Amendment began life in the U.S. Senate, which unanimously assented to its addition. It then proceeded to the House of Representatives, which quickly sent the measure to the states for ratification.

State legislatures or ratifying conventions hold the constitutional responsibility for affirming proposed amendments. A two-thirds majority of the states is required for a proposed amendment to be added to the Constitution. North Carolina became the thirty-eighth state to ratify the Twenty-Sixth Amendment on July 1, 1971. An additional five states approved the amendment after it had already achieved adequate support for adoption.

Historical Document

Twenty-Sixth Amendment to the Constitution

AMENDMENT XXVI

Passed by Congress March 23, 1971. Ratified July 1, 1971.

Section 1.

The right of citizens of the United States, who are eighteen years of age or older, to vote shall not be denied or abridged by the United States or by any State on account of age.

Section 2.

The Congress shall have power to enforce this article by appropriate legislation.

The Twenty-Sixth Amendment in the National Archives. Photo via Wikimedia Commons. [Public domain.]

Document Analysis

The Twenty-Sixth Amendment uses brief, direct language to establish the right of all citizens eighteen or older to vote in both state and federal elections. Divided into two sections, the amendment first asserts the right and then grants the federal government the power to ensure that the right is protected through "appropriate legislation."

The language of the Twenty-Sixth Amendment echoes that of earlier voting rights amendments. The Fifteenth Amendment and the Nineteenth Amendment both assert that the "right of citizens of the United States to vote shall not be denied or abridged by the United States or by any State," the former regarding race and the latter regarding sex. The Twenty-Sixth Amendment uses nearly the same phrasing, adding only the qualification that its protections apply to those eighteen years of age or older. The Twenty-Fourth Amendment, which bars the use of a poll tax, also uses similar wording. These four amendments thus share a common theme of broadly barring restrictions rather than extending rights in a more narrowly defined way.

Section 2 of the amendment provides Congress with the constitutional authority to make laws enforcing the amendment's provisions. Therefore, Congress now has the power to enact legislation similar to the amendment of the Voting Rights Act that the 1970 Supreme Court decision in *Oregon v. Mitchell* had overturned on the grounds that Congress lacked the authority to require states to set a particular voting age. Similar provisions exist in other voting rights amendments as well as in the Reconstruction era amendments barring slavery and establishing birthright citizenship in order to grant Congress powers that had not been directly addressed in the body of the Constitution.

Essential Themes

The Twenty-Sixth Amendment stands as part of the historical trend toward greater inclusion in the democratic process in the United States. Like other voting rights amendments before it, it expands the opportunity to have a say in the nation's representative government to more of the governed. It also reflects the support for civil rights for various groups that informed a great deal of federal action during the 1960s, such as the Voting Rights Act of 1965.

The legacy of the Twenty-Sixth Amendment has been somewhat clouded by the historically low voter turnout of the age group which it enfranchised, however. Young people vote at rates greatly below that of other Americans. Although about 55 percent of eligible youth cast votes in 1972, U.S. Census reports show that voting rates among those between the ages of eighteen and twenty-four have generally declined since the expansion of suffrage. By contrast, voting rates among Americans aged sixty-five and over are typically near 70 percent. Still, some elections galvanize the youth vote; Barack Obama's successful presidential campaign in 2008 brought out 49 percent of voters twenty-four and younger.

Some scholars have also argued for a broader reading of the Twenty-Sixth Amendment's impact. Eric S. Fish, for example, has asserted that the amendment protects the voting rights of the elderly and other groups who may face state-specific challenges to voting. For instance, requiring an older American to show a valid driving license in order to exercise the right to vote may be considered a form of age discrimination barred under the Twenty-Sixth Amendment. As states increasingly have passed laws strengthening voter identification requirements, possible constitutional challenges under the Twenty-Sixth Amendment—previously a rarity—may thus begin to reach the courts.

—*Vanessa E. Vaughn, MA*

Bibliography and Additional Reading

File, Thom. "Young-Adult Voting: An Analysis of Presidential Elections, 1964–2012." U.S. Census Bureau. U.S. Census Bureau, Apr. 2014.

Frost, Jennifer. *"Let Us Vote!": Youth Voting Rights and the 26th Amendment.* New York: NYU UP, 2022.

"Twenty-Sixth Amendment." Annenberg Classroom. Leonore Annenberg Inst. for Civics, n.d.

National Voter Registration Act of 1993 (NVRA)

Date: May 20, 1993
Author: 103rd U.S. Congress
Genre: legislation; law

Summary Overview

The National Voter Registration Act of 1993 (NVRA) is also called the Motor Voter Law because it permits eligible voters to register to vote when they apply for a state driver's license. The voter registration application was made part of the motor vehicle license application form by the new law. It also permitted voter registration forms to be submitted by mail. Individuals were free to refuse to sign the affidavit and were not required to register to vote, although the purpose of the law was to facilitate voter registrations and encourage more people to vote, especially in federal elections. The NVRA also designated state public assistance agencies and those dealing with persons with disabilities as voter registration agencies. Recruitment offices for the armed forces were included as locations for voter registration. While this law specifically dealt with federal elections, it encouraged states to apply these measures to state elections. However, the NVRA did not provide money for the implementation of the law, and that caused opposition from some lawmakers in some states.

Defining Moment

The declining number of voters in federal elections in the 1980s alarmed many in Congress. The Voting Rights Act of 1965 had helped reduce voting restrictions on racial minorities, with the goal of allowing all eligible Americans greater access to the vote. There followed in the 1970s attempts to establish a national postcard registration form, with the Census Bureau sending out mass mailings nationally. The effort stalled in Congress. During the Carter presidency (1977–1981) there was a proposal for same-day voter registration, but that also died in Congress. Some attempts to expand voting passed. Congress passed the Voting Accessibility for the Elderly and Handicapped Act in 1984, and the Uniformed and Overseas Citizens Absentee Voting Act in 1986. However, the percentage of voters participating in presidential elections declined from 62 percent in 1964 to 50 percent in 1988, and this prompted Congress to try again. Representative Al Swift (D-WA) introduced a "motor-voter" bill in 1990 but it did not reach the Senate. Later in the 102nd Congress Senators Wendell Ford (D-KY) and Mark Hatfield (R-OR) introduced the National Voter Registration Act of 1991. It passed in both the House and the Senate but was vetoed by President George H. W. Bush. Finally, in 1993 Representative Al Swift and Senator Wendell Ford

President Bill Clinton signing the National Voter Registration Act of 1993 into law. Photo via Wikimedia Commons. [Public domain.]

reintroduced many of the provisions of the 1991 legislation, which with some amendments was approved by both chambers and sent to President Bill Clinton. The president signed the legislation into law (as reproduced here, in synopsis) on May 20, 1993, although that was just the beginning. Opponents of the law argued that many factors influenced the number of voters in any one election and the motor-voter law would do little to increase voting nationwide. Others said that the cost of implementation would be in the millions and would create an unnecessary burden for states. One strong objection was that the ease of voter registration could allow noncitizens and ineligible individuals to register and vote. Proponents of the motor-voter law, in contrast, indicated that it would encourage voters and allow more to participate in elections. There were already measures in place at motor vehicle registration agencies to document a person's identity, they said, and the new law, moreover, made voter fraud a federal offense with strict penalties. It also said the motor-voter law did not apply to states that had no voter registration requirement for federal elections and/or allowed voters to register at the polling place at the time of a general election for federal office.

Author Biography

In the 103rd Congress, Representative Al Swift, a Democrat from Tacoma, Washington, cosponsored a motor-voter law. He was inspired to seek voter registration legislation when he chaired a committee hearing in 1988 in which Washington Secretary of State Ralph Monroe held up his driver's license and asked why it could not serve as voter registration. By 1992, Washington State passed a motor-voter law, even while national legislation was stalled. The other chief sponsors of motor-voter legislation were Wendell Ford, a Democratic senator from Kentucky, and Mark Hatfield, a Republican senator from Oregon. Together, they introduced the National Voter Registration Act of 1991. The bill allowed individuals to register to vote when applying for a driver's license, or by mail, or in person at designated locations. Despite the veto of President George H. W. Bush in 1992, the senators pushed through legislation in the next congress that was passed.

Historical Document

Major Provisions

The National Voter Registration Act of 1993 (NVRA, P.L. 103-31 [42 USC §1973gg et seq.]), the so-called "motor-voter" law, required that, for federal elections, states must establish procedures so that eligible citizens may register to vote:

"(1) by application made simultaneously with an application for a motor vehicle driver's license ... ;

(2) by mail application ... ; and

(3) by application in person (A) at the appropriate registration site designated with respect to the residence of the applicant in accordance with state law; and (B) at a federal, state, or nongovernmental office designated under Section 7 (required for state agencies providing public assistance and agencies primarily engaged in providing services to persons with disabilities)." (Sec. 4(a)(1)-(3))

States that had no voter registration requirement (North Dakota) or that allowed citizens to register to vote at polling places on election day, statewide (Minnesota, Wisconsin, and Wyoming), were exempted from the act. This exemption was also applied to New Hampshire and Idaho, which adopted election-day voter registration after the date specified in the original bill language, March 11, 1993. The cut-off date required for state election-day registration was changed (to August 4, 1994) in an amendment contained in P.L. 104-99, passed and signed into law January 26, 1996.

Some suggested that the law would transfer voting registration authority from local election authorities within a state to other state and local agencies. According to proponents, the law required other agencies to make available voter registration forms and materials and to collect completed applications for registering to vote. Only appropriate state election officials, proponents argued, determined whether applications were adequate and, if so, registered the applicants.

With respect to simultaneous application for voter registration and application for a motor vehicle driver's license (the "motor-voter" provision), the law covered new applications, renewals, and changes in address for drivers' licenses. Under the law, an application (or renewal) for a motor vehicle driver's license also served as an application for voter registration for federal elections, unless the applicant failed to sign the voter registration application (§5(a)(1)). The voter registration application form was to be a part of the motor vehicle license application form, but would not require any information that duplicated information required in the driver's license portion of the form (§5(c)(2)). The form could ask for only the minimum amount of information to prevent duplicate registrations and to enable state election officials to determine the eligibility of the applicant and to administer voter registration laws. Further, the law required that the form include a statement that listed each eligibility requirement (including citizenship), contained an attestation that applicants meet each requirement, and required the signature of the applicants, under penalty of perjury. The form also had to include a statement about penalties for the submission of a false voter registration application and a statement that information about either the declination or the office where the citizen registered would remain confidential. Similar language was required on the mail registration form (§9(b)). Proponents of P.L. 103-31 considered the "motor-voter" provisions to be the most important of the three procedures. Proponents expected that most voter registration eventually would occur via motor vehicle driver's license applications. Mail and agency registration were included to provide means for persons who did not normally acquire a driver's license.

P.L. 103-31 required the states to accept and use a mail registration application form, as developed by the Federal Election Commission (FEC) (§6(a)(1)). The mail registration application form, like the motor-vehicle form, could require only such identifying information (including the signature of the applicant) and other information (including data relating to previous registration by the applicant) as was necessary for state election officials to determine the eligibility of the applicant and to administer voter registration laws (§9(b)(1)). The state was required to make available mail registration forms to governmental and private entities for distribution, emphasizing availability to nongovernmental voter registration programs (§6(b)). Further, first-time voters who registered by mail might be required to vote in person if the person had not previously voted in that jurisdiction (§6(c)).

Under the NVRA, all state agencies involved in providing public assistance, as well as all offices in the state providing services to persons with disabilities, were to be designated as voter registration agencies (§7(a)). The state also was required to designate other offices within the state as voter registration agencies (might include public libraries, schools, offices of city and county governments, fishing and hunting license bureaus, and unemployment compensation offices). These voter registration agencies were required to distribute mail registration application forms to service applicants along with the agencies' own forms, unless the applicants declined to register to vote. The agencies were also to provide assistance in the completion of the mail voter registration application if requested. The agencies were not to attempt to influence applicants to register to vote in a certain way or to discourage the applicants from applying to register to vote. The designated agencies were also required to accept completed voter registration forms for transmittal to the appropriate state election official. Transmittal of completed forms was to occur not later than 10 days after the date of receipt or, if accepted within five days before the end of registration for an election, the application was to be transmitted to an election official not later than five days after receipt (§7(d)). Also, U.S. armed forces recruitment offices located within the state were designated as voter registration agencies under the NVRA (Sec.7(c)). In 1998, Congress passed and the President signed H.R. 6, the Higher Education Amendments of 1998. The bill, as signed into law, contained a provision that required institutions of higher learning in states covered by the NVRA to make "a good faith effort to distribute a mail voter registration form ... to each student enrolled in a degree or certified program." (See H.R. 6 §489(b), P.L. 105244, H.Rept. 105-481, H.Rept. 105-750.)

The NVRA required that, upon receipt and approval or disapproval by the appropriate state election official, each applicant would be sent a notice as to the disposition of the application (§8(a)(2)). A voter registrant's name was not to be removed from the voter registration list except at the request of the applicant, by reason of criminal conviction or mental incapacity, by the death of the applicant, or by the applicant moving out of the jurisdiction (§8(a)(3)-(4)). Registered voters could not be removed from the list for nonvoting (§8(b)(2)). A state's efforts at maintaining up-to-date voter registration rolls were to be conducted in a "uniform, nondiscriminatory" fashion and had to be in "compliance with the Voting Rights Act of 1965" (§8(b)(1)). A state could use the U.S. Postal Service's "National Change Of Address" program to help maintain accurate voter registration rolls (§8(c)(1)). A state could remove a person from its registration list if the registrant notified the election office that he/she had moved or if the registrant failed to respond to a notice sent by the registrar and failed to vote or appear to vote in two federal general elections (§8(d)(1)). That is, the registrant must respond to the notice within the period covered by two general elections—voting being a means of response.

P.L. 103-31 provided no funding to the states to carry out any of the prescribed features. The states could avail themselves of reduced postal rates for mailing for voter registration purposes (Section 8(h)). However, the U.S. Postal Service has stated that receipt of the reduced postal rates also meant a corresponding reduction in level of service. The FEC was to develop, in cooperation with the states, a mail registration form and to provide reports to Congress every two years on the impact of the act (§9(a)).9 Both the attorney general and any aggrieved citizen could seek relief under the act. If, after notification, the appropriate state election official failed to carry out the provisions of the act, an aggrieved citizen might bring a civil suit in a U.S. district court (§11(a)(b)). NVRA made a violation of the voter registration procedures as outlined in the law, either by persons or by election officials, a federal offense (§12). The act went into effect January 1, 1995, or, for states that needed to amend their state constitutions (Arkansas, Vermont, and Virginia), January 1, 1996, or 120 days after the amended state constitutions allowed the passage of the supporting legislation, whichever was later.

[Source: Congressional Research Service, Sept. 18, 2013. www.fas.org/sgp/crs/misc/R40609.pdf]

Document Analysis

The National Voter Registration Act of 1993 (NVRA) was passed by the 103rd Congress with bipartisan support after several years of unsuccessful attempts. The NVRA was aimed at increasing voter turnout by making the process for voter registration simpler and faster. The legislation exempted states that did not have a voter registration requirement or permitted eligible voters to register at a polling place on election day. All other states were required to allow eligible voters simultaneously to register to vote as they registered for a driver's license. It also required states to accept mail-in applications and permit state and federal agencies and those providing services to individuals with disabilities to serve as voter registration offices. The voter registration form was part of any request for renewal of a driver's license or a change of address. There was no requirement for the individual to register to vote while obtaining a driver's license. However, the information could be used for both functions as a way to make the process simple. The application form listed the requirements for voting and a place for the applicant to sign to authorize that they were eligible. To deter ineligible registrations, the form indicated that voter fraud was a federal crime and included a statement of punishment for same. Voter registration forms were also to be available at state welfare offices as well as armed forces recruitment offices. These offices were to function as places where citizens could register, but the information would then be sent to the appropriate state election officials to determine the validity of each application. All voter information was to remain confidential.

The NVRA was far-reaching in its effect. Among state agencies to be designated as voter registration offices were schools and libraries, city and county offices, fishing and hunting license bureaus, and offices of unemployment compensation. Staff in these agencies were expected to assist applicants, while not requiring them to register to vote. Applications from such agencies were required to transmit voter registration applications to state election officials in a timely manner: no later than ten days from receipt or five days if received during the last five days of the end of registration for an election. Although the new legislation supplied no funds for implementing the act, it did permit states to use reduced postage rates for mail registration forms.

Essential Themes

Support for, and opposition to, the NVRA reflected different views about the nature of the electorate in the United States, as well as the appropriate role of the federal government with regard to the states. Representative Al Swift and others who shepherded the NVRA through Congress believed that voting is a fundamental right of American democracy. Therefore, every eligible voter should be encouraged to vote, and any hindrances ought to be removed. The Voting Rights Act of 1965 addressed the obstacles some states had placed on minorities, especially African Americans who faced difficulties in registering and voting. Additional legislation made it easier for active duty military and for residents abroad to vote. The NVRA was designed to encourage voting by making the registration process easier by coupling it with something most Americans did on a regular basis, namely, obtaining or renewing a driver's license. Hence, the nickname the Motor-Voter Law.

Those who opposed this legislation believed that voting was a privilege that should not be abused by ineligible persons or those who had little interest for political candidates and their issues. This did not mean opponents wished to make voting more difficult, only that they feared that such a blanket registration process would make it easier for fraud to occur. Opponents also bristled at the lack of financial support for the implementation of the law. States would have to provide the funds to staff agencies to meet the requirement to provide voter registration assistance and pay for mass mailings of voter registration forms. They believed that the federal government should not impose undue burdens on the states, and that this was an instance of that. While some state attorneys general did file lawsuits to stop the new law, the NVRA prevailed, in the end, and state officials complied with the provisions of the law.

—*James A. Baer, PhD*

Bibliography and Additional Reading

Berman, Ari. *Give Us the Ballot: The Modern Struggle for Voting Rights in America.* New York: Farrar, Straus and Giroux, 2015.

Fife, Brian L. *Reforming the Electoral Process in America: Toward More Democracy in the 21st Century.* Santa Barbara, CA: Praeger, 2010.

Smith, Erin Geiger. *Thank You for Voting: The Maddening, Enlightening, Inspiring Truth About Voting in America.* New York: Harper, 2020.

Waldman, Michael. *The Fight to Vote.* New York: Simon & Schuster, 2016.

Help America Vote Act of 2002 (HAVA)

Date: October 29, 2002
Author: 107th U.S. Congress
Genre: legislation; law

Summary Overview

Confusion surrounding the 2000 presidential election led the U.S. Supreme Court of the United States to essentially decide the outcome, after weeks of reviews, legal suits, and countersuits. As a result, Congress proposed legislation to address problems with voting machines and systems. In October 2002, the 107th Congress passed the Help America Vote Act (HAVA), which was signed into law by President George W. Bush (who won the controversial 2000 election after the Supreme Court ruling). There were three basic elements to the act. The first created a new federal agency, the Election Assistance Commission (EAC), to serve as a national clearinghouse on election administration. The second provided funds for states to improve election administration and voting technology. Finally, the act created minimum standards for election administration.

Defining Moment

Presidential elections in the United States are often hard-fought campaigns that bring millions of citizens to the polls to vote. In 2000, Democratic Vice President Al Gore ran against George W. Bush, Republican governor of Texas. Polling suggested a close election, and as voting continued throughout the day on November 7, Gore won in the Northeast, the Upper Midwest, and the West Coast, garnering 255 electoral votes. Bush won much of the South and the Midwest, with 246 electoral votes. Initial tallies in New Mexico, Oregon, and Florida were too close to call. Some news organizations called the race one way, and then retracted. Al Gore at first publicly conceded, then retracted when it was not clear who won the election. It all came down to Florida and its twenty-five electoral votes. Voting machines and procedures in Florida led to confusion, with some punch cards in some districts deemed improperly marked. Voters in those districts had to line up names with paper tabs, that they were to punch, creating a hole that could be read as a vote. However, some cards had tabs that were only partially separated, which were called "hanging chads." Did this mean that the voter did not vote, or did the voter try to vote but did not punch the card hard enough? Which of the "hanging chads" should count and which should not? Because Bush initially led by 1,784 votes, a recount was ordered and it reduced that lead to 900 votes. Florida's electoral votes would decide the national election, and each political party poured additional resources into the effort to ensure that the recount was accurate and to keep the other side from gaining an advantage. With a lead of 327 votes after a recount in ten counties, Bush and his team proposed halting the recount and declared victory. Gore protested and said additional counties needed a manual recount. With weeks passing since the election, and dates for certification of the electoral count nearing, the U.S. Supreme Court declared an end to the recount, essentially giving the presidency to George Bush. The result pleased Republicans but angered many Democrats. No one believed that the convoluted voting system in Florida was appropriate or perfectly effective, and the mishap led to the Help America Vote Act of 2002 (HAVA).

Author Biography

The 107th U.S. Congress met from January 3, 2001, to November 22, 2002. It was a period of upheaval, beginning with the chaos of the 2000 presidential election, a Senate split 50–50 with shifting control, and a calamitous terrorist attack on September 11, 2001, on the World Trade Center in New York, the Pentagon outside Washington, and the crash of

United Airlines Flight 93 in Shanksville, Pennsylvania. With so much at stake, Congress resolved to improve the administration of voting in the United States, and the bipartisan legislation known as HAVA was passed 357–48 in the House of Representatives and 92–2 in the Senate. The bill was sponsored by Representative Robert Ney (R-OH) who served from 1995 to 2006.

Historical Document

Overview of Major Provisions

A defining image of the 2000 elections was a picture of a member of a Florida county canvassing board inspecting a punch card ballot with a magnifying glass. Florida's closely contested race would decide the 2000 presidential election. One of the issues highlighted by litigation and recounts in the state was the challenge of interpreting incompletely punched "hanging" and "dimpled" chads left by the punch card voting systems used in some Florida counties.

Hearings and reporting on the 2000 elections emphasized, however, that the election administration problems that year were not limited to Florida or to punch card voting systems. Those investigations identified other problems with voting systems. The lever voting machines used in some jurisdictions in 2000 could jam, for example, and did not produce paper trails that could be used to reconstruct votes cast on a jammed machine. Confusing ballot formats contributed to high rates of "overvoting"—or making more selections for a given contest than permitted—in some counties.

The investigations also revealed problems with other aspects of the administration of the 2000 elections, beyond voting systems. Eligible voters who had been erroneously removed from the voter registration rolls were turned away from the polls in some states, for example. Representatives of military and overseas citizens and of individuals with disabilities and older individuals reported particular obstacles to registration and voting by members of those groups.

Congress took three main approaches, in HAVA, to responding to issues highlighted by the 2000 elections: (1) setting requirements for the administration of federal elections, (2) authorizing elections grant programs, and (3) expanding agency support for election administration through creation of the EAC.

Requirements

Some states and localities had adopted policies or technologies before the 2000 elections that may have helped them avoid problems faced by other jurisdictions in 2000. Voting systems that alerted voters to multiple selections for a single office reportedly reduced overvoting in some cases, for example, and statewide voter registration databases may have helped election officials in some states maintain more accurate voter rolls. Provisional voting policies, which enabled voters whose eligibility was challenged at the polls to cast provisional ballots, may have helped mitigate some of the effects of voter registration list maintenance errors.

Other policy proposals were offered in post-2000 hearings and reports. Technology experts suggested setting national standards for voting system auditability, for example, and the U.S. Department of Defense's (DOD's) Federal Voting Assistance Program (FVAP), among others, proposed changes to military and overseas voting processes.

HAVA was designed, in part, to standardize use of some of those policies and technologies in federal elections. Title VII of the act amended existing law to incorporate some of the proposed changes to military and overseas voting, and Title III set requirements for other aspects of the conduct of federal elections. The Title III requirements are briefly summarized below...

- **Voting systems**. Require each state to set uniform standards for what counts as a vote on each type of voting system it uses, and require voting systems to offer voters the opportunity to check and correct their ballots; notify voters about overvoting; produce a manually auditable permanent paper record; provide for accessibility for individuals with disabilities; satisfy alternative language requirements of the Voting Rights Act of 1965 (VRA; P.L. 89-110), as amended; and meet specified error rate standards.

- **Provisional voting**. Require election officials to permit certain voters, including voters whose names do not appear on the voter rolls, to cast provisional ballots; count provisional ballots cast by voters who are found to be eligible under state law to vote; and provide voters with specified options for checking the status of their provisional ballots.

- **Voting information**. Require election officials to post the following information at the polls: a sample ballot, the date of the election, polling place hours, instructions for voting and for complying with HAVA's requirements for mail registrants and first-time voters, and general information about voting rights and prohibitions on fraud and misrepresentation.

- **Statewide voter registration databases**. Require states to implement centralized, computerized statewide voter registration lists and follow specified procedures for maintaining them.

- **Voter identification**. Require certain first-time voters who register by mail to provide one of a specified list of types of identification in order to cast a regular ballot.

- **Federal mail voter registration form**. Require questions about citizenship and age and statements about the new questions and HAVA's voter

ID requirement to be added to the federal mail voter registration form established by the National Voter Registration Act of 1993 (NVRA; P.L. 103-31; 52 U.S.C. §§20501-20511), and require election officials to offer voters who fail to answer the citizenship question an opportunity to complete the form.

HAVA left decisions about how to implement—and, to a certain extent, enforce—its Title III requirements to the states. The act directed the EAC to issue voluntary guidance for implementing the Title III requirements but left states discretion over exactly how to meet them. It assigned federal enforcement of the requirements to the U.S. Department of Justice (DOJ) but routed action by individual voters on violations through state-based administrative complaint procedures rather than an explicit private right of action.

[Source: Congressional Research Service, May 8, 2023. crsreports.congress.gov/product/pdf/R/R46949]

Document Analysis

The presidential election of 2000 shocked many Americans and led to hearings and investigations to discover what went wrong. The findings of these investigations showed that there were a variety of problems with the technology used in voting machines. Machines with pull levers occasionally jammed, leaving no trace of the voter's selection. In other cases, voters found it difficult to align the names of candidates with the place to record the vote. There were also serious issues with voting administration. In some cases, voters had been removed from voter rolls but not notified; when they came to vote, they were turned away. Voters with disabilities and active service military stationed abroad also complained of problems voting.

The 107th Congress addressed these problems with the Help America Vote Act of 2002 (HAVA). This legislation had three main parts. It set certain requirements for administering federal elections and provided grants for states to upgrade voting equipment and improve the administration of voting. It also created the Election Assistance Commission (EAC) to serve as a resource for voting administration. Since there were already many instances of voting machines that created a paper trail for auditing and voter registration databases, HAVA was designed to standardize these technologies and procedures. Title III of the Act set requirements for voting in federal elections. These included a requirement that each state set uniform standards for what counts as a vote, notify voters when they double voted, produce a paper record, and provide instructions in additional languages other than English. The act also permitted provisional voting: when a voter's registration was challenged, instead of being turned away the voter could cast a provisional ballot that would be checked and counted if the voter provided additional information to affirm eligibility. Additionally, sample ballots were to be provided, showing all the questions and candidates so that voters could review the ballot before voting. Finally, the act required specific forms of identification and made that requirement part of the federal voter registration form. The intent of the law was to improve the administration of elections.

Essential Themes

Voting procedures in the United States have evolved over time. In the early republic, only white men with property could vote. They stood before a judge and swore that they had not already voted and proved their identity. Then the voter called out the name of his candidate to the recording clerk. There was no privacy, and elections led to conflict. Property qualifications began to disappear after the 1820s; and then in 1870, the Fifteenth Amendments to the U.S. Constitution gave black men the vote. In 1920 the Nineteenth Amendment was ratified, allowing women to vote. In parts of the United States, especially in the South, there remained restrictions to keep African Americans from voting. Much of that was ended with the Voting Rights Act of 1965. The National Voter Registration Act of 1993 (NVRA), called the motor-voter law, made registering to vote easier.

The technology of voting has also evolved. The old voice vote was replaced by paper ballots, which at first were scraps of paper on which the voter printed the candidate's name. Eventually, political parties began to print a full list of their candidates, giving the voter a single "ticket" that encouraged party-line voting. In 1888 the so-called Australian ballot was adopted. It provided a modicum of secrecy to the voter. By the early twentieth century, a voting machine using levers emerged as a better way to record the vote. Voters stepped into a booth and pulled a small lever next to each name to indicate their choice. These voting machines had many moving parts, were cumbersome to move, and cost a lot of money to maintain. Nevertheless, they remained the most common method of voting through most of the twentieth century.

In the 1960s punch cards were introduced as a method of voting that could be instantaneously read by a computer, providing results more quickly. The problem with punch cards occurred when the small rectangle punched out by the voter, called a "chad," did not separate completely. When that occurred, punch cards had to be reviewed by hand, slowing the process. The difficulty in the 2000 election in Florida occurred when chads were not completely punched through, and the reviewer did not know whether that meant the voter had or had not chosen to vote. In response, Congress passed HAVA to encourage newer technologies for voting and better administrative procedures. One technology adopted by many states was the digital touch screen, where voters marked their vote by touching the name or election question presented. This solved one problem but created another when the possibility of computer hacking occurred and there were no paper backups. One compromise was the Scantron, where voters marked a small bubble to vote and put the paper ballot through a scanner that read it. This provided quick results with a paper backup and is widely used today.

The presidential election of 2020 during the COVID-19 pandemic created challenges for election officials. Many states issued changes to voting procedures, such as drop boxes and early voting. The losing Republican presidential candidate, Donald Trump, falsely claimed that the election was stolen and encouraged state officials to tighten requirements for voting and rely on hand counts of paper ballots. Election officials generally consider this unnecessary, although the debate continues. The 2002 act will not be the last attempt to improve the way Americans vote.

—*James A. Baer, PhD*

Bibliography and Additional Reading

de Nevers, Orion. "What Happened to HAVA? The Help America Vote Act Twenty Years On and Lessons for the Future." *Georgetown Law Journal Online*, www.law.georgetown.edu/georgetown-law-journal/wp content/uploads/sites/26/2022/01/de-Nevers_What-Happened-to-HAVA.pdf.

Fife, Brian L. *Reforming the Electoral Process in America: Toward More Democracy in the 21st Century*. Santa Barbara, CA: Praeger, 2010.

Haulley, Fletcher. *The Help America Vote Act of 2002: Legislation to Modernize America's Voting Systems*. New York: Rosen Central, 2005.

U.S. Congress House of Representatives. *Help America Vote Act of 2002*. Washington, DC: Bibliogov, 2010.

Americans with Disabilities Act (ADA) Polling Place Accessibility Checklist

Date: 2016
Author: U.S. Department of Justice
Genre: legal information; public guidance

Summary Overview

The Americans with Disabilities Act (ADA) is a 1990 federal civil rights law that provides protections to people with disabilities to ensure that they are treated equally in all aspects of life. Title II of the ADA requires state and local governments to ensure that people with disabilities have a full and equal opportunity to vote. The ADA's provisions apply to all aspects of voting, including ballot access and access to polling places (i.e., vote centers). Voting in person at one's designated polling place represents the quintessential American voting experience, although voting by mail has become an increasingly common alternative.

In communities large and small, people cast their ballots in a variety of facilities that temporarily serve as polling places, such as libraries, schools, and fire stations, or churches, stores, and other private buildings. Voters include people with a variety of disabilities, such as those who use wheelchairs, scooters, or other devices, those who have difficulty walking or using stairs, or those who are blind or have vision loss. They are people, young and old, who have come to their polling place to exercise their right to vote. Many localities report that their polling places are accessible. However, a review by the Government Accountability Office estimated in 2008 that only 27 percent of polling places were accessible to people with disabilities. According to the ADA, people with disabilities must have the opportunity to be full participants in a public civic event. The ADA requires that state and local governments ensure that people with disabilities can access and use all of their voting facilities.

Defining Moment

The Americans with Disabilities Act (ADA) regulations set out what makes a facility accessible. Because a mix of public and private facilities are used as polling places, district officials can ensure Election Day accessibility of a polling place by using low-cost temporary measures, such as portable ramps or doorstops, rather than necessarily making permanent modifications to a facility. In cases where temporary measures will not fix a barrier, and permanent modifications are infeasible (because of cost or use of the facility outside of polling), districts must locate an alternative, accessible polling place.

In the years following the institution of the ADA, the U.S. Department of Justice (DOJ) occasionally issued guidance to state and local governments regarding voting rights under the ADA. The document presented here, a checklist for polling officials to ensure compliance with the law, was released in 2016. The checklist is based on a fuller explanation of ADA regulations called the Standards for Accessible Design.

Author Biography

The ADA was put in place by a broad bipartisan coalition of legislators based on the recommendations of the National Council on Disabilities. It was signed into law in 1990 by President George H. W. Bush. Generally supported by the American public, it was initially opposed by business interests because of concerns over the cost of modifications. Since then it has become an ingrained part of business, education, and public life in communities throughout the United States.

The DOJ, an independent part of the executive branch of the U.S. government, is charged, among

Photo via iStock/shironosov. [Used under license.]

other things, with informing public entities about their rights and responsibilities concerning federal laws and regulations. In this instance, the DOJ issued (in 2016) specific guidance regarding the layout and use of polling places under the ADA. The guidance is based on the more comprehensive and authoritative ADA Standards for Accessibility Design. As noted in the document, those standards were established in 1991 and revised in 2010. The 2016 checklist reproduced here came out of DOJ's Civil Rights Division—specifically, its Disability Rights Section.

Historical Document

Part 3 : Polling Place Accessibility Checklist

Ward:_____ Precinct:_____ Staff:_____ Date:_____ Time:_____

Address:_____ Location name:_____

This checklist is designed to provide guidance for determining whether a polling place has basic accessibility features needed by voters with disabilities.

For each question below there are citations to the 2010 ADA Standards for Accessible Design (2010 Standards). Please review the 2010 Standards for all requirements.

There are some differences between the 1991 ADA Standards for Accessible Design (1991 Standards) and the 2010 Standards. Elements and spaces in a building constructed or altered before March 15, 2012, that complied with the 1991 Standards may remain in compliance with the 2010 Standards. See 28 C.F.R. §35.150(b)(2) for more information.

In completing the checklist, provide a measurement for every question with a "no" answer. Where a question asks about more than one element, provide a note in the comments explaining any noncompliant elements.

Status of Polling Place

____ All Elements Compliant

____ Non-Compliant Elements Remediable with Temporary Measures

____ Non-Compliant Elements Not Remediable with Temporary Measures (Relocate Polling Place)

Americans with Disabilities Act (ADA) Polling Place Accessibility Checklist

Ward:_____ Precinct:_____ Staff:_____ Date:_____ Time:_____

Address:_____ Location name:_____

| A | Parking

Only complete this section if off-street parking is provided to voters. If off-street parking is not provided to voters, go to Section B.

If more than 25 parking spaces are provided to voters, see the 2010 Standards for the number of accessible parking spaces required. (§208.2) | Yes | No | N/A | Comments/ Remedies |
|---|---|---|---|---|---|
| A1 | Is there at least one designated van accessible space with signage with the International Symbol of Accessibility and designated "van accessible"? (§§208.2, 208.2.4, 502.6) | | | | |
| A2 | Are the designated van accessible spaces at least 96" wide with a 96" wide access aisle, or 132" wide with a 60" wide access aisle? (§§502.2, 502.3)
Width of space _____
Width of access aisle _____ | | | | |
| A3 | For van accessible spaces (particularly in a garage or parking structure), is there vertical clearance of at least 98" for the vehicular route to the parking space, in the parking space and access aisle, and along the vehicular route to the exit? (§502.5) | | | | |
| A4 | Are designated accessible parking spaces and the access aisles serving them on a level surface, with slopes not exceeding 1:48 in all directions? (Note: Curb ramps may not be part of an access aisle since they include slopes greater than 1:48.) (§502.4) | | | | |
| A5 | Are the surfaces of the designated accessible parking spaces and access aisles stable, firm, and slip resistant? (§§502.4, 302.1) | | | | |
| A6 | Are the designated accessible parking spaces located on the shortest accessible route to the accessible entrance? (§208.3.1) | | | | |

Ward:_____ Precinct:_____ Staff:_____ Date:_____ Time:_____

Address:_____ Location name:_____

B	Passenger Drop-Off Area **Only complete this section if a passenger drop-off area is provided for voters. If a drop-off area is not provided to voters, go to Section C.**	Yes	No	N/A	Comments/ Remedies
B1	Is the vehicle pull-up space on a level surface, with slopes not exceeding 1:48 in all directions? (§503.4)				
B2	Is the access aisle next to the vehicle pull-up space on a level surface, with a slope not exceeding 1:48 in all directions? (§503.4)				
B3	Is there vertical clearance of at least 114" (9 feet 6 inches) from the site entrance to the vehicle pull-up area, in the access aisle, and along the vehicular route to the exit? (§503.5)				
B4	Is a curb ramp provided if a curb separates the access aisle from the accessible route to the accessible entrance? (§§206.2.1, 503.3)				
B5	Is the width of the curb ramp surface at least 36" (not counting the side flares)? (§405.5)				
B6	Does an accessible route connect the access aisle and curb ramp to the accessible entrance of the polling place? (§206.2)				

Ward:_____ Precinct:_____ Staff:_____ Date:_____ Time:_____

Address:_____ Location name:_____

C	Exterior Route to Accessible Entrance **Complete a separate Exterior Route form, when applicable, for the routes from 1) parking, 2) passenger drop-off areas, 3) public sidewalks and 4) public transportation stops.** **Exterior route location:** _____	Yes	No	N/A	Comments/ Remedies
C1	Is the route at least 36" wide? (§403.5.1)				
C2	Is the route free of abrupt changes in level greater than ½", including stairs? (§303)				
C3	Is the route free of surface openings greater than ½", such as grates or holes in the pavement? (§302.3)				
C4	Are walking surfaces stable, firm, and slip resistant? (§302.1)				
C5	Is the route free of wall mounted objects that protrude more than 4" into the path of travel and are between 27" and 80" high? (§307.2)				
C6	Is the route free of post mounted objects that protrude more than 12" into the path of travel and are between 27" and 80" high? (§307.3)				
C7	Are objects that hang over the pedestrian route 80" or higher, including the underside of exterior stairs? (§307.4)				
C8	If the route crosses a curb, is there a curb ramp that is at least 36" wide with a slope no more than 1:12? (§§303.4, 405.2, 405.5, 406.1)				
C9	Is the running slope of part of the route greater than 1:20? If yes, go to Section G. (§402.2)				
C10	Is the cross slope of the accessible route no greater than 1:48? (§§403.3, 405.3)				

Ward:_____ Precinct:_____ Staff:_____ Date:_____ Time:_____

Address:_____ Location name:_____

D	Polling Place Entrances	Yes	No	N/A	Comments/ Remedies
D1	Is the clear width of the door opening (one door or one active leaf of a double door) at least 32"? (§404.2.3)				
D2	Is each door hardware useable with one hand without tight grasping, pinching, or twisting of the wrist? (§§309.4, 404.2.7)				
D3	On the pull side of the door, is there at least 18" of clearance provided to the side of the latch? (§404.2.4)				
D4	Is the area in front of the door level, with slopes no greater than 1:48 in all directions? (§§404.2.4.4, 405.7.1)				
D5	If there are doors in a series, is the distance between the two hinged doors at least 48" plus the width of the door swinging into the space? (§404.2.6)				
D6	Can the second door (interior door) in the series be opened with no more than 5 pounds of force? (§309.4)				
D7	Does the second door (interior door) in the series comply with D2, D3, and D4, above?				
D8	Are door thresholds no higher than ½"? (Note: If the threshold is between ¼" and ½" it must be beveled.) (§404.2.5)				
D9	Do inaccessible entrances have signage directing voters to the accessible entrance? (§216.6)				
D10	If voters are directed to an alternative accessible entrance, is this entrance kept unlocked during voting hours? (28 C.F.R. §§35.130, 35.133)				

Ward:_____ Precinct:_____ Staff:_____ Date:_____ Time:_____

Address:_____ Location name:_____

E	Route from Entrance Into Voting Area	Yes	No	N/A	Comments/ Remedies
E1	Is the route at least 36" wide? (§403.5.1)				
E2	Is the route free of wall mounted objects that protrude more than 4" into the path of travel and are between 27" and 80" high? (§307.2)				
E3	Is the route free of post mounted objects that protrude more than 12" into the path of travel and are between 27" and 80" high? (§307.3)				
E4	Are objects that hang over the route 80" or higher, including the underside of stairs? (§307.4)				
E5	Is the route free of abrupt changes in level greater than ½", including stairs? (§303)				
E6	Is the running slope of part of the route greater than 1:20? If yes, go to Section G. (§303.4)				
E7	If the route to the voting area has stairs, is a platform lift or elevator provided? If yes, go to Section H (lifts) or Section I (elevators). (§402.2)				
E8	If doors are provided along the route to the voting area, is the clear width of each door opening (one door or one active leaf of a double door) at least 32"? (§404.2.3)				
E9	Is each door hardware useable with one hand without tight grasping, pinching, or twisting of the wrist? (§§309.4, 404.2.7)				
E10	Can each door be opened with no more than 5 pounds of force? (§309.4)				
E11	Is the threshold at each door no higher than ½"? (Note: If the threshold is between ¼" and ½" it must be beveled.) (§404.2.5)				
E12	On the pull side of each door, is there at least 18" of clearance provided to the side of the latch? (§404.2.4)				
E13	Is the area in front of each door level, with slopes no greater than 1:48 in all directions? (§§404.2.4.4, 405.7.1)				

Ward:_____ Precinct:_____ Staff:_____ Date:_____ Time:_____

Address:_____ Location name:_____

F	Within the Voting Area	Yes	No	N/A	Comments/ Remedies
F1	Are floor surfaces stable, firm, and slip resistant? (§302.1)				
F2	Is the route free of wall mounted objects that protrude more than 4" into the path of travel and are between 27" and 80" high? (§307.2)				
F3	Is the route free of post mounted objects that protrude more than 12" into the path of travel and are between 27" and 80" high? (§307.3)				
F4	Are objects that hang over the route 80" or higher, including the underside of stairs? (§307.4)				
F5	Is there enough room to provide a route at least 36" wide to the registration table and voting stations? (§403.5.1)				
F6	Is there enough room to provide a turning space in front of at least one voting station, such as a circle that is at least 60" in diameter? (§304.3)				
F7	Is there enough room to provide a turning space in front of at least one accessible voting machine, such as a circle that is at least 60" in diameter? (§304.3)				

Americans with Disabilities Act (ADA) Polling Place Accessibility Checklist • 279

Ward:_____ Precinct:_____ Staff:_____ Date:_____ Time:_____

Address:_____ Location name:_____

G	Ramps **Complete a separate ramp form for each ramp, whether exterior or interior.** **Ramp location:** _____	Yes	No	N/A	Comments/ Remedies
G1	Is the running slope of the ramp no greater than 1:12? (§405.2)				
G2	Is the cross slope of the ramp 1:48 or less? (§405.3)				
G3	Is the rise (height) for any ramp run 30" or less? (§405.6)				
G4	Is the ramp, measured between handrails, at least 36" wide? (§405.5)				
G5	Does the ramp have a level landing that is at least 60" long, at the top and bottom of each ramp section? (§405.7)				
G6	For every 30" of rise, is a level landing at least 60" long provided? (§§405.6, 405.7)				
G7	Is a level landing, at least 60" by 60" provided where the ramp changes direction? (§405.7.4)				
G8	If the rise of the ramp is greater than 6", are handrails provided that are between 34" and 38" above the ramp surface? (§§405.8, 505.4)				
G9	If the rise of the ramp is greater than 6" and the ramp or landing has a vertical drop-off on either side of the ramp, is edge protection provided? (§405.9)				

Ward:_____ Precinct:_____ Staff:_____ Date:_____ Time:_____

Address:_____ Location name:_____

H	Lifts	Yes	No	N/A	Comments/ Remedies
H1	Is the lift operational at the time of the survey? (28 C.F.R. §§35.130, 35.133)				
H2	Is the lift independently operable, or can it be made so during Election Day? (§410.1)				
H3	Is there 30" by 48" of clear floor space within the lift? (§§410.3, 305.3)				
H4	Are the controls for the lift no higher than 48"? (§§410.5, 309.3, 308)				
H5	Are the controls useable with one hand without tight grasping, pinching or twisting? (§§410.5, 309.4)				
H6	Is the clear width of the door opening/gate opening at the end of the lift at least 32"? If a side door/gate is provided, is the clear opening width at least 42"? (§410.6)				

Ward:_____ Precinct:_____ Staff:_____ Date:_____ Time:_____

Address:_____ Location name:_____

I	Elevators	Yes	No	N/A	Comments/ Remedies
I1	Is the elevator car door opening at least 36" wide? (§407.3.6, Table 407.4.1)				
I2	Is there space to maneuver within the elevator car, e.g., 51" deep and 68" wide; OR 80" deep and 54" wide; OR 60" deep and 60" wide? (§407.4.1)				
I3	Are hallway elevator call buttons 48" high or lower? (§§407.2.1.1, 308.2, 308.3)				
I4	Are elevator car controls 48" high or lower? (§§407.4.6.1, 308.2, 308.3)				
I5	Does the elevator have visible and audible signals in the hallway to indicate the arrival and direction of the elevator car? (§407.2.2.1)				
I6	Does the elevator have visible and audible signals within the elevator car to indicate the position of the car? (§407.4.8)				

Document Analysis and Themes

The checklist is broken down into nine sections: Parking, Passenger Drop-Off Areas, Exterior Route to Accessible Entrance, Polling Place Entrances, Route from Entrance into Voting Area, Within the Voting Area, Ramps, Lifts, and Elevators. Each section has a set of Yes or No questions to address in order to determine whether a space or facility is compliant. The user can also add comments or notes/measurements at the end of each question.

The checklist is designed to assist officials in determining whether a facility being considered for use as a polling place is accessible to people with mobility or vision disabilities, and, if not, whether modifications can be made to ensure accessibility or relocation to another accessible facility will be necessary. The checklist can be used to evaluate both new and existing polling places. Completing the checklist is a way to learn whether a facility is accessible for voters with disabilities, and to identify and help remedy any barriers that exist.

The evaluation of a polling place's accessibility is meant to bring to focus those areas of the facility that will be used by voters—specifically, voters with disabilities—on Election Day. The checklist leads one to examine parking area and passenger drop-off sites routes (both exterior and interior) the entrance to the polling place, and the voting area itself.

Each disability parking space must have an access aisle adjacent to it that is wide enough to allow voters with a mobility disability to get out of their car or van, and signage identifying it as an accessible parking space. After exiting the vehicle the voter with a disability must have an accessible route from the parking lot or passenger drop-off site (including from public transportation stops) to get to the entrance of the voting center. Inside the polling place, there must be an accessible route from the entrance through hallways, corridors, and interior rooms leading to the voting area. All such routes, exterior or interior, must be free of abrupt changes in level, steps, high thresholds, or steeply sloped walkways. Gradually sloping ramps can be added as necessary. Each polling place must have at least one accessible entrance with a minimum clearance width to allow wheelchairs through. If the voting area is not on the same level as the entrance, there must be a user-operable elevator or lift to provide an accessible route to individuals with disabilities. The voting area must have an accessible entrance and adequate circulation and maneuvering space for voters who use wheelchairs or scooters, or who walk with mobility devices, to get in to the voting area, sign in at the check-in table, and go to the voting stations or machines.

Although one person can complete a survey of a polling place, it is recommended elsewhere in the document (narrative portion; not shown) that two people work together to make the process go more quickly and easily. One can be responsible for taking the measurements and the other for recording the information and taking any photographs.

Some accessibility barriers at polling places can be addressed with temporary remedies. By visiting local hardware or home improvement stores, or shopping online, one may find such items as traffic cones, accessible parking signs, directional signs, portable ramps, doorstops, threshold wedges, and more. When temporary measures are insufficient, district officials will likely need to budget for building contractors to make the necessary changes to the facility. Many contractors specialize in accessible design and construction and can serve as a resource for local officials.

Bibliography and Additional Reading

"ADA Checklist for Polling Places." *U.S. Department of Justice*, 2016, archive.ada.gov/votingchecklist.pdf.

"ADA Standards for Accessible Design." *U.S. Department of Justice*, 2010, www.ada.gov/law-and-regs/design-standards.

Kent, Janice. *ADA in Detail: Interpreting the 2010 Americans with Disabilities Act Standards for Accessible Design*. Hoboken, NJ: Wiley, 2017.

"Voters with Disabilities: Challenges to Voting Accessibility." *U.S. Government Accountability Office*, 2013, www.gao.gov/products/gao-13-538sp.

Civics Test for Naturalization

Date: Revised January 2019
Author: U.S. Citizenship and Immigration Services
Genre: naturalization test

Summary Overview

The United States' naturalization process—the process by which noncitizens can become citizens—is about as old as the nation itself. In the late eighteenth century, the federal government codified the process. In these early years, the racial bias inherent in the nation's founding vision can be seen in the naturalization laws: among residency and character requirements, these early laws stipulated that individuals must be "free" and "white" in order to be naturalized. From the beginning, it was up to local judges to enforce the specifics of the laws and oversee the naturalization process. In 1802, the laws first required individuals seeking naturalization to be "attached to the principles of the Constitution." Many judges took this to mean that a civics test was required as part of the process. When the naturalization process was nationalized in the early twentieth century, the federal Bureau of Naturalization came to the same conclusion. The test was eventually standardized with study tests such as the one presented here published for those going through or about to go through the process. Test takers are asked up to ten of one hundred questions and must get six correct in order to pass this portion of the naturalization procedure. Many of the questions have to do with voting, elections, and related topics, reflecting the importance of elections in a democratic system.

Defining Moment

From the nation's birth, the government separated naturalization from immigration. For its first century or so, the nation had an open-borders policy regarding immigration: anyone with the means and will to do so could move to the United States, pay taxes, and even serve in the military. However, in order to vote or hold public office, an individual would need to be naturalized, which had stricter limits. Congress first attempted to codify the process in the Naturalization Act of 1790. This act stipulated that an individual could be naturalized as an American citizen provided that he or she were a "free white person," had lived in the United States for two years, and were "of good character." In successive iterations of the legislation (the

Local libraries may offer free resources to help naturalization applicants prepare for the American Civics Test. Photo by Jengod, via Wikimedia Commons.

Naturalizations Acts of 1795, 1798, and 1802), Congress tweaked the law, but it was not until the iteration of 1802 that Congress required any individual seeking naturalization to be "attached to the principles of the Constitution." This requirement served as the impetus for the civics test portion of the naturalization process.

Although requiring a familiarity with the U.S. Constitution," the naturalization process occurred at the local level through the nineteenth century. Local judges were charged with overseeing the process, and while some judges interpreted the "attachment clause" to call for a civics test, others did not. The tests that were administered varied widely in their content and difficulty. Beginning in 1906, the Bureau of Naturalization began to oversee and standardize the process from a federal standpoint. The test became an imbedded part of the process, and the bureau also began to provide educational services for those seeking to take the test. The questions themselves were eventually standardized, but the local administrators retained the ability to choose which questions to ask, and the test remained oral. In 1933, the Bureau of Naturalization was superseded by Immigration and Naturalization Service (INS), which in turn was superseded by multiple agencies in 2003. Among those was U.S. Citizenship and Immigration Services, which oversees the naturalization process—and therefore the civics test—till the present day.

Author Biography

The civics test, alone with the rest of the naturalization process, is administered by the U.S. Citizenship and Immigration Services (USCIS). The agency was formed in 2003 as part of the 2002 Homeland Security Act, which passed Congress under the administration of George W. Bush in the wake of the September 11 attacks of 2001. This act first created the Department of Homeland Security (DHS) and made its Secretary a cabinet position. Under the new agency, what had been Immigration and Naturalization Service (INS) from 1933 to 2003 became three new agencies: U.S. Citizenship and Immigration Services, U.S. Immigration and Customs Enforcement (ICE), and U.S. Customs and Border Protection (CBP). U.S. Citizenship and Immigration Services' mission statement reads, "U.S. Citizenship and Immigration Services administers the nation's lawful immigration system, safeguarding its integrity and promise by efficiently and fairly adjudicating requests for immigration benefits while protecting Americans, securing the homeland, and honoring our values." Upon its establishment, the agency inherited the civics test from INS and has been revising it regularly. Lee Cissna was the director of the USCIS when this most recent iteration (January 2019) was released.

Historical Document

Naturalization Test

(rev. 01/19)

Civics (History and Government) Questions for the Naturalization Test

The 100 civics (history and government) questions and answers for the naturalization test are listed below. The civics test is an oral test and the USCIS Officer will ask the applicant up to 10 of the 100 civics questions. An applicant must answer 6 out of 10 questions correctly to pass the civics portion of the naturalization test.

On the naturalization test, some answers may change because of elections or appointments. As you study for the test, make sure that you know the most current answers to these questions. Answer these questions with the name of the official who is serving at the time of your eligibility interview with USCIS. The USCIS Officer will not accept an incorrect answer.

Although USCIS is aware that there may be additional correct answers to the 100 civics questions, applicants are encouraged to respond to the civics questions using the answers provided below.

AMERICAN GOVERNMENT

A: Principles of American Democracy

1. What is the supreme law of the land?
   – the Constitution

2. What does the Constitution do?
   – sets up the government
   – defines the government
   – protects basic rights of Americans

3. The idea of self-government is in the first three words of the Constitution. What are these words?
   – We the People

4. What is an amendment?
   – a change (to the Constitution)
   – an addition (to the Constitution)

5. What do we call the first ten amendments to the Constitution?
    – the Bill of Rights

6. What is one right or freedom from the First Amendment?*
    – speech
    – religion
    – assembly
    – press
    – petition the government

7. How many amendments does the Constitution have?
    – twenty-seven (27)

8. What did the Declaration of Independence do?
    – announced our independence (from Great Britain)
    – declared our independence (from Great Britain)
    – said that the United States is free (from Great Britain)

9. What are two rights in the Declaration of Independence?
    – life
    – liberty
    – pursuit of happiness

10. What is freedom of religion?
    – You can practice any religion, or not practice a religion.

11. What is the economic system in the United States?*
    – capitalist economy
    – market economy

12. What is the "rule of law"?
    – Everyone must follow the law.
    – Leaders must obey the law.
    – Government must obey the law.
    – No one is above the law.

B: System of Government

13. Name one branch or part of the government.*
    – Congress legislative
    – President executive
    – the courts judicial

14. What stops one branch of government from becoming too powerful?
    – checks and balances
    – separation of powers

15. Who is in charge of the executive branch?
    – the President

16. Who makes federal laws?
    – Congress
    – Senate and House (of Representatives)
    – (U.S. or national) legislature

17. What are the two parts of the U.S. Congress?*
    – the Senate and House (of Representatives)

18. How many U.S. Senators are there?
    – one hundred (100)

19. We elect a U.S. Senator for how many years?
    – six (6)

20. Who is one of your state's U.S. Senators now?*
    – Answers will vary. [District of Columbia residents and residents of U.S. territories should answer that D.C. (or the territory where the applicant lives) has no U.S. Senators.]

21. The House of Representatives has how many voting members?
    – four hundred thirty-five (435)

22. We elect a U.S. Representative for how many years?
    – two (2)

23. Name your U.S. Representative.
    – Answers will vary. [Residents of territories with nonvoting Delegates or Resident Commissioners may provide the name of that Delegate or Commissioner. Also acceptable is any statement that the territory has no (voting) Representatives in Congress.]

24. Who does a U.S. Senator represent?
    – all people of the state

25. Why do some states have more Representatives than other states?
    – (because of) the state's population
    – (because) they have more people
    – (because) some states have more people

26. We elect a President for how many years?
    – four (4)

27. In what month do we vote for President?*
    – November

28. What is the name of the President of the United States now?*
    – Visit uscis.gov/citizenship/testupdates for the name of the President of the United States.

29. What is the name of the Vice President of the United States now?
    – Visit uscis.gov/citizenship/testupdates for the name of the Vice President of the United States.

30. If the President can no longer serve, who becomes President?
    – the Vice President

31. If both the President and the Vice President can no longer serve, who becomes President?
    – the Speaker of the House

32. Who is the Commander in Chief of the military?
    – the President

33. Who signs bills to become laws?
    – the President

34. Who vetoes bills?
    – the President

35. What does the President's Cabinet do?
    – advises the President

36. What are two Cabinet-level positions?
    – Secretary of Agriculture
    – Secretary of Commerce
    – Secretary of Defense
    – Secretary of Education
    – Secretary of Energy
    – Secretary of Health and Human Services
    – Secretary of Homeland Security
    – Secretary of Housing and Urban Development
    – Secretary of the Interior
    – Secretary of Labor
    – Secretary of State
    – Secretary of Transportation
    – Secretary of the Treasury
    – Secretary of Veterans Affairs
    – Attorney General
    – Vice President

37. What does the judicial branch do?
    – reviews laws

- explains laws
- resolves disputes (disagreements)
- decides if a law goes against the Constitution

38. What is the highest court in the United States?
    - the Supreme Court

39. How many justices are on the Supreme Court?
    - Visit uscis.gov/citizenship/testupdates for the number of justices on the Supreme Court.

40. Who is the Chief Justice of the United States now?
    - Visit uscis.gov/citizenship/testupdates for the name of the Chief Justice of the United States.

41. Under our Constitution, some powers belong to the federal government. What is one power of the federal government?
    - to print money
    - to declare war
    - to create an army
    - to make treaties

42. Under our Constitution, some powers belong to the states. What is one power of the states?
    - provide schooling and education
    - provide protection (police)
    - provide safety (fire departments)
    - give a driver's license
    - approve zoning and land use

43. Who is the Governor of your state now?
    - Answers will vary. [District of Columbia residents should answer that D.C. does not have a Governor.]

44. What is the capital of your state?*
    - Answers will vary. [District of Columbia residents should answer that D.C. is not a state and does not have a capital. Residents of U.S. territories should name the capital of the territory.]

45. What are the two major political parties in the United States?*
    - Democratic and Republican

46. What is the political party of the President now?
    - Visit uscis.gov/citizenship/testupdates for the political party of the President.

47. What is the name of the Speaker of the House of Representatives now?
    – Visit uscis.gov/citizenship/testupdates for the name of the Speaker of the House of Representatives.

C: Rights and Responsibilities

48. There are four amendments to the Constitution about who can vote. Describe one of them.
    – Citizens eighteen (18) and older (can vote).
    – You don't have to pay (a poll tax) to vote.
    – Any citizen can vote. (Women and men can vote.)
    – A male citizen of any race (can vote).

49. What is one responsibility that is only for United States citizens?*
    – serve on a jury
    – vote in a federal election

50. Name one right only for United States citizens.
    – vote in a federal election
    – run for federal office

51. What are two rights of everyone living in the United States?
    – freedom of expression
    – freedom of speech
    – freedom of assembly
    – freedom to petition the government
    – freedom of religion
    – the right to bear arms

52. What do we show loyalty to when we say the Pledge of Allegiance?
    – the United States
    – the flag

53. What is one promise you make when you become a United States citizen?
    – give up loyalty to other countries
    – defend the Constitution and laws of the United States
    – obey the laws of the United States
    – serve in the U.S. military (if needed)
    – serve (do important work for) the nation (if needed)
    – be loyal to the United States

54. How old do citizens have to be to vote for President?*
    – eighteen (18) and older

55. What are two ways that Americans can participate in their democracy?
    – vote

- join a political party
- help with a campaign
- join a civic group
- join a community group
- give an elected official your opinion on an issue
- call Senators and Representatives
- publicly support or oppose an issue or policy
- run for office
- write to a newspaper

56. When is the last day you can send in federal income tax forms?*
    - April 15

57. When must all men register for the Selective Service?
    - at age eighteen (18)
    - between eighteen (18) and twenty-six (26)

AMERICAN HISTORY

A: Colonial Period and Independence

58. What is one reason colonists came to America?
    - freedom
    - political liberty
    - religious freedom
    - economic opportunity
    - practice their religion
    - escape persecution

59. Who lived in America before the Europeans arrived?
    - American Indians
    - Native Americans

60. What group of people was taken to America and sold as slaves?
    - Africans
    - people from Africa

61. Why did the colonists fight the British?
    - because of high taxes (taxation without representation)
    - because the British army stayed in their houses (boarding, quartering)
    - because they didn't have self-government

62. Who wrote the Declaration of Independence?
    - (Thomas) Jefferson

63. When was the Declaration of Independence adopted?
    - July 4, 1776

64. There were 13 original states. Name three.
    – New Hampshire
    – Massachusetts
    – Rhode Island
    – Connecticut
    – New York
    – New Jersey
    – Pennsylvania
    – Delaware
    – Maryland
    – Virginia
    – North Carolina
    – South Carolina
    – Georgia

65. What happened at the Constitutional Convention?
    – The Constitution was written.
    – The Founding Fathers wrote the Constitution.

66. When was the Constitution written?
    – 1787

67. The Federalist Papers supported the passage of the U.S. Constitution. Name one of the writers.
    – (James) Madison
    – (Alexander) Hamilton
    – (John) Jay
    – Publius

68. What is one thing Benjamin Franklin is famous for?
    – U.S. diplomat
    – oldest member of the Constitutional Convention
    – first Postmaster General of the United States
    – writer of "Poor Richard's Almanac"
    – started the first free libraries

69. Who is the "Father of Our Country"?
    – (George) Washington

70. Who was the first President?*
    – (George) Washington

B: 1800s

71. What territory did the United States buy from France in 1803?
    – the Louisiana Territory
    – Louisiana

72. Name one war fought by the United States in the 1800s.
    – War of 1812
    – Mexican-American War
    – Civil War
    – Spanish-American War

73. Name the U.S. war between the North and the South.
    – the Civil War
    – the War between the States

74. Name one problem that led to the Civil War.
    – slavery
    – economic reasons
    – states' rights

75. What was one important thing that Abraham Lincoln did?*
    – freed the slaves (Emancipation Proclamation)
    – saved (or preserved) the Union
    – led the United States during the Civil War

76. What did the Emancipation Proclamation do?
    – freed the slaves
    – freed slaves in the Confederacy
    – freed slaves in the Confederate states
    – freed slaves in most Southern states

77. What did Susan B. Anthony do?
    – fought for women's rights
    – fought for civil rights

C: Recent American History and Other Important Historical Information

78. Name one war fought by the United States in the 1900s.*
    – World War I
    – World War II
    – Korean War
    – Vietnam War
    – (Persian) Gulf War

79. Who was President during World War I?
    – (Woodrow) Wilson

80. Who was President during the Great Depression and World War II?
    – (Franklin) Roosevelt

81. Who did the United States fight in World War II?
    – Japan, Germany, and Italy

82. Before he was President, Eisenhower was a general. What war was he in?
    – World War II

83. During the Cold War, what was the main concern of the United States?
    – Communism

84. What movement tried to end racial discrimination?
    – civil rights (movement)

85. What did Martin Luther King, Jr. do?*
    – fought for civil rights
    – worked for equality for all Americans

86. What major event happened on September 11, 2001, in the United States?
    – Terrorists attacked the United States.

87. Name one American Indian tribe in the United States.
[USCIS Officers will be supplied with a list of federally recognized American Indian tribes.]
    – Cherokee
    – Navajo
    – Sioux
    – Chippewa
    – Choctaw
    – Pueblo
    – Apache
    – Iroquois
    – Creek
    – Blackfeet
    – Seminole
    – Cheyenne
    – Arawak
    – Shawnee
    – Mohegan
    – Huron
    – Oneida
    – Lakota
    – Crow
    – Teton
    – Hopi
    – Inuit

INTEGRATED CIVICS

A: Geography

88. Name one of the two longest rivers in the United States.
    - Missouri (River)
    - Mississippi (River)

89. What ocean is on the West Coast of the United States?
    - Pacific (Ocean)

90. What ocean is on the East Coast of the United States?
    - Atlantic (Ocean)

91. Name one U.S. territory.
    - Puerto Rico
    - U.S. Virgin Islands
    - American Samoa
    - Northern Mariana Islands
    - Guam

92. Name one state that borders Canada.
    - Maine
    - New Hampshire
    - Vermont
    - New York
    - Pennsylvania
    - Ohio
    - Michigan
    - Minnesota
    - North Dakota
    - Montana
    - Idaho
    - Washington
    - Alaska

93. Name one state that borders Mexico.
    - California
    - Arizona
    - New Mexico
    - Texas

94. What is the capital of the United States?*
    - Washington, D.C.

95. Where is the Statue of Liberty?*
    - New York (Harbor)
    - Liberty Island
    - [Also acceptable are New Jersey, near New York City, and on the Hudson (River).]

B: Symbols

96. Why does the flag have 13 stripes?
 – because there were 13 original colonies
 – because the stripes represent the original colonies

97. Why does the flag have 50 stars?*
 – because there is one star for each state
 – because each star represents a state
 – because there are 50 states

98. What is the name of the national anthem?
 – The Star-Spangled Banner

C: Holidays

99. When do we celebrate Independence Day?*
 – July 4

100. Name two national U.S. holidays.
 – New Year's Day
 – Martin Luther King, Jr. Day
 – Presidents' Day
 – Memorial Day
 – Independence Day
 – Labor Day
 – Columbus Day
 – Veterans Day
 – Thanksgiving
 – Christmas

* If you are 65 years old or older and have been a legal permanent resident of the United States for 20 or more years, you may study just the questions that have been marked with an asterisk."

Document Analysis

This document provides the possible questions for the civics test taken as part of the U.S. naturalization process. It is meant as a study tool for those planning on taking the test and therefore provides the correct answers with their respective questions. The document is straightforward, with a brief introduction and then the one hundred questions and answers. The questions are divided into three sections, each with its own three subsections.

The introduction provides basic information on the test and then a couple of caveats. The first paragraph includes the primary information that an individual planning on taking the test would need. The test is oral and includes up to ten of the following questions. Moreover, "An applicant must answer 6 out of 10 questions correctly to pass the civics portion of the naturalization test." The introduction also includes two caveats. First, the document warns that some answers are subject to change because of elections or appointments. For examples, question twenty-eight asks, "What is the name of the President of the United States now?" Rather than listing answers that are susceptible to go out-of-date for this type of question, the document recommends the reader, "Visit uscis.gov/citizenship/testupdates..." The second caveat reads: "Although USCIS is aware that there may be additional correct answers to the 100 civics questions, applicants are encouraged to respond to the civics questions using the answers provided below." The oral nature of the exam gives the administrator a little leeway in granting credit; however, the document suggests that the test takers focus on the answers given to be safe.

The question-and-answer section is divided into three major sections: American Government, American History, and Integrated Civics. These three sections each have three subsections: American Government is divided into Principles of American Democracy, System of Government, and Rights and Responsibilities. American History is separated into time periods: Colonial Period and Independence, 1800s, and Recent American History and Other Important Historical Information. Finally, Integrated Civics contains Geography, Symbols, and Holidays. The number of questions granted to each section offers a glimpse of the importance the test setters place on each subject. The American Government section is by far the largest with fifty-seven questions, whereas the American History section has thirty and Integrated Civics has only thirteen. Some questions are marked with an asterisk. A footer explains, "If you are 65 years old or older and have been a legal permanent resident of the United States for 20 or more years, you may study just the questions that have been marked with an asterisk." These asterisks, therefore, mark the questions and answers that the authors deem especially important.

Essential Themes

The theme of this document is an implicit one: knowledge of one's governmental system and national history is an essential tool for a citizen. This test has been a staple of the naturalization process as well as one of its more famous components. Its inception can be found in the Naturalization Act of 1802, which required those seeking naturalization be "attached to the principles of the Constitution." The civics test exists in order to affirm that attachment, yet it does not really fulfill this end. Attachment to the principles of the Constitution requires a working knowledge of American civics, but this knowledge does not necessarily signify an attachment.

That is not to say the test is useless, however. Knowledge of one's government and history can be a meaningful end unto itself. In 1789, Thomas Jefferson wrote, "Whenever the people are well-informed, they can be trusted with their own government." He and many other democratic thinkers conceptualized a well-informed populace as a prerequisite for democracy. As the United States' democracy has come under siege in the twenty-first century, some of the largest underlying causes are misinformation and the general ignorance of the public. The wide-ranging questions of this exam stand in stark contrast to the increasing governmental illiteracy of the American public. The result is that naturalized citizens, who must pass this exam to complete the naturalization process, are necessarily more well-versed in civics than the average American citizen.

—*Anthony Vivian, PhD*

Bibliography and Additional Reading

Aleinikoff, Thomas, David Martin, Hiroshi Motomura Maryellen Fullerton, and Juliet Stumpf. *Immigration and Citizenship: Process and Policy*. St. Paul, MN: West Academic Publishing, 2016.

Aptekar, Sofya. *The Road to Citizenship: What Naturalization Means for Immigrants and the United States*. New Brunswick, NJ: Rutgers UP, 2015.

Bellamy, Richard. *Citizenship: A Very Short Introduction*. Oxford: Oxford UP, 2008.

Shklar, Judith N. *American Citizenship: The Quest for Inclusion*. Cambridge, MA: Harvard UP, 1998.

■ Electoral Count Reform Act of 2022

Date: July 20, 2022
Author: Susan M. Collins
Genre: legislation

Summary Overview

The turmoil after the 2020 U.S. presidential election created chaos in the nation's capital and beyond. Although it was clear that Joseph R. Biden had won the election, the loser, Donald J. Trump, and his allies, refused to accept the loss. As such, they tried several approaches to overturning the results, including making use of possible weaknesses in the system of having electors choose the president and vice president, and having the official count of the electors by Congress delayed by occupying the Capitol Building on January 6, 2021. This bill introduced by Senator Susan Collins two years later was designed to clarify and strengthen the Electoral Count Act of 1887, including setting a higher threshold as to the number of members of Congress that were needed to dispute the results of any presidential election.

Defining Moment

There have been times in the recent past when questions were raised regarding the results of an election—even a presidential election. This occurred in 2000, for example, when following a close race a recount of ballots was begun in selected districts in Florida. In most all such cases, once the results have been made clear, the losing candidate inevitably concedes to the victorious one in a public statement. This occurred in 2000 and in virtually every race before and after it in the modern era.

However, that tradition fell by the wayside in 2020, when Joe Biden defeated incumbent president Donald Trump and Trump not only refused to publicly concede to Biden, but Trump's lawyers filed dozens of lawsuits (all unsuccessful) across the country to try to change the results. His allies created fake slates of electors in several states where the vote had been close and tried to get Congress to accept them, rather than the legitimate electors. The most dramatic effort to stop the transition of presidential administrations after the election was the storming of the Capitol by Trump's supporters on January 6, 2021. Ultimately, none of these radical maneuvers succeeded, and Joe Biden was duly inaugurated as the forty-sixth president of the United States on January 20, 2021.

Sen. Susan Collins. Photo via Wikimedia Commons. [Public domain.]

While Trump's efforts failed, both Democrats and Republicans sought ways in which to keep a future disgruntled loser from being able to use potential weak points in the Electoral College to sabotage an election. Susan Collins, along with several other senators and representatives, developed and introduced bills to bring about systemic changes. Support coalesced around her bill, which was officially the Electoral Count Reform and Presidential Transition Improvement Act of 2022. The bill was designed to increase the number of senators and representatives needed to raise objections during the counting of the electoral votes; to clarify that the vice president, who conducted the count, had no power to raise objections to the results; and to specify who certified the slate of a state's electors after the election. All of these reflected means by which Trump had attempted to block Biden from becoming president. Because the bill was introduced during the last six months of the Congressional Session, a way had to be found to advance it more quickly than is the norm. This was done by making it part of the Consolidated Appropriations Act of 2023. The latter bill, which was primarily a means to fund the government, passed the Senate by 68–29 and the House 225–201, becoming law on December 22, 2022.

Author Biography

Susan Margaret Collins was born in Caribou, Maine, in 1952. Both of her parents were active in state and local politics, with each having the distinction of serving as mayor of Caribou. After graduating from St. Lawrence University, she became a member of Representative and later Senator Bill Cohen's staff. In 1987, she became commissioner of Maine's Department of Professional and Financial Regulation. In 1992, she moved to the federal Small Business Administration, as director of a regional office.

Entering electoral politics, she successfully ran for the U.S. Senate in 1996 and in 2020 became he first Republican woman to be elected to a fifth term, as well as the first senator from Maine to achieve that distinction. Following up on her belief that public servants should strive to faithfully serve the public, she not only has spearheaded many bipartisan bills, but as of March 2024, she had the longest perfect voting record in Senate history, having participated in more than 8,500 consecutive votes.

Historical Document

Electoral Count Reform Act of 2022

Summary

ECRA [Electoral Count Reform Act] would reform and modernize the outdated 1887 Electoral Count Act to ensure that electoral votes tallied by Congress accurately reflect each state's public vote for President. It would replace ambiguous provisions of the 19th-century law with clear procedures that maintain appropriate state and federal roles in selecting the President and Vice President of the United States as set forth in the U.S. Constitution.

KEY PROVISIONS INCLUDE:

- Single, Conclusive Slate of Electors. Includes a number of important reforms aimed at ensuring that Congress can identify a single, conclusive slate of electors from each state:

    - Identifies Official to Submit Slate. Identifies each state's Governor, unless otherwise specified in the laws or constitution of a state in effect on Election Day, as responsible for submitting the certificate of ascertainment identifying that state's electors. Congress could not accept a slate submitted by a different official. This reform would address the potential for multiple state officials to send Congress competing slates.

    - Provides for Expedited Judicial Review. Provides for expedited review, including a three-judge panel with a direct appeal to the Supreme Court, of certain claims related to a state's certificate identifying its electors. This accelerated process is available only for aggrieved presidential candidates and allows for challenges made under existing federal law and the U.S. Constitution to be resolved more quickly.

    - Modernizes Rules for Counting Electoral Votes. Requires Congress to defer to slates of electors submitted by a state's executive pursuant to the judgments of state or federal courts.

- Role of the Vice President.

    - Affirmatively states that the constitutional role of the Vice President, as the presiding officer of the joint meeting of Congress, is solely ministerial and that he or she does not have any power to solely determine, accept, reject, or otherwise adjudicate disputes over electors.

- Higher Objection Threshold. Raises the threshold to lodge an objection to electors to at least one-fifth of the duly chosen and sworn members of both the House of Representatives and the Senate. This change would reduce the likelihood of frivolous objections by ensuring that objections are broadly supported. Currently, only a single member of both chambers is needed to object to an elector or slate of electors.

- Protection of Each State's Popular Vote. Strikes a provision of an archaic 1845 law that could be used by state legislatures to override the popular vote in their states by declaring a "failed election"—a term that is not defined in the law. Instead, this legislation specifies that a state could move its presidential election day, which otherwise would remain the Tuesday immediately following the first Monday in November every four years, only if necessitated by "extraordinary and catastrophic" events.

[Source: Office of Senator Susan Collins (R-ME), www.collins.senate.gov/imo/media/doc/one_pager_on_electoral_count_reform_act_of_2022.pdf]

Glossary

certificate of ascertainment: the official form identifying the certified slate of electors from a state

elector: an individual selected by a state political party to vote for the party's candidate, if that candidate received a plurality of the popular vote in a state/district

ministerial: here, meaning serving as an instrument only, with no power of its own

"Stop the Steal" protest in Minnesota, November 2020. Photo by Chad Davis, via Wikimedia Commons.

Document Analysis

In the summary of the legislation put forward by Senator Collins's office, the text outlines several important points that could affect the confirmation of electoral votes in future presidential elections. Although the text does not refer to the fact that only one of the presidential elections held under the system created by the Twelfth Amendment had been challenged, the one exception was strongly embedded in people's minds. The desperate lengths to which Trump and his allies went to contest the 2020 election, after the fact, was seen as a warning of what might lie in the future. While some believed Congress should take stronger steps to remedy this type of situation, Collins's bill was understood to be a means for clarifying some basic issues that had been raised.

Even without the delay caused by the illegal entry into the Capitol building by the crowd hoping to stop the confirmation of Biden's election as president, the official actions taken on January 6, 2021, to receive the electoral votes from the various states, took a much longer time than in previous elections. The outcomes for two states (Arizona and Pennsylvania) came with objections raised by an individual in each chamber, resulting in floor debates and votes by the House and the Senate. Four other states' results came with objections raised by only one person, which did not meet the threshold to hold a vote. Collins's 2022 bill changed the threshold for debating the outcome and holding a vote from one member of each chamber to one-fifth of each chamber. If this had been in effect in 2021, neither of the two states over which debates took place would have had the opportunity to open a debate, because at the time neither had even one-tenth of the senators supporting the action. Under the new law, neither could any claim be advanced, as the Trump supporters were attempting to do, to have the vice president arbitrarily reject electors in favor of other, "alternative" electors. The Electoral Count Reform Act ensures that the vice president merely oversees the process while having no power to challenge the election results.

As for the slates of "fake electors" that were organized (in support of Trump) in some states, this new bill makes it clear that all valid electors must be named by a state's governor, unless state law has previously given such power to some other official. Thus, there cannot be two slates of electors sent to Congress by two different state officials. If a losing candidate has objections to a slate sent by a governor, or to any other electoral matters, a new process for hearing such potential grievances is established under the law, one that would get such a case heard more quickly than it would be by bringing it to the Supreme Court. Another point, one that was not a major issue in the 2020 controversy, simply confirms the date on which presidential elections are to be held. While that date has always been the Tuesday following the first Monday in November, in theory states might seek to set a different date for the vote. This bill makes it clear that the traditional date for presidential elections applies in all states unless there is an "extraordinary and catastrophic" event. Thus, while not a complex or extensive piece of legislation, the Electoral Count Reform Act has the potential to smooth the transition to a new presidential administration.

Essential Themes

Although it is too early to know exactly how this law will affect disagreements over the outcome of future presidential elections, real or perceived, it does clarify some issues that were raised following the 2020 election. The desire of Senator Collins, and the majority of both chambers who voted for this bill, was that spurious charges and challenges should not hold up the confirmation of a presidential election. Thus, the matter of who appoints electors is clarified. By increasing the number of congressional members needed to challenge a state's slate of electors from one in each chamber to twenty senators and eighty-seven representatives (using 2024 numbers), means that there must be a much broader group questioning the vote than in the past. By specifically indicating that the vice president had no power to challenge electors, it has become clear that only having this broader support among members of Congress can initiate a debate.

By early 2024, with another Biden–Trump presidential race in the offing, it was unclear whether the provisions of this new law might come into play following the upcoming vote. However, it has been assumed by most observers that 2020 (and maybe 2024) was an extraordinary exception to the smooth and peaceful acceptance of valid election results. By streamlining the process for affirming the outcome of the vote through the Electoral College, one hope is that Trump or similar individuals will not be able to impede the process of certification. The hope is that more people will have confidence in the electoral system and reject attempts by any losing candidate to question the validity of the electoral process.

—*Donald A. Watt, PhD*

Bibliography and Additional Reading

Capparell, Jessica Jones. "Reforming the Electoral Count Act." *League of Women Voters*, 2023, www.lwv.org/blog/reforming-electoral-count-act.

Hamilton, Kate. "State Implementation of the Electoral Count Reform Act and the Mitigation of Election-Subversion Risk in 2024 and Beyond." *The Yale Law Journal: Forum* 133 (Nov. 2023).

Prokop, Andrew. "The Bill to Prevent Trump from Stealing the Next Election, Explained." *Vox*, December 21, 2022, www.vox.com/policy-and-politics/2022/12/21/23520649/electoral-count-reform-act-omnibus-trump.

Whitaker, I. Paige, and Elizabeth Rybicki. "The Electoral Count Act and Presidential Elections." *Congressional Research Service*, December 19, 2022, crsreports.congress.gov/product/pdf/IN/IN12065.

Voting in Dispute

The subject of federal election law covers a body of constitutional provisions and legislative enactments governing federal elections in the United States. Today, the U.S. Constitution provides for the election of the president, vice president, senators, and representatives. As we saw in earlier sections, however, originally the only federal officials directly elected by the voters were members of the House of Representatives. The president and the vice president were chosen by the Electoral College, and members of the Senate were elected by state legislatures. The overall framework reflected the patrician atmosphere of the early era, when landholding was a requirement to vote and only adult white men could cast a ballot. The Seventeenth Amendment (1913) provided for the popular election of senators. Although the president and the vice president are still technically elected by the members of the Electoral College, the members of the college commonly carry out the mandate of the voters who have selected them.

The original electoral system for the presidency and the vice presidency did not contemplate competing candidates. It was instead the rise and development of political parties that supplied the mechanism by which election to the Executive Office and to Congress is conducted. Parties have also come to control much else besides, establishing themselves as the dominant players in the political field (along with wealthy donors and, in the recent era, political action committees or PACs).

For the most part, the system of primary elections and nominations based on them has been left to the control of the states. Congress has specified only the time of elections and has prohibited certain corrupt practices, retaining the right to determine the eligibility of a successful candidate to take his or her seat in either the Senate or the House. Congress has also passed legislation protecting the right of citizens to vote by making it a criminal offense to conspire to deprive any citizen of his or her constitutional rights and privileges. The U.S. Supreme Court has variously aided and stymied this "federalist" (or "states' rights") approach to elections.

Older statutes passed by Congress stipulating the election of representatives from districts that were to be "compact, contiguous, and equal in population" were allowed to lapse in 1929. The new landscape permitted the states to arrange their districts as they saw fit (a process called apportionment), even to the extent of selecting representatives at large from the entire state. The process of gerrymandering, which by now is common, is the process whereby a state legislature under the majority leadership of one or the other of the two major political parties, undertakes to redraw legislative districts to favor candidates from that same majority party. The result is a "hardening" of partisan politics centered on "red" (Republican) and "blue" (Democratic) districts, where once districts had been more broadly encompassing of voters from both parties.

Congress has also passed laws concerning corrupt practices in electoral politics. No national bank or public corporation organized under federal law may contribute directly to any political campaign, although they may donate indirectly through a PAC, which under federal law may be generally "aligned" with a political candidate but cannot "coordinate" its activities with those of the campaign. Reforms in the 1970s laid out some of the basic campaign finance regulations, but these have since been greatly altered by both legislation and Supreme Court decisions. The reforms also established the Federal Elections Commission (FEC) to oversee election activities and ensure their compliance. Laws remain in place that require candidates to disclose information about their contributions and expenditures. A law that sought to limit the amount a campaign could spend, however, was struck down by the Supreme Court (in *Buckley v. Valeo,* 1976) as a violation of the Constitution's free speech provision. The equating of money with speech has arisen a number of times since, notably in the case known as *Citizens United v. Federal Election Commission* (2010).

To get around funding restrictions, special interest groups began to form PACs that were eligible to receive unlimited amounts in private and corporate donations. These committees typically spend the money on elaborate "issue ads" on television and other media; the ads promote a particular candidate while technically remaining separate from the official campaign organization. In its ruling in *Citizens United*, the Supreme Court held that a federal law barring corporations and unions from using their general treasury money for campaign advertisement was unconstitutional. In effect, the Court ruled that the government cannot regulate political speech, even when that speech is largely in the form of money. The decision greatly expanded the role of "dark money" in U.S. politics, so-called because PAC money is not subject to the same disclosure requirements as regular campaign funds.

In the section that follows we look at landmark Supreme Court decisions in the area of election law: the construction of voting districts (apportionment); who is allowed to vote (voting rights); campaign finance; and other relevant issues.

■ Baker v. Carr

Date: March 26, 1962
Author: Justice William J. Brennan, Jr.
Genre: court opinion

Summary Overview

This case, in which the plaintiff sought changes to the voting districts in Tennessee, was appealed to the Supreme Court because the District Court would not hear the case. In his majority opinion, Justice William J. Brennan did not directly address the complaint filed by Charles Baker; that is, it did not mandate any changes in the voting districts. However, the ruling clearly stated that the federal courts did have the power to review state legislative districts. The results of this assertion not only included the District Court being ordered to hear the suit, but similar suits were filed in more than thirty states. These suits resulted in later Supreme Court rulings, such as Gray v. Sanders *and* Reynolds v. Sims, *which did force states to create electoral districts essentially equal in population. Thus, during the 1960s, state legislatures were transformed, generally increasing representation from urban areas so that, on a per capita basis, it was proportional with that from rural regions of a state.*

Defining Moment

From the foundation of the United States until the 1920s, the rural population was greater than the urban. Thus, in the early years of most states, creating legislative districts based upon land area, or the population distribution at that time, did not result in many major instances of disproportionate representation of people from one region of the state. However over the years, there was strong inertia, and desire by those in power, to keep at least part of the political system tilted in favor of rural regions of the state. This was partially because these regions would have had to give up political power, which they did not want to do, and partially because many viewed cities as suspect, being contaminated by non-American ideas and people. As the decades passed, the per capita disparity changed dramatically with increased urbanization. The rural sections of the various states would not willingly give up the political power they had as a result of having a greater land area, or from previous censuses. Many, in the growing urban areas, felt disenfranchised by having relatively fewer representatives in state legislatures. In one earlier Supreme Court non-ruling, as the result of a tie vote and a swing vote not clearly addressing the situation, federal judicial review of state

Justice William J. Brennan wrote the opinion. Photo via Wikimedia Commons. [Public domain.]

307

electoral processes did not seem to be allowed. However, this did not deter Baker from filing a suit seeking changes in the legislative district which had been created for the Tennessee legislature.

Baker v. Carr came to the Supreme Court during the 1960-61 term, but no consensus was reached by the justices at that time. It was re-argued during the next Court term, on October 9, 1961, with Brennan taking the lead in trying to create a consensus in favor of federal court jurisdiction over state elections and electoral districts. Eventually, this resulted in a 6-2 decision supporting his position. Although *Baker v. Carr* did not establish the principle of "one person, one vote," (which would come the following year with William O. Douglas's opinion in *Gray v. Sanders*), Brennan's opinion for the Court certainly set the stage for what came to be known as the "reapportionment revolution." Prior to Baker, state-mandated legislative districts normally continued to favor rural voters, even after populations had shifted to urban areas. In Baker, for example, residents of Memphis, Nashville, and Knoxville, Tennessee, sued Joe C. Carr, the Tennessee secretary of state, to force him to redraw the state's existing legislative districts. The boundaries of these districts had remained unchanged since 1901. As a result, the votes of those inhabiting rural districts in Tennessee carried more weight, individually and collectively, than did those of their more numerous urban counterparts, including those in Shelby County where Baker resided.

Author Biography

William J. Brennan, Jr. was the son of William and Agnes Brennan, both of whom had emigrated from Ireland. Born on April 25, 1906, in Newark, New Jersey, William Brennan, Jr. was raised a Catholic, which was an issue when he was nominated for the Supreme Court. He attended public schools and then the University of Pennsylvania, during which time he married Marjorie Leonard, whom he had known in high school. Brennan attended and, in 1931, graduated from Harvard Law School.

Prior to becoming a judge, Brennan was in private practice, except during World War II when he served in the Army as a judge advocate general. In 1949, Albert Driscoll, the Republican governor of New Jersey, appointed Brennan (a Democrat) to the Superior Court, a trial court. Then, in 1951, the same governor appointed Brennan to the New Jersey Supreme Court. At that time there was no indication that Brennan would become a liberal judicial leader, although he was not as conservative as he seemed to those advising President Eisenhower when a U.S. Supreme Court vacancy occurred in 1956.

To demonstrate his bipartisanship, Eisenhower appointed Brennan to the court during a 1956 Congressional recess, so he began serving immediately. His name was submitted for Senate approval during the next Congressional session and he was approved with only ultra-conservative Sen. Joseph McCarthy voting against him. For many of the other senators, Brennan's confirmation was only possible because he had made it clear that his decisions would be based on U.S. law, not on Catholic doctrines.

In his first term, it would seem that McCarthy's view of him was confirmed because in twelve cases Brennan was the swing vote supporting the individual rights of Communists against government intrusion. Within a few years, Brennan was seen as the leading liberal intellectual force on the Supreme Court. During his term, which lasted until 1990, Brennan put forward strong arguments generally on the liberal side of court cases. Currently, Brennan holds second place in the number of opinions written (1,360). After retirement for health reasons, he was moderately active in legal and academic circles, until his death on July 24, 1997.

Historical Document

Baker v. Carr

The District Court was uncertain whether our cases withholding federal judicial relief rested upon a lack of federal jurisdiction or upon the inappropriateness of the subject matter for judicial consideration—what we have designated "nonjusticiability." The distinction between the two grounds is significant. In the instance of nonjusticiability, consideration of the cause is not wholly and immediately foreclosed; rather, the Court's inquiry necessarily proceeds to the point of deciding whether the duty asserted can be judicially identified and its breach judicially determined, and whether protection for the right asserted can be judicially molded. In the instance of lack of jurisdiction the cause either does not "arise under" the Federal Constitution, laws or treaties (or fall within one of the other enumerated categories of Art. III, 2), or is not a "case or controversy" within the meaning of that section; or the cause is not one described by any jurisdictional statute. Our conclusion ... that this cause presents no nonjusticiable "political question" settles the only possible doubt that it is a case or controversy....

It is clear that the cause of action is one which "arises under" the Federal Constitution. The complaint alleges that the 1901 statute effects an apportionment that deprives the appellants of the equal protection of the laws in violation of the Fourteenth Amendment. Dismissal of the complaint upon the ground of lack of jurisdiction of the subject matter would, therefore, be justified only if that claim were "so attenuated and unsubstantial as to be absolutely devoid of merit."... Since the complaint plainly sets forth a case arising under the Constitution, the subject matter is within the federal judicial power defined in Art. III, 2, and so within the power of Congress to assign to the jurisdiction of the District Courts....

The appellees refer to *Colegrove v. Green* ... as authority that the District Court lacked jurisdiction of the subject matter. Appellees misconceive the holding of that case. The holding was precisely contrary to their reading of it. Seven members of the Court participated in the decision. Unlike many other cases in this field which have assumed without discussion that there was jurisdiction, all three opinions filed in *Colegrove* discussed the question....

We hold that the District Court has jurisdiction of the subject matter of the federal constitutional claim asserted in the complaint....

Have the appellants alleged such a personal stake in the outcome of the controversy as to assure that concrete adverseness which sharpens the presentation of issues upon which the court so largely depends for illumination of difficult constitutional questions? This is the gist of the question of standing. It is, of course, a question of federal law....

We hold that the appellants do have standing to maintain this suit.... These appellants seek relief in order to protect or vindicate an interest of their own, and of those similarly situated. Their constitutional claim is, in substance, that the 1901 statute constitutes arbitrary and capricious state action, offensive to the Fourteenth Amendment in its irrational disregard of the standard of apportionment prescribed by the State's Constitution or of any standard, effecting a gross disproportion of representation to voting population. The injury which appellants assert is that this classification disfavors the voters in the counties in which they reside, placing them in a position of constitutionally unjustifiable inequality vis-a-vis voters ... in irrationally favored counties. A citizen's right to a vote free of arbitrary impairment by state action has been judicially recognized as a right secured by the Constitution....

It would not be necessary to decide whether appellants' allegations of impairment of their votes by the 1901 apportionment will, ultimately, entitle them to any relief, in order to hold that they have standing to seek it. If such impairment does produce a legally cognizable injury, they are among those who have sustained it.... They are entitled to a hearing and to the District Court's decision on their claims....

In holding that the subject matter of this suit was not justiciable, the District Court relied on *Colegrove v. Green* .... We understand the District Court to have read the cited cases as compelling the conclusion that since the appellants sought to have a legislative apportionment held unconstitutional, their suit presented a "political question" and was therefore nonjusticiable. We hold that this challenge to an apportionment presents no nonjusticiable "political question."...

We come, finally, to the ultimate inquiry whether our precedents as to what constitutes a nonjusticiable "political question" bring the case before us under the umbrella of that doctrine.... The question here is the consistency of state action with the Federal Constitution. We have no question decided, or to be decided, by a political branch of government coequal with this Court. Nor do we risk embarrassment of our government abroad, or grave disturbance at home if we take issue with Tennessee as to the constitutionality of her action here challenged. Nor need the appellants, in order to succeed in this action, ask the Court to enter upon policy determinations for which judicially manageable standards are lacking. Judicial standards under the Equal Protection Clause are well developed and familiar, and it has been open to courts since the enactment of the Fourteenth Amendment to determine, if on the particular facts they must, that a discrimination reflects no policy, but simply arbitrary and capricious action.

We conclude that the complaint's allegations of a denial of equal protection present a justiciable constitutional cause of action upon which appellants are entitled to a trial and a decision. The right asserted is within the reach of judicial protection under the Fourteenth Amendment.

The judgment of the District Court is reversed and the cause is remanded for further proceedings consistent with this opinion.

Glossary

appellants: persons bringing a case on appeal to the Supreme Court

appellees: persons against whom a case is appealed to the Supreme Court

holding: the Supreme Court's ruling

judicial relief: the means by which a court applies a judicial remedy—that is, a solution to the problem presented to it by a given case

nonjusticiability: issues which do not fall within the purview of the court's power

offensive to: in violation of

relief: judicial relief

remanded: sent back to a lower court

standing: legal right to bring a lawsuit, which in the United States requires, among other things, clear proof that the party bringing the suit is directly and materially affected by the issue at hand

Document Analysis

Possible judicial review by federal courts of all laws passed by Congress and all actions taken by the executive branch of the federal government had been clearly stated in an 1803 Supreme Court decision (*Marbury v. Madison*). However, even though one of the issues related to the Civil War was the supremacy of the federal government in certain areas, it was unclear whether or not the federal courts had the power to mandate actions in what were seen as state "political activities." This included drawing the borders for state legislative districts. As the District Court had ruled that it did not have jurisdiction in this type of case, the Supreme Court initially dealt with this matter. If it ruled that federal courts had jurisdiction (which it ultimately did), only then would it deal with other questions, such as to whether the plaintiff had standing to file the suit and whether the issue was significant enough to warrant a trial by the District Court. Once the case was brought to the Supreme Court, Brennan became the leader in supporting the plaintiff's assertion that federal courts did have jurisdiction, while Justice Felix Frankfurter argued strongly against this position. After a second hearing of the case, Brennan was able to obtain support from a majority of the justices, that Section 1 of the Fourteenth Amendment did apply to laws regulating state elections, thereby giving federal courts the right of judicial review, which resulted in the case being remanded to the District Court, restarting the process of determining the merits of the case.

The plaintiffs, believing that only a federal forum could bring redress, brought their suit in federal district court, asking that the Tennessee apportionment act, which required reapportionment of the state's ninety-five counties only every ten years (a directive that had plainly been disregarded since 1901) be declared unconstitutional and that state officials be enjoined from conducting further elections under the existing act. The district court, citing the principle requiring that so-called legal questions were for legislatures, rather than courts to decide, dismissed the case. The plaintiffs then appealed directly to the U.S. Supreme Court, claiming, as they had in the lower court, that their right to equal protection under the laws, granted by the Fourteenth Amendment, had been violated.

The ostensible issue before the high bench was whether federal courts could mandate equality among legislative districts, however, this was not the specific issue coming to the Supreme Court. At its core, Baker concerned the scope and power of the Supreme Court itself. Seventeen years earlier, in *Colegrove v. Green* (1946), Frankfurter had written a plurality opinion for a seven-member Court (one justice was absent, and a recent vacancy had not been filled) declaring that the high court had no authority to entertain cases concerning apportionment of state legislatures. Now, in the last opinion he would write before retiring from the Court, Frankfurter—always the advocate for judicial restraint—dissented from the majority, once again warning against the Court's entry into a "political thicket." Colegrove had been decided by a vote of three to three to one, with Justice Wiley B. Rutledge concurring in the result but not with Frankfurter's reasoning. Because of the unusual circumstances surrounding that decision, the status of Colegrove as precedent had always been shaky. Brennan's opinion for the Court in Baker destroyed that status entirely.

The appellants in Baker had appealed to the Supreme Court for a writ of certiorari, meaning that Court review was discretionary and requiring the justices to vote first on the issue of hearing the case. When this vote was taken, a bare majority of the justices (five) supported Frankfurter's contention that Baker was a political case outside Court jurisdiction. Only four justices are required to grant certiorari, however, and thus the Court agreed to hear the case. After two days of oral argument, on April 19 and 20, 1961, the Court was still split four to four on the merits of the appeal, with Justice Potter Stewart undecided. Chief Justice Earl Warren, cognizant of Baker's significance and potential for overturning Colegrove, held the case over for re-argument in the next Court term. When Baker was reargued on October 9, 1961, neither side introduced anything new. Afterward Frankfurter attacked the plaintiffs' case with a sixty-page memorandum written to his colleagues. Only Brennan responded in kind, and his lengthy memo, addressing the injustice of malapportionment but asking only that Tennessee be obliged to defend its apportionment system (and intending to convince the still recalcitrant Stewart), carried the day. For his part, Warren, too, was convinced by Brennan's argument, and he assigned Brennan to write an opinion for what would eventually be a six-member majority (two justices dissented, and one did not participate) to overturn Colegrove and grant the Tennessee plaintiffs their day in court.

Brennan's opinion, though ultimately supporting the appellants' contention that Tennessee had acted unconstitutionally, comes at the matter tangentially. After rehearsing the facts of the case, Brennan addresses more technical matters. The lower court had dismissed the case on grounds that federal courts lacked jurisdiction and that Baker presented a question that could not be resolved by judicial means. Brennan carefully distinguishes between these two arguments: Whereas a case that is nonjusticiable can still be considered by a court up to the point of decision, the court is barred from entertaining a case over which it lacks jurisdiction. In Baker the court ruled that the complaint clearly sets forth a case that arises under the Constitution; therefore, the district court unquestionably has jurisdiction. What is more, the appellants have sufficient interest in the value of their votes to be granted standing to sue. Justiciability presents a knottier problem for Brennan, who nonetheless succeeds in distinguishing this case, which concerns a question of federalism, from one raising a political question about the relationship among the three branches of government. The appellants, Brennan concludes, have a cause of action, and he sends their case back to the lower court "for further proceedings consistent with this opinion."

Baker was decided on very narrow grounds, but it was nonetheless hard fought. Justice Charles Whittaker found the pressure put on him by some of his colleagues during the Court's consideration of the case too much to bear. He was hospitalized for exhaustion before Baker was decided, and he took no part in its decision. A week after Baker was handed down on March 26, 1962, Whittaker resigned from the Court. Frankfurter, embittered by his defeat, suffered a debilitating stroke a few weeks later. On August 28, 1962, he, too, resigned from the Court.

For urban residents of Tennessee—and other states—Baker had a happier aftermath. Within a year of its decision, thirty-six other states were involved in reapportionment suits. A string of Supreme Court cases that followed effectively declared the apportionment of every state legislature unconstitutional. Soon population equality was required of virtually all electoral districts, and even state senate seats were apportioned on the basis of population.

Earl Warren often referred to *Baker v. Carr* as the most interesting and important case decided during his tenure. Because the case succeeded in transferring political power from the largely landowning, largely conservative rural population to the more heterogeneous populace of the cities, Baker can be said to have opened the door to the major social restructuring America underwent during the Warren era as well as, perhaps, the conservative backlash that ensued decades later. This ruling also partially laid the legal foundation for various federal voter rights laws as they applied to state elections.

Essential Themes

Although the formal result of *Baker v. Carr* was the case being remanded to the District Court to hear the merits of the complaint by Baker, the case's impact went far beyond voting districts in Tennessee. The six justices who supported Brennan's majority opinion, in effect supported the extension of federal judicial review into an area of state politics not specifically mentioned in Article III of the Constitution or the Fourteenth Amendment. They did this on the grounds that the "equal protection" section of the 14th Amendment applied to legislative districts beyond those of the House of Representatives. The creation of these districts, according to this opinion, was not just a political decision by state leaders, but rather it was an action through which a state could demonstrate the equality of all of its citizens. However, in remanding the case to the District Court for a hearing upon its merits, the Supreme Court was also saying that it was possible that states might, contrary to Constitutional principles, illegally create different classes of citizenship based upon the location of a person's residence. For this reason, the case should be heard by the District Court.

After the adoption of several amendments soon after the Civil War, federal judicial review was extended into some areas of state government which had previously been ignored. The decision of *Baker v. Carr* made a clear statement that the federal courts had the right to intervene into the political systems of states, when those systems did not uphold the principle of equality for all citizens of the state. This is what made *Baker v. Carr* such an important case, not the fact that Tennessee ultimately had to deal with legislative redistricting, which it had put off for sixty years. The statement that states could "not deny . . . the equal protection of the laws" was found to apply to all areas of governmental (and thereby political) activity. This clearly included establishing the composition of state legislatures.

In finding that the "appellants are entitled to a trial and a decision" the Court indicated that citizens of a state had standing to bring suit regarding the legislative districts. While Brennan's opinion did not specifically say whether or not a thing could be solely a "political question," he clearly stated that the creation of state legislative districts was not a "political question," but rather a question of the equal treatment of a state's citizens.

Thus, as outlined in the parts of Brennan's opinion contained in this essay: the federal courts have broader powers of judicial review than previously thought; the plaintiffs (appellants) had standing to file a suit; there was the possibility that the plaintiffs were being treated unequally (although no ruling was made on this issue); and, therefore, the full case should be heard by the district court. In line with the philosophy contained in this ruling, not only did the district judge rule that Tennessee needed to update its legislative districts, but people in the majority of states filed similar suits to bring greater equity within their legislative elections.

Baker v. Carr has faced some challenges in more recent years. Although not directly overturned by *Rucho v. Common Cause* (2019), the conservative court's ruling in the latter case took a different approach to the partisan gerrymandering of legislative districts, viewing the matter as a political affair that state legislatures have a right to oversee without undue interference of the courts. (See "*Rucho v. Common Cause*" in the present volume.)

—Donald A. Watt, PhD

Bibliography and Additional Reading

Digital History. "Baker v. Carr." Digital History. Houston: Digital History, 2016.

Hansen, Richard. *The Supreme Court and Election Law: Judging from Baker v. Carr to Bush v. Gore.* New edition. New York: New York UP, 2006.

Legal Information Institute. "Baker v. Carr." Cornell: Cornell Law School, 2017.

C-SPAN with Theodore Olson and J. Douglas Smith. "Baker v. Carr, 1962." *Landmark Cases*. Washington: National Cable Satellite Corporation, 2017.

Stern, Seth, and Stephen Wermiel. *Justice Brennan: Liberal Champion.* New York: Houghton Mifflin Harcourt, 2013.

Washington Secretary of State. "Baker v. Carr et al., March 2, 1962." *Shifting Boundaries: Redistricting in Washington State.* Olympia: Office of the Secretary of State, 2017.

■ Reynolds v. Sims

Date: Decided June 15, 1964
Author: Justice Earl Warren
Genre: court opinion

Summary Overview

The case of Reynolds v. Sims *addressed disenfranchisement of blacks in the South, which was ongoing despite the protections offered by the Fourteenth Amendment. A group of voters challenged legislative reapportionment in Alabama, which left urban counties drastically underrepresented. In its decision the Court ruled that state legislative districts had to be roughly equal in population, based on the principle of "one person, one vote."*

Earl Warren led the U.S. Supreme Court during the turbulent years of the 1950s and 1960s. Driven by his own moral compass rather than politics, Warren shocked those on the left and right as he made the transition from crime-fighting district attorney to liberal chief justice. He became known as a protector of the rights of minorities and the oppressed, a stance reflected in many of his rulings.

Defining Moment

Starting as early as the 1950's, there was a movement within the United States encouraging political leaders to do something to ensure the fair apportionment of state legislative districts. Because cities and suburbs were experiencing periods of extreme growth in terms of population counts, many did not believe it was fair to continue allowing the government to be controlled primarily by those coming from rural districts. More specifically, there was growing concern that the system of apportionment being used was a major cause for the disenfranchisement of black voters. In particular, within the state of Alabama there were huge discrepancies between the number of voters in various districts, which lead to the underrepresentation of large portions of the Alabama population. In one shocking example, the number of eligible voters casting their votes for one senator was 41 times the number of voters in another district. Upon examination, it was evident the districts in Alabama still reflected the population counts from the 1900 census report. To challenge the existing apportionment practices of their state legislatures, many reapportionment cases came before the Supreme Court of the United States, with the case of *Reynolds v. Sims* stemming from the Alabama legislature, taking the spotlight as the lead case.

Justice Earl Warren gave the majority opinion, joined by five other justices. Photo via Wikimedia Commons. [Public domain.]

In an 8-1 decision, the Supreme Court decided state legislatures must undergo a system of reapportionment that would align with the population of the state. Noting the right to vote as being a fundamental right, the inequalities promoted in the faulty apportionment of legislative districts was struck down by the Court, causing a nationwide change in the political scene. Redrawing district maps was mandated, a call for districts to be drawn as equally as possible according to population, and the reign of rural lawmakers in states with increasingly urban populations was effectively ended.

About the Author

As governor of California and chief justice of the United States, Earl Warren defied political categorization, confounding his supporters and critics alike. Although he proved to be a notoriously "liberal" judge, he had been head of the Republican Party in California and had won the vice presidential nomination on the Republican ticket in 1948. Prominent in California politics during the reformist Progressive Era, Warren pursued an agenda as district attorney and later as governor that included elimination of corruption within law enforcement, cracking down on gambling rings, and prison reform. Under his leadership as chief justice, the Supreme Court issued several landmark rulings, among them, decisions on religious freedom, criminal law procedure, civil rights and equal protection under the law, and freedom of speech and obscenity. With a long career spanning the years of the Progressive Era, the Great Depression, World War II, the cold war, and the civil rights movement, Warren epitomizes the American struggle to answer many of the moral questions of the twentieth century.

Warren was born on March 19, 1891, and grew up in the booming oil town of Bakersfield, California, where his father worked as a handyman. He graduated from Kern County High School in 1908 and enrolled at the University of California, Berkeley, where he earned both a bachelor's and a law degree. Following President Woodrow Wilson's call for a congressional declaration of war against Germany on April 2, 1917, Warren joined the army and completed officer training. In 1919 a college friend helped him secure a position as clerk of the California State Assembly Judiciary Committee. Warren soon became deputy city attorney of Oakland, working his way up to the position of district attorney of Alameda County in 1925.

His professional reputation growing, Warren was elected state chairman of the Republican Party in 1934, despite his belief in nonpartisanship; he repeatedly campaigned as a political independent. In 1938 he was elected attorney general and, in 1942, governor of California. As governor, Warren irked the Republican right when he called for compulsory medical insurance, but his record of fiscal responsibility pleased most conservatives. Under Warren's watch, the University of California system expanded, the teachers' retirement fund regained solvency, and the state began developing its massive highway system. Perhaps the most notorious act of Warren's gubernatorial stint was his support for the evacuation and internment of Japanese residents, including U.S. citizens, following the attack on Pearl Harbor, Hawaii.

After his decisive reelection victory in 1946, Warren was considered a candidate for president. He was nominated for vice president on the Republican ticket in the 1948 election, in which the Republican Thomas Dewey lost to the Democrat Harry Truman. He then lost the presidential nomination to Dwight Eisenhower in 1952. When Chief Justice Fred Vinson died of a heart attack in 1953, Eisenhower named Warren as Vinson's replacement. Under Warren's leadership, the Supreme Court handed down several historic decisions. One of the first and most important of these cases was *Brown v. Board of Education of Topeka* (1954), which paved the way for school desegregation. The chief justice wrote dissenting opinions in four separate obscenity cases, arguing that pornographers did not deserve First Amendment protection. Nevertheless, decisions such as *Engel v. Vitale* (1962), which ruled school prayer unconstitutional, fueled public outcry against the liberal nature of the Warren Court. The Court addressed the issue of voting rights in *Baker v. Carr* (1962) and the subsequent case, *Reynolds v. Sims* (1964), handing down the famous "one man, one vote" edict, which essentially extended the Court's power to the legislative branch of government. The obligation of law enforcement officials to advise criminal suspects of their rights was confirmed by the Court's 1966 ruling in *Miranda v. Arizona*. Perhaps Warren's most well-known activity, however, was his investigation into the 1963 assassination of President John F. Kennedy. The President's Commission on the Assassination of President Kennedy, popularly known as the Warren Commission, produced a report that received enormous public scrutiny and has been the subject of ongoing debate into the twenty-first century. Warren retired from the Court in 1969. He died on July 9, 1974, in Washington, D.C.

Historical Document

Reynolds v. Sims

Undeniably, the Constitution of the United States protects the right of all qualified citizens to vote, in state as well as in federal, elections. A consistent line of decisions by this Court in cases involving attempts to deny or restrict the right of suffrage has made this indelibly clear. It has been repeatedly recognized that all qualified voters have a constitutionally protected right to vote, *Ex parte Yarbrough*, and to have their votes counted, *United States v. Mosley*. In *Mosley*, the Court stated that it is "as equally unquestionable that the right to have one's vote counted is as open to protection... as the right to put a ballot in a box." The right to vote can neither be denied outright, *Guinn v. United States*, *Lane v. Wilson*, nor destroyed by alteration of ballots, *see United States v. Classic*, nor diluted by ballot box stuffing, *Ex parte Siebold*, *United States v. Saylor*. As the Court stated in *Classic*, "Obviously included within the right to choose, secured by the Constitution, is the right of qualified voters within a state to cast their ballots and have them counted."

Racially based gerrymandering... and the conducting of white primaries,... both of which result in denying to some citizens their right to vote, have been held to be constitutionally impermissible. And history has seen a continuing expansion of the scope of the right of suffrage in this country. The right to vote freely for the candidate of one's choice is of the essence of a democratic society, and any restrictions on that right strike at the heart of representative government. And the right of suffrage can be denied by a debasement or dilution of the weight of a citizen's vote just as effectively as by wholly prohibiting the free exercise of the franchise.

In *Baker v. Carr*, we held that a claim asserted under the Equal Protection Clause challenging the constitutionality of a State's apportionment of seats in its legislature, on the ground that the right to vote of certain citizens was effectively impaired, since debased and diluted, in effect presented a justiciable controversy subject to adjudication by federal courts. The spate of similar cases filed and decided by lower courts since our decision in *Baker* amply shows that the problem of state legislative malapportionment is one that is perceived to exist in a large number of the States. In *Baker*, a suit involving an attack on the apportionment of seats in the Tennessee Legislature, we remanded to the District Court, which had dismissed the action, for consideration on the merits. We intimated no view as to the proper constitutional standards for evaluating the validity of a state legislative apportionment scheme. Nor did we give any consideration to the question of appropriate remedies. Rather, we simply stated: "Beyond noting that we have no cause at this stage to doubt the District Court will be able to fashion relief if violations of constitutional rights are found, it is improper now to consider what remedy would be most appropriate if appellants prevail at the trial."

We indicated in *Baker*, however, that the Equal Protection Clause provides discoverable and manageable standards for use by lower courts in determining the constitutionality of a state legislative apportionment scheme, and we stated:

"Nor need the appellants, in order to succeed in this action, ask the Court to enter upon policy determinations for which judicially manageable standards are lacking. Judicial standards under the Equal Protection Clause are well developed and familiar, and it has been open to courts since the enactment of the Fourteenth Amendment to determine if, on the particular facts they must, that a discrimination reflects no policy, but simply arbitrary and capricious action."

Subsequent to *Baker*, we remanded several cases to the courts below for reconsideration in light of that decision....

Legislators represent people, not trees or acres. Legislators are elected by voters, not farms or cities or economic interests. As long as ours is a representative form of government, and our legislatures are those instruments of government elected directly by and directly representative of the people, the right to elect legislators in a free and unimpaired fashion is a bedrock of our political system. It could hardly be gainsaid that a constitutional claim had been asserted by an allegation that certain otherwise qualified voters had been entirely prohibited from voting for members of their state legislature. And, if a State should provide that the votes of citizens in one part of the State should be given two times, or five times, or 10 times the weight of votes of citizens in another part of the State, it could hardly be contended that the right to vote of those residing in the disfavored areas had not been effectively diluted. It would appear extraordinary to suggest that a State could be constitutionally permitted to enact a law providing that certain of the State's voters could vote two, five, or 10 times for their legislative representatives, while voters living elsewhere could vote only once. And it is inconceivable that a state law to the effect that, in counting votes for legislators, the votes of citizens in one part of the State would be multiplied by two, five, or 10, while the votes of persons in another area would be counted only at face value, could be constitutionally sustainable. Of course, the effect of state legislative districting schemes which give the same number of representatives to unequal numbers of constituents is identical. Overweighting and overvaluation of the votes of those living here has the certain effect of dilution and undervaluation of the votes of those living there. The resulting discrimination against those individual voters living in disfavored areas is easily demonstrable mathematically. Their right to vote is simply not the same right to vote as that of those living in a favored part of the State. Two, five, or 10 of them must vote before the effect of their voting is equivalent to that of their favored neighbor. Weighting the votes of citizens differently, by any method or means, merely because of where they happen to reside, hardly seems justifiable. One must be ever aware that the Constitution forbids "sophisticated, as well as simpleminded, modes of discrimination."...

State legislatures are, historically, the fountainhead of representative government in this country. A number of them have their roots in colonial times, and substantially antedate the creation of our Nation and our Federal Government. In fact, the first formal stirrings of American political independence are to be found, in large part, in the views and actions of several of the colonial legislative bodies. With the birth of our National Government, and the adoption and ratification of the Federal Constitution, state legislatures retained a most important place in our Nation's governmental structure. But representative government is, in essence, self-government through the medium of elected representatives of the people, and each and every citizen has an inalienable right to full and effective participation in the political processes of his State's legislative bodies. Most citizens can achieve this participation only as qualified voters through the election of legislators to represent them. Full and effective participation by all citizens in state government requires, therefore, that each citizen have an equally effective voice in the election of members of his state legislature. Modern and viable state government needs, and the Constitution demands, no less.

Logically, in a society ostensibly grounded on representative government, it would seem reasonable that a majority of the people of a State could elect a majority of that State's legislators. To conclude differently, and to sanction minority control of state legislative bodies, would appear to deny majority rights in a way that far surpasses any possible denial of minority rights that might otherwise be thought to result. Since legislatures are responsible for enacting laws by which all citizens are to be governed, they should be bodies which are collectively responsive to the popular will. And the concept of equal protection has been traditionally viewed as requiring the uniform treatment of persons standing in the same relation to the governmental action questioned or challenged. With respect to the allocation of legislative representation, all voters, as citizens of a State, stand in the same relation regardless of where they live. Any suggested criteria for the differentiation of citizens are insufficient to justify any discrimination, as to the weight of their votes, unless relevant to the permissible purposes of legislative apportionment. Since the achieving of fair and effective representation for all citizens is concededly the basic aim of legislative apportionment, we conclude that the Equal Protection Clause guarantees the opportunity for equal participation by all voters in the election of state legislators. Diluting the weight of votes because of place of residence impairs basic constitutional rights under the Fourteenth Amendment just as much as invidious discriminations based upon factors such as race, *Brown v.*

Board of Education, or economic status, *Griffin v. Illinois, Douglas v. California*. Our constitutional system amply provides for the protection of minorities by means other than giving them majority control of state legislatures. And the democratic ideals of equality and majority rule, which have served this Nation so well in the past, are hardly of any less significance for the present and the future.

We are told that the matter of apportioning representation in a state legislature is a complex and many-faceted one. We are advised that States can rationally consider factors other than population in apportioning legislative representation. We are admonished not to restrict the power of the States to impose differing views as to political philosophy on their citizens. We are cautioned about the dangers of entering into political thickets and mathematical quagmires. Our answer is this: a denial of constitutionally protected rights demands judicial protection; our oath and our office require no less of us....

We hold that, as a basic constitutional standard, the Equal Protection Clause requires that the seats in both houses of a bicameral state legislature must be apportioned on a population basis. Simply stated, an individual's right to vote for state legislators is unconstitutionally impaired when its weight is in a substantial fashion diluted when compared with votes of citizens living in other parts of the State....

By holding that, as a federal constitutional requisite, both houses of a state legislature must be apportioned on a population basis, we mean that the Equal Protection Clause requires that a State make an honest and good faith effort to construct districts, in both houses of its legislature, as nearly of equal population as is practicable....

History indicates, however, that many States have deviated, to a greater or lesser degree, from the equal population principle in the apportionment of seats in at least one house of their legislatures. So long as the divergences from a strict population standard are based on legitimate considerations incident to the effectuation of a rational state policy, some deviations from the equal population principle are constitutionally permissible with respect to the apportionment of seats in either or both of the two houses of a bicameral state legislature. But neither history alone, nor economic or other sorts of group interests, are permissible factors in attempting to justify disparities from population-based representation. Citizens, not history or economic interests, cast votes.

Glossary

bicameral: consisting of two legislative bodies, generally one made up of state-wide representatives and the other of local representatives

concededly: admittedly

gainsaid: denied

gerrymandering: the act of drawing congressional boundary lines for the purpose of giving an advantage to a party, group of constituents, or candidate in an election

justiciable: able to be evaluated and ruled on in the courts

remanded: returned to a lower court for further consideration

Document Analysis

Despite the protections of the Fourteenth Amendment, black voters continued to be disenfranchised in the South through the 1950s. Disenfranchisement took many forms, including literacy tests and poll taxes. The process of apportionment, which determined the boundaries of congressional districts, also effectively disenfranchised voters, particularly those who lived in urban areas. Even though many states' populations were shifting from the country to the city, most states continued to allocate representatives by county, which effectively robbed urban voters of proportional representation in their legislatures. Rural interests thus governed increasingly urban populations.

In 1959 Charles Baker and nine other urban residents sued the Tennessee secretary of state, Joe C. Carr, noting that the state had not reapportioned its districts since 1901 and had thus effectively denied its urban voters their Fourteenth Amendment rights. *Baker v. Carr* represented a challenge to the Warren Court. First of all, the courts had traditionally shied away from matters involving political districting, concerned that judicial rulings in this area could be construed as a violation of separation of powers; legislative questions were considered political matters not appropriate for Court involvement. Furthermore, the right to vote is not clearly established by the Constitution. The Founders had a restrictive view of who should be able to vote: Slaves, women, and unpropertied males were not considered eligible. In considering *Baker v. Carr*, the Court was entering new territory. Written by William J. Brennan, the 1962 *Baker* decision was carefully worded, stating only that reapportionment could be taken up in the courts. The ruling thus let individual federal district courts decide how they would solve problems of malapportionment. Soon after the decision was announced, attorneys filed cases challenging apportionments in several states. By the end of 1962, the Supreme Court had twelve cases pending that related to redistricting. These state cases were decided collectively under *Reynolds v. Sims* on June 15, 1964.

In *Reynolds v. Sims*, several voters in Alabama sued state election officials, charging that their Fourteenth Amendment rights, as well as their rights under the Alabama Constitution, had been violated by the state's existing legislative apportionment. The case also involved a dispute over proposed reapportionment plans, which the plaintiffs argued were unconstitutional. Having established in *Baker v. Carr* that the courts did, in fact, have jurisdiction over such matters, the Warren Court now needed to address specific cases handed up by the federal district courts.

In the first paragraph of the excerpt of Warren's decision, he makes clear his opinion that the Court has jurisdiction over questions of redistricting. One of the roles of the Supreme Court is to evaluate the constitutionality of state and federal laws; by stating that the Constitution protects the right of qualified voters, Warren establishes the Court's role in striking down laws that violate those rights.

As was the case in *Brown v. Board*, Warren's decision in this case was strongly influenced by his attitude toward racial discrimination. He mentions the practice of "gerrymandering," which is the manipulation of election district boundaries in order to influence election results. The term derives from Elbridge Gerry, governor of Massachusetts from 1810 to 1812, who redistricted the state to benefit his political party. Warren refers to racial gerrymandering, which was practiced in both southern and northern states; by redrawing legislative district lines, politicians could create segregated, all-black districts or, in some cases, eliminate black voters from an area when it was expedient. Warren points out that malapportionment disenfranchises voters just as effectively as prohibiting them from voting at all.

Warren's decisions are noteworthy for their clear, straightforward language. This particular document contains an especially unusual and oft-quoted passage: "Legislators represent people, not trees or acres. Legislators are elected by voters, not farms or cities or economic interests." This verbiage was actually crafted by the law clerk Francis X. Beytagh, who worked on the case with Warren. Warren read this in the draft statement and thought that the language captured the essence of his "one man, one vote" argument. The passage stands out for the very reason that its tone differs from that of the rest of the document.

A key component of Warren's decision is his statement that "seats in both houses of a bicameral state legislature must be apportioned on a population basis." Important here is the assertion that both houses had to use population as a means of determining representation. Following *Baker v. Carr*, many states refused to reapportion their districts, instead using what was known as the "federal plan," in which one house of the legislature was apportioned geographically and the other by population. *Reynolds v. Sims* made clear that the federal plan was no longer an option. Warren allowed for some flexibility in redistricting in order to prevent gerrymandering or to provide for fair representation in more rural states with many counties. However, he reiterates in his decision that population is the overriding factor that should determine the number of representatives.

Reynolds v. Sims was a much broader decision than *Baker v. Carr* in the sense that it had a dramatic and lasting impact on the political landscape. By specifically defining constitutional districting plans in terms of population rather than geography, Warren summarily eliminated the jobs of many powerful rural senators and assemblymen; rural districts disappeared as states redrew boundaries to conform to the new requirements. Today, Congress and state legislatures are overwhelmingly filled with lawmakers from cities and suburbs. In addition to reshaping the makeup of legislatures and the state level, *Reynolds v. Sims* is cited as helping end one method of black voter disenfranchisement in America.

Essential Themes

According to the majority opinion of the Court on the *Reynolds* case, the principle of democracy was clearly based on the Equal Protection Clause of the Fourteenth Amendment. The concept of democracy in America, in large part, hinges on the right to vote in democratic elections. By ruling to create more equal legislative districts throughout the nation, the Court established the standard of "one person, one vote". In other words, each person voting in an election should have equal weight in determining the result of the election they voted in.

The Court's decision to end the unfair apportionment of legislative districts was a move to uphold the new "one person, one vote" standard, and simultaneously caused a major shakeup in the political landscape of America. Because the Court insisted upon reapportionment on the basis of population by calling for districts to be made as equal as possible, state legislative districts were overhauled across the country. The redrawing of state legislative districts meant there would be an end to the legislative stronghold held by rural lawmakers, and instead legislatures would be dominated by elected officials from cities and suburbs. The roughly 2% of Americans still living on farms would experience a loss of power in terms of their legislative representation. This was a seriously controversial ruling at the time, with many claiming the Supreme Court had no right to interfere in state politics. A constitutional amendment was proposed to combat the Court's ruling, but this attempt to reverse the decision was unsuccessful. Regardless of the pushback, the Court, and Justice Warren in particular, were confident this was the only fair ruling according to the Constitution. While the Court certainly has respect for states' rights, they must also fiercely defend individuals' rights and they ruling of *Reynolds* emphasizes that stance.

—*Karen Linkletter, PhD, Amber R. Dickinson, PhD*

Bibliography and Additional Reading

Douglas, Joshua, and Eugene Mazeo. *Election Law Stories*. Foundation Press, 2016.

Irons, Peter. *A People's History of the Supreme Court*. New York, NY: Penguin, 1999.

McBride, Alex. "Landmark Cases: Reynolds V. Sims." PBS, Public Broadcasting Services, www.pbs.org/wnet/supremecourt/rights/landmark_reynolds.html.

McClosky, Robert G. *The American Supreme Court*. Fourth Edition. University of Chicago Press, 2005.

■ Red Lion Broadcasting v. FCC

Date: June 8, 1969
Authors: U.S. Supreme Court; Justice Byron White
Genre: court opinion

Summary Overview

In the Supreme Court case Red Lion Broadcasting v. FCC, *the Court heard arguments against the Federal Communications Commission (FCC) policy known as the "Fairness Doctrine," a rule which stated that broadcasters had an obligation to provide equal time to advocates for either side of controversial issues. The doctrine gave the opportunity to political opponents, for example, to state their views and rebut any negative comments made about them by their rivals, thus permitting voters to decide for themselves which candidates they preferred. It also applied to "issues" campaigns concerning policy choices facing voters in the form of ballot questions.*

Red Lion Broadcasting claimed that this was an unfair infringement of its rights to free speech under the First Amendment; but in a unanimous decision, the Supreme Court declared that the FCC's observance of the Fairness Doctrine was justified and that broadcasters were required by the nature of their licenses to serve the public. While the Fairness Doctrine was repealed in the 1980s, the Court's defense of it in this 1969 decision presents readers with a strong case for the idea that the media has a duty to inform the public. The Red Lion Broadcasting case presents citizens with a question: what responsibilities should the media be required to observe, and what role can the media play in disseminating varied viewpoints to the public?

Defining Moment

When radio broadcasting first emerged in the late 1910s and 1920s, the unregulated airwaves quickly became unusable as different companies competed for the ability to broadcast programming over the air. A station broadcasting with too powerful a signal could interfere with stations in the same location; if two competing stations tried to broadcast on similar frequencies, they would cancel each other out and create static. As Justice Byron White later explained, "chaos ... ensued"—until the federal government got involved as a mediator.

In 1927, Congress passed the Radio Act of 1927, which established the government's role in issuing licenses for broadcasters to use radio frequencies; this was further strengthened by the "Communications Act of 1934," which established the Federal Communications Commission to regulate telegraph, telephone, and radio communications. These acts rested on the belief that the airwaves were owned by the

Photograph of investigative journalist Fred J. Cook (1911–2003), whose book, Goldwater–Extremist on the Right, *became part of the Red Lion case when Cook asked for equal airtime to respond to attacks made by Hargis.*

public. In practice, this meant that licenses would be offered only to those stations that could prove they would provide programming "in the public interest, convenience, or necessity." To properly serve the public, licensees had a duty to share time with members of the community who wished to espouse a particular point of view.

In 1949, the FCC further codified the "public interest" requirement. In a memorandum entitled "In the Matter of Editorializing by Broadcast Licenses," the regulating agency explained that "The Commission has consequently recognized the necessity for licensees to devote a reasonable percentage of their broadcast time to the presentation of news and programs devoted to the consideration of public issues of interest ... the paramount right of the public in a free society [is] to be informed and to have presented to it for acceptance and rejection ... different attitudes and viewpoints concerning ... vital and often controversial issues." It furthermore required that stations make time available for spokespersons of competing views as well as for people who had been publicly attacked on the air, so as to give each a fair hearing. Although the exact wording of this principle went through several changes over the years, the overarching idea became known as the "Fairness Doctrine." Each side in a public debate must be give their time on air to comment.

Broadcasters often balked at these requirements. In Red Lion Broadcasting v FCC, the Supreme Court upheld the Fairness Doctrine by offering a restatement of the basic philosophy underpinning the FCC's creation: because the FCC was created to facilitate communication over the airwaves in ways that furthered the public interest, the Fairness Doctrine was an acceptable way of balancing opposing views. However, despite the defense of the Fairness Doctrine in Red Lion Broadcasting v FCC, the doctrine was abandoned in 1987, at the urging of conservative activists who believed that the doctrine was a burden on the rights of broadcasters. After that change, partisan talk radio took off and began proliferating on the airwaves, giving rise to "entertainment" journalism that seeks not to inform but to drive audiences to the market and make profits.

Author Biographies

Supreme Court justice Byron White, who delivered the majority opinion in this case, served more than thirty years on the Court, from April 1962 to June 1993. In this time, White left an uncertain legacy that fails to place him in any one place on the political spectrum. Justice White was generally skeptical of sweeping judicial claims that created vast legal precedent; instead, he hoped that cases would be decided narrowly, based on the particular facts of a case. Implicit in this judicial path was White's belief that the

The Court ruling that upheld the Fair Doctrine spelled the end of the first Golden Age of Television, along with programming such as Playhouse 90 on CBS. (Note that the ad for this repeat, a production adapted from William Faulkner's story, makes no mention of Faulkner.)

rights of the individual must be balanced by the interests of the state. White was skeptical of rights not explicitly delineated in the Constitution and believed that the state's interests could overrule the needs of the individual in some cases.

During Byron White's tenure, the Court heard a succession of important cases that greatly expanded the rights of the individual. In 1965, the Court decided, in *Griswold v Connecticut* (a case concerning the right of states to ban the sale of birth control), that the Constitution implied a "right of privacy" for individuals. White, however, resisted the creation of the "right of privacy," instead deciding the *Griswold* case narrowly in a concurring opinion: he observed that while the government had a right to discourage extramarital affairs, which contraceptives might facilitate, laws that also limited a married couple's access to these pills impeded their freedom without a compelling state interest in doing so. In *Roe v. Wade* (1973), White famously dissented, arguing that there was no right to abortion; the law should rationally weigh the rights of communities to ban the practice with the rights of individuals to terminate pregnancies. He continued this line of thought in *Bowers v Hardwick* (1986), when he wrote for the majority that the individual has no more right to engage in homosexual acts than the state has in banning those acts. Despite these decisions showing a decided social conservatism, White's belief in the importance of balancing state interests often led him to more liberal positions as well; for instance, he consistently voted to uphold federal school desegregation laws, arguing that the state's interest in creating integrated schools and accommodations was more fundamental than the right of individuals to refuse service to African Americans.

In *Red Lion Broadcasting v FCC*, White similarly tried to balance the rights of competing actors. Here, he found that the public had a vested interest in regulating radio airwaves—one more fundamental than the right of radio stations to freely determine their own broadcasting. Thus, as in a number of such cases, White concerns himself not with fundamentally protected rights but rather with balancing the good of the community with the good of the individual.

Historical Document

Red Lion Broadcasting v. FCC

RED LION BROADCASTING CO., INC., ET AL. v. FEDERAL COMMUNICATIONS COMMISSION ET AL.

SUPREME COURT OF THE UNITED STATES

395 U.S. 367

June 9, 1969, Decided

MR. JUSTICE WHITE delivered the opinion of the Court.

The Federal Communications Commission has for many years imposed on radio and television broadcasters the requirement that discussion of public issues be presented on broadcast stations, and that each side of those issues must be given fair coverage. This is known as the fairness doctrine, which originated very early in the history of broadcasting and has maintained its present outlines for some time. It is an obligation whose content has been defined in a long series of FCC rulings in particular cases, and which is distinct from the statutory requirement of § 315 of the Communications Act that equal time be allotted all qualified candidates for public office. Two aspects of the fairness doctrine, relating to personal attacks in the context of controversial public issues and to political editorializing, were codified more precisely in the form of FCC regulations in 1967. The two cases before us now, which were decided separately below, challenge the constitutional and statutory bases of the doctrine and component rules. *Red Lion* involves the application of the fairness doctrine to a particular broadcast, and *RTNDA* arises as an action to review the FCC's 1967 promulgation of the personal attack and political editorializing regulations, which were laid down after the *Red Lion* litigation had begun.

I

A

The Red Lion Broadcasting Company is licensed to operate a Pennsylvania radio station, WGCB. On November 27, 1964, WGCB carried a 15-minute broadcast by the Reverend Billy James Hargis as part of a "Christian Crusade" series. A book by Fred J. Cook entitled "Goldwater — Extremist on the Right" was discussed by Hargis, who said that Cook had been fired by a newspaper for making false charges against city officials; that Cook had then worked for a

Communist-affiliated publication; that he had defended Alger Hiss and attacked J. Edgar Hoover and the Central Intelligence Agency; and that he had now written a "book to smear and destroy Barry Goldwater." When Cook heard of the broadcast he concluded that he had been personally attacked and demanded free reply time, which the station refused. After an exchange of letters among Cook, Red Lion, and the FCC, the FCC declared that the Hargis broadcast constituted a personal attack on Cook; that Red Lion had failed to meet its obligation under the fairness doctrine to send a tape, transcript, or summary of the broadcast to Cook and offer him reply time; and that the station must provide reply time whether or not Cook would pay for it. On review in the Court of Appeals for the District of Columbia Circuit, the FCC's position was upheld as constitutional and otherwise proper.

B

Not long after the *Red Lion* litigation was begun, the FCC issued a Notice of Proposed Rule Making with an eye to making the personal attack aspect of the fairness doctrine more precise and more readily enforceable, and to specifying its rules relating to political editorials. After considering written comments supporting and opposing the rules, the FCC adopted them substantially as proposed. As they now stand amended, the regulations read as follows: "Personal attacks; political editorials.

"(a) When, during the presentation of views on a controversial issue of public importance, an attack is made upon the honesty, character, integrity or like personal qualities of an identified person or group, the licensee shall, within a reasonable time and in no event later than 1 week after the attack, transmit to the person or group attacked (1) notification of the date, time and identification of the broadcast; (2) a script or tape (or an accurate summary if a script or tape is not available) of the attack; and (3) an offer of a reasonable opportunity to respond over the licensee's facilities....

C

Believing that the specific application of the fairness doctrine in *Red Lion*, and the promulgation of the regulations in *RTNDA*, are both authorized by Congress and enhance rather than abridge the freedoms of speech and press protected by the First Amendment, we hold them valid and constitutional, reversing the judgment below in *RTNDA* and affirming the judgment below in *Red Lion*.

II

The history of the emergence of the fairness doctrine and of the related legislation shows that the Commission's action in the *Red Lion* case did not exceed its authority, and that in adopting the new regulations the Commission was implementing congressional policy rather than embarking on a frolic of its own.... The statutory authority of the FCC to promulgate these regulations derives from the mandate to the "Commission from time to time, as public convenience, interest, or necessity requires" to promulgate "such rules and regulations and prescribe such restrictions and conditions ... as may be necessary to carry out the provisions of this chapter ...."

We cannot say that the FCC's declaratory ruling in *Red Lion*, or the regulations at issue in *RTNDA*, are beyond the scope of the congressionally conferred power to assure that stations are operated by those whose possession of a license serves "the public interest."

III

The broadcasters challenge the fairness doctrine and its specific manifestations in the personal attack and political editorial rules on conventional First Amendment grounds, alleging that the rules abridge their freedom of speech and press. Their contention is that the First Amendment protects their desire to use their allotted frequencies continuously to broadcast whatever they choose, and to exclude whomever they choose from ever using that frequency. No man may be prevented from saying or publishing what he thinks, or from refusing in his speech or other utterances to give equal weight to the views of his opponents. This right, they say, applies equally to broadcasters.

A

Although broadcasting is clearly a medium affected by a First Amendment interest, differences in the characteristics of new media justify differences in the First Amendment standards applied to them. For example, the ability of new technology to produce sounds more raucous than those of the human voice justifies restrictions on the sound level, and on the hours and places of use, of sound trucks so long as the restrictions are reasonable and applied without discrimination.

Just as the Government may limit the use of sound-amplifying equipment potentially so noisy that it drowns out civilized private speech, so may the Government limit the use of broadcast equipment. The right of free speech of a broadcaster, the user of a sound truck, or any other individual does not embrace a right to snuff out the free speech of others.

When two people converse face to face, both should not speak at once if either is to be clearly understood. But the range of the human voice is so limited that there could be meaningful communications if half the people in the United States were talking and the other half listening. Just as clearly, half the people might publish and the other half read. But the reach of radio signals is incomparably greater than the range of the human voice and the problem of interference is a massive reality. The lack of know-how and equipment may keep many from the air, but only a tiny fraction of those with resources and intelligence can hope to communicate by radio at the same time if intelligible communication is to be had, even if the entire radio spectrum is utilized in the present state of commercially acceptable technology.

It was this fact, and the chaos which ensued from permitting anyone to use any frequency at whatever power level he wished, which made necessary the enactment of the Radio Act of 1927 and the Communications Act of 1934, as the Court has noted at length before. It was this reality which at the very least necessitated first the division of the radio spectrum into portions reserved respectively for public broadcasting and for other important radio uses such as amateur operation, aircraft, police, defense, and navigation; and then the subdivision of each portion, and assignment of specific frequencies to individual users or groups of users. Beyond this, however, because the frequencies reserved for public broadcasting were limited in number, it was essential for the Government to tell some applicants that they could not broadcast at all because there was room for only a few.

Where there are substantially more individuals who want to broadcast than there are frequencies to allocate, it is idle to posit an unabridgeable First Amendment right to broadcast comparable to the right of every individual to speak, write, or publish. If 100 persons want broadcast licenses but there are only 10 frequencies to allocate, all of them may have the same "right" to a license; but if there is to be any effective communication by radio, only a few can be licensed and the rest must be barred from the airwaves. It would be strange if the First Amendment, aimed at protecting and furthering communications, prevented the Government from making radio communication possible by requiring licenses to broadcast and by limiting the number of licenses so as not to overcrowd the spectrum.

This has been the consistent view of the Court. Congress unquestionably has the power to grant and deny licenses and to eliminate existing stations. No one has a First Amendment right to a license or to monopolize a radio frequency; to deny a station license because "the public interest" requires it "is not a denial of free speech."

By the same token, as far as the First Amendment is concerned those who are licensed stand no better than those to whom licenses are refused. A license permits broadcasting, but the licensee has no constitutional right to be the one who holds the license or to monopolize a radio frequency to the exclusion of his fellow citizens. There is nothing in the First Amendment which prevents the Government from requiring a licensee to share his frequency with others and to conduct himself as a proxy or fiduciary with obligations to present those views and voices which are representative of his community and which would otherwise, by necessity, be barred from the airwaves.

This is not to say that the First Amendment is irrelevant to public broadcasting. On the contrary, it has a major role to play as the Congress itself recognized in § 326, which forbids FCC interference with "the right of free speech by means of radio communication." Because of the scarcity of radio frequencies, the Government is permitted to put restraints on licensees in favor of others whose views should be expressed on this unique medium. But the people as a whole retain their interest in free speech by radio and their collective right to have the medium function consistently with the ends and purposes of the First Amendment. It is the right of the viewers and listeners, not the right of the broadcasters, which is paramount. It is the purpose of the First Amendment to preserve an uninhibited marketplace of ideas in which truth will ultimately prevail, rather than to countenance monopolization of that market, whether it be by the Government itself or a private licensee. It is the right of the public to receive suitable access to social, political, esthetic, moral, and other ideas and experiences which is crucial here. That right may not constitutionally be abridged either by Congress or by the FCC.

B

Rather than confer frequency monopolies on a relatively small number of licensees, in a Nation of 200,000,000, the Government could surely have decreed that each frequency should be shared among all or some of those who wish to use it, each being assigned a portion of the broadcast day or the broadcast week. The ruling and regulations at issue here do not go quite so far. They assert that under specified circumstances, a licensee must offer to make available a reasonable amount of broadcast time to those who have a view different from that which has already been expressed on his station. The expression of a political endorsement, or of a personal attack while dealing with a controversial public issue, simply triggers this time sharing. As we have said, the First Amendment confers no right on licensees to prevent others from broadcasting on "their" frequencies and no right to an unconditional monopoly of a scarce resource which the Government has denied others the right to use....

Nor can we say that it is inconsistent with the First Amendment goal of producing an informed public capable of conducting its own affairs to require a broadcaster to permit answers to personal attacks occurring in the course of discussing controversial issues, or to require that the political opponents of those endorsed by the station be given a chance to communicate with the public. Otherwise, station owners and a few networks would have unfettered power to make time available only to the highest bidders, to communicate only their own views on public issues, people and candidates, and to permit on the air only those with whom they agreed. There is no sanctuary in the First Amendment for unlimited private censorship operating in a medium not open to all. "Freedom of the press from governmental interference under the

First Amendment does not sanction repression of that freedom by private interests."

C

It is strenuously argued, however, that if political editorials or personal attacks will trigger an obligation in broadcasters to afford the opportunity for expression to speakers who need not pay for time and whose views are unpalatable to the licensees, then broadcasters will be irresistibly forced to self-censorship and their coverage of controversial public issues will be eliminated or at least rendered wholly ineffective. Such a result would indeed be a serious matter, for should licensees actually eliminate their coverage of controversial issues, the purposes of the doctrine would be stifled.

At this point, however, as the Federal Communications Commission has indicated, that possibility is at best speculative. The communications industry, and in particular the networks, have taken pains to present controversial issues in the past, and even now they do not assert that they intend to abandon their efforts in this regard. It would be better if the FCC's encouragement were never necessary to induce the broadcasters to meet their responsibility. And if experience with the administration of these doctrines indicates that they have the net effect of reducing rather than enhancing the volume and quality of coverage, there will be time enough to reconsider the constitutional implications. The fairness doctrine in the past has had no such overall effect.

That this will occur now seems unlikely, however, since if present licensees should suddenly prove timorous, the Commission is not powerless to insist that they give adequate and fair attention to public issues. It does not violate the First Amendment to treat licensees given the privilege of using scarce radio frequencies as proxies for the entire community, obligated to give suitable time and attention to matters of great public concern....

D

The litigants embellish their First Amendment arguments with the contention that the regulations are so vague that their duties are impossible to discern. Of this point it is enough to say that, judging the validity of the regulations on their face as they are presented here, we cannot conclude that the FCC has been left a free hand to vindicate its own idiosyncratic conception of the public interest or of the requirements of free speech. Past adjudications by the FCC give added precision to the regulations; there was nothing vague about the FCC's specific ruling in *Red Lion* that Fred Cook should be provided an opportunity to reply. The regulations at issue in *RTNDA* could be employed in precisely the same way as the fairness doctrine was in *Red Lion*....

We need not and do not now ratify every past and future decision by the FCC with regard to programming. There is no question here of the Commission's refusal to permit the broadcaster to carry a particular program or to publish his own views; of a discriminatory refusal to require the licensee to broadcast certain views which have been denied access to the airwaves; of government censorship of a particular program contrary to § 326; or of the official government view dominating public broadcasting. Such questions would raise more serious First Amendment issues. But we do hold that the Congress and the Commission do not violate the First Amendment when they require a radio or television station to give reply time to answer personal attacks and political editorials.

In view of the scarcity of broadcast frequencies, the Government's role in allocating those frequencies, and the legitimate claims of those unable without governmental assistance to gain access to those frequencies for expression of their views, we hold the regulations and ruling at issue here are both authorized by statute and constitutional. The judgment of the Court of Appeals in *Red Lion* is affirmed and that in *RTNDA* reversed and the causes remanded for proceedings consistent with this opinion.

Document Analysis

In *Red Lion Broadcasting v FCC*, the Supreme Court heard a case in which a broadcaster sued the FCC on the basis that the Fairness Doctrine was a violation of the first amendment. The Fairness Doctrine was an FCC rule that required radio stations to devote equal time to both sides of partisan or generally divisive issues; Red Lion Broadcasting had refused to offer time to an individual who was publicly defamed on air, thus violating the rule.

The Supreme Court disagreed with Red Lion Broadcasting and laid out principles that justified the need for radio broadcasts to be more regulated than other forms of speech. First, because radio wavelengths were limited, the medium could allow only a limited number of voices to be heard. Unlike human speech, or writing, in which an unlimited number of speakers could communicate at essentially the same time, the prospect of letting everyone freely take advantage of the airwaves would lead to interference, and the silencing of many voices. Regulation of the airwaves, therefore, actually increased the amount of free speech available. The Court further noted that radio licensees did not own an unlimited right to the frequency they licensed. Rather, licenses were regulated by the FCC, and because the public has an equal claim to the airwaves, licensees were compelled to offer equal space to the public. The Fairness Doctrine was a way to make sure that every voice was heard, within the constraints of radio broadcasting as a medium.

Finally, the Court made one last claim: that the First Amendment was not a vehicle to simply protect free speech, but rather also obliged the government to promote an informed public. As the Court explained, "It is the purpose of the First Amendment to preserve an uninhibited marketplace of ideas in which truth will ultimately prevail, rather than to countenance monopolization of that market, whether it be by the Government itself or a private licensee. It is the right of the public to receive suitable access to social, political, esthetic, moral, and other ideas and experiences which is crucial here." Because of these restrictions, broadcasters owed a duty to inform the public; thus, the rights of the individual to unregulated broadcasting were superseded by the rights of the public to access those airwaves.

For all these reasons, the Supreme Court upheld the right of the FCC to compel broadcasters to offer equal time to anyone who was personally attacked on air, or to compel broadcasters to cover all sides of important public issues.

Essential Themes

Although *Red Lion Broadcasting v. FCC* upheld the Fairness Doctrine, this policy had become unpopular by the 1980s; free-market conservatives began to challenge the claim that any private industry had a duty to the public good. At the heart of the issue surrounding the Doctrine was a disagreement over the role that media played in American society. On the one hand, advocates of the Fairness Doctrine believed that the media were stewards of American democracy; the media owed the public a debt because the public has lent out the airwaves to them; thus, the media needed to use those airwaves responsibly for the good of all.

Advocates of small government, on the other hand, began to argue that such government regulation was counterproductive. Milton Friedman, an influential libertarian economist, claimed that government regulation inhibited market forces and caused businesses to be less receptive to public concerns. Other advocates of the free market were less nuanced: government regulation intruded on the individual's freedoms, they said, and regulations such as the Fairness Doctrine inhibited the media from using their property as they wanted. Inherent in this point of view was the idea that the media was made up of private businesses; as a result, the media owed no particular duty to the American public.

In practice, the Fairness Doctrine rarely achieved the results that its advocates had wished. Most broadcasters avoided political content on air, hoping thereby to avoid being forced to give up airtime to the other side of an issue. While the Fairness Doctrine sometimes compelled stations to broadcast the speeches of both opposing sides or to give voice to minority opinions, most of the time broadcasters carefully avoided political controversy. In the end, the free-market conservatives had a point: broadcasters were often profit motivated and bypassed their responsibilities to inform the public in favor of making profits.

Repeal of the doctrine in 1987, however, created a different set of problems. Unencumbered by the threat of providing free airtime for opposing viewpoints, radio stations around the country began to produce a brand of radically partisan right-wing talk radio. New radio hosts, such as Rush Limbaugh, dispensed with the notion of objectivity and instead treated their shows like a business; learning that they could cultivate a devoted audience by making outrageous statements, these radio hosts began to change the media landscape, dispensing entirely with traditional journalistic tenets regarding fairly informing the public.

Since the 2016 presidential election, if not before, Americans have become increasingly worried that the partisan division of news outlets has degraded our ability to find common ground. In addition, fake news—i.e., fabricated stories created, on social media and elsewhere, to fuel partisan anger at their political enemies—proliferated during the election and likely played a role in tipping the election to the Republican nominee, Donald Trump. Seeing the dangers firsthand of partisan media, some Americans have begun to wonder: does the media owe the public a debt of objectivity and truthfulness in journalism? Or, alternatively, were the advocates in the 1980s right when they dispensed with the Fairness Doctrine as an incumbrance on business?

—*Aaron George, PhD*

Bibliography and Additional Reading

Baughman, James. *The Republic of Mass Culture: Journalism, Filmmaking, and Broadcasting in America since 1941.* Baltimore: John Hopkins UP, 2006.

Congressional Research Service. *Fairness Doctrine: History and Constitutional Issues.* Washington, DC: CRS, 2011.

Ides, Allan. "The Jurisprudence of Justice Byron White," *Yale Law Journal*, vol. 103, no. 2 (November, 1993), 419–461.

Zelizer, Julian. "How Washington Helped to Create the Modern Media: Ending the Fairness Doctrine," in *Media Nation: The Political History of News in Modern America*, ed. Bruce Schulman and Julian Zelizer. Philadelphia: University of Pennsylvania Press, 2017; pp. 176–189.

Richardson v. Ramirez

Date: June 24, 1974
Author: William Rehnquist
Genre: court opinion

Summary Overview

In different eras, U.S. Supreme Court rulings have fluctuated between conservative and liberal philosophies. In light of the transformative civil rights rulings during the previous twenty years, attorneys for three California men (Abran Ramirez, Albert Lee, and Larry Gill) who were convicted felons, believed that 1974 might be an optimal time in which to seek to overturn California's law that took away the right to vote for any individual who had been convicted of a felony.

However, the U.S. Supreme Court's strong 6–3 ruling upholding the right of California to extend the punishment of convicted felons beyond a time of incarceration and/or probation was a surprise for many, since the California Supreme Court had voided the law. Written by conservative Justice William J. Rehnquist, Richardson v. Ramirez *made it clear that the Fourteenth Amendment did not restrict a state from making the loss of voting rights a standard part of the punishment for a convicted felon.*

Defining Moment

From the founding of the Greek city-states into the twenty-first century, democracies and republics have taken away an individual's right to vote based on that individual having been convicted of certain crimes. This was true in the British North American colonies, and after the adoption of the U.S. Constitution, the scope of disfranchisement was expanded in numerous states. (The Constitution gave the states the role of defining the criteria for eligible voters.) Except for the Fifteenth Amendment, outlawing racial discrimination and giving the right to vote to former slaves, all the major state and federal legislation on this topic, prior to 1950, tightened the rules for voting eligibility, including disenfranchising an increasing number of individuals convicted of crimes.

Beginning in the 1950s, legislative action and judicial decisions tended to move things in the opposite direction. The Civil Rights Act of 1957 allowed the attorney general to sue states that were accused of denying African Americans the vote solely based on race. The Civil Rights Act of 1965 further decreased

Chief Justice Wiliam Rehnquist. Photo via Wikimedia Commons. [Public domain.]

barriers to voter registration and expanded the federal government's role in overseeing the electoral process. In addition, the Supreme Court issued a ruling expanding voting rights in 1966, and the California Supreme Court (1966) did the same, while the New York (1967) Court of Appeals (their supreme court) ruled disenfranchisement constitutional. In a 1972 voting rights case, the Ninth Circuit Court of Appeals ruled that law was not stagnant and suggested the disenfranchisement based on criminal convictions should be greatly limited.

Thus, the plaintiffs in *Richardson v. Ramirez* saw that there was a much greater chance of their plea being upheld than at any previous time in the history of the United States. The California Supreme Court agreed with them and ordered that they be allowed to register to vote. However, the U.S. Supreme Court saw things differently and ruled that disenfranchisement was constitutional. In the ruling, Justice Rehnquist was clear that states could handle the issue of felon's voting rights as desired. He, and the majority, did not believe there was any mandate that states limit, or not limit, a convicted felon's voting rights. Partially, as a result of this ruling, within five months California enacted a law that reinstated the voting rights of almost all felons after they completed serving their sentences.

Author Biography

William Hubbs Rehnquist (1924–2005) grew up in a suburb of Milwaukee, Wisconsin, in a middle-class family. His father was a sales manager, and his mother was on the board of an insurance company. After graduating from Shorewood High School, he earned a BA and an MA from Stanford University, an MA from Harvard University, and his law degree from Stanford Law School. (During this time he also spent three years in the Army Air Corps.)

While clerking in the Supreme Court (1952 to 1953), Rehnquist wrote a memo supporting segregation, which he later claimed reflected the view of Justice Robert H. Jackson, for whom he was clerking. He then went into private practice in Arizona and was active in Republican politics. In 1969, he served in the Office of Legal Counsel under President Nixon. Nixon nominated him to be an associate justice in 1971 and he was sworn in in 1972. His written opinions reflected his very conservative outlook on legal issues. In 1986, President Reagan nominated him to be chief justice, and he was confirmed after the first televised hearings for a Supreme Court Justice. He served in this position until his death in 2005.

Historical Document

United States Supreme Court

Richardson v. Ramirez (1974)

Argued: January 15, 1974
Decided: June 24, 1974

SYLLABUS

[NOTE: Where it is feasible, a syllabus (headnote) will be released, as is being done in connection with this case, at the time the opinion is issued. The syllabus constitutes no part of the opinion of the Court but has been prepared by the Reporter of Decisions for the convenience of the reader.]

After the three individual respondents, who had been convicted of felonies and had completed their sentences and paroles, were refused registration to vote in three different California counties respectively because of their felony convictions, they brought a class petition, on behalf of themselves and all other ex-felons similarly situated, for a writ of mandate in the California Supreme Court, naming as defendants the Secretary of State and the three county election officials who had denied them registration "individually and as representatives of the class of all other" county election officials in the State, and challenging the constitutionality of respondents' disenfranchisement on the ground, inter alia, that provisions of the California Constitution and the implementing statutes that disenfranchised ex-felons denied them equal protection. The three county officials named as defendants decided not to contest the action, and told the court they would henceforth register to vote ex-felons, including respondents, whose sentences and paroles had expired. Prior to the return date of the writ, the court added to the named defendants (instead of allowing her to intervene) another county election official (petitioner here) who was the defendant in a similar action by an ex-felon pending in the State Court of Appeal. After holding that the three first-named county officials' acquiescence did not render the case moot, the California Supreme Court went on to hold that the constitutional and statutory provisions in question, as applied to ex-felons whose sentences and paroles had expired, violated the Equal Protection Clause of the Fourteenth Amendment, but did not issue the peremptory writ.

Held:

1. In view of its unusual procedural history in the Supreme Court of California, the case is not moot.

(a) The State Supreme Court's action in adding petitioner as a named defendant after the other named county officials decided not to contest the action, and at a time when the Secretary of State (who did not join in the petition to this Court) was still a party defendant who had answered the complaint, indicates that the court considered the suit to be not only on behalf of the three named plaintiffs, but also on behalf of all ex-felons in California similarly situated, and also that the court regarded petitioner's opponent in the Court of Appeal suit, both as an unnamed member of the class of ex-felons referred to in the complaint and as one of a class actually seeking to register in petitioner's county, as a party to the Supreme Court action.

(b) Being rendered in a class action in which relief in the nature of declaratory relief was granted, the decision below is not only binding on petitioner, and thus dispositive of her other suit, but also decides the federal constitutional question presented for the unnamed members of the classes represented below by petitioner and respondents, whose continuing controversy in the State Supreme Court still continues in this Court. Brockington v. Rhodes, 396 U. S. 41, distinguished.

2. California, in disenfranchising convicted felons who have completed their sentences and paroles, does not violate the Equal Protection Clause.

(a) The understanding of the framers of the Fourteenth Amendment, as reflected in the express language of § 2 of the Amendment, which exempts from the sanction of reduced congressional representation resulting from the denial of citizens' right to vote the denial of such right for "participation in rebellion, or other crime," and in the historical and judicial interpretation of the Amendment's applicability to state laws disenfranchising felons, is of controlling significance in distinguishing such laws from those other state limitations on the franchise that this Court has held invalid under the Equal Protection Clause.

(b) Section 1 of the Fourteenth Amendment, which contains the Equal Protection Clause, in dealing with voting rights as it does, could not have been meant to bar outright a form of disenfranchisement that was expressly exempted from the less drastic sanction of reduced representation that § 2 imposed for other forms of disenfranchisement.

(c) Even if § 2 was made part of the Amendment "largely through the accident of political exigency, rather than for the relation which it bore to the other sections of Amendment,'" as respondents contend, this does not preclude looking to it for guidance in interpreting § 1, since § 2 is as much a part of the Amendment as any of the other sections, and how it became part of the Amendment is less important than what it says and what it means.

9 Cal. 3d 199, 507 P.2d 1345, reversed and remanded.

Glossary

disenfranchisement: taking away a person's right to vote

moot: not relevant; neither here nor there

reversed and remanded: the phrase used in Supreme Court rulings when the ruling of the lower court has not been accepted (reversed) and the case has been sent back (remanded) to the lower court for the implementation of the Supreme Court decision

Document Analysis

As individuals registered to vote in the 1972 elections, three individuals in California were among the thousands who were not allowed to register, because of having been convicted of a felony. Abran Ramirez, Albert Lee, and Larry Gill had served their time in prison and completed other aspects of their sentence, such as having been on probation. They tried to register in three different counties and each had been denied. However, when they filed their suits (which were combined into one class action suit), the county clerks allowed them to register. This made the hearing before the California and U.S. Supreme Courts unusual. Normally, when the situation has resolved itself prior to an appeals court hearing the case, it is ruled as being moot and no further judicial action is taken. However, as outlined in the opening section of the summary, both of these courts decided to hear the case and rule on it. This was due to the fact that the law was still on the books, and it was assumed that additional lawsuits would be filed. In addition, country clerks arbitrarily disregarding a voter registration law was not an acceptable practice.

At the heart of the complaint by Ramirez, Lee, and Gill (and others filing similar suits) was the belief that the guarantee of equal rights outlined in Section 1 of the Fourteenth Amendment was not being granted to the plaintiffs. Focusing on the wording of Section 1, the California Supreme Court agreed with the plaintiffs and ruled the disenfranchisement of convicted fellows unconstitutional, once those convicted had served the mandated sentence. However, the U.S. Supreme Court looked closely at Section 2 of the Fourteenth Amendment, which includes the statement that the right to vote would not be limited, "except for participation in rebellion, or other crime." Obviously, an individual convicted of a felony has committed something falling into the category of "other crime." Because of these two words, Rehnquist and the majority of the Court ruled that states have the right to deny voting rights to anyone convicted of a felony, even after the trial court's sentence had been carried out.

Because these two sections are part of the same amendment to the Constitution, the justices believed it was important to read it as a whole, rather than as separate items. While the justices did believe that due process was important and a vital part of the American political and judicial system, and because the loss of one's vote was specifically noted as a possibility in Section 2 for anyone who participated in a rebellion or "other crime," the majority kept intact the law mandating the loss of voting rights to individuals who had been convicted of a felony. Debate about the history of Section 2 was "less important than what it says and what it means."

Essential Themes

Although there have been many who believe that disenfranchising individuals who were convicted of a felony and served the appropriate sentence is wrong, change has generally come through actions at the state level. Since this 1974 ruling brought the issue to the attention of the general population, overall there has been a movement toward lessening the extent of this practice. Although California, the state in which the suits originated, was quick in its action, since that time over twenty states have moved to grant voting rights to people previously convicted of a felony. During the same period, only one passed a law delaying when a convicted felon could register to vote.

At the national level, only one major ruling was made that limited a state's right to deny the vote to someone convicted of a crime. In *Hunter v. Underwood*, with Rehnquist again writing the majority opinion in an 8–0 ruling, the Supreme Court stated that if a law was passed with the intention to deny the vote to members of racial minorities, it would be unconstitutional. In that case, the debate was whether Alabama had passed a law regulating conduct with the intent to "discriminate against blacks." Other than this ruling, the federal government and courts have done nothing to change the outcome of *Richardson v. Ramirez*.

The effect of this ruling, and the state laws that it upholds, is that just under 2 percent of the voting age population in the United States is ineligible to vote due to a previous criminal conviction. As with most things that are based on state laws, the number who are ineligible varies dramatically. Maine and Vermont allow everyone, including people in prison, to vote. At the other end of the spectrum, about 8 percent of adults in Tennessee and Alabama are ineligible to vote based on this type of law. Florida remains the state with the largest number of ineligible voters, with more than a million people falling into this category. Thus, in many states this ruling has had and could continue to have an effect on electoral outcomes.

—*Donald A. Watt, PhD*

Bibliography and Additional Reading

Hinchcliff, Abagail M. "The "Other" Side of Richardson v. Ramirez: A Textual Challenge to Felon Disenfranchisement." *The Yale Law Journal* 121, no. 1 (Oct. 2011): 194–236.

Nelson, Anne M. "Constitutional Law—Fourteenth Amendment—Equal Protection—Voting Rights of Ex-Felons." *Duquesne Law Review* 13, no. 1 (1974): 130+.

Powell, Lewis F., Jr. "10-1973: Richardson v. Ramirez." *Washington and Lee University School of Law*. Scholarly Commons: Supreme Court Case Files, 1974.

The Reconstruction Amendments." *The Yale Law Journal*, 121 (2012): 1584–1670.

Re, Richard M., and Christopher M. Re. "Voting and Vice: Criminal Disenfranchisement and "Richardson v. Ramirez, 418 U.S. 24 (1974)." *Justia: U.S. Supreme Court*, supreme.justia.com/cases/federal/us/418/24.

■ Buckley v. Valeo

Date: January 30, 1976
Author: U.S. Supreme Court
Genre: court opinion

Summary Overview

At issue in the Buckley v. Valeo *Supreme Court case was the authority of the government to regulate campaign finance in order to control the undue influence of money (corruption) in the outcome of elections. The Federal Election Campaign Act (FECA) of 1971 and the 1971 Revenue Act had made sweeping changes to existing campaign finance regulations, limiting some types of campaign spending and requiring full campaign finance reporting from candidates. The FECA also set up the framework for political action committees (PACs) that could accept corporate and union funds and use them for issue advocacy in political campaigns. The FECA was amended in 1974, establishing limits on campaign contributions and setting up the Federal Election Commission (FEC) to oversee compliance with the law. The FECA was challenged in court by James L. Buckley, a Republican senator from New York, and others, who filed a lawsuit against the secretary of the senate, Francis R. Valeo, an FEC member. This challenge was heard by the Supreme Court, which issued a ruling on January 30, 1976, striking down some portions of the law (such as limits on spending by political campaigns) and upholding others (such as limits on the size of individual contributions to campaigns).*

Defining Moment

The solicitation of donations to fund campaigns has been regulated in the United States since 1867, when a prohibition on soliciting money from workers in naval yards was added to an appropriations bill. Still, there were no regulations on how civil service positions were filled, and most government workers were expected to make contributions to secure or continue their posts. Sixteen years later, in the wake of the 1881 assassination of President James A. Garfield by a disgruntled man in search of a political appointment, the Pendleton Civil Service Reform Act was passed. This act made it illegal for officials to solicit money from civil service workers, and it also became illegal to award civil service positions in exchange for any sort of payment.

With fundraising curtailed by the Pendleton Civil Service Reform Act, candidates turned increasingly to corporations and businessmen with deep pockets and obvious pro-business agendas. These interactions, however, had the appearance of corruption, and in 1907, the Tillman Act was passed, outlawing

Senator James L. Buckley, c. 1970s. Buckley was the lead petitioner in Buckley v. Valeo (1976), which "shaped modern campaign-finance law." Photo via Wikimedia Commons. [Public domain.]

corporate contributions in federal elections. This legislation was largely ignored, however, as contributions did not have to be disclosed, and there was no effective oversight of campaign finance. In 1910 and 1911, the Federal Corrupt Practices Act required financial disclosures from congressional candidates; however, this act also proved difficult to enforce, as no penalties were in place for failing to submit the required reports, and loopholes for contributions made it fairly simple to avoid the regulations. In 1943, the Smith-Connally Act prohibited unions from using dues to raise funds for federal candidates and saw the first political action committee (PAC) set up by the Congress of Industrial Organizations (CIO) to circumnavigate the restriction. Four years later, the Taft-Hartley Act strengthened that restriction, making it illegal for corporations and unions to spend money of any kind, not just dues, on federal elections. PACs were still able to flourish, however, as they were technically separate from the union or corporation and could raise money from a variety of smaller contributors.

In 1971, the FECA and the Revenue Act of the same year made significant changes to previous campaign finance regulations, restricting some types of spending contributions and mandating full reporting from candidates. The FECA set limits for PACs that could accept corporate and union monies and use them for issue advocacy in political campaigns and set aside federal money to be used to publically fund presidential campaigns. After these new regulations proved difficult to enforce during the 1972 presidential election, the Federal Election Commission (FEC) was established in 1974 to ensure that campaign finance laws were followed, and significant amendments were made to the FECA. Buckley, a Republican senator from New York, and others subsequently challenged the constitutionality of the FECA and its 1974 alterations.

Document Information

This ruling was decided by the Burger Court (1969–86) per curiam, meaning that the opinion was shared by the eight presiding judges (Associate Justice John Paul Stevens did not take part). The justices who decided this case were Chief Justice Warren E. Burger and Associate Justices William J. Brennan Jr., Potter Stewart, Byron White, Thurgood Marshall, Harry Blackmun, Lewis F. Powell Jr., and William Rehnquist. The court heard oral arguments on November 10, 1975, and released their opinion on January 30, 1976.

Historical Document

Buckley v. Valeo

424 U.S. 1 (1976)

U.S. Supreme Court

Decided: January 30, 1976

PER CURIAM.

These appeals present constitutional challenges to the key provisions of the Federal Election Campaign Act of 1971 (Act), and related provisions of the Internal Revenue Code of 1954, all as amended in 1974.

The Court of Appeals, in sustaining the legislation in large part against various constitutional challenges, viewed it as "by far the most comprehensive reform legislation [ever] passed by Congress concerning the election of the President, Vice-President, and members of Congress." The statutes at issue summarized in broad terms, contain the following provisions: (a) individual political contributions are limited to $1,000 to any single candidate per election, with an overall annual limitation of $25,000 by any contributor; independent expenditures by individuals and groups "relative to a clearly identified candidate" are limited to $1,000 a year; campaign spending by candidates for various federal offices and spending for national conventions by political parties are subject to prescribed limits; (b) contributions and expenditures above certain threshold levels must be reported and publicly disclosed; (c) a system for public funding of Presidential campaign activities is established by Subtitle H of the Internal Revenue Code; and (d) a Federal Election Commission is established to administer and enforce the legislation.

This suit was originally filed by appellants in the United States District Court for the District of Columbia. Plaintiffs included a candidate for the Presidency of the United States, a United States Senator who is a candidate for re-election, a potential contributor, the Committee for a Constitutional Presidency—McCarthy '76, the Conservative Party of the State of New York, the Mississippi Republican Party, the Libertarian Party, the New York Civil Liberties Union, Inc., the American Conservative Union, the Conservative Victory Fund, and Human Events, Inc. The defendants included the Secretary of the United States Senate and the Clerk of the United States House of Representatives, both in their official capacities and as ex officio members of the Federal Election Commission. The Commission itself was named as a defendant.

Also named were the Attorney General of the United States and the Comptroller General of the United States. . . .

In this Court, appellants argue that the Court of Appeals failed to give this legislation the critical scrutiny demanded under accepted First Amendment and equal protection principles. In appellants' view, limiting the use of money for political purposes constitutes a restriction on communication violative of the First Amendment, since virtually all meaningful political communications in the modern setting involve the expenditure of money. Further, they argue that the reporting and disclosure provisions of the Act unconstitutionally impinge on their right to freedom of association. . . .

I. CONTRIBUTION AND EXPENDITURE LIMITATIONS

The intricate statutory scheme adopted by Congress to regulate federal election campaigns includes restrictions on political contributions and expenditures that apply broadly to all phases of and all participants in the election process. The major contribution and expenditure limitations in the Act prohibit individuals from contributing more than $25,000 in a single year or more than $1,000 to any single candidate for an election campaign and from spending more than $1,000 a year "relative to a clearly identified candidate." Other provisions restrict a candidate's use of personal and family resources in his campaign and limit the overall amount that can be spent by a candidate in campaigning for federal office.

The constitutional power of Congress to regulate federal elections is well established and is not questioned by any of the parties in this case. Thus, the critical constitutional questions presented here go not to the basic power of Congress to legislate in this area, but to whether the specific legislation that Congress has enacted interferes with First Amendment freedoms or invidiously discriminates against nonincumbent candidates and minor parties in contravention of the Fifth Amendment.

A. General Principles

The Act's contribution and expenditure limitations operate in an area of the most fundamental First Amendment activities. Discussion of public issues and debate on the qualifications of candidates are integral to the operation of the system of government established by our Constitution. The First Amendment affords the broadest protection to such political expression in order "to assure [the] unfettered interchange of ideas for the bringing about of political and social changes desired by the people." Although First Amendment protections are not confined to "the exposition of ideas," "there is practically universal agreement that a major purpose of that Amendment was to protect the free discussion of governmental affairs, . . . of course includ[ing] discussions of candidates . . . ." This no more than reflects our "profound national commitment to the principle that debate on public issues should be uninhibited, robust, and wide-open." In a republic where the people are sovereign, the ability of the citizenry to make informed choices among candidates for office is essential, for the identities of those who are elected will inevitably shape the course that we follow as a nation.

The First Amendment protects political association as well as political expression. The constitutional right of association explicated in NAACP v. Alabama (1958), stemmed from the Court's recognition that "[e]ffective advocacy of both public and private points of view, particularly controversial ones, is undeniably enhanced by group association." Subsequent decisions have made clear that the First and Fourteenth Amendments guarantee "'freedom to associate with others for the common advancement of political beliefs and ideas,'" a freedom that encompasses "'[t]he right to associate with the political party of one's choice.'"

It is with these principles in mind that we consider the primary contentions of the parties with respect to the Act's limitations upon the giving and spending of money in political campaigns. Those conflicting contentions could not more sharply define the basic issues before us. Appellees contend that what the Act regulates is conduct, and that its effect on speech and association is incidental at most. Appellants respond that contributions and expenditures are at the very core of political speech, and that the Act's limitations thus constitute restraints on First Amendment liberty that are both gross and direct.

In upholding the constitutional validity of the Act's contribution and expenditure provisions on the ground that those provisions should be viewed as regulating conduct, not speech, the Court of Appeals relied upon United States v. O'Brien (1968). The O'Brien case involved a defendant's claim that the First Amendment prohibited his prosecution for burning his draft card because his act was "symbolic speech" engaged in as a "demonstration against the war and against the draft." On the assumption that "the alleged communicative element in O'Brien's conduct [was] sufficient to bring into play the First Amendment," the Court sustained the conviction because it found "a sufficiently important governmental interest in regulating the non-speech element" that was "unrelated to the suppression of free expression" and that had an "incidental restriction on alleged First Amendment freedoms . . . no greater than [was] essential to the furtherance of that interest."

We cannot share the view that the present Act's contribution and expenditure limitations are comparable to the restrictions on conduct upheld in O'Brien. The expenditure of money simply cannot be equated with such conduct as destruction of a draft card. Some forms of communication made possible by the giving and spending of money involve speech alone, some involve conduct primarily, and some involve a combination of the two. Yet this Court has never suggested that the dependence of a communication on the expenditure of money operates itself to introduce a non speech element or to reduce the exacting scrutiny required by the First Amendment.

Even if the categorization of the expenditure of money as conduct were accepted, the limitations challenged here would not meet the O'Brien test because the governmental interests advanced in support of the Act involve "suppressing communication." The interests served by the Act include restricting the voices of people and interest groups who have money to spend and reducing the overall scope of federal election campaigns. Although the Act does not focus on the ideas expressed by persons or groups subject to its regulations, it is aimed in part at equalizing the relative ability of all voters to affect electoral outcomes by placing a ceiling on expenditures for political expression by citizens and groups. Unlike O'Brien, where the Selective Service System's administrative interest in the preservation of draft cards was wholly unrelated to their use as a means of communication, it is beyond dispute that the interest in regulating the alleged "conduct" of giving or spending money "arises in some measure because the communication allegedly integral to the conduct is itself thought to be harmful."

Nor can the Act's contribution and expenditure limitations be sustained, as some of the parties suggest, by reference to the constitutional principles reflected in such decisions as Cox v. Louisiana (1966)...Those cases stand for the proposition that the government may adopt reasonable time, place, and manner regulations, which do not discriminate among speakers or ideas, in order to further an important governmental interest unrelated to the restriction of communication. The critical difference between this case and those time, place, and manner cases is that the present Act's contribution and expenditure limitations impose direct quantity restrictions on political communication and association by persons, groups, candidates, and political parties in addition to any reasonable time, place, and manner regulations otherwise imposed.

A restriction on the amount of money a person or group can spend on political communication during a campaign necessarily reduces the quantity of expression by restricting the number of issues discussed, the depth of their exploration, and the size of the audience reached. This is because virtually every means of communicating ideas in today's mass society requires the expenditure of money. The distribution of the humblest handbill or leaflet entails printing, paper, and circulation costs. Speeches and rallies generally necessitate hiring a hall and publicizing the event. The electorate's increasing dependence on television, radio, and other mass media for news and information has made these expensive modes of communication indispensable instruments of effective political speech.

The expenditure limitations contained in the Act represent substantial rather than merely theoretical restraints on the quantity and diversity of political speech. The $1,000 ceiling on spending "relative to a clearly identified candidate," would appear to exclude all citizens and groups except candidates, political parties, and the institutional press from any significant use of the most effective modes of communication. Although the Act's limitations on expenditures by campaign organizations and political parties provide substantially greater room for discussion and debate, they would have required restrictions in the scope of a number of past congressional and Presidential campaigns and would operate to constrain campaigning by candidates who raise sums in excess of the spending ceiling.

By contrast with a limitation upon expenditures for political expression, a limitation upon the amount that any one person or group may contribute to a candidate or political committee entails only a marginal restriction upon the contributor's ability to engage in free communication. A contribution serves as a general expression of support for the candidate and his views, but does not communicate the underlying basis for the support. The quantity of communication by the contributor does not increase perceptibly with the size of his contribution, since the expression rests solely on the undifferentiated, symbolic act of contributing. At most, the size of the contribution provides a very rough index of the intensity of the contributor's support for the candidate. A limitation on the amount of money a person may give to a candidate or campaign organization thus involves little direct restraint on his political communication, for it permits the symbolic expression of support evidenced by a contribution but does not in any way infringe the contributor's freedom to discuss candidates and issues. While contributions may result in political expression if spent by a candidate or an association to present views to the voters, the transformation of contributions into political debate involves speech by someone other than the contributor.

Given the important role of contributions in financing political campaigns, contribution restrictions could have a severe impact on political dialogue if the limitations prevented candidates and political committees from amassing the resources necessary for effective advocacy. There is no indication, however, that the contribution limitations imposed by the Act would have any dramatic adverse effect on the funding of campaigns and political associations. The overall effect of the Act's contribution ceilings is merely to require candidates and political committees to raise funds from a greater number of persons and to compel people who would otherwise contribute amounts greater than the statutory limits to expend such funds on direct political expression, rather than to reduce the total amount of money potentially available to promote political expression.

The Act's contribution and expenditure limitations also impinge on protected associational freedoms. Making a contribution, like joining a political party, serves to affiliate a person with a candidate. In addition, it enables like-minded persons to pool their resources in furtherance of common political goals. The Act's contribution ceilings thus limit one important means of associating with a candidate or committee, but leave the contributor free to become a member of any political association and to assist personally in the association's efforts on behalf of candidates. And the Act's contribution limitations permit associations and candidates to aggregate large sums of money to promote effective advocacy. By contrast, the Act's $1,000 limitation on independent expenditures "relative to a clearly identified candidate" precludes most associations from effectively amplifying the voice of their adherents, the original basis for the recognition of First Amendment protection of the freedom of association.

In sum, although the Act's contribution and expenditure limitations both implicate fundamental First Amendment interests, its expenditure ceilings impose significantly more severe restrictions on protected freedoms of political expression and association than do its limitations on financial contributions.

B. Contribution Limitations

1. The $1,000 Limitation on Contributions by Individuals and Groups to Candidates and Authorized Campaign Committees

Section 608 (b) provides, with certain limited exceptions, that "no person shall make contributions to any candidate with respect to any election for Federal office which, in the aggregate, exceed $1,000." The statute defines "person" broadly to include "an individual, partnership, committee, association, corporation or any other organization or group of persons." 591 (g). The limitation reaches a gift, subscription, loan, advance, deposit of anything of value, or promise to give a contribution, made for the purpose of influencing a primary election, a Presidential preference primary, or a general election for any federal office. 591 (e) (1), (2). The $1,000 ceiling applies regardless of whether the contribution is given to the candidate, to a committee authorized in writing by the candidate to accept contributions on his behalf, or indirectly via earmarked gifts passed through an intermediary to the candidate. 608 (b) (4), (6). The restriction applies to aggregate amounts contributed to the candidate for each election—with primaries, runoff elections, and general elections counted separately, and all Presidential primaries held in any calendar year treated together as a single election campaign. 608 (b) (5).

Appellants contend that the $1,000 contribution ceiling unjustifiably burdens First Amendment freedoms, employs overbroad dollar limits, and discriminates against candidates opposing incumbent officeholders and against minor-party candidates in violation of the Fifth Amendment. We address each of these claims of invalidity in turn.

(a) As the general discussion in Part I-A, supra, indicated, the primary First Amendment problem raised by the Act's contribution limitations is their restriction of one aspect of the contributor's freedom of political association. The Court's decisions involving associational freedoms establish that the right of association is a "basic constitutional freedom," Kusper v. Pontikes, 414 U.S., at 57, that is "closely allied to freedom of speech and a right which, like free speech, lies at the foundation of a free society." Shelton v. Tucker, 364 U.S. 479, 486 (1960). See, e. g., Bates v. Little Rock, 361 U.S. 516, 522-523 (1960); NAACP v. Alabama, supra, at 460-461; NAACP v. Button, supra, at 452 (Harlan, J., dissenting). In view of the fundamental nature of the right to associate, governmental "action which may have the effect of curtailing the freedom to associate is subject to the closest scrutiny." NAACP v. Alabama, supra, at 460-461. Yet, it is clear that "[n]either the right to associate nor the right to participate in political activities is absolute." CSC v. Letter Carriers, 413 U.S. 548, 567 (1973). Even a "'significant interference' with protected rights of political association" may be sustained if the State demonstrates a sufficiently important interest and employs means closely drawn to avoid unnecessary abridgment of associational freedoms. Cousins v. Wigoda, supra, at 488; NAACP v. Button, supra, at 438; Shelton v. Tucker, supra, at 488.

Appellees argue that the Act's restrictions on large campaign contributions are justified by three governmental interests. According to the parties and amici, the primary interest served by the limitations and, indeed, by the Act as a whole, is the prevention of corruption and the appearance of corruption spawned by the real or imagined coercive influence of large financial contributions on candidates' positions and on their actions if elected to office. Two "ancillary" interests underlying the Act are also allegedly furthered by the $1,000 limits on contributions. First, the limits serve to mute the voices of affluent persons and groups in the election process and thereby to equalize the relative ability of all citizens to affect the outcome of elections. Second, it is argued, the ceilings may to some extent act as a brake on the skyrocketing cost of political campaigns and thereby serve to open the political system more widely to candidates without access to sources of large amounts of money.

Of almost equal concern as the danger of actual quid pro quo arrangements is the impact of the appearance of corruption stemming from public awareness of the opportunities for abuse inherent in a regime of large individual financial contributions. In CSC v. Letter Carriers, supra, the Court found that the danger to "fair and effective government" posed by partisan political conduct on the part of federal employees charged with administering the law was a sufficiently important concern to justify broad restrictions on the employees' right of partisan political association. Here, as there, Congress could legitimately conclude that the avoidance of the appearance of improper influence "is also critical . . . if confidence in the system of representative Government is not to be eroded to a disastrous extent."

Appellants contend that the contribution limitations must be invalidated because bribery laws and narrowly drawn disclosure requirements constitute a less restrictive means of dealing with "proven and suspected quid pro quo arrangements." But laws making criminal the giving and taking of bribes deal with only the most blatant and specific attempts of those with money to influence governmental action. And while disclosure requirements serve the many salutary purposes discussed elsewhere in this opinion, Congress was surely entitled to conclude that disclosure was only a partial measure, and that contribution ceilings were a necessary legislative concomitant to deal with the reality or appearance of corruption inherent in a system permitting unlimited financial contributions, even when the identities of the contributors and the amounts of their contributions are fully disclosed.

The Act's $1,000 contribution limitation focuses precisely on the problem of large campaign contributions —the narrow aspect of political association where the actuality and potential for corruption have been identified—while leaving persons free to engage in independent political expression, to associate actively through volunteering their services, and to assist to a limited but nonetheless substantial extent in supporting candidates and committees with financial resources. Significantly, the Act's contribution limitations in themselves do not undermine to any material degree the potential for robust and effective discussion of candidates and campaign issues by individual citizens, associations, the institutional press, candidates, and political parties.

We find that, under the rigorous standard of review established by our prior decisions, the weighty interests served by restricting the size of financial contributions to political candidates are sufficient to justify the limited effect upon First Amendment freedoms caused by the $1,000 contribution ceiling.

(b) Appellants' first overbreadth challenge to the contribution ceilings rests on the proposition that most large contributors do not seek improper influence over a candidate's position or an officeholder's action. Although the truth of that proposition may be assumed, it does not undercut the validity of the $1,000 contribution limitation. Not only is it difficult to isolate suspect contributions but, more importantly, Congress was justified in concluding that the interest in safeguarding against the appearance of impropriety requires that the opportunity for abuse inherent in the process of raising large monetary contributions be eliminated.

A second, related overbreadth claim is that the $1,000 restriction is unrealistically low because much more than that amount would still not be enough to enable an unscrupulous contributor to exercise improper influence over a candidate or officeholder, especially in campaigns for statewide or national office. While the contribution limitation provisions might well have been structured to take account of the graduated expenditure limitations for congressional and Presidential campaigns, Congress' failure to engage in such fine tuning does not invalidate the legislation. As the Court of Appeals observed, "[i]f it is satisfied that some limit on contributions is necessary, a court has no scalpel to probe, whether, say, a $2,000 ceiling might not serve as well as $1,000." 171 U.S. App. D.C., at 193, 519 F.2d, at 842. Such distinctions in degree become significant only when they can be said to amount to differences in kind. Compare Kusper v. Pontikes, 414 U.S. 51 (1973), with Rosario v. Rockefeller, 410 U.S. 752 (1973).

(c) Apart from these First Amendment concerns, appellants argue that the contribution limitations work such an invidious discrimination between incumbents and challengers that the statutory provisions must be declared unconstitutional on their face. In considering this contention, it is important at the outset to note that the Act applies the same limitations on contributions to all candidates regardless of their present occupations, ideological views, or party affiliations. Absent record evidence of invidious discrimination against challengers as a class, a court should generally be hesitant to invalidate legislation which on its face imposes evenhanded restrictions. Cf. James v. Valtierra, 402 U.S. 137 (1971).

There is no such evidence to support the claim that the contribution limitations in themselves discriminate against major-party challengers to incumbents. Challengers can and often do defeat incumbents in federal elections. Major-party challengers in federal elections are usually men and women who are well known and influential in their community or State. Often such challengers are themselves incumbents in important local, state, or federal offices. Statistics in the record indicate that major-party challengers as well as incumbents are capable of raising large sums for campaigning. Indeed, a small but nonetheless significant number of challengers have in recent elections outspent their incumbent rivals. And, to the extent that incumbents generally are more likely than challengers to attract very large contributions, the Act's $1,000 ceiling has the practical effect of benefiting challengers as a class. Contrary to the broad generalization drawn by the appellants, the practical impact of the contribution ceilings in any given election will clearly depend upon the amounts in excess of the ceilings that, for various reasons, the candidates in that election would otherwise have received and the utility of these additional amounts to the candidates. To be sure, the limitations may have a significant effect on particular challengers or incumbents, but the record provides no basis for predicting that such adventitious factors will invariably and invidiously benefit incumbents as a class. Since the danger of corruption and the appearance of corruption apply with equal force to challengers and to incumbents, Congress had ample justification for imposing the same fundraising constraints upon both.

The charge of discrimination against minor-party and independent candidates is more troubling, but the record provides no basis for concluding that the Act invidiously disadvantages such candidates. As noted above, the Act on its face treats all candidates equally with regard to contribution limitations. And the restriction would appear to benefit minor-party and independent candidates relative to their major-party opponents because major-party candidates receive far more money in large contributions. Although there is some force to appellants' response that minor-party candidates are primarily concerned with their ability to amass the resources necessary to reach the electorate rather than with their funding position relative to their major-party opponents, the record is virtually devoid of support for the claim that the $1,000 contribution limitation will have a serious effect on the initiation and scope of minor-party and independent candidacies. Moreover, any attempt to exclude minor parties and independents en masse from the Act's contribution limitations overlooks the fact that minor-party candidates may win elective office or have a substantial impact on the outcome of an election.

In view of these considerations, we conclude that the impact of the Act's $1,000 contribution limitation on major-party challengers and on minor-party candidates does not render the provision unconstitutional on its face.

2. The $5,000 Limitation on Contributions by Political Committees

Section 608 (b) (2) permits certain committees, designated as "political committees," to contribute up to $5,000 to any candidate with respect to any election for federal office. In order to qualify for the higher contribution ceiling, a group must have been registered with the Commission as a political committee under 2 U.S.C. 433 (1970 ed., Supp. IV) for not less than six months, have received contributions from more than 50 persons, and, except for state political party organizations, have contributed to five or more candidates for federal office. Appellants argue that these qualifications unconstitutionally discriminate against ad hoc organizations in favor of established interest groups and impermissibly burden free association. The argument is without merit. Rather than undermining freedom of association, the basic provision enhances the opportunity of bona fide groups to participate in the election process, and the registration, contribution, and candidate conditions serve the permissible purpose of preventing individuals from evading the applicable contribution limitations by labeling themselves committees.

3. Limitations on Volunteers' Incidental Expenses

The Act excludes from the definition of contribution "the value of services provided without compensation by individuals who volunteer a portion or all of their time on behalf of a candidate or political committee." 591 (e) (5) (A). Certain expenses incurred by persons in providing volunteer services to a candidate are exempt from the $1,000 ceiling only to the extent that they do not exceed $500. These expenses are expressly limited to (1) "the use of real or personal property and the cost of invitations, food, and beverages, voluntarily provided by an individual to a candidate in rendering voluntary personal services on the individual's residential premises for candidate-related activities." 591 (e) (5) (B); (2) "the sale of any food or beverage by a vendor for use in a candidate's campaign at a charge [at least equal to cost but] less than the normal comparable charge," 591 (e) (5) (C); and (3) "any unreimbursed payment for travel expenses made by an individual who on his own behalf volunteers his personal services to a candidate," 591 (e) (5) (D).

If, as we have held, the basic contribution limitations are constitutionally valid, then surely these provisions are a constitutionally acceptable accommodation of Congress' valid interest in encouraging citizen participation in political campaigns while continuing to guard against the corrupting potential of large financial contributions to candidates. The expenditure of resources at the candidate's direction for a fundraising event at a volunteer's residence or the provision of in-kind assistance in the form of food or beverages to be resold to raise funds or consumed by the participants in such an event provides material financial assistance to a candidate. The ultimate effect is the same as if the person had contributed the dollar amount to the candidate and the candidate had then used the contribution to pay for the fundraising event or the food. Similarly, travel undertaken as a volunteer at the direction of the candidate or his staff is an expense of the campaign and may properly be viewed as a contribution if the volunteer absorbs the fare. Treating these expenses as contributions when made to the candidate's campaign or at the direction of the candidate or his staff forecloses an avenue of abuse without limiting actions voluntarily undertaken by citizens independently of a candidate's campaign.

4. The $25,000 Limitation on Total Contributions During any Calendar Year

In addition to the $1,000 limitation on the nonexempt contributions that an individual may make to a particular candidate for any single election, the Act contains an overall $25,000 limitation on total contributions by an individual during any calendar year. 608 (b) (3). A contribution made in connection with an election is considered, for purposes of this subsection, to be made in the year the election is held. Although the constitutionality of this provision was drawn into question by appellants, it has not been separately addressed at length by the parties. The overall $25,000 ceiling does impose an ultimate restriction upon the number of candidates and committees with which an individual may associate himself by means of financial support. But this quite modest restraint upon protected political activity serves to prevent evasion of the $1,000 contribution limitation by a person who might otherwise contribute massive amounts of money to a particular candidate through the use of unearmarked contributions to political committees likely to contribute to that candidate, or huge contributions to the candidate's political party. The limited, additional restriction on associational freedom imposed by the overall ceiling is thus no more than a corollary of the basic individual contribution limitation that we have found to be constitutionally valid.

C. Expenditure Limitations

The Act's expenditure ceilings impose direct and substantial restraints on the quantity of political speech. The most drastic of the limitations restricts individuals and groups, including political parties that fail to place a candidate on the ballot, to an expenditure of $1,000 "relative to a clearly identified candidate during a calendar year." 608 (e) (1). Other expenditure ceilings limit spending by candidates, 608 (a), their campaigns, 608 (c), and political parties in connection with election campaigns, 608 (f). It is clear that a primary effect of these expenditure limitations is to restrict the quantity of campaign speech by individuals, groups, and candidates. The restrictions, while neutral as to the ideas expressed, limit political expression "at the core of our electoral process and of the First Amendment freedoms." Williams v. Rhodes, 393 U.S. 23, 32 (1968).

1. The $1,000 Limitation on Expenditures "Relative to a Clearly Identified Candidate"

Section 608 (e) (1) provides that "[n]o person may make any expenditure . . . relative to a clearly identified candidate during a calendar year which, when added to all other expenditures made by such person during the year advocating the election or defeat of such candidate, exceeds $1,000." The plain effect of 608 (e) (1) is to prohibit all individuals, who are neither candidates nor owners of institutional press facilities, and all groups, except political parties and campaign organizations, from voicing their views "relative to a clearly identified candidate" through means that entail aggregate expenditures of more than $1,000 during a calendar year. The provision, for example, would make it a federal criminal offense for a person or association to place a single one-quarter page advertisement "relative to a clearly identified candidate" in a major metropolitan newspaper.

Before examining the interests advanced in support of 608 (e) (1)'s expenditure ceiling, consideration must be given to appellants' contention that the provision is unconstitutionally vague. Close examination of the specificity of the statutory limitation is required where, as here, the legislation imposes criminal penalties in an area permeated by First Amendment interests. The test is whether the language of 608 (e) (1) affords the "[p]recision of regulation [that] must be the touchstone in an area so closely touching our most precious freedoms."

The key operative language of the provision limits "any expenditure . . . relative to a clearly identified candidate." Although "expenditure," "clearly identified," and "candidate" are defined in the Act, there is no definition clarifying what expenditures are "relative to" a candidate. The use of so indefinite a phrase as "relative to" a candidate fails to clearly mark the boundary between permissible and impermissible speech, unless other portions of 608 (e) (1) make sufficiently explicit the range of expenditures covered by the limitation. The section prohibits "any expenditure . . . relative to a clearly identified candidate during a calendar year which, when added to all other expenditures . . . advocating the election or defeat of such candidate, exceeds $1,000." (Emphasis added.) This context clearly permits, if indeed it does not require, the phrase "relative to" a candidate to be read to mean "advocating the election or defeat of" a candidate.

But while such a construction of 608 (e) (1) refocuses the vagueness question, the Court of Appeals was mistaken in thinking that this construction eliminates the problem of unconstitutional vagueness altogether. For the distinction between discussion of issues and candidates and advocacy of election or defeat of candidates may often dissolve in practical application. Candidates, especially incumbents, are intimately tied to public issues involving legislative proposals and governmental actions. Not only do candidates campaign on the basis of their positions on various public issues, but campaigns themselves generate issues of public interest. In an analogous context, this Court in Thomas v. Collins, 323 U.S. 516 (1945), observed:

"[W]hether words intended and designed to fall short of invitation would miss that mark is a question both of intent and of effect. No speaker, in such circumstances, safely could assume that anything he might say upon the general subject would not be understood by some as an invitation. In short, the supposedly clear-cut distinction between discussion, laudation, general advocacy, and solicitation puts the speaker in these circumstances wholly at the mercy of the varied understanding of his hearers and consequently of whatever inference may be drawn as to his intent and meaning.

"Such a distinction offers no security for free discussion. In these conditions it blankets with uncertainty whatever may be said. It compels the speaker to hedge and trim."

The constitutional deficiencies described in Thomas v. Collins can be avoided only by reading 608 (e) (1) as limited to communications that include explicit words of advocacy of election or defeat of a candidate, much as the definition of "clearly identified" in 608 (e) (2) requires that an explicit and unambiguous reference to the candidate appear as part of the communication. This is the reading of the provision suggested by the non-governmental appellees in arguing that "[f]unds spent to propagate one's views on issues without expressly calling for a candidate's election or defeat are thus not covered." We agree that in order to preserve the provision against invalidation on vagueness grounds, 608 (e) (1) must be construed to apply only to expenditures for communications that in express terms advocate the election or defeat of a clearly identified candidate for federal office.

We turn then to the basic First Amendment question—whether 608 (e) (1), even as thus narrowly and explicitly construed, impermissibly burdens the constitutional right of free expression. The Court of Appeals summarily held the provision constitutionally valid on the ground that "section 608 (e) is a loophole-closing provision only" that is necessary to prevent circumvention of the contribution limitations. We cannot agree.

The discussion in Part I-A, supra, explains why the Act's expenditure limitations impose far greater restraints on the freedom of speech and association than do its contribution limitations. The markedly greater burden on basic freedoms caused by 608 (e) (1) thus cannot be sustained simply by invoking the interest in maximizing the effectiveness of the less intrusive contribution limitations. Rather, the constitutionality of 608 (e) (1) turns on whether the governmental interests advanced in its support satisfy the exacting scrutiny applicable to limitations on core First Amendment rights of political expression.

We find that the governmental interest in preventing corruption and the appearance of corruption is inadequate to justify 608 (e) (1)'s ceiling on independent expenditures. First, assuming, arguendo, that large independent expenditures pose the same dangers of actual or apparent quid pro quo arrangements as do large contributions, 608 (e) (1) does not provide an answer that sufficiently relates to the elimination of those dangers. Unlike the contribution limitations' total ban on the giving of large amounts of money to candidates, 608 (e) (1) prevents only some large expenditures. So long as persons and groups eschew expenditures that in express terms advocate the election or defeat of a clearly identified candidate, they are free to spend as much as they want to promote the candidate and his views. The exacting interpretation of the statutory language necessary to avoid unconstitutional vagueness thus undermines the limitation's effectiveness as a loophole-closing provision by facilitating circumvention by those seeking to exert improper influence upon a candidate or office-holder. It would naively underestimate the ingenuity and resourcefulness of persons and groups desiring to buy influence to believe that they would have much difficulty devising expenditures that skirted the restriction on express advocacy of election or defeat but nevertheless benefited the candidate's campaign. Yet no substantial societal interest would be served by a loophole-closing provision designed to check corruption that permitted unscrupulous persons and organizations to expend unlimited sums of money in order to obtain improper influence over candidates for elective office. Cf. Mills v. Alabama, 384 U.S., at 220.

Second, quite apart from the shortcomings of 608 (e) (1) in preventing any abuses generated by large independent expenditures, the independent advocacy restricted by the provision does not presently appear to pose dangers of real or apparent corruption comparable to those identified with large campaign contributions. The parties defending 608 (e) (1) contend that it is necessary to prevent would-be contributors from avoiding the contribution limitations by the simple expedient of paying directly for media advertisements or for other portions of the candidate's campaign activities. They argue that expenditures controlled by or coordinated with the candidate and his campaign might well have virtually the same value to the candidate as a contribution and would pose similar dangers of abuse. Yet such controlled or coordinated expenditures are treated as contributions rather than expenditures under the Act. Section 608 (b)'s contribution ceilings rather than 608 (e) (1)'s independent expenditure limitation prevent attempts to circumvent the Act through prearranged or coordinated expenditures amounting to disguised contributions. By contrast, 608 (e) (1) limits expenditures for express advocacy of candidates made totally independently of the candidate and his campaign. Unlike contributions, such independent expenditures may well provide little assistance to the candidate's campaign and indeed may prove counterproductive. The absence of prearrangement and coordination of an expenditure with the candidate or his agent not only undermines the value of the expenditure to the candidate, but also alleviates the danger that expenditures will be given as a quid pro quo for improper commitments from the candidate. Rather than preventing circumvention of the contribution limitations, 608 (e) (1) severely restricts all independent advocacy despite its substantially diminished potential for abuse.

While the independent expenditure ceiling thus fails to serve any substantial governmental interest in stemming the reality or appearance of corruption in the electoral process, it heavily burdens core First Amendment expression. For the First Amendment right to "'speak one's mind . . . on all public institutions'" includes the right to engage in "'vigorous advocacy' no less than 'abstract discussion.'" Advocacy of the election or defeat of candidates for federal office is no less entitled to protection under the First Amendment than the discussion of political policy generally or advocacy of the passage or defeat of legislation.

It is argued, however, that the ancillary governmental interest in equalizing the relative ability of individuals and groups to influence the outcome of elections serves to justify the limitation on express advocacy of the election or defeat of candidates imposed by 608 (e) (1)'s expenditure ceiling. But the concept that government may restrict the speech of some elements of our society in order to enhance the relative voice of others is wholly foreign to the First Amendment, which was designed "to secure 'the widest possible dissemination of information from diverse and antagonistic sources,'" and "'to assure unfettered interchange of ideas for the bringing about of political and social changes desired by the people.'" The First Amendment's protection against governmental abridgment of free expression cannot properly be made to depend on a person's financial ability to engage in public discussion.

The Court's decisions in Mills v. Alabama, 384 U.S. 214 (1966), and Miami Herald Publishing Co. v. Tornillo, 418 U.S. 241 (1974), held that legislative restrictions on advocacy of the election or defeat of political candidates are wholly at odds with the guarantees of the First Amendment. In Mills, the Court addressed the question whether "a State, consistently with the United States Constitution, can make it a crime for the editor of a daily newspaper to write and publish an editorial on election day urging people to vote a certain way on issues submitted to them." 384 U.S., at 215 (emphasis in original). We held that "no test of reasonableness can save [such] a state law from invalidation as a violation of the First Amendment." Id., at 220. Yet the prohibition of election-day editorials invalidated in Mills is clearly a lesser intrusion on constitutional freedom than a $1,000 limitation on the amount of money any person or association can spend during an entire election year in advocating the election or defeat of a candidate for public office. More recently in Tornillo, the Court held that Florida could not constitutionally require a newspaper to make space available for a political candidate to reply to its criticism. Yet under the Florida statute, every newspaper was free to criticize any candidate as much as it pleased so long as it undertook the modest burden of printing his reply. See 418 U.S., at 256-257. The legislative restraint involved in Tornillo thus also pales in comparison to the limitations imposed by 608 (e) (1).

For the reasons stated, we conclude that 608 (e) (1)'s independent expenditure limitation is unconstitutional under the First Amendment.

2. Limitation on Expenditures by Candidates from Personal or Family Resources

The Act also sets limits on expenditures by a candidate "from his personal funds, or the personal funds of his immediate family, in connection with his campaigns during any calendar year." 608 (a) (1). These ceilings vary from $50,000 for Presidential or Vice Presidential candidates to $35,000 for senatorial candidates, and $25,000 for most candidates for the House of Representatives.

The ceiling on personal expenditures by candidates on their own behalf, like the limitations on independent expenditures contained in 608 (e) (1), imposes a substantial restraint on the ability of persons to engage in protected First Amendment expression. The candidate, no less than any other person, has a First Amendment right to engage in the discussion of public issues and vigorously and tirelessly to advocate his own election and the election of other candidates. Indeed, it is of particular importance that candidates have the unfettered opportunity to make their views known so that the electorate may intelligently evaluate the candidates' personal qualities and their positions on vital public issues before choosing among them on election day. Mr. Justice Brandeis' observation that in our country "public discussion is a political duty," Whitney v. California, 274 U.S. 357, 375 (1927) (concurring opinion), applies with special force to candidates for public office. Section 608 (a)'s ceiling on personal expenditures by a candidate in furtherance of his own candidacy thus clearly and directly interferes with constitutionally protected freedoms.

The primary governmental interest served by the Act—the prevention of actual and apparent corruption of the political process—does not support the limitation on the candidate's expenditure of his own personal funds. As the Court of Appeals concluded: "Manifestly, the core problem of avoiding undisclosed and undue influence on candidates from outside interests has lesser application when the monies involved come from the candidate himself or from his immediate family." 171 U.S. App. D.C., at 206, 519 F.2d, at 855. Indeed, the use of personal funds reduces the candidate's dependence on outside contributions and thereby counteracts the coercive pressures and attendant risks of abuse to which the Act's contribution limitations are directed.

The ancillary interest in equalizing the relative financial resources of candidates competing for elective office, therefore, provides the sole relevant rationale for 608 (a)'s expenditure ceiling. That interest is clearly not sufficient to justify the provision's infringement of fundamental First Amendment rights. First, the limitation may fail to promote financial equality among candidates. A candidate who spends less of his personal resources on his campaign may nonetheless outspend his rival as a result of more successful fundraising efforts. Indeed, a candidate's personal wealth may impede his efforts to persuade others that he needs their financial contributions or volunteer efforts to conduct an effective campaign. Second, and more fundamentally, the First Amendment simply cannot tolerate 608 (a)'s restriction upon the freedom of a candidate to speak without legislative limit on behalf of his own candidacy. We therefore hold that 608 (a)'s restriction on a candidate's personal expenditures is unconstitutional.

3. Limitations on Campaign Expenditures

Section 608 (c) places limitations on overall campaign expenditures by candidates seeking nomination for election and election to federal office. Presidential candidates may spend $10,000,000 in seeking nomination for office and an additional $20,000,000 in the general election campaign. 608 (c) (1) (A), (B). The ceiling on senatorial campaigns is pegged to the size of the voting-age population of the State with minimum dollar amounts applicable to campaigns in States with small populations. In senatorial primary elections, the limit is the greater of eight cents multiplied by the voting-age population or $100,000, and in the general election the limit is increased to 12 cents multiplied by the voting-age population or $150,000. 608 (c) (1) (C), (D). The Act imposes blanket $70,000 limitations on both primary campaigns and general election campaigns for the House of Representatives with the exception that the senatorial ceiling applies to campaigns in States entitled to only one Representative. 608 (c) (1) (C)-(E). These ceilings are to be adjusted upwards at the beginning of each calendar year by the average percentage rise in the consumer price index for the 12 preceding months. 608 (d).

No governmental interest that has been suggested is sufficient to justify the restriction on the quantity of political expression imposed by 608 (c)'s campaign expenditure limitations. The major evil associated with rapidly increasing campaign expenditures is the danger of candidate dependence on large contributions. The interest in alleviating the corrupting influence of large contributions is served by the Act's contribution limitations and disclosure provisions rather than by 608 (c)'s campaign expenditure ceilings. The Court of Appeals' assertion that the expenditure restrictions are necessary to reduce the incentive to circumvent direct contribution limits is not persuasive. See 171 U.S. App. D.C., at 210, 519 F.2d, at 859. There is no indication that the substantial criminal penalties for violating the contribution ceilings combined with the political repercussion of such violations will be insufficient to police the contribution provisions. Extensive reporting, auditing, and disclosure requirements applicable to both contributions and expenditures by political campaigns are designed to facilitate the detection of illegal contributions. Moreover, as the Court of Appeals noted, the Act permits an officeholder or successful candidate to retain contributions in excess of the expenditure ceiling and to use these funds for "any other lawful purpose." 2 U.S.C. 439a (1970 ed., Supp. IV). This provision undercuts whatever marginal role the expenditure limitations might otherwise play in enforcing the contribution ceilings.

The interest in equalizing the financial resources of candidates competing for federal office is no more convincing a justification for restricting the scope of federal election campaigns. Given the limitation on the size of outside contributions, the financial resources available to a candidate's campaign, like the number of volunteers recruited, will normally vary with the size and intensity of the candidate's support. There is nothing invidious, improper, or unhealthy in permitting such funds to be spent to carry the candidate's message to the electorate. Moreover, the equalization of permissible campaign expenditures might serve not to equalize the opportunities of all candidates, but to handicap a candidate who lacked substantial name recognition or exposure of his views before the start of the campaign.

The campaign expenditure ceilings appear to be designed primarily to serve the governmental interests in reducing the allegedly skyrocketing costs of political campaigns. Appellees and the Court of Appeals stressed statistics indicating that spending for federal election campaigns increased almost 300% between 1952 and 1972 in comparison with a 57.6% rise in the consumer price index during the same period. Appellants respond that during these years the rise in campaign spending lagged behind the percentage increase in total expenditures for commercial advertising and the size of the gross national product. In any event, the mere growth in the cost of federal election campaigns in and of itself provides no basis for governmental restrictions on the quantity of campaign spending and the resulting limitation on the scope of federal campaigns. The First Amendment denies government the power to determine that spending to promote one's political views is wasteful, excessive, or unwise. In the free society ordained by our Constitution it is not the government, but the people—individually as citizens and candidates and collectively as associations and political committees—who must retain control over the quantity and range of debate on public issues in a political campaign.

For these reasons we hold that 608 (c) is constitutionally invalid.

In sum, the provisions of the Act that impose a $1,000 limitation on contributions to a single candidate, 608 (b) (1), a $5,000 limitation on contributions by a political committee to a single candidate, 608 (b) (2), and a $25,000 limitation on total contributions by an individual during any calendar year, 608 (b) (3), are constitutionally valid. These limitations, along with the disclosure provisions, constitute the Act's primary weapons against the reality or appearance of improper influence stemming from the dependence of candidates on large campaign contributions. The contribution ceilings thus serve the basic governmental interest in safeguarding the integrity of the electoral process without directly impinging upon the rights of individual citizens and candidates to engage in political debate and discussion. By contrast, the First Amendment requires the invalidation of the Act's independent expenditure ceiling, 608 (e) (1), its limitation on a candidate's expenditures from his own personal funds, 608 (a), and its ceilings on overall campaign expenditures, 608 (c). These provisions place substantial and direct restrictions on the ability of candidates, citizens, and associations to engage in protected political expression, restrictions that the First Amendment cannot tolerate.

II. REPORTING AND DISCLOSURE REQUIREMENTS

Unlike the limitations on contributions and expenditures imposed by 18 U.S.C. 608 (1970 ed., Supp. IV), the disclosure requirements of the Act, 2 U.S.C. 431 et seq. (1970 ed., Supp. IV), are not challenged by appellants as per se unconstitutional restrictions on the exercise of First Amendment freedoms of speech and association. Indeed, appellants argue that "narrowly drawn disclosure requirements are the proper solution to virtually all of the evils Congress sought to remedy." Brief for Appellants 171. The particular requirements embodied in the Act are attacked as overbroad—both in their application to minor-party and independent candidates and in their extension to contributions as small as $11 or $101. Appellants also challenge the provision for disclosure by those who make independent contributions and expenditures, 434 (e). The Court of Appeals found no constitutional infirmities in the provisions challenged here. We affirm the determination on overbreadth and hold that 434 (e), if narrowly construed, also is within constitutional bounds.

The first federal disclosure law was enacted in 1910. Act of June 25, 1910, c. 392, 36 Stat. 822. It required political committees, defined as national committees and national congressional campaign committees of parties, and organizations operating to influence congressional elections in two or more States, to disclose names of all contributors of $100 or more; identification of recipients of expenditures of $10 or more was also required. 1, 5-6, 36 Stat. 822 824. Annual expenditures of $50 or more "for the purpose of influencing or controlling, in two or more States, the result of" a congressional election had to be reported independently if they were not made through a political committee. 7, 36 Stat. 824. In 1911 the Act was revised to include prenomination transactions such as those involved in conventions and primary campaigns. Act of Aug. 19, 1911, 2, 37 Stat. 26. See United States v. Auto. Workers, 352 U.S., at 575-576.

Disclosure requirements were broadened in the Federal Corrupt Practices Act of 1925 (Title III of the Act of Feb. 28, 1925), 43 Stat. 1070. That Act required political committees, defined as organizations that accept contributions or make expenditures "for the purpose of influencing or attempting to influence" the Presidential or Vice Presidential elections (a) in two or more States or (b) as a subsidiary of a national committee, 302 (c), 43 Stat. 1070, to report total contributions and expenditures, including the names and addresses of contributors of $100 or more and recipients of $10 or more in a calendar year. 305 (a), 43 Stat. 1071. The Act was upheld against a challenge that it infringed upon the prerogatives of the States in Burroughs v. United States, 290 U.S. 534 (1934). The Court held that it was within the power of Congress "to pass appropriate legislation to safeguard [a Presidential] election from the improper use of money to influence the result." Id., at 545. Although the disclosure requirements were widely circumvented, no further attempts were made to tighten them until 1960, when the Senate passed a bill that would have closed some existing loopholes. S. 2436, 106 Cong. Rec. 1193. The attempt aborted because no similar effort was made in the House.

The Act presently under review replaced all prior disclosure laws. Its primary disclosure provisions impose reporting obligations on "political committees" and candidates. "Political committee" is defined in 431 (d) as a group of persons that receives "contributions" or makes "expenditures" of over $1,000 in a calendar year. "Contributions" and "expenditures" are defined in lengthy parallel provisions similar to those in Title 18, discussed above. Both definitions focus on the use of money or other objects of value "for the purpose of . . . influencing" the nomination or election of any person to federal office. 431 (e) (1), (f) (1).

Each political committee is required to register with the Commission, 433, and to keep detailed records of both contributions and expenditures, 432 (c), (d). These records must include the name and address of everyone making a contribution in excess of $10, along with the date and amount of the contribution. If a person's contributions aggregate more than $100, his occupation and principal place of business are also to be included. 432 (c) (2). These files are subject to periodic audits and field investigations by the Commission. 438 (a) (8).

Each committee and each candidate also is required to file quarterly reports. 434 (a). The reports are to contain detailed financial information, including the full name, mailing address, occupation, and principal place of business of each person who has contributed over $100 in a calendar year, as well as the amount and date of the contributions. 434 (b). They are to be made available by the Commission "for public inspection and copying." 438 (a) (4). Every candidate for federal office is required to designate a "principal campaign committee," which is to receive reports of contributions and expenditures made on the candidate's behalf from other political committees and to compile and file these reports, together with its own statements, with the Commission. 432 (f).

Every individual or group, other than a political committee or candidate, who makes "contributions" or "expenditures" of over $100 in a calendar year "other than by contribution to a political committee or candidate" is required to file a statement with the Commission. 434 (e). Any violation of these recordkeeping and reporting provisions is punishable by a fine of not more than $1,000 or a prison term of not more than a year, or both. 441 (a).

A. General Principles

Unlike the overall limitations on contributions and expenditures, the disclosure requirements impose no ceiling on campaign-related activities. But we have repeatedly found that compelled disclosure, in itself, can seriously infringe on privacy of association and belief guaranteed by the First Amendment. E. g., Gibson v. Florida Legislative Comm., 372 U.S. 539 (1963); NAACP v. Button, 371 U.S. 415 (1963); Shelton v. Tucker, 364 U.S. 479 (1960); Bates v. Little Rock, 361 U.S. 516 (1960); NAACP v. Alabama, 357 U.S. 449 (1958).

We long have recognized that significant encroachments on First Amendment rights of the sort that compelled disclosure imposes cannot be justified by a mere showing of some legitimate governmental interest. Since NAACP v. Alabama we have required that the subordinating interests of the State must survive exacting scrutiny. We also have insisted that there be a "relevant correlation" or "substantial relation" between the governmental interest and the information required to be disclosed. See Pollard v. Roberts, 283 F. Supp. 248,

257 (ED Ark.) (three-judge court), aff'd, 393 U.S. 14 (1968) (per curiam). This type of scrutiny is necessary even if any deterrent effect on the exercise of First Amendment rights arises, not through direct government action, but indirectly as an unintended but inevitable result of the government's conduct in requiring disclosure. NAACP v. Alabama, supra, at 461. Cf. Kusper v. Pontikes, 414 U.S., at 57-58.

Appellees argue that the disclosure requirements of the Act differ significantly from those at issue in NAACP v. Alabama and its progeny because the Act only requires disclosure of the names of contributors and does not compel political organizations to submit the names of their members.

As we have seen, group association is protected because it enhances "[e]ffective advocacy." NAACP v. Alabama, supra, at 460. The right to join together "for the advancement of beliefs and ideas," ibid., is diluted if it does not include the right to pool money through contributions, for funds are often essential if "advocacy" is to be truly or optimally "effective." Moreover, the invasion of privacy of belief may be as great when the information sought concerns the giving and spending of money as when it concerns the joining of organizations, for "[f]inancial transactions can reveal much about a person's activities, associations, and beliefs." California Bankers Assn. v. Shultz, 416 U.S. 21, 78-79 (1974) (POWELL, J., concurring). Our past decisions have not drawn fine lines between contributors and members but have treated them interchangeably. In Bates, for example, we applied the principles of NAACP v. Alabama and reversed convictions for failure to comply with a city ordinance that required the disclosure of "dues, assessments, and contributions paid, by whom and when paid." 361 U.S., at 518. See also United States v. Rumely, 345 U.S. 41 (1953) (setting aside a contempt conviction of an organization official who refused to disclose names of those who made bulk purchases of books sold by the organization).

The strict test established by NAACP v. Alabama is necessary because compelled disclosure has the potential for substantially infringing the exercise of First Amendment rights. But we have acknowledged that there are governmental interests sufficiently important to outweigh the possibility of infringement, particularly when the "free functioning of our national institutions" is involved. Communist Party v. Subversive Activities Control Bd., 367 U.S. 1, 97 (1961).

The governmental interests sought to be vindicated by the disclosure requirements are of this magnitude. They fall into three categories. First, disclosure provides the electorate with information "as to where political campaign money comes from and how it is spent by the candidate" in order to aid the voters in evaluating those who seek federal office. It allows voters to place each candidate in the political spectrum more precisely than is often possible solely on the basis of party labels and campaign speeches. The sources of a candidate's financial support also alert the voter to the interests to which a candidate is most likely to be responsive and thus facilitate predictions of future performance in office.

Second, disclosure requirements deter actual corruption and avoid the appearance of corruption by exposing large contributions and expenditures to the light of publicity. This exposure may discourage those who would use money for improper purposes either before or after the election. A public armed with information about a candidate's most generous supporters is better able to detect any post-election special favors that may be given in return. And, as we recognized in Burroughs v. United States, 290 U.S., at 548, Congress could reasonably conclude that full disclosure during an election campaign tends "to prevent the corrupt use of money to affect elections." In enacting these requirements it may have been mindful of Mr. Justice Brandeis' advice:

"Publicity is justly commended as a remedy for social and industrial diseases. Sunlight is said to be the best of disinfectants; electric light the most efficient policeman."

Third, and not least significant, recordkeeping, reporting, and disclosure requirements are an essential means of gathering the data necessary to detect violations of the contribution limitations described above.

The disclosure requirements, as a general matter, directly serve substantial governmental interests. In determining whether these interests are sufficient to justify the requirements we must look to the extent of the burden that they place on individual rights.

It is undoubtedly true that public disclosure of contributions to candidates and political parties will deter some individuals who otherwise might contribute. In some instances, disclosure may even expose contributors to harassment or retaliation. These are not insignificant burdens on individual rights, and they must be weighed carefully against the interests which Congress has sought to promote by this legislation. In this process, we note and agree with appellants' concession that disclosure requirements—certainly in most applications—appear to be the least restrictive means of curbing the evils of campaign ignorance and corruption that Congress found to exist. Appellants argue, however, that the balance tips against disclosure when it is required of contributors to certain parties and candidates. We turn now to this contention.

B. Application to Minor Parties and Independents

Appellants contend that the Act's requirements are overbroad insofar as they apply to contributions to minor parties and independent candidates because the governmental interest in this information is minimal and the danger of significant infringement on First Amendment rights is greatly increased.

1. Requisite Factual Showing

In NAACP v. Alabama the organization had "made an uncontroverted showing that on past occasions revelation of the identity of its rank-and-file members [had] exposed these members to economic reprisal, loss of employment, threat of physical coercion, and other manifestations of public hostility," 357 U.S., at 462, and the State was unable to show that the disclosure it sought had a "substantial bearing" on the issues it sought to clarify, id., at 464. Under those circumstances, the Court held that "whatever interest the State may have in [disclosure] has not been shown to be sufficient to overcome petitioner's constitutional objections." Id., at 465.

The Court of Appeals rejected appellants' suggestion that this case fits into the NAACP v. Alabama mold. It concluded that substantial governmental interests in "informing the electorate and preventing the corruption of the political process" were furthered by requiring disclosure of minor parties and independent candidates, 171 U.S. App. D.C., at 218, 519 F.2d, at 867, and therefore found no "tenable rationale for assuming that the public interest in minority party disclosure of contributions above a reasonable cutoff point is uniformly outweighed by potential contributors' associational rights," id., at 219, 519 F.2d, at 868. The court left open the question of the application of the disclosure requirements to candidates (and parties) who could demonstrate injury of the sort at stake in NAACP v. Alabama. No record of harassment on a similar scale was found in this case. We agree with the Court of Appeals' conclusion that NAACP v. Alabama is inapposite where, as here, any serious infringement on First Amendment rights brought about by the compelled disclosure of contributors is highly speculative.

It is true that the governmental interest in disclosure is diminished when the contribution in question is made to a minor party with little chance of winning an election. As minor parties usually represent definite and publicized viewpoints, there may be less need to inform the voters of the interests that specific candidates represent. Major parties encompass candidates of greater diversity. In many situations the label "Republican" or "Democrat" tells a voter little. The candidate who bears it may be supported by funds from the far right, the far left, or any place in between on the political spectrum. It is less likely that a candidate of, say, the Socialist Labor Party will represent interests that cannot be discerned from the party's ideological position.

The Government's interest in deterring the "buying" of elections and the undue influence of large contributors on officeholders also may be reduced where contributions to a minor party or an independent candidate are concerned, for it is less likely that the candidate will be victorious. But a minor party sometimes can play a significant role in an election. Even when a minor-party candidate has little or no chance of winning, he may be encouraged by major-party interests in order to divert votes from other major-party contenders.

We are not unmindful that the damage done by disclosure to the associational interests of the minor parties and their members and to supporters of independents could be significant. These movements are less likely to have a sound financial base and thus are more vulnerable to falloffs in contributions. In some instances fears of reprisal may deter contributions to the point where the movement cannot survive. The public interest also suffers if that result comes to pass, for there is a consequent reduction in the free circulation of ideas both within and without the political arena.

There could well be a case, similar to those before the Court in NAACP v. Alabama and Bates, where the threat to the exercise of First Amendment rights is so serious and the state interest furthered by disclosure so insubstantial that the Act's requirements cannot be constitutionally applied. But no appellant in this case has tendered record evidence of the sort proffered in NAACP v. Alabama. Instead, appellants primarily rely on "the clearly articulated fears of individuals, well experienced in the political process." Brief for Appellants 173. At best they offer the testimony of several minor-party officials that one or two persons refused to make contributions because of the possibility of disclosure. On this record, the substantial public interest in disclosure identified by the legislative history of this Act outweighs the harm generally alleged.

2. Blanket Exemption

Appellants agree that "the record here does not reflect the kind of focused and insistent harassment of contributors and members that existed in the NAACP cases." Ibid. They argue, however, that a blanket exemption for minor parties is necessary lest irreparable injury be done before the required evidence can be gathered.

Those parties that would be sufficiently "minor" to be exempted from the requirements of 434 could be defined, appellants suggest, along the lines used for public-financing purposes, see Part III-A, infra, as those who received less than 25% of the vote in past elections. Appellants do not argue that this line is constitutionally required. They suggest as an alternative defining "minor parties" as those that do not qualify for automatic ballot access under state law. Presumably, other criteria, such as current political strength (measured by polls or petition), age, or degree of organization, could also be used.

The difficulty with these suggestions is that they reflect only a party's past or present political strength and that is only one of the factors that must be considered. Some of the criteria are not precisely indicative of even that factor.

Age, or past political success, for instance, may typically be associated with parties that have a high probability of success. But not all long-established parties are winners—some are consistent losers— and a new party may garner a great deal of support if it can associate itself with an issue that has captured the public's imagination. None of the criteria suggested is precisely related to the other critical factor that must be considered, the possibility that disclosure will impinge upon protected associational activity.

An opinion dissenting in part from the Court of Appeals' decision concedes that no one line is "constitutionally required." It argues, however, that a flat exemption for minor parties must be carved out, even along arbitrary lines, if groups that would suffer impermissibly from disclosure are to be given any real protection. An approach that requires minor parties to submit evidence that the disclosure requirements cannot constitutionally be applied to them offers only an illusory safeguard, the argument goes, because the "evils" of "chill and harassment . . . are largely incapable of formal proof." This dissent expressed its concern that a minor party, particularly a new party, may never be able to prove a substantial threat of harassment, however real that threat may be, because it would be required to come forward with witnesses who are too fearful to contribute but not too fearful to testify about their fear. A strict requirement that chill and harassment be directly attributable to the specific disclosure from which the exemption is sought would make the task even more difficult.

We recognize that unduly strict requirements of proof could impose a heavy burden, but it does not follow that a blanket exemption for minor parties is necessary. Minor parties must be allowed sufficient flexibility in the proof of injury to assure a fair consideration of their claim. The evidence offered need show only a reasonable probability that the compelled disclosure of a party's contributors' names will subject them to threats, harassment, or reprisals from either Government officials or private parties. The proof may include, for example, specific evidence of past or present harassment of members due to their associational ties, or of harassment directed against the organization itself. A pattern of threats or specific manifestations of public hostility may be sufficient. New parties that have no history upon which to draw may be able to offer evidence of reprisals and threats directed against individuals or organizations holding similar views.

Where it exists the type of chill and harassment identified in NAACP v. Alabama can be shown. We cannot assume that courts will be insensitive to similar showings when made in future cases. We therefore conclude that a blanket exemption is not required.

C. Section 434 (e)

Section 434 (e) requires "[e]very person (other than a political committee or candidate) who makes contributions or expenditures" aggregating over $100 in a calendar year "other than by contribution to a political committee or candidate" to file a statement with the Commission. Unlike the other disclosure provisions, this section does not seek the contribution list of any association. Instead, it requires direct disclosure of what an individual or group contributes or spends.

In considering this provision we must apply the same strict standard of scrutiny, for the right of associational privacy developed in NAACP v. Alabama derives from the rights of the organization's members to advocate their personal points of view in the most effective way. 357 U.S., at 458, 460. See also NAACP v. Button, 371 U.S., at 429-431; Sweezy v. New Hampshire, 354 U.S., at 250.

Appellants attack 434 (e) as a direct intrusion on privacy of belief, in violation of Talley v. California, 362 U.S. 60 (1960), and as imposing "very real, practical burdens . . . certain to deter individuals from making expenditures for their independent political speech" analogous to those held to be impermissible in Thomas v. Collins, 323 U.S. 516 (1945).

1. The Role of 434 (e)

The Court of Appeals upheld 434 (e) as necessary to enforce the independent-expenditure ceiling imposed by 18 U.S.C. 608 (e) (1) (1970 ed., Supp. IV). It said:

"If . . . Congress has both the authority and a compelling interest to regulate independent expenditures under section 608 (e), surely it can require that there be disclosure to prevent misuse of the spending channel." 171 U.S. App. D.C., at 220 519 F.2d, at 869.

We have found that 608 (e) (1) unconstitutionally infringes upon First Amendment rights. If the sole function of 434 (e) were to aid in the enforcement of that provision, it would no longer serve any governmental purpose.

But the two provisions are not so intimately tied. The legislative history on the function of 434 (e) is bare, but it was clearly intended to stand independently of 608 (e) (1). It was enacted with the general disclosure provisions in 1971 as part of the original Act, while 608 (e) (1) was part of the 1974 amendments. Like the other disclosure provisions, 434 (e) could play a role in the enforcement of the expanded contribution and expenditure limitations included in the 1974 amendments, but it also has independent functions. Section 434 (e) is part of Congress' effort to achieve "total disclosure" by reaching "every kind of political activity" in order to insure that the voters are fully informed and to achieve through publicity the maximum deterrence to corruption and undue influence possible. The provision is responsive to the legitimate fear that efforts would be made, as they had been in the past, to avoid the disclosure requirements by routing financial support of candidates through avenues not explicitly covered by the general provisions of the Act.

2. Vagueness Problems

In its effort to be all-inclusive, however, the provision raises serious problems of vagueness, particularly treacherous where, as here, the violation of its terms carries criminal penalties and fear of incurring these sanctions may deter those who seek to exercise protected First Amendment rights.

Section 434 (e) applies to "[e]very person . . . who makes contributions or expenditures." "Contributions" and "expenditures" are defined in parallel provisions in terms of the use of money or other valuable assets "for the purpose of . . . influencing" the nomination or election of candidates for federal office. It is the ambiguity of this phrase that poses constitutional problems.

Due process requires that a criminal statute provide adequate notice to a person of ordinary intelligence that his contemplated conduct is illegal, for "no man shall be held criminally responsible for conduct which he could not reasonably understand to be proscribed." United States v. Harriss, 347 U.S. 612, 617 (1954). See also Papachristou v. City of Jacksonville, 405 U.S. 156 (1972). Where First Amendment rights are involved, an even "greater degree of specificity" is required. Smith v. Goguen, 415 U.S., at 573. See Grayned v. City of Rockford, 408 U.S. 104, 109 (1972); Kunz v. New York, 340 U.S. 290 (1951).

There is no legislative history to guide us in determining the scope of the critical phrase "for the purpose of . . . influencing." It appears to have been adopted without comment from earlier disclosure Acts. Congress "has voiced its wishes in [most] muted strains," leaving us to draw upon "those common-sense assumptions that must be made in determining direction without a compass." Rosado v. Wyman, 397 U.S. 397, 412 (1970). Where the constitutional requirement of definiteness is at stake, we have the further obligation to construe the statute, if that can be done consistent with the legislature's purpose, to avoid the shoals of vagueness. United States v. Harriss, supra, at 618; United States v. Rumely, 345 U.S., at 45.

In enacting the legislation under review Congress addressed broadly the problem of political campaign financing. It wished to promote full disclosure of campaign-oriented spending to insure both the reality and the appearance of the purity and openness of the federal election process. Our task is to construe "for the purpose of . . . influencing," incorporated in 434 (e) through the definitions of "contributions" and "expenditures," in a manner that precisely furthers this goal.

In Part I we discussed what constituted a "contribution" for purposes of the contribution limitations set forth in 18 U.S.C. 608 (b) (1970 ed., Supp. IV). We construed that term to include not only contributions made directly or indirectly to a candidate, political party, or campaign committee, and contributions made to other organizations or individuals but earmarked for political purposes, but also all expenditures placed in cooperation with or with the consent of a candidate, his agents, or an authorized committee of the candidate. The definition of "contribution" in 431 (e) for disclosure purposes parallels the definition in Title 18 almost word for word, and we construe the former provision as we have the latter. So defined, "contributions" have a sufficiently close relationship to the goals of the Act, for they are connected with a candidate or his campaign.

When we attempt to define "expenditure" in a similarly narrow way we encounter line-drawing problems of the sort we faced in 18 U.S.C. 608 (e) (1) (1970 ed., Supp. IV). Although the phrase, "for the purpose of . . . influencing" an election or nomination, differs from the language used in 608 (e) (1), it shares the same potential for encompassing both issue discussion and advocacy of a political result. The general requirement that "political committees" and candidates disclose their expenditures could raise similar vagueness problems, for "political committee" is defined only in terms of amount of annual "contributions" and "expenditures," and could be interpreted to reach groups engaged purely in issue discussion. The lower courts have construed the words "political committee" more narrowly. To fulfill the purposes of the Act they need only encompass organizations that are under the control of a candidate or the major purpose of which is the nomination or election of a candidate. Expenditures of candidates and of "political committees" so construed can be assumed to fall within the core area sought to be addressed by Congress. They are, by definition, campaign related.

But when the maker of the expenditure is not within these categories—when it is an individual other than a candidate or a group other than a "political committee"—the relation of the information sought to the purposes of the Act may be too remote. To insure that the reach of 434 (e) is not impermissibly broad, we construe "expenditure" for purposes of that section in the same way we construed the terms of 608 (e)—to reach only funds used for communications that expressly advocate the election or defeat of a clearly identified candidate. This reading is directed precisely to that spending that is unambiguously related to the campaign of a particular federal candidate.

In summary, 434 (e), as construed, imposes independent reporting requirements on individuals and groups that are not candidates or political committees only in the following circumstances: (1) when they make contributions earmarked for political purposes or authorized or requested by a candidate or his agent, to some person other than a candidate or political committee, and

(2) when they make expenditures for communications that expressly advocate the election or defeat of a clearly identified candidate.

Unlike 18 U.S.C. 608 (e) (1) (1970 ed., Supp. IV), 434 (e), as construed, bears a sufficient relationship to a substantial governmental interest. As narrowed, 434 (e), like 608 (e) (1), does not reach all partisan discussion for it only requires disclosure of those expenditures that expressly advocate a particular election result. This might have been fatal if the only purpose of 434 (e) were to stem corruption or its appearance by closing a loophole in the general disclosure requirements. But the disclosure provisions, including 434 (e), serve another, informational interest, and even as construed 434 (e) increases the fund of information concerning those who support the candidates. It goes beyond the general disclosure requirements to shed the light of publicity on spending that is unambiguously campaign related but would not otherwise be reported because it takes the form of independent expenditures or of contributions to an individual or group not itself required to report the names of its contributors. By the same token, it is not fatal that 434 (e) encompasses purely independent expenditures uncoordinated with a particular candidate or his agent. The corruption potential of these expenditures may be significantly different, but the informational interest can be as strong as it is in coordinated spending, for disclosure helps voters to define more of the candidates' constituencies.

Section 434 (e), as we have construed it, does not contain the infirmities of the provisions before the Court in Talley v. California, 362 U.S. 60 (1960), and Thomas v. Collins, 323 U.S. 516 (1945). The ordinance found wanting in Talley forbade all distribution of handbills that did not contain the name of the printer, author, or manufacturer, and the name of the distributor. The city urged that the ordinance was aimed at identifying those responsible for fraud, false advertising, and libel, but the Court found that it was "in no manner so limited." 362 U.S., at 64. Here, as we have seen, the disclosure requirement is narrowly limited to those situations where the information sought has a substantial connection with the governmental interests sought to be advanced. Thomas held unconstitutional a prior restraint in the form of a registration requirement for labor organizers. The Court found the State's interest insufficient to justify the restrictive effect of the statute. The burden imposed by 434 (e) is no prior restraint, but a reasonable and minimally restrictive method of furthering First Amendment values by opening the basic processes of our federal election system to public view.

D. Thresholds

Appellants' third contention, based on alleged overbreadth, is that the monetary thresholds in the recordkeeping and reporting provisions lack a substantial nexus with the claimed governmental interests, for the amounts involved are too low even to attract the attention of the candidate, much less have a corrupting influence.

The provisions contain two thresholds. Records are to be kept by political committees of the names and addresses of those who make contributions in excess of $10, 432 (c) (2), and these records are subject to Commission audit, 438 (a) (8). If a person's contributions to a committee or candidate aggregate more than $100, his name and address, as well as his occupation and principal place of business, are to be included in reports filed by committees and candidates with the Commission, 434 (b) (2), and made available for public inspection, 438 (a) (4).

The Court of Appeals rejected appellants' contention that these thresholds are unconstitutional. It found the challenge on First Amendment grounds to the $10 threshold to be premature, for it could "discern no basis in the statute for authorizing disclosure outside the Commission . . . , and hence no substantial 'inhibitory effect' operating upon" appellants. 171 U.S. App. D.C., at 216, 519 F.2d, at 865. The $100 threshold was found to be within the "reasonable latitude" given the legislature "as to where to draw the line." Ibid. We agree.

The $10 and $100 thresholds are indeed low. Contributors of relatively small amounts are likely to be especially sensitive to recording or disclosure of their political preferences. These strict requirements may well discourage participation by some citizens in the political process, a result that Congress hardly could have intended. Indeed, there is little in the legislative history to indicate that Congress focused carefully on the appropriate level at which to require recording and disclosure. Rather, it seems merely to have adopted the thresholds existing in similar disclosure laws since 1910. But we cannot require Congress to establish that it has chosen the highest reasonable threshold. The line is necessarily a judgmental decision, best left in the context of this complex legislation to congressional discretion. We cannot say, on this bare record, that the limits designated are wholly without rationality.

We are mindful that disclosure serves informational functions, as well as the prevention of corruption and the enforcement of the contribution limitations. Congress is not required to set a threshold that is tailored only to the latter goals. In addition, the enforcement goal can never be well served if the threshold is so high that disclosure becomes equivalent to admitting violation of the contribution limitations.

The $10 recordkeeping threshold, in a somewhat similar fashion, facilitates the enforcement of the disclosure provisions by making it relatively difficult to aggregate secret contributions in amounts that surpass the $100 limit. We agree with the Court of Appeals that there is no warrant for assuming that public disclosure of contributions between $10 and $100 is authorized by the Act. Accordingly, we do not reach the question whether information concerning gifts of this size can be made available to the public without trespassing impermissibly on First Amendment rights. Cf. California Bankers Assn. v. Shultz, 416 U.S., at 56-57.

In summary, we find no constitutional infirmities in the recordkeeping, reporting, and disclosure provisions of the Act.

III. PUBLIC FINANCING OF PRESIDENTIAL ELECTION CAMPAIGNS

A series of statutes for the public financing of Presidential election campaigns produced the scheme now found in 6096 and Subtitle H of the Internal Revenue Code of 1954, 26 U.S.C. 6096, 9001-9012, 9031-9042 (1970 ed., Supp. IV). Both the District Court, 401 F. Supp. 1235, and the Court of Appeals, 171 U.S. App. D.C., at 229-238, 519 F.2d, at 878-887, sustained Subtitle H against a constitutional attack. Appellants renew their challenge here, contending that the legislation violates the First and Fifth Amendments. We find no merit in their claims and affirm.

A. Summary of Subtitle H

Section 9006 establishes a Presidential Election Campaign Fund (Fund), financed from general revenues in the aggregate amount designated by individual taxpayers, under 6096, who on their income tax returns may authorize payment to the Fund of one dollar of their tax liability in the case of an individual return or two dollars in the case of a joint return. The Fund consists of three separate accounts to finance (1) party nominating conventions, 9008 (a), (2) general election campaigns, 9006 (a), and (3) primary campaigns, 9037 (a).

Chapter 95 of Title 26, which concerns financing of party nominating conventions and general election campaigns, distinguishes among "major," "minor," and "new" parties. A major party is defined as a party whose candidate for President in the most recent election received 25% or more of the popular vote. 9002 (6). A minor party is defined as a party whose candidate received at least 5% but less than 25% of the vote at the most recent election. 9002 (7). All other parties are new parties, 9002 (8), including both newly created parties and those receiving less than 5% of the vote in the last election.

Major parties are entitled to $2,000,000 to defray their national committee Presidential nominating convention expenses, must limit total expenditures to that amount, 9008 (d), and may not use any of this money to benefit a particular candidate or delegate, 9008 (c). A minor party receives a portion of the major-party entitlement determined by the ratio of the votes received by the party's candidate in the last election to the average of the votes received by the major parties' candidates. 9008 (b) (2). The amounts given to the parties and the expenditure limit are adjusted for inflation, using 1974 as the base year. 9008 (b) (5). No financing is provided for new parties, nor is there any express provision for financing independent candidates or parties not holding a convention.

For expenses in the general election campaign, 9004 (a) (1) entitles each major-party candidate to $20,000,000. This amount is also adjusted for inflation. See 9004 (a) (1). To be eligible for funds the candidate must pledge not to incur expenses in excess of the entitlement under 9004 (a) (1) and not to accept private contributions except to the extent that the fund is insufficient to provide the full entitlement. 9003 (b) Minor-party candidates are also entitled to funding, again based on the ratio of the vote received by the party's candidate in the preceding election to the average of the major-party candidates. 9004 (a) (2) (A). Minor-party candidates must certify that they will not incur campaign expenses in excess of the major-party entitlement and that they will accept private contributions only to the extent needed to make up the difference between that amount and the public funding grant. 9003 (c). New-party candidates receive no money prior to the general election, but any candidate receiving 5% or more of the popular vote in the election is entitled to post-election payments according to the formula applicable to minor-party candidates. 9004 (a) (3). Similarly, minor-party candidates are entitled to post-election funds if they receive a greater percentage of the average major-party vote than their party's candidate did in the preceding election; the amount of such payments is the difference between the entitlement based on the preceding election and that based on the actual vote in the current election. 9004 (a) (3). A further eligibility requirement for minor- and new-party candidates is that the candidate's name must appear on the ballot, or electors pledged to the candidate must be on the ballot, in at least 10 States. 9002 (2) (B).

Chapter 96 establishes a third account in the Fund, the Presidential Primary Matching Payment Account. 9037 (a). This funding is intended to aid campaigns by candidates seeking Presidential nomination "by a political party," 9033 (b) (2), in "primary elections," 9032 (7). The threshold eligibility requirement is that the candidate raise at least $5,000 in each of 20 States, counting only the first $250 from each person contributing to the candidate. 9033 (b) (3), (4). In addition, the candidate must agree to abide by the spending limits in 9035. See 9033 (b) (1). Funding is provided according to a matching formula: each qualified candidate is entitled to a sum equal to the total private contributions received, disregarding contributions from any person to the extent that total contributions to the candidate by that person exceed $250. 9034 (a). Payments to any candidate under Chapter 96 may not exceed 50% of the overall expenditure ceiling accepted by the candidate. 9034 (b).

B. Constitutionality of Subtitle H

Appellants argue that Subtitle H is invalid (1) as "contrary to the 'general welfare,'" Art. I, 8, (2) because any scheme of public financing of election campaigns is inconsistent with the First Amendment, and (3) because Subtitle H invidiously discriminates against certain interests in violation of the Due

Process Clause of the Fifth Amendment. We find no merit in these contentions.

Appellants' "general welfare" contention erroneously treats the General Welfare Clause as a limitation upon congressional power. It is rather a grant of power, the scope of which is quite expansive, particularly in view of the enlargement of power by the Necessary and Proper Clause. M'Culloch v. Maryland, 4 Wheat. 316, 420 (1819). Congress has power to regulate Presidential elections and primaries, United States v. Classic, 313 U.S. 299 (1941); Burroughs v. United States, 290 U.S. 534 (1934); and public financing of Presidential elections as a means to reform the electoral process was clearly a choice within the granted power. It is for Congress to decide which expenditures will promote the general welfare: "[T]he power of Congress to authorize expenditure of public moneys for public purposes is not limited by the direct grants of legislative power found in the Constitution." United States v. Butler, 297 U.S. 1, 66 (1936). See Helvering v. Davis, 301 U.S. 619, 640-641 (1937). Any limitations upon the exercise of that granted power must be found elsewhere in the Constitution. In this case, Congress was legislating for the "general welfare"—to reduce the deleterious influence of large contributions on our political process, to facilitate communication by candidates with the electorate, and to free candidates from the rigors of fundraising. See S. Rep. No. 93-689, Pp. 1-10 (1974). Whether the chosen means appear "bad," "unwise," or "unworkable" to us is irrelevant; Congress has concluded that the means are "necessary and proper" to promote the general welfare, and we thus decline to find this legislation without the grant of power in Art. I, 8.

Appellants' challenge to the dollar check-off provision (6096) fails for the same reason. They maintain that Congress is required to permit taxpayers to designate particular candidates or parties as recipients of their money. But the appropriation to the Fund in 9006 is like any other appropriation from the general revenue except that its amount is determined by reference to the aggregate of the one-and two-dollar authorization on taxpayers' income tax returns. This detail does not constitute the appropriation any less an appropriation by Congress. The fallacy of appellants' argument is therefore apparent; every appropriation made by Congress uses public money in a manner to which some taxpayers object.

Appellants next argue that "by analogy" to the Religion Clauses of the First Amendment public financing of election campaigns, however meritorious, violates the First Amendment. We have, of course, held that the Religion Clauses—"Congress shall make no law respecting an establishment of religion, or prohibiting the free exercise thereof"—require Congress, and the States through the Fourteenth Amendment, to remain neutral in matters of religion. E. g., Abington School Dist. v. Schempp, 374 U.S. 203, 222-226 (1963). The government may not aid one religion to the detriment of others or impose a burden on one religion that is not imposed on others, and may not even aid all religions. E. g., Everson v. Board of Education, 330 U.S. 1, 15-16 (1947). See Kurland, Of Church and State and the Supreme Court, 29 U. Chi. L. Rev. 1, 96 (1961). But the analogy is patently inapplicable to our issue here. Although "Congress shall make no law . . . abridging the freedom of speech, or the press," Subtitle H is a congressional effort, not to abridge, restrict, or censor speech, but rather to use public money to facilitate and enlarge public discussion and participation in the electoral process, goals vital to a self-governing people. Thus, Subtitle H furthers, not abridges, pertinent First Amendment values. Appellants argue, however, that as constructed public financing invidiously discriminates in violation of the Fifth Amendment. We turn therefore to that argument.

Equal protection analysis in the Fifth Amendment area is the same as that under the Fourteenth Amendment. Weinberger v. Wiesenfeld, 420 U.S. 636, 638 n. 2 (1975), and cases cited. In several situations concerning the electoral process, the principle has been developed that restrictions on access to the electoral process must survive exacting scrutiny. The restriction can be sustained only if it furthers a "vital" governmental interest, American Party of Texas v. White, 415 U.S. 767, 780-781 (1974), that is "achieved by a means that does not unfairly or unnecessarily burden either a minority party's or an individual candidate's equally important interest in the continued availability of political opportunity." Lubin v. Panish, 415 U.S. 709, 716 (1974). See American Party of Texas v. White, supra, at 780; Storer v. Brown, 415 U.S. 724, 729-730 (1974). These cases, however, dealt primarily with state laws requiring a candidate to satisfy certain requirements in order to have his name appear on the ballot. These were, of course, direct burdens not only on the candidate's ability to run for office but also on the voter's ability to voice preferences regarding representative government and contemporary issues. In contrast, the denial of public financing to some Presidential candidates is not restrictive of voters' rights and less restrictive of candidates'. Subtitle H does not prevent any candidate from getting on the ballot or any voter from casting a vote for the candidate of his choice; the inability, if any, of minor-party candidates to wage effective campaigns will derive not from lack of public funding but from their inability to raise private contributions. Any disadvantage suffered by operation of the eligibility formulae under Subtitle H is thus limited to the claimed denial of the enhancement of opportunity to communicate with the electorate that the formulae afford eligible candidates. But eligible candidates suffer a countervailing denial. As we more fully develop later, acceptance of public financing entails voluntary acceptance of an expenditure ceiling. Non-eligible candidates are not subject to that limitation. Accordingly, we conclude that public financing is generally less restrictive of access to the electoral process than the ballot-access regulations dealt with in prior cases. In any event, Congress enacted Subtitle H in furtherance of sufficiently important governmental interests and has not unfairly or unnecessarily burdened the political opportunity of any party or candidate.

It cannot be gainsaid that public financing as a means of eliminating the improper influence of large private contributions furthers a significant governmental interest. In addition, the limits on contributions necessarily increase the burden of fundraising, and Congress properly regarded public financing as an appropriate means of relieving major-party Presidential candidates from the rigors of soliciting private contributions. The States have also been held to have important interests in limiting places on the ballot to those candidates who demonstrate substantial popular support. Congress' interest in not funding hopeless candidacies with large sums of public money, necessarily justifies the withholding of public assistance from candidates without significant public support. Thus, Congress may legitimately require "some preliminary showing of a significant modicum of support," as an eligibility requirement for public funds. This requirement also serves the important public interest against providing artificial incentives to "splintered parties and unrestrained factionalism."

CONCLUSION

In summary, we sustain the individual contribution limits, the disclosure and reporting provisions, and the public financing scheme. We conclude, however, that the limitations on campaign expenditures, on independent expenditures by individuals and groups, and on expenditures by a candidate from his personal funds are constitutionally infirm. . . .

The Burger Court in 1976, with Chief Justice Warren E. Burger (center) presiding. Photo via Wikimedia Commons. [Public domain.]

Document Analysis

This complex case begins with a review of the FECA and its 1974 amendments, focusing on the limits it imposes on contributions to federal campaigns that are allowed by an individual or political action committee. The court also analyzes how the Federal Election Commission is constituted and how public funding for general elections is dispersed.

There are three primary issues that the rest of this opinion covers in detail. Firstly, the court agrees that limits on contributions to individual candidates are appropriate because it serves the public interest by protecting elections from corruption. The justices do not agree that the same purpose is served by limiting campaign spending, however, arguing that to limit the ability of a candidate to campaign, which often involves spending money to secure media coverage, will "limit political expression at the core of our electoral process and of First Amendment freedoms." Further emphasizing the protection of the constitutional freedom of speech, the court argues that monetary restrictions would inevitably lead to a restriction on that very freedom because "virtually every means of communicating ideas in today's mass society requires the expenditure of money." The court deems that campaign expenditure limits as established in the FECA are, therefore, an unnecessary violation of freedom of speech and freedom of association, and strikes them down. In addition, limits to spending personal or family money and limits on independent expenditures are also eliminated. The court concludes that when candidates accept public funds, however, the public interest in the limiting of expenditures still applies, and is also not overly burdensome on the candidate, since they could choose to forego public funding and spend as much money as they choose.

The court also rules that the structure of the FEC is unconstitutional, since four of the commissioners of this executive agency are appointed directly by Congress rather than nominated by the president and then approved by Congress.

Essential Themes

The FEC spent four months adjusting its activities to the new ruling and was back in full operation in May 1976.

One of the most important results of the *Buckley v. Valeo* opinion was the court's determination that so-called issue groups and their expenditures were not subject to campaign contribution regulations. As long as the advocacy that these groups engaged in did not openly promote the election of a named candidate, they could spend unlimited money to support an issue, even one clearly associated with a candidate. This decision led to a huge increase in PAC advertising, as well as contributions to political parties not earmarked specifically for campaigns, known as soft money. Within two decades, both major political parties were raising more soft money than direct campaign contributions.

However, debates over whether the protection of democracy or the protection of the First Amendment should take precedence in regard to possible regulations of campaign financing continued. In 2002, the Bipartisan Campaign Reform Act (BCRA) limited soft money contributions and tightened restrictions on advertising paid for by corporations close to an election. However, in 2010, the Supreme Court declared the provisions of the BCRA unconstitutional in the case of *Citizens United v. Federal Election Commission*. In its opinion, the court also ruled on communications paid for by independent groups that advocate directly for a candidate, overturning limits specified in *Buckley v. Valeo*. This led to the rise of "super PACs," organizations that can raise and spend unrestricted amounts to advocate directly for or against political candidates. Four years later, a Supreme Court decision in *McCutcheon v. Federal Election Commission* struck down the limit on the amount of money that an individual can contribute to federal candidates during a two-year period.

—Bethany Groff Dorau, MA

Bibliography and Additional Reading

Burdette, Robert B. *Buckley v. Valeo: The Opinion of the United States Supreme Court in the Election Campaign Case; Summary and Commentary.* Washington, DC: Library of Congress, 1976.

Collins, Ronald K. L., and David M. Skover. *When Money Speaks: The McCutcheon Decision, Campaign Finance Laws and the First Amendment.* Oak Park: Top Five, 2014.

Fuller, Jaime. "From George Washington to Shaun McCutcheon: A Brief-ish History of Campaign Finance Reform." *Washington Post*, 3 Apr. 2014.

Urofsky, Melvin I. *The Campaign Finance Cases: Buckley, McConnell, Citizens United, and McCutcheon.* Lawrence: University of Kansas Press, 2020.

Shaw v. Reno

Date: June 28, 1993
Authors: Justice Sandra Day O'Connor
Genre: court opinion

Summary Overview

The landmark U.S. Supreme Court decision in Shaw v. Reno *(1993) struck a blow against the practice of drawing electoral-district boundaries that create "majority-minority" districts based on race. The court ruled in a 5–4 decision that redistricting based on race must be held to a standard of strict scrutiny under the equal protection clause. This decision created tension with the Voting Rights Act of 1965, which requires redistricting bodies to be conscious of race.*

The redistricting that occurred after the 2000 census, which was required to reflect population changes, was the first nationwide redistricting to apply the rule set forth in Shaw v. Reno. *Shaw served as a watershed in the contest between advocates of racial representation and those who champion a "color-blind" electoral system. It came at a time when various racial issues that had for years remained largely outside sharp political debate—affirmative action, welfare reform, and so forth—had been thrust into the center stage of American political discourse. Although Shaw by no means resolved these debates, it helped to delineate the battle lines.*

Defining Moment

After the 1990 census, North Carolina became entitled to a twelfth seat in the U.S. House of Representatives. The state legislature reapportioned, or re-drew, its electoral districts to create the new district. To comply with Section 5 of the Voting Rights Act of 1965, North Carolina submitted a map to the Department of Justice with a single district with a black majority. The U.S. attorney general, who was tasked with reviewing the plan under the Voting Rights Act, rejected it, stating that a second district with a majority of minority group voters could be created in the southeastern part of the state using lines that were similar to those of other districts.

To respond to the attorney general's comments, and to meet provisions of the Voting Rights Act, the legislature revised their map to create two majority-nonwhite districts. To avoid disturbing incumbents' districts, the legislature drew the proposed Twelfth District largely along an interstate 85, snaking 160 miles through the north-central part of the state connecting various areas that had large black populations. In some places, the district was no wider than

Justice Sandra Day O'Connor wrote the majority opinion. Photo via Wikimedia Commons. [Public domain.]

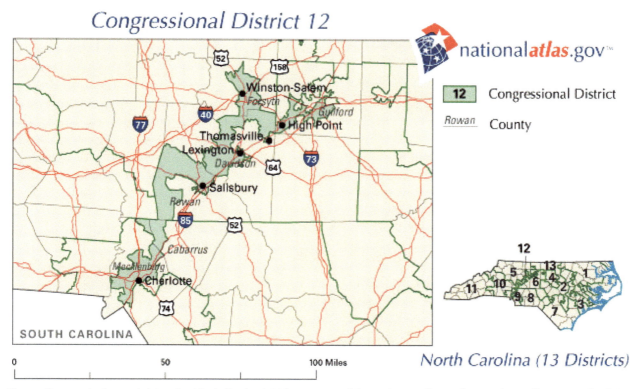

Shaw v. Reno revolved around claims that North Carolina's 12th congressional district (pictured) was affirmatively racially gerrymandered. Image via Wikimedia Commons. [Public domain.]

the I-85 corridor. The resulting district was 53 percent black.

Five voters who lived in the new district filed suit against state and federal officials, arguing that the revised plan created a racial gerrymander in violation of the Equal Protection Clause of the Fourteenth Amendment. The lawsuit alleged that the two districts created a concentration of black voters without regard to common redistricting concerns such as compactness, contiguousness, geographical boundaries, or political subdivisions. Instead, the goal appeared to be solely to create two districts along racial lines to ensure the election of two black representatives.

The three judge District Court held that it lacked subject matter jurisdiction over the federal appellees. It also dismissed the lawsuit against the state appellees, because under *United Jewish Organizations of Williamsburgh v. Carey* (1977). The court said the appellants had no equal protection claim because favoring minority voters was not discriminatory and neither the Fourteenth nor the Fifteenth Amendment prohibit the use of racial factors when creating electoral districts. The case was then appealed to the Supreme Court, which granted certiorari.

A 5–4 majority reversed the District Court, finding that the appellants had a claim under the Equal Protection Clause. In her majority opinion, Justice Sandra Day O'Connor wrote, "a plaintiff challenging a reapportionment statute under the Equal Protection Clause may state a claim by alleging that the legislation, though race neutral on its face, rationally cannot be understood as anything other than an effort to separate voters into different districts on the basis of race, and that the separation lacks sufficient justification."

The Court pointed out that electoral districts are created solely based on race reinforces racial stereotypes and undermines "our system of representative democracy by signaling to elected officials that they represent a particular racial group rather than their constituency as a whole." They also threaten "special harms that are not present in vote-dilution cases," such as *United Jewish Organizations*. The Court found that when a redistricting map is "so bizarre on its face that it is unexplainable on grounds other than race," that a claim for relief under the Fourteenth Amendment to the U.S. Constitution is available to plaintiffs.

When the *Shaw* case was subsequently returned to North Carolina, a federal panel upheld the reapportionment plan after finding that the state did indeed have a compelling interest in complying with the Voting Rights Act. Nevertheless, the Supreme Court's *Shaw* decision has been the basis for other important decisions concerning racially defined districts.

Author Biography

Sandra Day O'Connor was born in El Paso, Texas, on March 26, 1930. She grew up on a ranch near Duncan, Arizona. Both her undergraduate (1950) and law (1952) degrees are from Stanford University. After graduating from law school, she married her classmate and fellow lawyer, John Jay O'Connor III (1930-2009). They had three sons, Scott, Brian, and Jay.

After graduating from law school at the top of her class, O'Connor applied for a position as a lawyer with Gibson, Dunn & Crutcher. They said they might hire her as a legal secretary, but only if she could type fast enough. Instead, she became a deputy district attorney in San Mateo County, California.

John O'Connor was a member of the U.S. Army Judge Advocate General Corps (JAG Corps). When he was stationed in Frankfurt from 1954 to 1957, Justice O'Connor accompanied him and worked as a civilian attorney for the Army. After they were discharged, they spent a year living at a ski resort in Austria.

When the couple returned to the United States, Justice O'Connor was in private practice until 1960, when she took a five-year leave from the practice of law to care for her three children. She remained involved in a number of civic and social organizations, as well as providing pro bono legal services. In 1965, she became the assistant attorney general for Arizona. However, her children were still young, and she wanted to be home when they arrived from school, so she negotiated a deal where she worked two-thirds time for half the salary.

In 1969, the Maricopa County Board of Supervisors appointed Justice O'Connor to the Arizona Senate. The next year, she ran for and won the election for the seat. By 1973, she was rose to the position of senate majority leader—the first time a woman held this type of leadership role in a state legislature anywhere in the United States.

In 1975, she was elected as a Superior Court judge in Maricopa County. In 1979, she was appointed to the Arizona Court of Appeals in Phoenix. In July 1981, U.S. Supreme Court Justice Potter Stewart retired, and President Ronald Reagan nominated O'Connor to fill the vacancy. Reagan described her as a "person for all seasons" and she was unanimously confirmed by the Senate. She was sworn in as the first female U.S. Supreme Court justice on September 25, 1981. In January 2006, O'Connor retired from the Supreme Court and was replaced by Justice Samuel Alito. Three years after her retirement, she was awarded the Presidential Medal of Freedom.

O'Connor published a number of books, including a memoir about her family's ranch called *Lazy B* (2002, cowritten with her brother, Alan Day). She also wrote several children's books based on adventures from her childhood and in 2013 she published *Out of Order: Stories from the History of the Supreme Court*, which is a collection of stories about the evolution of the Supreme Court.

In addition to writing, Justice O'Connor was concerned about the lack of understanding about our government. She founded iCivics, an online tool that offers games and other resources to teach students civic education. Justice O'Connor believed iCivics to be "her most important work and greatest legacy."

In October 2018, the U.S. Supreme Court released a letter that said Justice O'Connor had been diagnosed with dementia, likely Alzheimer's disease, and she would withdraw from public life.

Historical Document

Shaw v. Reno

SYLLABUS
OCTOBER TERM, 1992

SHAW ET AL. *v.* RENO, ATTORNEY GENERAL, ET AL.

APPEAL FROM THE UNITED STATES DISTRICT COURT FOR THE EASTERN DISTRICT OF NORTH CAROLINA

No. 92-357. Argued April 20, 1993-Decided June 28,1993

To comply with § 5 of the Voting Rights Act of 1965—which prohibits a covered jurisdiction from implementing changes in a "standard, practice, or procedure with respect to voting" without federal authorization—North Carolina submitted to the Attorney General a congressional reapportionment plan with one majority-black district. The Attorney General objected to the plan on the ground that a second district could have been created to give effect to minority voting strength in the State's south-central to southeastern region. The State's revised plan contained a second majority-black district in the north-central region. The new district stretches approximately 160 miles along Interstate 85 and, for much of its length, is no wider than the 1-85 corridor. Appellants, five North Carolina residents, filed this action against appellee state and federal officials, claiming that the State had created an unconstitutional racial gerrymander in violation of, among other things, the Fourteenth Amendment. They alleged that the two districts concentrated a majority of black voters arbitrarily without regard to considerations such as compactness, contiguousness, geographical boundaries, or political subdivisions, in order to create congressional districts along racial lines and to assure the election of two black representatives. The three-judge District Court held that it lacked subject matter jurisdiction over the federal appellees. It also dismissed the complaint against the state appellees, finding, among other things, that, under *United Jewish Organizations of Williams burgh, Inc. v. Carey,* 430 U. S. 144 *(UJO),* appellants had failed to state an equal protection claim because favoring minority voters was not discriminatory in the constitutional sense and the plan did not lead to proportional underrepresentation of white voters statewide.

Held:

Appellants have stated a claim under the Equal Protection Clause by alleging that the reapportionment scheme is so irrational on its face that it can be understood only as an effort to segregate voters into separate districts on the basis of race, and that the separation lacks sufficient justification. Pp. 639-652.

(a) The District Court properly dismissed the claims against the federal appellees. Appellants' racial gerrymandering claims must be examined against the backdrop of this country's long history of racial discrimination in voting. Pp. 639-642.

(b) Classifications of citizens based solely on race are by their nature odious to a free people whose institutions are founded upon the doctrine of equality, because they threaten to stigmatize persons by reason of their membership in a racial group and to incite racial hostility. Thus, state legislation that expressly distinguishes among citizens on account of race-whether it contains an explicit distinction or is "unexplainable on grounds other than race," *Arlington Heights* v. *Metropolitan Housing Development Corp.*, 429 U. S. 252, 266—must be narrowly tailored to further a compelling governmental interest. See, *e. g.*, Wygant v. *Jackson Ed. of Ed.*, 476 U. S. 267, 277-278 (plurality opinion). Redistricting legislation that is alleged to be so bizarre on its face that it is unexplainable on grounds other than race demands the same close scrutiny, regardless of the motivations underlying its adoption. See, *e. g.*, *Gomillion* v. *Lightfoot,* 364 U. S. 339,341. That it may be difficult to determine from the face of a single-member districting plan that it makes such a distinction does not mean that a racial gerrymander, once established, should receive less scrutiny than other legislation classifying citizens by race. By perpetuating stereotypical notions about members of the same racial group—that they think alike, share the same political interests, and prefer the same candidates—a racial gerrymander may exacerbate the very patterns of racial bloc voting that majority-minority districting is sometimes said to counteract. It also sends to elected representatives the message that their primary obligation is to represent only that group's members, rather than their constituency as a whole. Since the holding here makes it unnecessary to decide whether or how a reapportionment plan that, on its face, can be explained in nonracial terms successfully could be challenged, the Court expresses no view on whether the intentional creation of majority-minority districts, without more, always gives rise to an equal protection claim. Pp. 642-649.

(c) The classification of citizens by race threatens special harms that are not present in this Court's vote-dilution cases and thus warrants an analysis different from that used in assessing the validity of at-large and multimember gerrymandering schemes. In addition, nothing in the Court's decisions compels the conclusion that racial and political gerrymanders are subject to the same constitutional scrutiny; in fact, this country's long and persistent history of racial discrimination in voting and the Court's Fourteenth Amendment jurisprudence would seem to compel the opposite conclusion. Nor is there any support for the argument that racial gerrymandering poses no constitutional difficulties when the lines drawn favor the minority, since equal protection analysis is not dependent on the race of those burdened or benefited by a particular classification, *Richmond* v. *J. A. Croson Co.*, 488 U. S. 469,494 (plurality opinion). Finally, the highly fractured decision in *UJO* does not foreclose the claim recognized here, which is analytically distinct from the vote-dilution claim made there. Pp. 649-652.

2. If, on remand, the allegations of a racial gerrymander are not contradicted, the District Court must determine whether the plan is narrowly tailored to further a compelling governmental interest. A covered jurisdiction's interest in creating majority-minority districts in order to comply with the nonretrogression rule under § 5 of the Voting Rights Act does not give it *carte blanche* to engage in racial gerrymandering. The parties' arguments about whether the plan was necessary to avoid dilution of black voting strength in violation of § 2 of the Act and whether the State's interpretation of § 2 is unconstitutional were not developed below, and the issues remain open for consideration on remand. It is also unnecessary to decide at this stage of the litigation whether the plan advances a state interest distinct from the Act: eradicating the effects of past racial discrimination. Although the State argues that it had a strong basis for concluding that remedial action was warranted, only three Justices in *UJO* were prepared to say that States have a significant interest in minimizing the consequences of racial bloc voting apart from the Act's requirements and without regard for sound districting principles. Pp. 653-657.

3. The Court expresses no view on whether appellants successfully could have challenged a district such as that suggested by the Attorney General or whether their complaint stated a claim under other constitutional provisions. Pp. 657-658.

808 F. Supp. 461, reversed and remanded.

O'CONNOR, J., delivered the opinion of the Court, in which REHNQUIST, C. J., and SCALIA, KENNEDY, and THOMAS, JJ., joined. WHITE, J., filed a dissenting opinion, in which BLACKMUN and STEVENS, JJ., joined, *post,* p. 658. BLACKMUN, J., *post,* p. 676, STEVENS, J., *post,* p. 676, and SOUTER, J., *post,* p. 679, filed dissenting opinions.

Glossary

Equal Protection Clause: a part of the text of the Fourteenth Amendment to the U.S. Constitution requiring states to govern impartially and treat people equally; states are not allowed to differentiate between individuals on differences that are not relevant to a legitimate government objective

Fourteenth Amendment: an amendment to the U.S. Constitution that discusses many aspects of citizenship and the rights of citizens; among other things, it includes the equal protection and due process clauses

gerrymandering: manipulating the boundaries of an electoral district to favor a party or class of people

plurality opinion: an appellate opinion that does not have enough judges' votes to constitute a majority

Document Themes

The term "gerrymandering" is derived from the name of Massachusetts Governor Elbridge Gerry, whose administration enacted a law in 1812 defining new election districts. The law consolidated most of the Federalist Party votes into a few districts, giving Democratic-Republicans the lion's share of representation. One of the district outlines looked like a salamander and inspired a satirical cartoon in the *Boston Gazette* that showed the districts in the shape of a winged animal called a "Gerry-mander."

Gerrymandering is used to draw electoral district boundaries to give one political party an advantage over others or to dilute the voting power of members of ethnic or racial groups. It was generally thought that disputes regarding political gerrymandering could not be decided by federal courts but had to appeal to the legislative or executive branches. However, in the 1986 case *Davis v. Bandemer*, a plurality of the Supreme held that political gerrymanders could be declared unconstitutional under the Equal Protection Clause if the resulting system "will consistently degrade a voter's or a group of voters' influence in the political process as a whole."

Shaw v. Reno (1993) was the first racial gerrymander case heard by the Supreme Court. In *Shaw*, the Court held that electoral districts with boundaries that can only be explained based on race can be challenged as violating the Equal Protection Clause. *Shaw*'s holding appeared to place limits on the traditionally broad interpretation of the Voting Rights Act of 1965.

The Voting Rights Act (VRA) is landmark legislation that prohibits racial discrimination in voting. At the height of the civil rights movement, it was signed into law by President Lyndon B. Johnson. It provides a means to enforce the voting rights guaranteed by the Fourteenth and Fifteenth Amendments to the U.S. Constitution. It is one of the most far-reaching pieces of civil rights legislation in U.S. history.

Sections 2 and 5 of the VRA prohibit the creation of electoral districts that dilute the votes of protected minorities. In addition, the Supreme Court held that the Equal Protection Clause of the Fourteenth Amendment also can prevent creating districts that favor protected minorities. In 1993, *Shaw* was the first case that recognized affirmative "racial gerrymandering" claims were also valid.

In the 1995 case *Miller v. Johnson*, the Supreme Court extended *Shaw*'s admonitions about racial reapportionment to argue that voters' rights are violated whenever "race was the predominant factor motivating the legislature's decision to place a significant number of voters within or without a particular district," irrespective of shape. If a court determines that racial considerations were the dominant factor, the redistricting plan is "racially gerrymandered" and is subject to strict scrutiny review. Under strict scrutiny, the plan will only be considered constitutional if it is narrowly tailored to advance a compelling state interest.

In 1996's *Bush v. Vera*, a plurality of the Court indicated that complying with Sections 2 or 5 of the VRA constituted "compelling interests." Since *Bush*, lower courts have only allowed racial gerrymandering when complying with one of these sections.

In *Shelby County v. Holder* (2013), however, a more conservative Court overturned key section of the VRA, leaving issues involving racial gerrymandering an open question, or at least less subject to a high level of scrutiny than before.

—*Noëlle Sinclair, JD, MLS*

Bibliography and Additional Reading

Aleinikoff, T. Alexander, and Samuel Issacharoff. "Race and Redistricting: Drawing Constitutional Lines After *Shaw v. Reno*." *Michigan Law Review* 92, no. 588 (1993).

Curtis, Robert A. "Race-Based Equal Protection Claims After *Shaw v. Reno*." *Duke Law Journal* 44, no. 298 (1994), scholarship.law.duke.edu/dlj/vol44/iss2/3.

Grofman, Bernard. "Would Vince Lombardi Have Been Right if He Had Said, 'When It Comes to Redistricting, Race isn't Everything, It's the Only Thing'?" *Cardozo Law Review* 14, no. 1237 (1993).

Keena, Alex, et al. *Gerrymandering the States: Partisanship, Race, and the Transformation of American Federalism.* New York: Cambridge UP, 2021.

Lublin, David. *The Paradox of Representation: Racial Gerrymandering and Minority Interests in Congress.* Princeton, NJ: Princeton UP, 2020.

Pildes, Richard H., and Richard G. Niemi. "Expressive Harms, 'Bizarre Districts,' and Voting Rights: Evaluating Election District Appearances after *Shaw v. Reno.*" *Michigan Law Review* 92, no. 483 (1993).

Rush, Mark E. "From *Shaw v. Reno* to *Miller v. Johnson*: Minority Representation and State Compliance with the Voting Rights Act." *Publius* 25, no. 155 (1995), www.jstor.org/stable/3330692.

■ Bush v. Gore

Date: December 12, 2000
Author: Per curiam
Genre: court opinion

Summary Overview

In the well-known case Bush v. Gore, *the U.S. Supreme Court reversed a Florida Supreme Court's authorization to proceed with a selective manual recount of that state's U.S. presidential election ballots, following problems in tallying ballots in some counties there. The 5–4 decision to stop the recount effort effectively awarded Florida's 25 electoral votes—and thus the presidential election itself—to Republican candidate George W. Bush, who was just slightly ahead in the tally prior to the start of the recount.*

Defining Moment

It was the evening of November 7, 2000, and a clear winner had yet to emerge in the United States presidential election between George W. Bush and Al Gore. Broadcast and print media supplied contradictor exit polling information and it became increasingly clear that races in Oregon and New Mexico would remain too close to call a clear winner for some days. The election ultimately came down to the voting results in Florida. Gore was initially projected to the winner in Florida but it was later reported that Bush had an insurmountable lead. Gore called Bush to concede the election. However, by early the following morning it was revealed that the vote count was much closer than Gore's staff had originally predicted. There were fewer than 600 votes separating the two candidates and the margin was narrowing. At approximately 3:00 a.m. Gore called Bush to retract his earlier concession. Pursuant to Florida election law, a machine recount of all votes cast was required when the margin of victory was less than 0.5%. Here the gap appeared to be approximately 0.01%, or less than 600 votes.

Both campaigns put a legal team in action in Florida, both filing lawsuits contending conflicts of interest. Notably, Bush's brother, Jeb Bush, was the governor of Florida and Florida secretary of state, Katherine Harris, was the co-chair of Bush's Florida campaign. Alternatively, Florida Attorney General Bob Butterworth, chaired Gore's campaign. A machine recount was completed on November 10, 2000, and the Bush campaign led by 327 votes out of the six million votes cast. Court challenges were filed regarding the legality of hand recounting ballots that was occurring in certain Florida counties.

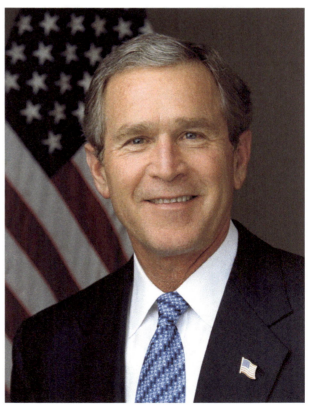

George W. Bush. Photo via Wikimedia Commons. [Public domain.]

Al Gore. Photo via Wikimedia Commons. [Public domain.]

Meanwhile, the broadcast and print media nationally were running stories regarding voter fraud, and inaccurate tallying of votes. Issues with paper ballots including "hanging chads" (where paper ballots were not completely punched) and "pregnant chads" (where paper ballots had been dimpled but not pierced during voting) were issues in the forefront. There were also allegations of "overvoting," where an individual ballot recorded multiple votes for the same elected office as well as "undervoting", where a ballot contained no votes for a particular elected office. Palm Beach County had a particular problem with a butterfly ballot design which caused confusion with Gore voters, prompting an alleged 3,400 inadvertent votes for a third-party candidate because of the name layout on the ballot.

Harris initially sought to certify the state election results on November 14 but the Florida Supreme Court ruled that hand recounts of any questionable ballots should proceed in the four counties at issue and that those results should be included in the state's final count. There were approximately 50 individual lawsuits in the following month, all relating to the vote counting, recounting and certification deadlines.

On December 4, 2000, the Florida Supreme Court ruled that hand recounts should continue in all the counties where a statistically significant number of undervotes existed. The Bush campaign responded by filing a lawsuit in the United States Supreme Court.

The Court granted a writ of certiorari, agreeing to hear the matter. On December 9, 2000, in an unprecedented time period, the U S Supreme Court ruled in a 5-4 decision that the hand recounts must stop and it agreed to hear oral arguments from both parties. On December 11, 2000, the arguments took place and both sides presented their cases. The Bush team contended the Florida Supreme Court exceeded its authority by authorizing the hand recounts. The Gore team argued that the matter had been settled at the state level and it was not a matter for the federal courts to decide. The following day, the Court, in a 7-2 vote, overruled the Florida decision and held that the various methods and standards used for the recount process violated the Equal Protection clause of the U.S. Constitution. The court ruled 5-4 on the remedy that should be provided, with the majority holding that the Florida Supreme Court's decision had created new election law which was a right only for the Florida legislature and that no recount could be held in time to satisfy a federal deadline for the selection of state electors. The majority's opinion was heavily criticized by the minority justices. The dissent argued that, while the recount process was somewhat flawed, it should be permitted to proceed, ensuring the constitutional protection of each vote and should not be subjected to an arbitrary deadline. Notably, Justice Ruth Bader Ginsburg noted in her dissent, "I dissent" rather than the traditional "I respectfully dissent." As a result of the decision, the hand recounting process was terminated and Gore officially conceded the election on December 13, 2000, noting, "While I strongly disagree with the court's decision, I accept it."

Legal scholars believe that without the United States Supreme Court intervening, the Florida election decision would have most likely worked itself out on the floor of the Florida legislature and most likely with the election of Bush. The Supreme Court's decision to take part in the process has been seen by some as either the Supreme Court risking its reputation for being apolitical in order to avoid an election crisis and by others as overstepping its bounds by unnecessarily intervening and creating an equal protection right for essentially one individual as the court noted in its opinion, "[o]ur consideration is limited to our present circumstances." In any event, although the Court noted the limited precedential value of its decision, the effects of *Bush v. Gore* have been noted in several federal appellate court cases as having precedence in election law in issues from a challenge to voting systems in Ohio, to voting recount litigation in Minnesota.

Author Biography

Unlike most U.S. Supreme Court opinions, the ruling in *Bush v. Gore* was not signed by a single justice as author. Rather, the opinion was issued as a per curiam ruling, or an unsigned ruling—written by one or more justices but presented as merely being "from the court." Supreme Court justices often issue a per curiam ruling when they wish to express a result that enjoyed the full and total institutional support of all nine justices. At other times, they issue such a ruling when a case is so lacking in complexity that no member of the Court wishes to commit the time to draft and sign his or her own opinion. Per curiam rulings also can provide cover in politically sensitive cases, shielding the writing justice within the protecting arms of the whole Court. Last, a per curiam ruling, especially in a case featuring dissent among the nine justices, can be a means of expressing the barest measure of consensus.

Most likely, the Court adopted the per curiam approach to authorship in *Bush v. Gore* for all of these reasons. With little time to spare, the opinion was probably written in different chambers and later

Protest at the Supreme Court, December 2000. Photo by Elvert Barnes, via Wikimedia Commons.

Protestors, 2000. Photo by David from Washington, D.C., via Wikimedia Commons.

cobbled together to form a whole—n point of fact, the evidence that exists suggests that most of this ruling was written by Justices Anthony Kennedy and Sandra Day O'Connor working in tandem. The per curiam approach also served as a means to consensus, permitting the members of the 7-2 majority in agreement on equal protection to reach a rough accord on the basic proposition that the Florida recount was flawed and unconstitutional; with this accord expressed in the per curiam statement, the justices were free to write separate concurring and dissenting opinions further detailing their personal views. Of course, the per curiam ruling also spared one of the justices from having to sign his or her name to an opinion that, owing to severe time constraints, was less coherent than the authors might have wished. So, too, it provided protection from the ruling's politically explosive impact. Perhaps above all, the per curiam statement gave the Court's ruling an air of consensus that actually did not exist, implied that the ruling was of modest scope, and supported the assertion that the Court was only reluctantly entering the fray to fulfill its constitutional role.

Historical Document

Bush v. Gore

531 U.S. 98, 148 L. Ed. 2d 388, 121 S. Ct. 525 (2000)

Wednesday, Dec. 13, 2000

[Here are excerpts from the U.S. Supreme Court decision in *Bush v. Gore*, from the per curiam opinion of seven justices.]

The closeness of this election, and the multitude of legal challenges which have followed in its wake, have brought into sharp focus a common, if heretofore unnoticed, phenomenon. Nationwide statistics reveal that an estimated 2% of ballots cast do not register a vote for President for whatever reason, including deliberately choosing no candidate at all or some voter error, such as voting for two candidates or insufficiently marking a ballot... In certifying election results, the votes eligible for inclusion in the certification are the votes meeting the properly established legal requirements.

This case has shown that punch card balloting machines can produce an unfortunate number of ballots which are not punched in a clean, complete way by the voter. After the current counting, it is likely legislative bodies nationwide will examine ways to improve the mechanisms and machinery for voting...

The individual citizen has no federal constitutional right to vote for electors for the President of the United States unless and until the state legislature chooses a statewide election as the means to implement its power to appoint members of the Electoral College. U.S. Const., Art. II, §1. This is the source for the statement in McPherson v. Blacker, 146 U.S. 1, 35 (1892), that the State legislature's power to select the manner for appointing electors is plenary; it may, if it so chooses, select the electors itself, which indeed was the manner used by State legislatures in several States for many years after the Framing of our Constitution. Id., at 28-33. History has now favored the voter, and in each of the several States the citizens themselves vote for Presidential electors. When the state legislature vests the right to vote for President in its people, the right to vote as the legislature has prescribed is fundamental; and one source of its fundamental nature lies in the equal weight accorded to each vote and the equal dignity owed to each voter. The State, of course, after granting the franchise in the special context of Article II, can take back the power to appoint electors. See id., at 35 ("[T]here is no doubt of the right of the legislature to resume the power at any time, for it can neither be taken away nor abdicated") (quoting S. Rep. No. 395, 43d Cong., 1st Sess.).

The right to vote is protected in more than the initial allocation of the franchise. Equal protection applies as well to the manner of its exercise. Having once granted the right to vote on equal terms, the State may not, by later arbitrary and disparate treatment, value one person's vote over that of another. See, e.g., Harper v. Virginia Bd. of Elections, 383 U.S. 663, 665 (1966) ("[O]nce the franchise is granted to the electorate, lines may not be drawn which are inconsistent with the Equal Protection Clause of the Fourteenth Amendment"). It must be remembered that "the right of suffrage can be denied by a debasement or dilution of the weight of a citizen's vote just as effectively as by wholly prohibiting the free exercise of the franchise." Reynolds v. Sims, 377 U.S. 533, 555 (1964).

There is no difference between the two sides of the present controversy on these basic propositions. Respondents say that the very purpose of vindicating the right to vote justifies the recount procedures now at issue. The question before us, however, is whether the recount procedures the Florida Supreme Court has adopted are consistent with its obligation to avoid arbitrary and disparate treatment of the members of its electorate...

The Supreme Court of Florida has said that the legislature intended the State's electors to "participate fully in the federal electoral process" ... as provided in 3 U.S.C. 5.

That statute, in turn, requires that any controversy or contest that is designed to lead to a conclusive selection of electors be completed by December 12. That date is upon us, and there is no recount procedure in place under the State Supreme Court's order that comports with minimal constitutional standards.

Because it is evident that any recount seeking to meet the December 12 date will be unconstitutional for the reasons we have discussed, we reverse the judgment of the Supreme Court of Florida ordering a recount to proceed. Seven Justices of the Court agree that there are constitutional problems with the recount ordered by the Florida Supreme Court that demand a remedy.... The only disagreement is as to the remedy.

Because the Florida Supreme Court has said that the Florida Legislature intended to obtain the safe-harbor benefits of 3 U. S. C. 5, Justice Breyer's proposed remedy remanding to the Florida Supreme Court for its ordering of a constitutionally proper contest until December 18—contemplates action in violation of the Florida election code, and hence could not be part of an "appropriate" order ....

None are more conscious of the vital limits on judicial authority than are the members of this Court, and none stand more in admiration of the Constitution's design to leave the selection of the President to the people, through their legislatures, and to the political sphere. When contending parties invoke the process of the courts, however, it becomes our unsought responsibility to resolve the federal and constitutional issues the judicial system has been forced to confront.

The judgment of the Supreme Court of Florida is reversed, and the case is remanded for further proceedings not inconsistent with this opinion.

———

From Chief Justice Rehnquist, with whom Justice Scalia and Justice Thomas join, concurring:

We join the per curiam opinion. We write separately because we believe there are additional grounds that require us to reverse the Florida Supreme Court's decision. We deal here not with an ordinary election, but with an election for the President of the United States ...

In most cases, comity and respect for federalism compel us to defer to the decisions of state courts on issues of state law. That practice reflects our understanding that the decisions of state courts are definitive pronouncements of the will of the States as sovereigns ... Of course, in ordinary cases, the distribution of powers among the branches of a State's government raises no questions of federal constitutional law, subject to the requirement that the government be republican in character.... But there are a few exceptional cases in which the Constitution imposes a duty or confers a power on a particular branch of a State's government. This is one of them.

———

From Justice Stevens, with whom Justice Ginsburg and Justice Breyer join, dissenting:

When questions arise about the meaning of state laws, including election laws, it is our settled practice to accept the opinions of the highest courts of the States as providing the final answers. On rare occasions, however, either federal statutes or the Federal Constitution may require federal judicial intervention in state elections. This is not such an occasion. The federal questions that ultimately emerged in this case are not substantial. ...

Nor are petitioners correct in asserting that the failure of the Florida Supreme Court to specify in detail the precise manner in which the intent of the voter, Fla. Stat. 101.5614(5) (Supp. 2001), is to be determined rises to the level of a constitutional violation. ...

The Florida statutory standard is consistent with the practice of the majority of States, which apply either an 'intent of the voter' standard or an impossible to determine the elector's choice standard in ballot recounts. ...

Admittedly, the use of differing substandards for determining voter intent in different counties employing similar voting systems may raise serious concerns. Those concerns are alleviated, if not eliminated, by the fact that a single impartial magistrate will ultimately adjudicate all objections arising from the recount process. ...

In the interest of finality, however, the majority effectively orders the disenfranchisement of an unknown number of voters whose ballots reveal their intent, and are therefore legal votes under state law, but were for some reason rejected by ballot-counting machines.

Finally, neither in this case, nor in its earlier opinion in *Palm Beach County Canvassing Bd. v. Harris* ... did the Florida Supreme Court make any substantive change in Florida electoral law. Its decisions were rooted in long-established precedent and were consistent with the relevant statutory provisions, taken as a whole. It did what courts do—it decided the case before it in light of the legislature's intent to leave no legally cast vote uncounted. ...

What must underlie petitioners' entire federal assault on the Florida election procedures is an unstated lack of confidence in the impartiality and capacity of the state judges who would make the critical decisions if the vote count were to proceed. Otherwise, their position is wholly without merit. The endorsement of that position by the majority of this Court can only lend credence to the most cynical appraisal of the work of judges throughout the land. It is confidence in the men and women who administer the judicial system that is the true backbone of the rule of law. Time will one day heal the wound to that confidence that will be inflicted by today's decision.

Glossary

judicial review: a constitutional doctrine which allows a court to review legislative or executive acts to determine whether they are constitutional

Equal Protection: part of the Fourteenth Amendment of the U.S. Constitution which took effect in 1868 and provides that no state should deny any person within its jurisdiction "the equal protection of the laws."

Presidential Electors: when voting for a candidate on a presidential ballot, voters are actually choosing electors when they vote for a president and vice president. Those electors in turn cast votes for those respective offices.

Protestors, 2000. Photo by David from Washington, D.C., via Wikimedia Commons.

Document Analysis

The United States Supreme Court granted certiorari in *Bush v. Gore* to address the argument that there had been a violation of the Fourteenth Amendment's equal protection clause in the manual recounts that had been ordered in Florida. It is undisputed that Art. II, § 1, cl. 2 of the U.S. Constitution clearly specifies that it is the sole right and responsibility of the state legislatures to provide for the selection of Presidential electors. Under Florida law, this had been accomplished by providing for a popular vote, the winner of which was to receive all of the state's electoral votes. Since this right had been extended to the people of Florida, the equal protection clause mandates that the right to vote not be infringed either by preventing the act of voting or by unequal treatment of votes after they have been cast. Regarding the Florida recount, the majority opinion concluded that equal protection was violated due to the lack of uniform standards on assessing voter intent on a ballot. The Court also concluded that there would not be enough time to conduct an acceptable recount before the "safe harbor" provision of the federal statute expired so that hand recount had to be terminated.

The Court was presented with several options for addressing an equal protection problem. It could have held that legal votes are defined as those that were marked correctly and counted mechanically which was the remedy argued for by Florida secretary of state Harris. However, the Florida election law as written did not support that solution. Therefore, the Court accepted the Florida Supreme Court's

President George W. Bush delivers his Inaugural Address following his swearing-in ceremony in Washington, D.C., Jan. 20, 2001.

definition of a legal vote being one that clearly shows the intention of the voter. Having accepted that a vote tabulation should seek out the intent of each voter, the court majority found that arbitrary and inconsistent state-wide standards for assessing voter intent constituted a violation of equal protection, making the Florida recount unconstitutional as it had been ordered.

In its decision, the majority did not deny that a legal recount was possible. However, it found that circumstances would not permit such a recount before the expiration of the "safe harbor" afforded by 3 U.S.C. § 5. This clause essentially guarantees that the electors selected in the general election to represent a state will be counted in the Electoral College so long as they are selected under legislation that predates the election and are chosen at least six days before the Electoral College convenes. Since Florida law is designed to take advantage of 3 U.S.C. § 5, the court majority ruled that the selection of electors could not extend past that safe harbor time without ignoring the Florida statutes, which in turn would violate Art. II, § 1, cl. 2 of the U.S. Constitution. By invoking this restricted time frame, the court majority made it infeasible to conduct a constitutional recount and concluded that it was appropriate to order the cessation of all recounts in Florida.

Several of the dissenting Justices argue persuasively that in this case, the safe harbor clause can be ignored without causing any harm. Justice Stevens noted in his dissent that the Hawaiian slate of electors counted in the 1960 election was not certified until January 4, 1961 but was still counted by Congress. This effectively refutes the argument that missing the safe harbor deadline would risk the disenfranchisement of millions of Florida voters who cast mechanically-recordable ballots. If, as the Court defined, the undervotes and overvotes in Florida represent potential legal votes, it is a violation of equal protection for these votes not to be counted. In the majority's own words, "Having once granted the right to vote on equal terms, the State may not, by later arbitrary and disparate treatment, value one person's vote over that of another." The largest criticism by the dissent was that counting only those legal votes that happen to be easily tabulated by mechanical equipment to fulfill an unnecessary time limit for vote certification is the very definition of arbitrary and disparate treatment and by refusing to allow a legal recount to go on for as long as possible, the court majority supported the very abuses that the equal protection clause is designed to prevent, even as it claimed to be ruling in the spirit of equal protection.

The Court found itself in a very difficult situation as it tried to reach a decision in *Bush v. Gore*. Regardless of the outcome, half the voting public was likely to come out feeling that their candidate had been treated unfairly. Disagreement over judicial interpretations of the law is to be expected, especially in a complicated case like *Bush v. Gore*. As the court noted it considered the case itself to be of limited precedential value based upon the facts of the particular case.

Essential Themes

In *Bush v. Gore* the Supreme Court of the United States reversed a Florida Supreme Court request for a selective manual recount of that state's U.S. presidential election ballots and ordered the hand recounting of the Florida to be halted. The Court concluded that no constitutionally adequate recount could take place prior to the safe harbor deadline set forth in federal election law. The 5–4 decision effectively awarded Florida's 25 votes in the electoral college to Republican candidate George W. Bush.

—*Michele McBride Simonelli, JD*

Bibliography and Additional Reading

Bush v. Gore, 121 S.Ct. 525 (2000). Justia: U.S. Supreme Court. supreme.justia.com/cases/federal/us/531/98/.

Edward Foley. "Voting Rules and Constitutional Law," *George Washington Law Review,* 81 Geo. Wash. L. Rev. 1836, 2013.

Hasen, Richard L. *The Supreme Court and Election Law: Judging Equality from* Baker v. Carr *to* Bush v. Gore. New York: New York UP, 2003.

Mark Tushnet. "Renorm*alizing Bush v. Gore: An Anticipatory Intellectual History,"* Georgetown Law Journal, 90 Geo. L.J. 113, 2001.

Patterson, James T. *Restless Giant: The United States from Watergate to* Bush v. Gore. New York: Oxford UP, 2005.

■ Citizens United v. Federal Election Commission

Date: January 21, 2010
Author: Justice Anthony Kennedy
Genre: court opinion

Summary Overview

Citizens United v. Federal Election Commission *transformed the electoral landscape, as well as strength-ened organizations' legal standing as regards the First Amendment. Justice Anthony Kennedy, considered a moderate on the Supreme Court, wrote a lengthy opinion that overturned portions of the 2002 Bipartisan Campaign Reform Act (BCRA), as well as portions of two earlier Supreme Court rulings. While since 1853 the Court had treated organizations as "persons" for certain legal purposes, in the 1970s certain restrictions were placed on organizations when it came to donations to political campaigns. In* Buckley v. Valeo (1976) *the Court ruled that money is effectively "speech" and, as such, its use in the political forum was protected by the First Amendment. However, even though earlier Watergate-inspired campaign finance reforms were curbed by this ruling, Congress continued to seek ways to regulate campaign fundraising and expenditures in order to control the influence of big money. One result was the BCRA, which established a prohibition on "soft money" (money given to a political party but not for direct campaign expenses), a limitation on electioneering communication, a prohibition on using general funds from a for-profit corporation or a labor union for campaign donations, and a ban on contributions by minors.*

When Citizens United came before the Supreme Court, the Court used this case to examine all of the BCRA, not just those provisions that Citizens United *claimed were unconstitutional. In its ruling, the Court held that most of the BCRA was unconstitutional and put forward the assertion that all organizations had total freedom of speech in the electoral process.*

The organization Citizens United is a conservative non-profit entity that has produced a substantial number of documentary, and documentary-style, films. It was a controversy with the Federal Election Commission (FEC) over a film critical of Hillary Clinton, prior to the 2008 election, that led to the court case. Citizens United *wanted the freedom to distribute and promote the film without interference from the FEC. Ultimately, the ruling by the Supreme Court went far beyond what might have been necessary to deal with the specific case. The Court not only ruled that films such as this were protected under the First Amendment, it ruled that all campaign expenditures by organizations were also protected. Thus,* Citizens United *facilitated a massive expansion of campaign spending on ads for or against candidates, or initiatives, the only proviso being that organizations sponsoring such ads must clearly state that they are behind them.*

Justice Anthony Kennedy wrote the majority opinion. Photo via Wikimedia Commons. [Public domain.]

Defining Moment

Throughout the history of the United States, free speech has been one aspect of life that has been held in high esteem. While those involved with the adoption of the Bill of Rights may have had people in mind when it was written, the rights granted through freedom of speech and of the press were not specified as applying only to citizens, or even to people. While mega-corporations did not exist at that time, newspapers, and similar publications, were businesses, even if wholly owned by one person. Thus, the right of expression was broadly conferred to people and companies within the American society. The type of speech historically most protected was politically-oriented assertions and discussions.

In the slightly more than two hundred and twenty years between when the First Amendment was written and the *Citizens United v. Federal Election Commission* ruling was made, the technology available for communicating ideas, including political ideas, changed tremendously. However, it was the changes that had been made in the fifty years prior to the ruling that created the circumstances from which the case was derived. While in the mid-twentieth century electronic communication, radio or television, was only offered through a few networks and local channels, by the first decade of the twenty-first century, audio and video communications could be "broadcast" by almost anyone. The technology to create and "transmit" ideas and information of all types was relatively inexpensive and available to the public. Thus, when individuals or organizations wanted to support, or hinder, a political campaign, it could be done relatively easily via the internet or a cable company, and the potential audience for each "broadcast" could be in the millions.

Concern over groups, or rich individuals, having too much power within the political system had developed throughout the history of the United States. In 1907, the Tillman Act outlawed corporations giving money to individuals running for federal office. In 1947, a similar law was passed outlawing contributions by labor unions. At the end of the twentieth century, many rich individuals and interest groups (including corporations and unions) started greatly

Hillary: The Movie, *a film made by Citizens United that was critical of Presidential candidate Hillary Clinton, figured largely in the case. Photo via Wikimedia Commons. [Public domain.]*

increasing the amount they were spending in support of their preferred candidates through unregulated support. As a result, in 2002 the BCRA was passed, which made campaign contribution and expenditure regulations more restrictive for individuals and organizations. Another provision outlawed electronic "electioneering" by corporations in the period of 60 days prior to a general election, or 30 days prior to a primary election. Citizens United had produced a video critical of Senator Hillary Clinton, which it wanted to distribute during the prohibited period around the 2008 primaries, when Clinton was running for the Democratic nomination for president. Because the FEC was charged with overseeing the regulations established by the BCRA, Citizens United filed a suit against it to block enforcement of the law.

The Court, with the majority opinion written by Justice Kennedy, took a broad view of the issue and the ruling it made went far beyond the specifics of the

President Barack Obama stated that "this ruling strikes at our democracy itself" and "I can't think of anything more devastating to the public interest." Photo by Ari Levinson, via Wikimedia Commons.

case or what was needed to remedy the issue. Thus, the ruling did away with the ban on "broadcasting" political message by corporations and much more. It went beyond BCRA to the law that had established the FEC, doing away with restrictions that had been in place since 1971. The Court ruled that while the government had a need to inhibit corruption, the BCRA, and other laws and previous rulings, were too broad, so they were mainly overturned. However, the part of the BCRA that mandated identifying which group created the electronic communication was held as constitutional. Thus, beginning in 2010, all types of corporations were free to independently engage in political campaigning for, or against, a specific candidate or cause. Some have seen this as a disaster for American democracy, while others believe it has given all legal entities, individuals or corporations, the same right to fully participate in the electoral process through the free speech guaranteed in the First Amendment.

Author Biography

Born July 23, 1936, Anthony McLeod Kennedy became a member of the Supreme Court in 1988. Having been raised in Sacramento, California, by politically active parents, Anthony J. and Gladys Kennedy, he attended Stanford University and then Harvard Law School. Following in his father's footsteps, Kennedy went into private practice in 1961, and then returned to Sacramento in 1963, when his father died. During that time he also joined the law school faculty at the University of the Pacific's McGeorge School of Law, serving until 1988. During the 1970s, while working in Sacramento, Kennedy helped Gov. Ronald Reagan rewrite the California tax code.

In 1975, President Gerald Ford nominated Kennedy to a position on the Ninth Circuit of the Court of Appeals. Confirmed in this position, Kennedy ended his private practice. During 1987, a vacancy occurred on the Supreme Court and President Reagan nominated two individuals, Robert Bork and Douglas Ginsburg, who failed to be confirmed. In November, Kennedy was nominated by Reagan for that position and in February, 1988, Kennedy was confirmed by a vote of 97-0. Since joining the court, he has often been seen as a moderate, the swing vote on many cases. In 2017, rumors of a pending retirement have circulated although have not been confirmed. However, given his age and length of service it can be anticipated that a retirement in the near future is not out of the realm of possibility.

Historical Document

Justice Kennedy delivered the opinion of the Court.

Federal law prohibits corporations and unions from using their general treasury funds to make independent expenditures for speech defined as an "electioneering communication" or for speech expressly advocating the election or defeat of a candidate....

I

A

Citizens United is a nonprofit corporation. It brought this action in the United States District Court for the District of Columbia. A three-judge court later convened to hear the cause. The resulting judgment gives rise to this appeal.

Citizens United has an annual budget of about $12 million. Most of its funds are from donations by individuals; but, in addition, it accepts a small portion of its funds from for-profit corporations.

In January 2008, Citizens United released a film entitled *Hillary: The Movie*.... It is a 90-minute documentary about then-Senator Hillary Clinton, who was a candidate in the Democratic Party's 2008 Presidential primary elections. *Hillary* mentions Senator Clinton by name and depicts interviews with political commentators and other persons, most of them quite critical of Senator Clinton. *Hillary* was released in theaters and on DVD, but Citizens United wanted to increase distribution by making it available through video-on-demand.

... In December 2007, a cable company offered, for a payment of $1.2 million, to make *Hillary* available on a video-on-demand channel called "Elections '08." Some video-on-demand services require viewers to pay a small fee to view a selected program, but here the proposal was to make *Hillary* available to viewers free of charge.

To implement the proposal, Citizens United was prepared to pay for the video-on-demand; and to promote the film, it produced two 10-second ads and one 30-second ad for *Hillary*. Each ad includes a short (and, in our view, pejorative) statement about Senator Clinton, followed by the name of the movie and the movie's Website address. Citizens United desired to promote the video-on-demand offering by running advertisements on broadcast and cable television.

B

Before the Bipartisan Campaign Reform Act of 2002 (BCRA), federal law prohibited—and still does prohibit—corporations and unions from using general treasury funds to make direct contributions to candidates or independent expenditures that expressly advocate the election or defeat of a candidate, through any form of media, in connection with certain qualified federal elections.... An electioneering communication is defined as "any broadcast, cable, or satellite communication" that "refers to a clearly identified candidate for Federal office" and is made within 30 days of a primary or 60 days of a general election. The Federal Election Commission's (FEC) regulations further define an electioneering communication as a communication that is "publicly distributed."... Corporations and unions are barred from using their general treasury funds for express advocacy or electioneering communications. They may establish, however, a "separate segregated fund" (known as a political action committee, or PAC) for these purposes. The moneys received by the segregated fund are limited to donations from stockholders and employees of the corporation or, in the case of unions, members of the union.

C

Citizens United wanted to make *Hillary* available through video-on-demand within 30 days of the 2008 primary elections. It feared, however, that both the film and the ads would be covered by §441b's ban on corporate-funded independent expenditures, thus subjecting the corporation to civil and criminal penalties under §437g. In December 2007, Citizens United sought declaratory and injunctive relief against the FEC. It argued that (1) §441b is unconstitutional as applied to *Hillary*; and (2) BCRA's disclaimer and disclosure requirements, BCRA §§201 and 311, are unconstitutional as applied to *Hillary* and to the three ads for the movie.

The District Court denied Citizens United's motion for a preliminary injunction... and then granted the FEC's motion for summary judgment.... The court held that §441b was facially constitutional under *McConnell*, and that §441b was constitutional as applied to *Hillary* because it was "susceptible of no other interpretation than to inform the electorate that Senator Clinton is unfit for office, that the United States would be a dangerous place in a President Hillary Clinton world, and that viewers should vote against her." The court also rejected Citizens United's challenge to BCRA's disclaimer and disclosure requirements. It noted that "the Supreme Court has written approvingly of disclosure provisions triggered by political speech even though the speech itself was constitutionally protected under the First Amendment."

We noted probable jurisdiction. 555 U. S. ___ (2008). The case was reargued in this Court after the Court asked the parties to file supplemental briefs addressing whether we should overrule either or both *Austin* and the part of *McConnell* which addresses the facial validity of 2 U. S. C. §441b.

II

Before considering whether *Austin* should be overruled, we first address whether Citizens United's claim that §441b cannot be applied to *Hillary* may be resolved on other, narrower grounds.

A

Citizens United contends that §441b does not cover *Hillary*, as a matter of statutory interpretation, because the film does not qualify as an "electioneering communication."... Under the definition of electioneering communication, the video-on-demand showing of *Hillary* on cable television would have been a "cable... communication" that "refer[red] to a clearly identified candidate for Federal office" and that was made within 30 days of a primary election. Citizens United, however, argues that *Hillary* was not "publicly distributed," because a single video-on-demand transmission is sent only to a requesting cable converter box and each separate transmission, in most instances, will be seen by just one household—not 50,000 or more persons.

This argument ignores the regulation's instruction on how to determine whether a cable transmission "[c]an be received by 50,000 or more persons." The regulation provides that the number of people who can receive a cable transmission is determined by the number of cable subscribers in the relevant area. Here, Citizens United wanted to use a cable video-on-demand system that had 34.5 million subscribers nationwide. Thus, *Hillary* could have been received by 50,000 persons or more.

One *amici* brief asks us, alternatively, to construe the condition that the communication "[c]an be received by 50,000 or more persons," to require "a plausible likelihood that the communication will be viewed by 50,000 or more potential voters"—as opposed to requiring only that the communication is "technologically capable" of being seen by that many people. Whether the population and demographic statistics in a proposed viewing area consisted of 50,000 registered voters—but not "infants, pre-teens, or otherwise electorally ineligible recipients"—would be a required determination, subject to judicial challenge and review, in any case where the issue was in doubt.

In our view the statute cannot be saved by limiting the reach of 2 U. S. C. §441b through this suggested interpretation. In addition to the costs and burdens of litigation, this result would require a calculation as to the number of people a particular communication is likely to reach, with an inaccurate estimate potentially subjecting the speaker to criminal sanctions. The First Amendment does not permit laws that force speakers to retain a campaign finance attorney, conduct demographic marketing research, or seek declaratory rulings before discussing the most salient political issues of our day. Prolix laws chill speech for the same reason that vague laws chill speech: People "of common intelligence must necessarily guess at [the law's] meaning and differ as to its application."... The Government may not render a ban on political speech constitutional by carving out a limited exemption through an amorphous regulatory interpretation....

B

Citizens United next argues that §441b may not be applied to *Hillary* under the approach taken in WRTL. *McConnell* decided that §441b(b)(2)'s definition of an "electioneering communication" was facially constitutional insofar as it restricted speech that was "the functional equivalent of express advocacy" for or against a specific candidate. WRTL then found an unconstitutional application of §441b where the speech was not "express advocacy or its functional equivalent." As explained by The Chief Justice's controlling opinion in *WRTL*, the functional-equivalent test is objective: "a court should find that [a communication] is the functional equivalent of express advocacy only if [it] is susceptible of no reasonable interpretation other than as an appeal to vote for or against a specific candidate."

Under this test, *Hillary* is equivalent to express advocacy. The movie, in essence, is a feature-length negative advertisement that urges viewers to vote against Senator Clinton for President. In light of historical footage, interviews with persons critical of her, and voiceover narration, the film would be understood by most viewers as an extended criticism of Senator Clinton's character and her fitness for the office of the Presidency....

Citizens United argues that *Hillary* is just "a documentary film that examines certain historical events." We disagree. The movie's consistent emphasis is on the relevance of these events to Senator Clinton's candidacy for President....

As the District Court found, there is no reasonable interpretation of *Hillary* other than as an appeal to vote against Senator Clinton. Under the standard stated in *McConnell* and further elaborated in *WRTL*, the film qualifies as the functional equivalent of express advocacy.

C

Citizens United further contends that §441b should be invalidated as applied to movies shown through video-on-demand, arguing that this delivery system has a lower risk of distorting the political process than do television ads. On what we might call conventional television, advertising spots reach viewers who have chosen a channel or a program for reasons unrelated to the advertising. With video-on-demand, by contrast, the viewer selects a program after taking "a series of affirmative steps": subscribing to cable; navigating through various menus; and selecting the program....

While some means of communication may be less effective than others at influencing the public in different contexts, any effort by the Judiciary to decide which means of communications are to be preferred for the particular type of message and speaker would raise questions as to the courts' own lawful authority. Substantial questions would arise if courts were to begin saying what means of speech should be preferred or disfavored. And in all events, those differentiations might soon prove to be irrelevant or outdated by technologies that are in rapid flux....

Courts, too, are bound by the First Amendment. We must decline to draw, and then redraw, constitutional lines based on the particular media or technology used to disseminate political speech from a particular speaker.... The interpretive process itself would create an inevitable, pervasive, and serious risk of chilling protected speech pending the drawing of fine distinctions that, in the end, would themselves be questionable. First Amendment standards, however, "must give the benefit of any doubt to protecting rather than stifling speech."...

D

Citizens United also asks us to carve out an exception to §441b's expenditure ban for nonprofit corporate political speech funded overwhelmingly by individuals. As an alternative to reconsidering *Austin*, the Government also seems to prefer this approach. This line of analysis, however, would be unavailing.

In *MCFL*, the Court found unconstitutional §441b's restrictions on corporate expenditures as applied to nonprofit corporations that were formed for the sole purpose of promoting political ideas, did not engage in business activities, and did not accept contributions from for-profit corporations or labor unions.... Citizens United does not qualify for the *MCFL* exemption, however, since some funds used to make the movie were donations from for-profit corporations.

The Government suggests we could find BCRA's Wellstone Amendment unconstitutional, sever it from the statute, and hold that Citizens United's speech is exempt from §441b's ban under BCRA's Snowe-Jeffords Amendment.... Citizens United would not qualify for the Snowe-Jeffords exemption, under its terms as written, because *Hillary* was funded in part with donations from for-profit corporations.

Consequently, to hold for Citizens United on this argument, the Court would be required to revise the text of MCFL, sever BCRA's Wellstone Amendment, §441b(c)(6), and ignore the plain text of BCRA's Snowe-Jeffords Amendment.... There is no principled basis for doing this without rewriting Austin's holding that the Government can restrict corporate independent expenditures for political speech.

...

E

As the foregoing analysis confirms, the Court cannot resolve this case on a narrower ground without chilling political speech, speech that is central to the meaning and purpose of the First Amendment....

Citizens United has preserved its First Amendment challenge to §441b as applied to the facts of its case; and given all the circumstances, we cannot easily address that issue without assuming a premise—the permissibility of restricting corporate political speech—that is itself in doubt....

As noted above, Citizens United's narrower arguments are not sustainable under a fair reading of the statute. In the exercise of its judicial responsibility, it is necessary then for the Court to consider the facial validity of §441b. Any other course of decision would prolong the substantial, nation-wide chilling effect caused by §441b's prohibitions on corporate expenditures....

The ongoing chill upon speech that is beyond all doubt protected makes it necessary in this case to invoke the earlier precedents that a statute which chills speech can and must be invalidated where its facial invalidity has been demonstrated....

III

The First Amendment provides that "Congress shall make no law... abridging the freedom of speech."...

The law before us is an outright ban, backed by criminal sanctions. Section 441b makes it a felony for all corporations—including nonprofit advocacy corporations—either to expressly advocate the election or defeat of candidates or to broadcast electioneering communications within 30 days of a primary election and 60 days of a general election. Thus, the following acts would all be felonies under §441b: The Sierra Club runs an ad, within the crucial phase of 60 days before the general election, that exhorts the public to disapprove of a Congressman who favors logging in national forests; the National Rifle Association publishes a book urging the public to vote for the challenger because the incumbent U.S. Senator supports a handgun ban;

and the American Civil Liberties Union creates a Web site telling the public to vote for a Presidential candidate in light of that candidate's defense of free speech. These prohibitions are classic examples of censorship.

Section 441b is a ban on corporate speech notwithstanding the fact that a PAC created by a corporation can still speak.... So the PAC exemption from §441b's expenditure ban, §441b(b)(2), does not allow corporations to speak. Even if a PAC could somehow allow a corporation to speak—and it does not—the option to form PACs does not alleviate the First Amendment problems with §441b....

Given the onerous restrictions, a corporation may not be able to establish a PAC in time to make its views known regarding candidates and issues in a current campaign.

Section 441b's prohibition on corporate independent expenditures is thus a ban on speech....

Speech is an essential mechanism of democracy, for it is the means to hold officials accountable to the people....

For these reasons, political speech must prevail against laws that would suppress it, whether by design or inadvertence. Laws that burden political speech are "subject to strict scrutiny," which requires the Government to prove that the restriction "furthers a compelling interest and is narrowly tailored to achieve that interest."...

Premised on mistrust of governmental power, the First Amendment stands against attempts to disfavor certain subjects or viewpoints.... As instruments to censor, these categories are interrelated: Speech restrictions based on the identity of the speaker are all too often simply a means to control content.

Quite apart from the purpose or effect of regulating content, moreover, the Government may commit a constitutional wrong when by law it identifies certain preferred speakers. By taking the right to speak from some and giving it to others, the Government deprives the disadvantaged person or class of the right to use speech to strive to establish worth, standing, and respect for the speaker's voice. The Government may not by these means deprive the public of the right and privilege to determine for itself what speech and speakers are worthy of consideration. The First Amendment protects speech and speaker, and the ideas that flow from each.

...

We find no basis for the proposition that, in the context of political speech, the Government may impose restrictions on certain disfavored speakers. Both history and logic lead us to this conclusion.

A

1

...

At least since the latter part of the 19th century, the laws of some States and of the United States imposed a ban on corporate direct contributions to candidates.... Yet not until 1947 did Congress first prohibit independent expenditures by corporations and labor unions in §304 of the Labor Management Relations Act 1947....

For almost three decades thereafter, the Court did not reach the question whether restrictions on corporate and union expenditures are constitutional....

2

In *Buckley*, the Court addressed various challenges to the Federal Election Campaign Act of 1971 (FECA) as amended in 1974....

The *Buckley* Court recognized a "sufficiently important" governmental interest in "the prevention of corruption and the appearance of corruption." This followed from the Court's concern that large contributions could be given "to secure a political *quid pro quo*."

The *Buckley* Court explained that the potential for *quid pro quo* corruption distinguished direct contributions to candidates from independent expenditures. The Court emphasized that "the independent expenditure ceiling... fails to serve any substantial governmental interest in stemming the reality or appearance of corruption in the electoral process," because "[t]he absence of prearrangement and coordination... alleviates the danger that expenditures will be given as a *quid pro quo* for improper commitments from the candidate."...

3

Thus the law stood until *Austin*. *Austin* "uph[eld] a direct restriction on the independent expenditure of funds for political speech for the first time in [this Court's] history." There, the Michigan Chamber of Commerce sought to use general treasury funds to run a newspaper ad supporting a specific candidate. Michigan law, however, prohibited corporate independent expenditures that supported or opposed any candidate for state office. A violation of the law was punishable as a felony. The Court sustained the speech prohibition.

...

B

The Court is thus confronted with conflicting lines of precedent: a pre-*Austin* line that forbids restrictions on political speech based on the speaker's corporate identity and a post-*Austin* line that permits them. No case before *Austin* had held that Congress could prohibit independent expenditures for political speech based on the speaker's corporate identity.

...

1

...

Austin's antidistortion rationale would produce the dangerous, and unacceptable, consequence that Congress could ban political speech of media corporations....

Media corporations are now exempt from §441b's ban on corporate expenditures.... Yet media corporations accumulate wealth with the help of the corporate form, the largest media corporations have "immense aggregations of wealth," and the views expressed by media corporations often "have little or no correlation to the public's support" for those views. Thus, under the Government's reasoning, wealthy media corporations could have their voices diminished to put them on par with other media entities. There is no precedent for permitting this under the First Amendment.

The media exemption discloses further difficulties with the law now under consideration. There is no precedent supporting laws that attempt to distinguish between corporations which are deemed to be exempt as media corporations and those which are not.... With the advent of the Internet and the decline of print and broadcast media, moreover, the line between the media and others who wish to comment on political and social issues becomes far more blurred.

The law's exception for media corporations is, on its own terms, all but an admission of the invalidity of the antidistortion rationale. And the exemption results in a further, separate reason for finding this law invalid: Again by its own terms, the law exempts some corporations but covers others, even though both have the need or the motive to communicate their views. The exemption applies to media corporations owned or controlled by corporations that have diverse and substantial investments and participate in endeavors other than news. So even assuming the most doubtful proposition that a news organization has a right to speak when others do not, the exemption would allow a conglomerate that owns both a media business and an unrelated business to influence or control the media in order to advance its overall business interest. At the same time, some other corporation, with an identical business interest but no media outlet in its ownership structure, would be forbidden to speak or inform the public about the same issue. This differential treatment cannot be squared with the First Amendment.

There is simply no support for the view that the First Amendment, as originally understood, would permit the suppression of political speech by media corporations. The Framers may not have anticipated modern business and media corporations....

The great debates between the Federalists and the Anti-Federalists over our founding document were published and expressed in the most important means of mass communication of that era—newspapers owned by individuals.... At the founding, speech was open, comprehensive, and vital to society's definition of itself; there were no limits on the sources of speech and knowledge.... The Framers may have been unaware of certain types of speakers or forms of communication, but that does not mean that those speakers and media are entitled to less First Amendment protection than those types of speakers and media that provided the means of communicating political ideas when the Bill of Rights was adopted.

...

The censorship we now confront is vast in its reach. The Government has "muffle[d] the voices that best represent the most significant segments of the economy."... And "the electorate [has been] deprived of information, knowledge and opinion vital to its function."... By suppressing the speech of manifold corporations, both for-profit and nonprofit, the Government prevents their voices and viewpoints from reaching the public and advising voters on which persons or entities are hostile to their interests. Factions will necessarily form in our Republic, but the remedy of "destroying the liberty" of some factions is "worse than the disease."...

The purpose and effect of this law is to prevent corporations, including small and nonprofit corporations, from presenting both facts and opinions to the public. This makes *Austin*'s antidistortion rationale all the more an aberration....

When Government seeks to use its full power, including the criminal law, to command where a person may get his or her information or what distrusted source he or she may not hear, it uses censorship to control thought. This is unlawful. The First Amendment confirms the freedom to think for ourselves.

...

C

...

Austin is undermined by experience since its announcement. Political speech is so ingrained in our culture that speakers find ways to circumvent campaign finance laws.... Our Nation's speech dynamic is changing, and informative voices should not have to circumvent onerous restrictions to exercise their First Amendment rights. Speakers have become adept at presenting citizens with sound bites, talking points, and scripted messages that dominate the 24-hour news cycle. Corporations, like individuals, do not have monolithic views. On certain topics corporations may possess valuable expertise, leaving them the best equipped to point out errors or fallacies in speech of all sorts, including the speech of candidates and elected officials.

Rapid changes in technology—and the creative dynamic inherent in the concept of free expression—counsel against upholding a law that restricts political speech in certain media or by certain speakers.... The First Amendment does not permit Congress to make these categorical distinctions based on the corporate identity of the speaker and the content of the political speech.

...

Due consideration leads to this conclusion: *Austin* should be and now is overruled. We return to the principle established in *Buckley* and *Bellotti* that the Government may not suppress political speech on the basis of the speaker's corporate identity. No sufficient governmental interest justifies limits on the political speech of nonprofit or for-profit corporations.

D

Austin is overruled, so it provides no basis for allowing the Government to limit corporate independent expenditures....

IV

A

Citizens United next challenges BCRA's disclaimer and disclosure provisions as applied to *Hillary* and the three advertisements for the movie. Under BCRA §311, televised electioneering communications funded by anyone other than a candidate must include a disclaimer that "'_____ is responsible for the content of this advertising.'" The required statement must be made in a "clearly spoken manner," and displayed on the screen in a "clearly readable manner" for at least four seconds. It must state that the communication "is not authorized by any candidate or candidate's committee"; it must also display the name and address (or Web site address) of the person or group that funded the advertisement. Under BCRA §201, any person who spends more than $10,000 on electioneering communications within a calendar year must file a disclosure statement with the FEC. 2 U. S. C. §434(f)(1). That statement must identify the person making the expenditure, the amount of the expenditure, the election to which the communication was directed, and the names of certain contributors. §434(f)(2).

Disclaimer and disclosure requirements may burden the ability to speak, but they "impose no ceiling on campaign-related activities" and "do not prevent anyone from speaking."...

B

Citizens United sought to broadcast one 30-second and two 10-second ads to promote *Hillary*. Under FEC regulations, a communication that "[p]roposes a commercial transaction" was not subject to 2 U. S. C. §441b's restrictions on corporate or union funding of electioneering communications. The regulations, however, do not exempt those communications from the disclaimer and disclosure requirements in BCRA §§201 and 311....

Citizens United argues that the disclaimer requirements in §311 are unconstitutional as applied to its ads. It contends that the governmental interest in providing information to the electorate does not justify requiring disclaimers for any commercial advertisements, including the ones at issue here. We disagree. The ads fall within BCRA's definition of an "electioneering communication": They referred to then-Senator Clinton by name shortly before a primary and contained pejorative references to her candidacy.... The disclaimers required by §311 "provid[e] the electorate with information" and "insure that the voters are fully informed" about the person or group who is speaking.... At the very least, the disclaimers avoid confusion by making clear that the ads are not funded by a candidate or political party....

The First Amendment protects political speech; and disclosure permits citizens and shareholders to react to the speech of corporate entities in a proper way. This transparency enables the electorate to make informed decisions and give proper weight to different speakers and messages.

C

For the same reasons we uphold the application of BCRA §§201 and 311 to the ads, we affirm their application to *Hillary*. We find no constitutional impediment to the application of BCRA's disclaimer and disclosure requirements to a movie broadcast via video-on-demand. And there has been no showing that, as applied in this case, these requirements would impose a chill on speech or expression.

V

...

Modern day movies, television comedies, or skits on Youtube.com might portray public officials or public policies in unflattering ways. Yet if a covered transmission during the blackout period creates the background for candidate endorsement or opposition, a felony occurs solely because a corporation, other than an exempt media corporation, has made the "purchase, payment, distribution, loan, advance, deposit, or gift of money or anything of value" in order to engage in political speech. Speech would be suppressed in the realm where its necessity is most evident: in the public dialogue preceding a real election. Governments are often hostile to speech, but under our law and our tradition it seems stranger than fiction for our Government to make this political speech a crime. Yet this is the statute's purpose and design.

Some members of the public might consider *Hillary* to be insightful and instructive; some might find it to be neither high art nor a fair discussion on how to set the Nation's course; still others simply might suspend judgment on these points but decide to think more about issues and candidates. Those choices and assessments, however, are not for the Government to make. "The First Amendment underwrites the freedom to experiment and to create in the realm of thought and speech. Citizens must be free to use new forms, and new forums, for the expression of ideas. The civic discourse belongs to the people, and the Government may not prescribe the means used to conduct it."...

The judgment of the District Court is reversed with respect to the constitutionality of 2 U. S. C. §441b's restrictions on corporate independent expenditures. The judgment is affirmed with respect to BCRA's disclaimer and disclosure requirements. The case is remanded for further proceedings consistent with this opinion.

It is so ordered.

Glossary

Austin: *Austin v. Michigan Chamber of Commerce*, a case in which the Court upheld a prohibition against corporations spending funds to support a candidate or issue

Bipartisan Campaign Reform Act of 2002: Also known as the McCain-Feingold Act, which sought to regulate the financing of political campaigns, passed in response to a rapid increase in the use of soft money, money raised outside previously regulated times and sources

facial validity: valid on the surface

McConnell: *McConnell v. Federal Election Commission*, a previous case in which the BCRA was upheld as constitutional

prolix laws: wordy, written in an extended length that confuses, causing un-clarity rather than clarity

Document Analysis

Writing for the five-member majority of the Court, Justice Kennedy ruled that limitations on the speech of corporations in order to decrease the chance of corruption, or the perception of corruption, was an overly broad remedy for the problem. Without a compelling interest, he wrote, the government should refrain from attempting to create boundaries on what corporations (and individuals) can say about an election or a candidate and when they can say it. For Kennedy, anything short of total freedom in this area would be too burdensome upon the groups, as these entities tried to ascertain what were, and what were not legally made statements about a candidate or issue. However, by an 8 – 1 vote, the Court did kept intact the provision requiring the group, or individual, doing the speaking to be identified. Otherwise, the major provisions of the BCRA were ruled unconstitutional, as were certain provisions of the 1971 law that created the FEC.

Citizens United, having previously distributed the film *Hillary: The Movie*, wanted to show it through a pay-per-view system into 2008, an election year. Knowing that this anti-Clinton film would be seen as electoral-related communications, Citizens United filed suit to keep the FEC from fining them. They sought to either have the film confirmed as not related to the election, because it did not express a view on the election, or to have a determination that the film fell outside the "electioneering communication" section of the BCRA. The logic behind this was the fact that to see it on a pay-per-view system, an individual had to request it be sent to their cable box. In the initial sections of his opinion, Kennedy made it clear that neither of these assertions by Citizens United could be upheld. Kennedy stated that the film focused on a "clearly identified candidate." In addition, he interpreted the content as a "feature-length negative advertisement" about Senator Clinton. For Kennedy, and the others on the Court, it was definitely "electioneering communication."

Kennedy also rejected the concept that an offer for a pay-per-view showing of the film did not constitute a public showing, because it was for one person at a time, not a large group. While Kennedy understood the difference between a regular, over the air or cable, broadcast and pay-per-view, this was not significant in terms of the number of people who could be reached. As he noted, the system being used had the potential for up to 34.5 million viewers of the film. As a result, Kennedy rejected the Citizens United claim that the breadth of distribution caused this film to not be covered by the BCRA.

However, after rejecting the narrow arguments presented by Citizens United, Kennedy and others on the majority moved to the broader issue regarding regulating political speech. Here they went far beyond what Citizens United was asking, although giving Citizens United the victory that it sought. Further examining the BCRA, Kennedy wrote that "Section 441b's prohibition on corporate independent expenditures is thus a ban on speech." He went on to assert, "political speech must prevail against laws that would suppress it," as he ruled that the limitations put in place by the BCRA were unconstitutional. In his examination of the BCRA, Kennedy presented hypothetical situations in which it might be unclear whether or not an organization was violating the law by its activities. Uncertainty, in his eyes, created a burden upon an individual or organization which decreased the ability and likelihood of their participation in the electoral system. This was unacceptable for him.

Kennedy and the Court's majority understood that their action would overturn precedents that had guided the lower courts, as well as parts of two laws. *Austin v. Michigan Chamber of Commerce* had guided lower courts since 1990 when the Court had accepted a Michigan law prohibiting the use of general funds in a corporation's treasury for political purposes. Within that ruling, and within the BCRA itself, an exception had been created for media companies, since the distribution of news was a part of the reason these corporations existed. In addition, the Court had ruled in *McConnell v. Federal Election Commission*, 2003, stating that the law creating the BCRA was constitutional, as the focus of the law was on money not directly used in campaigning, but on auxiliary activities. In *Citizens United v. Federal Election Commission,* the heart of these two rulings were overturned for the broader interpretation of free speech in the electoral process put forward by

Kennedy. In *Austin*, it was, in Kennedy's mind, too great a limit upon the free speech of the corporation. In addition, with innovations such as the internet, a media company, according to his thought process, could no longer be defined. As regarded the *McConnell* case, Kennedy asserted that the need for free speech overrode the logic that had led to that decision.

The major point of the BCRA that was upheld was the need for corporations to identify themselves, within the piece being distributed, as the producers/speakers of the material that was being distributed. These organizations must also make regular reports regarding donors to the organizations. This, Kennedy and the others believed, would act as a check on the power of the corporations when they entered the electoral process. Admitting that the requirements of publicly stating who was responsible for the ad and compiling a list of donors, were a type of burden, the majority of justices did not see them as being arduous enough to be a limiting factor on what was said, or the means by which it was communicated to the public.

Toward the end of his opinion, Kennedy wrote, "The civic discourse belongs to the people, and the Government may not prescribe the means used to conduct it." This was the majority view of the situation and the foundation of why they voted to extend the right of corporate free speech to all issues, and to all days on the calendar. However, for those who believed unfettered money (represented by corporate interests) was a corrupting influence on the electoral process, this ruling was major tragedy for the democratic system.

Essential Themes

When the Supreme Court rules on cases, there are times when it takes a narrow approach to the appeal with which it is dealing, while at others the justices take the opportunity to explore the possible broad ramifications of the case before them. In *Citizens United v. Federal Election Commission* they took the latter approach. They chose to examine the implications of limitations upon the speech of corporations in the electoral process. Since corporations, whether for-profit or non-profit, are composed of and owned by people, the majority of the justices believed that by limiting the speech of corporations, the government was limiting the speech of a particular group of people. They ruled this to be unconstitutional, by allowing any corporation to express the political views of its members via any means and at any time in the electoral process. The only boundary on the free expression of the "corporation's" ideas, was that, within the electoral related message, the corporation, or organization, must identify itself as the source of the material. This is true no matter what format is used to communicate the opinion or facts to the general public. Secondary requirements were that the corporation must identify the source of its funds and must act independently from the official campaign of the candidate or political party.

In the *Citizens United* ruling, the Court did not do away with limits on campaign contributions to the official campaign funds of the various candidates by individuals, nor the prohibition against corporations or unions make contributions to official campaign committees. Thus, it could be argued that for the official campaigns, the ruling had no effect. However, it allowed many more unofficial, non-affiliated campaign organizations to emerge with the potential to have a great impact upon the races.

In light of the *Citizens United* ruling, SpeechNOW.org expanded a suit it had filed against the FEC, hoping to do away with the contribution limits and the reporting requirements that the FEC had instructed them to follow prior to the *Citizens United* ruling. The United States Court of Appeals for the District of Columbia Circuit upheld the reporting requirement mandated by the FEC, just as the reporting requirements remained in *Citizens United*. However, following the logic of *Citizens United* the appeals court did away with any limitations on the amount of money individuals or groups could give to political groups not formally affiliated with political candidates or parties. The Supreme Court refused to hear the case, leaving the appeals court's *SpeechNOW.org* ruling as the precedent for other groups. This resulted in these independent political action committees' income growing from $62 million, in 2010, to $1.1 billion in 2016.

As a result of *Citizens United*, and the case filed by SpeechNOW.org, there has been a substantial increase in the amount of money pumped into political campaigns. In accordance with the rulings, this has not been money donated to the formal political party or candidate organizations; rather these are donations given to what are supposed to be independent advocates for or against candidates. The ruling has resulted in much more information being shared with the general public, and many more opinions being expressed. However, the quality and veracity of the independently sponsored ads have not generally been held to the same standards as the official ads, and for some this is troubling. It is unclear whether in the long run, the optimistic view of the majority of the Court justices, that more ideas and greater freedom of speech will be better for the nation, or the pessimistic view of the minority, that a few rich individuals and groups will dominate the political system, will be upheld.

In addition, this ruling, granting corporations a fuller type of personhood, through the First Amendment rights of speech, has been used by other corporations to seek other rights. Thus, when Hobby Lobby refused to abide by all the provisions of Obamacare, which ended up as *Burwell v. Hobby Lobby Stores,* Hobby Lobby cited the *Citizens United* case as Hobby Lobby successfully sought protection from certain provisions of the Affordable Care Act on the basis of the closely held corporation's religious freedom. This has raised questions in many people's minds, regarding how far a corporation's legal personhood will extend.

—Donald A. Watt, PhD

Bibliography and Additional Reading

Barnes, Robert and Dan Eggen. "Supreme Court rejects limits on corporate spending on political campaigns." Washingtonpost.com. Washington: The Washington Post Company, 2010.

Clements, Jeffrey D. with Bill Moyers. *Corporations Are Not People: Reclaiming Democracy from Big Money and Global Corporations.* (2nd ed.) San Francisco: Berett-Koehler Publishers, 2014.

Mayer, Jane. *Dark Money: The Hidden History of the Billionaires behind the Rise of the Radical Right.* New York: Doubleday, 2016.

Moyers, Bill with Floyd Abrams and Trevor Potter. ""Citizens United v. FEC." *Bill Moyers Journal.* (including *Frontline* September 4, 2009 broadcast) Washington: Public Affairs Television, 2017.

Oyez. "Citizens United v. Federal Election Commission." *Oyez.* Chicago: Kent College of Law at Illinois Tech, 2017.

Post, Robert C. with Pamela S. Karlan, Lawrence Lessing, Frank I. Michelman, and Nadia Urbinati. *Citizens Divided: Campaign Finance Reform and the Constitution.* (The Tanner Lectures on Human Values) Cambridge: Harvard UP, 2014.

Spakovsky, Hans von. "Citizens United and the Restoration of the First Amendment." *The Heritage Foundation.* Washington: The Heritage Foundation, 2010.

Youn, Monica (ed.) *Money, Politics, and the Constitution: Beyond Citizens United.* New York: The Century Foundation, 2011.

■ Shelby County v. Holder

Date: June 25, 2013
Author: Chief Justice John Roberts
Genre: court opinion

Summary Overview

At issue in Shelby County v. Holder *were two key provisions of the Voting Rights Act (VRA) of 1965, a law passed to prohibit racial discrimination in voter registration and election laws. The parties to the case were Shelby County, Alabama, and Eric Holder, the attorney general of the United States at the time. One of the VRA provisions in question was Section 5, which required jurisdictions with histories of voter discrimination in the area of race to obtain federal "preclearance" before making any changes in their voting laws or procedures to ensure that such practices were not repeated. The other provision was Section 4(b), which provided a "formula" to determine which jurisdictions were subject to the preclearance requirement. As of 2008, when this decision came down, the preclearance provisions largely applied to states throughout the South, as well as to Alaska, Arizona, and much of Virginia, along with selected counties and townships in states including North Carolina, Florida, California, and South Dakota. In its 5–4 decision, the conservative Roberts Court held that the preclearance formula was based on an outdated perspective that was no longer pertinent. Thus, it was held that the VRA imposed an unconstitutional burden by violating the principles of federalism and the equal sovereignty of the states. In the view of many Court observers, the Court's decision effectively gutted the VRA.*

Defining Moment

The U.S. Constitution gives each state the authority to determine voter qualifications and voting procedures. In the wake of the Civil War, however, it was apparent that in some states, various obstacles were depriving African Americans of their voting rights, among them literacy tests, poll taxes, property-ownership requirements, proofs of good moral character, the ability to read and interpret documents, and the like. In response, the Fifteenth Amendment, ratified in 1870, affirmed that "the right of citizens of the United States to vote shall not be denied or abridged by the United States or by any State on account of race, color, or previous condition of servitude." To put teeth into the amendments, Congress passed a series of Enforcement Acts in the 1870s to grant the federal government authority to intervene in states where African Americans were being denied their right to vote. The Supreme Court, however, ruled that various provisions of the acts were unconstitutional, and in time

Chief Justice John Roberts. Photo via Wikimedia Commons. [Public domain.]

Congress repealed many of the acts' provisions. In a 1903 case, *Giles v. Harris*, the Court ruled that the judiciary did not have the authority to force states to register minorities to vote.

The issue lay dormant through much of the twentieth century until the civil rights movement gathered steam in the 1950s and 1960s, putting pressure on Congress to pass legislation to protect the voting rights of minorities. In response, Congress passed the Civil Rights Act of 1957 and the Civil Rights Act of 1960. This legislation, however, proved unequal to the task, for various legal standards made it extremely difficult for the U.S. Justice Department to litigate claims of voter discrimination. Additionally, the Justice Department found local officials unwilling to cooperate with federal investigations into charges of voter discrimination. The Civil Rights Act of 1964 contained voter protections, but again the act as it pertained to voting rights proved ineffective and difficult to enforce. Congress responded with the Voting Rights Act of 1965.

The VRA prohibited "voter denial," that is, preventing a person from casting a ballot or from having that ballot counted, particularly through imposition of a "test or device," such as literacy tests, that had the effect of discriminating against classes of voters. It also prohibited "voter dilution," referring to efforts to diminish the strength or effectiveness of a vote by, for example, gerrymandering voting districts. But the act also contained two key provisions that would be challenged in Shelby County. The first of these was Section 5, which required covered jurisdictions—those with a history of voter discrimination—to obtain "preclearance" from the federal government before enacting any changes in its voting requirements or procedures. This provision required the jurisdiction to demonstrate that any proposed change did not have the effect of discriminating against racial minorities. If the jurisdiction was unable to do meet this burden, the change would not be allowed to take effect. The other provision, Section 4(b), consisted of a "coverage formula" that was to be used to determine which "political subdivisions" would require preclearance. Essentially, the coverage formula consisted of two prongs. First, the jurisdiction made use of a "test or device" to qualify voters: educational requirements, literacy tests, tests of moral character, or requirements that a person be vouched for before voting. Additionally, this provision prohibited the use of English-only registration and election materials when a jurisdiction had a significant population of a non-English-speaking minority group. The second prong of the coverage formula applied to any jurisdiction where half of its eligible citizens were not registered to vote or did not vote in recent presidential elections; the specifics of this provision evolved as time passed and further national elections were held.

When the VRA came up for reauthorization, Shelby County brought suit against the U.S. attorney general asking for a permanent injunction against enforcement of these provisions of the act, arguing that they were unconstitutional. Both the district court and the U.S. Court of Appeals upheld the constitutionality of the provisions. The U.S. Supreme Court agreed to hear the case on appeal, and on June 25, 2013, the Court issued its decision. By a 5–4, the Court struck down Section 4(b), holding that it exceeded the enforcement powers of Congress under the Fourteenth and Fifteenth Amendments to the Constitution. The Court reasoned that the formula violates the constitutional principal of federalism and that it treats states in a disparate fashion on the basis of decades-old conditions that have "no logical relationship to the present day." The Court did not rule on the constitutionality of Section 5, for without a coverage formula, Section 5 was rendered moot.

About the Author

The Court's decision in *Shelby County v. Holder* was written by Chief Justice John Roberts. Joining him in the majority opinion were Justices Antonin Scalia, Anthony Kennedy, Clarence Thomas, and Samuel Alito; the majority was generally regarded as the more conservative wing of the Supreme Court. Dissenting were Justices Ruth Bader Ginsburg, Stephen Breyer, Sonia Sotomayor, and Elena Kagan, generally thought of as the Court's more liberal wing. Roberts was born in Buffalo, New York, on January 27, 1955, although his family later settled in Indiana. He attended Harvard University, then graduated from Harvard Law School in 1979. In the years that followed, he held various clerkship positions, including one for Supreme Court Justice William Rehnquist; he also worked in private practice. From 2003 to 2005 he was a judge for the U.S. District Court of Appeals for the District of Columbia. President George W. Bush nominated him to the U.S. Supreme Court to replace Justice Sandra Day O'Connor after her retirement, but before Roberts's confirmation hearings, Chief Justice Rehnquist died. Accordingly, President Bush nominated Roberts to the chief justice position. On September 29, 2005, he took his seat, the youngest chief justice in a century.

Historical Document

Shelby County v. Holder

Chief Justice Roberts delivered the opinion of the Court.

The Voting Rights Act of 1965 employed extraordinary measures to address an extraordinary problem. Section 5 of the Act required States to obtain federal permission before enacting any law related to voting—a drastic departure from basic principles of federalism. And §4 of the Act applied that requirement only to some States—an equally dramatic departure from the principle that all States enjoy equal sovereignty. This was strong medicine, but Congress determined it was needed to address entrenched racial discrimination in voting, "an insidious and pervasive evil which had been perpetuated in certain parts of our country through unremitting and ingenious defiance of the Constitution." *South Carolina v. Katzenbach*, 383 U. S. 301, 309 (1966) . As we explained in upholding the law, "exceptional conditions can justify legislative measures not otherwise appropriate." Id., at 334. Reflecting the unprecedented nature of these measures, they were scheduled to expire after five years. See Voting Rights Act of 1965, §4(a), 79Stat. 438.

Nearly 50 years later, they are still in effect; indeed, they have been made more stringent, and are now scheduled to last until 2031. There is no denying, however, that the conditions that originally justified these measures no longer characterize voting in the covered jurisdictions. By 2009, "the racial gap in voter registration and turnout [was] lower in the States originally covered by §5 than it [was] nationwide." *Northwest Austin Municipal Util. Dist. No. One v. Holder*, 557 U. S. 193 –204 (2009). Since that time, Census Bureau data indicate that African-American voter turnout has come to exceed white voter turnout in five of the six States originally covered by §5, with a gap in the sixth State of less than one half of one percent. See Dept. of Commerce, Census Bureau, Reported Voting and Registration, by Sex, Race and Hispanic Origin, for States (Nov. 2012) (Table 4b).

At the same time, voting discrimination still exists; no one doubts that. The question is whether the Act's extraordinary measures, including its disparate treatment of the States, continue to satisfy constitutional requirements. As we put it a short time ago, "the Act imposes current burdens and must be justified by current needs." Northwest Austin, 557 U. S., at 203.

I

A

The Fifteenth Amendment was ratified in 1870, in the wake of the Civil War. It provides that "[t]he right of citizens of the United States to vote shall not be denied or abridged by the United States or by any State on account of race, color, or previous condition of servitude," and it gives Congress the "power to enforce this article by appropriate legislation."

"The first century of congressional enforcement of the Amendment, however, can only be regarded as a failure." Id., at 197. In the 1890s, Alabama, Georgia, Louisiana, Mississippi, North Carolina, South Carolina, and Virginia began to enact literacy tests for voter registration and to employ other methods designed to prevent African-Americans from voting. *Katzenbach*, 383 U. S., at 310. Congress passed statutes outlawing some of these practices and facilitating litigation against them, but litigation remained slow and expensive, and the States came up with new ways to discriminate as soon as existing ones were struck down. Voter registration of African-Americans barely improved. Id., at 313–314.

Inspired to action by the civil rights movement, Congress responded in 1965 with the Voting Rights Act. Section 2 was enacted to forbid, in all 50 States, any "standard, practice, or procedure . . . imposed or applied . . . to deny or abridge the right of any citizen of the United States to vote on account of race or color." 79Stat. 437. The current version forbids any "standard, practice, or procedure" that "results in a denial or abridgement of the right of any citizen of the United States to vote on account of race or color." 42 U. S. C. §1973(a). Both the Federal Government and individuals have sued to enforce §2, see, e.g., *Johnson v. De Grandy*, 512 U. S. 997 (1994), and injunctive relief is available in appropriate cases to block voting laws from going into effect, see 42 U. S. C. §1973j(d). Section 2 is permanent, applies nationwide, and is not at issue in this case.

Other sections targeted only some parts of the country. At the time of the Act's passage, these "covered" jurisdictions were those States or political subdivisions that had maintained a test or device as a prerequisite to voting as of November 1, 1964, and had less than 50 percent voter registration or turnout in the 1964 Presidential election. §4(b), 79Stat. 438. Such tests or devices included literacy and knowledge tests, good moral character requirements, the need for vouchers from registered voters, and the like. §4(c), id., at 438–439. A covered jurisdiction could "bail out" of coverage if it had not used a test or device in the preceding five years "for the purpose or with the effect of denying or abridging the right to vote on account of race or color." §4(a), id., at 438. In 1965, the covered States included Alabama, Georgia, Louisiana, Mississippi, South Carolina, and Virginia. The additional covered subdivisions included 39 counties in North Carolina and one in Arizona. See 28 CFR pt. 51, App. (2012).

In those jurisdictions, §4 of the Act banned all such tests or devices. §4(a), 79Stat. 438. Section 5 provided that no change in voting procedures could take effect until it was approved by federal authorities in Washington, D. C.—either the Attorney General or a court of three judges. Id., at 439. A jurisdiction could obtain such "preclearance" only by proving that the change had neither "the purpose [nor] the effect of denying or abridging the right to vote on account of race or color." Ibid.

Sections 4 and 5 were intended to be temporary; they were set to expire after five years. See §4(a), id., at 438; Northwest Austin, supra, at 199. In *South Carolina v. Katzenbach*, we upheld the 1965 Act against constitutional challenge, explaining that it was justified to address "voting discrimination where it persists on a pervasive scale." 383 U. S., at 308.

In 1970, Congress reauthorized the Act for another five years, and extended the coverage formula in §4(b) to jurisdictions that had a voting test and less than 50 percent voter registration or turnout as of 1968. Voting Rights Act Amendments of 1970, §§3–4, 84Stat. 315. That swept in several counties in California, New Hampshire, and New York. See 28 CFR pt. 51, App. Congress also extended the ban in §4(a) on tests and devices nationwide. §6, 84Stat. 315.

In 1975, Congress reauthorized the Act for seven more years, and extended its coverage to jurisdictions that had a voting test and less than 50 percent voter registration or turnout as of 1972. Voting Rights Act Amendments of 1975, §§101, 202, 89Stat. 400, 401. Congress also amended the definition of "test or device" to include the practice of providing English-only voting materials in places where over five percent of voting-age citizens spoke a single language other than English. §203, id., at 401–402. As a result of these amendments, the States of Alaska, Arizona, and Texas, as well as several counties in California, Florida, Michigan, New York, North Carolina, and South Dakota, became covered jurisdictions. See 28 CFR pt. 51, App. Congress correspondingly amended sections 2 and 5 to forbid voting discrimination on the basis of membership in a language minority group, in addition to discrimination on the basis of race or color. §§203, 206, 89Stat. 401, 402. Finally, Congress made the nationwide ban on tests and devices permanent. §102, id., at 400.

In 1982, Congress reauthorized the Act for 25 years, but did not alter its coverage formula. See Voting Rights Act Amendments, 96Stat. 131. Congress did, however, amend the bailout provisions, allowing political subdivisions of covered jurisdictions to bail out. Among other prerequisites for bailout, jurisdictions and their subdivisions must not have used a forbidden test or device, failed to receive preclearance, or lost a §2 suit, in the ten years prior to seeking bailout. §2, id., at 131–133.

We upheld each of these reauthorizations against constitutional challenge. See *Georgia v. United States*, 411 U. S. 526 (1973) ; *City of Rome v. United States*, 446 U. S. 156 (1980) ; *Lopez v. Monterey County*, 525 U. S. 266 (1999) .

In 2006, Congress again reauthorized the Voting Rights Act for 25 years, again without change to its coverage formula. Fannie Lou Hamer, Rosa Parks, and Coretta Scott King Voting Rights Act Reauthorization and Amendments Act, 120Stat. 577. Congress also amended §5 to prohibit more conduct than before. §5, id., at 580– 581; see *Reno v. Bossier Parish School Bd.*, 528 U. S. 320, 341 (2000) (Bossier II); *Georgia v. Ashcroft*, 539 U. S. 461, 479 (2003) . Section 5 now forbids voting changes with "any discriminatory purpose" as well as voting changes that diminish the ability of citizens, on account of race, color, or language minority status, "to elect their preferred candidates of choice." 42 U. S. C. §§1973c(b)–(d).

Shortly after this reauthorization, a Texas utility district brought suit, seeking to bail out from the Act's coverage and, in the alternative, challenging the Act's constitutionality. See Northwest Austin, 557 U. S., at 200–201. A three-judge District Court explained that only a State or political subdivision was eligible to seek bailout under the statute, and concluded that the utility district was not a political subdivision, a term that encompassed only "counties, parishes, and voter-registering subunits." *Northwest Austin Municipal Util. Dist. No. One v. Mukasey*, 573 F. Supp. 2d 221, 232 (DC 2008). The District Court also rejected the constitutional challenge. Id., at 283.

We reversed. We explained that "'normally the Court will not decide a constitutional question if there is some other ground upon which to dispose of the case.'" Northwest Austin, supra, at 205 (quoting *Escambia County v. McMillan*, 466 U. S. 48, 51 (1984) (per curiam)). Concluding that "underlying constitutional concerns," among other things, "compel[led] a broader reading of the bailout provision," we construed the statute to allow the utility district to seek bailout. Northwest Austin, 557 U. S., at 207. In doing so we expressed serious doubts about the Act's continued constitutionality.

We explained that §5 "imposes substantial federalism costs" and "differentiates between the States, despite our historic tradition that all the States enjoy equal sovereignty." Id., at 202, 203 (internal quotation marks omitted). We also noted that "[t]hings have changed in the South. Voter turnout and registration rates now approach parity. Blatantly discriminatory evasions of federal decrees are rare. And minority candidates hold office at unprecedented levels." Id., at 202. Finally, we questioned whether the problems that §5 meant to address were still "concentrated in the jurisdictions singled out for preclearance." Id., at 203.

Eight Members of the Court subscribed to these views, and the remaining Member would have held the Act unconstitutional. Ultimately, however, the

Court's construction of the bailout provision left the constitutional issues for another day.

B

Shelby County is located in Alabama, a covered jurisdiction. It has not sought bailout, as the Attorney General has recently objected to voting changes proposed from within the county. See App. 87a–92a. Instead, in 2010, the county sued the Attorney General in Federal District Court in Washington, D. C., seeking a declaratory judgment that sections 4(b) and 5 of the Voting Rights Act are facially unconstitutional, as well as a permanent injunction against their enforcement. The District Court ruled against the county and upheld the Act. 811 F. Supp. 2d 424, 508 (2011). The court found that the evidence before Congress in 2006 was sufficient to justify reauthorizing §5 and continuing the §4(b) coverage formula.

The Court of Appeals for the D. C. Circuit affirmed. In assessing §5, the D. C. Circuit considered six primary categories of evidence: Attorney General objections to voting changes, Attorney General requests for more information regarding voting changes, successful §2 suits in covered jurisdictions, the dispatching of federal observers to monitor elections in covered jurisdictions, §5 preclearance suits involving covered jurisdictions, and the deterrent effect of §5. See 679 F. 3d 848, 862–863 (2012). After extensive analysis of the record, the court accepted Congress's conclusion that §2 litigation remained inadequate in the covered jurisdictions to protect the rights of minority voters, and that §5 was therefore still necessary. Id., at 873.

Turning to §4, the D. C. Circuit noted that the evidence for singling out the covered jurisdictions was "less robust" and that the issue presented "a close question." Id., at 879. But the court looked to data comparing the number of successful §2 suits in the different parts of the country. Coupling that evidence with the deterrent effect of §5, the court concluded that the statute continued "to single out the jurisdictions in which discrimination is concentrated," and thus held that the coverage formula passed constitutional muster. Id., at 883.

Judge Williams dissented. He found "no positive correlation between inclusion in §4(b)'s coverage formula and low black registration or turnout." Id., at 891. Rather, to the extent there was any correlation, it actually went the other way: "condemnation under §4(b) is a marker of higher black registration and turnout." Ibid. (emphasis added). Judge Williams also found that "[c]overed jurisdictions have far more black officeholders as a proportion of the black population than do uncovered ones." Id., at 892. As to the evidence of successful §2 suits, Judge Williams disaggregated the reported cases by State, and concluded that "[t]he five worst uncovered jurisdictions . . . have worse records than eight of the covered jurisdictions." Id., at 897. He also noted that two covered jurisdictions—Arizona and Alaska—had not had any successful reported §2 suit brought against them during the entire 24 years covered by the data. Ibid. Judge Williams would have held the coverage formula of §4(b) "irrational" and unconstitutional. Id., at 885.

We granted certiorari. 568 U. S. ___ (2012).

II

In Northwest Austin, we stated that "the Act imposes current burdens and must be justified by current needs." 557 U. S., at 203. And we concluded that "a departure from the fundamental principle of equal sovereignty requires a showing that a statute's disparate geographic coverage is sufficiently related to the problem that it targets." Ibid. These basic principles guide our review of the question before us. [1]

A

The Constitution and laws of the United States are "the supreme Law of the Land." U. S. Const., Art. VI, cl. 2. State legislation may not contravene federal law. The Federal Government does not, however, have a general right to review and veto state enactments before they go into effect. A proposal to grant such authority to "negative" state laws was considered at the Constitutional Convention, but rejected in favor of allowing state laws to take effect, subject to later challenge under the Supremacy Clause. See 1 Records of the Federal Convention of 1787, pp. 21, 164–168 (M. Farrand ed. 1911); 2 id., at 27–29, 390–392.

Outside the strictures of the Supremacy Clause, States retain broad autonomy in structuring their governments and pursuing legislative objectives. Indeed, the Constitution provides that all powers not specifically granted to the Federal Government are reserved to the States or citizens. Amdt. 10. This "allocation of powers in our federal system preserves the integrity, dignity, and residual sovereignty of the States." *Bond v. United States*, 564 U. S. ___, ___ (2011) (slip op., at 9). But the federal balance "is not just an end in itself: Rather, federalism secures to citizens the liberties that derive from the diffusion of sovereign power." Ibid. (internal quotation marks omitted).

More specifically, " 'the Framers of the Constitution intended the States to keep for themselves, as provided in the Tenth Amendment, the power to regulate elections.' " *Gregory v. Ashcroft*, 501 U. S. 452 –462 (1991) (quoting *Sugarman v. Dougall*, 413 U. S. 634, 647 (1973) ; some internal quotation marks omitted). Of course, the Federal Government retains significant control over federal elections. For instance, the Constitution authorizes Congress to establish the time and manner for electing Senators and Representatives. Art. I, §4, cl. 1; see also *Arizona v. Inter Tribal Council of Ariz., Inc.*, ante, at

4–6. But States have "broad powers to determine the conditions under which the right of suffrage may be exercised." *Carrington v. Rash*, 380 U. S. 89, 91 (1965) (internal quotation marks omitted); see also Arizona, ante, at 13–15. And "[e]ach State has the power to prescribe the qualifications of its officers and the manner in which they shall be chosen." *Boyd v. Nebraska ex rel. Thayer*, 143 U. S. 135, 161 (1892). Drawing lines for congressional districts is likewise "primarily the duty and responsibility of the State." *Perry v. Perez*, 565 U. S. ___, ___ (2012) (per curiam) (slip op., at 3) (internal quotation marks omitted).

Not only do States retain sovereignty under the Constitution, there is also a "fundamental principle of equal sovereignty" among the States. Northwest Austin, supra, at 203 (citing *United States v. Louisiana*, 363 U. S. 1, 16 (1960); *Lessee of Pollard v. Hagan*, 3 How. 212, 223 (1845); and *Texas v. White*, 7 Wall. 700, 725–726 (1869); emphasis added). Over a hundred years ago, this Court explained that our Nation "was and is a union of States, equal in power, dignity and authority." *Coyle v. Smith*, 221 U. S. 559, 567 (1911). Indeed, "the constitutional equality of the States is essential to the harmonious operation of the scheme upon which the Republic was organized." Id., at 580. Coyle concerned the admission of new States, and *Katzenbach* rejected the notion that the principle operated as a bar on differential treatment outside that context. 383 U. S., at 328–329. At the same time, as we made clear in Northwest Austin, the fundamental principle of equal sovereignty remains highly pertinent in assessing subsequent disparate treatment of States. 557 U. S., at 203.

The Voting Rights Act sharply departs from these basic principles. It suspends "all changes to state election law—however innocuous—until they have been precleared by federal authorities in Washington, D. C." Id., at 202. States must beseech the Federal Government for permission to implement laws that they would otherwise have the right to enact and execute on their own, subject of course to any injunction in a §2 action. The Attorney General has 60 days to object to a preclearance request, longer if he requests more information. See 28 CFR §§51.9, 51.37. If a State seeks preclearance from a three-judge court, the process can take years.

And despite the tradition of equal sovereignty, the Act applies to only nine States (and several additional counties). While one State waits months or years and expends funds to implement a validly enacted law, its neighbor can typically put the same law into effect immediately, through the normal legislative process. Even if a noncovered jurisdiction is sued, there are important differences between those proceedings and preclearance proceedings; the preclearance proceeding "not only switches the burden of proof to the supplicant jurisdiction, but also applies substantive standards quite different from those governing the rest of the nation." 679 F. 3d, at 884 (Williams, J., dissenting) (case below).

All this explains why, when we first upheld the Act in 1966, we described it as "stringent" and "potent." Katzenbach, 383 U. S., at 308, 315, 337. We recognized that it "may have been an uncommon exercise of congressional power," but concluded that "legislative measures not otherwise appropriate" could be justified by "exceptional conditions." Id., at 334. We have since noted that the Act "authorizes federal intrusion into sensitive areas of state and local policymaking," Lopez, 525 U. S., at 282, and represents an "extraordinary departure from the traditional course of relations between the States and the Federal Government," *Presley v. Etowah County Comm'n*, 502 U. S. 491–501 (1992). As we reiterated in *Northwest Austin*, the Act constitutes "extraordinary legislation otherwise unfamiliar to our federal system." 557 U. S., at 211.

B

In 1966, we found these departures from the basic features of our system of government justified. The "blight of racial discrimination in voting" had "infected the electoral process in parts of our country for nearly a century." Katzenbach, 383 U. S., at 308. Several States had enacted a variety of requirements and tests "specifically designed to prevent" African-Americans from voting. Id., at 310. Case-by-case litigation had proved inadequate to prevent such racial discrimination in voting, in part because States "merely switched to discriminatory devices not covered by the federal decrees," "enacted difficult new tests," or simply "defied and evaded court orders." Id., at 314. Shortly before enactment of the Voting Rights Act, only 19.4 percent of African-Americans of voting age were registered to vote in Alabama, only 31.8 percent in Louisiana, and only 6.4 percent in Mississippi. Id., at 313. Those figures were roughly 50 percentage points or more below the figures for whites. Ibid.

In short, we concluded that "[u]nder the compulsion of these unique circumstances, Congress responded in a permissibly decisive manner." Id., at 334, 335. We also noted then and have emphasized since that this extraordinary legislation was intended to be temporary, set to expire after five years. Id., at 333; Northwest Austin, supra, at 199.

At the time, the coverage formula—the means of linking the exercise of the unprecedented authority with the problem that warranted it—made sense. We found that "Congress chose to limit its attention to the geographic areas where immediate action seemed necessary." Katzenbach, 383 U. S., at 328. The areas where Congress found "evidence of actual voting discrimination" shared two characteristics: "the use of tests and devices for voter registration, and a voting rate in the 1964 presidential election at least 12 points below the national average." Id., at 330. We explained that "[t]ests and devices are relevant to voting discrimination because of their long history as a tool for perpetrating the evil; a low voting rate is pertinent for the obvious reason that widespread disenfranchisement must inevitably affect the number of actual voters." Ibid. We therefore concluded that "the coverage formula [was] rational in both practice and theory." Ibid. It accurately reflected those jurisdictions uniquely characterized by voting discrimination "on a pervasive scale," linking coverage to the devices used to effectuate discrimination and to the resulting disenfranchisement. Id., at 308. The formula ensured that the "stringent remedies [were] aimed at areas where voting discrimination ha[d] been most flagrant." Id., at 315.

C

Nearly 50 years later, things have changed dramatically. Shelby County contends that the preclearance requirement, even without regard to its disparate coverage, is now unconstitutional. Its arguments have a good deal of force. In the covered jurisdictions, "[v]oter turnout and registration rates now approach parity. Blatantly discriminatory evasions of federal decrees are rare. And minority candidates hold office at unprecedented levels." Northwest Austin, 557 U. S., at 202. The tests and devices that blocked access to the ballot have been forbidden nationwide for over 40 years. See §6, 84Stat. 315; §102, 89Stat. 400.

Those conclusions are not ours alone. Congress said the same when it reauthorized the Act in 2006, writing that "[s]ignificant progress has been made in eliminating first generation barriers experienced by minority voters, including increased numbers of registered minority voters, minority voter turnout, and minority representation in Congress, State legislatures, and local elected offices." §2(b)(1), 120Stat. 577. The House Report elaborated that "the number of African-Americans who are registered and who turn out to cast ballots has increased significantly over the last 40 years, particularly since 1982," and noted that "[i]n some circumstances, minorities register to vote and cast ballots at levels that surpass those of white voters." H. R. Rep. No. 109–478, p. 12 (2006). That Report also explained that there have been "significant increases in the number of African-Americans serving in elected offices"; more specifically, there has been approximately a 1,000 percent increase since 1965 in the number of African-American elected officials in the six States originally covered by the Voting Rights Act. Id., at 18.

The following chart, compiled from the Senate and House Reports, compares voter registration numbers from 1965 to those from 2004 in the six originally covered States. These are the numbers that were before Congress when it reauthorized the Act in 2006: See S. Rep. No. 109–295, p. 11 (2006); H. R. Rep. No. 109–478, at 12. The 2004 figures come from the Census Bureau. Census Bureau data from the most recent election indicate that African-American voter turnout exceeded white voter turnout in five of the six States originally covered by §5, with a gap in the sixth State of less than one half of one percent. See Dept. of Commerce, Census Bureau, Reported Voting and Registration, by Sex, Race and Hispanic Origin, for States (Table 4b).

The preclearance statistics are also illuminating. In the first decade after enactment of §5, the Attorney General objected to 14.2 percent of proposed voting changes. H. R Rep. No. 109–478, at 22. In the last decade before reenactment, the Attorney General objected to a mere 0.16 percent. S. Rep. No. 109–295, at 13.

There is no doubt that these improvements are in large part because of the Voting Rights Act. The Act has proved immensely successful at redressing racial discrimination and integrating the voting process. See §2(b)(1), 120Stat. 577. During the "Freedom Summer" of 1964, in Philadelphia, Mississippi, three men were murdered while working in the area to register African-American voters. See *United States v. Price*, 383 U. S. 787, 790 (1966). On "Bloody Sunday" in 1965, in Selma, Alabama, police beat and used tear gas against hundreds marching in support of African-American enfranchisement. See Northwest Austin, supra, at 220, n. 3 (Thomas, J., concurring in judgment in part and dissenting in part). Today both of those towns are governed by African-American mayors. Problems remain in these States and others, but there is no denying that, due to the Voting Rights Act, our Nation has made great strides.

Yet the Act has not eased the restrictions in §5 or narrowed the scope of the coverage formula in §4(b) along the way. Those extraordinary and unprecedented features were reauthorized—as if nothing had changed. In fact, the Act's unusual remedies have grown even stronger. When Congress reauthorized the Act in 2006, it did so for another 25 years on top of the previous 40—a far cry from the initial five-year period. See 42 U. S. C. §1973b(a)(8). Congress also expanded the prohibitions in §5. We had previously interpreted §5 to prohibit only those redistricting plans that would have the purpose or effect of worsening the position of minority groups. See Bossier II, 528 U. S., at 324, 335–336. In 2006, Congress amended §5 to prohibit laws that could have favored such groups but did not do so because of a discriminatory purpose, see 42 U. S. C. §1973c(c), even though we had stated that such broadening of §5 coverage would "exacerbate the substantial federalism costs that the preclearance procedure already exacts, perhaps to the extent of raising concerns about §5's constitutionality," Bossier II, supra, at 336 (citation and internal quotation marks omitted). In addition, Congress expanded §5 to prohibit any voting law "that has the purpose of or will have the effect of diminishing the ability of any citizens of the United States," on account of race, color, or language minority status, "to elect their preferred candidates of choice." §1973c(b). In light of those two amendments, the bar that covered jurisdictions must clear has been raised even as the conditions justifying that requirement have dramatically improved.

We have also previously highlighted the concern that "the preclearance requirements in one State [might] be unconstitutional in another." Northwest Austin, 557 U. S., at 203; see *Georgia v. Ashcroft*, 539 U. S., at 491 (Kennedy,

J., concurring) ("considerations of race that would doom a redistricting plan under the Fourteenth Amendment or §2 [of the Voting Rights Act] seem to be what save it under §5"). Nothing has happened since to alleviate this troubling concern about the current application of §5.

Respondents do not deny that there have been improvements on the ground, but argue that much of this can be attributed to the deterrent effect of §5, which dissuades covered jurisdictions from engaging in discrimination that they would resume should §5 be struck down. Under this theory, however, §5 would be effectively immune from scrutiny; no matter how "clean" the record of covered jurisdictions, the argument could always be made that it was deterrence that accounted for the good behavior.

The provisions of §5 apply only to those jurisdictions singled out by §4. We now consider whether that coverage formula is constitutional in light of current conditions.

III

A

When upholding the constitutionality of the coverage formula in 1966, we concluded that it was "rational in both practice and theory." Katzenbach, 383 U. S., at 330. The formula looked to cause (discriminatory tests) and effect (low voter registration and turnout), and tailored the remedy (preclearance) to those jurisdictions exhibiting both.

By 2009, however, we concluded that the "coverage formula raise[d] serious constitutional questions." Northwest Austin, 557 U. S., at 204. As we explained, a statute's "current burdens" must be justified by "current needs," and any "disparate geographic coverage" must be "sufficiently related to the problem that it targets." Id., at 203. The coverage formula met that test in 1965, but no longer does so.

Coverage today is based on decades-old data and eradicated practices. The formula captures States by reference to literacy tests and low voter registration and turnout in the 1960s and early 1970s. But such tests have been banned nationwide for over 40 years. §6, 84Stat. 315; §102, 89Stat. 400. And voter registration and turnout numbers in the covered States have risen dramatically in the years since. H. R. Rep. No. 109–478, at 12. Racial disparity in those numbers was compelling evidence justifying the preclearance remedy and the coverage formula. See, e.g., Katzenbach, supra, at 313, 329–330. There is no longer such a disparity.

In 1965, the States could be divided into two groups: those with a recent history of voting tests and low voter registration and turnout, and those without those characteristics. Congress based its coverage formula on that distinction. Today the Nation is no longer divided along those lines, yet the Voting Rights Act continues to treat it as if it were.

B

The Government's defense of the formula is limited. First, the Government contends that the formula is "reverse-engineered": Congress identified the jurisdictions to be covered and then came up with criteria to describe them. Brief for Federal Respondent 48–49. Under that reasoning, there need not be any logical relationship between the criteria in the formula and the reason for coverage; all that is necessary is that the formula happen to capture the jurisdictions Congress wanted to single out.

The Government suggests that Katzenbach sanctioned such an approach, but the analysis in Katzenbach was quite different. Katzenbach reasoned that the coverage formula was rational because the "formula . . . was relevant to the problem": "Tests and devices are relevant to voting discrimination because of their long history as a tool for perpetrating the evil; a low voting rate is pertinent for the obvious reason that widespread disenfranchisement must inevitably affect the number of actual voters." 383 U. S., at 329, 330.

Here, by contrast, the Government's reverse-engineering argument does not even attempt to demonstrate the continued relevance of the formula to the problem it targets. And in the context of a decision as significant as this one—subjecting a disfavored subset of States to "extraordinary legislation otherwise unfamiliar to our federal system," Northwest Austin, supra, at 211—that failure to establish even relevance is fatal.

The Government falls back to the argument that because the formula was relevant in 1965, its continued use is permissible so long as any discrimination remains in the States Congress identified back then—regardless of how that discrimination compares to discrimination in States unburdened by coverage. Brief for Federal Respondent 49–50. This argument does not look to "current political conditions," Northwest Austin, supra, at 203, but instead relies on a comparison between the States in 1965. That comparison reflected the different histories of the North and South. It was in the South that slavery was upheld by law until uprooted by the Civil War, that the reign of Jim Crow denied African-Americans the most basic freedoms, and that state and local governments worked tirelessly to disenfranchise citizens on the basis of race. The Court invoked that history—rightly so—in sustaining the disparate coverage of the Voting Rights Act in 1966. See Katzenbach, supra, at 308 ("The constitutional propriety of the Voting Rights Act of 1965 must be judged with reference to the historical experience which it reflects.").

But history did not end in 1965. By the time the Act was reauthorized in 2006, there had been 40 more years of it. In assessing the "current need[ ]" for a preclearance system that treats States differently from one another today, that history cannot be ignored. During that time, largely because of the Voting Rights Act, voting tests were abolished, disparities in voter registration and turnout due to race were erased, and African-Americans attained political office in record numbers. And yet the coverage formula that Congress reauthorized in 2006 ignores these developments, keeping the focus on decades-old data relevant to decades-old problems, rather than current data reflecting current needs.

The Fifteenth Amendment commands that the right to vote shall not be denied or abridged on account of race or color, and it gives Congress the power to enforce that command. The Amendment is not designed to punish for the past; its purpose is to ensure a better future. See *Rice v. Cayetano*, 528 U. S. 495, 512 (2000) ("Consistent with the design of the Constitution, the [Fifteenth] Amendment is cast in fundamental terms, terms transcending the particular controversy which was the immediate impetus for its enactment."). To serve that purpose, Congress—if it is to divide the States—must identify those jurisdictions to be singled out on a basis that makes sense in light of current conditions. It cannot rely simply on the past. We made that clear in Northwest Austin, and we make it clear again today....

Striking down an Act of Congress "is the gravest and most delicate duty that this Court is called on to perform." *Blodgett v. Holden*, 275 U. S. 142, 148 (1927) (Holmes, J., concurring). We do not do so lightly. That is why, in 2009, we took care to avoid ruling on the constitutionality of the Voting Rights Act when asked to do so, and instead resolved the case then before us on statutory grounds. But in issuing that decision, we expressed our broader concerns about the constitutionality of the Act. Congress could have updated the coverage formula at that time, but did not do so. Its failure to act leaves us today with no choice but to declare §4(b) unconstitutional. The formula in that section can no longer be used as a basis for subjecting jurisdictions to preclearance.

Our decision in no way affects the permanent, nationwide ban on racial discrimination in voting found in §2. We issue no holding on §5 itself, only on the coverage formula. Congress may draft another formula based on current conditions. Such a formula is an initial prerequisite to a determination that exceptional conditions still exist justifying such an "extraordinary departure from the traditional course of relations between the States and the Federal Government." Presley, 502 U. S., at 500–501. Our country has changed, and while any racial discrimination in voting is too much, Congress must ensure that the legislation it passes to remedy that problem speaks to current conditions.

The judgment of the Court of Appeals is reversed.

It is so ordered.

Glossary

"covered" jurisdictions: states or political subdivisions that had maintained a test or device as a prerequisite to voting that had the effect of discriminating against minority groups

preclearance: a provision of the Voting Rights Act of 1965 requiring political subdivisions that wanted to enact a change in voting requirements or procedures to obtain authorization from the federal government

test or device: any requirement used to prevent minorities from registering to vote or from voting, including such requirements as poll taxes and literacy tests

Document Analysis

Justice Roberts begins with a historical overview, examining not only the Voting Rights Act of 1965 but also the Fifteenth Amendment, which guaranteed to all citizens, including African Americans, the right to vote. He discusses the "covered" jurisdictions of the VRA, the "tests or devices" that had the effect of denying African Americans the right to vote, and the concept of "preclearance," requiring a jurisdiction that wanted to enact a change in voting requirements or procedures to obtain federal approval, which it could obtain only if it could prove that the change did not have "the purpose [nor] the effect of denying or abridging the right to vote on account of race or color." He notes that both Sections 4 and 5 of the VRA were intended to be temporary, and in fact they needed to be reauthorized at various points in the intervening years; as part of that reauthorization, various jurisdictions were added to Section 5. The coverage formula contained in Section 4(b), however, remained unchanged. After summarizing the history of the case in the district court and the U.S. Court of Appeals, Roberts turns to the constitutional issues raised.

At issue are the Supremacy Clause of Constitution (Article VI, Section 2) and the Tenth Amendment to the Constitution. This amendment has proven to be a knotty one, for it has to do with the balance between the powers delegated to the federal government and those retained by the states. Under the Constitution, states retain sovereignty, giving them broad authority to enact laws, including election laws. The federal government will presumably intervene only when a state law runs counter to the Constitution. Further, the Constitution requires that states be treated equally; states cannot be subjected to disparate treatment by the federal government. Roberts then states that "the Voting Rights Act sharply departs from these basic principles." He explains that the circumstances that existed at the time of the passage of the VRA warranted federal intervention, for the "blight of racial discrimination in voting" had "infected the electoral process in parts of our country for nearly a century." He further notes that the coverage formula at that time made sense. However, he writes: "Nearly 50 years later, things have changed dramatically."

Roberts goes on to note, first, that the "tests and devices" that inhibited black voter participation are things of the past. Further, he provides data to show that black voter registration is very much on a par with white voter registration in the covered states. In 1965, for example, 69 percent of whites but only 19 percent of blacks were registered to vote in Alabama, one of the covered jurisdictions. In 2004, 73.8 percent of whites and 72.9 percent of blacks were registered, a gap of less than 1 percent. Despite these significant improvements on the ground, the relevant provisions of the VRA were reauthorized as if nothing had changed. Roberts notes that "the bar that covered jurisdictions must clear has been raised even as the conditions justifying that requirement have dramatically improved." He goes on to state: "Coverage today is based on decades-old data and eradicated practices. The formula captures States by reference to literacy tests and low voter registration and turnout in the 1960s and early 1970s." Roberts acknowledges the historical argument: that for decades, a system of Jim Crow laws disenfranchised African Americans, particularly in the South. He argues, however, that history did not end in 1965 and that the law as it stands keeps "the focus on decades-old data relevant to decades-old problems, rather than current data reflecting current needs." He concludes: "Our country has changed, and while any racial discrimination in voting is too much, Congress must ensure that the legislation it passes to remedy that problem speaks to current conditions."

Essential Themes

After the Court's ruling, several states that had been affected by the preclearance provision of the VRA—and several that had not—changed voter registration procedures in their states. Among the changes was removal of online voter registration, early voting, Sunday voting, same-day (i.e., election day) registration, preregistration for those about to turn age eighteen, and "Souls to the Polls" programs designed to allow congregations at African American churches to vote as a community of faith after church services. Also, various states proposed tougher voter identification laws and took firm steps to purge ineligible voters from their registration rolls. One such state was Wisconsin, which passed a voter ID law that was challenged by the American Civil Liberties Union and the Advancement Project (a civil rights organization), which argued that the law would disproportionately affect minority voters. In a broader sense, many observers, including the nation's president at the time, Barack Obama, along with civil rights activists, condemned the ruling, calling it a setback in the ongoing struggle for civil rights. In 2014, a bill to remedy the defects of the VRA, titled the Voting Rights Amendment Act of 2014, was proposed in Congress, but the bill died in the Senate and House Judiciary Committees. A later bill, the Voting Rights Amendment Act of 2015, similarly died in committee.

—Michael J. O'Neal, PhD

Bibliography and Additional Reading

Barnes, Robert. "Supreme Court Stops Use of Key Part of Voting Rights Act," *Washington Post,* June 25, 2013.

Bullock, Charles S. III, Ronald Keith Gaddie, and Justin J. Wert, eds. *The Rise and Fall of the Voting Rights Act.* Norman, OK: University of Oklahoma Press, 2016.

Davidson, Chandler. *Quiet Revolution in the South: The Impact of the Voting Rights Act, 1965–1990.* Princeton, NJ: Princeton UP, 1994.

Gillette, William. *The Right to Vote: Politics and the Passage of the Fifteenth Amendment.* Baltimore, MD: Johns Hopkins Press, 1969.

Liptak, Adam. "Supreme Court Invalidates Key Part of Voting Rights Act," *New York Times,* June 25, 2013, p. A1

Supreme Court of the United States, Shelby County, *Alabama v. Holder,* Attorney General, www.supremecourt.gov/opinions/12pdf/12-96_6k47.pdf.

U.S. Department of Justice. "About Section 5 of the Voting Rights Act," www.justice.gov/crt/about-section-5-voting-rights-act.

Waldman, Michael. *The Fight to Vote.* New York: Simon and Schuster, 2016.

■ Cooper v. Harris

Date: May 22, 2017
Author: Elena Kagan
Genre: court opinion

Summary Overview

The case of Cooper v. Harris *involved a challenge to the redrawing of voting districts in North Carolina on the basis of an alleged violation of the Voting Rights Act of 1965. In its opinion, the U.S. Supreme Court upheld the lower Federal court's ruling that North Carolina state legislators had illegally packed districts with African American voters, which in turn reduced the influence of African American voters in other North Carolina districts. The litigants in the case were Roy Cooper, then governor of North Carolina, and David Harris, a resident of the state who brought the case. The majority opinion was written by Justice Elena Kagan.*

Defining Moment

A number of redistricting cases have come before the United States Supreme Court alleging violations of the Voting Rights Act. The majority of the cases have involved states in the southern United States, including Alabama, Virginia and North Carolina, which have a long history of voter suppression and utilizing redistricting (gerrymandering) as a means of diluting and minimizing the impact of African-American and Latino votes. *Cooper v. Harris* is the latest gerrymandering case heard by the Supreme Court in an attempt to provide guidance and to further shape federal law under the Voting Rights Act.

In 1993 the Supreme Court enumerated a general rule in another North Carolina gerrymandering case, *State v. Reno*, in which it held that race could not normally be the predominant factor considered in redistricting, as that would be a violation of the Equal Protection Clause of the U.S. Constitution. However, the Court concluded that race could be one of many factors considered in order to ensure compliance with the Voting Rights Act. If race was deemed to be a predominant factor in the redistricting, then a stringent level of review called strict scrutiny was applied which then required the state in question to show that the redistricting plan served a "compelling interest" and was "narrowly tailored" to meet that interest. *Shaw v. Reno* came before the Supreme Court in 1996 and in that case the Court established that the Voting

Justice Elena Kagan wrote the majority opinion. Photo by Steve Petteway, Collection of the Supreme Court of the United States, via Wikimedia Commons.

Rights Act was considered to be a "compelling interest" under the strict scrutiny standard.

In this latest challenge to a redistricting plan by the North Carolina legislature, Justice Elena Kagan, writing for the Court majority, held that race was a predominant factor in drawing the districts. However, North Carolina lacked a strong basis in evidence for believing that it needed a minority-dominated district in order to avoid any liability under Section 2 of the Voting Rights Act. Rather, Kagan's opinion held that racial gerrymandering, rather than political gerrymandering, was the predominant factor in drawing the other district as a minority-dominated district.

The case arises from two North Carolina congressional districts, District 1 and District 12 which have a long legislative history before the Supreme Court. The two districts have been the basis of four earlier racial gerrymandering cases at the Court. In 2016 a three-judge federal district court in North Carolina invalidated both districts, holding that the state legislators had illegally packed the districts with African-American voters, which had the effect of reducing the influence of African-American voters in other districts. District 1 has been likened to an octopus in its geographical shape, with a body that starts at the North Carolina/Virginia border with tentacles that stretch out west, south and east. District 12 is more serpentine in shape; as the court noted it "begins in the south-central part of the State (where it takes in a large part of Charlotte) and then travels northeast, zig-zagging much of the way to the State's northern border."

The Supreme Court granted certiorari to hear the matter and upheld the district court decision by a 5-3 decision, in a major ruling on racial gerrymandering. Justice Kagan wrote for the majority. Justice Clarence Thomas wrote a concurring opinion. Justice Samuel Alito filed an opinion concurring in the judgment in part and dissenting in part, in which Chief Justice John Roberts and Justice Anthony Kennedy joined. Justice Gorsuch took no part in the consideration or decision of the case.

About the Author

Elena Kagan is an Associate Justice on the Supreme Court. She was born on April 28, 1960 in New York City. Kagan studied history at Princeton before attending Harvard Law School, where she was supervising editor of the *Harvard Law Review*. Kagan was a law clerk for Judge Abner Mikva of the U.S. Court of Appeals for the District of Columbia Circuit after which she served as a law clerk for Justice Thurgood Marshall. She moved into the private sector working as an associate for the Washington D.C. law firm Williams & Connolly.

In 1991 Kagan began teaching at the University of Chicago Law School and by 1995 was a tenured professor of law. Kagan began working as associate counsel for President Bill Clinton later that year and spent four years working in the White House, first as Deputy Assistant to the President for Domestic Policy before taking the role of Deputy Director of the Domestic Policy Council.

President Clinton nominated Kagan to serve on the U.S. Court of Appeals D.C. Circuit. Her nomination languished in the Senate Judiciary Committee and, in 1999 Kagan returned to academia, beginning as a visiting professor at Harvard Law before eventually becoming Dean of Harvard Law in 2003. When President Barack Obama, a fellow Harvard alumnus, won the 2008 presidential election, Kagan was selected as solicitor general. She was confirmed in that position by the Senate on March 19, 2009, becoming the first woman to serve as solicitor general of the United States. Two months after being confirmed, President Obama nominated Kagan to replace Justice John Paul Stevens on the Supreme Court after his retirement. Kagan was confirmed by the Senate in a 63-37 vote, making her the fourth woman to sit on the Supreme Court. Kagan was also the youngest Justice at 50 years old and the only one without previous experience as a sitting judge.

During her tenure on the Supreme Court, Kagan sided with the majority on two landmark Supreme Court rulings. First, she was one of six justices to uphold a critical component of the 2010 Affordable Care Act (Obamacare) in *King v. Burwell*. That decision allowed the federal government to keep providing subsidies to Americans who purchased healthcare insurance through exchanges regardless of whether they were operated by state or federal government. Second, Kagan again joined the majority in a 5-4 ruling in *Obergefell v. Hodges* that made same sex marriage legal in all 50 states.

Historical Document

Cooper v. Harris

ROY COOPER, GOVERNOR OF NORTH CAROLINA, ET AL., APPELLANTS v. DAVID HARRIS, ET AL.

ON APPEAL FROM THE UNITED STATES DISTRICT COURT FOR THE MIDDLE DISTRICT OF NORTH CAROLINA

[May 22, 2017]

JUSTICE KAGAN delivered the opinion of the Court.

The Constitution entrusts States with the job of designing congressional districts. But it also imposes an important constraint: A State may not use race as the predominant factor in drawing district lines unless it has a compelling reason. In this case, a three-judge District Court ruled that North Carolina officials violated that bar when they created two districts whose voting-age populations were majority black. Applying a deferential standard of review to the factual findings underlying that decision, we affirm.

I

A

The Equal Protection Clause of the Fourteenth Amendment limits racial gerrymanders in legislative districting plans. It prevents a State, in the absence of "sufficient justification," from "separating its citizens into different voting districts on the basis of race." .... When a voter sues state officials for drawing such race-based lines, our decisions call for a two-step analysis.

First, the plaintiff must prove that "race was the predominant factor motivating the legislature's decision to place a significant number of voters within or without a particular district." ...

Second, if racial considerations predominated over others, the design of the district must withstand strict scrutiny. ...The burden thus shifts to the State to prove that its race-based sorting of voters serves a "compelling interest" and is "narrowly tailored" to that end. ...

Two provisions of the VRA—§2 and §5—are involved in this case. ... Section 2 prohibits any "standard, practice, or procedure" that "results in a denial or abridgement of the right . . . to vote on account of race." §10301(a). .... Section 5, at the time of the districting in dispute, worked through a different mechanism. Before this Court invalidated its coverage formula, see *Shelby County* v. *Holder*, ... that section required certain jurisdictions (including various North Carolina counties) to pre-clear voting changes with the Department of Justice, so as to forestall "retrogression" in the ability of racial minorities to elect their preferred candidates, *Beer* v. *United States*....

When a State invokes the VRA to justify race-based districting, it must show (to meet the "narrow tailoring" requirement) that it had "a strong basis in evidence" for concluding that the statute required its action. ... Or said otherwise, the State must establish that it had "good reasons" to think that it would transgress the Act if it did *not* draw race-based district lines. .... That "strong basis" (or "good reasons") standard gives States "breathing room" to adopt reasonable compliance measures that may prove, in perfect hindsight, not to have been needed. ...

B

This case concerns North Carolina's most recent redrawing of two congressional districts, both of which have long included substantial populations of black voters. In its current incarnation, District 1 is anchored in the northeastern part of the State, with appendages stretching both south and west (the latter into Durham). District 12 begins in the south-central part of the State (where it takes in a large part of Charlotte) and then travels northeast, zig-zagging much of the way to the State's northern border. ... The design of that "serpentine" district, we held, was nothing if not race-centric, and could not be justified as a reasonable attempt to comply with the VRA.

The next year, the State responded with a new districting plan, including a new District 12—and residents of that district brought another lawsuit alleging an impermissible racial gerrymander. A District Court sustained the claim twice, but both times this Court reversed. ... Racial considerations, we held, did not predominate in designing the revised District 12. Rather, that district was the result of a *political* gerrymander—an effort to engineer, mostly "without regard to race," a safe Democratic seat. ...

The State redrew its congressional districts again in 2001, to account for population changes revealed in the prior year's census. Under the 2001 map, which went unchallenged in court, neither District 1 nor District 12 had a black voting-age population (called a "BVAP") that was a majority of the whole: The former had a BVAP of around 48%, the latter a BVAP of around 43%. .... Nonetheless, in five successive general elections conducted in those reconfigured districts, all the candidates preferred by most African-American voters won their contests—and by some handy margins. In District 1, black voters' candidates of choice garnered as much as 70% of the total vote, and never less than 59%. ...

Another census, in 2010, necessitated yet another congressional map—(finally) the one at issue in this case. ...

The new map (among other things) significantly altered both District 1 and District 12. The 2010 census had revealed District 1 to be substantially underpopulated: To comply with the Constitution's one-person-one-vote principle, the State needed to place almost 100,000 new people within the district's boundaries. ... Rucho, Lewis, and Hofeller chose to take most of those people from heavily black areas of Durham, requiring a finger-like extension of the district's western line. ... With that addition, District 1's BVAP rose from 48.6% to 52.7%. ...District 12, for its part, had no need for significant total-population changes: It was overpopulated by fewer than 3,000 people out of over 730,000. ... Still, Rucho, Lewis, and Hofeller decided to reconfigure the district, further narrowing its already snakelike body while adding areas at either end—most relevantly here, in Guilford County. ...Those changes appreciably shifted the racial composition of District 12: As the district gained some 35,000 African-Americans of voting age and lost some 50,000 whites of that age, its BVAP increased from 43.8% to 50.7%. ...

... a three-judge District Court held both districts unconstitutional. All the judges agreed that racial considerations predominated in the design of District 1... all rejected the State's argument that it had a "strong basis" for thinking that the VRA compelled such a race-based drawing of District 1's lines. ... the court explained that the State had failed to put forward any reason, compelling or otherwise, for its attention to race in designing that district.

The State filed a notice of appeal, and we noted probable jurisdiction. *McCrory v. Harris*, 579 U. S. ___ (2016).

II

We address at the outset North Carolina's contention that a victory it won in a very similar state-court lawsuit should dictate (or at least influence) our disposition of this case. As the State explains, the North Carolina NAACP and several other civil rights groups challenged Districts 1 and 12 in state court immediately after their enactment, charging that they were unlawful racial gerrymanders. ... By the time the plaintiffs before us filed this action, the state trial court, in *Dickson v. Rucho*, had rejected those claims... The North Carolina Supreme Court then affirmed that decision by a 4–3 vote, applying the state-court equivalent of clear error review. ...In this Court, North Carolina makes two related arguments based on the *Dickson* litigation: first, that the state trial court's judgment should have barred this case altogether, under familiar principles of claim and issue preclusion; and second, that the state court's conclusions should cause us to conduct a "searching review" of the decision below, rather than deferring (as usual) to its factual findings. ....

The State's preclusion theory rests on an assertion about how the plaintiffs in the two cases are affiliated. ...

But North Carolina never satisfied the District Court that the alleged affiliation really existed. ... Because of those unresolved "factual disputes," the District Court denied North Carolina's motion for summary judgment. ...

That conclusion defeats North Carolina's attempt to argue for claim or issue preclusion here. We have no basis for assessing the factual assertions underlying the State's argument any differently than the District Court did. Nothing in the State's evidence clearly rebuts Harris's and Bowser's testimony that they never joined any of the *Dickson* groups. We need not decide whether the alleged memberships would have supported preclusion if they had been proved. It is enough that the District Court reasonably thought they had not.

...

III

With that out of the way, we turn to the merits of this case, ... We uphold both conclusions.

A

Uncontested evidence in the record shows that the State's mapmakers, in considering District 1, purposefully established a racial target: African-Americans should make up no less than a majority of the voting-age population. ... Senator Rucho and Representative Lewis were not coy in expressing that goal. They repeatedly told their colleagues that District 1 had to be majority-minority, so as to comply with the VRA. ... Dr. Hofeller testified multiple times at trial that Rucho and Lewis instructed him "to draw [District 1] with a [BVAP] in excess of 50 percent." ...

Hofeller followed those directions to the letter, such that the 50%-plus racial target "had a direct and significant impact" on District 1's configuration. ...

Faced with this body of evidence...the District Court did not clearly err in finding that race predominated in drawing District 1. Indeed, as all three judges recognized, the court could hardly have concluded anything but. ...

B

The more substantial question is whether District 1 can survive the strict scrutiny applied to racial gerrymanders. ...

This Court identified, in *Thornburg* v. *Gingles*, three threshold conditions for proving vote dilution under §2 of the VRA...First, a "minority group" must be "sufficiently large and geographically compact to constitute a majority" in some reasonably configured legislative district. ... Second, the minority group must be "politically cohesive." ... And third, a district's white majority must "vote sufficiently as a bloc" to usually "defeat the minority's preferred candidate." ... ...If a State has good reason to think that all the "*Gingles* preconditions" are met, then so too it has good reason to believe that §2 requires drawing a majority-minority district. ...But if not, then not.

Here, electoral history provided no evidence that a §2 plaintiff could demonstrate the third *Gingles* prerequisite—effective white bloc-voting. ... In the lingo of voting law, District 1 functioned, election year in and election year out, as a "crossover" district, in which members of the majority help a "large enough" minority to elect its candidate of choice. ...

The State counters that, in this context, past performance is no guarantee of future results... So, North Carolina contends, the question facing the state mapmakers was not whether the *then-existing* District 1 violated §2. Rather, the question was whether the *future* District 1 would do so if drawn without regard to race. And that issue, the State claims, could not be resolved by "focusing myopically on past elections."

... The prospect of a significant population increase in a district only raises—it does not answer—the question whether §2 requires deliberate measures to augment the district's BVAP. (...State must carefully evaluate whether a plaintiff could establish the *Gingles* preconditions—including effective white bloc-voting—in a new district created without those measures. We see nothing in the legislative record that fits that description.

...Over and over in the legislative record, Rucho and Lewis cited *Strickland* as mandating a 50%-plus BVAP in District 1. ... In effect, they concluded, whenever a legislature *can* draw a majority-minority district, it *must* do so— even if a crossover district would also allow the minority group to elect its favored candidates. ...

That idea, though, is at war with our §2 jurisprudence— *Strickland* included. Under the State's view, the third *Gingles* condition is no condition at all, because even in the absence of effective white bloc-voting, a §2 claim could succeed in a district (like the old District 1) with an under 50% BVAP. But this

Court has made clear that unless *each* of the three *Gingles* prerequisites is established, "there neither has been a wrong nor can be a remedy." ...

In sum: Although States enjoy leeway to take race-based actions reasonably judged necessary under a proper interpretation of the VRA, that latitude cannot rescue District 1. ... But neither will we approve a racial gerrymander whose necessity is supported by no evidence and whose *raison d'être* is a legal mistake. Accordingly, we uphold the District Court's conclusion that North Carolina's use of race as the predominant factor in designing District 1 does not withstand strict scrutiny.

IV

We now look west to District 12, making its fifth (!) appearance before this Court. This time, the district's legality turns, and turns solely, on which of two possible reasons predominantly explains its most recent reconfiguration. The plaintiffs contended at trial that the General Assembly chose voters for District 12, as for District 1, because of their race; more particularly, they urged that the Assembly intentionally increased District 12's BVAP in the name of ensuring preclearance under the VRA's §5. But North Carolina declined to mount any defense ...The mapmakers drew their lines, in other words, to "pack" District 12 with Democrats, not African-Americans. After hearing evidence supporting both parties' accounts, the District Court accepted the plaintiffs'.

... In *Shaw II*, for example, this Court emphasized the "highly irregular" shape of then-District 12 in concluding that race predominated in its design. ... But such evidence loses much of its value when the State asserts partisanship as a defense, because a bizarre shape—as of the new District 12—can arise from a "political motivation" as well as a racial one...

...

... we uphold the District Court's finding of racial predominance respecting District 12. The evidence offered at trial, including live witness testimony subject to credibility determinations, adequately supports the conclusion that race, not politics, accounted for the district's reconfiguration. And no error of law infected that judgment...the District Court had no call to dismiss this challenge just because the plaintiffs did not proffer an alternative design for District 12 as circumstantial evidence of the legislature's intent.

A

Begin with some facts and figures, showing how the redistricting of District 12 affected its racial composition. ...

As the plaintiffs pointed out at trial, Rucho and Lewis had publicly stated that racial considerations lay behind District 12's augmented BVAP. ... Thus, the District Court found, Rucho's and Lewis's own account "evince[d] intentionality" as to District 12's racial composition: *Because of* the VRA, they increased the number of African-Americans. ....

Hofeller confirmed that intent ...Before the redistricting, Hofeller testified, some black residents of Guilford County fell within District 12 while others fell within neighboring District 13. The legislators, he continued, "decided to reunite the black community in Guilford County into the Twelfth." ..."[M]indful that Guilford County was covered" by §5, Hofeller explained, the legislature "determined that it was prudent to reunify [the county's] African-American community" into District 12. ... It would "avoid the possibility of a [VRA]charge" that would "inhibit preclearance." ...

...

... Congressman Mel Watt ...recounted a conversation he had with Rucho in 2011 ..., Rucho said that "his leadership had told him that he had to ramp the minority percentage in [District 12] up to over 50 percent to comply with the Voting Rights Law." ...In the court's view, Watt's account was of a piece with all the other evidence—including the redistricters' on-the-nose attainment of a 50% BVAP—indicating that the General Assembly, in the name of VRA compliance, deliberately redrew District 12 as a majority-minority district. ...

The State's contrary story—that politics alone drove decision making—came into the trial mostly through Hofeller's testimony. Hofeller explained that Rucho and Lewis instructed him, first and foremost, to make the map as a whole "more favorable to Republican candidates." ...In part of his testimony, Hofeller further stated that the Obama-McCain election data explained (among other things) his incorporation of the black, but not the white, parts of Guilford County then located in District 13. ...

The District Court, however, disbelieved Hofeller's asserted indifference to the new district's racial composition. The court recalled Hofeller's contrary deposition testimony—his statement (repeated in only slightly different words in his expert report) that Rucho and Lewis "decided" to shift African-American voters into District 12 "in order to" ensure preclearance under §5...Right after asserting that Rucho and Lewis had told him "[not] to use race" in designing District 12, Hofeller added a qualification: "except perhaps with regard to Guilford County." ...As the District Court understood, that is the kind of "exception" that goes pretty far toward swallowing the rule. ...

Finally, an expert report by Dr. Stephen ... looked at the six counties overlapping with District 12.... The question he asked was: Who from those counties actually ended up in District 12? The answer he found was: Only 16% of the region's white registered voters, but 64% of the black ones. ... Those stark disparities led Ansolabehere to conclude that "race, and not party," was "the dominant factor"....

The District Court's assessment that all this evidence proved racial predominance clears the bar of clear error review. The court emphasized that the districting plan's own architects had repeatedly described the influx of African-Americans into District 12 as a §5 compliance measure, not a side-effect of political gerrymandering...—that Watt told the truth when he recounted Rucho's resolve to hit a majority-BVAP target; and conversely that Hofeller skirted the truth (especially as to Guilford County) when he claimed to have followed only race-blind criteria in drawing district lines. We cannot disrespect such credibility judgments. ...

B

The State mounts a final, legal rather than factual, attack on the District Court's finding of racial predominance. When race and politics are competing explanations of a district's lines, argues North Carolina, the party challenging the district must introduce a particular kind of circumstantial evidence: "an alternative [map] that achieves the legislature's political objectives while improving racial balance." ...

...

A plaintiff's task... is simply to persuade the trial court—without any special evidentiary prerequisite—that race (not politics) was the "predominant consideration in deciding to place a significant number of voters within or without a particular district." ...that burden of proof, we have often held, is "demanding." ... And because that is so, a plaintiff will sometimes need an alternative map, as a practical matter, to make his case. But in no area of our equal protection law have we forced plaintiffs to submit one particular form of proof to prevail. ...Nor would it make sense to do so here. ...

...

V

Applying a clear error standard, we uphold the District Court's conclusions that racial considerations predominated in designing both District 1 and District 12. For District 12, that is all we must do, because North Carolina has made no attempt to justify race-based districting there. For District 1, we further uphold the District Court's decision that §2 of the VRA gave North Carolina no good reason to reshuffle voters because of their race. We accordingly affirm the judgment of the District Court.

It is so ordered.

JUSTICE GORSUCH took no part in the consideration or decision of this case.

Glossary

gerrymandering: purposefully dividing a geographical region into electoral districts with intent to allow one political party to have a majority of sympathetic voters

judicial review: a constitutional doctrine which allows a court to review legislative or executive acts to determine whether they are constitutional

strict scrutiny: the highest level of judicial review, applied by the Supreme Court to a law that is alleged to violate equal protection rights under the U.S. Constitution and to determine if the law is narrowly tailored to serve a compelling state interest

Voting Rights Act of 1965: a landmark federal law that seeks to prohibit racial discrimination in voting

Document Analysis

In the majority opinion, Justice Kagan noted that the crux of a racial gerrymandering case amounts to answering two questions. The first is whether race was the predominant factor behind the state legislature's decision to move particular voters in or out of a particular district. The second question is, if race was the predominant factor, can the state show that it had "good reasons" to believe that the Voting Rights Act would be violated if the legislature did not use race to draw the districts?

The Supreme Court's inquiry into the first question is limited because it can only review the district court's findings of fact to determine if they are clearly wrong, a very high threshold. Thus, a district court's factual findings on whether race was the predominant factor will not be overturned if the findings are "plausible," even if the justices might reach a different conclusion. In analyzing the first question, Kagan noted that before drawing the boundary lines for District 1, the gerrymandering map "purposefully established a racial target: African Americans should make up no less than a majority of the voting-age population." Kagan noted that in fulfilling this goal, the gerrymandering plan resulted in a "district with stark racial borders. Within the same counties, the portions that fall inside District 1 have black populations two to three times larger than the portions placed in neighboring districts." Kagan concluded that the federal district court was not clearly wrong in finding that "race predominated in drawing District 1."

Regarding the second question in the analysis, Kagan found the state did not have "good reasons" to believe that it had to either consider race or risk violating the Voting Rights Act with its redistricting plan. To the contrary, the opinion concludes that the state provided "no reason" to show that it needed to increase the number of African American voters in District 1 because the district had consistently been electing minority members of Congress.

The state attempted to argue that race wasn't a factor but, rather, that party affiliation was a predominant factor and many Democrats happened to be African American. The district court had concluded that although race and party affiliation were closely aligned, it was race that was the predominant factor. Kagan's opinion acknowledged it was not an easy task for the district court to make the determination on whether race was a predominant factor in drawing the redistricting maps but that the Supreme Court had to find the district court's determination to be "clearly wrong" in its determination, and that in the instant case it was not.

Thus, the majority concluded that race was a predominant factor; that the district wrong was not "clearly wrong" in making that finding; and, that the state failed to make any showing of a "good reason" demonstrating the Voting Rights Act would be violated if race had not been used to draw the redistricting map.

Justices Alito, Chief Justice Roberts, and Justice Kennedy disagreed with the majority opinion about District 12 being invalidated. Justice Thomas provided the needed fifth vote to uphold the district court's invalidating of District 12, somewhat surprising as he traditionally is regarded as a more conservative jurist.

In his opinion, Justice Alito concurred in part with Kagan's opinion, and dissented in part as well. He believed that the challengers to the racial gerrymandering should have been required to provide their own redistricting map, stating that an alternative map "is a logical response to the difficult problem of distinguishing between racial and political motivations when race and political party preference closely correlate." Alito further asserted that the majority opinion risked confusing "a political gerrymander for a racial gerrymander" and that the opinion "invades a traditional domain of state authority."

Essential Themes

Although *Cooper v. Harris* did not definitively create new law on the issue, its interpretation of state legislature motives in drawing up redistricting maps in coordination with the Voting Rights Act was regarded as a major ruling on racial gerrymandering. Particularly, Cooper made clear that the Supreme Court took a common-sense approach to the idea that legislatures that utilize race in drawing districts, even if race is used as a proxy for political affiliation, would be seen as highly suspect. It provided guidance and a road map for what challengers to redistricting needed to prove in order to establish that race was a predominant factor in the drawing of districts.

—Michele McBride Simonelli, JD

Bibliography and Additional Reading

Cooper v. Harris, 137 S.Ct. 1455 (2017). Justia: U.S. Supreme Court, supreme.justia.com/cases/federal/us/581/15-1262/

Curtis, Michael Kent. "Using the Voting Rights Act to Discriminate: North Carolina's Use of Racial Gerrymanders, Two Racial Quotas, Safe Harbors, Shields, and Inoculations to Undermine Multiracial Coalitions and Black Political Power," *Wake Forest Law Review*, 51 (2016): 421-492.

Daley, David. *Ratf**ked : The True Story Behind the Secret Plan to Steal America's Democracy*. New York: Liveright Publishing, 2016.

"The Future of Majority-Minority Districts in Light of Declining Racially Polarized Voting," *Harvard Law Review*, 116 (2003): 2208-2229.

Grofman, Bernard, editor. *Race and Redistricting in the 1990s*. New York: Agathon Press, 1998.

Shaw v. Reno, 113 S.Ct. 2816 (1993). Justia: U.S. Supreme Court, supreme.justia.com/cases/federal/us/509/630/

■ *Rucho v. Common Cause*

Date: June 27, 2019
Author: Chief Justice John Roberts (with Syllabus compiled by Christine Luchok Fallon)
Genre: court opinion

Summary Overview

When Chief Justice John Roberts wrote the majority opinion in Rucho v. Common Cause, *he, and the four other conservative justices who concurred, created the foundation for a transformation of the process of electing members of state legislatures and the House of Representatives. His majority opinion basically took the federal judiciary out of picture, if and when a political party believed that a legislative district had been drawn to grossly favor the opposition. Thus, each state was given free rein to create districts according to the wishes of those assigned that task. As long as districts were approximately the same size and not based on race, Roberts did not see any reason for the federal courts to become involved. This was a major departure from previous practice in the modern era.*

Defining Moment

Although the term "gerrymandering" goes back to the elections of 1812, as noted in this case's opinion, the practice had existed even before that. In the eighteenth and early nineteenth centuries, most areas did not have a set time for redistricting, so the districts were often changed the next time a different political party came to power. (For example, the famous 1812 map of Massachusetts for which the term was created, was redrawn in 1813 after new elections changed the party in power.) Although strong steps, via gerrymandering, were taken by some states in the late 1800s to keep the new African American voters from wielding any substantial power, other means were used in the early twentieth century. Federal court involvement in redistricting oversight was not a major consideration until the rulings by the Warren Court in the 1960s set certain standards for legislative districts. However, this did not directly address partisan gerrymandering. With the 1960s rulings forcing similar-sized districts and full redistricting after every census, many called on the skills of political operatives to create districts advantageous to their party through partisan gerrymandering. The biggest change was in those states that had a state senate patterned after the U.S. Senate, where districts were based on state political units not population. Because the wholesale creation of districts had been mandated by the U.S. Supreme Court, those who felt aggrieved by the new district turned to the federal courts to obtain relief from the perceived injustice. This was the reason that *Rucho v. Common Cause* had been taken to the federal Middle District Court of North Carolina and ultimately to the Supreme Court.

In the decades leading up to *Rucho*, both major political parties had undertaken concerted efforts to create legislative districts favorable to themselves, although the Republican Party seemed to have been more successful at this than the Democrats. Although not specifically part of this ruling, one of the issues that had been growing in strength since the time of the Warren Court, was the desire by many conservatives to have more power vested at the state level and less at the federal level. This ruling was in line with those desires, and was well received by this part of the population.

Author Biography

Chief Justice John Roberts (b. 1955) did his undergraduate studies at Harvard University and then attended and graduated from Harvard Law School. He has served as Chief Justice of the Supreme Court since 2005, having been an appeals court judge for the four years prior to that. He had served in the Justice Department in the Reagan and George H.W. Bush administrations, and worked in private practice between that time and 2001, when he became a judge.

Christine Luchok Fallon (b. 1952) was the first woman to hold the position of Reporter of Decisions for the U.S. Supreme Court. She was a graduate of West Virginia University and then the Columbus School of Law, which is part of Catholic University of America. She served in this post from 2011 until late 2020. Just prior to this, she had been Deputy Reporter of Decisions for twenty-two years.

Printed in March 1812, this political cartoon was drawn in reaction to the newly drawn congressional electoral district of South Essex County drawn by the Massachusetts legislature to favor the Democratic-Republican Party candidates of Governor Elbridge Gerry over the Federalists. The caricature satirizes the bizarre shape of a district in Essex County, Massachusetts, as a dragon-like "monster." Federalist newspapers' editors and others at the time likened the district shape to a salamander, and the word gerrymander was born out of a portmanteau of that word and Governor Gerry's surname. Image via Wikimedia Commons. [Public domain.]

Historical Document

Rucho v. Common Cause

SUPREME COURT OF THE UNITED STATES

Syllabus

RUCHO ET AL. v. COMMON CAUSE ET AL.

Appeal from the United States District Court for the Middle District of North Carolina

No. 18-422. Argued March 26, 2019—Decided June 27, 2019

Voters and other plaintiffs in North Carolina and Maryland filed suits challenging their States' congressional districting maps as unconstitutional partisan gerrymanders. The North Carolina plaintiffs claimed that the State's districting plan discriminated against Democrats, while the Maryland plaintiffs claimed that their State's plan discriminated against Republicans. The plaintiffs alleged violations of the First Amendment, the Equal Protection Clause of the Fourteenth Amendment, the Elections Clause, and Article I, §2. The District Courts in both cases ruled in favor of the plaintiffs, and the defendants appealed directly to this Court.

Held: Partisan gerrymandering claims present political questions beyond the reach of the federal courts. Pp. 6-34.

(a) In these cases, the Court is asked to decide an important question of constitutional law. Before it does so, the Court "must find that the question is presented in a 'case' or 'controversy' that is...'of a Judiciary Nature.'" *DaimlerChrysler Corp. v. Cuno*, 547 U. S. 332, 342. While it is "the province and duty of the judicial department to say what the law is," *Marbury v. Madison*, 1 Cranch 137, 177, sometimes the law is that the Judiciary cannot entertain a claim because it presents a nonjusticiable "political question," *Baker v. Carr*, 369 U. S. 186, 217. Among the political question cases this Court has identified are those that lack "judicially discoverable and manageable standards for resolving [them]." *Ibid*. This Court's partisan gerrymandering cases have left unresolved the question whether such claims are claims of *legal* right, resolvable according to *legal* principles, or political questions that must find their resolution elsewhere. See *Gill v. Whitford*, 585 U. S. ___, ___.

Partisan gerrymandering was known in the Colonies prior to Independence, and the Framers were familiar with it at the time of the drafting and ratification of the Constitution. They addressed the election of Representatives to Congress in the Elections Clause, Art. I, §4, cl. 1, assigning to state legislatures the power to prescribe the "Times, Places and Manner of holding Elections" for Members of Congress, while giving Congress the power to "make or alter" any such regulations. Congress has regularly exercised its Elections Clause power, including to address partisan gerrymandering. But the Framers did not set aside all electoral issues as questions that only Congress can resolve. In two areas—one-person, one-vote and racial gerrymandering—this Court has held that there is a role for the courts with respect to at least some issues that could arise from a State's drawing of congressional districts. But the history of partisan gerrymandering is not irrelevant. Aware of electoral districting problems, the Framers chose a characteristic approach, assigning the issue to the state legislatures, expressly checked and balanced by the Federal Congress, with no suggestion that the federal courts had a role to play.

Courts have nonetheless been called upon to resolve a variety of questions surrounding districting. The claim of population inequality among districts in *Baker v. Carr*, for example, could be decided under basic equal protection principles. 369 U. S., at 226. Racial discrimination in districting also raises constitutional issues that can be addressed by the federal courts. See *Gomillion v. Lightfoot*, 364 U. S. 339, 340. Partisan gerrymandering claims have proved far more difficult to adjudicate, in part because "a jurisdiction may engage in constitutional political gerrymandering." *Hunt v. Cromartie*, 526 U. S. 541, 551. To hold that legislators cannot take their partisan interests into account when drawing district lines would essentially countermand the Framers' decision to entrust districting to political entities. The "central problem" is "determining when political gerrymandering has gone too far." *Vieth v. Jubelirer*, 541 U. S. 267, 296 (plurality opinion). Despite considerable efforts in *Gaffney v. Cummings*, 412 U. S. 735, 753; *Davis v. Bandemer*, 478 U. S. 109, 116-117; *Vieth*, 541 U. S., at 272-273; and *League of United Latin American Citizens v. Perry*, 548 U. S. 399, 414 (*LULAC*), this Court's prior cases have left "unresolved whether…claims [of legal right] may be brought in cases involving allegations of partisan gerrymandering," *Gill*, 585 U. S., at ___. Two "threshold questions" remained: standing, which was addressed in *Gill*, and "whether [such] claims are justiciable." *Ibid*. Pp. 6-14.

(b) Any standard for resolving partisan gerrymandering claims must be grounded in a "limited and precise rationale" and be "clear, manageable, and politically neutral." *Vieth,* 541 U. S., at 306-308 (Kennedy, J., concurring in judgment). The question is one of degree: How to "provid[e] a standard for deciding how much partisan dominance is too much." *LULAC,* 548 U. S., at 420 (opinion of Kennedy, J.). Partisan gerrymandering claims rest on an instinct that groups with a certain level of political support should enjoy a commensurate level of political power and influence. Such claims invariably sound in a desire for proportional representation, but the Constitution does not require proportional representation, and federal courts are neither equipped nor authorized to apportion political power as a matter of fairness. It is not even clear what fairness looks like in this context. It may mean achieving a greater number of competitive districts by undoing packing and cracking so that supporters of the disadvantaged party have a better shot at electing their preferred candidates. But it could mean engaging in cracking and packing to ensure each party its "appropriate" share of "safe" seats. Or perhaps it should be measured by adherence to "traditional" districting criteria. Deciding among those different visions of fairness poses basic questions that are political, not legal. There are no legal standards discernible in the Constitution for making such judgments. And it is only after determining how to define fairness that one can even begin to answer the determinative question: "How much is too much?"

The fact that the Court can adjudicate one-person, one-vote claims does not mean that partisan gerrymandering claims are justiciable. This Court's one-person, one-vote cases recognize that each person is entitled to an equal say in the election of representatives. It hardly follows from that principle that a person is entitled to have his political party achieve representation commensurate to its share of statewide support. Vote dilution in the one-person, one-vote cases refers to the idea that each vote must carry equal weight. That requirement does not extend to political parties; it does not mean that each party must be influential in proportion to the number of its supporters. The racial gerrymandering cases are also inapposite: They call for the elimination of a racial classification, but a partisan gerrymandering claim cannot ask for the elimination of partisanship. Pp. 15-21.

(c) None of the proposed "tests" for evaluating partisan gerrymandering claims meets the need for a limited and precise standard that is judicially discernible and manageable. Pp. 22-30.

(1) The *Common Cause* District Court concluded that all but one of the districts in North Carolina's 2016 Plan violated the Equal Protection Clause by intentionally diluting the voting strength of Democrats. It applied a three-part test, examining intent, effects, and causation. The District Court's "predominant intent" prong is borrowed from the test used in racial gerrymandering cases. However, unlike race-based decision making, which is "inherently suspect," *Miller* v. *Johnson*, 515 U. S. 900, 915, districting for some level of partisan advantage is not unconstitutional. Determining that lines were drawn on the basis of partisanship does not indicate that districting was constitutionally impermissible. The *Common Cause* District Court also required the plaintiffs to show that vote dilution is "likely to persist" to such a degree that the elected representatives will feel free to ignore the concerns of the supporters of the minority party. Experience proves that accurately predicting electoral

outcomes is not simple, and asking judges to predict how a particular districting map will perform in future elections risks basing constitutional holdings on unstable ground outside judicial expertise. The District Court's third prong—which gave the defendants an opportunity to show that discriminatory effects were due to a "legitimate redistricting objective"—just restates the question asked at the "predominant intent" prong. Pp. 22-25.

(2) The District Courts also found partisan gerrymandering claims justiciable under the First Amendment, coalescing around a basic three-part test: proof of intent to burden individuals based on their voting history or party affiliation, an actual burden on political speech or associational rights, and a causal link between the invidious intent and actual burden. But their analysis offers no "clear" and "manageable" way of distinguishing permissible from impermissible partisan motivation. Pp. 25-27.

(3) Using a State's own districting criteria as a baseline from which to measure how extreme a partisan gerrymander is would be indeterminate and arbitrary. Doing so would still leave open the question of how much political motivation and effect is too much. Pp. 27-29.

(4) The North Carolina District Court further held that the 2016 Plan violated Article I, §2, and the Elections Clause, Art. I, §4, cl. 1. But the *Vieth* plurality concluded—without objection from any other Justice—that neither §2 nor §4 "provides a judicially enforceable limit on the political considerations that the States and Congress may take into account when districting." 541 U. S., at 305. Any assertion that partisan gerrymanders violate the core right of voters to choose their representatives is an objection more likely grounded in the Guarantee Clause of Article IV, §4, which "guarantee[s] to every State in [the] Union a Republican Form of Government." This Court has several times concluded that the Guarantee Clause does not provide the basis for a justiciable claim. See, *e.g., Pacific States Telephone & Telegraph Co. v. Oregon*, 223 U. S. 118. Pp. 29-30.

(d) The conclusion that partisan gerrymandering claims are not justiciable neither condones excessive partisan gerrymandering nor condemns complaints about districting to echo into a void. Numerous States are actively addressing the issue through state constitutional amendments and legislation placing power to draw electoral districts in the hands of independent commissions, mandating particular districting criteria for their mapmakers, or prohibiting drawing district lines for partisan advantage. The Framers also gave Congress the power to do something about partisan gerrymandering in the Elections Clause. That avenue for reform established by the Framers, and used by Congress in the past, remains open. Pp. 30-34.

318 F. Supp. 3d 777 and 348 F. Supp. 3d 493, vacated and remanded.

Roberts, C. J., delivered the opinion of the Court, in which Thomas, Alito, Gorsuch, and Kavanaugh, JJ., joined. Kagan, J., filed a dissenting opinion, in which Ginsburg, Breyer, and Sotomayor, JJ., joined.

Glossary

justiciable: capable of being resolved by a court of law

partisan gerrymandering: the drawing of legislative district lines based on the political party affiliations of its residents

Document Analysis

In *Rucho v. Common Cause*, Chief Justice Roberts makes it clear that there is a division between politics and political decisions, on the one hand, and the judiciary, on the other; he observes that the line of separation should be crossed only in the most extreme situations. Roberts, and the four other conservative justices who voted in favor of this ruling, states that the drawing of legislative boundaries with the goal of gaining political advantage does not meet the high threshold of an extreme situation, and thus all federal courts should refrain from intervening. Only if it is clear that equal representation is threatened should the courts enter into the political process. Thus, the courts could rule on the need for legislative districts to be approximately the same size, but not on the distribution of members of various political parties among the districts. In Robert's mind, any regulation of how members of political parties are divided among legislative districts is up to Congress or the states.

Examining the issues that the Court has faced in partisan redistricting cases, Roberts looks at the various provisions in the Constitution cited by those who have previously alleged that partisan gerrymandering adversely affected them. He quickly dismisses arguments based on the First Amendment, as he does not see any relevance of this amendment to charges of partisan gerrymandering. Roberts is more open to complaints about redistricting based on the Fourteenth Amendment, because in extreme cases, he believes that this amendment applies. Thus, he refers to *Baker v. Carr* as an example of when the Court correctly stepped in to force states to have the number of people in each legislative district approximately equal. He similarly understood redistricting based on racial discrimination to be inherently unjust under this amendment. However, beyond these situations, Roberts goes back to the original Constitution, where Article I, Sections 2 and 4, gives the power to regulate elections to the states and to Congress. For him, this is the key to understanding who should regulate the redistricting process.

In addition, as regards possible partisan gerrymandering, Roberts maintains that nowhere in the Constitution is it made clear "How much is too much." Thus, there is no guidance given to the courts on which a rule could be made about partisan gerrymandering in the redistricting process. Because of this, Roberts firmly states that the courts could not rule on proposed plans for redistricting because there are no "legal standards." Given this, a "precise statement" regarding what is permissible and what is not cannot not be given as guidance to states on the matter of creating appropriate legislative districts. This second factor, for Roberts, strengthens the argument that the courts should not generally be involved in the redistricting process. He could be said to appear optimistic about the ability of the states to do the right thing and reduce the possibility of partisan districts, as he believes that "numerous states" are addressing the issue in good faith. If this turns out not to be the case, Roberts observes that the "Framers also gave Congress the power to do something," which for him would be the ultimate remedy if the states abuse their power. Either way, for Roberts the Court should not enter into an area that is "not justiciable" no matter how much, or how little, partisan gerrymandering is evident in a redistricting plan.

Essential Themes

Justice Roberts makes it clear that he has an understanding that limits the extension of judicial powers into the realm of politics. Although he is clear that in some areas, such as equal representation and processes that were blatantly discriminatory against racial minorities, there is a role for the courts to intervene, these are the exception rather than the rule. For him, the general rule is that electoral politics has its own process for determining the desired outcome. This includes the determination of legislative districts. As he states, "Partisan gerrymandering claims present political questions beyond the reach of the federal courts." Unlike what he sees as the problematic rulings that previously had been made by various federal courts, this ruling is quite clear. Roberts refers to Article 1, Sections 2 and 4, as, in his opinion, clearly giving Congress and the states the power to conduct elections. Thus, for him, the courts have no business regulating the electoral process, except in extreme cases that show evidence of undercutting the equal protection portion of the Fourteenth Amendment.

In addition to Roberts' argument about the Constitution as having granted power over elections to the states and to Congress, he examines the types of cases and solutions that had previously come before the various federal courts. These cases illustrate, for the majority in *Rucho*, the fact that there is no one ideal solution that a court can mandate in the determination of legislative districts. Referring to three "prongs" of the arguments used by those seeking redress from the courts against proposed legislative boundaries ("intent, effects, and causation"), Roberts understands that the plaintiffs believe that an illegal burden was being placed on them based on their voting history. However, he does not see such complaints rising to the level where it becomes necessary for the Court to intervene to preserve people's rights. As to the desired outcome from redistricting, Roberts states that it is not clear whether the ideal is to have safe districts for each political party in numbers consistent with the number of party members, or to have as many competitive districts as possible within a state. Without clear constitutional guidance on this, Roberts writes that the matter is "not justiciable." Given that, he says that the Court is not judging whether the proposed districts in North Carolina (or any state) are ideal or suboptimal. He means to state only that unless Congress acts to the contrary, each state is essentially free to create legislative districts according to the standards outlined in its own laws.

—Donald A. Watt, PhD

Bibliography and Additional Reading

Bitzer, J. Michael. *Redistricting and Gerrymandering in North Carolina.* (Palgrave Studies in U.S. Elections.) Cham, Switzerland: Palgrave-MacMillan, 2021.

Court Case Tracker. "*Rucho v. Common Cause.*" *Brennan Center for Justice.* New York: Brennan Center for Justice at the NYU Law, 2019.

Harvard Law Review. "*Rucho v. Common Cause.*" *Harvard Law Review.* Cambridge, MA: Harvard Law Review, 2019.

LWV Guest. "The Woman Who Argued 'Rucho v. Common Cause' Looks Back." *League of Women Voters.* Washington, D.C.: League of Women Voters of the United States, 2022.

Supreme Court. "*Rucho v. Common Cause.*" *Legal Information Institute.* Ithaca, NY: Cornell Law School, 2019.

Voting and Political Division Today

The 2016 U.S. presidential election was one of both great moment and great controversy. Taking place in an atmosphere of increasing political partisanship in the nation generally, it pitted former Secretary of State (and former First Lady) Hillary Clinton, on the Democratic side, against businessman (and political novice) Donald Trump, on the Republican side. Trump's right-wing populist, nationalist campaign promised to "Make America Great Again" and opposed illegal immigration, "endless wars," trade with China, and the supposed decline of the United States as a power on the world stage. Clinton ran on a campaign of extending President Barack Obama's policies of "diversity and inclusion" at home, maintaining strong international alliances, and fostering a form of inclusive capitalism. The tone of the campaign was considered to be harsh, negative, and generally off-putting to many voters.

There were also major scandals. Throughout his campaign Trump would rally his supporters with the line "Lock her up!"—referring to Clinton and her use of a private server for some of her official emails. The Federal Bureau of Investigation looked into the matter but concluded in July 2016 that there were no grounds for prosecuting Clinton. Yet, in late October, just over a week before election day, the FBI director announced that the agency was investigating a new set of classified emails that were said to have been lost by Clinton. The timing of the announcement could hardly have been worse for the Clinton campaign. (Clinton was later cleared of any deliberate malfeasance, and no important state secrets were thought to have been revealed in the exchanges.)

Meanwhile, the Trump campaign was facing some serious difficulties of its own. Key among them was alleged collusion with Russian state actors seeking to undermine Clinton and get Trump elected. The story stewed for over a year and remained unresolved by election day, though Trump denied any such collusion. It was later found, after several investigations, that Russia had indeed engaged in various forms of political manipulation during the 2016 election campaign, but neither Trump nor his top campaign aides could be proved to have been involved.

It was in this environment that a related scandal connected to Trump unfolded. A data analysis company called Cambridge Analytica, run by a wealthy supporter of Trump, was found to be illegally using private data from Facebook to aid the Trump campaign by targeting ads to users. A 2017 report on the matter stated that Russian propaganda and advertising may have been spread through the company's targeting abilities. The Trump campaign's digital operations relied heavily on Facebook, along with other tech platforms. The head of Cambridge Analytica's political wing was recorded speaking about other unethical means the firm used to influence elections, such as bribery and prostitution. In the grand scheme of things, however, the Cambridge Analytica scandal seemed to blow past many voters as being both too technical and part of the general aura of scandal surrounding Trump. (There were several others besides this one.) In the end, Trump was elected president in one of the greatest upsets in U.S. history.

Political divisiveness only got worse under his presidency. Indeed, by the time of the 2020 election, which saw Trump running against former vice president Joseph R. Biden, Trump could rely on his hardcore MAGA ("Make America Great Again") supporters to take it to his opponents *physically*, as a crowd of MAGA people did in the U.S. Capitol district on January 6, 2021, the day Congress was set to certify that Trump had lost the November 2020 election to Biden in a close race. Trump, denying that he had lost, encouraged the armed crowd to march to the Capitol Building, where Congress was gathered, and "fight like hell" to "stop the steal" of the election. Liberal and old-line conservative observers would see the ensuing violence as an insurrection, a "high crime" for which Trump would face impeachment for a second time. (A majority in the Senate voted to impeach but not enough to reach the necessary two-thirds mark.) A year later, now in the presidency, Biden delivered a speech in which he recalled the events of the day and warned against the continuing political dangers facing the nation from the extremists who supported the "Big Lie" that Trump had not lost the election.

Nevertheless, Trump and his MAGA Republicans only grew stronger in the Republican Party and eventually came to dominate it, casting all alternative viewpoints aside. Hardline governors and/or legislatures in many states passed laws aimed at suppressing broad participation in the voting process, hoping to limit access to the ballot box and thus give an edge to dedicated political troopers of the kind who back Trump. We include two examples of such voter suppression efforts, from Texas and Arizona, in the present section. The 2024 presidential election, a rematch between Trump and Biden, was, as of mid-2024, shaping up to be every bit as momentous (and possibly as calamitous) as the one in 2020.

■ Statement to the U.S. Senate Judiciary Committee concerning Cambridge Analytica

Date: May 16, 2018
Author: Christopher Wylie
Genre: written testimony

Summary Overview

Christopher Wylie is the former Research Director of Cambridge Analytica, a political consulting firm specializing in data analysis. In this written statement to the U.S. Senate, Wylie outlines his concerns regarding his former employer's use of inappropriately obtained Facebook data in connection with the 2016 presidential election. Wylie was called to testify in front of lawmakers in both the United States and the United Kingdom, after his interviews with the Guardian, *the* Observer, *and the* New York Times. *He told the press that Cambridge Analytica based its work on an unauthorized data set containing the private information of about 87 million Facebook users. The data was purchased from a Cambridge-based scientist named Aleksandr Kogan. Kogan had violated Facebook's terms of service by selling the information he collected to the company. Wylie reveals the practices of the data analytics firm he helped to create, stating the data was used to create psychographic profiles of Facebook users in order to serve them pro-Trump advertisements during the 2016 election campaign. Wylie's revelations shone a spotlight on Facebook programs that monetized user data through targeted advertising. Facebook and other technology companies were subsequently forced to change their practices regarding privacy. In his statement, Wylie urges lawmakers to recognize the importance of creating protections for people's private data and calls for a higher level of scrutiny around the use of personal data by social media companies such as Facebook.*

Defining Moment

Cambridge Analytica was founded in 2013 by conservative businesspersons Steve Bannon, an executive at *Breitbart News*, and Robert Mercer, an American hedge fund manager. The company was headquartered in London, but also had offices in New York and Washington, D.C. Mercer invested $15 million in the venture. Bannon divested his holdings in the company in April 2017, due to his role as White House chief strategist for the Trump administration.

In 2014, SCL Group, the parent company of Cambridge Analytica, became interested in the work of Michal Kosinski, a researcher at the Psychometrics Centre of Cambridge University. Kosinski and his colleagues had created a psychographic profiling system based on Facebook data such as likes and interests that predicted behavior better than real-life friends. Psychographics is the study and classification of people by psychological attributes, such as emotions,

Christopher Wylie. Photo by Simon Fraser University - Communications & Marketing, via Wikimedia Commons.

values, and aspirations. Psychographic targeting uses these profiles to craft and market advertising that delivers comparatively effective results. Since psychographic marketing requires abundant personal data in order to be effective, Facebook, with its social network of about 2 billion users internationally, is an important data source. Cambridge Analytica tried to hire Kosinski and purchase his algorithms and data sets, but negotiations fell through.

Cambridge Analytica then turned to Aleksandr Kogan, a psychology professor who was also at Cambridge. Kogan created a Facebook app called "This Is Your Digital Life." About 320,000 Facebook users were paid to take a personality quiz (with Cambridge Analytica's money) and allowed Kogan to collect their Facebook data. In addition, the app was able to scrape data from the friends of those taking the quizzes without their knowledge if their privacy settings allowed it. In this manner, Kogan was able to collect data on 87 million people. In 2010, Facebook allowed this type of friends-network data collection. In 2014, Facebook made accessing the data of an app user's friends without their knowledge or permission against its rules. This rule change was not retroactive, so Kogan did not delete the data he had collected. Kogan told Facebook that he was acquiring the data solely for academic purposes and did not disclose that he was selling it to Cambridge Analytica.

Cambridge Analytica combined Kogan's Facebook data with voter lists and data purchased from commercial brokers that included names, ages, religious affiliations, work and educational histories, and preferences for news stories, products, and other online posts. This gave them a very precise picture of a large number of American voters. Wylie stated, "We exploited Facebook to harvest millions of people's profiles. And built models to exploit what we knew about them and target their inner demons."

Wylie left Cambridge Analytica in 2014, but the company continued to expand upon the profiling and targeting work he did for them. In 2015, the *Guardian* reported that presidential candidate Ted Cruz hired Cambridge Analytica to provide psychological targeting based on research on millions of Facebook users to win the election. After this story broke, Facebook banned Kogan's app and demanded Kogan and

Photo by Book Catalog, via Wikimedia Commons.

Cambridge Analytica erase the data they acquired improperly. Facebook did not inform users whose data had been harvested. Though the United Kingdom and many U.S. states have laws that require disclosure of any data breach, Facebook argued that no breach had occurred as "no systems were infiltrated, no passwords or information were stolen or hacked."

After Wylie left, Cambridge Analytica continued working in elections across the globe. According to chief executive officer (CEO) Alexander Nix, Cambridge Analytica was hired to work in forty-four U.S. political elections in 2014. In 2015, they provided data analysis and advertising strategies for Ted Cruz's presidential campaign. In 2018, the company worked in over 200 elections across the globe, including those in Nigeria, the Czech Republic, and Argentina.

In May 2017, *Time* reported that Congress was investigating Cambridge Analytica in relation to Russian interference in the 2016 presidential election. The report states that Russian propaganda and advertising may have been spread through the company's targeting abilities. The Trump campaign's digital operations chief said Cambridge Analytica worked closely with employees from Facebook, Alphabet Inc. (parent company of Google), and Twitter in relation to Trump's online campaign efforts. By this time, Wylie was growing concerned that the applications he created at Cambridge Analytica were being used inappropriately. He began talking with a reporter for the *Observer*, Carole Cadwalladr, and hired an attorney. Channel 4 also ran a surreptitiously recorded video in which Nix spoke about using unethical means to influence elections, such as bribery and prostitution. Wylie claims that he helped set up the station's sting operation.

In March 2018, Wylie provided interviews to reporters from the *Guardian*, the *Observer*, and the *New York Times*. In these interviews, he discussed his profiling work and his concerns about the use of inappropriately obtained data. His revelations spurred investigations in both the United States and the United Kingdom. Though Cambridge Analytica insists it did not use Facebook data in its work on Donald Trump's 2016 presidential campaign, its role has remained controversial. In the United Kingdom, Cambridge Analytica's work for Leave.EU during the 2016 Brexit referendum has also spurred concern. Currently, there are criminal investigations underway regarding the firm's work in both the United States and the United Kingdom.

The scandal over the data collection forced the company to close and declare bankruptcy in May 2018. However, that was not the end for Cambridge Analytica, as many of its executives started their own companies. Alexander Taylor, a former director of Cambridge Analytica, became director of Emerdata in March 2018. Data Propria was created in May 2018, and July 2018 saw the launch of Auspex International, a company focusing on influencing politics and culture in Africa and the Middle East.

Author Biography

Christopher Wylie (born on June 19, 1989) described himself to *Observer* reporter Carole Cadwalladr as "the gay Canadian vegan who somehow ended up creating 'Steve Bannon's psychological warfare ... tool.'" Wylie grew up in British Columbia, Canada, the son of a physician and a psychiatrist. He was diagnosed with attention-deficit/hyperactivity disorder and dyslexia as a teen. In 2005, he dropped out of his elite secondary school, Pearson College, without graduating.

After leaving school, he moved to Ottawa and volunteered for various members of the Liberal Party. There he pursued his interest in working with political data. In 2009, he lost his job for pitching an early form of a controversial data-harvesting technique to candidates that the politicians deemed "too invasive." He also volunteered for the Obama campaign in 2008, where he learned more about the role data plays in the election process and microtargeting. Wylie says he taught himself to code during this time.

Wylie moved to London in 2010 at the age of 20 to study law at the London School of Economics. He graduated in 2013 with his LLB, specializing in technology, media, and intellectual property law. While a law student, he worked as a "microtargeting and digital campaigns strategist" for the Liberal Democrats in the United Kingdom.

After law school, Wylie began working on a PhD in fashion trend forecasting at the University of the Arts London. Wylie stated "to change politics you need to change culture. And fashion trends are a useful proxy for that." He later received a master's degree in political management from George Washington University in Washington, D.C. In 2013, he left his PhD program to accept a job at SCL Group, the parent company of Cambridge Analytica. SCL specialized in data-driven psychographic targeting for elections all over the globe. Wylie left SCL in 2014 and founded his own company, Eunoia Technologies, which closed in 2017.

In December 2018, Wylie joined Swedish fashion-giant H&M as director of research. Working closely with H&M's head of artificial intelligence and advanced analytics, he is exploring how artificial intelligence might help tackle ethical and sustainability issues.

Historical Document

Written Statement to the United States Senate Committee on the Judiciary in the Matter of Cambridge Analytica and Other Related Issues

OPENING REMARKS

Mr. Chairman, Senators—Thank you for your invitation and opportunity to speak to your committee.

American democracy matters. It matters not just to the American citizens who vote, organise, protest, run for office or to those who just speak their minds. American democracy matters to the world which so often looks to the United States for leadership in defending and promoting democratic ideals. But to defend democracy around the world, the United States must defend its own at home. As Ronald Reagan cautioned, democracy is not a fragile flower, but still it needs cultivating.

Democracy is a bipartisan issue. I do not intend to make this a partisan testimony and I welcome questions from all members. Although Cambridge Analytica may have supported particular candidates in US elections, I am not here to point fingers. The firm's political leanings are far less relevant than the broader vulnerabilities this scandal has exposed. It should also be said that the actions of one rogue company are not necessarily reflective of the character of its past clients or candidates.

This should be about moving forward to protect democratic institutions from rogue actors and hostile foreign interference, as well as ensuring the safety of Americans online, which is something I know both Democrats and Republicans care deeply about.

I am a Canadian citizen who is resident in the United Kingdom. I have come here today voluntarily as a witness and as a whistleblower. I reported these matters to the responsible UK authorities months before the stories were made public by the *Guardian*, *New York Times* and Channel 4, and it should be made clear that I am considered a witness by both the British and American authorities.

On 26 March 2018, the UK Information Commissioner personally confirmed in writing that I am "not a subject of [their] investigation."

Company Origins

I was the Director of Research for SCL and Cambridge Analytica from mid-2013 to late 2014. SCL Group was a UK based military contractor, which worked for the US and UK militaries and also worked at the NATO StratComm Centre in the Baltic region.

Cambridge Analytica ("CA") was created by SCL Group with funding from Robert Mercer, an American billionaire based in New York. Robert Mercer installed Steve Bannon as CA's Vice President with responsibilities to manage the company day-to-day. Mr. Mercer's daughter, Rebekah Mercer, also played a role in the company.

Mr. Bannon is a follower of the Breitbart Doctrine, which posits that politics flows downstream from culture. Therefore, Mr. Bannon sees cultural warfare as the means to create enduring change in American politics. It was for this reason Mr. Bannon engaged SCL, a foreign military contractor, to build an arsenal of informational weapons he could deploy on the American population. Mr. Bannon wanted to use the same kinds of information operations tactics used by the military for his political aims in the United States and elsewhere.

CA was created as the front-facing American brand to allow SCL to work in the USA. I was informed that this setup was largely to get around various electoral compliance and foreign agent restrictions in the USA. CA did not have any employed staff, only an intellectual property agreement and data assets it received from SCL. SCL assigned all its intellectual property ("IP") to CA and in return, CA licensed back this same IP and all CA clients would be handed to SCL staff.

SCL and Mr. Mercer's lawyers decided upon the setup. I later learned that one advantage of this complicated setup was that funds invested by Mr. Mercer and his investment vehicles would not necessarily be considered declarable campaign contributions. Rather, monies transferred for the firm's research and development ("R&D") would be classed investments not donations, even if that R&D ended up supporting political clients. This allowed the firm to develop IP worth far more than the value of each client contract it had with the campaigns it was supporting.

The majority of SCL staff were not American citizens. Although Mr. Bannon was formally warned about the implications of using foreign citizens in US elections in a legal memorandum, the firm disregarded this advice and proceeded to install Alexander Nix, a British national resident in London, as CEO, and sent non-US citizens to play strategic roles embedded in American campaigns. To be clear, during my time at CA, I never directly worked in any of the firm's supported American campaigns, nor did I exert strategic or managerial influence on those campaigns, nor was I responsible for those SCL/CA staff hiring and deployment decisions.

The ethos of the firm was 'anything goes'. I witnessed some senior staff even going so far as attempting to divert health ministry funds in a struggling African country to support a politician's re-election campaign. To be clear, I was not myself involved in inducing any public official to misuse their position.

By taking advantage of countries with still-developing civic institutions, the firm was a corrupting force in the world and became the face of what colonialism looks like in the 21st century.

Use of Hacked Materials

When I was at SCL and CA, I was made aware of the firm's "black ops" capacity, which I understood to include using hackers to break into computer systems to acquire kompromat or other intelligence for its clients. The firm referred to these operations as "special intelligence services" or "special IT services." I have been told about and seen documents relating to several instances where SCL or CA procured hacked material for the benefit of its clients. Some of the targets of these intelligence operations are currently heads of state in various countries. Of concern, some of the former CA staff who worked on these projects currently hold senior positions in the British government. I have also seen internal CA documents that make reference to using specialised technologies and intelligence gathering services from former members of Israeli and Russian state security services. Mr. Bannon was Vice President at the time of some of these events.

Of further concern is CA's links to people closely associated with Wikileaks and Julian Assange. The firm hired two senior staff, both of whom were previously aides to John Jones QC in London. Mr. Jones was the British lawyer who represented Julian Assange, Wikileaks and members of the Gaddafi regime. He later killed himself by walking in front of a train in 2016. I believe that part of the appeal of hiring these staff members was their previous work with Mr. Jones, including the association with Mr. Assange. At least one of these staff members was involved in a project that procured and used hacked materials on an election campaign. Although the firm claimed only brief contact with Mr. Assange, recordings of SCL Group's former CEO suggest that contact with Wikileaks began 18 months prior to the US election.

I realise these are very serious allegations, and to be clear, I have already reported the matter to the UK National Crime Agency, which is co-ordinating a multijurisdictional investigation with their American colleagues in the Federal Bureau of Investigation ("FBI"). I have also been contacted directly by the FBI and the US Department of Justice, and I intend to fully co-operate with their investigations.

To be clear, I have never authorised, facilitated or otherwise procured the services of hackers for CA or anyone else. I have therefore been informed by both British and American authorities that I am not a target of these investigations.

Facebook Data Harvesting

Between 2013 and 2015, CA funded a multi-million dollar operation called Project Ripon. This project was overseen by Mr. Bannon and was based upon research that was originally conducted by psychologists at the University of Cambridge.

It should be noted that some of the profiling research used as the basis of CA operations had declared funding from the US Defense Advanced Research Projects Agency ("DARPA").

The purpose of Ripon was to develop and scale psychological profiling algorithms for use in American political campaigns. To be clear, the work of CA and SCL is not equivalent to traditional marketing, as has been claimed by some. This false equivalence is misleading. CA specialised in disinformation, spreading rumours, kompromat and propaganda. Using machine learning algorithms, CA worked on moving these tactics beyond its operations in Africa or Asia and into American cyberspace.

CA sought to identify mental and emotional vulnerabilities in certain subsets of the American population and worked to exploit those vulnerabilities by targeting information designed to activate some of the worst characteristics in people, such as neuroticism, paranoia and racial biases. This was targeted at narrow segments of the population.

For those who claim that profiling does not work, this contradicts copious amounts of peer-reviewed literature in top scientific journals, including the Proceedings of the National Academy of Science ("PNAS"), *Psychological Science* and the *Journal of Personality and Individual Differences*. Even Facebook itself has applied for a US patent on "determining user personality characteristics from social networking system communications and characteristics."

The Russian-American researcher Dr. Aleksandr Kogan was selected to lead the data harvesting operation, as he offered the use of Facebook apps which he had developed in his academic role to collect personal data about Facebook users and their friends. However, I later learned that Dr. Kogan did not have permission from Facebook to exploit the app's privileged access for commercial or political activities. This has been confirmed to me in legal correspondence with Facebook.

Dr. Kogan developed data harvesting applications that would capture not only the original app user but would harvest all the personal data of that user's Facebook friends and connections—without their knowledge or explicit consent.

CA did not conduct due diligence to ensure that Dr. Kogan had authorisation before spending circa 1 million US dollars on this scheme. However, CA has a history of seeking out data with dubious provenance. For example, the company contracted a partner firm in an attempt to acquire live Internet service provider ("ISP") data to tacitly monitor the Internet browsing habits of voters in the Caribbean without their knowledge or consent.

As Facebook has now confirmed, over 80 million data subjects had their personal data misappropriated in the Ripon programme, many of whom were American citizens. Given this scale, Ripon could be one of the largest breaches of Facebook's data.

CA often stored or transmitted data in insecure formats, including files of hundreds of thousands of Americans' data being passed around via unencrypted e-mails. CA also allowed access to its American datasets to external contractors, including senior staff from the company Palantir, which is a contractor to the US National Security Agency ("NSA"). To be clear, Palantir denies having any formal relationship with CA and states this work was apparently done in a "personal capacity."

SCL has a documented history of poor handling of sensitive data. In 2014, SCL Group, the parent of CA, was criticised by the UK Defence Science and Technology Laboratory for its inability to properly handle sensitive Ministry of Defence information. This Ministry of Defence assessment was conducted the same year as the Facebook data harvesting scheme.

Russian Contact

At the time, Dr. Kogan was also working on Russian state-funded research projects. He was based at times in St Petersburg and also would fly to Moscow. The Russian team at St Petersburg was also building similar algorithms using Facebook data for psychological profiling. The Russian project had a particular focus on the "dark triad" traits of narcissism, Machiavellianism and psychopathy. The Russian project also conducted behavioural research on online trolling.

It should be noted that CA was very much aware of this work going on in Russia and in fact sought to pitch "the interesting work Alex Kogan has been doing for the Russians" to its other clients.

Contemporaneous to Dr. Kogan's data profiling work in Russia, CA was also in close contact with senior executives at Lukoil, one of Russia's largest oil companies. After receiving a request for information from Lukoil executives in the spring of 2014, CA discussed with Lukoil its experience with foreign disinformation, rumour campaigns, microtargeting and its American data assets. Mr. Nix also emailed me to say that he was passing on a white paper I wrote outlining the US project to the CEO of Lukoil.

It should be noted that Lukoil has formal information sharing agreements with the Russian Federal Security Service ("FSB") and is known to conduct intelligence gathering on behalf of the FSB.

It should also be noted that CA's parent company, SCL Group, has managed information operations projects in Eastern Europe and the Baltic region and may have been an intelligence target at the time.

This means that in addition to Facebook data being accessed in Russia, there are reasonable grounds to suspect that (1) CA may have been an intelligence target of Russian security services at the time of Project Ripon, (2) that Russian security services may have been notified of the existence of CA's Facebook data and/or methods through CA's frequent contact with Russian companies, and (3) that it was made known that certain data assets could have been accessed inside Russia or via accessing Dr. Kogan's work and computers using something as simple as a keylogger device (with or without his knowledge or consent).

Other CA contractors have worked on pro-Russian political operations in Eastern Europe, including work in Ukraine with suspected Russian intelligence agents. This may have influenced some of CA's research in the USA. During its research projects in 2014, CA also set up focus groups, message testing and polling on Americans' views on the leadership of Vladimir Putin and Russian expansionism in Eastern Europe. Of note, Vladimir Putin was the only foreign leader tested by CA.

In short, Cambridge Analytica (1) used Russian researchers to gather its data, (2) openly shared information on "rumour campaigns" and "attitudinal inoculation" with FSB-linked Russian companies and executives, (3) pitched Russian-led profiling projects to its other clients, (4) contracted people who worked for pro-Russian parties in Eastern Europe with suspected Russian intelligence operatives, (5) referenced the use of former Russian intelligence agents in internal documents, and (6) went as far as to test Americans' views on Vladimir Putin's leadership.

CA's behaviour is more disconcerting given that its parent company SCL had extensive experience working in counter-extremism and military projects for the British and American governments. It should have known better.

To be clear, no allegation is being made that any CA personnel, including Mr. Nix or Dr. Kogan, knowingly colluded with the FSB, GRU or other Russian agencies. However, what is clear is the gross risk of data breaches and foreign intelligence gathering created by CA's recklessness in the face of skilled intelligence and cyber operations.

Voter Disengagement

CA did not operate in elections to promote democratic ideals. Oftentimes, CA worked to interfere with voter participation, including by weaponising fear. In one country, CA produced videos intended to suppress turnout by showing voters sadistic images of victims being burned alive, undergoing forced amputations with machetes and having their throats cut in a ditch. These videos also conveyed Islamophobic messages. It was created with a clear intent to intimidate certain communities, catalyse religious hatred, portray Muslims as terrorists and deny certain voters of their democratic rights. I have seen this video, but to be clear, I had no part in its creation, editing or deployment, and I left before the company made use of it in the field.

If it suited the client's objective, the firm was eager to capitalise on discontent and to stoke ethnic tensions. This was not just on its projects in Africa. As the CEO of SCL said in a recorded conversation about the firm's work in the USA in 2016: "It's the things that resonate, sometimes to attack the other group and know that you are going to lose them is going to reinforce and resonate your group. Which is why [...] Hitler attacked the Jews, because he didn't have a problem with the Jews at all, but the people didn't like the Jews [...] So he just leveraged an artificial enemy. Well that's exactly what Trump did. He leveraged a Muslim [...] Trump had the balls, and I mean, really the balls, to say what people wanted to hear."

I am aware that CA clients requested voter suppression as part of their contracts. CA offered "voter disengagement" as a service in the United States and there are internal documents that I have seen that make reference to this tactic. My understanding of these projects, which I did not personally participate in, was that the firm would target African American voters and discourage them from participating in elections. Mr. Bannon was Vice President of the company at the time of these voter disengagement projects.

Facebook's Response

Facebook was first notified of CA's harvesting scheme in 2015. It did not warn users then, and it only took action to warn affected users three weeks after the *Guardian, New York Times* and Channel 4 made the story public.

Facebook's behaviour before the story broke was to threaten to sue the *Guardian*. Facebook's lawyers also tried to intimidate me with aggressive legal notices. Facebook tried to shut down this story from going public when it knew it was true. At the British parliamentary inquiry, the CTO of Facebook recently explained, to the surprise of many in the inquiry, that the company had assumed "that this is common practice in the UK."

Credit should therefore be given to the international team of journalists who supported me as a whistleblower, stood up to these threats and nonetheless dared to publish: Carole Cadwalladr, Sarah Donaldson, Emma Graham-Harrison, Paul Webster, John Mulholland and Gill Phillips at the *Guardian*; Matt Rosenberg, Nick Confessore, Gabriel Dance and Danny Hakim at the *New York Times*; Job Rabkin and Ben de Pear at Channel 4.

I am disappointed that Facebook has not acted constructively in the wake of this scandal. Before the story broke, I offered to help Facebook. One of Facebook's Vice Presidents explicitly told my lawyer that they would welcome a collaborative engagement, but at the last minute, they instead announced in a press release that they had banned me from their platform. I believe I was banned in a bungled attempt to re-frame the story and cast Facebook as the victim.

But it did not work. Facebook's decision to ban me from their platform was recently debated in the UK Parliament. Responding on behalf of the British Government, the UK Secretary of State for Culture, Media and Sport said on the floor of Parliament that: "Of all the different things that have surprised me and shocked me in this revelation, the decision by Facebook to take down the whistleblower's Facebook account, and the removal of their WhatsApp account and the Instagram account, was the most surprising".

The Secretary of State went further to call the ban "outrageous"—because the ban is outrageous. It reveals the unrestrained power technology companies have over users when a person's entire online presence can be so quickly and so thoroughly eliminated from existence. There is no due process or check on this power and my ban raises a serious question for Republicans and Democrats alike: what happens to our democracy when these companies can delete people at will who dissent, scrutinise or speak out?

Silicon Valley has this power now. I know because Facebook used it on me. They sought to make me a digital pariah.

Facebook's actions against me also show the serious consequences of Silicon Valley's rush to consolidate the ownership of different platforms. Although this scandal had nothing to do with Instagram, my account on Instagram was also eliminated in what I can only assume was a punitive move by Facebook, which now owns Instagram. This unchecked monopoly on digital space presents a serious risk to people's rights.

Facebook also demanded that I hand over my personal computer and phone after the story broke. The company disregarded that I had already handed over evidence to the responsible British authorities with jurisdiction over the investigation. In effect, Facebook was demanding that I let them acquire and handle evidence relevant to an ongoing investigation it was a party to. The company did not seem to understand or care about due process or respecting the integrity of an ongoing investigation by a competent legal authority.

I remain banned from Facebook despite the UK Information Commissioner's Office confirming in writing that I am "not a subject of [their] investigation."

I would like to be able to discuss the data security and digital privacy issues raised by my evidence with Facebook in a non-confrontational manner and help it figure out how to move forward. I came out as a whistleblower to help the authorities uncover what happened. But I also want to work towards finding solutions and Facebook is a key player in finding those solutions. Platforms like Facebook are still huge public assets that do a lot of amazing work, but we should not shy away from the real problems that exist.

The Cambridge Analytica scandal has exposed that social platforms are no longer safe for users. We have to face up to this fact. These platforms are critical parts of American cyberspace in desperate need of protection and oversight.

In the context of information operations from hostile foreign actors, we cannot keep relying on the promises, apologies or good intentions of these firms to protect American citizens. We protect our borders at land, sea and air with dedicated public agencies. We do not leave this critical public service to private companies or land owners. We should protect our digital spaces with the same level of care.

The security of American communities online is one of the most pressing national security issues in the 21st century. This is not an emerging problem on the horizon. This is not a niche issue. This is a problem today, in the here and now, affecting the 260 million Americans who use social media.

But it is not just Americans who have been affected. The rest of the world uses and often depends on American technology. But as we have seen with Mark Zuckerberg's continual refusal to attend the British Parliament's inquiry, it is impossible for other countries like the UK to hold these companies to account. To highlight the seriousness of the matter, the British parliamentary inquiry is now considering issuing a standing summons on Mark Zuckerberg after the company failed to answer of the inquiry's questions.

Moving Forward

What I bore witness to at Cambridge Analytica should alarm everyone. Cambridge Analytica is the canary in the coal mine to a new Cold War emerging online.

If a foreign actor dropped propaganda leaflets by aeroplane over Florida or Michigan, that would universally be condemned a hostile act. But this is what is happening online. We must address these issues before disinformation and information warfare become pervasive in American cyberspace.

We also must address the digital echo chambers that are being exploited to algorithmically segregate American society. Online communities should unite us, not divide us.

But we cannot keep deferring to the technology sector with the defeatist mantra that 'the law cannot keep up with technology'. We need a different mentality. Technology should not be exempt from public oversight or debate simply because it relates to software. If we can regulate the safety standards of aeroplanes, medicines or nuclear power plants, we can create safety standards for software.

Every year, Americans are buying more and more Internet-enabled devices and appliances. Soon the so-called 'Internet of Things' will become the norm in American households. Algorithms will soon be driving our cars and organising our lives.

This is not just about technology today, we have to seriously consider the implications for tomorrow. To put it bluntly, we risk walking into the future blind and unprepared.

What happens when your cousin's DNA profile affects your insurance because an algorithm has used someone else's data to infer risks about you? What happens when an algorithm targets ads that provoke your daughter's body image issues because it has inferred this is the optimal way to sell her a product? What happens when our appliances and physical spaces are influenced by algorithms that start to make decisions about what you can eat, see or experience? What happens when an innocent person is stopped on the street because the police used a biased dataset? What happens when monolithic technology platforms start taking sides and distort our elections?

Some of us worry about big government robbing us of our freedom—but what about big data?

Data is the new electricity of our digital economy. And just like electricity, we cannot escape data. It is nearly impossible for the average American to stop using social media, search engines, apps and e-mail, but still be functional in the workplace and in society. We should therefore be wary of any company that presents a false dichotomy between our privacy rights and living in a modern digitised society. Online platforms' terms and conditions present users with a false choice because using the Internet is no longer a choice. Americans cannot opt out of the 21st century.

Data protection is a consumer safety issue and we cannot continue putting the burden on consumers by using this false narrative of choice. We don't allow buildings to lack fire exits as long as there are terms and conditions posted on the wall. We do not allow automotive companies to build unsafe cars as long as they include warning labels. In every other sector, we empower public regulators to create safety standards. Because safety matters. So why should software and online platforms be any different?

Legislators have an opportunity to create expert-led technology safety authorities to enforce standards for user safety, just as we already do for everything else we value: our cars, electricity, appliances, medicines, buildings and food. Regulators do not need to be the adversaries of innovation, but innovation must always put the safety of people first.

Technology companies may claim that rules inhibit growth in the sector. But car safety standards have not inhibited innovation or demand, nor have they unreasonably inhibited profit. Seat belts do not stop people from buying cars and privacy engineered software will not stop people from using online platforms.

Technology is a social issue. Technology is a national security issue. Technology is a consumer rights issue. Everyone has a stake in this, not just engineers. My generation's future will involve technology in almost every space and part of our lives.

I am still optimistic about the future of technology. But we should not walk into the future blind, and it is the job of lawmakers to ensure that technology serves citizens and not the other way around.

CHRISTOPHER WYLIE

16 MAY 2018

Glossary

Channel 4: a British public television network

Guardian: a British newspaper

kompromat: a Russian term, short for "compromising material" that is damaging to a public figure's reputation

Observer: a sister publication to the Guardian, it is a British newspaper published on Sundays

Ripon program: a software program built by AggregateIQ (named after Ripon, Wisconsin, where the Republican party was founded) for Cambridge Analytica used by Ted Cruz's 2016 campaign for the Republication presidential nomination

WhatsApp: an app owned by Facebook that allows users to send messages, make calls, and share information and other media

Document Themes

Regret over the use of his technology and research was the primary reason Wylie choose to act as a whistle-blower. In 2014, he left Cambridge Analytica because he became concerned about the increasingly conservative political causes the researchers were supporting in their work. He also thought Alexander Nix was a "bully." Wylie said that when he turned in his resignation, Nix told him, "You're going to leave, and we're going to be in the White House." When Nix's prediction came true, whether due to Cambridge Analytica or not, Wylie became concerned. He said that his true failure was not recognizing the "potential misuse" of the technology and research he created. Wylie did not know if Cambridge Analytica was involved in Trump's successful 2016 presidential bid, but he recognized many of the themes that the company was using in 2014, such as building a wall to keep immigrants out. While he did not take part in this work, he felt responsible for his role in the intrusion of privacy and manipulative use of data. He believes cooperating with legal authorities in both the United States and United Kingdom is a first step in repairing the damage he may have caused.

Though Wylie had initially hoped that Facebook would be a powerful partner in creating greater security for private data, Wylie was disappointed. Facebook instead denied there was a breach and refused to be transparent about how they were using or making this data available to researchers. Wylie's whistle-blowing triggered a plunge in Facebook stock and triggered government investigations in both the United States and the United Kingdom. Facebook's CEO, Mark Zuckerberg, was called to explain how the data of 87 million Facebook users came to be in the hands of Cambridge Analytica.

The lax security surrounding Facebook's data is another concern in Wylie's testimony. Wylie suspected that Russia may have also obtained access to the Facebook data set. The data at Cambridge Analytica was stored on nonencrypted servers and the regulations and requirements for the protection of the data were loose. Wylie points out that while he does not know if the data was shared, he emphasizes that it could have been. He outlines Dr. Kogan's frequent trips to Russia and the briefing that Cambridge Analytica employees provided to Lukoil, a Russian oil company, on its American voter research.

Wylie ends his written testimony with a call for greater government protection and oversight of social media companies and the data they hold. In our current culture, social media is an essential component of social discourse. Wylie is concerned about the power that social media and technology companies have, and the danger disinformation relayed along these channels presents to democratic principles. He believes these companies have a responsibility if they are going to create and support communities to be transparent and submit to government oversight to ensure both data and democracy remain safe. Wylie wants to continue to educate the public about how data is gathered and used for political purposes, as well as a push for regulation of technology and data. Wylie believes the "security of our digital spaces" should not be left to private companies who have no accountability, but that the government needs to regulate the space.

—Noëlle Sinclair, JD, MLS

Bibliography and Additional Reading

Amer, Karim, and Jehane Noujaim. *The Great Hack*. Netflix documentary, released January 26, 2019.

"Cambridge Analytica and Data Privacy." C-Span, May 16, 2018. Videotaped testimony of Christopher Wylie before the Senate Committee on the Judiciary, along with related video from the Facebook and Cambridge Analytica hearings.

"The Cambridge Analytica Files." March 17, 2018. *The Guardian/The Observer*. www.theguardian.com/news/series/cambrdige-analytica-files.

Granville, Kevin. "Facebook and Cambridge Analytica: What You Need to Know as Fallout Widens." *New York Times*, March 19, 2018. www.nytimes.com/2018/03/19/technology/facebook-cambridge-analytica-explained.html.

Kaiser, Brittany. *Targeted: The Cambridge Analytica Whistleblower's Inside Story of How Big Data, Trump, and Facebook Broke Democracy and How It Can Happen Again*. New York: Harper, 2019.

Lapowsky, Issie. "Senators Grill Whistleblower on Cambridge Analytica's Inner Workings." *Wired*, May 16, 2018.

Remarks by President Biden One Year after the January 6 Assault on the U.S. Capitol

Date: January 6, 2022
Author: Joseph R. Biden
Genre: speech

Summary Overview

January 6, 2021, was a historic day at the Capitol Building in Washington, D.C., as hundreds of rioters broke into the building, seeking to stop the certification of the election of Joseph R. Biden as president of the United States and Kamala Harris as vice president. The rioters attacked Capitol police, threatened legislators, and chanted "Hang Mike Pence"—President Donald Trump's vice president—because of Pence's role in carrying out the certification process. Over the course of the year following the event, President Biden had harsh words for the rioters and called for their prosecution; however, he seemed reluctant to clearly state the cause of the violence. On the one-year anniversary of the event, Biden spoke to the nation and directly attributed the attack to the former president (whose name he never used), Donald J. Trump. Biden outlined how Trump's lies and the misinformation spread by his supporters gave rise to the movement that culminated in the violent attack on the Capitol and Congress on January 6, 2021.

Defining Moment

Historically, American presidents often change the policies of their predecessors, but rarely do they speak out about their predecessor's personal choices and actions. Up until January 6, 2022, Biden basically followed this precedent and did not criticize Trump personally. In the months leading up to the 2020 election, Donald Trump had claimed that the election was not going to be fair, in that the Democrats and various other groups/forces would tamper with the vote. This was not based on solid evidence but helped to prepare his supporters for a possible loss, since the polls were tight between the two candidates. Once it was clear that Biden had won the 2020 election, Trump forcefully advanced the idea that Biden's supporters had cheated in various ways and the he (Trump) had actually won the election. This became known in media circles as "The Big Lie," and for more than a year after the election it was continuously repeated by Trump and his supporters. When Trump's lawyers tried to take legal action to block the results from being certified, filing numerous lawsuits in key states, the cases were quickly thrown out of court for lack of evidence and

A crowd-erected gallows hangs near the United States Capitol during the 2021 storming of the United States Capitol. Photo by Tyler Merbler, via Wikimedia Commons.

unsupported claims. Some state legislatures initiated recounts, and all official recounts demonstrated that Biden had won the states in question. This created a situation in which Trump's supporters, and seemingly Trump himself, believed that the only way Biden could be stopped from taking office was to interfere with Congress' final certification of the vote on January 6, 2021. This was precisely what the rioters were attempting to do when they assaulted the Capitol after hearing Trump speak nearby that same day. In his speech, Trump had made a number of provocative statements—"Never concede"; "fight like hell"; "walk down to the Capitol"; "we can't let this happen"—that suggested a link between what happened before and what happened during the riot.

While the Capitol Police made certain that members of Congress were safe, they were restrained in their use of force to repel those breaking into the building and vandalizing portions of it. This kept the number of casualties to a minimum, but it also made it more difficult for the police to deal effectively with the attackers until other federal departments sent reinforcements and the building was cleared. After this intense conflict, in which one rioter was killed and numerous police suffered wounds, the counting of the electors' votes and the certification of the election by the Congress continued. The Biden-Harris ticket was duly certified as the winner.

A year after the attack, Biden spoke to all citizens of the United States and called for unity against forces that would disrupt American democracy. This speech marked the anniversary of the attack and was a major change in the way Biden spoke about those who had encouraged the crowd to go beyond a peaceful demonstration to a riot and violent attack. With Trump still not accepting the outcome of the election, and claiming that

"I have said it many times, and it is no more true or real than when we think about the events of January 6: We are in a battle for the soul of America. A battle that by the grace of God, and by the goodness and greatness of this nation, we will win." President Joe Biden in the Capitol Building, January 6, 2022. Photo courtesy of The White House, via Wikimedia Commons. [Public domain]

Rioters outside the Capitol, January 6, 2021. Photo by Tyler Merbler, via Wikimedia Commons.

the rioters were "special people" whom he respected, Biden was forced to ignore precedent and begin speaking directly about his predecessor and the harm he believed Trump had inflicted on the nation.

Author Biography

Joseph Robinette Biden, Jr. (born 1942) was elected the forty-sixth president of the United States in 2020. Born in Scranton, Pennsylvania, his family moved to Delaware while he was a youth. He graduated from high school there, then the University of Delaware, followed by the Syracuse Law School. In 1971 he was elected to the U.S. Senate, serving from 1972 until elected vice president in 2008. He was chair or ranking member of the judiciary and foreign relations committees. Serving as vice president from 2009 until 2017, he then defeated the incumbent president, Donald Trump, and became the president in 2021. Family tragedies have affected his career, as his first wife and a daughter died in an auto accident, when Biden had just been elected to the Senate and this started his lifestyle of commuting from Delaware to Washington each day, so he could help take care of his sons. When considering an earlier run for the presidency, Biden stepped aside due to one son having just died of cancer.

Historical Document

Remarks by President Biden One Year after the January 6 Assault on the U.S. Capitol

JANUARY 06, 2022

South Court Auditorium
Eisenhower Executive Office Building

9:16 A.M. EST

THE PRESIDENT: Madam Vice President, my fellow Americans: To state the obvious, one year ago today, in this sacred place, democracy was attacked—simply attacked. The will of the people was under assault. The Constitution—our Constitution—faced the gravest of threats.

Outnumbered and in the face of a brutal attack, the Capitol Police, the D.C. Metropolitan Police Department, the National Guard, and other brave law enforcement officials saved the rule of law.

Our democracy held. We the people endured. And we the people prevailed.

For the first time in our history, a president had not just lost an election, he tried to prevent the peaceful transfer of power as a violent mob breached the Capitol.

But they failed. They failed.

And on this day of remembrance, we must make sure that such an attack never, never happens again.

I'm speaking to you today from Statuary Hall in the United States Capitol. This is where the House of Representatives met for 50 years in the decades leading up to the Civil War. This is—on this floor is where a young congressman of Illinois, Abraham Lincoln, sat at desk 191.

Above him—above us, over that door leading into the Rotunda—is a sculpture depicting Clio, the muse of history. In her hands, an open book in which she records the events taking place in this chamber below.

Clio stood watch over this hall one year ago today, as she has for more than 200 years. She recorded what took place. The real history. The real facts. The real truth. The facts and the truth that Vice President Harris just shared and that you and I and the whole world saw with our own eyes.

The Bible tells us that we shall know the truth, and the truth shall make us free. We shall know the truth.

Well, here is the God's truth about January 6th, 2021:

Close your eyes. Go back to that day. What do you see? Rioters rampaging, waving for the first time inside this Capitol a Confederate flag that symbolized the cause to destroy America, to rip us apart.

Even during the Civil War, that never, ever happened. But it happened here in 2021.

What else do you see? A mob breaking windows, kicking in doors, breaching the Capitol. American flags on poles being used as weapons, as spears. Fire extinguishers being thrown at the heads of police officers.

A crowd that professes their love for law enforcement assaulted those police officers, dragged them, sprayed them, stomped on them.

Over 140 police officers were injured.

We've all heard the police officers who were there that day testify to what happened. One officer called it, quote, a med—"medieval" battle, and that he was more afraid that day than he was fighting the war in Iraq.

They've repeatedly asked since that day: How dare anyone—anyone—diminish, belittle, or deny the hell they were put through?

We saw it with our own eyes. Rioters menaced these halls, threatening the life of the Speaker of the House, literally erecting gallows to hang the Vice President of the United States of America.

But what did we not see?

We didn't see a former president, who had just rallied the mob to attack—sitting in the private dining room off the Oval Office in the White House, watching it all on television and doing nothing for hours as police were assaulted, lives at risk, and the nation's capital under siege.

This wasn't a group of tourists. This was an armed insurrection.

They weren't looking to uphold the will of the people. They were looking to deny the will of the people.

They were looking to uphold—they weren't looking to uphold a free and fair election. They were looking to overturn one.

They weren't looking to save the cause of America. They were looking to subvert the Constitution.

This isn't about being bogged down in the past. This is about making sure the past isn't buried.

That's the only way forward. That's what great nations do. They don't bury the truth, they face up to it. Sounds like hyperbole, but that's the truth: They face up to it.

We are a great nation.

My fellow Americans, in life, there's truth and, tragically, there are lies—lies conceived and spread for profit and power.

We must be absolutely clear about what is true and what is a lie.

And here is the truth: The former president of the United States of America has created and spread a web of lies about the 2020 election. He's done so because he values power over principle, because he sees his own interests as more important than his country's interests and America's interests, and because his bruised ego matters more to him than our democracy or our Constitution.

He can't accept he lost, even though that's what 93 United States senators, his own Attorney General, his own Vice President, governors and state officials in every battleground state have all said: He lost.

That's what 81 million of you did as you voted for a new way forward.

He has done what no president in American history—the history of this country—has ever, ever done: He refused to accept the results of an election and the will of the American people.

While some courageous men and women in the Republican Party are standing against it, trying to uphold the principles of that party, too many others are transforming that party into something else. They seem no longer to want to be the party—the party of Lincoln, Eisenhower, Reagan, the Bushes.

But whatever my other disagreements are with Republicans who support the rule of law and not the rule of a single man, I will always seek to work together with them to find shared solutions where possible. Because if we have a shared belief in democracy, then anything is possible—anything.

And so, at this moment, we must decide: What kind of nation are we going to be?

Are we going to be a nation that accepts political violence as a norm?

Are we going to be a nation where we allow partisan election officials to overturn the legally expressed will of the people?

Are we going to be a nation that lives not by the light of the truth but in the shadow of lies?

We cannot allow ourselves to be that kind of nation. The way forward is to recognize the truth and to live by it.

The Big Lie being told by the former president and many Republicans who fear his wrath is that the insurrection in this country actually took place on Election Day—November 3rd, 2020.

Think about that. Is that what you thought? Is that what you thought when you voted that day? Taking part in an insurrection? Is that what you thought you were doing? Or did you think you were carrying out your highest duty as a citizen and voting?

The former president and his supporters are trying to rewrite history. They want you to see Election Day as the day of insurrection and the riot that took place here on January 6th as the true expression of the will of the people.

Can you think of a more twisted way to look at this country—to look at America? I cannot.

Here's the truth: The election of 2020 was the greatest demonstration of democracy in the history of this country.

More of you voted in that election than have ever voted in all of American history. Over 150 million Americans went to the polls and voted that day in a pandemic—some at grea—-great risk to their lives. They should be applauded, not attacked.

Right now, in state after state, new laws are being written—not to protect the vote, but to deny it; not only to suppress the vote, but to subvert it; not to strengthen or protect our democracy, but because the former president lost.

Instead of looking at the election results from 2020 and saying they need new ideas or better ideas to win more votes, the former president and his supporters have decided the only way for them to win is to suppress your vote and subvert our elections.

It's wrong. It's undemocratic. And frankly, it's un-American.

The second Big Lie being told by the former President and his supporters is that the results of the election of 2020 can't be trusted.

The truth is that no election—no election in American history has been more closely scrutinized or more carefully counted.

Every legal challenge questioning the results in every court in this country that could have been made was made and was rejected—often rejected by Republican-appointed judges, including judges appointed by the former president himself, from state courts to the United States Supreme Court.

Recounts were undertaken in state after state. Georgia—Georgia counted its results three times, with one recount by hand.

Phony partisan audits were undertaken long after the election in several states. None changed the results. And in some of them, the irony is the margin of victory actually grew slightly.

So, let's speak plainly about what happened in 2020. Even before the first ballot was cast, the former president was preemptively sowing doubt about the election results. He built his lie over months. It wasn't based on any facts. He was just looking for an excuse—a pretext—to cover for the truth.

He's not just a former president. He's a defeated former president—defeated by a margin of over 7 million of your votes in a full and free and fair election.

There is simply zero proof the election results were inaccurate. In fact, in every venue where evidence had to be produced and an oath to tell the truth had to be taken, the former president failed to make his case.

Just think about this: The former president and his supporters have never been able to explain how they accept as accurate the other election results that took place on November 3rd—the elections for governor, United States Senate, the House of Representatives—elections in which they closed the gap in the House.

They challenge none of that. The President's name was first, then we went down the line—governors, senators, House of Representatives. Somehow, those results were accurate on the same ballot, but the presidential race was flawed?

And on the same ballot, the same day, cast by the same voters.

The only difference: The former President didn't lose those races; he just lost the one that was his own.

Finally, the third Big Lie being told by a former President and his supporters is that the mob who sought to impose their will through violence are the nation's true patriots.

Is that what you thought when you looked at the mob ransacking the Capitol, destroying property, literally defecating in the hallways, rifling through desks of senators and representatives, hunting down members of congress? Patriots? Not in my view.

To me, the true patriots were the more than 150 [million] Americans who peacefully expressed their vote at the ballot box, the election workers who protected the integrity of the vote, and the heroes who defended this Capitol.

You can't love your country only when you win.

You can't obey the law only when it's convenient.

You can't be patriotic when you embrace and enable lies.

Those who stormed this Capitol and those who instigated and incited and those who called on them to do so held a dagger at the throat of America—at American democracy.

They didn't come here out of patriotism or principle. They came here in rage—not in service of America, but rather in service of one man.

Those who incited the mob—the real plotters—who were desperate to deny the certification of the election and defy the will of the voters.

But their plot was foiled. Congressmen—Democrats and Republicans—stayed. Senators, representatives, staff—they finished their work the Constitution demanded. They honored their oath to defend the Constitution against all enemies, foreign and domestic.

Look, folks, now it's up to all of us—to "We the People"—o stand for the rule of law, to preserve the flame of democracy, to keep the promise of America alive.

That promise is at risk, targeted by the forces that value brute strength over the sanctity of democracy, fear over hope, personal gain over public good.

Make no mistake about it: We're living at an inflection point in history.

Both at home and abroad, we're engaged anew in a struggle between democracy and autocracy, between the aspirations of the many and the greed of the few, between the people's right of self-determination and self—the self-seeking autocrat.

From China to Russia and beyond, they're betting that democracy's days are numbered. They've actually told me democracy is too slow, too bogged down by division to succeed in today's rapidly changing, complicated world.

And they're betting—they're betting America will become more like them and less like us. They're betting that America is a place for the autocrat, the dictator, the strongman.

I do not believe that. That is not who we are. That is not who we have ever been. And that is not who we should ever, ever be.

Our Founding Fathers, as imperfect as they were, set in motion an experiment that changed the world—literally changed the world.

Here in America, the people would rule, power would be transferred peacefully—never at the tip of a spear or the barrel of a gun.

And they committed to paper an idea that couldn't live up to—they couldn't live up to but an idea that couldn't be constrained: Yes, in America all people are created equal.

We reject the view that if you succeed, I fail; if you get ahead, I fall behind; if I hold you down, I somehow lift myself up.

The former President, who lies about this election, and the mob that attacked this Capitol could not be further away from the core American values.

They want to rule or they will ruin—ruin what our country fought for at Lexington and Concord; at Gettysburg; at Omaha Beach; Seneca Falls; Selma, Alabama. What—and what we were fighting for: the right to vote, the right to govern ourselves, the right to determine our own destiny.

And with rights come responsibilities: the responsibility to see each other as neighbors—maybe we disagree with that neighbor, but they're not an adversary; the responsibility to accept defeat then get back in the arena and try again the next time to make your case; the responsibility to see that America is an idea—an idea that requires vigilant stewardship.

As we stand here today—one year since January 6th, 2021—the lies that drove the anger and madness we saw in this place, they have not abated.

So, we have to be firm, resolute, and unyielding in our defense of the right to vote and to have that vote counted.

Some have already made the ultimate sacrifice in this sacred effort.

Jill and I have mourned police officers in this Capitol Rotunda not once but twice in the wake of January 6th: once to honor Officer Brian Sicknick, who lost his life the day after the attack, and a second time to honor Officer Billy Evans, who lost his life defending this Capitol as well.

We think about the others who lost their lives and were injured and everyone living with the trauma of that day—from those defending this Capitol to members of Congress in both parties and their staffs, to reporters, cafeteria workers, custodial workers, and their families.

Don't kid yourself: The pain and scars from that day run deep.

I said it many times and it's no more true or real than when we think about the events of January 6th: We are in a battle for the soul of America. A battle that, by the grace of God and the goodness and gracious—and greatness of this nation, we will win.

Believe me, I know how difficult democracy is. And I'm crystal clear about the threats America faces. But I also know that our darkest days can lead to light and hope.

From the death and destruction, as the Vice President referenced, in Pearl Harbor came the triumph over the forces of fascism.

From the brutality of Bloody Sunday on the Edmund Pettus Bridge came historic voting rights legislation.

So, now let us step up, write the next chapter in American history where January 6th marks not the end of democracy, but the beginning of a renaissance of liberty and fair play.

I did not seek this fight brought to this Capitol one year ago today, but I will not shrink from it either.

I will stand in this breach. I will defend this nation. And I will allow no one to place a dagger at the throat of our democracy.

We will make sure the will of the people is heard; that the ballot prevails, not violence; that authority in this nation will always be peacefully transferred.

I believe the power of the presidency and the purpose is to unite this nation, not divide it; to lift us up, not tear us apart; to be about us—about us, not about "me."

Deep in the heart of America burns a flame lit almost 250 years ago—of liberty, freedom, and equality.

This is not a land of kings or dictators or autocrats. We're a nation of laws; of order, not chaos; of peace, not violence.

Here in America, the people rule through the ballot, and their will prevails.

So, let us remember: Together, we're one nation, under God, indivisible; that today, tomorrow, and forever, at our best, we are the United States of America.

God bless you all. May God protect our troops. And may God bless those who stand watch over our democracy.

Glossary

Capitol Police: a police department established in the early nineteenth century to safeguard Congress and the Capitol; it is under the control of Congressional leaders

Omaha Beach: the location where American troops landed in France during World War II

Selma, Alabama (Bloody Sunday—Edmond Pettus Bridge): Selma was the scene of many Civil Rights protests, and a march from Selma to Montgomery was organized for Sunday, March 7, 1965, which was brutally turned back by Alabama State Police at the bridge

Seneca Falls: reference to an 1848 conference to promote women's rights and suffrage

Document Analysis

Using the anniversary of the attack on the Capitol Building as the focal point for the speech, President Joe Biden calls for people to not only remember what they had seen on TV, but to understand the results of the government's yearlong investigation into the riot. Biden speaks about American democracy being under attack by the rioters, whom he clearly identifies as supporters of the former president, Donald Trump. Not only that, but for the first time in a systematic way, Biden argues that the attack was instigated by the former president, with Trump's "Big Lie" having convinced the rioters that they were patriots rather than criminals.

Although Trump, and his supporters, would dispute the statements made by Biden, and his interpretation of events, Biden bases his speech on facts that had been verified by independent researchers as well as the courts. At the heart of this speech is what Biden identifies as "the truth." This is that Trump "has created and spread a web of lies about the 2020 election." This was, according to Biden, the basis for the attack on democracy by the Trump supporters who rioted, attacked police officers, and rampaged through the Capitol on January 6, 2021.

Biden then goes on to outline and refute three parts of the post-January 6 Big Lie that Trump had been disseminating. Biden says that Trump was pushing the idea that the insurrection had happened on Election Day, not on January 6, a claim that would make Biden the insurrectionist and Trump the victim. This is an astonishing claim for any former president to make, even, perhaps, one so prone to untruths as Donald Trump. As for the accuracy of the election results, numerous recounts and court cases made it clear the outcome was accurate. Trump's unwillingness to accept his own defeat, and his ongoing effort to rewrite the history of the January 6 attack, clearly irk Biden and are founded on personal animosity, not legal evidence or concrete fact. Biden made it clear that the real patriots were the voters who went to the polls and cast their ballots, not the rioters who attacked the Capitol and tried to overturn an election.

Biden applauds the work of the various police who protected members of Congress and defeated the mob attacking the Capitol. He sees them as representative of America, not those who carried the Confederate battle flag into the Capitol while Trump watched on TV. Biden urges all citizens to work together as neighbors who know what truth is and uphold it, rather than separating themselves from one another through acceptance of the Big Lie. According to Biden, patriots are voters who participate in the democratic process, not those who violently attack American institutions because they lost the election.

Essential Themes

In this well-written speech, President Biden made it clear that the events on January 6, 2021, represented an attack on democracy in the United States, and that this was the result of former President Trump spreading "a web of lies about the 2020 election." Although the entire U.S. population and a few foreign leaders were the audience for the speech, Biden was focused on trying to sway political independents and moderate Republicans (not devoted supporters of Trump). Although the facts regarding what happened in 2021 were not generally in dispute, the interpretation of the events was; and so, throughout this speech, Biden tried to make his point clear that what happened a year earlier was totally un-American, nondemocratic and had been instigated by Trump, who was dissatisfied because he lost the election.

Although it is uncertain if Biden achieved his goal of changing people's minds, he clearly did go on record to lay the blame for the riot/insurrection at the feet of his predecessor. He did this in a dismissive manner, by never using Trump's name, only his title as the "former president." His forthright statement that the rioters were not patriots but rather were subservient to one man, made it clear that Biden was not going to allow history to be distorted by Trump and his supporters.

—*Donald A. Watt, PhD*

Bibliography and Additional Reading

Cillizza, Chris. "The Single Most Important—And Powerful—Line from Joe Biden's 1/6 Speech." *CNN Politics.* New York: Cable News Network, 2022.

Committee on Homeland Security and Governmental Affairs and Committee on Rules and Administration, Staff. *Examining the U.S. Capitol Attack: A Review of the Security, Planning, and Response Failures on January 6*. Washington, D.C.: U.S. Senate, 2021.

Raskin, Jamie. *Unthinkable: Trauma, Truth, and the Trials of American Democracy*. New York: Harper, 2022.

Wray, Christopher. "Examining the January 6 Attack on the U.S. Capitol." *FBI*. Washington, D.C.: Federal Bureau of Investigation, 2021.

■ "Texas Limits Mail Voting, Adds ID Requirements After Surge in Turnout"

Date: October 6, 2022
Author: Karen Juanita Carrillo, *Public Integrity*
Genre: news article

Summary Overview

Voter suppression is a political strategy that uses various methods to limit the impact of votes from certain groups or subsets of people within a society, or to generally discourage voting in order to limit turnout for a specific election. Voter suppression is an undemocratic practice, as it unnecessarily places limits on the popular will in any democratic system.

Voter suppression can take many forms, and Americans have been engaging in this kind of unethical electoral behavior since the very beginning. While any political party can and has attempted to suppress votes for opposing parties, voter suppression is a tactic most often associated with American conservative political parties, including the Federalists (in the Early Era), the Democrats of the American Civil War era, and the modern Republican Party.

In recent years, especially following the election of the right-wing populist Republican president Donald J. Trump in 2016, hardline Republican governors and state legislatures have been busy setting up election protocols and procedures that serve to limit voters' access to the ballot. It has long been believed that higher-voter turnout will favor progressive or liberal candidates, and that lower voter turnout favors conservatives. This is based on the perception that conservatives already vote at relatively high numbers, so that any expansion in turnout will likely favor the party or candidates that have lower-average turnout— which is typically the progressive or liberal party of the era. There is some historic justification for this belief, because groups that have been barred or prevented from exercising voting rights, such as African Americans and women, tend to favor more liberal or progressive candidates because these were in favor of expanding their rights and privileges.

This dynamic can be seen today in the efforts by many Republican-majority states to restrict the vote through a variety of means. The present example looks at the state of Texas through the lens of an October 2022 news article prepared by a writer from the Center for Public Integrity, a nonprofit investigative journalism organization.

Defining Moment

Restrictions on the right to vote in the United States are nothing new. Questions about who could vote and how votes were to be counted in the United States date back to the original framing of the Constitution and the "Three-Fifths Compromise," which determined that enslaved people were counted as three-fifths of a person when determining a state's population for taxation and representation in the federal government. The end of the Civil War meant the end of enslavement for black Americans, which theoretically meant that the formerly enslaved people would be recognized as full citizens and gain the right to vote. However, attempts to prevent black people and other minorities from exercising their right to vote continued in the twentieth century through poll taxes, reading and writing tests, and other discriminatory practices.

While the 1965 Voting Rights Act prohibited racial discrimination in voting, many tactics continue to be used that are designed to make it more difficult to vote. Proponents of measures such as voter ID laws or requiring individuals to register to vote months in advance of an election argue that these laws ensure that elections are free and fair. In practice, these measures tend to prevent individuals with lower incomes and those who are not the most committed voters from voting. As a broad statement, these groups tend to favor candidates who are more centrist in their political positions than the right-wing legislators and governors who seek to curtail access to the vote. Today, it is typically hard-right Republican governors and lawmakers who most often push for stricter voter laws and tighter regulations around who can vote and how.

Texas has a long history of voting restriction. After poll taxes were made unconstitutional in 1965, residents in Texas had improved access to exercising their right to vote. However, in 2013, the Supreme Court struck down a key segment of the Voting Rights Act. That section had required certain areas of the country—those with a strong history of discriminatory voting practices—to have changes to their election laws approved by the federal government prior to enacting them. When Texas regained the ability to change its election rules without supervision after the 2013 court decision, it immediately began to implement restrictive voter ID laws and to remove programs such as same-day registration and mail-in voting, which tend to favor those who vote for Democratic candidates.

Another way that Texas Republicans have sought to suppress voting is by closing or "consolidating" polling places in strategic areas. Conservative legislators in many different states have closed hundreds of polling places in poor, underserved, or predominantly non-white parts of cities and towns. Making it more difficult to vote in those areas, discourages voting, and also limits voting by people of color and working-class urban residents, who tend to favor progressive politicians. The closure of polling places is often presented to voters as a budgetary issue, but the selection of which polling places to close and which to continue funding reflects partisan efforts to obtain an advantage by disadvantaging voters who tend to favor progressive or liberal candidates or policies.

While these programs were rapidly expanding in the late 2010s, Donald Trump's election loss in 2020, his unsupported claims of widespread election fraud, and the attempted insurrection in the Capitol on January 6, 2021, have been followed by extreme changes in voting laws that seem explicitly designed to target urban black and Latino voters and lower-income voters generally, that is, voters who often lean toward voting for Democratic candidates.

Author Biography

The Center for Public Integrity is, according to its mission statement, a "nonprofit newsroom investigation inequality and holding powerful interests accountable." It publishes a journal, *Public Integrity*, containing the results of its work. The journal is made available free to all and relies on contributions from donors rather than paid advertising to support it and the Center. The Center states that it maintains an editorial "firewall" between its donors and its content; that is, donors contribute to its work but do not directly influence the content it publishes. Founded in

In 2021, Republican Gov. Greg Abbott signed into law a massive elections overhaul that rolled back extended voting hours and drive-through voting, restricted voting by mail, added new voter ID requirements, banned some forms of organizing voter turnout and increased criminal penalties for violating election laws. Photo by J Dimas, via Wikimedia Commons.

A vote-by-mail ballot being placed in a ballot drop box. Photo by Chris Phan, via Wikimedia Commons.

1989 in Washington, D.C., *Public Integrity* won the Pulitzer Prize for Investigative Journalism in 2014 and the Edward R. Murrow Award for General Excellence in 2023. The Center is considered a trusted independent watchdog group whose aim is "to protect democracy" and expose "betrayals of the public trust by powerful interests."

The author of this article, Karen Juanita Carrillo, is a Brooklyn, New York–based author and photographer. She is a frequent speaker on African American and Afro Latinx history and politics. Her news reporting has won awards from the New York Association of Black Journalists, New California Media Awards, and the National Newspapers Publishers Association.

Historical Document

Texas Limits Mail Voting, Adds ID Requirements After Surge in Turnout

by Karen Juanita Carrillo

Public Integrity

October 6, 2022

Texas has vacillated between occasionally prying open a smidgen of expanded access to the ballot box and then constraining it. It's a state with a long history of voter intimidation and suppression — recorded since at least 1902, when it enacted an annual poll tax, designed to discourage Mexican-Americans, African Americans and poor whites from voting.

Those disenfranchised saw voting access open up with the ratification of the 24th Amendment in 1964 — prohibiting the use of poll taxes — and the signing of the Voting Rights Act of 1965. But after the law's "preclearance" provision was struck down by the U.S. Supreme Court in 2013, Texas again implemented some of the most restrictive voter ID laws in the country. Previously, it was among states with a long history of discrimination that were required by preclearance to get approval from the U.S. Justice Department before implementing election changes that could create voting inequities.

Several factors have fueled the Republican-controlled Texas legislature to enact new voting restrictions in the past two years: President Donald Trump's re-election loss in 2020 and his false claims of widespread fraud costing him the elction; surging turnout, thanks in part to voting by mail; and shifting demographics that threaten their grip on power. In 2021, Republican Gov. Greg Abbott signed into law a massive elections overhaul that rolled back extended voting hours and drive-through voting, restricted voting by mail, added new voter ID requirements, banned some forms of organizing voter turnout and increased criminal penalties for violating election laws.

Civil rights groups immediately mounted a court challenge, claiming SB1 violates the federal Voting Rights Act by intentionally discriminating against voters of color, voters with disabilities, those who are more comfortable with a language other than English, and those who have no option but to vote by mail. While the case won't go to trial until July of 2023, the law has taken effect. [A federal judge in 2023 invalidated a portion of the law concerning minor errors in mail-in ballots. –Ed.]

In 2020, election officials in Harris County, home to Houston, experimented with "drive-through voting" as a way to encourage turnout amid concerns about COVID-19. It survived a court challenge from Republicans, but SB1 banned the practice.

"More than anything else, SB1 was a response to the efforts to facilitate voting in 2020," said J. Morgan Kousser, a professor of history and social science at Caltech. Houston, Dallas, San Antonio and Austin "tried to make it easier to vote in 2020, particularly because of the particular conditions of voting in the midst of a pandemic."

"Harris County, for example, set up 24-hour-voting for two days—in a limited number of places, but still, you could vote at any time. They also set up—and again this was quite constrained as to time—drive-through voting: You still had to show identification, but you could sit in your car, and they would give you a tablet that you could vote on," Kousser said. "They kept statistics on that by race and we know that that was extraordinarily likely to be used by Blacks and Latinos. Texas has had early voting for a long time, [but] the legislature is likely to constrain early voting more in the next legislative session because Democrats—particularly Black and Latino Democrats, particularly in urban areas—are likely to engage in early voting."

A new requirement in SB1 that a driver's license or last four digits of a voter's Social Security number be included with absentee ballots and that they match applications on file led to the rejection of 25,000 mail-in ballots in Texas' April primary. That was more than 12% of total votes cast, according to a Bloomberg report, compared to the average rate across the country of 1%.

The law makes it a felony for local election officials to send out "unsolicited" absentee ballot applications—a common practice in other states—or to assist an outside group in distributing them.

One portion of the new law was struck down this summer by a federal judge. It would have placed restrictions and possible criminal penalties on people who assist others with casting a ballot, including those with limited English skills or a disability, requiring them to fill out paperwork disclosing their relationship to the voter and whether they are being paid in some way to assist them. They are also required to recite an oath pledging not to "pressure or coerce" the voter. Advocates with disability rights organizations had expressed worry about the ambiguity of the criminal penalty portion of the law, and worry that it will prevent people from voting.

Stephanie Gómez, political director of advocacy group MOVE Texas, said the new law has hampered her organization's efforts to engage underrepresented youth in the political process.

"Our field team encountered young people who were attempting to vote by mail and unable to or had to maneuver a really confusing process," she said. "Another issue that we're running into is that we have some young people who are interested in getting their friends to the polls (when there is no easily accessible campus polling option) and will be unable to do so without signing an affidavit due to changes from SB1!"

Other limits

There is no online voter registration in Texas, and the deadline is 30 days before Election Day—so, for the Nov. 8 midterm elections, that date is Oct. 11. When voting in person at the polls, seven acceptable forms of ID can be presented. Voters who don't have any of the approved forms of photo ID can fill out a "Reasonable Impediment Declaration" form and submit an alternative form of ID, such as a utility bill or bank statement.

In addition to SB1, Texas legislators approved bills after the 2020 election that bar local officials from accepting grants from private foundations to supplement the cost of running elections; prohibit people from establishing residence in the state for the sole purpose of swaying an election; and strip state funding from local officials who refuse or fail to comply with some aspects of the state's election laws.

Election workers targeted

With a hotly contested gubernatorial race and congressional seats, calls for gun control legislation, and abortion rights all up for grabs on Nov. 8, threats against election administrators and county clerks have increased throughout Texas. In one county, the entire elections staff quit after being stalked and having faced threats of violence from Trump supporters echoing false conspiracy theories he's advanced about the 2020 election. Trump won Texas in 2020. The county that lost its election staff voted for Trump in 2020 as well.

Texas Republicans in Congress voted against certification of federal election results after Trump lost. The Texas Republican Party adopted a resolution at its state convention rejecting President Joe Biden as the winner of the 2020 election.

During testimony to the U.S. House of Representatives Aug. 11, Texas elections administrators spoke of how "'personal attacks on national media outlets' led to alarming threats against an election administrator, including a social media call to 'hang him when convicted for fraud and let his lifeless body hang in public until maggots drip out of his mouth' and messages threatening his children."

Felony disenfranchisement

Texas strips voting rights from people who are in prison on a felony conviction or on parole. Those rights can't be restored until someone has "fully discharged" their sentence or has been pardoned. A 2019 Georgetown Law Civil Rights Clinic report describes Texas as having an "implicit" requirement that fines and fees associated with a conviction must be paid before rights are restored, because of its requirement that parole and probation be completed first.

In 2020, more than 500,000 Texas residents were unable to vote because of felony disenfranchisement. Nearly 28% of those barred from voting were Black, despite representing only 12% of the state's population.

As a recent Public Integrity report detailed, people incarcerated awaiting trial or on misdemeanor convictions are eligible to vote but can be "de facto disenfranchised" if state and local officials don't provide a mechanism for them to cast ballots.

Activists are pushing to have more of the state's jails serve as voting sites after Houston's Harris County Jail was used as a polling place for eligible incarcerated voters. "The pilot program allows people arrested on or after Oct. 22 to vote in a secure area of the jail," Houston Public Media reported. "An unsecured part of the jail is available for the public to vote."

[Source: publicintegrity.org/politics/elections/who-counts/texas-limits-mail-voting-adds-id-requirements-after-surge-in-turnout/]

Document Analysis

Voter suppression strategies typically impact people of color and poor voters more than affluent or white voters, and racism and classism continue to play a role in motivating attitudes about voting rights and the ethics of legislation and policies that suppress the vote. Those who embrace white supremacist ideology are more likely to approve of measures that would limit the influence of black voters and studies indicate that white Republican voters are far more likely to embrace prejudicial attitudes about race and gender than voters in any other party. The fact that white supremacists tend to identify more closely with the Republican Party (or other conservative groups) helps to explain why America's conservative parties have become more closely associated with efforts to suppress voting among certain facets of the population.

This article lays out the basic background of voter suppression efforts before moving on to the latest (as of late 2022) efforts in Texas, by a Republican-majority government, to limit access to the ballot in order to favor voters opposed to broad access by minority communities. Measures such as extended voting hours, mail-in ballots, drive-through voting, and low-level identity requirements are banned under the new law, Senate Bill 1, or SB1. A set of criminal penalties for any violations of the new law are also put in place, in order to discourage voting by such communities generally. The disconnect between what civil liberties groups see as progress in voting access before the law's enactment, and the burden placed on voters after the law, are likewise noted. A number of liberal commentators are quoted describing how SB1 is essentially an antidemocratic law, setting up restrictions, such as IDs and perfectly completed registration forms, that many voters would be hard-pressed to meet, especially in the mere one-month timeframe before the midterm elections of November 2022. The law makes some formerly used practices, such as sending out unsolicited absentee ballot applications, a felony. (Ironically, the data shows that many Republican voters in the United States have made good use of absentee and/or mail-in ballots, and to a degree favor them over on-site voting; Donald Trump himself has utilized mail-in ballots.) The prospect of simply confusing voters, so that there is limited turnout in an election, is also part of laws such as SB1, and that seems to be true in the Texas case. It is noted that hardline Texas lawmakers voted *not* to certify the results of the 2020 presidential election, in which Trump lost to his opponent, Joe Biden. This suggests the far-right mindset of the Republican majority in the Texas statehouse. One outcome of such extreme measures is a targeting of local election officials by far-right supporters of voter restriction. The article mentions a couple of cases of such abuse. SB1 also strips the right to vote from those in prison or on parole—a practice known as felony disenfranchisement. This is a controversial topic and also ties in with the effort to restrict minority voters generally.

Allegations that there has been widespread "election fraud" in Texas, or any other state, are simply incorrect. The Heritage Foundation, a conservative think tank, maintains a record of prosecuted and convicted election crimes; between 2019 and 2022, just six instances are listed, with most of them tied to one candidate's fraudulent attempts to manipulate votes in a local primary election.

For many years, demographics in Texas have been shifting. The Latino and Black populations in the state are increasing, and the state is rapidly becoming more "purple" (politically mixed) rather than "red" (Republican) or "blue" (Democrat), especially around urban areas such as Austin and Houston. Most of the current political establishment in Texas is controlled by the far-right of the Republican Party. Without the intense voter suppression acts currently underway, it is not unlikely that a shift in power in the state would occur favoring more centrist Republican or Democratic policies and candidates.

This shift is visible when considering recent presidential elections in Texas. According to *Politico*, Donald Trump won Texas over Hillary Clinton by more than 800,000 votes, with wide disparities in most districts. In 2020, however, CNN showed that Joe Biden lost the state to Donald Trump by around 500,000 votes, a modest decline in the Republican edge. When considering the state district by district, many counties showed much closer races between the two

In 2020, election officials in Harris County, home to Houston, experimented with "drive-through voting" as a way to encourage turnout amid concerns about COVID-19. Photo via iStock/J. Michael Jones. [Used under license.]

parties. Overall, this arguably represents the changing landscape beginning to affect Texas politics.

Essential Themes

In 2023, federal courts struck down two of the provisions of SB1; these provisions were related to circumstances that required election officials to discard mail-in ballots in certain situations. While this benefits future voting, broadly considered, there have been hundreds of thousands of ballots that were discarded in ways that would be illegal if the same vote were carried out today. This hints at the real danger of restrictive voting laws; they are often addressed in court long after the relevant elections have come and gone. Lawmakers who created situations designed to keep themselves in power do not lose their positions; they remain in office and continue to create hostile voting environments that prevent challengers from gaining power.

The greater threat to voting in environments like Texas's may come less from the actual laws and more from the culture of caution and fear that has come to surround voting. This is a deliberate exercise in fomenting confusion by far-right politicians. Texas is on the front lines of the national fight around undocumented immigration and asylum seeking. Many legal citizens and documented immigrants in Texas have understandable fears that they will be unlawfully detained and deported if they catch the attention of certain officials, and therefore they may stay away from the polls to maintain their safety as a result. Those with lower income may not be able to vote during convenient voting hours, and without the ability to mail in their ballot, they quite simply may not be able to visit the polls. As voting rights cases bounce back and forth between the courts, even election officials who have every intention of ensuring a fair and honest election to the best of their ability may struggle to keep up with who does and does not have the right to vote. Because Texas has implemented severe penalties for those who do not follow voting laws, the consequences of making a mistake are steep.

Texans may struggle to see a path forward in this situation. The current Roberts' Supreme Court, one of the most conservative in the court's history, has been largely unfriendly to voters' rights issues, evidenced by its elimination of the preclearance rules in the Voting Rights Act in 2013 (*Shelby County v. Holder*) and its 2018 ruling that Ohio could purge infrequent voters from its rolls without notification, among other decisions. A 2019 ruling by the Court about partisan gerrymandering, where districts are redrawn along strictly political lines to favor the party in power, declared the practice a legitimate exercise in democracy. Thus, when in 2023 the Court forced Alabama to redraw its district maps in a less overtly discriminatory way, observers were surprised by the decision as it seemed to go in the opposite direction.

Over the past several elections, the Republican candidate has received fewer and fewer votes in Texas. The odds of Texas "flipping" and voting for a Democratic Party candidate for president in 2024, providing that the election is free and fair, seem not unplausible. Meanwhile, the current hard-right government in Texas is deeply committed to preventing such an outcome from occurring and works to ensure that it stays in power, largely regardless of the will of an increasing number of Texans.

—*Kay Lemay, MA*

Bibliography and Additional Reading

"2016 Texas Presidential Election Results." *Politico*, December 13, 2016, www.politico.com/2016-election/results/map/president/texas.

Bullock, Charles S., Keith Gaddle, and Justin Wert. *The Rise and Fall of the Voting Rights Act*. Norman: University of Oklahoma Press, 2016.

Center for Public Integrity, publicintegrity.org.

Daniels, Gilda R. *Uncounted: The Crisis of Voter Suppression in America*. New York: NYU Press, 2020.

"Election Fraud Cases: Texas." *Heritage Foundation*, n.d., www.heritage.org/voterfraud/search? state=TX.

Meyerson, Harold. "How Racist Are Republicans? Very." *The American Prospect*, October 22, 2020, prospect.org/blogs-and-newsletters/tap/how-racist-are-republicans-very.

Silver, Nate, and Allison McCann. "Are White Republicans More Racist Than White Democrats?" *FiveThirtyEight*, April 30, 2014, fivethirtyeight.com/features/are-white-republicans-more-racist-than-white-democrats.

"Texas President Results." February 22, 2021. *CNN*, www.cnn.com/election/2020/results/state/texas/president.

■ "Republican Resolution Would Declare Trump the Winner in 2024, Regardless of What Voters Say"

Date: February 15, 2024
Author: Caitlin Sievers, *AZ Mirror*
Genre: news article

Summary Overview

Since Donald Trump lost the presidential election in 2020 to Joe Biden, Trump has argued, loudly and publicly, that the election was "rigged," that votes were miscounted, and that he was the actual winner of the election. This reached a peak on January 6, 2021, when a group of armed insurrectionists, after listening to a speech by Trump, attempted to stop Congress from certifying the national vote that would finalize the election results and officially declare Joe Biden to be the next president of the United States.

In subsequent years, Trump has continued to make these false accusations of voter fraud and illegitimate elections, and right-wing government officials throughout the United States have taken advantage of these claims to tighten voter ID laws, remove mail-in ballot options, and make it more difficult in general to vote. These measures tend to disenfranchise voters who are younger, people of color, and those who have lower economic status, all of whom are more likely to vote for Democratic Party candidates or, perhaps, centrist Republicans. Those tightening the restrictions are almost always hard-right Republicans. It is almost impossible to see their work in this area as anything but a raw attempt to consolidate and retain power, often regardless of the desires of the voters in their districts and states.

The attempt by a far-right Arizona state representative to declare that Donald Trump is the winner of the 2024 presidential election before the vote has even taken place—indeed, before Trump has even secured the official Republican Party presidential nomination—is among the more bizarre and chilling events to have occurred following Trump's exit from the White House. This resolution seems designed to cast so much doubt on the election process as to say that voting is a waste of time. Not only does the proposed bill seek to declare Trump the winner of Arizona's electoral votes prior to the election, but it also is seen as a ploy to force the (Democratic) governor in the state to agree to a series of radical voter suppression measures, such as the elimination of early voting and mail-in ballots, the reliance on one-day-only in-person voting, and a hand count of all ballots. The measure was so extreme that even some right-leaning Republicans doubted its merits and questioned whether it could pass.

Donald Trump. Photo via Wikimedia Commons. [Public domain.]

Defining Moment

There have been times in American history where voter fraud was common, but most of these occurred in the 1800s. At that time, people tended to vote publicly, sometimes by declaring their vote out loud during a roll call, and sometimes by writing down their vote and putting it into a glass box where everyone could see who the person had voted for. In other districts, voters handed their ballots directly to an election official, which allowed the ballot to be changed to favor a particular candidate. Corrupt officials could also "buy" votes by the thousands (often for $1 or less), driving an election in a direction that suited them and their financial backers.

In the 1890s, however, a "secret ballot" (imported from Australia via England) began to be used in northern cities. This ballot allowed voters to cast their votes privately, which removed many of the opportunities for voter tampering. Elections began to be run in more democratic ways.

In the southern states, however, deliberate suppression of black and lower-income voters continued through poll taxes and requirements that Black (but not white) voters be able to read, answer various civics questions, and provide birth certificates and other documents that often were not available to black people. The Voting Rights Act of 1965 barred states from discriminating against voters along racial lines. While this did not completely put an end to discriminatory voting practices, it did limit them and brought more free and fair elections.

Modern concerns about election fraud specifically resurfaced in the presidential election in 2000, where George W. Bush defeated Al Gore by a small number of votes in a few counties in Florida. The entire country watched as Florida's ballots were determined to be hard to read, difficult to use, and easy to misinterpret. The country learned the meaning of the phrase "hanging chad" (the small bit of paper left attached to a punch-card ballot when it is not fully punched through). Al Gore ultimately conceded the election to George W. Bush, but because Gore had won the popular vote (while losing the electoral vote), many voters were left frustrated.

In 2020 the incumbent presidential candidate on the Republican side, Donald J. Trump, lost to Joseph R. Biden from the Democratic side. Despite losing the race, Trump immediately began to claim that the election had been rigged and that Biden had won only because of massive voter fraud on the part of the Democrats. His claims had no proof behind them and went nowhere in court on multiple occasions, but his followers came to embrace the "Big Lie," as it came to be known. Increasingly, in fact, Republican candidates to office were expected to state their support of Trump's claims of fraud before getting themselves onto a ticket; only then would Trump deign to endorse them. By 2024, when this Arizona "declaration for Trump" resolution was put forth, hundreds if not thousands of far-right lawmakers throughout the nation had passed the Trump litmus test and announced themselves as believers in Trump's false claims. They almost always supported harsh voter suppression measures as well.

Arizona has a long history of voter suppression, particularly against Native Americans and Latino voters. It has been a battleground state for many years, and Joe Biden was only the third Democratic presidential candidate (after Harry Truman and Bill Clinton) to win the electoral votes from Arizona in its history. While the Supreme Court did strike down a 2024 Arizona law that forced voters to prove their state residency as well as their place of birth, it upheld a 2020 law that a lower court had ruled as intentional discrimination in that the state was well aware that the law would disenfranchise Native American voters.

Author Biography

The source of this article, the *AZ Mirror,* or *Arizona Mirror,* is part of a national tax-exempt news consortium called States Newsroom. Members of the consortium focus on state news and have a liberal or progressive editorial outlook. Having launched in 2019, States Newsroom encompassed all fifty states by 2024 with a team of 220 journalists. Its logo is "Fair. Fearless. Free."

Caitlin Sievers joined the *Arizona Mirror* in 2022, having nearly ten years of experience as a reporter and editor. She has won statewide awards in Nebraska, Indiana, and Wisconsin for reporting, photography, and commentary.

Historical Document

Republican Resolution Would Declare Trump the Winner in 2024, Regardless of What Voters Say

by Caitlin Sievers

AZ Mirror

FEBRUARY 15, 2024

A Republican state representative wants to completely invalidate the votes of Arizonans in the upcoming presidential election as a bargaining tool to force Democrat Gov. Katie Hobbs to agree to a Republican wishlist of election reforms.

Rep. Rachel Jones, of Tucson, is the sponsor of House Concurrent Resolution 2055, a declaration saying that the state legislature already has the power — via the U.S. Constitution — to pre-appoint Arizona's electors for the 2024 presidential election, to ensure that they would vote for former President Donald Trump, regardless of the results of the popular vote.

The Legislature would then use the threat of ignoring the votes of millions of Arizonans to strong-arm Hobbs into signing an election reform bill that would eliminate early voting and allow only in-person voting and only on Election Day with no mail-in ballots, to be completely counted by hand. Hobbs would not have the power to veto the measure since the resolution does not have the power of law, but simply declares its backers' intentions and what they already believe to be true, per federal law.

While the Republican members of the House Municipal Oversight and Elections Committee almost always vote along party lines to approve proposed legislation from their own party, Jones' resolution went too far, even for them. Committee Chairwoman Jacqueline Parker, R-Mesa, opted not to take a vote on the resolution and to table discussion on it for the moment, after an impassioned debate among lawmakers and members of the public.

Rep. Alexander Kolodin, R-Scottsdale, said he did not believe the U.S. Supreme Court would side with the Arizona legislature if it decided to appoint electors to vote for Trump, regardless of the will of the voters. He added that passing this resolution would put a bullseye on Republicans for accusations of stealing the election from Democrats.

"Wouldn't we be guilty of exactly what we accuse the other side of doing?" he asked. "Wouldn't that be just as bad as what we imagine they have been doing?"

Josh Barnett, who sued then-Secretary of State Hobbs after he lost the Republican primary for Arizona's first congressional district for U.S. House in August 2022, spoke passionately in favor of the resolution.

"Do you not think 2020 was illegally run?" Barnett asked the legislators. "I'm confused here."

In the suit, which was rapidly dismissed, Barnett asked the judge to annul the results of the 2022 general election because it was "illegally run."

Barnett also has a history of making posts to social media about the QAnon conspiracy theories.

Barnett was adamant that the 2020 and 2022 general elections in Arizona were illegally run, without providing any evidence, adding that Republicans had not accomplished any significant election reforms since then, and that he was sure the 2024 election would be illegally run as well.

When Rep. Justin Heap, R-Mesa, asked Barnett if he was really asking for the legislators to appoint electors to vote for Trump regardless of the will of the voters, Barnett answered that the voters elected a Republican majority in the Legislature and that means they want a conservative agenda.

Republicans have a slim one-vote majority in both the state House and Senate, and in 2022 voters elected Democrats to several of the state's top offices, including governor, secretary of state and attorney general.

Barnett added that with Republicans in control of the Legislature there was no need for a presidential election this year.

Ruthee Goldkorn, a local activist, argued that the only illegal activity surrounding the 2020 election was the attempt in several states to use fake electors to supersede the will of the voters, who elected Democrat President Joe Biden.

"Why this bill is in conversation, I have no idea," she said. "There's no way on God's green acres that this should ever come to fruition."

Melissa Price, a former Carefree Town Council member, told the lawmakers that members of the public think the legislators don't care enough to ensure a safe and secure election this year.

"This next election could change the course of our lives," she said.

Price added that if the legislators couldn't stomach disenfranchising the entire electorate, they could run their own separate presidential election on one day, with paper ballots and to be counted by hand.

Jones did not provide any conclusive reason that she believes the votes of Arizonans should not count — something she's accused Democrats of doing behind the scenes for years — other than that many Republicans and some Democrats have lost faith in the elections system.

She also claimed that a recent trend toward more Democrats being elected into office in Arizona somehow indicated that the state's elections are rigged or "maladministered."

Some of Jones' reasoning included that until 2020, Arizonans had not backed a Democrat for president since Harry Truman in 1948 — with the exception of Bill Clinton in 1996.

While this is true, demographics in the state have changed substantially over the past 20 years, and the state's presidential elections have trended purple since 2000.

She added that George W. Bush won Arizona with a record vote gain of more than 300,000 votes and Trump surpassed that in 2020 with a gain of more than 400,000 votes, calling these "interesting anomalies" and implying that the numbers indicate fraud.

Jones' thesis ignores the massive population increase from 2000 to 2020, with around 2 million people moving into the state, and the increase in voter turnout in the same timeframe.

The voter turnout for the 2000 presidential election in Arizona was almost 72%. That increased to 77% in 2004 and 80% in 2020.

Both Kolodin and Heap said they had misgivings about the resolution, with Kolodin saying if it were passed, it would guarantee that the Legislature would flip to Democratic control after the 2024 election.

[Source: azmirror.com/2024/02/15/republican-resolution-shows-intent-to-bypass-voters-in-the-2024-presidential-election]

[Update Feb. 18, 2024. The bill did not advance to a full House vote because of reservations on the part of some Republicans. –Ed.]

Document Analysis

The history of voter suppression has always been tied to power. Those in power make laws to restrict those who can vote to ensure that they remain in power. This is particularly necessary when politicians fear that they will not remain in power without voter imposing targeted restrictions.

Like many states in the Western United States, the population in Arizona has been rapidly shifting as more Latino voters join the polls. These voters often vote for Democratic candidates, or centrist candidates generally, threatening the post–Trump Republican governors and state lawmakers who have controlled their states and continue to support Trump. The flip in the presidential election in 2020 clearly created a sense of concern in Arizona that this trend would continue and the power in the state would continue to shift. Midterm elections in 2022 brought a Democratic governor, secretary of state, and attorney general into office.

The resolution presented here is an extreme attempt to bypass the election process and deliver all the state's eleven electoral votes to Trump. In its brazenness, it suggests a deep worry over the outcome of any actual election and a fear that Republicans might lose their majority. The idea of "pre-appointing" state electors is unprecedented, and did not go down well with all of the Republican lawmakers in the Arizona legislature. A few of them voiced concerns or disagree with the idea, seeing it as "placing a target on their backs" as they seek to be reelected in the future. One of the strongest supporters of the bill, on the other hand, is noted as being someone who lost an earlier race for the U.S. House of Representatives and, as a result, attempted to sue the Democratic secretary of state (and now governor) for conducting an "illegal" election; the complainant is also characterized as participating in QAnon conspiracy theories—in other words, just the kind of person who would see a normal, legitimate election as amounting to a secret cabal.

As the article points out, the Republicans currently control both the state House and Senate by one vote; endorsing extreme measures such as doing away with a presidential election in favor of assigning all electoral votes to Trump would likely get them thrown out of office in the next cycle. One Arizona Republican doubter worries, in fact, that such an effort would only mark Republicans as *facilitators* of election fraud, not opponents of it. For her part, the main sponsor of the bill, Representative Rachel Jones, regards the fact that Democrats have won top offices in the state as itself evidence that elections have been rigged or "maladministered." It is notable that when this story spread in the national news media, it was often presented as an instance of fact being stranger than fiction.

Essential Themes

Ultimately, Representative Jones's extreme resolution did not get the benefit of a House vote. The committee chairperson did not allow it to be voted or discussed in the legislature. Although at the federal level the Roberts' Supreme Court has not, in general, ruled in favor of voting rights, it has made a number of decisions in 2023 and 2024 that determined various laws and rules to be too discriminatory and too likely to create unnecessary obstacles for voters. But these decisions have rarely been tied to groups' minority status —as shown in the sole 2020 decision regarding obstructions to voting for Native Americans. In any case, a likely state and/or federal Supreme Court case would surely have come in the wake of the resolution had it passed.

It has got to be reassuring when a state legislature, presented with the idea of pre-declaring a candidate the victor of an election that has not even occurred yet, finds it to too ludicrous to debate or vote on. Yet it is concerning that such a concept can be presented at all, and find numerous backers besides. The essence of democracy is allowing all voters to vote for their preferred candidate, the person they believe will best represent their wishes. Restrictions on voter laws try to tightly contain whose vote counts and to prevent votes from people who generally favor broad access to the ballot and candidates who do too. These restrictions are regarded by liberal opponents—and most political scientists—as inherently undemocratic.

For obvious reasons, politicians do not typically state that their intentions—with regard to some new policy or ordinance—is to suppress votes from certain demographics. If a politician were to admit, openly, that they were trying to limit voting access to black voters, Latino voters, or poor voters, the result would likely be public outrage and a loss of political support for the politician who openly espoused such undemocratic ideals. Typically, politicians justify policies that limit voting access as a matter of election security or budgetary concerns. This resolution is a rather rare example of open hostility toward anyone who is not a hardline supporter of Donald Trump. As such, it was questioned even by some of those same supporters as being too baldly stated and a clear "target" for critics.

There are now several sitting members of the U.S. Congress who have actively participated in claims that the 2020 election was "stolen" (even though it was sometimes the same election that brought them to power). Since his election loss that year, Trump has continued to make highly controversial political statements on social media and continued to endorse candidates who publicly agree that the results of the 2020 election were invalid. Given that 2024 has shaped up to be another race between Joe Biden and Donald Trump, it seems clear that the groundwork has already been laid on the Republican side to mount another claim of voter fraud, regardless of the outcome. Voters are understandably concerned about what might then happen in Washington, D.C., during the next electoral vote count. (A 2022 law did regularize the procedure, but one cannot preclude the possibility of violent protest in any case.)

Current methods for detecting and preventing fraud are highly effective, the result of decades of conscious effort to protect elections. Online registration, digital and computerized vote tabulation, and other technological advances have greatly reduced the potential for voter fraud and make it far easier for authorities to see when fraud has been committed. It is important, however, for Americans to remain vigilant. Fraud delegitimizes the democratic process and so it is in the interest of every American to take voter fraud seriously and to continue to take steps to eliminate fraud in whatever form it takes. However, it is also important for politicians to counter efforts to use fear and propaganda to suggest threats to election integrity where threats do not exist, because this practice damages trust in the election system and may ultimately pose as serious a threat to American democracy as any form of electoral fraud.

—*Kay Lemay, MA*

Bibliography and Additional Reading

Blakemore, Erin. "Voter Fraud Used to Be Rampant: Now It's an Anomaly." *National Geographic*, November 11, 2020, www.nationalgeographic.com/history/article/voter-fraud-used-to-be-rampant-now-an-anomaly.

Cooper, Jonathan L., and Christie, Bob. "Democrats Win Big in Arizona, Now a Former GOP Stronghold." *AP News,* November 4, 2020, apnews.com/article/election-2020-joe-biden-donald-trump-race-and-ethnicity-mark-kelly-6841e27210770f59418bdc13a60ccec7.

Downs, Jim, ed. *Voter Suppression in U.S. Elections.* Athens: University of Georgia Press, 2020.

Herman, Alice, et al. "The Election-Denying Republicans Who Aided Trump's 'Big Lie' and Got Promoted." *The Guardian,* March 9, 2023, www.theguardian.com/us-news/ng-interactive/2023/mar/09/trump-big-lie-2020-election-republican-supporters-congress.

"Voting Rights: A Short History." *Carnegie Corporation of America*, November 18, 2019, www.carnegie.org/our-work/article/voting-rights-timeline.

■ Chronological List

1788: *Federalist Paper* No. 52 2
June 15, 1804: Twelfth Amendment to the U.S. Constitution 10
1841-1842: The "People's Constitution" and Dorr's Rebellion 17
July 19-20, 1848: Seneca Falls Convention: Declaration of Sentiments 36
1849: Henry David Thoreau: "Civil Disobedience" 22
July 9, 1868: Fourteenth and Fifteenth Amendments to the Constitution 120
February 3, 1870: Fourteenth and Fifteenth Amendments to the Constitution 120
February 11, 1870: A Contested Election: Report to Congress on the Activities of the Ku Klux Klan 131
1873: Susan B. Anthony: "Is It a Crime for a Citizen of the United States to Vote?" 49
January 12, 1874: Petition to U.S. Congress for Women's Suffrage 62
1903: Booker T. Washington: "Statement on Suffrage" 144
1910: Jane Addams: "Why Women Should Vote" 70
April 8, 1913: Seventeenth Amendment to the U.S. Constitution 244
1915: *Guinn v. United States* 154
June 21, 1915: Anna Howard Shaw: "Women's Suffrage in a Democratic Republic" 91
December 16, 1915: Alice Paul: Testimony before the House Judiciary Committee 79
1920 (describing events of 1917): Prison Writings of a Radical Suffragist 102
August 18, 1920: Nineteenth Amendment to the U.S. Constitution 108
June 2, 1924: Indian Citizenship Act 172
1927: Alice Moore Dunbar-Nelson: "The Negro Woman and the Ballot" 176
April 3, 1944: *Smith v. Allwright* 186
March 26, 1962: *Baker v. Carr* 307
January 23, 1964: Twenty-Fourth Amendment to the U.S. Constitution 218
April 3, 1964: Malcolm X: "The Ballot or the Bullet" 198
June 15, 1964: *Reynolds v. Sims* 315
March 15, 1965: Speech before Congress on Voting Rights 224
August 6, 1965: Voting Rights Act of 1965 237
June 8, 1969: *Red Lion Broadcasting v. FCC* 325
July 1, 1971: Twenty-Sixth Amendment to the U.S. Constitution 250
June 24, 1974: *Richardson v. Ramirez* 337
January 30, 1976: *Buckley v. Valeo* 344
May 20, 1993: National Voter Registration Act of 1993 (NVRA) 255
June 28, 1993: *Shaw v. Reno* 384
December 12, 2000: *Bush v. Gore* 393
October 29, 2002: Help America Vote Act of 2002 (HAVA) 263
January 21, 2010: *Citizens United v. Federal Election Commission* 404
June 25, 2013: *Shelby County v. Holder* 424
2016: Americans with Disabilities Act (ADA) Polling Place Accessibility Checklist 270
May 22, 2017: *Cooper v. Harris* 443
May 16, 2018: Statement to the U.S. Senate Judiciary Committee concerning Cambridge Analytica ... 467

January 2019: Civics Test for Naturalization 283
June 27, 2019: *Rucho v. Common Cause* 456
January 6, 2022: Remarks by President Biden One Year after the January 6 Assault on the U.S. Capitol. . 483
July 20, 2022: Electoral Count Reform Act of 2022. 299
October 6, 2022: "Texas Limits Mail Voting, Adds ID Requirements After Surge in Turnout". 497
February 15, 2024: "Republican Resolution Would Declare Trump the Winner in 2024,
    Regardless of What Voters Say". 507

■ Web Resources

American Civil Liberties Union (ACLU): Know Your Voting Rights
www.aclu.org/know-your-rights/voting-rights
Users can learn more about how to exercise their voting rights, resist voter intimidation efforts, and access disability-related accommodations and language assistance at the polls.

Ben's Guide to U.S. Government for Kids
bensguide.gpo.gov
The educational component the U.S. Government Printing Office's service, called GPO Access, provides the official online version of legislative and regulatory information. This site provides learning tools for K-12 students, parents, and teachers.

The Center for Civic Education
www.civiced.org
A nonprofit, nonpartisan educational corporation dedicated to promoting an enlightened and responsible citizenry committed to democratic principles and actively engaged in the practice of democracy in the United States and other countries.

Civil Rights in America—Racial Voting Rights, A Study by the National Park Service
www.nps.gov/subjects/tellingallamericansstories/upload/CivilRights_VotingRights.pdf
An extensive and in-depth look at African American voting rights over the nation's history, as well as the rights of American Indian, Hispanic, and Asian American voting rights. Explores historic landmarks and identifies properties associated with events considered nationally significant within the history of racial voting discrimination.

Crusade for the Vote—A History of Women's Suffrage, by The National Women's History Museum
www.crusadeforthevote.org
Traces the history of the women's suffrage movement, using primary source documents from each phase of the 72-year campaign that illustrate the incremental progress towards equal voting opportunity.

Federal Voting Assistance Program (FVAP)
www.fvap.gov
This government site provides resources for service members, their families, and eligible voters living abroad.

The History of Voting Rights—An Interactive Timeline by PBS Learning Media
ny.pbslearningmedia.org/resource/ush22-soc-votinghistory/the-history-of-voting-rights-interactive-timeline
Analyze the evolution of voting rights in the United States, starting with the ratification of the U.S. Constitution and ending with the current competing efforts to suppress voting rights and improve voting access in this interactive timeline. Students learn about key events that have either expanded or suppressed voting rights as well as the roles that both government institutions and ordinary citizens have played in effecting these changes.

I Side With...
www.isidewith.com
This is a great tool if you are unsure about candidate views on various issues. It provides an enormous amount of useful data for undecided voters.

League of Women Voters
www.lwv.org
The League of Women Voters is a nonpartisan, grassroots organization working to protect and expand voting rights and ensure everyone is represented democratically, through means such as advocacy, education, and litigation, at the local, state, and national levels.

Library of Congress: Voting Rights
www.loc.gov/collections/civil-rights-history-project/articles-and-essays/voting-rights
A brief examination of the history of voting rights in America, from the Library of Congress.

The Living Room Candidate
livingroomcandidate.org
From the Museum of the Modern Image in New York City, The Living Room Candidate is an online exhibition containing more than 300 commercials for presidential candidates since 1952, when the first TV campaign ads aired. The site includes a searchable database, and features commentary, historical background, election results, and navigation organized by year, type of ad, and issue.

National Archives: Teacher Resources
www.archives.gov/education
Includes civic education and history, primary and secondary sources, lesson plans, and professional development workshops and activities.

Politifact
www.politifact.com
This tool rates the accuracy of claims made by political and cultural figures. It is a nonpartisan organization owned by the Poynter Institute, a nonprofit journalism school.

ProCon.org
www.procon.org
The award-winning ProCon.org website promotes critical thinking, education, and informed citizenship by presenting the pro and con arguments to controversial issues in a straightforward, nonpartisan, freely accessible way. Examples of issues addressed on this site include the presidential election, defunding the police, medical marijuana, gun control, homework, the electoral college, and illegal immigration. ProCon.org is a part of the Britannica® Group of companies.

Rock the Vote
www.rockthevote.org
Through registering new young voters, the group aims to "channel the energy among young people around racial, economic, and health justice into one of the most powerful actions they can take: voting." The organization was founded in 1990 to encourage young Americans to vote. It is geared toward increasing voter turnout among voters ages 18 to 24. Rock the Vote is known for its celebrity spokespeople and its partnership with MTV.

United States Election Assistance Commission (EAC)
www.eac.gov
The U.S. Election Assistance Commission (EAC) is an independent, bipartisan commission whose mission is to help election officials improve the administration of elections and help Americans participate in the voting process.

U.S. Vote Foundation
www.usvotefoundation.org
Develops and provides online tools to assist U.S. citizens living anywhere in the world to register to vote and request their absentee ballot using their state's specific voter forms. This includes citizens living within the U.S., living abroad, or serving in the military.

USA.gov: Voting Rights Laws and Constitutional Amendments
www.usa.gov/voting-rights
Federal laws govern voting rights. Here, readers can learn about the laws and how they protect voters' rights, and make it easier to vote.

Vote.gov
vote.gov
An official website of the General Services Administration, Vote.gov helps citizens register to vote; find voter registration deadlines; check registration; register after moving; change party affiliation; and learn how to get a voter registration card.

Vote.org
www.vote.org
This site provides various election resources but also includes extensive guides to voting in each state.

Vote411.org
www.vote411.org
Launched by the League of Women Voters Education Fund (LWVEF) in October of 2006, VOTE411.org is a "one-stop-shop" for election-related information. It provides nonpartisan information to the public with both general and state-specific information on the following aspects of the election process: absentee ballot information; early voting options (where applicable); election dates; factual data on candidates in various federal, state and local races; ID requirements; polling place locations; voting machines; and more.

VoteSmart
justfacts.votesmart.org
Vote Smart's mission is to provide free, factual, unbiased information on candidates and elected officials to all Americans.

Voting Rights: A Short History—by the Carnegie Corporation of New York
www.carnegie.org/our-work/article/voting-rights-timeline
An informative article that traces the history of U.S. voting rights, from the 1700s to the present day.

When We All Vote
whenweallvote.org
When We All Vote is a leading national, nonpartisan initiative on a mission to change the culture around voting and to increase participation in elections by helping to close the race and age gap. Created by Michelle Obama, When We All Vote brings together individuals, institutions, brands, and organizations to register new voters across the country and advance civic education for the entire family and voters of every age to build an informed and engaged electorate for today and generations to come.

WhiteHouse.gov: Elections and Voting
www.whitehouse.gov/about-the-white-house/our-government/elections-and-voting
A brief examination of how the voting process works, as well as the history of voting rights.

■ Bibliography

"100 Milestone Documents: Voting Rights Act (1965)." *OurDocuments.Gov.* National Archives and Records Administration, 2015.

"2016 Texas Presidential Election Results." *Politico*, December 13, 2016, www.politico.com/2016-election/results/map/president/texas.

"ADA Checklist for Polling Places." *U.S. Department of Justice*, 2016, archive.ada.gov/votingchecklist.pdf.

"ADA Standards for Accessible Design." *U.S. Department of Justice*, 2010, www.ada.gov/law-and-regs/design-standards.

Aleinikoff, T. Alexander, and Samuel Issacharoff. "Race and Redistricting: Drawing Constitutional Lines After *Shaw v. Reno*." *Michigan Law Review* 92, no. 588 (1993).

Aleinikoff, Thomas, David Martin, Hiroshi Motomura Maryellen Fullerton, and Juliet Stumpf. *Immigration and Citizenship: Process and Policy*. St. Paul, MN: West Academic Publishing, 2016.

Allen, W. B., with Kevin A. Cloonan. *The Federalist Papers: A Commentary*. New York: Peter Lang, 2000.

Amer, Karim, and Jehane Noujaim. *The Great Hack*. Netflix documentary, released January 26, 2019.

Anderson, Carol. *One Person, No Vote: How Voter Suppression Is Destroying Our Democracy*. New York: Bloomsbury Publishing, 2018.

Aptekar, Sofya. *The Road to Citizenship: What Naturalization Means for Immigrants and the United States*. New Brunswick, NJ: Rutgers UP, 2015.

Baker, Jean H., ed. *Votes for Women: The Struggle for Suffrage Revisited*. New York: Oxford UP, 2002.

Barber, Lucy G. *Marching on Washington: the Forging of an American Political Tradition*. Berkeley: University of California Press, 2002.

Barnes, Robert and Dan Eggen. "Supreme Court rejects limits on corporate spending on political campaigns." Washingtonpost.com. Washington: The Washington Post Company, 2010.

Barnes, Robert. "Supreme Court Stops Use of Key Part of Voting Rights Act," *Washington Post*, June 25, 2013.

Barnett, Randy E., and Evan D. Bernick. *The Original Meaning of the Fourteenth Amendment: Its Letter and Spirit*. Cambridge, MA: Belknap Press/Harvard UP, 2021.

Barry, Kathleen. *Susan B. Anthony: A Biography of a Singular Feminist*. New York: NYUP, 1988.

Baughman, James. *The Republic of Mass Culture: Journalism, Filmmaking, and Broadcasting in America since 1941*. Baltimore: John Hopkins UP, 2006.

Bausum, Ann. *With Courage and Cloth: Winning the Fight for a Woman's Right to Vote*. Washington, DC: Natl. Geographic, 2004.

Bellamy, Richard. *Citizenship: A Very Short Introduction*. Oxford: Oxford UP, 2008.

Bergeron, Paul H., Stephen V. Ash, and Jeanette Keith. *Tennesseans and Their History*. Knoxville: U of Tennessee P, 1999.

Berman, Ari. *Give Us the Ballot: The Modern Struggle for Voting Rights in America*. New York: Farrar, Straus and Giroux, 2015.

Bitzer, J. Michael. *Redistricting and Gerrymandering in North Carolina*. (Palgrave Studies in U.S. Elections.) Cham, Switzerland: Palgrave-MacMillan, 2021.

Blakemore, Erin. "Voter Fraud Used to Be Rampant: Now It's an Anomaly." *National Geographic*, November 11, 2020, www.nationalgeographic.com/history/article/voter-fraud-used-to-be-rampant-now-an-anomaly.

Brundage, W. Fitzhugh, ed. *Booker T. Washington and Black Progress: Up from Slavery 100 Years Later.* Gainesville: UP of Florida, 2003.

Buchanan, Paul D. *The American Women's Rights Movement: A Chronology of Events and Opportunities from 1600 to 2008.* Boston: Branden, 2009.

Budiansky, Stephen. *The Bloody Shirt: Terror after Appomattox.* New York: Viking, 2008.

Bullock, Charles S. III, Ronald Keith Gaddie, and Justin J. Wert, eds. *The Rise and Fall of the Voting Rights Act.* Norman, OK: University of Oklahoma Press, 2016.

Bunting, Luke, ed. *Symposium Commemorating the 100th Anniversary of the Nineteenth Amendment.* Special issue of Georgetown Journal of Law & Public Policy 20, no. 1 (2022).

Burdette, Robert B. *Buckley v. Valeo: The Opinion of the United States Supreme Court in the Election Campaign Case; Summary and Commentary.* Washington, DC: Library of Congress, 1976.

Burns, Ken and Paul Barnes. "United States vs. Anthony." *Not for Ourselves Alone.* Washington: PBS and WETA, 1999.

Bush v. Gore, 121 S.Ct. 525 (2000). Justia: U.S. Supreme Court

Bybee, Jay S. "Ulysses at the Mast: Democracy, Federalism, and the Sirens' Song of the Seventeenth Amendment." *Scholarly Works,* 1997. 350. scholars.law.unlv.edu/facpub/350.

Cahill, Bernadette. *Alice Paul, the National Women's Party and the Vote.* Jefferson, NC: McFarland & Company, 2015.

Cain, William. *A Historical Guide to Henry David Thoreau.* Oxford: Oxford UP, 2000.

"Cambridge Analytica and Data Privacy." C-Span, May 16, 2018. Videotaped testimony of Christopher Wylie before the Senate Committee on the Judiciary, along with related video from the Facebook and Cambridge Analytica hearings.

"The Cambridge Analytica Files." March 17, 2018. The Guardian/*The Observer.* www.theguardian.com/news/series/cambrdige-analytica-files.

Capparell, Jessica Jones. "Reforming the Electoral Count Act." *League of Women Voters,* 2023, www.lwv.org/blog/reforming-electoral-count-act.

Center for Public Integrity, publicintegrity.org.

Chafe, William H. *The Paradox of Change: American Women in the Twentieth Century.* New York: Oxford UP, 1991.

Chaput, Erik J. *The People's Martyr: Thomas Wilson Dorr and His 1842 Rhode Island Rebellion.* Lawrence: UP of Kansas, 2013.

Cillizza, Chris. "The Single Most Important-And Powerful-Line from Joe Biden's 1/6 Speech." *CNN Politics.* New York: Cable News Network, 2022.

Clements, Jeffrey D. with Bill Moyers. *Corporations Are Not People: Reclaiming Democracy from Big Money and Global Corporations.* (2nd ed.) San Francisco: Berett-Koehler Publishers, 2014.

Clift, Eleanor. *Founding Sisters and the Nineteenth Amendment.* New York: Wiley, 2003.

Coenen, Dan T. *The Story of* The Federalist: *How Hamilton and Madison Reconceived America.* New York: Twelve Tables Press, 2007.

Collins, Ronald K. L., and David M. Skover. *When Money Speaks: The McCutcheon Decision, Campaign Finance Laws and the First Amendment.* Oak Park: Top Five, 2014.

Committee on Homeland Security and Governmental Affairs and Committee on Rules and Administration, Staff. *Examining the U.S. Capitol Attack: A Review of the Security, Planning, and Response Failures on January 6.* Washington, D.C.: U.S. Senate, 2021.

Congressional Research Service. *Fairness Doctrine: History and Constitutional Issues.* Washington, DC: CRS, 2011.

_____. *The Electoral College: How It Works in Contemporary Presidential Elections.* Washington, DC: CRS, 2024.

Cooper v. Harris, 137 S.Ct. 1455 (2017). Justia: US Supreme Court, supreme.justia.com/cases/federal/us/581/15-1262/

Cooper, Jonathan L., and Christie, Bob. "Democrats Win Big in Arizona, Now a Former GOP Stronghold." *AP News,* November 4, 2020, apnews.com/

article/election-2020-joe-biden-donald-trump-race-and-ethnicity-mark-kelly-6841e27210770f59418bdc13a60ccec7.

Cott, Nancy F. *The Grounding of Modern Feminism.* New Haven, Conn.: Yale UP, 1987.

Court Case Tracker. "*Rucho v. Common Cause.*" *Brennan Center for Justice.* New York: Brennan Center for Justice at the NYU Law, 2019.

Crawford, Elizabeth. *The Women's Suffrage Movement: A Reference Guide, 1866-1928.* London: Routledge, 2001.

C-SPAN with Theodore Olson and J. Douglas Smith. "Baker v. Carr, 1962." *Landmark Cases.* Washington: National Cable Satellite Corporation, 2017.

Curtis, Robert A. "Race-Based Equal Protection Claims After *Shaw v. Reno.*" *Duke Law Journal* 44, no. 298 (1994), scholarship.law.duke.edu/dlj/vol44/iss2/3.

Daley, David. *Ratf**ked : The True Story Behind the Secret Plan to Steal America's Democracy.* New York: Liveright Publishing, 2016.

Daniels, Gilda R. *Uncounted: The Crisis of Voter Suppression in America.* New York: NYU Press, 2020.

Dassow, Laura. *Henry David Thoreau: A Life.* Chicago: University of Chicago Press, 2017.

Davidson, Chandler. *Quiet Revolution in the South: The Impact of the Voting Rights Act, 1965-1990.* Princeton, NJ: Princeton UP, 1994.

_____, and Bernard Grofman, eds. *Quiet Revolution in the South: The Impact of the Voting Rights Act, 1965-1990.* Princeton, NJ: Princeton UP, 1994.

de Nevers, Orion. "What Happened to HAVA? The Help America Vote Act Twenty Years On and Lessons for the Future." *Georgetown Law Journal Online,* www.law.georgetown.edu/georgetown-law-journal/wp content/uploads/sites/26/2022/01/de-Nevers_What-Happened-to-HAVA.pdf.

Delahunty, Robert J., and John Yoo. "Who Counts? The Twelfth Amendment, the Vice President, and the Electoral College." *Case Western Reserve Law Review* 73, no. 1 (2022): 27-138.

Deloria, Vine, Jr., ed. *American Indian Policy in the Twentieth Century.* Norman: University of Oklahoma Press, 1985.

_____, and Clifford M. Lytle. *The Nations Within: The Past and Future of American Indian Sovereignty.* Austin: University of Texas Press, 1984.

_____, and David E. Wilkins. *Tribes, Treaties, and Constitutional Tribulations.* Austin: University of Texas Press, 1999.

Digital History. "Baker v. Carr." Digital History. Houston: Digital History, 2016.

Douglas, Joshua, and Eugene Mazeo. *Election Law Stories.* Foundation Press, 2016.

Downs, Jim, ed. *Voter Suppression in U.S. Elections.* Athens: University of Georgia Press, 2020.

Dray, Philip. *At the Hands of Persons Unknown: The Lynching of Black America.* New York: Random House, 2002.

DuBois, Ellen Carol. *Feminism and Suffrage: The Emergence of an Independent Women's Movement in the United States, 1848-1869.* Revised edition. Ithaca, N.Y.: Cornell UP, 1999.

Dunbar-Nelson, Alice. *Give Us Each Day: The Diary of Alice Dunbar-Nelson,* ed. Gloria T. Hull. New York: W. W. Norton, 1984.

Edward Foley. "Voting Rules and Constitutional Law," *George Washington Law Review,* 81 Geo. Wash. L. Rev. 1836, 2013.

"Election Fraud Cases: Texas." *Heritage Foundation,* n.d., www.heritage.org/voterfraud/search?state=TX.

Ellis, Sylvia. Freedom's Pragmatist: Lyndon Johnson and Civil Rights. Gainesville: University of Florida Press, 2013.

Epps, Garrett. *Democracy Reborn: The Fourteenth Amendment and the Fight for Equal Rights in Post-Civil War America.* New York: Holt, 2006.

Fife, Brian L. *Reforming the Electoral Process in America: Toward More Democracy in the 21st Century.* Santa Barbara, CA: Praeger, 2010.

File, Thom. "Young-Adult Voting: An Analysis of Presidential Elections, 1964-2012." US Census Bureau. US Census Bureau, Apr. 2014.

Flexner, Eleanor, and Ellen Fitzpatrick. *Century of Struggle: The Woman's Rights Movement in the*

United States. Enlarged edition. Cambridge, Mass.: Belknap Press of Harvard UP, 1996.

Flexner, Eleanor. *Century of Struggle: The Woman's Rights Movement in the United States.* Cambridge: Belknap, 1996.

Foner, Eric. *Reconstruction: America's Unfinished Revolution, 1863-1877.* New York: Harper, 1988.

_____. *Reconstruction: America's Unfinished Revolution, 1863-1877.* New York: Perennial, 2002.

Ford, Linda G. *Iron-Jawed Angels: The Suffrage Militancy of the National Women's Party, 1912-1920.* Lanham, NY: UP of America, 1991.

Fradin, Judith Bloom and Dennis Brindell Fradin. *Jane Addams: Champion of Democracy.* New York: Clarion, 2006.

Franzen, Trisha. *Anna Howard Shaw: The Work of Woman Suffrage.* Champaign: U of Illinois P, 2014.

Frost, Jennifer. *"Let Us Vote!": Youth Voting Rights and the 26th Amendment.* New York: NYU UP, 2022.

Frost-Knappman, Elizabeth, and Kathryn Cullen-DuPont. *Women's Suffrage in America: An Eyewitness History.* New York: Facts on File, 1992.

Fuller, Jaime. "From George Washington to Shaun McCutcheon: A Brief-ish History of Campaign Finance Reform." *Washington Post*, 3 Apr. 2014.

"The Future of Majority-Minority Districts in Light of Declining Racially Polarized Voting," *Harvard Law Review*, 116 (2003): 2208-2229.

Gettleman, Marvin E. *The Dorr Rebellion: A Study in American Radicalism, 1833-1849.* New York: Random House, 1973.

Gillette, William. *The Right to Vote: Politics and the Passage of the Fifteenth Amendment.* Baltimore, MD: Johns Hopkins Press, 1969.

Ginzberg, Lori. *Untidy Origins: A Story of Woman's Rights in Antebellum New York.* Chapel Hill: University of North Carolina Press, 2005.

Goldstone, Lawrence. *Inherently Unequal: The Betrayal of Equal Rights by the Supreme Court, 1865-1903.* New York: Walker, 2011.

_____. *Stolen Justice: The Struggle for African American Voting Rights.* New York: Scholastic Focus, 2020.

Gordon, Ann D., ed. *The Elizabeth Cady Stanton & Susan B. Anthony Papers Project.* New Brunswick NJ: Rutgers, The State University of New Jersey, 2012.

_____. *The Selected Papers of Elizabeth Cady Stanton and Susan B. Anthony.* 6 Vols. New Brunswick: Rutgers UP, 1997-2013.

_____. *The Trial of Susan B. Anthony.* Washington, DC: Federal Judicial Center, 2005.

_____, et al., eds. *African American Women and the Vote, 1837-1965.* Amherst: University of Massachusetts Press, 1997.

Granville, Kevin. "Facebook and Cambridge Analytica: What You Need to Know as Fallout Widens." *New York Times*, March 19, 2018. www.nytimes.com/2018/03/19/technology/facebook-cambridge-analytica-explained.html.

Griffith, Elisabeth. *In Her Own Right: The Life of Elizabeth Cady Stanton.* New York: Oxford UP, 1985.

Grofman, Bernard, ed. *Race and Redistricting in the 1990s.* New York: Agathon Press, 1998.

_____. "Would Vince Lombardi Have Been Right if He Had Said, 'When It Comes to Redistricting, Race isn't Everything, It's the Only Thing'?" *Cardozo Law Review* 14, no. 1237 (1993).

Hamilton, Kate. "State Implementation of the Electoral Count Reform Act and the Mitigation of Election-Subversion Risk in 2024 and Beyond." *The Yale Law Journal: Forum* 133 (Nov. 2023).

Hamington, Maurice. *The Social Philosophy of Jane Addams.* Chicago: University of Illinois Press, 2009.

Hansen, Richard. *The Supreme Court and Election Law: Judging from Baker v. Carr to Bush v. Gore.* New edition. New York: New York UP, 2006.

Harlan, Louis R. *Booker T. Washington: The Wizard of Tuskegee, 1901-1915.* Vol. 2. Oxford, UK: Oxford UP, 1983.

Harvard Law Review. "*Rucho v. Common Cause.*" *Harvard Law Review.* Cambridge, MA: Harvard Law Review, 2019.

Hasen, Richard L. *The Supreme Court and Election Law: Judging Equality from* Baker v. Carr *to* Bush v. Gore. New York: New York UP, 2003.

Haulley, Fletcher. *The Help America Vote Act of 2002: Legislation to Modernize America's Voting Systems.* New York: Rosen Central, 2005.

Herman, Alice, et al. "The Election-Denying Republicans Who Aided Trump's 'Big Lie' and Got Promoted." *The Guardian*, March 9, 2023, www.theguardian.com/us-news/ng-interactive/2023/mar/09/trump-big-lie-2020-election-republican-supporters-congress.

Hinchcliff, Abagail M. "The "Other" Side of Richardson v. Ramirez: A Textual Challenge to Felon Disenfranchisement." *The Yale Law Journal* 121, no. 1 (Oct. 2011): 194-236.

Hine, Darlene Clark, William C. Hine, and Stanley C. Harrold. *African Americans: A Concise History*, Combined Volume. Boston: Pearson, 2011.

Hull, Gloria T. "Alice Dunbar-Nelson (1875-1935)." Cengage Learning Web site. college.cengage.com/dunbarnelson_al.html.

Hull, N. E. H. *The Woman Who Dared to Vote: The Trial of Susan B. Anthony.* Lawrence KS: The UP of Kansas, 2012.

Ides, Allan. "The Jurisprudence of Justice Byron White," *Yale Law Journal*, vol. 103, no. 2 (November, 1993), 419-461.

Irons, Peter. *A People's History of the Supreme Court.* New York, NY: Penguin, 1999.

Isenberg, Nancy. *Sex and Citizenship in Antebellum America.* Chapel Hill: University of North Carolina Press, 1998.

Johnson, Wilma J. "Dunbar-Nelson, Alice Ruth Moore (1875-1935)." BlackPast.org Web site. blackpast.com/dunbar-nelson-alice-ruth-moore-1875-1935.

Kaiser, Brittany. *Targeted: The Cambridge Analytica Whistleblower's Inside Story of How Big Data, Trump, and Facebook Broke Democracy and How It Can Happen Again.* New York: Harper, 2019.

Kearns, Doris. Lyndon Johnson and the American Dream. New York: St. Martins Griffin, 1991.

Keena, Alex, et al. *Gerrymandering the States: Partisanship, Race, and the Transformation of American Federalism.* New York: Cambridge UP, 2021.

Kent, Janice. *ADA in Detail: Interpreting the 2010 Americans with Disabilities Act Standards for Accessible Design.* Hoboken, NJ: Wiley, 2017.

Kotz, Nick. *Judgment Days: Lyndon Baines Johnson, Martin Luther King, Jr., and the Laws That Changed America.* Boston: Houghton Mifflin, 2005.

Kraditor, Aileen S. *The Ideas of the Woman Suffrage Movement, 1890-1920.* New York: Anchor, 1971.

Kuroda, Tadahisa. *The Origins of the Twelfth Amendment: The Electoral College in the Early Republic, 1787-1804.* Westport, CT: Praeger, 1994.

Landsberg, Brian K. *Free at Last to Vote: The Alabama Origins of the 1965 Voting Rights Act.* Lawrence: UP of Kansas, 2007.

Lapowsky, Issie. "Senators Grill Whistleblower on Cambridge Analytica's Inner Workings." *Wired*, May 16, 2018.

Lasch, Christopher, ed. *The Social Thought of Jane Addams.* 2nd ed. New York: Irvington, 1997.

Lawson, Steven F. *Black Ballots: Voting Rights in the South, 1944-1969.* New York: Columbia UP, 1976.

_____. *Black Ballots: Voting Rights in the South, 1944-1969.* Lanham, MD: Lexington Books, 1999.

"LBJ and Civil Rights." *Lyndon Baines Johnson Library and Museum.* LBJ Presidential Library, 2015.

Legal Information Institute. "Baker v. Carr." Cornell: Cornell Law School, 2017.

Library of Congress. "Profiles: Selected Leaders of the National Woman's Party." *Library of Congress.* Library of Congress, n.d.

Liptak, Adam. "Supreme Court Invalidates Key Part of Voting Rights Act," *New York Times*, June 25, 2013, p. A1

Lublin, David. *The Paradox of Representation: Racial Gerrymandering and Minority Interests in Congress.* Princeton, NJ: Princeton UP, 2020.

LWV Guest. "The Woman Who Argued 'Rucho v. Common Cause' Looks Back." *League of Women Voters.* Washington, D.C.: League of Women Voters of the United States, 2022.

Malcolm X, and Alex Haley. *The Autobiography of Malcolm X.* 1965. New York: Ballantine, 2015.

Marable, Manning, and Leith Mullings, eds. *Let Nobody Turn Us Around: An African American Anthology.* Lanham, Md: Rowman & Littlefield, 2009.

Mark Tushnet. "Renormalizing Bush v. Gore: An Anticipatory Intellectual History," *Georgetown Law Journal*, 90 Geo. L.J. 113, 2001.

Martinez, J. Michael. *Carpetbaggers, Cavalry, and the Ku Klux Klan: Exposing the Invisible Empire during Reconstruction.* Lanham: Rowman, 2007.

Mayer, Jane. *Dark Money: The Hidden History of the Billionaires behind the Rise of the Radical Right.* New York: Doubleday, 2016.

McBride, Alex. "Landmark Cases: Reynolds V. Sims." PBS, Public Broadcasting Services, www.pbs.org/wnet/supremecourt/rights/landmark_reynolds.html.

McClosky, Robert G. *The American Supreme Court.* Fourth Edition. University of Chicago Press, 2005.

McCool, Daniel, ed. *The Most Fundamental Right: Contrasting Perspectives on the Voting Rights Act.* Bloomington: Indiana UP, 2012.

_____, Susan M. Olson, and Jennifer L. Robinson. *Native Vote: American Indians, the Voting Rights Act, and the Right to Vote.* New York: Cambridge UP, 2007.

McGerr, Michael. *A Fierce Discontent: The Rise and Fall of the Progressive Movement in America, 1870-1920.* New York: Free Press, 2003.

McKenzie, Jonathan. *The Political Thought of Henry David Thoreau: Privatism and the Practice of Philosophy.* Lexington: UP of Kentucky, 2016.

McMillen, Sally. *Seneca Falls and the Origins of the Women's Rights Movement.* New York: Oxford UP, 2008.

Meyer, Howard N. *The Amendment That Refused to Die: Equality and Justice Deferred: The History of the Fourteenth Amendment.* Lanham: Madison, 2000.

Meyerson, Harold. "How Racist Are Republicans? Very." *The American Prospect*, October 22, 2020, prospect.org/blogs-and-newsletters/tap/how-racist-are-republicans-very.

Michael Kent Curtis, "Using the Voting Rights Act to Discriminate: North Carolina's Use of Racial Gerrymanders, Two Racial Quotas, Safe Harbors, Shields, and Inoculations to Undermine Multiracial Coalitions and Black Political Power," *Wake Forest Law Review*, 51 (2016): 421-492.

Moller, Mary Elkins. *Thoreau in the Human Community.* Amherst: University of Massachusetts Press 1980.

Moyers, Bill with Floyd Abrams and Trevor Potter. ""Citizens United v. FEC." *Bill Moyers Journal.* (including *Frontline* September 4, 2009 broadcast) Washington: Public Affairs Television, 2017.

Muller, Derek T. "The President of the Senate, the Original Public Meaning of the Twelfth Amendment, and the Electoral Count Reform Act." *Case Western Reserve Law Review* 73, no. 4 (2023): 1023-1046.

Mungarro, Angelica, et al. "How Did Black Women in the NAACP Promote the Dyer Anti-Lynching Bill, 1918-1923?" Women and Social Movements in the United States, 1600-2000, Web site. womhist.alexanderstreet.com/lynch/intro.htm.

National Park Service. "Notable Women's Rights Leaders." Women's Rights National Historical Park. Washington: National Park Service, 2017.

Nelson, Anne M. "Constitutional Law-Fourteenth Amendment-Equal Protection-Voting Rights of Ex-Felons." *Duquesne Law Review* 13, no. 1 (1974): 130+.

Newton, Michael. *The Ku Klux Klan: History, Organization, Language, Influence, and Activities of America's Most Notorious Secret Society.* Jefferson: McFarland, 2007.

Norrell, Robert J. *Up from History: The Life of Booker T. Washington.* Cambridge, MA: Harvard UP, 2009.

Oyez. "Citizens United v. Federal Election Commission." *Oyez.* Chicago: Kent College of Law at Illinois Tech, 2017.

Parsons, Elaine Frantz. *Ku Klux: The Birth of the Klan during Reconstruction.* Chapel Hill: U of North Carolina P, 2016.

Patterson, James T. *Restless Giant: The United States from Watergate to Bush v. Gore.* New York: Oxford UP, 2005.

Payne, Charles M. *I've Got the Light of Freedom: The Organizing Tradition and the Mississippi Freedom Struggle.* Berkeley: University of California Press, 1995.

Perman, Michael. *Struggle for Mastery: Disfranchisement in the South, 1888-1908.* Chapel Hill: University of North Carolina Press, 2001.

Perry, Michael J. *We the People: The Fourteenth Amendment and the Supreme Court.* New York: Oxford UP, 1999.

Perry, Theresa, ed. *Teaching Malcolm X.* New York: Routledge, 1996.

Pildes, Richard H., and Richard G. Niemi. "Expressive Harms, 'Bizarre Districts,' and Voting Rights: Evaluating Election District Appearances after *Shaw v. Reno*." *Michigan Law Review* 92, no. 483 (1993).

Pinkney, Alphonso. *Red, Black, and Green: Black Nationalism in the United States.* New York: Cambridge UP, 1976.

Post, Robert C. with Pamela S. Karlan, Lawrence Lessing, Frank I. Michelman, and Nadia Urbinati. *Citizens Divided: Campaign Finance Reform and the Constitution.* (The Tanner Lectures on Human Values) Cambridge: Harvard UP, 2014.

Powell, Lewis F., Jr. "10-1973: Richardson v. Ramirez." *Washington and Lee University School of Law.* Scholarly Commons: Supreme Court Case Files, 1974.

Pratt, Walter F., Jr. *The Supreme Court under Edward Douglass White, 1910-1921.* Columbia: University of South Carolina Press, 1999.

Prokop, Andrew. "The Bill to Prevent Trump from Stealing the Next Election, Explained." *Vox,* December 21, 2022, www.vox.com/policy-and-politics/2022/12/21/23520649/electoral-count-reform-act-omnibus-trump.

Prucha, Francis Paul. *American Indian Policy in Crisis: Christian Reformers and the Indian, 1865-1900.* Norman: University of Oklahoma Press, 1964.

_____. *The Great Father: The United States Government and the American Indians.* Lincoln: University of Nebraska Press, 1984.

Rable, George C. *But There Was No Peace: The Role of Violence in the Politics of Reconstruction.* Athens: U of Georgia P, 2007.

Rakove, Jack N. "The Great Compromise: Ideas, Interests, and the Politics of Constitution Making." *William and Mary Quarterly* 44 (1987): 424-457.

Raskin, Jamie. *Unthinkable: Trauma, Truth, and the Trials of American Democracy.* New York: Harper, 2022.

Raven, Rory. *The Dorr War: Treason, Rebellion, and the Fight for Reform in Rhode Island.* Charleston, SC: Arcadia Publishing, 2015.

The Reconstruction Amendments." *The Yale Law Journal,* 121 (2012): 1584-1670.

Re, Richard M., and Christopher M. Re. "Voting and Vice: Criminal Disenfranchisement and Reconstruction: The Second Civil War." *American Experience.* PBS Online/WGBH, 2004.

"Richardson v. Ramirez, 418 U.S. 24 (1974)." *Justia: U.S. Supreme Court,* supreme.justia.com/cases/federal/us/418/24.

Riker, William H. "The Senate and American Federalism." *American Political Science Review* 49, no. 2 (1955): 452-69.

Roydhouse, Marion W. *Votes for Women! The American Suffrage Movement and the Nineteenth Amendment: A Reference Guide.* Santa Barbara, CA: ABC-CLIO, 2020.

Rush, Mark E. "From *Shaw v. Reno* to *Miller v. Johnson*: Minority Representation and State Compliance with the Voting Rights Act." *Publius* 25, no. 155 (1995), www.jstor.org/stable/3330692.

_____, ed. *Voting Rights and Redistricting in the United States.* Westport, Conn.: Praeger, 1998.

Schiller, Wendy J., and Charles Stewart III. *Electing the Senate: Indirect Democracy before the Seventeenth Amendment.* Princeton, NJ: Princeton UP, 2014.

Schneider, Dorothy and Carl J. Schneider. *American Women in the Progressive Era, 1900-1920.* New York: Facts on File, 1993.

"Selma Movement." *National Voting Rights Museum and Institute.* National Voting Rights Museum and Institute, 2015.

Shaw v. Reno, 113 S.Ct. 2816 (1993). Justia: US Supreme Court, supreme.justia.com/cases/federal/us/509/630/

Shaw, Anna Howard. The Story of a Pioneer. Teddington: Echo Lib., 2006.

Sherr, Lynn. *Failure Is Impossible: Susan B. Anthony in Her Own Words.* New York: Random House, 1995.

Shklar, Judith N. *American Citizenship: The Quest for Inclusion.* Cambridge, MA: Harvard UP, 1998.

Shoemaker, Rebecca S. *The White Court: Justices, Rulings, and Legacy.* Santa Barbara, Calif.: ABC-CLIO, 2004.

Silver, Nate, and Allison McCann. "Are White Republicans More Racist Than White Democrats?" *FiveThirtyEight*, April 30, 2014, fivethirtyeight.com/features/are-white-republicans-more-racist-than-white-democrats.

Smith, Erin Geiger. *Thank You for Voting: The Maddening, Enlightening, Inspiring Truth About Voting in America.* New York: Harper, 2020.

Smock, Raymond W. *Booker T. Washington: Black Leadership in the Age of Jim Crow.* Chicago: Ivan R. Dee, 2009.

Spakovsky, Hans von. "Citizens United and the Restoration of the First Amendment." *The Heritage Foundation.* Washington: The Heritage Foundation, 2010.

Stanton, Elizabeth Cady, and Susan Brownell Anthony. *The Elizabeth Cady Stanton-Susan B. Anthony Reader: Correspondence, Writings, Speeches.* Ed. Ellen Carol DuBois. Boston: Northeastern UP, 1992.

Stebner, Eleanor J. *The Women of Hull House: A Study in Spirituality, Vocation, and Friendship.* Albany: State University of New York Press, 1997.

Stern, Seth, and Stephen Wermiel. *Justice Brennan: Liberal Champion.* New York: Houghton Mifflin Harcourt, 2013.

Stevens, Doris. *Jailed for Freedom.* 1920: n.p. Project Gutenberg, 2003.

Storing, Herbert J. *What the Anti-Federalists Were For: The Political Thought of the Opponents of the Constitution.* Chicago: University of Chicago Press, 1981.

Summers, Mark W. *A Dangerous Stir: Fear, Paranoia, and the Making of Reconstruction.* Chapel Hill: U of North Carolina P, 2009.

_____. *Party Games: Getting, Keeping, and Using Power in the Gilded Age.* Chapel Hill: University of North Carolina Press, 2004.

Supreme Court of the United States, Shelby County, *Alabama v. Holder,* Attorney General, www.supremecourt.gov/opinions/12pdf/12-96_6k47.pdf.

_____. "Rucho v. Common Cause." *Legal Information Institute.* Ithaca, NY: Cornell Law School, 2019. supreme.justia.com/cases/federal/us/531/98.

Susan B. Anthony House. "Biography of Susan B. Anthony." National Susan B. Anthony Museum & House. Rochester NY: Susan B. Anthony House, 2013.

Terrill, Robert E., ed. *The Cambridge Companion to Malcolm X.* New York: Cambridge UP, 2010.

"Texas President Results." February 22, 2021. *CNN*, www.cnn.com/election/2020/results/state/texas/president.

Tilly, Louise A., and Patricia Gurin, eds. *Women, Politics, and Change.* New York: Russell Sage Foundation, 1990.

Toller, Eric T. "A More Perfect Electoral College: Challenging Winner-Take-All Provisions under the Twelfth Amendment." *Legislation & Policy Brief* 9, no. 1 (2020): 4-36.

"Twenty-Sixth Amendment." Annenberg Classroom. Leonore Annenberg Inst. for Civics, n.d.

U.S. Congress House of Representatives. *Help America Vote Act of 2002.* Washington, DC: Bibliogov, 2010.

U.S. Department of Justice. "About Section 5 of the Voting Rights Act," www.justice.gov/crt/about-section-5-voting-rights-act.

Urofsky, Melvin I. *The Campaign Finance Cases: Buckley, McConnell, Citizens United, and McCutcheon*. Lawrence: University of Kansas Press, 2020.

Valelly, Richard M., ed. *The Voting Rights Act: Securing the Ballot*. Washington, DC: CQ Press, 2006.

———. *The Two Reconstructions: The Struggle for Black Enfranchisement*. Chicago: University of Chicago Press, 2004.

"Voters with Disabilities: Challenges to Voting Accessibility." *U.S. Government Accountability Office*, 2013, www.gao.gov/products/gao-13-538sp.

"Voting Rights: A Short History." *Carnegie Corporation of America*, November 18, 2019, www.carnegie.org/our-work/article/voting-rights-timeline.

Waldman, Michael. *The Fight to Vote*. New York: Simon & Schuster, 2016.

Walton, Mary. *A Woman's Crusade: Alice Paul and the Battle for the Ballot*. New York: Palgrave MacMillan, 2010.

Ward, Geoffrey C. [based on a documentary film by Ken Burns and Paul Barnes]. *Not for Ourselves Alone: The Story of Elizabeth Cady Stanton and Susan B. Anthony: An Illustrated History*. New York. Alfred A. Knopf, 1999.

Washington Secretary of State. "Baker v. Carr et al., March 2, 1962." *Shifting Boundaries: Redistricting in Washington State*. Olympia: Office of the Secretary of State, 2017.

Washington, Booker T. *Up from Slavery*. Mineola, NY: Dover Publications, 1995.

Wellman, Judith. *The Road to Seneca Falls: Elizabeth Cady Stanton and the First Woman's Rights Convention*. Urbana: University of Illinois Press, 2004.

Whitaker, I. Paige, and Elizabeth Rybicki. "The Electoral Count Act and Presidential Elections." *Congressional Research Service*, December 19, 2022, crsreports.congress.gov/product/pdf/IN/IN12065.

Woloch, Nancy. *Women and the American Experience*. New York: Alfred A. Knopf, 1984.

Woodward, C. Vann. *The Strange Career of Jim Crow: A Commemorative Edition*. New York and Oxford: Oxford UP, 2002.

Wray, Christopher. "Examining the January 6 Attack on the U.S. Capitol." *FBI*. Washington, D.C.: Federal Bureau of Investigation, 2021.

Youn, Monica, ed. *Money, Politics, and the Constitution: Beyond Citizens United*. New York: The Century Foundation, 2011.

Zelden, Charles Z. *Voting Rights on Trial*. Indianapolis, Ind.: Hackett, 2004.

———. *The Battle for the Black Ballot: Smith v. Allwright and the Defeat of the Texas All-White Primary*. Lawrence: UP of Kansas, 2004.

Zelizer, Julian. "How Washington Helped to Create the Modern Media: Ending the Fairness Doctrine," in *Media Nation: The Political History of News in Modern America*, ed. Bruce Schulman and Julian Zelizer. Philadelphia: University of Pennsylvania Press, 2017; pp. 176-189.

Zywicki, Todd J. "Beyond the Shell and Husk of History: The History of the Seventeenth Amendment and its Implications for Current Reform Proposals." *Cleveland State Law Review* 45, no. 1 (1997). mason.gmu.edu/~tzywick2/Cleveland%20State%20Senators.pdf.

Index

1971 Revenue Act, 344, 345
2002 Bipartisan Campaign Reform Act (BCRA), 383, 404, 408, 420
2016 presidential election, 336, 465, 467, 468
2020 presidential election, 299, 504
2024 presidential election, 466, 507, 509, 511

A
Abernathy, Ralph, 118
abolition of slavery, 28, 38, 51, 109
Adams, John, 10, 109
Addams, Jane, 70-78, 116
African Americans, 1, 34, 49, 51, 59, 60, 110, 117, 118, 120, 127, 129, 131, 132, 133, 139, 140, 141, 143, 144, 145, 151, 152, 153, 154, 155, 156, 168, 170, 171, 172, 176, 177, 178, 179, 183, 184, 186, 187, 196, 197, 198, 199, 209, 216, 217, 218, 223, 224, 237, 241, 250, 261, 268, 327, 337, 424, 428, 434, 435, 438, 439, 441, 447, 448, 450, 451, 452, 454, 497, 500
American Civil War, 20, 62, 497
American Indians, 172, 174, 291
American Revolution, 29, 73, 109
Americans with Disabilities Act (ADA), 243, 270-282
Anthony Amendment, 41, 51, 79, 83, 88, 90, 108, 110, 111, 112, 115
Anthony, Susan B., 35, 40, 41, 49-61, 62, 64, 68, 79, 80, 83, 88, 91, 94, 108, 111, 176, 293
Asian Americans, 118, 237
AZ Mirror, 507, 508, 509

B
Baker v. Carr, 307-314, 316, 318, 323, 324, 458, 459, 463
Baker, Charles, 307, 323
"Ballot or the Bullet, The," 198-217
Beal, J. J., 154, 156, 168
Biden, Joseph R., 243, 299, 465, 483, 508
Birmingham Bus Boycott of 1955-56, 225
black Americans, 120, 216, 497
black nationalists, 198, 206, 215
black voters, 145, 152, 155, 168, 169, 170, 186, 196, 218, 237, 238, 315, 323, 385, 387, 446, 504, 513
Blackmun, Harry, 345
Brennan, William J., Jr., 307, 308, 323, 345
Bristow, Joseph L., 244, 245
Brown v. Board of Education, 221, 224, 316
Brownlow, William, 131, 139
Buckley v. Valeo, 305, 344-383, 404
Buckley, James L., 344
Bureau of Naturalization, 283, 284
Burger, Warren E., 345
Burns, Lucy, 88, 90, 102
Bush v. Gore, 393-403
Bush, George H. W., 255, 256, 270, 457
Bush, George W., 14, 243, 263, 284, 393, 403, 426

C
Cambridge Analytica, 465, 467-482
Carrillo, Karen Juanita, 497, 499, 500
Catt, Carrie Chapman, 80, 88, 109
Caucasian Americans, 118
Center for Public Integrity, 497, 498
Cissna, Lee, 284
Citizens United v. Federal Election Commission, 305, 383, 404-423
Civics Test for Naturalization (2019), 243, 283-298
"Civil Disobedience," 22-34
Civil Rights Act of 1957, 117, 337, 425
Civil Rights Act of 1960, 117, 425
Civil Rights Act of 1964, 118, 216, 235, 237, 238, 425
Civil Rights Era, 243
civil rights legislation, 117, 201, 202, 237, 391

civil rights movement, 117, 129, 198, 216, 218, 236, 237, 238, 316, 391, 425, 428
Clinton, DeWitt, 10
Clinton, Hillary, 90, 404, 405, 407, 408, 465, 504
Coleman, J. P., 118
Collins, Susan M., 299, 300
Congress of Industrial Organizations (CIO), 345
Congressional Union for Woman Suffrage, 79, 81, 87, 88
Constitutional Convention, 2, 3, 18, 59, 251, 292, 432
Cooper v. Harris, 443-455
Cooper, Roy, 443, 445
Council of Federated Organizations (COFO), 118

D
Davis v. Bandemer, 391, 459
Declaration of Independence, 30, 36, 45, 46, 47, 51, 52, 59, 72, 235, 286, 291
Declaration of Sentiments, 36-48, 51, 72, 79, 110, 112
Democratic Party, 84, 85, 88, 89, 115, 135, 143, 155, 170, 178, 179, 186, 189, 190, 191, 192, 196, 202, 203, 204, 215, 237, 407, 506, 507
Democratic-Republican party, 10
Department of Homeland Security (DHS), 284
Dirksen, Everett, 117
Dorr, Thomas Wilson, 17, 18
Dorr's Rebellion, 1, 17-21
Driscoll, Albert, 308
driver's license, 243, 255, 256, 257, 258, 261, 289, 501
Dunbar-Nelson, Alice Moore, 176, 178
Dyer bill, 176, 177, 178, 179, 181, 182, 184

E
Election Assistance Commission (EAC), 263, 268
electoral college, 1, 10, 14, 15, 300, 304, 305, 397, 402, 403
Electoral Count Act of 1887, 15, 299
Electoral Count Reform Act of 2022, 299-304
Ellender, Allen, 118
Enforcement Acts, 424

Equal Protection Clause, 190, 191, 219, 310, 318, 319, 320, 321, 324, 339, 340, 384, 385, 387, 389, 391, 394, 398, 401, 403, 443, 445, 458, 460
Ervin, Sam, 118

F
Facebook data, 467, 468, 469, 473, 474, 475, 482
Fairness Doctrine, 325, 326, 328, 329, 330, 333, 335, 336
Fallon, Christine Luchok, 456, 457
Federal Bureau of Investigation, 465, 472
Federal Communications Commission (FCC), 325, 328, 333
Federal Election Campaign Act (FECA) of 1971, 344, 346, 414
Federal Election Commission (FEC), 258, 305, 344, 345, 346, 382, 383, 404-423
federalism, 128, 313, 399, 424, 425, 427, 430, 432, 436
Federalist Paper No. 52, 1, 2-9
Federalist Party, 10, 391
Fifteenth Amendment, 35, 40, 49, 51, 56, 59, 60, 63, 69, 91, 108, 110, 111, 112, 115, 117, 120-130, 152, 154, 155, 157, 158, 159, 160, 161, 162, 163, 164, 165, 166, 167, 168, 169, 170, 171, 176, 186, 190, 191, 193, 194, 195, 196, 218, 224, 225, 250, 254, 268, 337, 385, 391, 424, 425, 428, 439, 441
First Amendment, 286, 316, 325, 329, 330, 331, 332, 333, 334, 335, 347, 348, 349, 351, 352, 353, 354, 357, 359, 360, 361, 362, 364, 366, 367, 369, 370, 372, 373, 375, 376, 378, 379, 380, 382, 383, 404, 405, 406, 408, 410, 411, 412, 413, 415, 416, 417, 418, 419, 423, 458, 461, 463
Ford, Wendell, 255, 256
Fortieth and Forty-First Congresses, 120
Fourteenth Amendment, 35, 40, 49, 55, 56, 59, 60, 62, 69, 91, 110, 117, 120-130, 168, 169, 172, 174, 186, 188, 189, 190, 191, 196, 219, 223, 224, 309, 310, 311, 312, 313, 315, 319, 320, 323, 324, 337, 339, 340, 342, 348, 379, 380,

385, 386, 387, 388, 389, 390, 391, 398, 400, 401, 425, 437, 445, 458, 463
Frankfurter, Felix, 312

G
Gard, Warren, 79, 89
Garfield, James A., 344
Gerry, Elbridge, 323, 391
gerrymandering, 118, 205, 305, 314, 318, 322, 323, 324, 388, 389, 390, 391, 425, 443, 444, 452, 453, 454, 456, 458, 459, 460, 461, 462, 463, 506
Gill, Larry, 337, 342
Gore, Al, 14, 243, 263, 393, 508
Government Accountability Office, 270
Grant, Ulysses S., 120, 121, 143, 218
Gray v. Sanders, 307, 308
Grimké, Sarah, 109
Grovey v. Townsend, 186, 187, 188, 191, 192, 194, 195, 196
Guardian, The, 467, 468, 469, 470, 476, 477, 481
Guinn v. United States, 154-171, 192, 194, 318
Guinn, Frank, 154, 156, 168

H
Hamilton, Alexander, 1, 2, 292
"Hang Mike Pence," 16, 483
Harris, David, 443, 445
Harris, Kamala, 483
Harris, Katherine, 393
Hatfield, Mark, 255, 256
Help America Vote Act of 2002 (HAVA), 243, 263-269
Holder, Eric, 424
Homeland Security Act, 284
House Judiciary Committee, 79-90, 442
human rights, 168, 187, 198, 207, 208, 216, 217, 229
Humphrey, Hubert, 118
Hunt, Jane, 36, 38, 40

I
Immigration and Naturalization Service (INS), 284
Indian Citizenship Act (also Snyder Act), 172-175

investigative journalism, 497, 499
"Is It a Crime for a Citizen of the United States to Vote?," 49-61

J
Jefferson, Thomas, 3, 10, 30, 45, 47, 291, 297
Johnson, Andrew, 120, 121, 128
Johnson, Lyndon B., 117, 118, 215, 216, 223, 224, 239, 391

K
Kagan, Elena, 425, 443, 444
Kennedy, Anthony, 396, 404, 425, 444
King, Martin Luther, Jr., 34, 118, 199, 200, 239, 294, 296
Kogan, Aleksandr, 467, 468, 473
Ku Klux Klan, 117, 118, 131-143, 199, 218

L
Ladies' Home Journal, 70, 71, 77
Lee, Albert, 337, 342
literacy test, 117, 118, 154, 155, 157, 160, 161, 162, 164, 165, 166, 168, 169, 170, 171, 186, 218, 237, 238, 241, 323, 424, 425, 428, 437, 440, 441

M
Madison, James, 1, 2, 3, 51, 53, 59, 292
"Make America Great Again," 465
Marbury v. Madison, 312, 458
Marshall, Thurgood, 188, 345, 444
McClintock, Mary Ann, 36, 38, 40
McConnell v. Federal Election Commission, 420, 421
McCutcheon v. Federal Election Commission, 383
Messenger, The, 176
Mexican Americans, 118, 500
Mexican-American War (1846-1848), 1, 22, 23, 30, 31, 33, 293
minimum voting ages, 250
Mondell, Franklin Wheeler, 79
Monroe, Ralph, 256
Moss, Ralph, 79, 89

Mott, Lucretia Coffin, 36, 38, 39, 109

N

Nation of Islam, 198, 199, 216
National American Woman Suffrage Association (NAWSA), 41, 63, 77, 81, 88, 102, 108, 109
National Association for the Advancement of Colored People (NAACP), 72, 118, 145, 154, 177, 187, 219, 237
National Voter Registration Act of 1991, 255, 256
National Voter Registration Act of 1993 (also Motor Voter Law), 243, 255-262, 267, 268
National Women's Party (NWP), 80, 102, 115
National Women's Rights Convention, 62
Native Americans, 118, 177, 291, 508, 512
Naturalization Act of 1790, 174, 283, 297
naturalization laws, 283
naturalization process, 283, 284, 297
Naturalizations Acts of 1795, 1798, and 1802, 284
"Negro Woman and the Ballot, The," 176-185
New York Times, 467, 469, 470, 476, 477
Nineteenth Amendment, 35, 41, 49, 51, 60, 62, 77, 79, 81, 88, 90, 103, 108-116, 177, 183, 218, 219, 250, 254, 268
Northern Republicans, 120

O

O'Connor, Sandra Day, 384, 385, 386, 396, 426
Obama, Barack, 254, 442, 444, 465
Obergefell v. Hodges, 444
Observer, The, 467, 468, 469, 482

P

Paul, Alice, 48, 79-90, 102, 105, 106, 115, 116
Pence, Mike, 16, 483
Pendleton Civil Service Reform Act, 344
Plessy v. Ferguson, 129, 152, 156, 224
political action committee (PAC), 305, 344, 345, 382, 408, 422
poll taxes, 1, 22, 24, 33, 117, 118, 186, 187, 197, 218, 219, 223, 237, 238, 241, 323, 424, 440, 497, 498, 500, 508
Powell, Lewis F., Jr., 345

Progressive movement, 70
property rights, 36, 39, 45, 47, 110
Public Integrity, 497, 498, 499, 500, 503

R

racial violence, 144, 152, 156, 205
Radio Act of 1927, 325, 331
Ramirez, Abran, 337, 342
Reconstruction, 60, 62, 120, 121, 127, 128, 129, 131, 138, 143, 154, 177, 186, 187, 198, 218, 219, 224, 242, 254
Red Lion Broadcasting v. FCC, 325-336
Reed, Stanley F., 186, 187
Rehnquist, William, 337, 345, 426
Republican Party, 10, 55, 56, 112, 155, 168, 170, 176, 177, 182, 183, 184, 316, 346, 456, 466, 481, 488, 497, 502, 504, 507
Reynolds v. Sims, 307, 315-324, 398
Richardson v. Ramirez, 337-343
right to suffrage, 1, 165, 170
right to vote, 1, 2, 8, 18, 19, 20, 40, 44, 46, 49, 51, 52, 55, 56, 58, 59, 60, 62, 63, 64, 65, 66, 69, 72, 77, 80, 81, 88, 89, 102, 108, 113, 115, 116, 117, 118, 122, 129, 144, 151, 152, 154, 155, 158, 159, 160, 161, 168, 169, 176, 177, 178, 183, 184, 186, 190, 192, 195, 196, 204, 221, 224, 225, 227, 228, 229, 232, 235, 238, 239, 241, 248, 250, 251, 254, 270, 316, 318, 319, 321, 323, 324, 337, 340, 341, 342, 397, 398, 401, 403, 424, 428, 429, 439, 441, 492, 493, 497, 498, 504, 506
Ripon program, 474, 481
Roberts, John, 424, 425, 444, 456
Rogers, William P., 117
Rucho v. Common Cause, 314, 456-464

S

Sargent, Aaron Augustus, 108
Seneca County Courier, 36
Seneca Falls Convention, 36-48, 51, 62, 72, 79
Seventeenth Amendment, 190, 196, 243, 244-249, 305
Shaw v. Reno, 384-392, 443

Shaw, Anna Howard, 80, 91-101, 110
Sheafe, C. A., 131, 132, 134, 139
Shelby County v. Holder, 119, 242, 391, 424-442, 446, 506
Sievers, Caitlin, 507, 508, 509
Smith v. Allwright, 186-197
Smith, William L., 10
Snyder, Homer P., 172
Stanton, Elizabeth Cady, 36, 38, 39, 51, 60, 63, 72, 88, 91, 109, 112, 176
Staples, Sam, 22
"Statement on Suffrage," 144-153
Stevens, John Paul, 345, 444
Stewart, Potter, 312, 345, 386
student activism, 250
Student Nonviolent Coordinating Committee (SNCC), 118, 211
suffrage movement, 20, 40, 41, 63, 69, 80, 81, 88, 100, 112, 243
Sutherland, George, 79
Swift, Al, 255, 256, 261

T

Taft-Hartley Act, 345
Taggart, Joseph, 79, 89, 90
Thoreau, Henry David, 1, 22-34
Tillman Act, 344, 405
Tillman, Lewis, 131, 132, 134, 139
Trump, Donald J., 15, 243, 269, 299, 336, 465, 469, 483, 485, 495, 497, 498, 500, 504, 507, 508, 509, 513
Twelfth Amendment, 1, 10-16, 303
Twenty-Fourth Amendment, 1, 117, 197, 218-223, 254
Twenty-Sixth Amendment, 243, 250-254

U

U.S. Capitol, 243, 465, 483-496
U.S. citizenship, 62, 117, 172, 174, 283, 284
U.S. Citizenship and Immigration Services (USCIS), 283, 284
U.S. Commission on Civil Rights, 117, 238

U.S. Congress, 10, 62-69, 108, 115, 118, 120, 172, 218, 221, 237, 250, 255, 263, 287, 513
U.S. Constitution, 1, 2, 8, 10-16, 38, 40, 51, 59, 79, 108-116, 122, 155, 168, 186, 196, 198, 218-223, 243, 244-249, 250-254, 268, 284, 292, 301, 305, 337, 386, 389, 390, 391, 394, 400, 401, 402, 424, 443, 453, 509
U.S. Customs and Border Protection (CBP), 284
U.S. Department of Justice, 237, 267, 270, 384, 446, 472
U.S. House of Representatives, 2, 3, 4, 6, 7, 8, 9, 10, 12, 13, 14, 35, 53, 81, 83, 87, 88, 90, 108, 113, 115, 121, 127, 131, 132, 139, 140, 142, 172, 173, 177, 182, 188, 202, 221, 225, 244, 245, 246, 251, 264, 287, 290, 302, 305, 313, 346, 361, 362, 384, 456, 486, 490, 502, 512
U.S. Immigration and Customs Enforcement (ICE), 284
U.S. presidential election ballots, 393, 403
U.S. Senate Judiciary Committee, 444, 467-482
U.S. Supreme Court, 35, 154, 156, 168, 170, 171, 172, 174, 186, 187, 218, 224, 242, 243, 251, 263, 305, 308, 312, 315, 325, 337, 338, 342, 344, 346, 384, 386, 393, 395, 397, 425, 426, 443, 456, 457, 500, 509
United Jewish Organizations of Williamsburgh v. Carey, 385
United States v. Susan B. Anthony, 62

V

Valeo, Francis R., 344
Vietnam War, 216, 225, 250, 293
Vindication of the Rights of Woman, A, 109
Volstead, Andrew, 79, 89
voter discrimination, 80, 424, 425
voter ID laws, 497, 498, 500, 507
voter registration agencies, 255, 258, 259
voter registration application, 255, 258, 261
voter suppression, 223, 443, 466, 476, 497, 504, 507, 508, 512
Voting Rights Act of 1960, 117

Voting Rights Act of 1965, 117, 118, 170, 197, 223, 237-242, 254, 255, 259, 261, 266, 268, 384, 387, 391, 425, 427, 438, 440, 441, 443, 453, 500, 508
voting rights for African Americans, 60
voting rights for women, 77, 80, 102

W

Wallace, George, 118
Warren, Earl, 312, 313, 315, 316
Washington, Booker T., 144-153, 198
Webb, Edwin, 79, 89
White Citizens Council, 118
White, Byron, 325, 326, 327, 345
White, Edward Douglass, Jr., 154, 156
"Why Women Should Vote," 70-78
Williams, William Ezra, 79, 89
Wilson, Woodrow, 35, 81, 102, 109, 111, 115, 177, 293
Winslow, Rose, 102, 103
Wollstonecraft, Mary, 109
Women's Rights Convention, 35, 39, 40, 48, 51, 62, 109, 112
women's rights movement, 47, 62, 79, 80, 100, 109, 250
women's suffrage, 35, 49, 51, 59, 60, 62-69, 70, 72, 77, 78, 79, 80, 89, 90, 91-101, 108, 109, 176, 177, 178, 250
"Women's Suffrage in a Democratic Republic," 91-101
World Anti-Slavery Conference, 109
World War I, 35, 90, 91, 93, 100, 108, 111, 115, 172, 174, 187, 293
World War II, 187, 219, 250, 293, 294, 308, 316, 494
Wright, Martha, 36, 38, 40
Wylie, Christopher, 467, 469, 480

X

X, Malcolm, 198-217

The Defining Documents Series

Defining Documents in American History: Themes
American Citizenship
The American Economy
Business Ethics
Capital Punishment
The Constitution
Dissent & Protest
Domestic Terrorism & Extremism
Drug Policy
Environment & Conservation
Espionage & Intrigue
The First Amendment
The Free Press
The Great Depression
The Great Migration
The Gun Debate
Immigration & Immigrant Communities
The Legacy of 9/11
LGBTQ+
Native Americans
Political Campaigns, Candidates & Discourse
Prison Reform
Secrets, Leaks & Scandals
Slavery
Supreme Court Decisions
U.S. Involvement in the Middle East
Workers' Rights

Defining Documents in World History: Themes
Asia
Genocide & The Holocaust
Human Rights
The Middle East
Nationalism & Populism
The Nuclear Age
Pandemics, Plagues & Public Health
Religious Freedom & Religious Persecution
Revolutions
Treason
Women's Rights

SALEM PRESS   https://salempress.com   (800) 221-1592

Defining Documents in American History: Eras
Exploration and Colonial America (1492-1755)
The American Revolution (1754-1805)
Manifest Destiny and the New Nation (1803-1860)
The American West (1836-1900)
The Civil War (1860-1865)
The Reconstruction Era (1865-1877)
The Emergence of Modern America (1874-1917)
The 1900s (1900-1909)
The 1910s (1910-1919)
World War I (1914-1919)
The 1920s (1920-1929)
The Great Depression (1929-1941)
The 1930s (1930-1939)
World War II (1939-1946)
Postwar 1940s (1945-1949)
The Cold War (1945-1991)
The 1950s (1950-1959)
Civil Rights (1954-2015)
The Vietnam War (1956-1975)
The 1960s (1960-1969)
The 1970s (1970-1979)
The 1980s (1980-1989)

Defining Documents in World History: Eras
The Ancient World (2700 B.C.E. - 50 C.E.)
The Middle Ages (476-1500)
Renaissance & Early Modern Era, 1308-1600
The 17th Century (1601-1700)
The 18th Century (1701-1800)
The 19th Century (1801-1900)
The 20th Century (1900-1950)